Conspiracy Theories and the People Who Believe Them

Conspiracy Theories and the People Who Believe Them

EDITED BY
JOSEPH E. USCINSKI

OXFORD
UNIVERSITY PRESS

OXFORD
UNIVERSITY PRESS

Oxford University Press is a department of the University of Oxford. It furthers
the University's objective of excellence in research, scholarship, and education
by publishing worldwide. Oxford is a registered trade mark of Oxford University
Press in the UK and certain other countries.

Published in the United States of America by Oxford University Press
198 Madison Avenue, New York, NY 10016, United States of America.

Library of Congress Cataloging-in-Publication Data
Names: Uscinski, Joseph E., editor.
Title: Conspiracy theories and the people who believe them / edited by Joseph E. Uscinski.
Description: New York, NY : Oxford University Press, [2019] |
Includes bibliographical references and index.
Identifiers: LCCN 2018012939| ISBN 9780190844073 (hard cover) | ISBN 9780190844080 (pbk.)
Subjects: LCSH: Conspiracy theories. | Conspiracies.
Classification: LCC HV6275 .C6633 2019 | DDC 001.9—dc23
LC record available at https://lccn.loc.gov/2018012939

CONTENTS

SECTION VII   HOW SHOULD WE LIVE WITH
CONSPIRACY THEORIES?

JOSEPH E. USCINSKI

PREFACE

The study of conspiracy theories is multidisciplinary, and perspectives on the topic vary widely. This will become readily apparent should you read the volume from start to finish (which I recommend, of course!). To include as many perspectives as possible, 31 chapters written by 40 authors lie beyond. What I hope will make this volume valuable to readers is that all of the authors are not only experts but are passionate about the study of conspiracy theories. I hope this volume pushes forward the study of conspiracy theories and leads readers to a better understanding of their own beliefs.

I had no idea what I was getting into eight years ago. My friend and colleague at the University of Miami, Joe Parent, came to me with an idea for a paper: "Conspiracy theories!" he exclaimed, "the causes and consequences of conspiracy theories!" I didn't know if he was being serious or not, and I was inclined to turn him down, hoping that we could find something more mundane to work on together. At the time, conspiracy theories were well off the beaten path of political science. A few scholars were starting to collect data, but there had not been any major publications focusing on conspiracy theories in the discipline as far as I could tell, even going back decades. This meant there would likely be little readymade data available, and as a survey researcher this meant that there would likely not be any easy way to study changes over time. Moving forward with the project would require a serious investment of time and money just to collect data. Despite my misgivings, we moved forward and collected data for three years. What was supposed to be a one-off paper became a book project and then, for me, a research agenda.

In spring 2015 I organized and hosted a large conference on conspiracy theories. Fifty attendees from ten countries and fifteen disciplines attended. It was amazing to see just how varied the perspectives were, from the philosophers to the political scientists, the psychologists to the historians. Having read most of the literature on the topic, I knew that some scholars were more positively inclined toward conspiracy theories than others. I did not know that the dividing line between those who studied them and those who believed them might be so fuzzy at times! To wit, the conference was reported on by both *Reason Magazine* (an expressly anti–conspiracy theory outlet) and by *Global Research* (an outlet brimming with conspiracy theories.) Their viewpoints were obviously very different.

This volume springs partially from that conference. The discussions that took place provided firsthand evidence that more needed to be done to bring together scholars from the varied disciplines. But, it also provided evidence that any such attempt could easily end in disaster. Chasms separated the views of some scholars, and corralling them around shared themes would be akin to herding cats. Being a masochist, I decided to push forward anyway, and in late spring 2015 I fashioned a prospectus that included philosophers, journalists, historians, political scientists, sociologists, communication scholars, psychologists, social psychologists, religion scholars, American Studies scholars, international relations scholars, epistemologists, and a marine chemist.

Over the course of the two and a half years it took to sign the contract with Oxford University Press and deliver the volume, authors and chapters shuffled in and out of the project. Because of natural limitations there are some obvious gaps in the volume, nonetheless I think what is presented here represents a strong step forward. If I had my way, the volume would be more encompassing than it is now, with more authors and more chapters, but perhaps that's what a second edition is for.

Knowing what a challenge this project would be, the editorial board, delegates, and reviewers at Oxford were all adamant that I use a very heavy hand in editing the chapters. This was first and foremost to prevent needless overlap while keeping the chapters substantively tied together. But this was also to bring out the shared themes among the chapters, some of which lie beneath the surface but tie the volume together very nicely. While my university was very supportive of the project—they offered to fund another conference to bring the contributing authors together—these plans unfortunately could not be realized when my lovely wife was diagnosed with cancer. I am happy to report that she endured chemo-radiation like a champ and is on the road to a full recovery. I am grateful to all of this volume's authors, who were tremendously understanding and helpful as my wife and I went through this ordeal. I know I owe all of them a trip to Miami as I originally promised.

Regardless, it has been an overwhelming pleasure working with this group of scholars. Some chapters underwent dozens of revisions since 2015. I believe that readers will appreciate the work that the contributors invested. I certainly do!

The study of conspiracy theories is at a tipping point. The social sciences, in particular, have invested heavily into the topic during the last ten years, and psychologists have been publishing studies almost daily it seems. It is the ideal time for the various perspectives to come together and provide a springboard that will fuel the next ten years of inquiry.

Equally important, conspiracy theories are now a topic of prime social and political importance. Given events all over the world, but particularly in the United States, United Kingdom, and Russia, this volume is necessary. It is designed for those struggling to make sense of our chaotic public sphere. One goal throughout this project was to make the ideas as accessible as possible to the public. Ironically, there exist a lot of conspiracy theories, misinformation, and fake news about conspiracy theories, misinformation, and fake news. For example, it is a common trope on Twitter that the term *conspiracy theory* is itself part of a conspiracy. My hope is that by appealing to a crossover audience, we can make sure that the best information about conspiracy theories is available to the public. (And no, the CIA did not create the term *conspiracy theory* to stop JFK conspiracy theories. If they had, it would have been the worst plot ever, given that by the 1990s upwards of 80 percent of Americans believed those theories.)

I want to begin the acknowledgments by expressing my deepest gratitude to the 39 authors who were kind enough to join this project. The patience and good humor they have shown toward me is much appreciated and a model of professionalism. I have been lucky enough to build friendships with many of them over the last decade.

I need to recognize the scholars who attended my conference in Miami in 2015. The conversations at that meeting not only inspired this volume, but several research agendas. I am very grateful for everyone's participation.

Over the last few years I have had the privilege of associating with some very excellent funded projects which have greatly advanced the study of conspiracy theories. In particular, the Conspiracy & Democracy Project at CRASSH, University of Cambridge, was kind enough to invite Joe Parent and me to be visiting fellows in 2014; it was a pleasure to work with their PIs, postdocs, and staff. The friendships that developed from that experience have been incredibly rewarding. In 2015, Peter Knight and Michael Butter invited me to help brainstorm a proposal they were putting together for a large networking grant. Their proposal was successful (eCost Conspiracy), and it has been a pleasure being involved with Peter, Michael, and their excellent staff. Finally, I need to thank Karen Douglas and her team who I had the good fortune to work with at the University of Kent. It was a pleasure to be a small part of their CREST grant focusing on conspiracy theories and security. These projects have resulted in great scholarship and have done much to bring scholars together.

This is my second trip around the block with Oxford; I could not be more proud to publish in one of the world's most important academic presses. I owe much to Dave McBride and his team for shepherding this project, as well as *American Conspiracy Theories*. Thanks as always, Dave!!

At the University of Miami I need to thank the university administration and the College of Arts & Sciences who have been very supportive of this project. For funding the conference I need to thank Dean Leonidas Bachas, College of Arts & Sciences, and Jon West, Chair of Political Science. University of Miami is a great place to study, work, and live. And of course, I could not have completed this project without the help of my colleagues, particularly while my wife was sick: Casey Klofstad, Joe Parent, Greg Koger, Costa Pischedda, Mike Touchton, Cole Taratoot, Jennifer Connolly, Louise Davidson-Schmich, Merike Blofield, Art Simon, Elton Skendaj, Patrick Thompson, and Fred Frohock. I need to thank my family who have always supported my various enterprises, this being no different. I save my final thank yous, for my wife Leilany, and Benny and Ruby for their unending love and support.

—November 22, 2017

CONTRIBUTORS

Matthew D. Atkinson is an Assistant Professor of Political Science at Long Beach City College. He received his doctorate from UCLA, and his work has been published in the *Journal of Politics, British Journal of Political Science, Quarterly Journal of Political Science, Political Research Quarterly*, and *PS: Political Science & Politics.*

David C. Barker is Director of the Center for Congressional and Presidential Studies and Professor of Political Science, American University, author of *Rushed to Judgment: Talk Radio, Persuasion, and American Political Behavior* and *Representing Red and Blue: How the Culture Wars Change the Way Citizens Speak and Politicians Listen.*

Lee Basham is a Professor of Philosophy at South Texas College and the University of Texas, Rio Grande Valley. One of the first contemporary philosophers to defend the rational legitimacy of conspiracy theorizing, he is author of a number of journal articles and book chapters on epistemic issues in Western information hierarchies, as well as on social science assumptions and practices surrounding the evaluation of conspiracy theorizing and theorists.

Michał Bilewicz is an Associate Professor of Psychology at the University of Warsaw, Poland, where he chairs the Center for Research on Prejudice. His research interests include conspiracy theories, reconciliation processes, dehumanization, prejudice, and collective moral emotions. In 2013 he co-edited a special issue of *Journal of Social Issues* on the consequences of genocide, and in 2015 a volume *The Psychology of Conspiracy* (Routledge).

Preston R. Bost earned his Doctorate in Cognitive Psychology from Vanderbilt University in 1998. He joined the Wabash College faculty two years later, and for fifteen years has taught a wide range of courses focusing on cognitive processes such as visual perception, communication, decision making, and memory. For the last several years, he and his student collaborators have been conducting studies on the psychology of conspiracy beliefs; his most recent article on the topic appears in the January/February 2015 issue of *Skeptical Inquirer* magazine.

Michael Butter has been a Professor of American Literary and Cultural History at the University of Tübingen since 2014. He received his PhD from the University of Bonn in 2007 and his Habilitation from the University of Freiburg in 2012. He is the author of three monographs: *The Epitome of Evil: Hitler in American Fiction, 1939–2002* (New York: Palgrave, 2009), *Plots, Designs, and Schemes: American Conspiracy Theories from the Puritans to the Present* (Berlin/Boston: de Gruyter, 2014), and *Der »Washington-Code«: Zur Heroisierung amerikanischer Präsidenten, 1775–1865* (Göttingen: Wallstein, 2016). He is currently completing an introduction to conspiracy theories, to be published in German by Suhrkamp in 2018. Together with Peter Knight, he is the co-director of the EU COST Action COMPACT [Comparative Analysis of Conspiracy Theories], and co-editor of the Routledge series Research in Conspiracy Theories, and the forthcoming *Routledge Handbook of Conspiracy Theories*.

Aleksandra Cichocka is a Senior Lecturer in Political Psychology at the University of Kent, where she leads the Political Psychology Lab and the MSc in Political Psychology. She is a member of the Governing Council of the International Society of Political Psychology. Her research interests include group identification and inter-group relations (especially the role of collective narcissism), political ideology, and political behavior.

Jay T. Cullen is a Professor of Oceanography at the University of Victoria. His research specialty is the chemistry of metals and artificial radioactive isotopes in seawater and living organisms. He was awarded the Craigdarroch Research Award for Excellence in Knowledge Mobilization and named Provost's Engaged Scholar at the University in recognition of his efforts in science communication, education, and public outreach. Cullen is Project Lead of the Integrated Fukushima Ocean Radionuclide Monitoring project that is investigating the impact of the 2011 Fukushima nuclear disaster on ocean and public health in Canada. He was also shortlisted in the competition, but not ultimately selected, to become one of Canada's next astronauts during the Canadian Space Agency's 2016 Astronaut Recruitment campaign. He lives with his wife and three children in Victoria, British Columbia.

M R. X. Dentith received their PhD in Philosophy from the University of Auckland, where they wrote their dissertation on the epistemology of conspiracy theories. Author of the first single-author book on conspiracy theories by a philosopher (*The Philosophy of Conspiracy Theories*, Palgrave Macmillan 2014), their current research interest is in developing a framework for the investigation of conspiracy theories, focusing on the role of expertise and evidence evaluation in complex epistemic communities. They also have a side project developing an account of how we might talk about the epistemology of secrecy generally, which should probably be kept secret until such time it is ready to be leaked to the public.

Darin DeWitt is an Assistant Professor of Political Science at California State University, Long Beach. He received his PhD from UCLA, and his scholarship has been published in *Celebrity Studies, PS: Political Science and Politics,* and *Urban Affairs Review.*

Nicholas DiFonzo is Professor of Psychology at Rochester Institute of Technology. He has published over 40 articles, book chapters, encyclopedia entries, and technical reports on rumor, and given over 50 presentations and invited addresses at academic conferences on rumor. His books include *Rumor Psychology: Social & Organizational Approaches* (RumorPsychology.com; written with Prashant Bordia), and *The Watercooler Effect: A Psychologist Explores the Extraordinary Power of Rumors* (TheWaterCoolerEffect.com), which has been translated into six different languages. He has been interviewed by NPR, CNN, MSNBC, *The New York Times, The Boston Globe,* and *The Los Angeles Times,* and routinely assists the press in the analysis of rumor and gossip. Dr. DiFonzo has served as an expert trial witness for corporations and government entities on topics involving defamatory workplace rumors, malicious product rumors, and slanderous conspiracy rumors.

Karen M. Douglas is a Professor of Social Psychology at the University of Kent. She studies the psychology of conspiracy theories, including the psychological factors and processes associated with conspiracy belief and the consequences of conspiracy theories for people's political, health, and environmental decisions.

Hugo Drochon is a Postdoctoral Research Fellow on the the Conspiracy and Democracy Project at CRASSH, University of Cambridge. He is the author of *Nietzsche's Great Politics* (Princeton 2016) and is currently working on the history of elites and democracy in the twentieth century.

Asbjørn Dyrendal is Professor in History of Religions at the Norwegian University of Science and Technology. His primary research interests revolve around new religious movements and conspiracy culture, of which the latter currently takes most of his time. Recent work includes *The Invention of Satanism* (coauthor, Oxford University Press 2016) and the forthcoming *Handbook of Conspiracy Theory and Contemporary Religion* (co-editor, Brill 2018).

Adam M. Enders is an Assistant Professor of Political Science at the University of Louisville. He is the coauthor of articles on the interaction between conspiratorial thinking and partisanship appearing in the *British Journal of Political Science* and *Research and Politics,* as well as other articles on mass polarization and value orientations.

Tanya Filer is a Research Fellow at the University of Cambridge, based at the Centre for Research in the Arts, Social Sciences and Humanities (CRASSH). At CRASSH, she is a member of the Leverhulme Trust Conspiracy and Democracy Project. Her current research examines the intersections of media, political communications, and digital technologies, with a regional focus on Latin America. Her work appears in journals including *Information, Communication & Society, International Journal of Politics, Culture, and Society* and *Hispanic Research Journal.* Tanya serves on the Council on the Future of Information and Entertainment at the World Economic Forum.

Ted Goertzel is Emeritus Professor of Sociology at Rutgers University in Camden, NJ, and Adjunct Professor at Washington State Community College in Marietta, Ohio. His publications include "Belief in Conspiracy Theories," (*Political Psychology,* 1994), "The Conspiracy Meme," (*Skeptical Inquirer,* 2011), "Conspiracy Theories in Science" (*EMBO Reports,* 2010) and *Turncoats and True Believers* (Prometheus Press, 1992). He also publishes on Brazilian politics and on artificial general intelligence.

Ginna Husting is Associate Professor of Sociology and the Director of Gender Studies at Boise State University. Her research spans sociology, cultural studies, feminist political theory, and symbolic interaction, focusing on identity change, popular political culture, emotion, Hannah Arendt, and belonging/otherness.

Brian L. Keeley is Professor of Philosophy at Pitzer College in Claremont, California, where he also teaches in the Science, Technology & Society and Neuroscience Programs, in addition to serving as Extended Graduate Faculty in Philosophy at Claremont Graduate University. In addition to having edited a volume in the Cambridge University Press *Contemporary Philosophy in Focus* series on Paul Churchland, he has published over 40 articles, book chapters, and reviews on topics including the philosophy of neuroscience, the nature of the senses, artificial life, and the unusual epistemology of contemporary conspiracy theories.

Peter Knight is a Professor of American Studies at the University of Manchester, U.K., where he is Chair of the Department of English Literature, American Studies, and Creative Writing. He is the author of *Conspiracy Culture: From the Kennedy Assassination to "The X-Files"* (2000), *The Kennedy*

Assassination (2007) and *Reading the Market: Genres of Financial Capitalism in Gilded Age America* (2016), and the editor of *Conspiracy Nation: The Politics of Paranoia in Postwar America* (2002) and *Conspiracy Theories in American History: An Encyclopedia* (2004, 2 vols). Together with Michael Butter, he is the co-director of the EU COST Action COMPACT [Comparative Analysis of Conspiracy Theories], and co-editor of the Routledge series Research in Conspiracy Theories, and the forthcoming *Routledge Handbook of Conspiracy Theories*.

Stephan Lewandowsky is a Cognitive Scientist at the University of Bristol. He was an Australian Professorial Fellow from 2007 to 2012, and was awarded a Discovery Outstanding Researcher Award from the Australian Research Council in 2011. He held a Revesz Visiting Professorship at the University of Amsterdam in 2012, and received a Wolfson Research Merit Award from the Royal Society upon moving to the U.K. in 2013. His research examines people's memory, decision making, and knowledge structures, with a particular emphasis on how people update information in memory. He has published over 140 scholarly articles, chapters, and books, including numerous papers on how people respond to corrections of misinformation and what variables determine people's acceptance of scientific findings.

Marta Marchlewska is a Researcher at the University of Warsaw (Institute for Social Studies and Department of Psychology). Her main research interests focus on psychological underpinnings and consequences of beliefs in conspiracy theories (with particular emphasis on defensive self-esteem, defensive in-group identification, need for cognitive closure, and emotion regulation strategies).

Morgan Marietta is Associate Professor of Political Science, University of Massachusetts Lowell, author of *A Citizen's Guide to American Ideology: Conservatism and Liberalism in Contemporary Politics, The Politics of Sacred Rhetoric: Absolutist Appeals and Political Persuasion, A Citizen's Guide to the Constitution and the Supreme Court: Constitutional Conflict in American Politics,* and *One Nation, Two Realities: Dueling Facts in American Democracy* (forthcoming from Oxford University Press, with David Barker).

Andrew McKenzie-McHarg is a Research Fellow on the Leverhulme-funded project "Conspiracy and Democracy: History, Political Theory and Internet Research" at the University of Cambridge. His interests have extended from anti-Jesuit rhetoric in the Early Modern Period to radical streams of thought in late Enlightenment Germany. He is currently completing a book on the conceptual history of conspiracy theory.

Alfred Moore is a Lecturer in Political Theory at the University of York. He works on political theory, deliberative democracy, and the politics of expertise. He has taught philosophy at University College Cork, was a Marie Curie Research Fellow at the University of British Columbia, and a Democracy Fellow at the Ash Center at Harvard University. Until 2017 he was a research fellow at Cambridge University working on the Leverhulme Trust project "Conspiracy and Democracy: History, Political theory, Internet," which supported the writing of his chapter.

Türkay Salim Nefes completed his PhD at the Sociology Department of the University of Kent. Currently, he is a Research Fellow at the Sociology Department of the University of Oxford. He is also a William Golding Junior Research Fellow at the Brasenose College of the University of Oxford. His main research interest is the diffusion and impacts of conspiracy theories and anti-Semitism. Türkay has published his work on conspiracy rhetoric in various academic journals including *British Journal of Sociology*. On anti-Semitism, he published a book by Palgrave MacMillan, *Online Anti-Semitism in Turkey,* and various journal articles.

Kathryn S. Olmsted is a Professor of History at the University of California, Davis. She is the author of four books: *Right Out of California: The 1930s and the Big Business Roots of Modern Conservatism* (New Press, 2015); *Real Enemies: Conspiracy Theories and American Democracy, World War I to 9/11* (Oxford, 2009); *Red Spy Queen: A Biography of Elizabeth Bentley* (North Carolina, 2002); and *Challenging the Secret Government: The Post-Watergate Investigations of the CIA and FBI* (North Carolina, 1996). She has also co-edited a book on the history of the Central Intelligence Agency and published several journal articles and book chapters that highlight her overlapping areas of expertise: conspiracy theories, government secrecy, espionage, counterintelligence, and anticommunism.

Martin Orr is Professor of Sociology at Boise State University. His research and teaching interests include social inequality, political sociology, globalization, social movements, mass media, and the environment. He has published on anti-globalization movements, the role of oil in social development and foreign policy, sociological theory, and the politics of "conspiracy theory."

Josh Pasek is Assistant Professor of Communication Studies, Faculty Associate in the Center for Political Studies, and Core Faculty for the Michigan Institute for Data Science at the University of Michigan. His research explores how new media and psychological processes each shape political attitudes, public opinion, and political behaviors. Josh also examines issues in the measurement of public opinion including techniques for reducing measurement error and improving population inferences. His work has been published in *Public Opinion Quarterly, Political Communication, Communication Research*, and the *Journal of Communication* among other outlets.

Scott Radnitz is an Associate Professor in the Jackson School of International Studies and Director of the Ellison Center for Russian, East European, and Central Asian Studies at the University of Washington. He does research on post-Soviet politics, covering topics such as protests, authoritarianism, identity, and state building. His book, *Weapons of the Wealthy: Predatory Regimes and Elite-Led Protests in Central Asia*, was published by Cornell University Press in 2010. His publications include *Comparative Politics, Comparative Political Studies, British Journal of Political Science, Journal of Democracy, Foreign Policy*, and *Slate*.

Juha Räikkä is a Professor of Philosophy at the University of Turku, Finland. His research interests concern issues of privacy, justice, forgiveness, self-deception, and minority rights. He has published papers in journals such as *The Monist, Metaphilosophy, The Journal of Political Philosophy, Bioethics, Australasian Journal of Philosophy, Utilitas, Res Publica, The Journal of Value Inquiry*, and *Social Theory and Practice*.

David G. Robertson is Lecturer in Religious Studies at the Open University, and Co-founder of the Religious Studies Project. His work applies critical theory to the study of alternative and emerging religions and conspiracy theories. He is the author of *UFOs, the New Age and Conspiracy Theories: Millennial Conspiracism* (Bloomsbury 2016) and co-editor of the *Handbook of Conspiracy Theories and Contemporary Religion* (Brill 2018).

Steven M. Smallpage is an Assistant Professor of Political Science at Stetson University. He has coauthored work on conspiracy thinking and polarization. His main research areas are American political psychology and the history of political liberalism.

Wiktor Soral is a Researcher at the University of Warsaw (Institute for Social Studies and the Center for Research on Prejudice), Poland. His main research interest focus on the role of negative psychological factors (e.g., lack of control, uncertainty, threat) in processing of social information (related to self, in-group and out-group). In 2015 he co-edited a volume *The Psychology of Conspiracy* (Routledge).

Joseph E. Uscinski is associate professor of political science at the University of Miami College of Arts & Sciences in Coral Gables, FL and co-author of *American Conspiracy Theories* (Oxford, 2014).

Jan-Willem van Prooijen received his PhD from the Department of Social and Organizational Psychology at Leiden University in 2002 on a thesis about procedural justice. At present he is Associate Professor at the Department of Experimental and Applied Psychology at VU Amsterdam, and Senior Researcher at the Netherlands Institute for the Study of Crime and Law Enforcement. His current research interests include conspiracy theories, justice and morality, and ideological extremism.

Jesse Walker is books editor of *Reason Magazine* and author of *The United States of Paranoia: A Conspiracy Theory* (HarperCollins, 2013).

Drew Wegner is a JD Candidate at Harvard Law School.

Michael J. Wood is a Lecturer in Psychology at the University of Winchester. He completed his PhD at the University of Kent in 2013 in the psychology of conspiracy theories, and continues to study how conspiracy theories fit into broader worldviews and how they are communicated via social media and other online discussion platforms.

Ilya Yablokov received his doctoral degree from the University of Manchester in 2014. His research interests include conspiracy theories, nation building, and politics in post-Soviet Russia; the history of post-Soviet journalism; and international broadcasting. His work has been published in a number of peer-reviewed journals. In 2015 he won the British Association for Slavonic and East European Studies Prize for the best peer-reviewed article published by a postgraduate student. His book *Fortress Russia: Conspiracy Theories in the Post-Soviet World* (Cambridge: Polity) will be published in June 2018. Ilya teaches Russian politics, history, and media at the University of Leeds (U.K.).

Conspiracy Theories and
the People Who Believe Them

Down the Rabbit Hole We Go!

JOSEPH E. USCINSKI

Conspiracy theories are not fringe ideas, tucked neatly away in the dark corners of society. They are politically, economically, and socially relevant to all of us. They are intertwined with our everyday lives in countless ways. Conspiracy theories are everywhere, and, like other ideas, they have consequences.

When people believe conspiracy theories they may act on them. In democracies, conspiracy theories can drive majorities to make horrible decisions backed by the use of legitimate force. Conspiracy beliefs can conversely encourage abstention. Those who believe the system is rigged will be less willing to take part in it.[1] Conspiracy theories form the basis for some people's medical decisions; this can be dangerous not only for them but for others as well.[2] For a select few believers, conspiracy theories are instructions to use violence.[3]

There is no time in recorded history without conspiracy theories. Whether we are examining accounts of ancient Rome, medieval Europe, or twentieth century America, conspiracy theories have driven beliefs and action. Scares, panics, purges, and bloodshed have sometimes been the result.

Conspiracy theories are timeless, but this volume is driven by their timeliness. They have become a marker of the early twenty-first century. Conspiracy theories have dominated elite discourse in many parts of the world and have become the rallying cry of major political movements. While studies have yet to determine their salience and impact relative to previous eras, countless scholars and journalists are looking to conspiracy theories to explain our contemporary affairs.

The most alarming developments in world politics are closely interwoven with conspiracy theories. Recent displays of populism, nationalism, xenophobia, and racism are all accompanied by conspiracy narratives. Many world leaders have justified authoritarianism and the consolidation of power with scapegoating and accusations of conspiracy. The Internet, once touted as an instrument of democracy, has been used to manipulate the masses—for profit or power—with fake news consisting mainly of conspiracy theories constructed out of whole cloth. To break the current trends, scholars need to better understand how conspiracy theories create, reinforce, and give cover to humanity's worst impulses.

There are an infinite number of conspiracy theories for people to believe in. Even though it is possible for opinion polls to ask only about a few, current figures suggest that everyone—no matter where they are from—believes in at least one conspiracy theory.[4] I am willing to go further and suggest that everyone believes in at least a few. Some people believe in dozens if not hundreds of conspiracy theories. It is easy to look at the polls showing the numbers of people who believe in faked birth certificates, alien cover-ups, and false flags, and ask, "they don't all really believe in that stuff, do they?" They do.[5]

Our culture is awash in conspiracy theories. Blockbuster movie franchises such as the Jason Bourne series, and popular television shows such as *The Blacklist* and *Stranger Things*, sell fictional accounts of malevolent global conspiracies. One of the most popular shows to air on the Animal Planet network – a network supposedly about real animals – documents a government conspiracy to conceal and kill mermaids.[6] Likewise, the History Channel has seemingly ditched history in favor of *Ancient Aliens*, a show comprised of bizarre conspiracy narratives. Because of their cultural prominence, even society's more scientific spaces must address conspiracy theories. Public intellectuals and science communicators such as Bill Nye, Michael Shermer, Neil deGrasse Tyson, and Brian Dunning continually have to defend science and reason from popular conspiracy theories. Our less scientific spaces are rife with conspiracy theories as well. Social media like Facebook and Twitter, in some instances, favor conspiracy theories over more accurate information.[7] If this were not enough, there is now an annual Conspira-sea cruise where passengers can enjoy fun in the sun, pristine beaches, and nightly UFO watch parties, all while "taking back power from corrupt and greedy institutions."[8]

This volume is about conspiracy theories and the people who believe them. Thirty chapters by forty authors lay beyond this, each attempting to tackle an important aspect of a largely misunderstood phenomenon. Conspiracy theories have existed almost as long as recorded history, yet as Andrew McKenzie-McHarg will show in Chapter 4, the term *conspiracy theory* did not come to be associated with the concept of conspiracy theory until the late nineteenth century. Perhaps the only thing more sluggish than our vernacular has been scholars' efforts to address the topic. The historian Richard Hofstadter and a few other others studied conspiracy theories in the mid-twentieth century, but these efforts did not culminate into a sustained research agenda.[9] In the 1990s cultural scholars reopened the investigation, and as the new century approached, philosophers took an interest as well.[10] But, as Michael Butter and Peter Knight will make clear in the next chapter, a sustained interdisciplinary research agenda did not emerge until around 2007 when psychologists entered the field. Political scientists and other social scientists soon followed, and a decade later new studies addressing the topic are being published nearly every day.

Journalists appear equally interested. Until recently, prestigious news outlets treated conspiracy theories as fringe phenomena, but have since elevated them to top billing. For example, in November 2017, *The New York Times* published an article with the term *conspiracy theories* in it nearly every day. For comparison, the *Times* published zero such articles that same month forty years prior.

Now is the time for scholars to share what we know and to push our understanding of conspiracy theories forward. The following thirty chapters bring together the most promising perspectives with the hope of fueling the next decade of research. Perhaps just as important, each chapter was designed with accessibility in mind: little jargon, no regression tables, and clear concise writing. This volume is written for scholars, journalists, and students, but also for regular folks with an interest in the topic. Most of the chapters synthesize the most important ideas from the extant literature, and provide new directions for research. Other chapters provide riveting first-person accounts. I have taken great care to assemble many of the brightest scholars in the field, and I am quite proud of the results. Over the last decade, the stakes have increased. Current events have jettisoned what was once a cute research topic to prime global importance. To motivate the next thirty chapters, some specifics are in order.

The Election

In 2016, a person with no experience in government was elected president of the United States.[11] Characterizing Donald Trump's campaign were racist and xenophobic comments, Twitter rants, and an audio tape of him favorably discussing sexual assault with the phrase, "Grab'em by the pussy!"[12] But, more so than anything else, his campaign rhetoric was fueled by conspiracy theories.[13]

Among Donald Trump's most notorious conspiracy theories was his accusation that Senator Ted Cruz's father took part in the assassination of President John Kennedy in 1963.[14] In most election years such a bizarre claim would have been enough to disqualify a candidate from contention, but not this time. Trump's endorsement of conspiracy theories never seemed to hurt his chances of winning. He claimed that Syrian refugees were ISIS operatives, that Mexico was sending murderers and rapists to attack innocent Americans, and that President Obama was secretly sympathizing with terrorists. The list goes on.[15] While Trump's conspiracy theories addressed a range of seemingly unrelated matters, they could all be boiled down to one singular overarching conspiracy narrative: political elites sold out the interests of regular Americans to foreign interests.

Throughout the entire process, from the state primaries to the general election, Trump claimed it was rigged.[16] Even months after his unlikely general election victory, Trump continued to assert—despite his success—that the outcome had been sullied by millions of illegal voters.[17]

The conspiracy theories permeating the 2016 election were not due solely to Trump. Bernie Sanders, a socialist who ran for the Democratic nomination, used the word "rigged" frequently in his speeches,[18] claimed foul play when he lost a contest,[19] and campaigned on the idea that a small group of wealthy individuals—the "one percent"—rigged the entire political and economic systems.

Sanders' main conspiracy theory often contradicted itself. He claimed that the wealthy had on the one hand "rigged" the economy, but on the hand were "gambling" in the market.[20] These claims are mutually exclusive and can't both be right. This is the same style of rhetoric Nazi's used against the Jews—their propaganda attacked Jews for being greedy capitalists, but also for being subversive communists. These claims are again mutually exclusive. But, no matter one's economic grievance in Germany under the Nazi regime, one could scapegoat Jewish people (or currently in Sanders' case, wealthy people). Sanders' campaign rhetoric included explicit scapegoating just the same: of the wealthy he claimed, "their greed knows no end," and they "make it hard . . . to survive."[21] Interestingly, both Sanders and Donald Trump were able to garner about forty percent of their party's support during the primary contests (Trump was able to succeed with a plurality because twenty other Republican contenders split the remaining votes).

Sanders was not the only one on his side of the aisle to espouse conspiracy theories during the campaign. Hillary Clinton used conspiracy theories on occasion when it suited her. While she argued that Donald Trump was unfit to be president because he was a conspiracy theorist, Clinton also claimed that Trump was a part of a powerful Russian conspiracy.[22] "There's something he's hiding; we'll guess, we'll keep guessing at what it might be," she said during one of the presidential debates.[23]

Clinton's accusations of coordination between Russia and the Trump campaign have remained salient for more than two years since they first arose, and have become a rallying cry for Democrats who feel that the election was rigged against them. This is also ironic given that Democratic elites were certain going into the election that rigging could not possibly take place.[24] Despite their reassurances, a YouGov poll taken after the election in 2016 showed that an astounding fifty percent of Democrats believed that Russia had hacked the voting machines despite there being no evidence of such.[25]

Since Trump took office, he has been dogged by conspiracy theories. To some, this seems like karma: Trump made headlines in 2011 suggesting that Barack Obama was a foreign usurper with a phony birth certificate. Just as Obama had to spend time, effort, and precious political capital fighting off such accusations, Trump now has to do the same, the only difference being that this conspiracy theory could have serious legal ramifications due to the appointment of a special prosecutor, Robert Mueller. The investigation thus far (May 2018) has turned up little direct evidence to implicate Trump in a conspiracy to rig the election with Russia, but, as with other conspiracy theories, evidence is not one of the main factors driving the public's beliefs on this matter.

Like other conspiracy theorists, Trump–Russia conspiracy theorists have been playing tennis without a net. No matter what the special prosecutor eventually turns up, conspiracy theorists will claim that they were right all along (or, if nothing turns up, they will probably claim that Mueller is corrupt as well). They have put forward hundreds of different conspiracy theories, many of which are self-contradicting, and many of their predictions have already gone unfulfilled.[26] To name but two examples, immediately after the election, liberal economist Paul Krugman accused FBI Director James Comey and the FBI of conspiring with Russia to rig the election.[27] It was peculiar, then, that Krugman and other Democrats were upset when Trump eventually fired Comey. After he gave unflattering testimony about the president in front of Congress, the conspiracy theories accusing Comey were forgotten only to be replaced by new conspiracy theories in which Comey was a hero.[28] Democrats were delighted to uncover evidence showing that Jared Kushner had sought out a back channel to communicate with Russia in January 2017. The only problem was that if the Trump family was seeking a communication channel with Russia in January, it meant they did not have one prior to the election—as is usually alleged— in 2016.[29] Since it contradicted the collusion narrative, this story seemed to disappear. False predictions and demonstrably wrong theories continue to pile up, nonetheless Trump–Russia conspiracy theorists continue to froth at the mouth.

It is odd as well that Russia has become such a bogeyman for Democrats, given that in 2012 President Obama and other Democrats jeered Republican Presidential Candidate Mitt Romney for thinking that Russia posed a threat to the United States.[30] But, in consideration of the fact that their nominee accused Trump of collusion with Russia during the campaign, and that they lost control of the White House and Congress, it is no surprise that Democrats are prone to conspiracy theories about Trump–Russia. Being on the losing end of a power asymmetry makes people prone to conspiracy theorizing. Elite cues drive the specifics of those theories, and Democratic elites and liberal media outlets have been more than willing to take advantage of Democrats' anxieties.[31]

Trump and his supporters have fought the accusations of collusion with their own conspiracy theories: that Mueller's investigation is rigged, that Obama wiretapped Trump Tower during the campaign, that Clinton and the FBI conspired against the Trump campaign, and that the deep state allowed Clinton to escape responsibility for her poor handling of classified emails.[32] It might seem odd, given that they won, that Trump supporters have trafficked in so many conspiracy theories. However, Trump built a coalition by appealing more to conspiracy theory than to partisanship; therefore his supporters are naturally using conspiracy theories to fight what they see as a conspiracy against them.[33] Like tribbles, each new conspiracy theory spontaneously breeds more. The growing number of opposing conspiracy theories have piled up and obscured truth.

Reverberation

The numerous accusations of conspiracy since the election has sown discord and confusion. Conspiracy theories have been reverberating against each other, in some instances quite loudly. As if in a feedback loop, those accused of conspiracy turn to conspiracy theories as a defense mechanism. This makes judging the veracity of any one claim difficult. It has created an information environment that is at best unclear and at worst incomprehensible.

Election Rigging

When Democrats lost the 2000 presidential election in a contest decided by the Supreme Court, they believed they had been cheated.[34] Opinion polls showed that almost half of Democrats thought the process had been rigged against them. Another demoralizing loss in 2004 led Democrats to conclude again that they had been swindled, and polls showed that many Democrats thought Ohio, the pivotal state in the election, had been rigged.[35] In 2008, their herculean mobilization efforts were successful at bringing Barack Obama to the White House, but this led Republicans to believe that Obama's victory came at the hands of crooked registration practices.[36] There was strong evidence that ACORN, a community activist group associated with the Obama campaign, had turned in dubious registration forms, but no evidence that this was an attempt to influence the election.[37] After Obama's reelection in 2012, Republicans believed that ACORN had rigged that election even though, ironically, ACORN had been shuttered since 2010.[38]

Using conspiracy theories, Republicans were able to leverage Obama's successes into their own victories. Arguing that Obama's health care plan contained "death panels," Republicans gained control over the House and many governorships and state houses in 2010.[39] Republicans used this control to fight back against the supposed rigging by passing restrictive voter identification laws. Democrats, believing that these laws would disadvantage voters in their coalition, accused the Republicans of conspiring to disenfranchise citizens.[40]

As the 2016 general election approached, election integrity became an election issue. Trump argued that the election would be "rigged," and Democrats responding to Trump argued that it would not be rigged. But, after Trump's surprising victory, Democrats changed their minds and decided that the election had been rigged—by Trump and his family, Vladimir Putin, Russian hackers, WikiLeaks, fake news, social media outlets, James Comey, the FBI, the RT Channel, and third-party candidates. Those on the losing side immediately initiated a recount, claiming that Russia may have interfered with the voting machines in key states. Jill Stein, the nominee of the Green Party, spearheaded the effort which raised seven million dollars in a week.[41] In response to the demand for a recount, Trump tweeted that the election was indeed rigged, but that the rigging was done by three million illegal aliens who voted against him.[42] The recount did not proceed, and Democrats have gone on to accuse Jill Stein of being a Russian agent herself.[43] Now, ironically, Democrats seem to agree with Trump's campaign message that political elites had sold out the interests of regular Americans to foreign interests. In this case the foreign interests are Russia, and the elites are the Trump administration.

In this environment, conspiracy theories rebound off of each other, interact with actual events, and feed off of what seem like real attempts at conspiracy. Conspiracy theories about Hillary Clinton's health demonstrate how this can happen rapidly.

Clinton's Illness

During the 2016 election Donald Trump accused Hillary Clinton of being too old and weak to handle the rigors of office. To underscore these claims, Trump campaign surrogates claimed that Clinton was not only hiding severe illness such as AIDS, epilepsy, heart problems, and dysphasia, but was on the verge of death.[44] Roger Stone, a Trump advisor, claimed that Clinton had to be carted off the stage with an oxygen mask after the first presidential debate.[45] The insinuation was that the media was complicit in hiding Clinton's infirmity from the public so as to sway the election.

The accusations put Clinton on the defensive and led her to hide whatever normal health problems a presidential candidate might face. During a 9/11 memorial, for example, she fainted due to dehydration, heat exposure, and pneumonia. Rather than skip the event, the conspiracy theories led her to conceal her illness and attend an outdoor memorial in the heat. But, given an inch, conspiracy theorists took it a mile. Once her illness was exposed, further conspiracy theories claimed she was on the verge of death, had a body double, or was already dead.[46] Conspiracy theorists charged that the Clinton who emerged from care had a smaller hip size and different fitting pantsuit, and was therefore a doppelganger.

To address the rumors, Clinton booked an appearance on the late-night Jimmy Kimmel Show where she opened a pickle jar as a testament to her vigor. The next day, conspiracy theories contended that the pickle jar was already open.[47] Clinton had to continually respond to the conspiracy theories, sometimes in ways that seemed as if she was herself conspiring.

Bernie Sanders

While Bernie Sanders dismissed the salient Clinton email scandal, his rhetoric took on a decidedly conspiratorial tone during the primaries. Consonant with his "one percent" conspiracy theories, Sanders attacked Clinton's involvement with Wall Street interests, suggesting that she was hiding her true plans to enrich the wealthy interests. The Sanders campaign also argued that the Democratic establishment was intent on thwarting his candidacy with a "rigged" primary.[48]

Immediately prior to the Democratic nominating convention, WikiLeaks released a series of hacked emails detailing pro-Clinton sentiment within the DNC. These emails made the process appear "fixed" to many Sanders' supporters. To move discussion away from accusations of rigging, Sanders' opening speech at the convention was perhaps his first to exclude the word "rigged" (he used the clunkier term "oligarchy" instead.)

The email dump led Debbie Wasserman-Schultz, head of the DNC at the time, to step down. Clinton, rather than distancing herself from the scandal, immediately hired Wasserman-Schultz into her campaign. This gave the appearance of a quid pro quo. Adding to this, further emails were released showing that Donna Brazille, CNN commentator and DNC vice-chair who replaced Wasserman-Schultz as head of the DNC, had provided advance debate questions to the Clinton team during the primaries. When asked about giving such an unfair advantage to Clinton, Brazille claimed that the emails were a fraud: "As a Christian woman I understand persecution, but I will not stand here and be persecuted because your information is totally false."[49] A few weeks later Brazille copped to the accusations, saying, "[A]mong the many things I did in my role as a Democratic operative and DNC vice chair . . . was to share potential town hall topics with the Clinton campaign."[50] A year later, Brazille showed another change of heart when she claimed that the Clinton machine had dominated the DNC and rigged the primary process.[51] Brazille was, peculiarly, either vice-chair or chair of the DNC at the time of the supposed rigging and actively took part in it.

Republicans had concocted their own theories about the WikiLeaks hacks. They alleged that a DNC staffer named Seth Rich, who had died under mysterious circumstances, was actually a whistleblower who allowed the DNC's servers to be breached. Republicans, particularly Fox News Channel's Sean Hannity, pushed the theory that the Clintons had Rich murdered.

In the above instances, partisan animosities, political interests, fear, and actual events combined into a toxic soil that is fertile for little more than conspiracy theorizing. As the conspiracy theories take root, they pollenate the environment leading to more animosity, defensive actions, and anxiety, which then blossom into more conspiracy theories. These cycles have such an organic quality that one wonders how their growth can be impeded.

Conspiracy Theories across the Globe

The United States is not the only place where conspiracy theories have overtaken public discourse. Only months before the November American election, the United Kingdom held a referendum on its membership in the European Union

(EU). The "Brexit" vote was driven in part by conspiracy theories suggesting, among other things, that the EU was hiding further plans of integration, that the EU was building an army and that the referendum vote would be rigged. The political and economic impacts of leaving the EU were shrouded in an air of conspiracy; prominent Leavers told voters not to believe the experts. On the day of the vote, Leave voters were urged to vote in pen rather than pencil so their votes could not be erased. Hugo Drochon will demonstrate in Chapter 22 that EU conspiracy theories had been percolating for some time and laid the blueprint for the Brexit vote. Should the United Kingdom actually leave the EU (as it is currently poised to do), the conspiracy theories that motivated Leave voters will have shaken the very foundation of the international order.

Terror attacks in France and Germany provided fertile ground for conspiracy theories to blossom. The November 2015 attacks in Paris that left 130 dead, as well as the attack on Charlie Hebdo, led many to suspect that the attacks were not what they seemed. A sizable portion of French people continue to suspect that the government rather than Al-Qaeda was behind the attacks.[52] In response, the French government is currently looking to supplement children's education so as to inoculate them against conspiracy beliefs. In Germany, conspiracy theories have swirled around similar events, but rather than accusing the government of orchestrating attacks, some have accused Angela Merkel's government of covering up attacks by refugee Muslims because such attacks run counter to the government's immigration narrative.[53] Terror attacks attract conspiracy theories because they become salient in the information environment, so these instances are not extraordinary in that sense. But, the immigration and integration of Muslims is an important policy issue for all of Europe, and conspiracy theories play a large role in driving the politics behind it. Poland has eschewed all immigration from the Middle East and, as Wiktor Soral and colleagues will explain in Chapter 25, seems to be experiencing a conspiracy theory renaissance.

Since Russia's opening in the 1990s, scholars have observed conspiracy theorizing as a norm of understanding, where accusations of conspiracy are traded between conflicting elites. Chapters 24 and 25 by Scott Radnitz and Ilya Yablokov respectively, address conspiracy theorizing in Russia. Unlike more Westernized states, Russia retains many elements of a closed society, and their politics often justify conspiracy beliefs. For example, Russian agents conspired to rig athletic competitions using banned substances. When this plot was exposed, the actors who orchestrated the scheme turned up mysteriously dead.[54] This of course led to more accusations of conspiracy.

In Turkey, suspicions of political interference by outsiders (Jews, "the interest rate lobby," and foreign powers) are a part of mainstream politics and intertwined with Turkey's history. A failed attempt to overthrow the president in 2016 led to a government crackdown on all those suspected of taking part in the conspiracy. Unsurprisingly, the government is relying on conspiracy theories to justify its widening suppression of opposition parties and critical speech. Chapter 26 by Turkay Nefes examines Turkish politicians' rationale for using conspiracy rhetoric.

Moving south of the equator, Argentina's former president Kirchner recently turned to anti-Semitic conspiracy theories to explain away her alleged role in covering up the bombing of a Jewish community center in 1994. Tanya Filer expounds upon Kirchner's use of conspiracy theories in Chapter 27. Kirchner implied that Jews "contribute to financial attacks" and "destabilize governments."[55] The conspiracy theories, meant to deflect the accusations against her, did not stop a judge from signing an arrest warrant.

I could continue around the globe, but the point is made. Conspiracy theories are everywhere.

Policy Consequences

Conspiracy theories took an easily won American presidential election away from an experienced establishment candidate and gave it to a vulgar political novice, and they tilted the scales of the "Brexit" EU referendum away from the expected "stay" position to "leave." In both of these instances, conspiracy theories gained traction across traditional party lines confusing partisan elites and signaling the potential for realignment.

Conspiracy theories have been the rhetoric of choice for leaders in states moving toward (or already with) authoritarian control. Recent examples include Putin in Russia, Erdogan in Turkey, the Law and Justice Party in Poland, Nicolas Maduro in Venezuela, and Duerte in the Philippines.

Beyond shaping the composition and nature of governments, conspiracy theories exert a profound effect on policy choices. Sometimes this is a top-down process by which political elites use conspiracy rhetoric to justify or propagate particular policies; in other instances conspiracy theories can percolate from the bottom up, and affect policy through direct democracy or by influencing the actions of otherwise nonconspiratorial elites. Sometimes elites and the masses fall victim to conspiracy theories simultaneously. Regardless of their origin, policies driven by conspiracy theories can have horrible consequences.

That the climate is warming due to human activity is a scientific certainty, however political progress to address the problem has been stymied (particularly in the United States) by conspiracy theorists who believe climate change is a hoax concocted by scheming interests (i.e., scientists, communists, and the United Nations).[56] Given that the United States is one of the largest carbon polluters, how it addresses the conspiracy theories about climate change will determine if the world will be able to mitigate the looming catastrophe.

In many parts of the world, conspiracy theories about genetically modified foods (GMOs) have driven detrimental policies. In Europe, conspiracy theories and financial interests have succeeded in convincing governments to enact anti-GMO importation policies.[57] This has been a boon to local producers, but it has inhibited producers, particularly in Africa, who could increase crop yields significantly from the use of modified seeds. There is a cost to health and lives because of these policies. According to recent research, had Kenya adopted GM corn in 2006, between "440 and 4,000 lives could theoretically have been saved. Similarly, Uganda had the possibility in 2007 to introduce the black sigatoka–resistant banana, thereby potentially saving between 500 and 5,500 lives over the past decade."[58] Prior to this, Africa put millions of lives at risk because it would not accept GM crop donations from the United States, even though millions of people were facing extreme hunger.[59] Today in the United States, Vermont has implemented GM labeling regulations that have increased food cost while decreasing choice. As additional states consider bending to conspiracy theories, food is likely to become more costly, particularly for those who are already food-insecure.[60]

In Africa, the fear of AIDS has been eclipsed by the fear of medicines for preventing AIDS.[61] The former health minister of South Africa, Manto Tshabalala-Msimang, claimed that the country's AIDs crisis was caused by "a global conspiracy intent on reducing the continent's population."[62] The government supported the use of massage and vitamins as a more appropriate cure of the disease because, they contended, the pharmaceuticals intended to cure it were also part of a malevolent Western plot. Estimates suggest as many as 300,000 are needlessly dead because of these theories.[63]

Outbreaks of diseases once thought eradicated have recently experienced a resurgence. Unfounded fears of the MMR vaccine have driven communities in the United States, United Kingdom, and elsewhere to refuse vaccines for themselves and their children.[64] This has led to mounting deaths across the globe.[65] Parents are also eschewing the HPV vaccine for their daughters at the urging of unfounded conspiracy theories.[66] Michelle Bachman, a former Congresswoman and presidential candidate, wrongly claimed in a nationally televised debate that HPV vaccination policy was part of a conspiracy and that the vaccine made people "retarded."[67] Although a vaccine for the emerging Zika virus has yet to be developed, conspiracy theorists have already decided that it is part of a dark conspiracy, to defraud, experiment on, or poison the public.[68]

The introduction of fluoride into the water supply has long been a thorny issue for some, owing largely to conspiracy theories suggesting the government is using fluoride as a method for pacifying the populace to institute totalitarian or communist rule. In Canada, the Calgary City Council decided to remove fluoride from the local drinking water in 2011. This was against all of the scientific evidence and dire warnings from dentists (who have an obvious financial interest in creating more tooth decay.) Studies only a few years later showed that tooth decay in children had increased significantly compared to nearby Edmonton that continued to fluoridate.[69] In the United States, Portland, OR is one of the few major cities to not fluoridate.

When the city council voted to begin doing so, left-wing conspiracy theories became fuel for an intense political battle. Whereas opposition to fluoridation in the 1950s stemmed from antigovernment conservatives, Portland's opposition sprang from those on the left and included Ralph Nader, the NAACP, and the Sierra Club. Portland voted to overturn its city council in favor of jettisoning fluoride, much to the dismay of scientists, dentists, and teeth.[70] Nonetheless, Portland's longstanding resistance to fluoride is instructive. Going back to 1956, observers noted that science and experts were often powerless at the hands of conspiracy theories. As the *Oregonian* noted in 1956 after ten of twelve fluoridation measures across the state were defeated:

> It would appear the backers of this new aid to dental health made the classic military error of underestimating the enemy . . . They relied too heavily on the presumed confidence of voters in the AMA, ADA, U.S. Public Health Service, and state and local health authorities who have given fluoridation their blessing. . . . [but] after [fluoride opponents] fire their counterbarrage of speeches, leaflets, mailing pieces and newspaper ads, the poor voter is baffled and uncertain. The strategy of fluoridation's foes is to put its friends on the defensive, to create doubts in the voters' minds. Once this is accomplished, they know people are likely to vote to maintain the status quo.[71]

This episode fits a pattern of localities relying on conspiracy theories rather than authoritative sources of information. Bicycle sharing programs in Colorado, land-use policies in California, papaya regulations in Hawaii, and mosquito abatement programs in Florida have all faced backlash due to conspiracy beliefs.[72] In each of these cases, wrong information and underlying suspicion lead to casual accusations of conspiracy.

Violence

In June 2017, James Thomas Hodgkinson, a Democrat and supporter of left-wing causes, walked onto a baseball field where Republican members of Congress were practicing for a charity game and began firing a rifle. Majority Whip Steve Scalise was shot along with a few others. Hodgkinson, who died in the ensuing shootout, was purported to have been animated by Trump–Russia conspiracy theories. In December 2016 Edgar Maddison Welch fired a rifle inside a popular Washington DC pizza parlor. He was investigating "Pizzagate," a conspiracy theory alleging that DNC officials ran a child sex ring. Welch, who eventually pleaded guilty to weapons charges, was surprised not to find evidence supporting his theory.

Government agents can also fall victim to conspiracy theory–driven impulses. In the early 1990s, federal agents believed that Randy Weaver and his family were part of a conspiracy to overthrow the government.[73] So, they conspired against Weaver, first by sending in an informant to goad him into selling a sawed off shotgun in violation of law. After arresting and attempting, unsuccessfully, to turn him into an informant, the government released him. Sometime later in 1992, FBI agents began a surveillance effort which turned into an eleven-day siege at his residence in Ruby Ridge, Idaho. By the end of the siege (which included a military-size force complete with tanks), FBI agents had shot and killed Weaver's wife and young son. The FBI then conspired to cover up those crimes.[74] A more drawn-out episode is that of the drug war in the United States. President Richard Nixon began the government's war against drug users, dealers, and smugglers, partially for political reasons and partially due to his conspiracy beliefs.[75] Nixon believed that African Americans, Jews, college students, and antiwar protesters were conspiring against the country (and against him!).[76] So, he decided to conspire against them by starting a bloody and decades-long drug war. The cost is "about $40 billion a year at home and abroad. . . [it] has imprisoned currently up to 400,000 people on drug-related charges—the vast majority of them nonviolent offenders."[77]

In the above examples, conspiracy theories occasionally are the proximate reason for why their adherents commit violence. But in other instances, those who commit violence believe in conspiracy theories but are not necessarily motivated by them. Robert Dear killed three at a Planned Parenthood in Colorado Springs in 2015; he had encouraged his neighbors to install metal roofing on their houses to prevent government spying. The Boston Marathon bombers, Tamerlan and Dzhokhar Tsarnaev, who killed three and injured 264, accused the U.S. government of complicity in the 9/11 bombings. Jared Lee Loughner, who killed six and severely wounded Representative Gabrielle Giffords in 2011, held similar beliefs—as did John Patrick Bedell, who killed two police officers in 2010. Osama bin Laden's library included books about Illuminati, Federal Reserve, and, ironically, 9/11 conspiracy theories.[78]

The relationship between conspiracy theories and violent action is complicated, and researchers are only beginning to examine its complexity. Perhaps those who commit violence would do so regardless of their conspiracy beliefs. Maybe conspiracy theories are only one of many motivations for violence. Researchers don't yet know. But the latest findings suggest that those most likely to believe in conspiracy theories are also (1) more likely to support violence against the government, (2) more likely to oppose gun control measures, and (3) more likely to agree that it's acceptable to engage in conspiracies themselves to achieve goals.[79] It's not hard to see how the approval of violence, lax gun laws, and secret plotting could form a toxic combination driving some to fight fire with fire.

Conversely, violent events can inspire conspiracy theories. The assassinations of President Kennedy, the 9/11 and 7/7 attacks, and the mass shootings in Las Vegas, Aurora, and Sandy Hook Elementary School have all provided fodder for

committed conspiracy theorists. The conspiracy theorizing seems to be in proportion to the amount of news coverage an event receives, and can inspire further violence. The horrific shooting at Sandy Hook Elementary School in Newtown, CT,
took the lives of twenty-six students and teachers. Authorities reported that the
shooter was a disturbed lone gunman, but conspiracy theorists disagree. Some suggest that no one actually died at Sandy Hook and that the grieving families cashed
in on a phony tragedy.[80] Others suggested that the government staged the shooting
as a "false flag" attack to build support for gun control legislation. Some of these
conspiracy theorists took matters into their own hands by harassing the victims'
family members.[81]

Returning to Ruby Ridge, Randy Weaver believed the government was
conspiring against him, and government agents believed that Weaver was
conspiring against them. This led the government to actually conspire against
Weaver and his family by killing his innocent wife and son and then covering up
those activities. A year later, conspiracy theories drove the government siege on
the Branch Davidian compound in Waco, TX. The incidents at Ruby Ridge and
Waco drove Timothy McVeigh's conspiracy theories about government; these
conspiracy theories led McVeigh to destroy the Oklahoma City Federal Building.
Extremist groups to this day continue to use the incidents at Ruby Ridge and
Waco as evidence of their conspiracy theories and as justification for their sometimes violent actions.[82] This in turn drives government conspiracy theories about
these groups. The cycle is likely to continue.

The Battle of Ideas

Conspiracy theories face intense resistance from the establishment. They are generally criticized and condemned (unless those theories are themselves propagated
by the establishment). The vast majority of establishment news sources discredit conspiracy theories as crazy, outlandish, and bizarre.[83] While conspiracy
theories—especially in 2017—occupy significant news space, one of the more
frequent topics is "why do people believe this stuff?"[84] For example, mainstream
journalists and politicians did not investigate the supposed child sex ring after
finding out about the Pizzagate conspiracy theories. Instead, the establishment
condemned the theories as ludicrous and has been more concerned with those
who believe the theories.

Conspiracy theories, once they come into conflict with establishment accounts,
are engaging in a battle of ideas with mainstream institutions. It isn't just that conspiracy theorists have a different set of explanations, it is that their explanations
call into question our knowledge-generating and knowledge-disseminating
institutions. The establishment, in order to maintain control and function, must
specify the parameters under which society is to operate; this includes stipulating

the relevant facts and the methods of discovering those facts. Conspiracy theories undermine the establishment by providing alternative facts, realities, and ways of knowing.

The bedrock factual matters people should be able to agree upon—such as facts about how society is organized—are often contested by conspiracy theorists. Conspiracy theories posit alternative views in which politics is a conspiracy orchestrated by powerful string pullers and not a hodgepodge of competing groups vying for favorable treatment. Some versions of these theories are rather commonplace. Trump's espoused worldview is one in which political elites are the pawns of shadowy foreign interests. Bernie Sanders suggests that the entire political and economic systems have been rigged by a small number of wealthy individuals. For both Trump and Sanders, conspiracies determine political and economic outcomes. Many on the left contend that the billionaire Koch brothers control the entire Republican and Libertarian parties; many on the right believe that billionaire philanthropist George Soros controls the DNC and its affiliated left-wing groups. For many Brexiters, the EU was not an institutional arrangement that eased trade, immigration, and political disputes; it was a conspiracy to sap money from the United Kingdom to Brussels, construct an EU army, or help spread Islam across the continent. Readers may very well sympathize with a few of the preceding theories. But as we move toward the fringe, the conspiracy theories will, for most, seem more distant from reality.

American conspiracy theorist Alex Jones contends that a network of global elites control or are attempting to control the planet. Jones' relationship with Trump has brought his show, InfoWars, from being somewhat apolitical toward a pro-Trump, anti-left bend.[85] Author Jim Marrs agrees with Jones on the basics – he refers to these global elites as the GOD Syndicate (Guns, Oil, Drugs) – and argues that they are attempting to depopulate the planet. Marrs' account leans a bit to the left – he sees corporate owners as the villains and builds his argument by drawing on left-leaning economists Thomas Piketty and Paul Krugman.[86] From there he espouses a very dark outlook:

> We now live in a culture of death and decay that has been imposed upon us by a small group of wealthy elites that publicly espouses involuntary population reduction. We're being killed by chemicals, genetically modified organisms (GMO's), dyes, additives, plastics, tainted water, and polluted air, . . We are not aware of these things because precious few recognize that we are being psychologically programmed by a mass media controlled by a mere handful of corporate owners . . . [This] ensures that we cannot protest the population reduction that threatens our very lives.[87]

Former politician and political activist Lyndon LaRouche is just as concerned about the coming apocalypse, but posits a different set of elite conspirators. LaRouche has built a cult following with his conspiracy theories focusing on the Queen of England.[88] From LaRouchePAC:

> [T]he 9/11 attacks on Manhattan (and Washington) were run by the British system, and only the Queen, under that system, had the authority to give the go-ahead. But what supplements that case in a most fascinating way, is that Lyndon LaRouche was able in essence to forecast the 9/11 attacks a full eight months before they occurred.[89]

It is unfortunate that no one heeded LaRouche's prophetic warnings. Prior to this, LaRouche spent the 1980s spreading AIDS conspiracy theories, which were almost successful in urging California to adopt a measure that would have potentially quarantined those with HIV.[90]

British conspiracy theorist David Icke adds a touch of the paranormal. He begins with the rather mundane assertion (among conspiracy theorists) that a "sinister network of families" (including the Queen) secretly control humanity.

> The Republican and Democratic parties, and their equivalents around the world, are owned by Illuminati bloodlines through the 'transnational corporation' structure of the secret society web . . . The Rothschild Illuminati networks . . . run the government no matter who 'wins' an election.[91]

Icke then points to less mundane villains: "non-human entities" which he refers to as reptilian elites.

> It became clear to me that the Illuminati bloodlines are human-reptilian hybrids, and the offspring of a race of reptilian humanoids that are widely described in ancient legends and accounts. The Rothschilds and the bloodline family network obsessively and incessantly interbreed because they are seeking to retain their 'special' genetics which would be quickly diluted by breeding with the general population . . . The reptilian race covertly controlling human society is from a dimension of reality very close to this one, but beyond visible light and that's why we don't see them. They can move in and out of visible light, however, and there are reptilian 'cities' and bases inside the Earth. Some top-secret underground military bases connect with them. The hybrid bloodlines, like the Rothschilds, serve their agenda on the surface and within visible light.[92]

Icke's Reptilian Elite theory, while not convincing many in public opinion polls, has had a strong cultural impact.[93] Icke frequently sells out small arenas for day-long events in which the audience is invited to dance away the conspiracy. Former

Minnesota Governor Jesse Ventura's television show *Conspiracy Theory* featured an episode in which Jesse and his team attempted to find the underground reptilian base with the use of a Native American tracker and a psychic channeler. Their efforts were unsuccessful, even though they had tested weapons for shooting the reptilians should they have encountered them.[94]

The list of entities thought to rule the world in various conspiracy theories goes on. Many posit that pop stars such as Beyonce, Jay Z, or Kanye West are part of a secret group that rules the world.[95] Other theories believe that the lost city of Atlantis, aliens, secret societies, corporations, Jews, the United Nations, World Trade Organization, or some other group really rules the world. Obviously, all of these explanations run counter to authoritative accounts.

Other conspiracy theories accept the standard accounts of our basic political structures, but challenge the establishment in more specific areas. Some challenge accounts from government sources. Conspiracy theories about the Kennedy assassination, 9/11, and Sandy Hook contested the Warren Commission, 9/11 Commission, and the Connecticut State Attorney's office, respectively. Other conspiracy theories challenge scientific consensuses such as those around climate change, GM foods, and vaccines. When establishment accounts and conspiracy theories meet, there is a clash of ideas which have to battle for supremacy. The establishment is much better suited for these battles – it has money, power, visibility, and expertise on its side. With this said, conspiracy theories occasionally win the battle for public opinion; majorities consistently believe in JFK assassination theories and that GM foods are dangerous.[96]

These battles, however, can inflict incalculable collateral damage because conspiracy theorists are often wrong and therefore impede critical progress. Scientists who develop and study genetically modified foods agree that these foods are safe and better for the environment.[97] However, conspiracy theorists contend that the corporations that develop these foods are bad actors who conspire to hide the dangerous side-effects of their foods.[98] A common trope is that the biotechnology company Monsanto has bought off all of the researchers who study GM food so as to hide the true effects of consuming it.[99] Conspiracy theorists butt directly into government agencies who certify that the foods are safe; so conspiracy theorists expand their theories to claim that the government agencies have been captured by Monsanto.[100] As the evidence grows for the safety of GM foods, the conspiracy must get bigger and bigger so as to discount it.[101] This is no different with climate change. Conspiracy theorists claimed that climate change was a hoax by a few scientists who had scant evidence. Thirty years later, the evidence has only strengthened, and about ninety-seven percent of climate scientists agree that the climate is changing due to human activity.[102] Climate change conspiracy theorists originally claimed that there was no scientific agreement on climate change; when confronted with the size of the consensus, they claimed that the ninety-seven percent figure was faked.[103] Further, when studies showed that their denial of climate change was due to conspiracy thinking rather than evidence, conspiracy theorists claimed that those studies were faked.[104] The conspiracy theories necessarily had to enlarge and impugn more and more of the establishment. The debate over climate change has altered the discussion from "what should we do about climate change," to "are the scientists part of a hoax." Climate scientists are put on the defensive trying to answer charges of conspiracy.[105] In Chapter 10, Stephan Lewandowsky discusses his experiences with climate change conspiracy theorists, specifically how conspiracy theorists were able to strong-arm an academic journal into retracting an academic paper.[106] As Lewandowsky's account will show, conspiracy theorists occasionally lack self-awareness in that they deny being conspiracy theorists but freely accuse others of engaging in wide-ranging conspiracies. In Chapter 9, marine chemist Jay Cullen recounts how conspiracy theorists harassed him because he did not find evidence of radiation in the coastal waters of Canada. They were convinced that the Fukishima radiation leak had poisoned the ocean and that Cullen had engaged in a conspiracy to cover up the disaster.

On the other end, conspiracy theorists often find themselves underneath the heel of the establishment boot. As detailed in Chapter 12 by Steven Smallpage, vocal conspiracy theorists risk losing their friends, families, reputations, and livelihoods when challenging the establishment with their ideas. James Tracy, for example, claims that he was fired from his tenured position at Florida Atlantic University because of his advocacy of Sandy Hook conspiracy theories. Tracy sued the university in federal court, ironically, claiming it had conspired with the faculty union to violate his first amendment rights. He lost his case at trial and his initial appeal was denied.[107]

Those with a strong conspiracy worldview tend to make less money.[108] While the causal relationship between income and conspiracy thinking is not yet fully determined, James Tracy's ordeal suggests that high-profile employers that offer high incomes tend to eschew vocal conspiracy theorists. Imagine you were charged with hiring a public representative for a Fortune 500 company: would you hire a person who publicly espoused beliefs in Sandy Hook conspiracy theories?

This aversion varies across conspiracy theories and theorists: for example, espousing conspiracy theories about the Kennedy assassination will not arouse suspicion in most jobs because majorities of Americans believe in these largely benign theories (Kennedy theories may disqualify you from a job at the CIA, however). Some employers may even value certain conspiracy theories. Expressing anti-GMO conspiracy theories might get one hired and promoted at a health food chain, for example. But in general, the establishment sets the boundaries of acceptable ideas and excludes people and ideas that do not conform. There are, of course, good reasons for this.

How could a university biology department function with professors who believed that evolution was a conspiracy among scientists? How many people would invest their savings with a financial planner who believed the markets were rigged by the Jews? Would stock owners be willing to entrust a Fortune 500 company to a CEO who spouted conspiracy theories about big corporations? Would a hospital hire a doctor who espoused conspiracy theories about the medical establishment, vaccines, and pharmaceutical companies? Establishment institutions are designed to ensure stability; conspiracy theories, on the other hand, are instruments of disruption.

The disruptive nature of conspiracy theories allow them to change the terms of debate.[109] When major news sources reported accusations of sexual harassment against former Fox News host Bill O'Reilly, he responded that "This was a hit job to get me out of the marketplace. . . . Media Matters is involved, CNN is involved, that is beyond any doubt."[110] When numerous accusations of sexual harassment and assault against film producer Harvey Weinstein were made public, Weinstein allegedly claimed that the charges were nothing but a conspiracy against him.[111] When evidence surfaced that Weinstein had hired former Moussad spies to gather information on the women he harassed, his spokesperson claimed those charges were "inaccuracies and wild conspiracy theories."[112] After Syed Farook and Tashfeen Malik killed fourteen and injured twenty-one in San Bernadino, CA, their family lawyer invoked conspiracy theories about the Sandy Hook shooting to imply that U.S. government officials were behind events in San Bernadino.[113] In these cases, the accused use conspiracy theories to turn accusations back onto the accusers.

Focusing on political debates, Matthew Atkinson and Darin DeWitt in Chapter 8 argue that conspiracy theories are entrepreneurial because they shift how elites discuss issues and how the public understands them. For example, when Alabama Senatorial candidate Roy Moore was accused by multiple women of pedophilia and sexual harassment, Moore claimed that the accusers were part of grand conspiracy involving George Soros, the liberal media, and the "gay agenda."[114] When a woman came forward claiming to have been sexually assaulted by Moore when she was teenager, she provided his inscription in her high school yearbook as evidence of Moore's sexual interest in her. Moore's attorney suggested the inscription was fake and demanded that the yearbook be turned over to a handwriting expert to verify its authenticity. When the yearbook was not turned over, Moore's supporters began to view the accusations a part of a conspiracy and discounted the myriad legitimate accusations of sexual assault.[115] Even though Moore lost, the fact that he, an accused pedophile, almost won is a testament to how conspiracy theories can alter debate.

I should note that the establishment is not inherently "anti-conspiracy theory" per se. Establishment political leaders are often more than willing to promote their own conspiracy theories when it suits them. See in particular the excellent chapters in this volume by Alfred Moore (Chapter 7), Scott Radnitz (Chapter 23), Ilya Yablokov (Chapter 24), Turkay Nefes (Chapter 26), and Tanya Filer (Chapter 27). Scholars as well occasionally cross the line into conspiracy theory, even though they tend to vehemently deny it.[116] Ted Goertzel discusses the tendency of academics to sometimes enter conspiracy theory waters in Chapter 15.

The Positive Side of the Ledger

It is expected that scholars and mainstream reporters will focus on the negative aspects of conspiracy theories: conspiracy theories conflict with establishment accounts, and the costs of conspiracy theories are visible and sometimes great.[117] This does not mean that we should ignore their positive aspects.

While their costs are apparent, the benefits of conspiracy theories are more obscure. For example, if conspiracy theorists investigate a theory that eventually turns out to be true, that theory stops being labeled *conspiracy theory*. As a consequence, at any given time only the unverified remain in the well, giving the impression that no true theories spring from it.

Conspiracy theories can encourage transparency and good behavior by the powerful. They can foster a healthy skepticism in the public. Conspiracy theories can bring new information to light. Conspiracy theories are often used by the weak to balance against power. Therefore, to rid people of their conspiracy theories is to leave them without an important tool for thwarting potential abuse. Any conspiracy theory could, of course, be wrong, but how can we know an idea's strength unless it is allowed to compete in an open field? If conspiracy theorists do not test establishment truths, who will do it?

Plan of the Book

Since Richard Hofstadter's seminal work, hundreds of studies have moved beyond his original accounting of conspiracy theorists. But there have been few efforts to synthesize all of the disparate findings into a coherent statement. This is because integrating different disciplinary approaches and reconciling contradictory findings is no easy task. Among the many findings, we know that it is difficult to convince people that their conspiracy beliefs are wrong.[118] The release of President Obama's long-form birth certificate, for example, did little to quell the Birthers.[119] But, on the other hand, research also shows that conspiracy theorists sometimes believe logically irreconcilable accounts, such as that Osama bin Laden was dead before the Navy Seals killed him, and that Osama bin Laden is still alive.[120]

The contradictions go on. Some view conspiracy theorists as truth seekers, but on the other hand conspiracy theorists are prone not only to confabulation but to outright lies.[121] Much of the scholarship assumes that conspiracy theories travel indiscriminately convincing all in their path, but polls show that only a select few conspiracy theories can convince more than a minority of people. Studies by psychologists show that particular traits such as authoritarianism drive conspiracy theories, but other studies fail to find such effects.[122] This is not to suggest that the literature on conspiracy theories is incoherent; it's just that the inconsistencies are visible and occasionally difficult to overcome.

Some of the contradictions stem from the fact that scholars from varied disciplines start from different assumptions, literatures, and methods. But on top of this, the study of conspiracy theories is a worldwide venture. Poll results are often country-specific, and few efforts have been made to compile cross-cultural data. It's not clear if a finding from Poland has anything to say about conspiracy theorizing in France, for example. Also, the study of conspiracy theories has vastly expanded and accelerated in the last decade, but we don't know if the current findings are specific to this particular time period and perhaps the result of political and social phenomena that do not vary in cross-sectional studies. Would our current findings be different if we were to replicate our studies a decade from now? It's hard to know.

Nonetheless, this volume is one of several ongoing efforts to integrate the prevailing research. The Leverhulme-funded Conspiracy and Democracy project at University of Cambridge's Centre for Research in the Arts, Humanities, Social Sciences, and Humanities (CRASSH) has been integral to the study of conspiracy theories since 2013; it has brought together numerous scholars, pushed the literature forward in very creative ways, and made a large body of public talks available for the public. The EU-funded Comparative Analysis of Conspiracy Theories project managed by Peter Knight and Michael Butter has also been very successful, particularly at bringing together scholars from across Europe. The volume you are currently reading is the result of an effort I began in 2015 when I hosted more than forty scholars at the University of Miami. At that conference, many of the participants talked at cross-purposes, often past each other.[123] But these efforts have had their intended effect, and scholars have been more willing to engage a wider range of perspectives in their work. The scholarship is now at a tipping point, and it is time to springboard the next decade of research.

This volume focuses on seven overarching questions which comprise the seven sections of the volume.

What is a conspiracy theory? As Jesse Walker demonstrates in Chapter 3, the term *conspiracy theory* has been used to encompass not just theories involving conspiracies, but also those addressing the paranormal, supernatural, and mystical. For example, when the Malaysian jet airliner went missing in March 2014, CNN speculated that "a black hole – or some other conspiracy theory" might be to blame for the disappearance. Andrew McKenzie-McHarg examines the first appearances of the term *conspiracy theory* in the United States and how the term first became linked to the concept of conspiracy theory. Martin Orr and Ginna Husting show how *The New York Times* slurs people in other countries with the term *conspiracy theory*. Matthew Dentith then connects the varying definitions of conspiracy theory to the outcomes of social scientific research, arguing that researchers need to be very careful in how they decide what is and what is not a conspiracy theory.

How do conspiracy theorists and non–conspiracy theorists interact? Conspiracy theories have had a tenuous relationship with both the political and scientific establishments. Two chapters by Alfred Moore and by Darin DeWitt and Matthew Atkinson address the use of conspiracy theories as disruptive mechanisms in politics. Chapters 9 and 10 provide first-person accounts by two scientists – Jay Cullen, a marine chemist, and Stephan Lewandowsky, a psychologist – of how conspiracy theorists treated them when their scientific findings contradicted the conspiracy theories. Chapter 11, by Juha Raikka and Lee Basham, examines the irrational fear that some have of conspiracy theories, and Chapter 12 by Steven Smallpage provides a discussion of the tension between democratic tolerance and offending community sensibilities—this tension is particularly evident when college professors entertain conspiracy theories.

Are conspiracy theories "anti-science"? How do anti-science beliefs such as global warming skepticism, anti-vaccination attitudes, and fears of genetically modified food take root in spite of large scientific consensuses? How do anti-science conspiracy theories operate, and why is a scientific consensus not always enough to convince skeptics? Josh Pasek in Chapter 13 uses polling data to measure the public's agreement with a series of scientific consensuses; he shows that many people disagree with science even when they know that a consensus exists. Pasek points to the distrust of scientists as a reason why. Morgan Marietta and David Barker in Chapter 14 show that people's underlying partisanship, along with conspiracy thinking, drives people to agree or disagree with authoritative views. Ted Goertzel in Chapter 15 suggests that conspiracy theories about science can spread easily when high-profile elites endorse them.

What is the psychology of conspiracy theories? Michael Wood and Karen Douglas discuss the current perspectives from psychologists in Chapter 16, and Nicholas DiFonzo examines how the long-established research into rumors can help us better understand conspiracy theorizing in Chapter 17. In Chapter 18, Preston Bost poses a series of questions intended to set the stage for the next round of psychological research.

What do conspiracy theories look like in the United States? How many people believe in conspiracy theories in the United States, and how widespread are beliefs in individual conspiracy theories? Kathy Olmsted provides a historical overview of conspiracy theories in the United States; this is followed by Steven Smallpage and Adam Enders looking at contemporaneous levels of belief. Darin DeWitt, Matthew Atkinson, and Drew Wegner examine the ways in which conspiracy theories might travel in the United States and how we might better understand how they move from person to person.

What do conspiracy theories look like around the world? While most accounts of conspiracy theorizing are geographically bounded, this section provides chapters detailing conspiracy theorizing across the world. Hugo Drochon provides the results of polling from across the United Kingdom, European Union, and Argentina. Scott Radnitz and Ilya Yablokov look at how conspiracy theories flourish in institutionally weak post-Soviet states; then Wiktor Soral, Aleksandra Cichocka, Michał Bilewicz, and Marta Marchlewska look at the factors driving popular conspiracy theories in Poland. Turkay Nefes examines how legislators make use the "deep state" conspiracy theory in Turkey. Finally, Tanya Filer looks at how former President Cristina Fernández de Kirchner of Argentina benefited from the use of conspiracy theories.

How should we live with conspiracy theories? Asbjørn Dyrendal and David Robertson in Chapter 28 and Brian Keeley in Chapter 29 examine conspiracy thinking in relation to other forms of reasoning, such as scientific and religious. In Chapter 30 Jan-Willem van Prooijen suggests a framework for government transparency and inclusiveness that could limit the suspicions that drive conspiracy theorizing. In Chapter 31, I synthesize some of the main points from the volume to provide a few tips for journalists covering conspiracy theories.

There are, of course, questions this volume will not answer or even pose. This is a huge topic, and no treatment could cover it all. There are countries that we could unfortunately not study in this treatment, and substantive areas that we had no choice but to exclude. With this said, the ground covered here provides an adequate springboard for future inquiry.

Conclusion

Conspiracy theories are a timely and timeless subject, but recent events highlight their timeliness. This volume is intended to inspire the next decade of research and also to assist journalists attempting to grasp the latest conspiracy theory panic. Our knowledge-generating and knowledge-disseminating institutions need to need learn more about conspiracy theories and report what they learn in better ways. More importantly, this volume is an effort to help the public better understand their own beliefs. Perhaps the key to diffusing conflict and lessening violence is to help people appreciate that their beliefs did not come from up on high, but rather from a series of easily understandable processes that have little to do with truth. Regardless of what beliefs people hold, they likely all came to those beliefs in similar ways. Because of this, we should all be able to empathize with each other.

Notes

1. Uscinski, Joseph E., and Joseph M. Parent. 2014. *American Conspiracy Theories*. Oxford: Oxford University Press.
2. Broniatowski, David A., Karen M. Hilyard, and Mark Dredze. 2016. "Effective Vaccine Communication During the Disneyland Measles Outbreak." *Vaccine* 34(28): 3225–3228. DOI: 10.1016/j.vaccine.2016.04.044; Oliver, Eric, and Thomas Wood. 2014. "Medical Conspiracy Theories and Health Behaviors in the United States." *JAMA Internal Medicine* 174(5): 817–818. DOI: 10.1001/jamainternmed.2014.190.
3. Uscinski and Parent. *American Conspiracy Theories*.
4. Miller, Joanne M., Kyle L. Saunders, Christina E. Farhart. 2016. "Conspiracy Endorsement as Motivated Reasoning: The Moderating Roles of Political Knowledge and Trust." *American Journal of Political Science* 60(4): 824–844; Oliver, Eric, and Thomas Wood. 2014. "Conspiracy Theories and the Paranoid Style (S) of Mass Opinion." *American Journal of Political Science* 58(4): 952–966.
5. Berinsky, Adam J. 2017. "Telling the Truth About Believing the Lies? Evidence for the Limited Prevalence of Expressive Survey Responding." *The Journal of Politics* 80(1). DOI: 10.1086/694258.
6. Full episodes of Mermaids: The Body Found, can be found at: https://www.animalplanet.com/tv-shows/mermaids/ (Accessed December 27, 2017).
7. Bode, Leticia, and Emily K. Vraga. 2015. "In Related News, That Was Wrong: The Correction of Misinformation through Related Stories Functionality in Social Media." *Journal of Communication* 65(4): 619–638. DOI: 10.1111/jcom.12166; Broniatowski, Hilyard, and Dredze, "Effective Vaccine Communication During the Disneyland Measles Outbreak"; Sharma, Megha, Kapil Yadav, Nitika Yadav, Keith C. Ferdinand. 2017. "Zika Virus Pandemic: Analysis of Facebook as a Social Media Health Information Platform." *American Journal of Infection Control* 45(3): 301–302. DOI: 10.1016/j.ajic.2016.08.022; Thomson, Robert, Naoyo Ito, Hinako Suda, Fangyu Lin, Yafei Liu, Ryo Hayasaka, Ryuzo Isochi, and Zian Wang. 2012. "Trusting Tweets: The Fukushima Disaster and Information Source Credibility on Twitter." *Proceedings of the 9th International Conference on Information Systems for Crisis Response and Management*.
8. See Merlan, Ann. 2016. "Sail (Far) Away: At Sea with America's Largest Floating Gathering of Conspiracy Theorists." https://jezebel.com/sail-far-away-at-sea-with-americas-largest-floating-1760900554 (Accessed December 12, 2017); Dickey, Bronwen. 2016. "Come Aboard, Ye Who Seek Truth!" http://www.popularmechanics.com/culture/a21919/conspiracy-theory-cruise/ (Accessed December 12, 2017). Information on the 2019 Conspira-sea Cruise available at: http://www.divinetravels.com/ConspiraSeaCruise.html (Accessed December 12, 2017).
9. Davis, Brion David, ed. 1971. "Fear of Conspiracy: Images of Un-American Subversion from the Revolution to the Present." Ithica: Cornell University Press; Gribbin, William. 1974. "Antimasonry, Religious Radicalism, and the Paraniod Style of the 1820s." *History Teacher* 7(2): 239–254; Hofstadter, Richard. 1964. *The Paranoid Style in American Politics, and Other Essays*. Cambridge: Harvard University Press; Hogue, William M. 1976. "The Religious Conspiracy Theory of the American Revolution: Anglican Motive." *Church History* 4(3): 277–292.
10. Keeley, Brian. 1999. "Of Conspiracy Theories." *Journal of Philosophy* 96(3), 1999: 109–126; Knight, P.G. 1997. "Naming the Problem: Feminism and the Figuration of Conspiracy." *Cultural Studies* 11(1): 40–63. DOI: 10.1080/09502389700490031; Knight, Peter. 1999. "Everything Is Connected: Underworld's Secret History of Paranoia." *MFS Modern Fiction Studies* 45(3): 811–836.
11. Simon, Arthur M., and Joseph E. Uscinski. 2012. "Prior Experience Predicts Presidential Performance." *Presidential Studies Quarterly* 42(3): 514–548. DOI: 10.1111/j.1741–5705.2012.03991.x.

12. Trump now claims the tape is a fraud. West, Lindy. 2016. "Donald and Billy on the Bus." *The New York Times*, October 8, 2016.

13. DelReal, Jose A. 2016. "Here Are 10 More Conspiracy Theories Embraced by Donald Trump." *The Washington Post*. https://www.washingtonpost.com/news/post-politics/wp/2016/09/16/here-are-10-more-conspiracy-theories-embraced-by-donald-trump/?utm_term=.217633487e52 (Accessed December 27, 2017).

14. Borchers, Callum. 2016. "How on Earth Is the Media Supposed to Cover Trump's Wacky JFK-Cruz Conspiracy Theory?" *The Washington Post*. https://www.washingtonpost.com/news/the-fix/wp/2016/05/03/how-on-earth-is-the-media-supposed-to-cover-trumps-wacky-jfk-cruz-conspiracy-theory/?utm_term=.59bc512984ce (Accessed December 27, 2017).

15. Tani, Maxwell. 2016. "The Conspiracy Candidate? 13 Outlandish Theories Donald Trump Has Floated on the Campaign Trail." *Business Insider*. http://www.businessinsider.com/donald-trump-birther-conspiracy-theories-2016-9 (Accessed December 27, 2017).

16. Uscinski, Joseph E. 2016. "Lots of Americans Agree with Donald Trump About 'Rigged Elections.'" *The Washington Post*. https://www.washingtonpost.com/news/monkey-cage/wp/2016/08/08/lots-of-americans-agree-with-donald-trump-about-rigged-elections/?utm_term=.ed91fd2bdcd9 (Accessed December 27, 2017).

17. Shelbourne, Mallory. 2016. "Trump Claims Voter Fraud without Evidence, Says 'I Won the Popular Vote.'" *The Hill*. http://thehill.com/homenews/campaign/307622-trump-i-would-have-won-popular-vote-if-people-had-not-voted-illegally (Accessed December 27, 2017).

18. Dwyer, Paula. 2016. "Everything Is 'Rigged.'" *Chicago Tribune*. http://www.chicagotribune.com/news/opinion/commentary/ct-elizabeth-warren-bernie-sanders-system-rigged-20160204-story.html (Accessed December 27, 2017).

19. Berman, Ari. 2016. "The Democratic Primary Wasn't Rigged." *The Nation*. https://www.thenation.com/article/the-democratic-primary-wasnt-rigged/ (Accessed December 27, 2017).

20. Sanders, Bernie. N.d. "Issues: Reforming Wall Street." https://berniesanders.com/issues/reforming-wall-street/ (Accessed December 12, 2017); Wilkinson, Will. "Bernie Sanders Is Right the Economy Is Rigged. He's Dead Wrong About Why." *Vox.com*. https://www.vox.com/policy-and-politics/2016/7/15/12200990/bernie-sanders-economy-rigged (Accessed December 12, 2017).

21. Barkan, Ross. 2015. "'Their Greed Has No End': Bernie Sanders Makes a Surprise Appearance in Manhattan." *The Observer*. http://observer.com/2015/10/their-greed-has-no-end-bernie-sanders-makes-a-surprise-appearance-in-manhattan/ (Accessed December 27, 2017).

22. Ehrenfreund, Max. 2016. "What Is Hillary Clinton Trying to Say with This Ad About Donald Trump and Putin?" *Washington Post*. https://www.washingtonpost.com/news/wonk/wp/2016/08/07/what-is-hillary-clinton-trying-to-say-with-this-ad-about-donald-trump-and-putin/?utm_term=.593955d33239 (Accessed December 27, 2017).

23. Mathis-Lilley, Ben. 2016. "Watch Hillary Shred Trump on Releasing His Taxes." [Blog] *The Slatest*. Available at: http://www.slate.com/blogs/the_slatest/2016/09/26/hillary_clinton_s_effective_shot_at_trump_over_tax_releases.html (Accessed December 27, 2017).

24. Stewart III, Charles. 2016. "Donald Trump's 'Rigged Election' Talk Is Changing Minds. Democrats' Minds, That Is." [Blog] *The Monkey Cage*. Available at: https://www.washingtonpost.com/news/monkey-cage/wp/2016/10/19/donald-trumps-rigged-election-talk-is-changing-minds-democrats-minds-that-is/?utm_term=.5e072a8490ee (Accessed December 27, 2017).

25. Frankovic, Kathy. 2016. "Belief in Conspiracies Largely Depends on Political Identity." https://today.yougov.com/news/2016/12/27/belief-conspiracies-largely-depends-political-iden/ (Accessed December 27, 2017).

26. Walker, Jesse. 2016. "Donald Trump Loves Conspiracy Theories. So do His Foes." *Chicago Tribune* http://www.chicagotribune.com/news/opinion/commentary/ct-donald-trump-russia-conspiracy-theories-20160815-story.html (Accessed December 27, 2017); Beauchamp, Zack.

2017. "Democrats are Falling for Fake News About Russia: Why Liberal Conspiracy Theories are Flourishing in the Age of Trump." *Vox.com*. https://www.vox.com/world/2017/5/19/15561842/trump-russia-louise-mensch (Accessed December 27, 2017); Coppins, Mckay. 2017. "How the Left Lost its Mind." *The Atlantic*. https://www.theatlantic.com/politics/archive/2017/07/liberal-fever-swamps/530736/ (Accessed December 27, 2017); LaFrance, Adrienne. 2017. The Normalization of Conspiracy Theories: People Who Share Dangerous Ideas Don't Necessarily Believe Them." The Atlantic. https://www.theatlantic.com/technology/archive/2017/06/the-normalization-of-conspiracy-culture/530688/ (Accessed December 27, 2017).

27. Bryan, Bob. 2017. "Krugman: 'We Arguably do not Have a Legitimate President or Administration.'" *Business Insider*. http://www.businessinsider.com/paul-krugman-tweets-james-comey-trump-russia-investigation-2017-5 (Accessed December 27, 2017); Bryan, Bob. 2016. "Krugman: It's Looking More and More Like the Election was Swung by the FBI in Virtual 'Alliance with Putin.'" *Business Insider*. http://www.businessinsider.com/paul-krugman-fbi-putin-comey-2016-11 (Accessed December 27, 2017).

28. Bryan, "Krugman: 'We Arguably do not Have a Legitimate President or Administration.'"

29. Cordero, Carrie. 2017. "How to Understand Kushner's 'Back-Channel.'" Politico Magazine. https://www.politico.com/magazine/story/2017/06/06/how-to-understand-kushners-back-channel-215232 (Accessed December 27, 2017).

30. Drucker, David M. 2017. "Romney was Right About Russia." http://www.cnn.com/2017/07/31/opinions/obama-romney-russia-opinion-drucker/index.html (Accessed December 27, 2017).

31. Uscinski and Parent. *American Conspiracy Theories*.

32. Wolf, Bryon Z. 2017. "Trump Embraces Deep State Conspiracy Theory." http://www.cnn.com/2017/11/29/politics/donald-trump-deep-state/index.html (Accessed December 27, 2017); Jarrett, Gregg. 2017. "Did the FBI and the Justice Department, Plot to Clear Hillary Clinton, Bring Down Trump?" http://www.foxnews.com/opinion/2017/12/15/gregg-jarrett-did-fbi-and-justice-department-plot-to-clear-hillary-clinton-bring-down-trump.html (Accessed December 27, 2017); Investor's Business Daily. 2017. "Deep State Run Amok? Deomcrats and Hillary Clinton Paid for FBI's Dossier on Trump." https://www.investors.com/politics/editorials/deep-state-run-amok-democrats-and-hillary-paid-for-fbis-dossier-on-trump/ (Accessed December 27, 2017).

33. Atkinson, Matthew D., Darin DeWitt, and Joseph E. Uscinski. 2017. "How Conspiracy Theories Helped Power Trump's Disruptive Politics." *Vox.com*. https://www.vox.com/mischiefs-of-faction/2017/5/2/15517266/conspiracy-theories-trump-populism (Accessed December 27, 2017); Uscinski, Joseph E. 2016. "If Trump's Rhetoric around Conspiracy Theories Follows Him to the White House, It Could Lead to the Violation of Rights on a Massive Scale." [Blog] *Impact of American Politics & Policy Blog*. Available at: http://blogs.lse.ac.uk/usappblog/2016/03/30/if-trumps-rhetoric-around-conspiracy-theories-follows-him-to-the-white-house-it-could-lead-to-the-violation-of-rights-on-a-massive-scale/ (Accessed December 27, 2017).

34. Edelson, Jack, Alexander Alducin, Christopher Krewson, James A. Sieja, and Joseph E. Uscinski. 2017. "The Effect of Conspiratorial Thinking and Motivated Reasoning on Belief in Election Fraud." *Political Research Quarterly* 70(4). DOI: 10.1177/1065912917721061.

35. Jensen, Tom. 2013. "Democrats and Republicans Differ on Conspiracy Theory Beliefs." https://www.publicpolicypolling.com/polls/democrats-and-republicans-differ-on-conspiracy-theory-beliefs/ (Accessed December 27, 2017).

36. Edelson, Alducin, Krewson, Sieja, and Uscinski, "The Effect of Conspiratorial Thinking and Motivated Reasoning on Belief in Election Fraud."

37. Fox News. "ACORN Fires More Officials for Helping 'Pimp,' and 'Prostitute' in Washington Office." http://www.foxnews.com/story/2009/09/11/acorn-fires-more-officials-for-helping-pimp-prostitute-in-washington-office.html (Accessed December 27, 2017); Henig, Jess. 2008. "Acorn Accusations: McCain Makes Exaggerated Claims of 'Voter Fraud.' Obama

Soft-pedals His Connections." http://www.factcheck.org/2008/10/acorn-accusations/ (Accessed December 27, 2017).

38. Abad-Santos, Alexander. 2012. "Yes, Half of Republicans Think ACORN, Which Doesn't Exist, Stole the Election." *The Atlantic*. https://www.theatlantic.com/politics/archive/2012/12/yes-half-republicans-think-acorn-which-doesnt-exist-stole-election/320846/ (Accessed December 27, 2017).

39. Berinsky, Adam J. 2015. "Rumors and Health Care Reform: Experiments in Political Misinformation." *British Journal of Political Science* 47(2):241–262. DOI: 10.1017/S0007123415000186; Nyhan, Brendan, Eric McGhee, John Sides, Seth Masket, and Steven Greene. 2012. "One Vote out of Step? The Effects of Salient Roll Call Votes in the 2010 Election." *American Politics Research* 40(5): 844–879.

40. Some evidence does show that Republicans did pass voter identification laws with the intent of disenfranchising minority voters. But with that said a majority of voters do support voter ID laws and Republicans may have been responding as much to popular sentiment as to their crass electoral concerns. See Edelson, Alducin, Krewson, Sieja, and Uscinski, "The Effect of Conspiratorial Thinking and Motivated Reasoning on Belief in Election Fraud"; Graham, David A. 2016. "Deliberate Disenfranchisement of Black Voters." *The Atlantic*. https://www.theatlantic.com/politics/archive/2016/07/north-carolina-voting-rights-law/493649/ (Accessed December 27, 2017).

41. Schulteis, Emily. 2016. "Jill Stein Announces Plans for Leftover Recount Money." https://www.cbsnews.com/news/jill-stein-announces-plans-for-leftover-recount-money/ (Accessed December 27, 2017).

42. Shelbourne, Mallory. 2016. "Trump Claims Voter Fraud without Evidence, Says 'I Won the Popular Vote." *The Hill*. http://thehill.com/homenews/campaign/307622-trump-i-would-have-won-popular-vote-if-people-had-not-voted-illegally (Accessed December 27, 2017).

43. Nazaryan, Alexander. 2017. "Russian Plot to Elect Trump Included Jill Stein, According to Latest Gleeful Twitter Theory." *Newsweek*. http://www.newsweek.com/donald-trump-jr-jill-stein-putin-russia-senate-639422 (Accessed December 27, 2017).

44. Media Matters Staff. 2016. "Trump Ally Roger Stone on Hillary Clinton: "Bitch Can Hardly Stand UP."" [Blog] *Media Matters for America*. Available at: https://www.mediamatters.org/blog/2016/10/25/trump-ally-roger-stone-hillary-clinton-bitch-can-hardly-stand/214090 (Accessed December 27, 2017).

45. Media Matters Staff. 2016. "Trump Advisor Roger Stone Claims Clinton was Placed on "Oxygen Tank" Immediately After Presidential Debate." [Blog] *Media Matters for America*. Available at: https://www.mediamatters.org/video/2016/09/27/trump-adviser-roger-stone-claims-clinton-was-placed-oxygen-tank-immediately-after-presidential/213346 (Accessed December 27, 2017).

46. O'Grady, Siobhán. 2016. "Conspiracy Theorists Think Hillary Clinton Has a Body Double. She's Not Alone." *Foreign Policy*. http://foreignpolicy.com/2016/09/12/conspiracy-theorists-think-hillary-clinton-has-a-body-double-shes-not-alone/ (Accessed December 27, 2017).

47. Robison, Will. 2016. "Hillary Clinton: Jimmy Kimmel Discusses Pickle Jar Conspiracy." http://ew.com/article/2016/08/26/hillary-clinton-jimmy-kimmel-pickle-jar-conspiracy/ (Accessed December 27, 2017).

48. Stein, Jeff. 2017. "Donna Brazile's Bombshell About the DNC and Hillary Clinton Explained." *Vox.com*. https://www.vox.com/policy-and-politics/2017/11/2/16599036/donna-brazile-hillary-clinton-sanders (Accessed December 27, 2017).

49. Arnsdorf, Issac. 2016. "Kelly Corners Brazile on Leaked Town Hall Question." *Politico Magazine*. https://www.politico.com/story/2016/10/megyn-kelly-donna-brazile-wikileaks-230064 (Accessed December 27, 2017).

50. Caplan, David. 2017. "Donna Brazile: Passing Potential Town Hall Topics to Clinton Camp 'A Mistake I Will Forever Regret." http://abcnews.go.com/Politics/donna-brazile-passing-de-bate-questions-clinton-camp-mistake/story?id=46218677 (Accessed December 27, 2017).

51. Debenedetti, Gabriel. 2017. "Democrats Shaken and Angered by Brazile Book." *Politico Magazine.*   https://www.politico.com/story/2017/11/05/brazile-democrats-clinton-sanders-dnc-244574 (Accessed December 27, 2017).

52. Gee, Oliver. 2016. "Schools: France Vows to Fight Terror Conspiracy Theories." https://www.thelocal.fr/20160209/france-takes-up-fight-against-conspiracy-theories-in-schools (Accessed December 27, 2017).

53. Hjekmgaard, Kim. 2017. "How Fake News Could Put German Election at Serious Risk." *USA Today.* https://www.usatoday.com/story/news/world/2017/02/01/german-election-fake-news/97076608/ (Accessed December 27, 2017); Arpi, Ivar. 2016. "It's not Only Germany that Covers Up Mass Sex Attacks by Migrant Men. . . Sweden's Record is Shameful." [Blog] *Coffee House.* Available at: https://blogs.spectator.co.uk/2016/12/not-germany-covers-mass-sex-attacks-migrant-men-swedens-record-shameful/ (Accessed December 27, 2017).

54. Hurst, Sarah, Oren Dorell, and George Petras. 2017. "Suspicious Russian Deaths: Sacrifical Pawns or Coincidence?" *USA Today.* https://www.usatoday.com/pages/interactives/suspicious-russian-deaths-sacrificial-pawns-or-coincidence/ (Accessed December 27, 2017).

55. Editorial Board. 2015. "Argentina's President Resorts to Anti-Semitic Conspiracy Theories." *Washignton Post.* https://www.washingtonpost.com/opinions/conspiracy-theory/2015/04/23/0d2d07ca-e90b-11e4-aae1-d642717d8afa_story.html?utm_term=.5d938bcb85f7 (Accessed December 27, 2017).

56. Lewandowsky, Stephan, Gilles E. Gignac, and Klaus Oberauer. 2013. "The Role of Conspiracist Ideation and Worldviews in Predicting Rejection of Science." *PLoS ONE* 8(10). DOI: 10.1371/journal.pone.0075637.

57. Tupy, Marian. 2017. "Europe's Anti-GMO Stance Is Killing Africans." http://reason.com/archives/2017/09/05/europes-anti-gmo-stance-is-killing-afric   (Accessed   December 27, 2017).

58. Wesseler, Justus et al. 2017. "Foregone Benefits of Important Food Crop Improvements in Sub-Saharan Africa." *PLoS ONE* 12(7). DOI: 10.1371/journal.pone.0181353.

59. Michael, Meron Tesfa. 2002. "Africa Bites the Bullet on Genetically Modified Food Aid." http://www.worldpress.org/Africa/737.cfm (Accessed December 27, 2017).

60. Linnekin, Baylen, and Juie Kelly. 2016. "Unless a Federal Court Acts Fast, Vermont's GMO Labeling Law Will Wreak Havoc on the Nation's Food Supply Next Week." http://reason.com/archives/2016/06/25/court-must-put-a-halt-now-to-vermonts-gm   (Accessed December 27, 2017).

61. Chigwedere, Pride, George R. Seage III, Sofia Gruskin, Tun-Hou Lee, and M. Essex. 2008. "Estimating the Lost Benefits of Antiretroviral Drug Use in South Africa." *JAIDS Journal of Acquired Immune Deficiency Syndromes* 49(4): 410–415. DOI: 10.1097/QAI.0b013e31818a6cd5.

62. MacGregor, Karen. 2000. "Conspiracy Theories Fuel Row Over AIDs Crisis in South Africa." http://www.independent.co.uk/news/world/africa/conspiracy-theories-fuel-row-over-aids-crisis-in-south-africa-699302.html (Accessed December 27, 2017).

63. Nattrass, Nicoli. 2012. "How Bad Ideas Gain Social Traction." *The Lancet* 380(9839): 332–333. DOI: 10.1016/S1040-6736(12)61238-0; Nattrass, Nicoli. 2013. "Understanding the Origins and Prevalence of AIDS Conspiracy Beliefs in the United States and South Africa." *Sociology of Health & Illness* 35(1):113–129. DOI: 10.1111/j.1467-9566.2012.01480.x.

64. For example, Broniatowski, Hilyard, and Dredze, "Effective Vaccine Communication During the Disneyland Measles Outbreak."

65. For example, Plait, Phil. 2013. "Antivaccine Megachurch Linked to Texas Measles Outbreak." [Blog] *Bad Astronomy.* Avaiable at: http://www.slate.com/blogs/bad_astronomy/2013/08/26/antivax_communities_get_measles_outbreaks_linked_to_denial_of_vaccines.html (Accessed December 27, 2017).

66. Briones, Rowena, Xiaoli Nan, Kelly Madden, and Leah Waks. 2011. "When Vaccines Go Viral: An Analysis of HPV Vaccine Coverage on Youtube." *Health Communication*

27(5): 478–485. DOI:10.1080/10410236.2011.610258; Craciun, Catrinel, and Adriana Baban. 2012. "'Who Will Take the Blame?': Understanding the Reasons Why Romanian Mothers Decline HPV Vaccination for Their Daughters." *Vaccine* 30(48): 6789–6793. DOI: 10.1016/j.vaccine.2012.09.016; Madden, Kelly, Xiaoli Nan, Rowena Briones, and Leah Waks. 2012. "Sorting through Search Results: A Content Analysis of HPV Vaccine Information Online." *Vaccine* 30(25): 3741–3746. DOI: 10.1016/j.vaccine.2011.10.025.

67. Drobnic Holan, Angie, and Louis Jacobson. 2011. "Michele Bachmann Says HPV Vaccine can Cause Mental Retardation." http://www.politifact.com/truth-o-meter/statements/2011/sep/16/michele-bachmann/bachmann-hpv-vaccine-cause-mental-retardation/ (Accessed December 28, 2017).

68. Dredze, Mark, David A. Broniatowski, and Karen M. Hilyard. 2016. "Zika Vaccine Misconceptions: A Social Media Analysis." *Vaccine* 34(30): 3441–3442. DOI: 10.1016/j.vaccine.2016.05.008.

69. McLaren, Lindsay, Steven Patterson, Salima Thawer, Peter Faris, Deborah McNeil, Melissa Potestio, and Luke Shwart. 2016. "Measuring the Short-Term Impact of Fluoridation Cessation on Dental Caries in Grade 2 Children Using Tooth Surface Indices." *Community Dentistry and Oral Epidemiology* 44(3): 274–282. DOI: 10.1111/cdoe.12215.

70. Hill, Kyle. 2013. "Why Portland Is Wrong about Water Fluoridation." [Blog] *But Not Simpler*. Available at https://blogs.scientificamerican.com/but-not-simpler/why-portland-is-wrong-about-water-fluoridation/ (Accessed December 28, 2017).

71. Blumgart, Jake. 2013. "What's the Matter with Portland?" [Blog] *Medical Examiner*. Available at http://www.slate.com/articles/health_and_science/medical_examiner/2013/05/portland_fluoride_vote_will_medical_science_trump_fear_and_doubt.html (Accessed December 28, 2017).

72. Harmon, Amy. 2014. "A Lonely Quest for Facts on Genetically Modified Crops." *New York Times*. https://www.nytimes.com/2014/01/05/us/on-hawaii-a-lonely-quest-for-facts-about-gmos.html?_r=0 (Accessed December 28, 2017); Hurley, Patrick T., and Peter A. Walker. 2004. "Whose Vision? Conspiracy Theory and Land-Use Planning in Nevada County, California." *Environment and Planning* 36(9):1529–1547; Osher, Christopher N. 2010. "Bike Agenda Spins Cities toward U.N. Control, Maes Warns." *Denver Post*. https://www.denverpost.com/2010/08/03/bike-agenda-spins-cities-toward-u-n-control-maes-warns/ (Accessed December 28, 2017); Bloss, Cinnamon S., Justin Stoler, Kimberly C. Brouwer, and Cynthia Cheung. 2017. "Public Response to a Proposed Field Trial of Genetically Engineered Mosquitoes in the United States." *JAMA* 318(7): 662–664; Enders, Adam and Steven Smallpage. 2016. "Obama Was Right: Conspiracy Theorists are More Likely to Oppose Gun Control." [Blog] *Monkey Cage*. Available at https://www.washingtonpost.com/news/monkey-cage/wp/2016/01/19/obama-was-right-conspiracy-theorists-are-more-likely-to-oppose-gun-control/?utm_term=.c6bd7971f535 (Accessed December 28, 2017).

73. Bock, Alan W. 1993. "Ambush at Ruby Ridge." http://reason.com/archives/1993/10/01/ambush-at-ruby-ridge (Accessed December 28, 2017).

74. Ibid.

75. LoBianco, Tom. 2016. "Report: Aide Says Nixon's War on Drugs Targeted Blacks, Hippies." http://www.cnn.com/2016/03/23/politics/john-ehrlichman-richard-nixon-drug-war-blacks-hippie/index.html (Accessed December 28, 2017).

76. Hughes, Ken. n.d. "A Rough Guide to Richard Nixon's Conspiracy Theories." https://millercenter.org/the-presidency/educational-resources/a-rough-guide-to-richard-nixon-s-conspiracy-theories (Accessed December 28, 2017).

77. Conroy, Bill. 2012. "Drug-related Homicides in the US Average at Least 1,100 a Year." https://narcosphere.narconews.com/notebook/bill-conroy/2012/03/drug-war-related-homicides-us-average-least-1100-year (Accessed December 28, 2017).

78. Parent, Joseph, and Joseph Uscinski. 2016. "People Who Believe in Conspiracy Theories Are More Likely to Endorse Violence." [Blog] Monkey Cage. Available at https://www.

washingtonpost.com/news/monkey-cage/wp/2016/02/05/are-conspiracy-theorists-plotting-to-blow-up-the-u-s/?utm_term=.395c94e7c119 (Accessed December 28, 2017).

79. Douglas, Karen, and Robbie Sutton. 2011. "Does It Take One to Know One? Endorsement of Conspiracy Theories Is Influenced by Personal Willingness to Conspire." *British Journal of Social Psychology* 50(3): 544–552. DOI: 10.1111/j.2044-8309.2010.02018.x; Uscinski and Parent, *American Conspiracy Theories.*

80. Fetzer, Jim, and Mike Palecek. 2015. *Nobody Died at Sandy Hook.* Moon Rock Books.

81. Pesta, Abigail. 2016. "What Drives Someone to Confront Grieving Families?" http://www.cosmopolitan.com/politics/a58661/young-women-killed-gun-truthers/ (Accessed December 28, 2017).

82. Lind, Dara. "Waco and Ruby Ridge: The 1990s Standoffs Haunting the Oregon Takeover, Explained." *Vox.com.* https://www.vox.com/2016/1/5/10714746/waco-ruby-ridge-oregon (Accessed December 28, 2017).

83. Uscinski and Parent, *American Conspiracy Theories.*

84. Kluger, Jeffrey. 2017. "Why So Many People Believe Conspiracy Theories." *Time.* http://time.com/4965093/conspiracy-theories-beliefs/ (Accessed December 28, 2017).

85. Blake, Andrew. 2017. "Alex Jones Says He's Working with Secret Service to Protect Donald Trump from Assassination Plots." *The Washington Times.* https://www.washingtontimes.com/news/2017/dec/7/alex-jones-says-hes-working-secret-service-protect/ (Accessed December 28, 2017).

86. Marrs, Jim. 2015. *Population Control: How Corporate Owners Are Killing Us.* New York: William Morrow.

87. Ibid., 2.

88. LaRouchePac. 2012. "Britain's Thermonuclear War and Russia's Warning." [Blog] *LaRouchePac.* Available at http://archive.larouchepac.com/node/22617 (Accessed December 28, 2017).

89. LaRouchePac. 2016. "It Was Your Bloody Hand that Unleashed 9/11, Queen Elizabeth!" [Blog] *LaRouchePac.* Available at https://larouchepac.com/20160421/it-was-your-bloody-hand-unleashed-911-queen-elizabeth (Accessed December 28, 2017).

90. Shapiro, Dina. 2011. "The Risk of Disease Stigma: Threat and Support for Coercive Public Heath Policy." Presented at APSA Pre-Conference on Political Communication of Risk.

91. Icke, David. 2010. *Human Race Get Off Your Knees: The Lion Sleeps No More.* Isle of Wight, UK: David Icke Books: 142–143.

92. Ibid., 194–195

93. Time Magazine. n.d. "Conspiracy Theories." http://content.time.com/time/specials/packages/completelist/0,29569,1860871,00.html (Accessed December 28, 2017).

94. McGirk, James. 2012. "Jesse Ventura Suspects a Conspiracy About His Show About Conspiracies." *The Atlantic.* https://www.theatlantic.com/entertainment/archive/2012/12/jesse-ventura-suspects-a-conspiracy-about-his-show-about-conspiracies/266361/ (Accessed December 28, 2017).

95. Bryant, Kenzie. "The Celebrity Conspiracy Theories That Just Won't Quit." *Vanity Fair.* https://www.vanityfair.com/style/2017/02/best-celebrity-conspiracy-theories-2017 (Accessed December 28, 2017).

96. CBSNews.com Staff. 1998. "CBS Poll: JFK Conspiracy Lives." *CBSNews.com.* https://www.cbsnews.com/news/cbs-poll-jfk-conspiracy-lives/ (Accessed December 28, 2017); Swift, Art. 2013. "Majority in U.S. Still Believe JFK Killed in a Conspiracy." *Gallup.com.* http://news.gallup.com/poll/165893/majority-believe-jfk-killed-conspiracy.aspx (Accessed December 28, 2017); Anderson, Monica. 2015. "Amid Debate over Labeling GM Foods, Most Americans Believe They're Unsafe." *Pew Research Center.* http://www.pewresearch.org/fact-tank/2015/08/11/amid-debate-over-labeling-gm-foods-most-americans-believe-theyre-unsafe/ (Accessed December 28, 2017).

97. Hollingworth, Robert M., Leonard F. Bjeldanes, Michael Bolger, Ian Kimber, Barbara Jean Meade, Steve L. Taylor, and Kendall B. Wallace. 2003. "The Safety of Genetically Modified

Foods Produced through Biotechnology." *Toxicological Sciences* 71(1): 2–8. DOI: 10.1093/toxsci/71.1.2.

98. Saad, Lydia. 2015. "U.S. Views on Climate Change Stable after Extreme Winter." *Gallup* News. http://news.gallup.com/poll/182150/views-climate-change-stable-extreme-winter.aspx (Accessed December 28, 2017).

99. Harmon, "A Lonely Quest for Facts on Genetically Modified Crops."

100. Huff, Ethan A. 2016. "How Monsanto Invaded, Occupied and Now CONTROLS Government Regulators." https://www.naturalnews.com/054636_Monsanto_federal_regulators_corporate_collusion.html (Accessed December 28, 2017).

101. Boudry, Maarten, and Johan Braeckman. 2011. "Immunizing Strategies and Epistemic Mechanisms." *Philosophia* 39(1): 145–161.

102. Cook, John, Naomi Oreskes, Peter T. Dolan, William R.L. Anderegg, Bart Verheggen, Ed W. Maibach, J. Stuart Carlton, Stephan Lewandowsky, Andrew G. Skuce, and Sarah A. Green. 2016. "Consensus on Consensus: A Synthesis of Consensus Estimates on Human-Caused Global Warming." *Environmental Research Letters* 11(4): 1–8; Oreskes, Naomi. 2004. "The Scientific Consensus on Climate Change." *Science* 306(5702):1686. DOI: 10.1126/science.1103618.

103. Uscinski, Joseph E., Karen Douglas, and Stephan Lewandowsky. 2017. "Climate Change Conspiracy Theories." *Oxford Research Encyclopedia of Climate Science*: 1–43. DOI: 10.1093/acrefore/9780190228620.013.328.

104. Lewandowsky, Stephan, John Cook, Klaus Oberauer, Scott Brophy, Elisabeth Lloyd, and Michael Marriott. 2015. "Recurrent Fury: Conspiratorial Discourse in the Blogosphere Triggered by Research on the Role of Conspiracist Ideation in Climate Denial." *Journal of Social and Political Psychology* 3(1): 142–178. DOI: 10.5964/jspp.v3i1.443.

105. Lewandowsky, Stephan, Naomi Oreskes, James S. Risbey, Ben R. Newell, and Michael Smithson. 2015. "Seepage: Climate Change Denial and Its Effect on the Scientific Community." *Global Environmental Change* 33(July): 1–13. DOI: 10.1016/j.gloenvcha.2015.02.013.

106. Lewandowsky, Stephan, John Cook, Klaus Oberauer, and Michael Marriott. 2013. "Recursive Fury: Conspiracist Ideation in the Blogosphere in Response to Research on Conspiracist Ideation." *Frontiers in Psychology* 4(73). DOI: 10.3389/fpsyg.2013.00073.

107. Madan, Monique O. 2017. "Professor Who Said Sandy Hook Massacre was a Hoax Loses Suit to get His Job Back." *Miami Herald.* http://www.miamiherald.com/news/local/education/article189261704.html (Accessed December 28, 2017).

108. Freeman, Daniel, and Richard P. Bentall. 2017. "The Concomitants of Conspiracy Concerns." *Social Psychiatry and Psychiatric Epidemiology* 52(5): 595–604. DOI: 10.1007/s00127-017-1354-4; Uscinski and Parent, *American Conspiracy Theories.*

109. Atkinson, DeWitt, and Uscinski, "How Conspiracy Theories Helped Power Trump's Disruptive Politics."

110. Wilstein, Matt. 2017. "Bill O'Reilly Lashes Out at Critics in Conspiracy-Laden Glenn Beck Interview." *The Daily Beast.* https://www.thedailybeast.com/bill-oreilly-lashes-out-at-critics-in-conspiracy-laden-glenn-beck-interview (Accessed December 28, 2017).

111. Bates, Daniel. 2017. "EXCLUSIVE: Hillary Supporter Harvey Weinstein Thinks a 'Right Wing Conspiracy Out to Get Me' Is Reason He Has Been Revealed as Serial Sexual Harasser." *The Daily Mail.* http://www.dailymail.co.uk/news/article-4953450/Harvey-Weinstein-right-wing-conspiracy-sex-shame.html (Accessed December 28, 2017).

112. Maddaus, Gene. 2017. "Harvey Weinstein Hired Investigators to Spy on Accusers, New Yorker Reports." *Variety.* http://variety.com/2017/film/news/harvey-weinstein-spies-accusers-1202608495/ (Accessed December 28, 2017).

113. Atkinson, DeWitt, and Uscinski, "How Conspiracy Theories Helped Power Trump's Disruptive Politics."

114. Sacks, Brianna. 2017. "Roy Moore Just Blamed His Sexual Misconduct Allegations on Lesbians, Gays, and Socialists." https://www.buzzfeed.com/briannasacks/roy-moore-just-blamed-the-lgbt-community-for-the-sexual?utm_term=.uxQxLLdJN9#.arrAwwL5Gm (Accessed December 28, 2017).

115. Fredericks, Bob. 2017. "Roy Moore Accuser Admits Altering Yearbook Entry." *The New York Post.* https://nypost.com/2017/12/08/roy-moore-accuser-admits-altering-yearbook-entry/ (Accessed December 28, 2017).

116. Herman, Edward S., and Noam Chomsky. 1988. *Manufacturing Consent: The Political Economy of the Mass Media.* New York: Pantheon; deHaven-Smith, Lance. 2006. "When Political Crimes Are inside Jobs: Detecting State Crimes against Democracy." *Administrative Theory & Praxis* 28(3): 330–355; MacLean, Nancy. 2017. *Democracy in Chains: The Deep History of the Radical Right's Stealth Plan for America.* New York: Viking.

117. Sunstein, Cass R. 2014. *Conspiracy Theories and Other Dangerous Ideas.* New York: Simon and Schuster.

118. Nyhan, Brendan, and Jason Reifler. 2010. "When Corrections Fail: The Persistence of Political Misperceptions." *Political Behavior* 32(2): 303–330.

119. Berinsky, Adam. 2012. "The Birthers Are (Still) Back." *YouGov: What the World Thinks.* https://today.yougov.com/news/2012/07/11/birthers-are-still-back/ (Accessed December 28, 2017).

120. Wood, Michael et al. 2012. "Dead and Alive: Beliefs in Contradictory Conspiracy Theories." *Social Psychological and Personality Science* 3(6): 767–773. DOI: 10.1177/1948550611434786.

121. *Conspiracy Theorists Lie.* 2015. United States: nomagicbullets.org

122. Grzesiak-Feldman, Monika, and Monika Irzycka. 2009. "Right-Wing Authoritarianism and Conspiracy Thinking in a Polish Sample." *Psychological Reports* 105(2):389–393; Oliver and Wood, "Conspiracy Theories and the Paranoid Style (S) of Mass Opinion."

123. Walker, Jesse. 2015. "What I Saw at the Conspiracy Theory Conference." [Blog] *Hit and Run.* Available at http://reason.com/blog/2015/03/18/what-i-saw-at-the-conspiracy-theory-conf (Accessed December 28, 2017); Tracy, James F. 2015. "Among the 'Conspiracy Theory' Theorists." https://www.globalresearch.ca/among-the-conspiracy-theory-theorists/5436898 (Accessed December 28, 2017).

2

The History of Conspiracy Theory Research

A Review and Commentary

MICHAEL BUTTER AND PETER KNIGHT

Today conspiracy theories exist in all cultures and societies. While there are precursors in antiquity, there is evidence that their modern form emerged during the transition from the Early Modern period to the Enlightenment.[1] Conspiracy theory research, by contrast, is a relatively new phenomenon. While historians occasionally touched upon the subject already during the first decades of the twentieth century, "conspiracy theory" emerged as an identifiable category of scholarly discourse and an object of concern only during the second half, not least because— except for a few isolated examples—the very label did not enter wide circulation until that time.[2]

This chapter outlines the history of academic research on conspiracy theories in English. We begin with an account of early studies conducted in various disciplines which led to Richard Hofstadter's famous conceptualization of conspiracy theorizing as the manifestation of a "paranoid style" in the 1960s—a conceptualization that has both inspired and impeded research.[3] We then proceed systematically rather than chronologically, moving from disciplines that have not entirely overcome the pathologizing approach to conspiracy theories to those that have adopted alternative approaches. Accordingly, the second section is dedicated to studies in social psychology and political science. Scholars from these disciplines largely share Hofstadter's concern about conspiracy theories, but they have increasingly employed quantitative methods to pin down the factors that lead people to believe in conspiracy theories or to engage in underlying conspiracy thinking. The third section discusses the work of analytical philosophers, who have sought to provide more precise definitions of the term and to distinguish between warranted and unwarranted theories. The final section is devoted to the "cultural turn" in conspiracy theory research, whose proponents have been challenging the dominant pathologizing approach since the late 1990s. The chapter closes with an evaluation of the current state of the debate and makes some recommendations for future research.

The Emergence of the Pathologizing Paradigm: From the Beginnings to Richard Hofstadter (1930s to 1960s)

The early history of conspiracy theory research has been convincingly related by Katharina Thalmann, whose account builds on and expands earlier work by Jack Bratich and Mark Fenster.[4] According to Thalmann, scholarly interest in the phenomenon emerged during the 1930s and 1940s under the influence of the two world wars and the rise of totalitarianism.[5] Three different strands are discernible in the initial phase. Political psychologists like Harold Lasswell and Theodor Adorno identified personality types particularly prone to what they considered the irrational practice of conspiracy theorizing, "the agitator" in Lasswell and "the authoritarian personality" in Adorno.[6] While they thus focused on individual traits and psychological causes, sociologists Leo Loewenthal and Norbert Guterman related belief in conspiracy theories to the complexities of modernization and the emergence of mass societies.[7] Anticipating the work of cultural studies scholars fifty years later, in 1949 Loewenthal and Guterman regarded "conspiracy theorizing [as] a meaning-making cultural practice that was worth analyzing and studying."[8]

However, neither the political psychologists nor the sociologists came up with a label for the phenomenon they were studying. This task fell to Karl Popper, a historian of science, who described in the late 1940s what he called *the conspiracy theory of society* as an utterly simplistic and, more importantly, unscientific way of understanding social relations, which had emerged as a reaction and in opposition to the Enlightenment.[9] Although Popper acknowledged that Marx himself was careful to distance himself from what would later be called conspiracy theories, so-called Vulgar Marxism (but also other forms of "totalitarian" thinking such as Nazism) fell into the trap of attributing historical causation to conspiracies of, say, the ruling class or capital itself. If, for Popper, these simplistic forms of historicism committed the intellectual error of ascribing agency to impersonal forces, then the opposite tendency—blaming every unfortunate turn of events on an intentional conspiracy of powerful individuals behind the scenes—was equally guilty of misunderstanding how history works. Popper insisted that the kind of large-scale, coordinated action imagined by conspiracy theorists was impossible because of the inevitability of unintended consequences in complex societies. History, for Popper, should more properly be thought of as the product of an invisible hand (in Adam Smith's term) than a hidden hand.

While these scholars had looked primarily to Europe, the rise of McCarthyism during the 1950s focused the attention of the next generation of researchers on the United States. Scholars such as Edward Shils and Seymour Martin Lipset, and also journalists like Richard Rovere, regarded conspiracy theories as both irrational and unscientific and worried about their harmful effects on American politics.[10] These fears increased further when, during the 1960s, the most vocal proponents of conspiracy theories were no longer representatives of the two major parties and thus the political center, but the members of the John Birch Society.[11] As a result of this shift, consensus historians and pluralist political scientists like John Bunzel, Seymour Martin Lipset, and Earl Raab began to consider conspiracy theories as both symptoms and articulations of extremism.[12] Forging "a link between anti-democratic extremism on the one hand and irrational, unscientific conspiracy theories on the other," they cast conspiracy theories as dangerous to pluralist societies in general and the United States in particular, while simultaneously relegating them to the margins of society.[13]

This way of understanding conspiracy theories climaxed in Richard Hofstadter's famous concept of the "paranoid style," which synthesized most of the ideas put forth by the scholars discussed so far. First, like most scholars of the time, Hofstadter discarded the more neutral sociological perspective of Loewenthal and Guterman and projected conspiracy theories as a minority phenomenon that threatened the liberal-democratic consensus.[14] Second, by drawing on the concept of paranoia, Hofstadter, like Lasswell and Adorno, pathologized conspiracy theorists, even though he claimed not to.[15] Finally, like Popper, Hofstadter regarded conspiracy theories as unscientific.[16]

The impact of Hofstadter's conceptualization of conspiracy theory cannot be overestimated. While he did not coin the term *conspiracy theory* (and indeed, rarely used the phrase), his understanding of the phenomenon influences how considerable parts of the public, the media, and academics all over the world have conceived of the topic thus labeled ever since. Because of Hofstadter, paranoia and conspiracy theory have been almost inextricably linked. This has been beneficial to conspiracy theory research, because it has provided researchers across the board with an easy-to-grasp paradigm that can be applied to different historical and cultural contexts and that continues to be relevant in the present, not least with his focus on the connection between conspiracy belief and status anxiety. Moreover, Hofstadter's emphasis on the importance of "style" in conspiracy theorizing has helped pave the way not only for studies that focus on underlying conspiracy thinking as a "style" of thought, but also for those that focus on the aesthetic and narrative dimensions of conspiracy theories, their rhetorical transmission, or their dramatizations in films and novels.[17]

At the same time, however, Hofstadter's approach to conspiracy theories has impeded research because it pathologizes and marginalizes them. The consequences are particularly obvious in the field of history, where researchers have frequently encountered conspiracy theories that were clearly neither minority phenomena nor articulated by people who should be described as paranoid.[18] Since Hofstadter's theorization of conspiracy theory (the only one available for a long time) was unfit to capture what these scholars observed, most of them either did not refer at all to the theoretical research on the issue in their discussions of specific visions of conspiracy, or they drew on Hofstadter's concept of the paranoid style even though its implications obviously contradicted their findings. Consequently, the engagement of these scholars with the phenomenon was, despite their valuable contributions to scholarship, not as nuanced and productive as it surely would have been if a more neutral theorization of conspiracy theory had been available.

What is more, even scholars who reject or at least modify Hofstadter's premises often do not entirely escape his powerful conceptualization. Michael Pfau's *The Political Style of Conspiracy: Chase, Sumner, and Lincoln* rather unconvincingly distinguishes between a paranoid style of the fringe and a political style of the center in antebellum America to present the conspiracy theories that he focuses on as an exception to the rule.[19] In looking at eighteenth-century America, Gordon Wood makes a far more compelling case that conspiracy theorizing was a rational activity that was firmly rooted in the social mainstream and evidence of sophisticated Enlightenment thinking, but then suggests that this changed at the turn of century, implying that Hofstadter's paranoid style adequately describes conspiracy theories in the nineteenth and twentieth centuries.[20] However, as historian Geoffrey Cubitt has put it: "Quite simply, this recession [that Wood postulates] shows very little signs of having happened during the nineteenth and early twentieth centuries."[21]

Perpetuating and Carefully Challenging the Pathologizing Paradigm: Research in Psychology and Political Science (1990s to the Present)

Although there are, as we have seen, obvious ties to psychology and political science in early conspiracy theory research, both disciplines were initially slow to investigate the topic. A discussion of the reasons for this delayed engagement is beyond the scope of this chapter. Suffice it to say that scholars from both disciplines very likely regarded conspiracy theories for a long time as a fringe curiosity undeserving of serious discussion. What is more, in political science the focus on partisanship, ideology, and issue positions during the 1950s and 1960s, and later the dominance of the rational choice paradigm (which held that opinions were rational as opposed to purely social-psychological) was surely a factor, since conspiracy theories—cast by Hofstadter and most of his predecessors as irrational and unscientific—did not really fit either of these paradigms. However, as researchers from both disciplines recognized that the phenomenon is widespread and has potentially serious consequences, they began to engage with the issue. In psychology an interest in conspiracy theories began to emerge in the 1990s, while in political science it took longer. The widespread conspiracy theories surrounding Barack Obama appear to have motivated most research in this field. In recent years, there has been a significant flourishing of empirical studies in both disciplines.

Despite the increasing recognition that conspiracy theories are a mainstream phenomenon, most studies in psychology until today share at least some of Hofstadter's assumptions, even though they rarely refer to him in anything more than the most general way. Early research tended to take for granted that conspiracy theories are held by distinctive kinds of people with identifiable and flawed characteristics, and most work in the field holds that belief in conspiracy theories is irrational.[22] Ted Goertzel, who provided one of the first and most influential studies using survey data, came even closer to Hofstadter when he argued that conspiracy beliefs are "monological," that is, they serve as a complete worldview such that people who believe in one conspiracy theory tend to believe in them all.[23] This idea is still maintained by more recent studies but has also been challenged by other researchers, who find that sometimes conspiracy beliefs are topic-specific.[24]

Generally, work in psychology has sought to profile believers and to enumerate the personality and cognitive factors involved in underlying conspiracy thinking, what is sometimes termed—in a phrase that evokes an unwarranted level of diagnostic precision—"conspiracy ideation."[25] Once again following Hofstadter (albeit not always directly), some researchers have investigated the supposed link between conspiracy thinking and forms of psychopathology, but have reached little agreement. Psychologists have linked conspiracy thinking and belief in specific conspiracy theories to the traits of a "damaged" psyche including paranoia, schizotypy, distrust, suspiciousness, obsession with hidden motives, heightened threat sensitivity, anomie, feelings of alienation, cynicism, uncertainty, powerlessness, anxiety and perceived loss of control.[26] Although some researchers have found some correlations between conspiracy thinking and elements of the so-called Big Five personality differences (e.g., a negative relation to agreeableness, connected with a suspicion of others) and have suggested that individual differences in "conspiracy ideation" are stable over time, others have found that the conspiracy theorist does not have a distinctive personality and that circumstantial factors are needed to trigger the personality traits.[27]

In terms of methodology, many psychological studies employ questionnaires that rank the respondent on scales measuring conspiracy thinking or belief in a range of specific conspiracy theories, and then test out variables that might be associated with high or low rates. There has been a proliferation of different scales, such as the Belief in Conspiracy Theories Inventory, the Generic Conspiracist Beliefs Scale, and the Conspiracy Mentality Scale, but no agreement on a single measure yet.[28] Although most surveys measure belief in well-known conspiracy theories, some researchers make up conspiracy theories to measure endorsement.[29] Other researchers have also begun to move beyond surveys to experimental manipulation of attitudes in their quest to identify the variables and mechanisms involved in "conspiracy ideation." They find, for example, that people who have been induced into experiencing a sense of emotional uncertainty or a loss of control are more likely to draw on conspiratorial interpretations of events.[30] Many researchers are increasingly concerned with the harmful social and political effects of conspiracy theories, with findings that mere exposure makes it less likely, for example, for people to try to reduce their carbon footprint or have their children vaccinated.[31] Others have conducted experiments to show that belief in potentially harmful conspiracy theories can be reduced with a task that increases analytic thinking.[32]

Compared to the large body of psychological studies that have been published since *ca.* 2007, there is still comparatively little research in political science, where scholars now mainly rely on polling data to detect factors that fuel belief in conspiracy theories. All of the empirical studies have begun to converge on the result that conspiracy theorizing is not a fringe phenomenon but a rather a fairly normal pastime. For example, about 60%, 25%, and 25% of Americans believe in JFK assassination, birther, and truther conspiracy theories respectively.[33]

Studies differ, however, with regard to the causes researchers identify for the belief in conspiracy theories. Identified causal mechanisms range from epistemological problems to political asymmetries to feverish worldviews. Cass Sunstein and Adrian Vermeule hold that conspiracy theories are the result of "crippled epistemology"; that is, they arise when people either lack information or do not process it properly.[34] Uscinski and Parent argue that in the United States, "conspiracy theories are for losers," suggesting that they arise among groups who feel threatened, powerless, and insecure, most often as a result of being on the losing side of the partisan divide following an election.[35] By contrast, Oliver and Wood come closest to a psychological explanation by arguing that conspiracy theories are caused by the predisposition to attribute events to the machinations of invisible forces, and to perceive the world as a Manichean struggle between good and evil.[36] Finally, Sunstein and Vermeule argue that conspiracy theories are far more a matter of the political right than of the left, whereas Uscinski and Parent, Oliver and Wood, as well as Miller, Saunders, and Farhart reject this claim.[37] They all contend, though, that political convictions and situations determine which conspiracy theories individuals believe in.

Since these studies all hold that conspiracy theories are a widespread phenomenon in American culture, they all more or less explicitly reject the correlation between conspiracy theories and personality disorders that is so prominent in psychology. Because they identify a cause—misinformation—that, in theory, could be remedied, Sunstein and Vermeule openly reflect about possible cures for conspiracy beliefs. They suggest, however, that once people have begun to believe in a conspiracy theory, it is almost impossible to convince them otherwise. This finding has been recently corroborated in further studies.[38] Uscinski and Parent as well as Oliver and Wood largely refrain from offering remedies, largely because their findings suggest that conspiracy theories are such an integral part of American culture that they will not go away. Yet, they are still largely pessimistic about conspiracy theories. This distinguishes them from some of the analytical philosophers discussed below.

The Debate in Analytical Philosophy on Warranted and Unwarranted Conspiracy Beliefs (Mid-1990s to the Present)

Charles Pigden opened up a new set of debates in analytical philosophy by challenging Karl Popper's fundamental assumption that conspiracy theories are necessarily mistaken.[39] Pigden, along with subsequent contributions from David Coady and Lee Basham, insisted that conspiracy theories are not *prima facie* irrational, not least because there are many historical examples of conspiracy theories that could broadly be construed as successful.[40] Instead of dismissing all conspiracy theories out of hand, researchers must therefore examine them on a case-by-case basis for their potential validity. This argument has recently been reiterated by Matthew Dentith in the most comprehensive monograph so far in this subfield.[41]

In contrast, other philosophers such as Brian Keeley, Jeffrey Bale, and Juha Räikkä have sought to make sense of what they see as the common intuition that there is a distinction between plausible analyses of political conspiracies and unwarranted conspiracy theories, even if in practice the boundaries between the two are sometimes blurred at the edges.[42] For Keeley, even if there is not (in the mode of Popper) an a priori reason to dismiss all conspiracy theories, there is nevertheless a prima facie case to be made that unwarranted conspiracy theories—those, for example, which have grown too large to not be detected and exposed—are the result of flawed thinking. Steve Clarke, for example, looking to social psychology, identifies the "fundamental attributional error" as a key intellectual vice of conspiracy theorists.[43]

Although the debate in analytical philosophy has tended to revolve around the definition of conspiracy theory and the question of its rationality, it has often ignored the fact that the very term *conspiracy theory* is not a neutral, objective label but a pejorative dismissal of an allegedly "crippled epistemology."[44] Likewise, although philosophers have sought to determine the inherent justifiability of this way of viewing historical causality and (in some cases) to identify the intellectual flaws, there has been little interest in systematically considering the social, political, and cultural circumstances that might make conspiracy theories more warranted in some historical and geopolitical settings than others. In many of these essays, the same handful of familiar examples of conspiracy theories are cited, and the underlying assumption is that the phenomenon of conspiracy theory has a stable, identifiable logic that holds true in all times and places. This is simply not borne out by the historical record or anthropological studies of how conspiracy theories work in other cultures. The debate has also tended to be self-contained within the discipline of philosophy and rarely engages in a sustained way with discussions of conspiracy theories in other disciplines, while those other disciplines (especially social psychology) likewise have failed to take up some of the interesting challenges posed by the debate on distinguishing between warranted conspiracy theories (in the sense of better evidenced or reasoned, but not necessarily true) and unwarranted ones.

Challenging the Pathologizing Paradigm: Cultural History and Cultural Studies (Late 1990s to the Present)

Since the late 1990s, a number of important studies have been published in the fields of cultural history and cultural studies. Fueled by the pervasiveness of conspiracy discourses in American films and TV shows, on the media, and in early Internet newsgroups at the turn of the millennium, these works either focus exclusively on the contemporary period or make a larger historical argument in order to explain the prominence of conspiracy theorizing in the present. The most conservative of these studies is Michael Barkun's *A Culture of Conspiracy: Apocalyptical Visions in Contemporary America*.[45] Situated at the crossroads of historical analysis and qualitative political science, he observes that conspiracy theories have been moving from the fringe to the center of American culture, though he does not challenge the pathologization of conspiracy theory and even reaffirms the Hofstadterian link to paranoia. This distinguishes his study from those by Robert Goldberg and Kathryn Olmsted, who approach the topic more neutrally.[46] Goldberg explores the deep immersion of popular culture into conspiracy scenarios in recent decades and investigates how conspiracy theories allow many people to make sense of the world they are living in. Olmsted argues that American conspiracy theories have undergone a major shift at the time of World War I. While earlier versions had focused on external threats to the federal government, twentieth-century versions cast the government as conspiring against the people. The focus on the rhetorical and narrative qualities of conspiracy theories, and the refusal to pathologize their proponents—Olmsted explicitly sees conspiracy theories as "understandable responses to conspiratorial government rhetoric and actions"—aligns them with work in cultural studies.[47]

The first wave of the works in cultural studies comprises the work of Jodi Dean, Mark Fenster, Timothy Melley, and Peter Knight.[48] Without directly referencing them, these studies approach the topic in the tradition of Loewenthal and Guterman because they refuse to pathologize conspiracy theorists. Instead, like them, they hold that conspiracy theories are indicators of larger anxieties and concerns. They also agree that conspiracy theories are no longer a fringe phenomenon but became part of the mainstream after World War II.

For Dean, conspiracy theories about alien abduction are symptoms of a distrust in politicians and institutions that permeates American culture.[49] In similar fashion, Melley understands conspiracy theories as an expression of "agency panic," a concern about a loss of autonomy and challenges to traditional notions of identity in the present.[50] He also makes clear that the "paranoid" imagination of vast organizations and systems as conspiracies controlling individual and collective behavior, in both fictional and factual texts alike in the Cold War, share many assumptions with works of popular social theory from the period that likewise betray an anxiety about the controlling influence of social forces. Like Melley, the sociologist Luc Boltanski in his study of Anglo-American detective fiction draws attention to the potentially confounding similarities between the "hermeneutic of suspicion" (in Ricoeur's phrase) that is at the heart of most critical social theory and the operating assumption of conspiracy theory that nothing is as it seems.[51]

Like Melley and Dean, Knight also holds that under the conditions of post-modernity, conspiracy theories no longer simply affirm collective identities or scapegoat certain groups, but perform a variety of other functions. They articulate "increasing doubt and uncertainty" about power, identity, and agency.[52] Moreover, he observes that many Americans engage with conspiracy theories in self-conscious and ironic fashion, treating them "as if" they were true, rather than fully believing in them.

By contrast, Fenster focuses more on the ways in which conspiracy theories affect democratic politics. For him, conspiracy theories are "non-necessary element[s] of populist ideology" and thus posit a struggle between the people and those in power.[53] They misrepresent political realities but must be taken seriously because they hint at crises of representative democracy. They are not aberrations that threaten democracy from the extremist margins, but inherent components of all democratic societies.

The critique of pathologization central to these studies was taken up in a slightly different fashion by Jack Bratich. He argues that "conspiracy theory" as a category only exists to delegitimize certain forms of knowledge that are unwanted by elites or the public at large. He rightly points out that there are, even in the present, many conspiracy theories that escape this label such as the one forged by the Bush administration after 9/11 about the collaboration of al-Qaida and Saddam Hussein. Accordingly, conspiracy theories constitute a form of subjugated knowledge (in the Foucauldian sense) that is dismissed by experts and elites but which has never lost its "commonsensical appeal," which might explain why the anonymous polls conducted by political scientists find that so many Americans believe in conspiracy theories.[54] Clare Birchall is also interested in the status of conspiracy theories as knowledge and, like Bratich, she draws on Foucault and the sociology of knowledge to explain the status of conspiracy theories.[55] She describes conspiracy theories as a form of popular knowledge that circulates outside of official channels. However, unlike Bratich, she suggests that the distinction between official and subjugated forms of knowledge is eroding in the present, largely because of the influence of the Internet. Conspiracy theories in particular, she argues, have become more accepted because of 9/11.[56] And, like Knight, she emphasizes the playful way people engage with heterodox forms of knowledge. Finally, the status of conspiracy theories as knowledge is also at the center of Michael Butter's study of conspiracist visions from the seventeenth to the twentieth centuries in American culture. Synthesizing the work done by cultural studies scholars and the findings of the historians discussed at the end of the first section, he suggests that American conspiracy theories for a long time generated official knowledge, which changed only during the 1960s, exactly at the moment when the concerns about them reached the mainstream with the writings of Hofstadter.[57]

Conclusion: Plotting a Transdisciplinary and Transnational Future

As this overview shows, like conspiracy theories themselves, conspiracy theory research is currently mushrooming (or, perhaps more accurately, even if conspiracy theories are not necessarily more widespread than in the past, then conspiracy theories as a social problem have become prominent in part because both academic research and popular journalism have turned them into an object of inquiry). We have restricted ourselves here to fields that have already produced a substantial body of works, and have not discussed the ever more numerous contributions from scholars in disciplines that are just beginning to address the issue. Middle Eastern Studies, for example, where research had for a long time been impeded by Pipes' application of the pathologizing paradigm, has recently produced more nuanced studies.[58] Other disciplines, such as religious studies or ethnology, have also contributed at least a few studies to the understanding of conspiracy theory.[59] Moreover, we have also bypassed here the considerable body of research published in languages other than English.[60]

However, as our overview has also made clear, the various disciplines operate with vastly different conceptualizations of conspiracy theory. Research in psychology and research in cultural studies, for example, approach the subject from almost diametrically opposed premises, and there is little dialogue between the two. The fundamental assumptions of each discipline are at odds: Where psychologists are keen to find the *universal* predictors and drivers of conspiracy ideation beyond local difference, cultural historians are concerned to investigate the ways that conspiracy theory has functioned in *specific* historical, political, and media environments, arguing that even the very concept of "conspiracy theory" as a describable social and psychological phenomenon has its own history that cannot simply be taken for granted. It remains an open question whether more research into conspiracy theories in different cultures, regimes, and periods will produce a convergence on a single analytical model, or whether it will only reveal further complexities and contradictions.

Conversely, scholars from quantitative disciplines such as psychology and political science find the narrowness of the evidence base in cultural and historical studies frustrating, even if they find the hypotheses intriguing. Scholars in both camps sometimes point to work conducted in the other field in their introductions, but rarely ever seriously engage with it. Thus, there is no cross-disciplinary dialogue on contradictory findings and differing methodologies. Moreover, even those who draw on the findings of different disciplines are usually only aware of work published in the two or three languages they know. Due to the narrow perspectives of individual researchers, scholarship on conspiracy theory is fragmented and has not yet been able to answer various overarching questions and provide meaningful comparisons between the case studies. The enormous progress made over the last couple of years is thus in danger of being stalled, as scholars tend to reinvent the wheel instead of truly advancing knowledge.

Yet, whereas a decade ago there was a real lack of any detailed research, there is now a sufficient basis to push conspiracy theory research a step further. Research across the disciplines has reached a critical mass that now makes transdisciplinary and transnational research projects both feasible and desirable. Such projects, though, will demand intellectual openness from their practitioners. Researchers must be ready to seriously engage with colleagues who approach the topic from vastly different angles and with sometimes diametrically opposed assumptions. In other words, they must display exactly the openness to opposing ideas which conspiracy theorists are thought to lack.

Notes

1. Popper, Karl R. 2002. *Conjectures and Refutations: The Growth of Scientific Knowledge.* New York: Routledge; Wood, Gordon S. 1982. "Conspiracy and the Paranoid Style: Causality and Deceit in the Eighteenth Century." *William and Mary Quarterly* 39(3): 402–441; Zwierlein, Cornel, and Beatrice de Graaf. 2013. "Security and Conspiracy in Modern History." *Historical Social Research/Historische Sozialforschung* 38(1): 7–45; Pagán, Victoria E. 2012. *Conspiracy Theory in Latin Literature.* Austin: University of Texas Press; Roisman, Joseph. 2006. *The Rhetoric of Conspiracy in Ancient Athens.* Berkeley: University of California Press.
2. Cochin, Augustin. 1909. *La Crise de l'Histoire Révolutionnaire: Taine et M. Aulard.* Paris: Honoré Champion; Stauffer, Vernon. 1918. *New England and the Bavarian Illuminati.* Diss. New York: Columbia University Press; McKenzie-McHarg, Andrew. 2018. *The Hidden History of Conspiracy Theory.* Princeton: Princeton University Press.
3. Hofstadter, Richard. 1995. *The Paranoid Style in American Politics and Other Essays.* Cambridge: Harvard University Press.

4. Thalmann, Katharina. 2014. "'John Birch Blues': The Problematization of Conspiracy Theory in the Early Cold-War Era." *COPAS* 15(1). https://copas.uni-regensburg.de/article/view/182 (Accessed December 18, 2017); Bratich, Jack Z. 2008. *Conspiracy Panics: Political Rationality and Popular Culture*. Albany: State University of New York Press; Fenster, Mark. 2008. *Conspiracy Theories: Secrecy and Power in American Culture*. Rev. ed. Minneapolis: University of Minnesota Press.

5. Thalmann, "'John Birch Blues,'" 6.

6. Lasswell, Harold D. 1986. *Psychopathology and Politics*. Chicago: University of Chicago Press, 78; Adorno, Theodor W., Else Frenkel-Brunswik, Daniel J. Levinson, and R. Nevitt Sanford. 1950. *The Authoritarian Personality: Part Two*. New York: Wiley, 611.

7. Loewenthal, Leo and Norbert. Gutermann. 1949. *Prophets of Deceit: A Study of the Techniques of the American Agitator*. New York: Harper.

8. Thalmann, "'John Birch Blues,'" 7.

9. Popper, *Conjectures and Refutations*, 94. Italicized text in the original.

10. Shils, Edward. 1956. *The Torment of Secrecy: The Background and Consequences of American Security Politics*. New York: Free Press; Lipset, Seymour Martin. 1955. "The Sources of the Radical Right." In *The New American Right*, ed. Daniel Bell. New York: Criterion; Rovere, Richard H. 1959. *Senator Joe McCarthy*. New York: Harper Colophon.

11. Thalmann, "'John Birch Blues,'" 11.

12. Bunzel, John H. 1967. *Anti-Politics in America: Reflections on the Anti-Political Temper and Its Distortions of the Democratic Process*. New York: Knopf; Lipset, Seymour Martin, and Earl Raab. 1970. *The Politics of Unreason: Right-Wing Extremism in America, 1790–1970*. New York: Harper.

13. Thalmann, "'John Birch Blues,'" 11.

14. Hofstadter, *The Paranoid Style*, 7, 39.

15. Bratich, *Conspiracy Panics*, 31–32.

16. Hofstadter, *The Paranoid Style*, 36–37.

17. Fenster, *Conspiracy Theories*, 36.

18. Bailyn, Bernarnd. 1967. "Foreword." In *The Ideological Origins of the American Revolution*. Cambridge: Belknap; Davis, David Brion. 1970. *The Slave Power Conspiracy and the Paranoid Style*. Baton Rouge: Louisiana State University Press; Boyer, Paul, and Stephen Nissenbaum. 1974. *Salem Possessed: The Social Origins of Witchcraft*. Cambridge: Harvard University Press; Schwartz, Barry. 1987. *George Washington: The Making of an American Symbol*. New York: Free Press; Foner, Eric. 1995. *Free Soil, Free Labor, Free Men: The Ideology of the Republican Party before the Civil War*. New York: Oxford University Press.

19. Pfau, Michael. 2005. *The Political Style of Conspiracy: Chase, Sumner, and Lincoln*. East Lansing: Michigan State University Press.

20. Wood, "Conspiracy and the Paranoid Style."

21. Cubitt, Geoffrey. 1989. "Conspiracy Myths and Conspiracy Theories." *Journal of the Anthropological Society of Oxford* 20(1): 18.

22. Wood, Michael J., Karen M. Douglas, and Robbie M. Sutton. 2012. "Dead and Alive: Beliefs in Contradictory Conspiracy Theories." *Social Psychological and Personality Science* 3(6): 767–773.

23. Goertzel, Ted. 1994. "Belief in Conspiracy Theories." *Political Psychology* 15(4): 731–742.

24. Swami, Virna, Tomas Chamorro-Pemuzic, and Adrian Furnham. 2010. "Unanswered Questions: A Preliminary Investigation of Personality and Individual Difference Predictors of 9/11 Conspiracist Beliefs." *Applied Cognitive Psychology* 24(6): 749–761; Sutton, Robbie M., and Karen M. Douglas. 2014. "Examining the Monological Nature of Conspiracy Theories." In *Power, Politics, and Paranoia*. eds. Jan-Willem van Prooijen and Paul A. M. van Lange. Cambridge: Cambridge University Press.

25. Lewandowsky, Stephan, Gilles E. Gignac, and Klaus Oberauer. 2013. "The Role of Conspiracist Ideation and Worldviews in Predicting Rejection of Science." *PloS ONE* 8(10). https://doi.org/10.1371/journal.pone.0075637 (Accessed December 18, 2017).

26. Darwin, Hannah, Nick Neave, and Joni Holmes. 2011. "Belief in Conspiracy Theories: The Role of Paranormal Beliefs, Paranoid Ideation and Schizotypy." *Personal and Individual Differences* 50(8): 1289–1293; Baron, David, Kevin Morgan, Tony Towell, Boris Altemeyer, and Viren Swami. 2014. "Associations between Schizotypy and Belief in Conspiracist Ideation." *Personality and Individual Differences* 70(November): 156–159; Abakalina-Paap, Marina, Walter G. Stephan, Traci Craig, and W. Larry Gregory. 1999. "Beliefs in Conspiracies." *Political Psychology* 20(3): 637–647; Goertzel, "Belief in Conspiracy Theories"; Swami, Chamorro-Pemuzic, and Furnham, "Unanswered Questions"; Grzesiak-Feldman, Monika. 2013. "The Effect of High-Anxiety Situations on Conspiracy Thinking." *Current Psychology* 32(1): 100–118; Jolley, Daniel. 2013. "Are Conspiracy Theories Just Harmless Fun?" *The Psychologist* 26(1): 60–62.

27. Swami, Chamorro-Pemuzic, and Furnham, "Unanswered Questions"; Imhoff, Roland, and Martin Bruder. 2014. "Speaking Truth to (Un)Power: Conspiracy Mentality as a Generalised Political Attitude." *European Journal of Personality* 28(1): 25–43; Brotherton, Robert, Christopher C. French, and Alan D. Pickering. 2013. "Measuring Belief in Conspiracy Theories: The Generic Conspiracist Beliefs Scale." *Frontiers in Psychology* 4 (May). https://doi.org/10.3389/fpsyg.2013.00279 (Accessed December 18, 2017).

28. Swami, Viren, Martin Voracek, Stefan Stieger, Ulrich S. Tran, and Adrian Furnham. 2014. "Analytical Thinking Reduces Belief in Conspiracy Theories." *Cognition* 133.3(3): 572–585; Brotherton, French, and Pickering, "Measuring Belief in Conspiracy Theories"; Imhoff and Bruder, "Speaking Truth to (Un)Power."

29. Leman, Patrick J., and Marco Cinnirella. 2013. "Beliefs in Conspiracy Theories and the Need for Cognitive Closure." *Frontiers in Psychology* 4(June). https://doi.org/10.3389/fpsyg.2013.00378 (Accessed December 18, 2017).

30. Whitson, Jennifer A., Adam D. Galinsky, and A. Kay. 2015. "The Emotional Roots of Conspiratorial Perceptions, System Justification, and the Belief in the Paranormal." *Journal of Experimental Social Psychology* 56(January): 89–95.

31. Jolley, Daniel, and Karen M. Douglas. 2014. "The Effects of Anti-Vaccine Conspiracy Theories on Vaccination Intentions." *PLoS ONE* 9(2). https://doi.org/10.1371/journal.pone.0089177 (Accessed December 18, 2017); Jolley, Daniel, and Karen M. Douglas. 2014. "The Social Consequences of Conspiracism: Exposure to Conspiracy Theories Decrease Intentions to Engage in Politics and to Reduce One's Carbon Footprint." *British Journal of Psychology* 105(1): 35–56.

32. Swami, Voracek, Stieger, Tran, and Furnham, "Analytical Thinking Reduces Belief in Conspiracy Theories."

33. Oliver, J. Eric, and Thomas J. Wood. 2014. "Conspiracy Theories and the Paranoid Style(s) of Mass Opinion." *American Journal of Political Science* 58(4): 952–966; Sunstein, Cass R., and Adrian Vermeule. 2009. "Conspiracy Theories: Causes and Cures." *Journal of Political Philosophy* 17(2): 202–227; Uscinski, Joseph E., and Joseph M. Parent. 2014. *American Conspiracy Theories*. Oxford: Oxford University Press.

34. Sunstein and Vermeule, "Conspiracy Theories: Causes and Cures," 211.

35. Uscinski and Parent, *American Conspiracy Theories*, 130.

36. Oliver and Wood, "Conspiracy Theories and the Paranoid Style(s) of Mass Opinion," 953.

37. Miller, Joanne M., Kyle L. Saunders, and Christina E. Farhart. 2015. "Conspiracy Endorsement as Motivated Reasoning: The Moderating Roles of Political Knowledge and Trust." *American Journal of Political Science* 60(4): 824–844.

38. Nyhan, Brendan, Jason Reifler, and Peter A. Ubel. 2013. "The Hazards of Correcting Myths about Health Care Reform." *Medical Care* 51(2):127–132; Nyhan, Brendan, and Jason Reifler. 2015. "Does Correcting Myths about the Flu Vaccine Work? An Experimental Evaluation of the Effects of Corrective Information." *Vaccine* 33(3): 459–464.

39. Pigden, Charles. 1995. "Popper Revisited, or What is Wrong with Conspiracy Theories?" *Philosophy of the Social Sciences* 25(1): 3–34.

40. Ibid.; Coady, David. 2013. "Conspiracy Theories and Official Stories." *International Journal of Applied Philosophy* 17(2): 197–209; Basham, Lee. 2003. "Malevolent Global Conspiracy." *Journal of Social Philosophy* 34(1): 91–103.

41. Dentith, Matthew R.X. 2014. *The Philosophy of Conspiracy Theories.* New York: Palgrave Macmillan.

42. Keeley, Brian L. 1999. "Of Conspiracy Theories." *The Journal of Philosophy* 96(3): 109–126; Bale, Jeffrey M. 2017. "Political Paranoia vs. Political Realism: On Distinguishing between Bogus Conspiracy Theories and Genuine Conspiratorial Politics." *Patterns of Prejudice* 41(1): 45–60; Räikkä, Juha. 2009. "On Political Conspiracy Theories." *Journal of Political Philosophy* 17(2): 185–201.

43. Clarke, Steve. 2002. "Conspiracy Theories and Conspiracy Theorizing." *Philosophy of the Social Sciences* 32(3): 131–150.

44. Husting, Ginna and Martin Orr. 2007. "Dangerous Machinery: 'Conspiracy Theorist' as a Transpersonal Strategy of Exclusion." *Symbolic Interaction* 30(2): 127–150.

45. Barkun, Michael. A 2003. *Culture of Conspiracy: Apocalyptical Visions in Contemporary America.* Berkeley: University of California Press.

46. Goldberg, Robert Alan. 2001. *Enemies Within: The Culture of Conspiracy in Modern America.* New Haven: Yale University Press; Olmsted, Kathryn S. 2009. *Real Enemies: Conspiracy Theories and American Democracy, World War I to 9/11.* Oxford: Oxford University Press.

47. Ibid., 11.

48. Dean, Jodi. 1998. *Aliens in America: Conspiracy Cultures from Outerspace to Cyberspace.* Ithaca: Cornell University Press; Fenster, *Conspiracy Theories*; Melley, Timothy. 2000. *Empire of Conspiracy: The Culture of Paranoia in Postwar America.* Ithaca: Cornell University Press; Knight, Peter. 2000. *Conspiracy Culture: From Kennedy to the X-Files.* London: Routledge.

49. Dean, *Aliens in America*, 17.

50. Melley, *Empire of Conspiracy*, 7.

51. Boltanski, Luc. 2014. *Mysteries and Conspiracies: Detective Stories, Spy Novels and the Making of Modern Societies.* Trans. C. Potter. Cambridge: Polity Press.

52. Knight, *Conspiracy Culture*, 10.

53. Fenster, *Conspiracy Theories*, 84.

54. Bratich, *Conspiracy Panics*, 7.

55. Birchall, Clare. 2006. *Knowledge Goes Pop: From Conspiracy Theory to Gossip.* Oxford: Berg.

56. Ibid., 33.

57. Butter, Michael. 2014. *Plots, Designs, and Schemes: American Conspiracy Theories from the Puritans to the Present.* Berlin/Boston: de Gruyter.

58. Pipes, Daniel. 1996. *The Hidden Hand: Middle East Fears of Conspiracy.* Basingstoke: Macmillan; Gray, Matt C. 2010. *Conspiracy Theories in the Arab World: Sources and Politics.* London: Routledge; Butter, Michael, and Maurus Reinkowski, eds. 2014. *Conspiracy Theories in the United States and the Middle East: A Comparative Approach.* Berlin/Boston: de Gruyter.

59. West, Harry G. and Todd Sanders, eds. 2003. *Transparency and Conspiracy: Ethnographies of Suspicion in the New World Order.* Durham: Duke University Press; Dyrendal, Asbjorn. 2015. "Confluence of Spirituality and Conspiracy Theory?" *Journal of Contemporary Religion* 30(3): 367–382.

60. Taguieff, Pierre-André. 2005. *La Foire aux illumines. Ésotérisme, théorie du complot, extrémisme.* Paris: Mille et une nuits; Klausnitzer, Ralf. 2007. *Poesie und Konspiration: Beziehungssinn und Zeichenökonomie von Verschwörungsszenarien in Publizistik, Literatur und Wissenschaft 1750–1850.* Berlin: de Gruyter; Blanusa, Nebojsa. 2011. *Teorije zavjera I hrvatska politicka zbilja 1980–2007.* Zagreb: Plejada.

WHAT IS A CONSPIRACY THEORY?

JOSEPH E. USCINSKI

Definitions are particularly important when discussing conspiracy theories, because what we count as a conspiracy theory determines how we view that theory's veracity. Also, our definition of *conspiracy theory* determines who the conspiracy theorists are. If one's use of *conspiracy theory* excludes ideas believed by the left, for example, then people on the right will always appear as conspiracy theorists, and the characteristics shared by the right will always be found to predict conspiracy theorizing. Skewing the definition biases all findings. We have therefore agreed to a broad neutral definition of *conspiracy theory* that should not bias our discussions. The term *conspiracy theory* and its derivatives can evoke strong emotional responses; therefore we want to be clear that our terminology is intended in the most impartial way and without pejorative connotation. This issue is of such importance that we have dedicated four chapters to it.

Beyond *conspiracy* and *conspiracy theory*, there are a range of terms used throughout the volume. Authors have taken great care to define their terms. Readers will note that there is some disagreement among researchers about the best term to use and about the concepts tied to particular terms. For example, to refer to a similar concept, Alfred Moore uses the term *conspiracy politics* while Matthew Atkinson and Darin DeWitt use the term *conspiracy theory politics*. These sorts of disagreements will be settled over time in the marketplace of ideas. But for now, I provide definitions for *conspiracy, conspiracy theory, conspiracy belief, conspiracy thinking*, and *conspiracy theorist*.

Conspiracy

We define *conspiracy* as a secret arrangement between two or more actors to usurp political or economic power, violate established rights, hoard vital secrets, or unlawfully alter government institutions to benefit themselves at the expense of the common good. Known conspiracies include Watergate and the Tuskegee Experiments. Our definition refers to plots that typically go beyond criminal conspiracies, such as plans to knock over the local 7/11 or a scheme to kill grandma for the inheritance.

Conspiracies happen too regularly and are no doubt happening now. But because conspiracies are difficult to execute and conceal, they tend to fail. As the size and scope of a scheme increases, the number of actors who can either get caught in the act or "spill the beans" increases, making exposure more imminent. With this said, it is difficult to discuss conspiracies as a whole, because we only know about the ones that have been exposed and not the ones that have yet to be exposed. When conspiracies are exposed, they become deemed by the appropriate epistemological institutions as having actually occurred. Thus, *conspiracy*—when compared to *conspiracy theory*—refers to events that have been determined by the proper institutions to have actually happened. With this said, the proper authorities can be wrong or just late in their assessment.

Conspiracy Theory

Conspiracy theory refers to an explanation of past, ongoing, or future events or circumstances that cites as a main causal factor a small group of powerful persons, the conspirators, acting in secret for their own benefit and against the common good. The conspirators could be foreign or domestic governments, nongovernmental actors, scientists, religious and fraternal organizations, or any other group perceived as powerful and treacherous. Conspiracy theories are at their core about power: who has it and what do they do with it when no one can see.

While *conspiracy* refers to events that our appropriate institutions have determined to be true, *conspiracy theory* refers to an accusatory perception which may or may not be true, and usually conflicts with the appropriate authorities. Perhaps the best standard for differentiating between *conspiracy* and *conspiracy theory* is put forward by Neil Levy. He argues that properly constituted distributed networks of inquirers trained in assessing knowledge claims, with methods and results made public and available for scrutiny, are best suited for determining the existence of conspiracies.[1]

For example, theories suggesting that President John Kennedy was killed as part of a vast conspiracy, as opposed to by a single deranged gunman, are conspiracy theories because they have not been adopted by the proper epistemic authorities. Thus, such theories remain as *conspiracy theories*: accusatory and suspect, rather than as accepted knowledge. A conspiracy theory today can become accepted by authoritative institutions tomorrow and thus be deemed a conspiracy.

Telling which conspiracy theories are most likely to be true can be difficult, and epistemologists have yet to settle on standard tests by which to judge. Some philosophers are rather dismissive of conspiracy theories.[2] Others are more accepting of conspiracy theories; for example see the chapter by Matthew Dentith in this section. Because conspiracy theories address the use of secrecy, researchers should expect to find little indication of their existence and instead, plenty of disconfirming evidence and red herrings. We should therefore expect a lack of evidence and a preponderance of disconfirming evidence to count in favor of conspiracy theories, rendering them non-falsifiable. All conspiracy theories have a positive probability of being true, therefore researchers should not consider conspiracy theories within a true/false dichotomy. Instead, conspiracy theories should be considered in probabilistic terms: what is the likelihood a given conspiracy theory is true? Brian Keeley, for example, suggests that as a conspiracy theory becomes bigger (i.e., more actors and institutions are added to the plot to explain why it has yet to be exposed), should be considered less likely to be true.[3] On the other hand, the factual claims used to support a conspiracy theory can be deemed true and false (i.e., did World Trade Center Building 7 fall directly down or to the side). It is with these claims of fact that "debunking" should take place. It is impossible to prove a secret plot is not at work; it's much easier to show that the factual claims presented in favor of the secret group's plot are manufactured.

Explanations including strictly paranormal and supernatural phenomena are excluded. For example, Bigfoot, Loch Ness, and chupacabra are not conspiracy theories. If they exist, then they are just animals wandering around undetected. If one posited that the government was hiding evidence of Bigfoot from the public, then that would be a conspiracy theory. Aliens are not a conspiracy theory. If a theory claimed that the aliens were plotting with the government to kidnap and experiment on people, then that would be a conspiracy theory. ESP is not a conspiracy theory, but if one posited that malevolent groups were secretly reading our minds with it, then yes, that would be a conspiracy theory. Fan theories about fictional movies or television shows (i.e., the plot of Grease is really just Sandy's dying hallucination as she drowns in the ocean) do not meet our definition of *conspiracy theory*. It is interesting how the term is sometimes stretched and other times very selectively applied in popular usage; Jesse Walker's account in Chapter 3 is instructive on this point. In this volume, we try to keep our usage narrow and apply it as evenly as possible.

Conspiracy Belief

Conspiracy belief, sometimes *conspiricist belief* or *conspiratorial belief*, refers to a person's belief in a specific conspiracy theory or specific set of conspiracy theories. Included in this definition are beliefs that climate change is a hoax, that the Jews secretly manipulate the economy, that the CIA assassinated President Kennedy, that the Freemasons, Illuminati, or Bilderbergers rule the world, and that Monsanto wants to poison the world's population. There are, of course, an infinite number of conspiracy beliefs that one could hold.

Conspiracy Thinking

Sometimes referred to as *conspiratorial predispositions, conspiracist ideation, conspiracy ideology, conspiracy mindset, conspiratorial worldview,* or *conspiricism, conspiracy thinking* refers to an underlying worldview or disposition, similar to political ideology, toward viewing events and circumstances as the product of conspiracies. Those with high levels of this latent trait are more likely to believe in specific conspiracy theories than people with lower levels, all else being equal.

This concept of conspiracy thinking stems from two strands of literature. First, numerous studies in psychology and political science identify this latent tendency. While there is some disagreement about how to measure it and what its causes are, researchers seem to be in agreement that this generalized latent unique dimension of opinion exists to one degree or another within people.[4] It could be thought of as a bias against powerful actors that leads people to accuse those actors of collusion.[5] Second, traditional theories of public opinion formation suggest that underlying worldviews are likely the cause of observable and more specific opinions. In writing about information, predispositions, and opinion, John Zaller argues, "Every opinion is a marriage of information and predisposition: information to form a mental picture of the given issue, and predisposition to motivate some conclusion about it," and that "[Citizens] possess a variety of interests, values, and experiences that may greatly affect their willingness to accept—or alternatively, their resolve to resist—persuasive influence."[6] Just as citizens interpret events and circumstances with their underlying political predispositions such as partisanship and political ideology,[7] citizens also interpret the world through their underlying view about how much conspiracies determine events and circumstances.[8] In the United States, conspiracy thinking occupies its own dimension of opinion and is spread evenly across political ideology and partisanship.[9]

Researchers have yet to fully determine the factors that cause individuals to possess particular levels of conspiratorial thinking. Political socialization likely plays a large role, much the way many researchers argue partisanship and political ideology are determined by processes occurring during one's formative years. Psychological factors could play a role as well. Chapter 16 by Michael Wood and Karen Douglas address this concept more in depth.

Conspiracy Theorist

Conspiracy theorist is a term that has never been well defined. Given that everyone believes in a conspiracy theory or two, the term could apply to everyone, but this would render the term meaningless. Sometimes *conspiracy theorist* is used to denote people who believe in a specific conspiracy theory, or to people who believe in many conspiracy theories. The term is used at times to denote professionals who spread conspiracy theories for a living, like Alex Jones, or amateurs who improve upon particular theories. *Conspiracy theorist* could also mean a person with a high level of conspiracy thinking. Because of the ambiguity, the authors in this volume have limited the use of this term and when they do use it, they use it so that its meaning is obvious.

Notes

1. Levy, Neil. 2007. "Radically Socialized Knowledge and Conspiracy Theories." *Episteme* 4(2): 181–192. DOI: 10.3366/epi.2007.4.2.181.
2. Cassam, Quassim. 2016. "Vice Epistemology." *The Monist* 99(2): 159–180. DOI: 10.1093/monist/onv034; Mandik, Pete. 2007. "Shit Happens." *Episteme* 4(2): 205–218. DOI: 10.3366/epi.2007.4.2.205; Popper, Karl R. 1972. *Conjectures and Refutations*. London and New York: Routledge & Kegan Paul; Popper, Karl R. 1966. *The Open Society and Its Enemies, Vol. 2: The High Tide of Prophecy: Hegel, Marx, and the Aftermath*. 5th edition. London and New York: Routledge & Kegan Paul.

3. Keeley, Brian. 1999. "Of Conspiracy Theories." *Journal of Philosophy* 96(3): 109–126.

4. Brotherton, Robert, Christopher C. French, and Alan D. Pickering. 2013. "Measuring Belief in Conspiracy Theories: The Generic Conspiracist Beliefs Scale." *Frontiers in Psychology* 4(May). DOI: 10.3389/fpsyg.2013.00279; Bruder, Martin, Peter Haffke, Nina Nouripanah, and Roland Imhoff. 2013. "Measuring Individual Differences in Generic Beliefs in Conspiracy Theories across Cultures: The Conspiracy Mentality Questionnaire." *Frontiers in Psychology* 4(April). DOI: 10.3389/fpsyg.2013.00225; Imhoff, Roland and Martin Bruder. 2013. "Speaking (Un-)Truth to Power: Conspiracy Mentality as a Generalised Political Attitude." *European Journal of Personality* 28(1): 25–43. DOI: 10.1002/per.1930.

5. Brotherton, French, and Pickering, "Measuring Belief in Conspiracy Theories"; Bruder, Haffke, Nouripanah, and Imhoff, "Measuring Individual Differences in Generic Beliefs in Conspiracy Theories across Cultures"; Imhoff and Bruder, "Speaking (Un-)Truth to Power."

6. Zaller, John. 1992. *The Nature and Origins of Mass Opinion* Cambridge: Cambridge University Press.

7. Berinsky, Adam. 2009. *In Time of War: Understanding American Public Opinion from World War Ii to Iraq.* Chicago: University of Chicago Press; Converse, Philip E. 2006. "The Nature of Belief Systems in Mass Publics (1964)." *Critical Review* 18(1–3): 1–74.

8. Uscinski, Joseph E., Casey Klofstad, and Matthew Atkinson. 2016. "What Drives Conspiratorial Beliefs? The Role of Informational Cues and Predispositions." *Political Research Quarterly* 69(1): 57–71.

9. Uscinski, Joseph E. and Joseph M. Parent. 2014. *American Conspiracy Theories.* Oxford: Oxford University Press; Uscinski, Joseph E., and Santiago Olivella. 2017. "The Conditional Effect of Conspiracy Thinking on Attitudes toward Climate Change." *Research & Politics* 4(4). DOI: 10.1177/2053168017743105.

3

What We Mean When We Say "Conspiracy Theory"

JESSE WALKER

What exactly do we mean by the term *conspiracy theory*? The problem is vexing enough in the academic literature, where scholars have made countless attempts to formulate a firm definition.[1] In everyday usage, the expression is even more slippery: Its meaning constantly stretches and narrows, particularly when it is used as a pejorative. What follows is more impressionistic than systematic—not a complete study of the way the words *conspiracy theory* are used, but some observations about the way it bends to include or not include certain stories, and a hypothesis about why that might be so.

Let's begin with the great vaccine debate of February 2015. That month, New Jersey Governor Chris Christie, Kentucky Senator Rand Paul, and White House Press Secretary Josh Earnest all suggested, to one degree or another, that when it comes to childhood vaccines, public health should be balanced with parental choice. Christie, who we'll focus on here, called vaccinations "an important part of being sure we protect" children's health but added that "parents need to have some measure of choice in things as well."[2]

Christie's critics immediately started digging for anything else he might have said on the subject. They found he had a history of courting voters who believe there might be a causal link between vaccines and autism. In 2009, for example, he put his signature on a letter that said:

> I have met with families affected by autism from across the state and have been struck by their incredible grace and courage. Many of these families have expressed their concern over New Jersey's highest-in-the-nation vaccine mandates. I stand with them now, and will stand with them as their governor in their fight for greater parental involvement in vaccination decisions that affect their children.[3]

One prominent liberal site, *ThinkProgress*, reported this news under the headline "Chris Christie's Long Flirtation with Anti-Vaccine Conspiracy Theories."[4] Another, *The Daily Kos*, used the title "In 2009, Chris Christie sent letter endorsing anti-vaxxer conspiracy theory."[5] Watching discussions of the story on social media, I repeatedly saw the phrase "conspiracy theory" attached to Christie's claims. Yet Christie didn't explicitly say anything about a conspiracy.

Perhaps the slippage is understandable in this case. After all, many people who believe these discredited claims about vaccines also believe that there is a conspiracy to conceal the shots' supposed ill effects. But the idea of a vaccine/autism connection is not innately conspiratorial, and the attempts I've seen to argue otherwise fall flat. An article in *Salon*, for instance, claimed that anti-vaxxers "are, at their core, conspiracy theorists" because they must "believe that all major health organizations in the world are colluding to cover up the supposed dangers of vaccines."[6] But of course there's no reason to assume a vaccine skeptic is actually aware of how strong the scientific consensus on the question is. Indeed, when powerful figures like Christie—and, the year before Christie wrote that letter, Barack Obama, John McCain, and Hillary Clinton—throw around phrases like "the science right now is inconclusive,"[7] that creates the illusion not of a conspiracy but of an open question.

This is not unusual. In other domains, such as climate change, denial of the scientific consensus is often automatically equated with conspiracy theory. The two do often go hand in hand. One could deny climate change because one believes scientists are deliberately faking data, just as one could deny the safety of vaccines because one believes pharmaceutical companies are covering up a product's side effects. But a conspiracy theory is not a necessary condition of denying either climate change or vaccine safety.

A year before the vaccine debate flared up, the phrase "conspiracy theory" was invoked in an even odder context. At one moment during CNN's heavy coverage of the disappearance of Malaysia Airlines Flight 370, host Don Lemon claimed that some people had suggested the plane had been swallowed by a black hole, an idea he categorized with "all of these conspiracy theories."[8]

As with the supposed vaccination/autism link, there are conspiracy theories about the missing airplane. But this surely was not one of them, since a black hole is not a secret plot. Yet Lemon wasn't the only person to make that category error. A video at *The Daily Beast*, for example, claimed to list the "kookiest conspiracy theories" about the plane.[9] It did indeed list a lot of conspiracy theories, but it also included the black hole, along with the idea that the plane had been hit by a meteor—no, not a meteor controlled by a conspiracy—and the notion that it had landed on an isolated island.

Another recent example: In 2014 *Technology Review* published an article headlined "Data Mining Reveals How Conspiracy Theories Emerge on Facebook."[10] This article covered an interesting piece of research from Italy, where a quintet of scholars were observing how a large sample of Facebook users engaged with different sorts of stories.[11] One of the tales the team tackled was a satiric article claiming the country had passed a bill giving legislators 134 billion Euros "to find a job in case of defeat." Many readers had mistaken this spoof for an actual news report, and thousands of people signed a petition against the imaginary law. The *Technology Review* article led with this tale, which it used to argue that "Conspiracy theories seem to come about by a process in which ordinary satirical commentary or obviously false content somehow jumps the credulity barrier."

Yet again, we see the term being applied in a strange way. The rumor involved a bill supposedly passed in public by the Italian senate, not a secret plan hatched by a hidden cabal. Nor did the original group of scholars claim the rumor was a conspiracy theory. Their concern was the transmission of *false* stories, whether or not they involve covert plotting. (The word *conspiracy* and its variants appear only four times in their study.) But for the *Technology Review* writer, "false story" and "conspiracy theory" apparently were synonyms.

So on the one hand there is this habit of using the phrase "conspiracy theory" to describe dubious claims that do not actually include conspiracies. Couple that now with another trend: the tendency *not* to use the phrase "conspiracy theory" to describe conspiratorial stories embraced by the mainstream.

When I say "embraced by the mainstream," I'm not referring to beliefs that are widely held but still somewhat disreputable, like some of the JFK assassination theories. Nor do I mean those events, such as Watergate or Iran–Contra, where a conspiracy clearly did take place. I mean things like these:

Terrorism

Real terrorist conspiracies obviously do exist, but recent history is also filled with purported plots that failed to materialize. Furthermore, when terror plots do occur, people often assume they're part of a larger organized effort even when the evidence for such centralization is scarce. (In the wake of 9/11, for example, the White House reportedly pushed the FBI to prove that Al Qaeda was responsible for the anthrax mailings.[12]) And where there really is a larger organized effort, there is a tendency to imagine it in ways that have more in common with paranoid pulp fiction than with asymmetric warfare as it is conducted in the real world.

Consider this November 2001 report in *The Independent*, which purported to describe Osama bin Laden's Tor Bora base:

> It has its own ventilation system and its own power, created by a hydroelectric generator. Its walls and floors in the rooms are smooth and finished and it extends 350 yards beneath a solid mountain. It is so well defended and concealed that—short of poison gas or a tactical nuclear weapon—it is immune to outside attack. And it is filled with heavily armed followers

of Osama bin Laden, with a suicidal commitment to their cause and with nothing left to lose.

Yesterday, for the first time, a witness spoke about one of the greatest remaining challenges for the effort to destroy al-Qa'ida—its underground cave complex in the Tora Bora area of the White Mountains of eastern Afghanistan. He described a purpose-built guerrilla lair, in and around which as many as 2,000 Arab and foreign fighters and remnants of the Taliban are reported to be preparing for a guerrilla battle.[13]

As the story was picked up by outlets across the United States, another British paper—the London *Times*—ran this imaginative illustration of bin Laden's Bond-villain lair (Figure 3.1): [14]

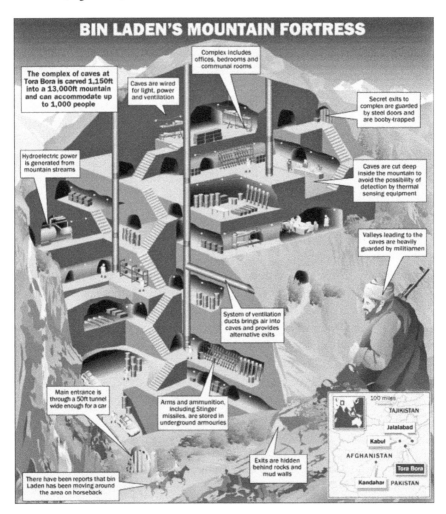

Figure 3.1 Bin Laden

This vision received an official endorsement of sorts when it was mentioned on *Meet the Press*. Shown the *Times'* diagram, Defense Secretary Donald Rumsfeld declared that "there's not *one* of those. There are *many* of those."[15]

When American forces arrived at Osama's actual base, they found that the *Independent* report was a fantasy, something better suited for a legend about Hassan i Sabbah than a realistic assessment of bin Laden's methods and capabilities. Yet the incident is rarely raised during discussions of conspiracism.

Gangs

In his 1999 book *Random Violence*, the sociologist Joel Best explained how criminal gangs are typically imagined in contemporary America: They "are secretive; they are large (and spreading); their business is calculated, deliberate, and structured; dealing in drugs, violence, and other crime, they form great, powerful hierarchies through supergang alliances; and their members have a rich, secretive culture of colors, gang signs, and initiation rites."[16] There are obvious similarities between this image and many traditional conspiracy theories, and indeed Best goes on to explore those parallels. But ordinary discussions of "conspiracy theories" rarely cite such tales of tightly organized supergangs, even though they are surely among the most popular and influential conspiracy stories in the United States today.

As with terrorism, there are multiple layers here. First there are the times people see a gang where one doesn't exist. This typically happens when reporters or officials encounter an unfamiliar subculture. A recent example would be the FBI's 2011 decision to include the Juggalos—that is, the fans of the band Insane Clown Posse—in its National Gang Threat Assessment, a periodically published report on gang activities.[17] This is roughly comparable to looking at the LSD sales outside Grateful Dead concerts and concluding that the Deadheads are a drug-trafficking ring.

The second layer comes when a decentralized criminal network is perceived as a centralized criminal hierarchy. Much of the rhetoric around human trafficking follows this pattern, particularly when politicians and the press conflate voluntary migration with involuntary trafficking. The anthropologist Laura Agustín has noted, for example, that people crossing borders illicitly need "access to social networks providing knowledge, contacts and expertise. Migrants find them amongst friends, families and small-time entrepreneurs, most of whom would not qualify as organised crime, with its demonic overtones, or even as gangsters."[18] Yet that is how the media and the law often treat them.

And the third layer, as with terrorism, is the tendency to inflame these stories with imagery out of pulp fiction. (Pulp-fiction imagery is also common with human trafficking—unsurprisingly, given the long tradition of lurid "white slavery" tales to draw on.[19]) These pulpy notions often kick in with stories that do not come from official sources (though occasionally a policeman or politician will gullibly repeat them) but are passed around as urban legends.

This email, for example, circulated online in 2005:

> Gang Initiation Weekend. (Please Read Very Important!!!)
>
> Police officers working with the DARE program has issued this warning: If you are driving after dark and see an on-coming car with no headlights on, DO NOT FLASH YOUR LIGHTS AT THEM! This is a common Bloods gang member "initiation game" that goes like this:
>
> The new gang member under initiation drives along with no headlights, and the first car to flash their headlights at him is now his "target". He is now required to turn around and chase that car, then shoot and kill every individual in the vehicle in order to complete his initiation requirements.
>
> Police Depts. across the nation are being warned that September 23rd and 24th is the "Blood" initiation weekend. Their intent is to have all the new bloods nationwide drive around on Friday and Saturday nights with their headlights off. In order to be accepted into the gang, they have to shoot and kill all individuals in the first auto that does a courtesy flash to warn them that their lights are off. Make sure you share this information with all your friends and family who are drivers.[20]

Needless to say, the warning did not actually originate with the DARE program. And needless to say, the weekend came and went without a bloody mass initiation into a secret society. That did not keep the rumor from taking off again a few years later. Indeed, different incarnations of the story have been circulating since the 1980s, if not earlier.

Such stories can be particularly influential at times of heightened tensions. Consider the Baltimore riots of April 2015. On the day the bulk of the violence erupted, the city police department announced that it had "received credible information" that the Bloods, the Crips, and the Black Guerilla Family—three gangs that had called a truce to march against police brutality—had secretly "entered into a partnership to 'take-out' law enforcement officers."[21] News of this alleged entente moved quickly through the media and helped shape the public response to the unrest, but no further evidence for the plot emerged. Indeed, during the actual riot the gangs wound up helping cops keep the crowds calm, not assassinating officers.

It later emerged that it had taken the FBI only a few hours to decide that this "credible information" wasn't all that credible after all. But that was not reported until much later.[22]

"Cults"

There is a long history of conspiracy theories about new religious movements. The Mormons, to give a prominent example, inspired some intensely paranoid folklore. For that matter, there is a long history of conspiracy theories about *old* religious movements, notably Catholics, Jews, and lately Muslims. Discussions of conspiracy theories frequently include these.

Yet sometimes they don't. It's easy to throw around phrases like "the paranoid style" when looking back at, say, the cult scare of the 1970s, given some of the stories that circulated then: Secretive groups controlled by powerful puppetmasters were said to be recruiting young people through a form of mind control. But while that scare was actually underway, you weren't likely to hear such phrases unless the alleged conspiracy also involved, say, the CIA.

There was a similar lack of self-awareness in the following decade, when those anxieties about real religions helped fan a fear of fictional Satanic conspiracies. In the 1980s and early 1990s, countless reporters, prosecutors, and jurors convinced themselves that a network of devil worshippers was infiltrating day care centers and other institutions, then engaging in the ritual rape and murder of children. (Geraldo Rivera summed up the supposed situation on one of his TV specials: "Satanic cults! Every hour, every day, their ranks are growing. Estimates are there are over one million Satanists in this country. The majority of them are linked in a highly organized, very secret network. . . . The odds are this is happening in your town."[23])

At times this was described as a conspiracy theory, particularly after skeptical journalists started to debunk these ideas. A 1989 article in *Police Chief* magazine, for example, complained about the dubious claims the author was hearing at law enforcement seminars devoted to occult crimes; among other things, the author cited stories about "satanic groups involved in organized conspiracies, such as taking over day care centers, infiltrating police departments, and trafficking in human sacrifice victims."[24] Even so, when Americans in the 1980s discussed conspiracy theories as a general phenomenon, it's remarkable how rarely the idea of Satanic ritual abuse was included, even though those fears were surely far more widespread than many of the other conspiracy stories under discussion at the time.

Why Has This Happened?

So this is the rough direction in which our language has been evolving. People started using the phrase *conspiracy theory* to mean "implausible conspiracy theory," then "implausible theory, whether or not it involves a conspiracy." Meanwhile, they leave out those implausible theories that have a lot of cultural cachet, such as these stories about cults, gangs, and terrorists.

Why has this happened? For now one can only speculate; it's a question researchers should explore. Criminal, terrorist, and Satanic gangs would fit most standard definitions of conspiracy theory (depending on the activity they are accused of), while stories of the paranormal are often lumped into the *conspiracy theory* category even when they do not contain anything conspiratorial. Perhaps cultural representations of conspiracy theory such as *The X-Files* and *Coast to Coast AM*, which draw audiences with fantastic ideas that often go well beyond conspiracy theories, have blurred the lines. Or perhaps the lines were never drawn that well to begin with.

It is surely notable, though, that the combined effect is to underline the idea that conspiracy theories are something for *those* people, way out on the periphery of society. Conspiratorial thinking is perceived not as a widespread human trait but as the province of a peculiar personality type, not as a mass phenomenon but as a fringe phenomenon. "Conspiracy" starts to *mean* "fringe."

Many people may find that a comforting thought. But it does not have the advantage of being true.

Notes

1. Uscinski, Joseph E., and Joseph M. Parent. 2014. *American Conspiracy Theories*. Oxford: Oxford University Press, Chapter 2. For a broad discussion of conspiracy theories in American history, see Walker, Jesse. 2013. *The United States of Paranoia*. New York, Harper Collins.
2. Earnest said "the science on this is really clear" but "the president certainly believes that these kinds of decisions are decisions that should be made by parents." Earnest, Josh. 2015. "Press Briefing by Press Secretary Josh Earnest." The White House, February 3, 2015. https://obamawhitehouse.archives.gov/the-press-office/2015/02/03/press-briefing-press-secretary-josh-earnest-232015 (Accessed December 17, 2017). Paul said, "I'm not arguing vaccines are a bad idea. I think they're a good thing, but I think the parent should have some input." Quoted in Jaffe, Alexandra. 2015. "Paul: Vaccines can cause 'profound mental disorders.'" http://www.cnn.com/2015/02/02/politics/rand-paul-vaccine-effects/index.html (Accessed December 17, 2017). Christie quoted in Topaz, Jonathan. 2015. "Christie causes stir with vaccination comments." https://www.politico.com/story/2015/02/chris-christie-vaccinations-114825 (Accessed December 17, 2015).
3. Christie, Chris. n.d. http://www.rescuepost.com/Files/Christie.pdf (December 17, 2017).
4. The headline was later softened to "How Chris Christie Became a Hero of the Anti-Vax Movement." Culp-Ressler, Tara. 2015. https://thinkprogress.org/how-chris-christie-became-a-hero-of-the-anti-vax-movement-43c61a9563ae/ (Accessed December 17, 2017).
5. Hunter. 2015. "In 2009, Chris Christie sent letter endorsing anti-vaxxer conspiracy theory." https://dailykos.com/story/2015/02/02/1361766/-In-2009-Chris-Christie-sent-letter-endorsinganti-vaxxer-conspiracy-theory (Accessed February 2, 2015).
6. Marcotte, Amanda. 2015. "4 Reasons Right-wingers are Embracing Vaccine Trutherism." https://www.salon.com/2015/02/07/4_reasons_right_wingers_are_embracing_vaccine_trutherism_partner/ (Accessed December 17, 2017).
7. That particular quote comes from Obama, who said it at a rally in 2008. Dobbs, Michael. 2008. "Dr. Obama and Dr. McCain," *Washington Post*, April 22, 2008.
8. This may have been a garbled account of the theory that the plane had entered an "aeronautical black hole" where its transponder system ceases to function. See Lemon, Don. 2014.

"The Mystery of Flight 370: The Theory of Black Holes." YouTube, 1:02. Talking Points Memo TV. Available at: https://www.youtube.com/watch?v=ZpVd7k1Uw6A (Accessed December 17, 2017).

9. The Daily Beast. 2014. "MH370's Kookiest Conspiracies." https://www.thedailybeast.com/mh370s-kookiest-conspiracies (December 17, 2017).

10. MIT Technology Review. 2014. "Data Mining Reveals How Conspiracy Theories Emerge on Facebook," *Technology Review*. [Blog] *arXiv*. Available at https://www.technologyreview.com/s/525616/data-mining-reveals-how-conspiracy-theories-emerge-on-facebook/ (Accessed December 17, 2017).

11. Mocanu, Delia, Luca Rossi, Qian Zhang, Marton Karsai, and Walter Quattrociocchi. 2015. "Collective Attention in the Age of (Mis)information." *Computers in Human Behavior* 51: 1198–1204.

12. Meek, James Gordon. 2008. "FBI Was Told to Blame Anthrax Scare on Al Qaeda by White House Officials," *New York Daily News*, August 2, 2008.

13. Parry, Richard Lloyd. 2001. "Al-Qa'ida Almost 'immune to attack' Inside its Hi-tech Underground Lair," *The Independent*, November 27, 2001.

14. Unknown. 2001. "Bin Laden's Mountain Fortress." *Times of London*, November 29, 2001.

15. Rumsfeld, Donald. 2001. *Meet the Press*. By Tim Russert. NBC, December 2, 2001.

16. Best, Joel. 1999. *Random Violence: How We Talk about New Crimes and New Victims*. London: University of California Press, 82.

17. U.S. Federal Bureau of Investigations. 2011. *National Gang Threat Assessment: Emerging Trends*, National Gang Intelligence Center, Washington, D.C.: 22–23. While the FBI report wavered between acknowledging the Juggalos' "disorganization and lack of structure" and declaring them a "gang," police agencies were soon willing to declare a suspect a "gang member" with no more basis than his Juggalo lifestyle.

18. Agustín, Laura. 2008. "The Shadowy World of Sex Across Borders," *The Guardian*, November 19, 2008. For a more in-depth discussion, see Agustín, Laura. 2007. *Sex at the Margins: Migration, Labour Markets and the Rescue Industry*. New York, NY: Zed Books. A very similar alchemy allows police, politicians, and the press to treat decentralized and consensual prostitution as though it's a product of a centralized sex-slavery conspiracy; see Brown, Elizabeth. 2015. "The War on Sex Trafficking Is the New War on Drugs." https://reason.com/archives/2015/09/30/the-war-on-sex-trafficking-is (Accessed December 17, 2015).

19. There is a whole genre of viral Facebook posts dedicated to the idea that the author's young child just narrowly escaped being seized by sex traffickers at the supermarket or some similarly public place.

20. Mikkelson, Barbara. 2014. "Flashing Headlights Gang Initiation." https://snopes.com/crime/gangs/lightsout.asp (Accessed December 17, 2017).

21. Baltimore Police Department. 2015. "Credible Threat to Law Enforcement." https://scribd.com/doc/263262264/Credible-Threat (Accessed December 17, 2017).

22. Leopold, Jason. 2015. "Fearing a 'Catastrophic Incident,' 400 Federal Officers Descended on the Baltimore Protests." https://news.vice.com/article/fearing-a-catastrophic-incident-400-federal-officers-descended-on-the-baltimore-protests (Accessed December 17, 2017).

23. Quoted in Alexander, David. 1990. "Giving the Devil More Than His Due." *The Humanist*, March/April, 5–15.

24. Lanning, Kenneth V. 1989. "Satanic, Occult, Ritualistic Crime: A Law Enforcement Perspective." *The Police Chief*, October, 62–84.

4

Conspiracy Theory

The Nineteenth-Century Prehistory of a Twentieth-Century Concept

ANDREW MCKENZIE-MCHARG

Conspiracy theories have been around for a long time, though how long is a matter of debate. As for the concept itself, it might seem reasonable to expect a more exact answer about the moment of its emergence. When do we first find people talking and writing about *conspiracy theories*?

Ironically enough, it is possible to find an answer to this question in the form of a conspiracy theory. According to the political scientist Lance deHaven-Smith, the currency that *conspiracy theory* enjoys in our contemporary conceptual vocabulary can be traced back to CIA Dispatch 1035-906, an internal directive issued in 1967 in an effort to push back against growing skepticism of the official account of President Kennedy's assassination and to offset the speculation about the real circumstances behind the events of November 1963—speculation that, it hardly need be said, often impugned the integrity of American intelligence agencies.[1] It requires, however, a highly tendentious reading of this dispatch to arrive at deHaven-Smith's conclusion that the CIA decided to pursue this goal by tarring such speculation through use of the pejorative label of *conspiracy theory*.

DeHaven-Smith is furthermore aware that the CIA cannot take the credit for having invented the concept. As he notes, an earlier example of its usage can be found in *The Open Society and its Enemies* (1945), the famous denunciation of age-old proto-totalitarian strains of thought penned by the Austrian-English philosopher Karl Popper and conceived by him as his contribution to the war effort. Much of the literature on conspiracy theories has tended to point readers to this ambitious work of social philosophy for the origins of the term.[2] Yet we can easily predate Popper's discussion of the "conspiracy theory of society" by consulting the *Oxford English Dictionary* (OED), which uncovers an appearance of the term in the *American Historical Review* in 1909. This citation prompted the inclusion of *conspiracy theory* in *Twentieth-Century Words* (1999), a compilation of approximately

5,000 words and terms that were drawn from the OED and that were absorbed into the general vocabulary of the English language in the course of the twentieth century.[3]

New databases, especially those that have digitized huge masses of nineteenth-century newspaper materials, allow us, however, to locate even earlier occurrences of *conspiracy theory*. In particular they reveal a usage of the term in newspaper reports on crime from the 1870s onward; a setting that is conspicuously different from the musing on social philosophy where we later find use of the term by Popper and others. As ever more of this material is digitized and becomes searchable, it will undoubtedly be possible to find the odd earlier usage here and there.

I would like, however, to go beyond the rather trivial game of one-upmanship whose goal is to find ever earlier usages of a term by putting forward some reasons why the 1870s were a particularly germane period for the semantic union of *conspiracy* and *theory*. As we will see, laying bare some of the semantic shifts that encouraged the creation of the term can yield genuine insights into the phenomenon to which the term is applied.

First though, a caveat: early occurrences of the term are *not* instantiations of the concept. Concepts form part of a conceptual vocabulary. As such, they belong to a collective semantic memory from which they can be retrieved for use on repeated occasions. This in turn implies that a certain generality inheres to concepts; they can be recruited again and again for deployment in different situations. While undoubtedly both *conspiracy* and *theory* were concepts in nineteenth-century America (from where we will be drawing our material), there is no indication that *conspiracy theory* had attained this status at this time. Instead each time the term appears during this century (and well into the twentieth century), we are dealing with a one-off kind of event: it appears like a blip and then disappears back into the welter of communication that society produces (and that in turn reproduces society).

A good indicator of this is that we practically never find talk in the nineteenth century of *conspiracy theories*, that is, *conspiracy theory* in the plural. Table 4.1 displays the results of an inquiry that was conducted by using a number of databases. For each database a simple search was undertaken for the terms *conspiracy theory, conspiracy theories*, and *conspiracy theorist*. The table shows the year of the first occurrence (with the adjacent column recording the number of occurrences from this date onward within the database). The story related to the third term, which marks the creation of a type of person, namely the conspiracy theorist, is a story located in the latter part of the twentieth century, and, interesting as it might be, it is a story for another day. More pertinent for present purposes is the fact that the plural form *conspiracy theories* appears so much later than the singular form. In fact, the earliest example reveals itself to be a perfect example of a false positive: a sub-headline in the June 25, 1875 edition of the *Chicago Daily Tribune* reads: "The Blackmail and Conspiracy Theories Knocked Out of Court." Obviously it was informing its readers of a blackmail theory plus a conspiracy theory.

Table 4.1 **First Occurrences of the Term** Conspiracy Theory **(CT),** Conspiracy Theories **(CTs), and** Conspiracy Theorist(s) **(CTist(s)).**

Database	1st CT	No. CT	1st CTs	No. CTs	1st CTist(s)	No. CTist(s)
America's Historical Newspapers (1690–1922)	1874	110	1881*	1*	—	0
British Periodicals Collection I and II (17th C.–21st C.)	1868	13	—	0	—	0
Chronicling America (1836–1922)	1875**	202**	1875†**	>1†**	—	0
The Economist (1843–2011)	1963	154	1966	238	1976	232
Financial Times (1888–2010)	1988	12	1986	18	1990	9
Historical Newspapers (Proquest) (1791–1922)	1875**	75**	—**	—**	—	0
JSTOR	1909	4021	1951	3327	1962	549
Nineteenth-Century British Newspapers (1800–1900)	1869	7	—	0	—	0
Nineteenth-Century U.S. Newspapers (1800–1899)	1873	57	—	0	—	0
The Times (1785–1985)	1873	95	1968	56	1972	22
TLS (1902–2011)	1903	158	1967	133	1983	70

CT = conspiracy theory
CTs = conspiracy theories
CTist(s) = conspiracy theorist(s)
(checked: May 2016)

* First occurrence of CTs related to assassination of Garfield: "One of the conspiracy theories has been exploded," Boston Journal, July 12, 1881.

† "The Blackmail and Conspiracy Theories Knocked Out of Court," Chicago Daily Tribune, June 25, 1875.

** Does not distinguish between CT and CTs.

How are we to interpret this almost complete absence of the plural form in the nineteenth century? The answer is simple and is borne out by actually delving into the context of each occurrence registered by the search of the database: whenever the term *conspiracy theory* appeared, it referred to the specific, narrowly circumscribed case at hand. Of course, today the situation is completely different. *Conspiracy theory* has a generic status, meaning that in talking about *conspiracy theories* today, we can collect under this rubric a startlingly wide array of sub-phenomena—allegations of Jewish world domination, assassinations of American Presidents, the alleged foreknowledge about the Japanese bombing Pearl Harbor, faked moon landings, alien abductions, etc. In fact the diversity is so bewildering that we feel moved to ask how such disparate themes can possibly congeal to create the cohesive super-phenomenon we know as *conspiracy theory* (see, for example, Chapter 3 in this volume by Jesse Walker). In particular, the connection of these phenomena to *conspiracy* in its old meaning, of a covert assault on the seat of political sovereignty, is often not immediately clear. *Conspiracy* seems to have become short hand for cover-up or, more generally, secrecy and deception.

By contrast, the connection to *theory* in the generalized sense of a possible or tentative explanation might seem more apparent. This article will, however, focus its efforts to excavate the history of the term at precisely this point. Why are we speaking of *theories* when we talk of *conspiracy theories*?

Much of the material in what follows focuses on assassinations. In the wake of an assassination, conspiracy obviously offers itself as one explanation competing with an alternative explanation that posits a lone assassin. Thus, when Henri IV was killed in Paris in 1610, there were suspicions that his assassin Ravaillac had not acted alone. But no one at this time thought to characterize the suspicion of a conspiracy in terms of a *theory*. Why in modern times have we taken to calling such explanations *theories*?

The basic contention of this article is that the appeal to *theory* in this context reflects a process that has recently been called *scientization*.[4] Admittedly the term is somewhat unfamiliar. (My spellcheck is refusing to recognize it.) Yet it simply denotes a social process like many others that have reshaped society, such as urbanization or industrialization (both of which my spellcheck does recognize). Scientization unfolded as certain non-scientific sectors of society began, particularly in the nineteenth century, to recognize the authority and to envy the prestige of science. For this reason, they attempted to adopt scientific methods and align themselves with scientific principles. Scientization thus implies the social ascendancy of science—an ascendancy that was often tied to a devaluation of religious or theological knowledge.

Scientization, however, denotes more than secularization. This can be appreciated by observing how, throughout the nineteenth and into the twentieth century, journalists began to espouse standards and norms that can be subsumed under the concept of objectivity. Aspiring to objectivity was not necessarily connected to a disdain of institutionalized religion. It was, however, an expression of a wish shared among certain journalists to overhaul their own practices in the interest of making them more scientific. Furthermore, scientists for their part had no interest in conducting their research in a manner that was more journalistic. The journalists were looking to the scientists, and not the other way around. This asymmetry entitles us to speak of scientization.

Thus scientization was not just a case of a growing ideological preference for scientific knowledge over religious knowledge. Its impact extended much farther. Numerous sectors of society were increasingly dependent upon scientific expertise in maintaining their technical infrastructure, in assessing the performance of their respective institutions, in identifying problem areas, and in formulating future-oriented programs for improvement. For present purposes, I am interested in its influence on a semantic level. In this regard the scientization of society was discernible in the manner in which a scientific vocabulary begins to permeate non-scientific parts of society. The most pertinent example of this process is the newspaper.

Reading a newspaper is not a scientific activity. Nevertheless, by the 1880s readers of a newspaper found themselves often encountering notions of *evidence, proof, refutation, fact,* and—most significantly for present purposes—*theory.* Admittedly many of these concepts do not have a purely scientific provenance. In her book *The Culture of Fact. England, 1550–1720* (2000) Barbara Shapiro reminds readers that the concept of the *fact* was originally at home in legal discourse (think, for example, of expressions such as "accessory after the fact") before it was transferred and integrated into programs of scientific inquiry. The scientific provenance is, however, clearer when it comes to *theory.*[5] In what follows, we will have occasion to examine its use in response to the assassination of the American president James Garfield in 1881.

The Assassination of Garfield

On July 2, 1881, Garfield was walking through a Washington train station when he was shot by Charles Guiteau.[6] For years, Guiteau had been prone to notions of a higher calling. At first these had found an outlet in bouts of evangelical enthusiasm. But he later became convinced that he was destined for a diplomatic career, even though the years spent living in semi-vagrancy hardly qualified him for the post in Paris that he desired. When, after countless rejections, Guiteau finally realized that the administration was not receptive to his solicitations, he decided that the president had to be removed.[7]

Garfield lived on for six weeks after being shot. In the days immediately following the attempt on his life, at a time when the mental instability of the assassin had not been fully ascertained, a reporter from the Washington-based newspaper *The Evening Star* asked attorney general William A. Cook the following question:

> Reporter—What is your theory of the assassination?
>
> Mr. Cook—I have no definite or final theory in reference to it, and it would be both unjust and unwise to form a theory. To do so is inconsistent with a full, fair and impartial examination of the case. All theories should be temporarily entertained, so as to be considered in connection with all the facts that may be ultimately elicited.[8]

It is worth first noting the interview format. In 1881 such a format represented a still relatively new innovation in the practice of journalism. In the words of the historian of journalism Michal Schudson, the interview became "a common activity for reporters in the 1870s and 1880s." The exchange between the reporter and the attorney general testifies to Schudson's observation that "by the 1880s the interview was a well accepted and institutionalized 'media event,' an occasion created by journalists from which they could then craft a story."[9] Because an interview occurs between an interviewer and an interviewee, the excerpt also reminds us that, in explaining the uptake of *theory*, there are two sides to the story. We need to consider both (1) those investigating crime and (2) those reporting on it. Both had their reasons for integrating *theory* into their vocabulary.

Theory in the Context of Forensics

If we begin with Cook as a representative of the first group, it is noticeable how his answer betrays a curious inconsistency in its appeal to *theory*, even if the intended meaning remains clear. The first two sentences suggest that a theory represents the result of a foregoing investigation. By contrast, Cook's insistence in the third sentence that "all theories should be temporarily entertained" ascribes a speculative, open-ended character to them. *Theory* becomes no longer the endpoint aimed at in an investigation but rather the means of arriving at this endpoint. Yet the manner in which Cook fudges his answer is akin to a pencil smudging a paper pad; it reveals the imprint of far older jottings. The ambiguities and equivocations in Cook's answer raise age-old and even perennial questions about the need and the means to discipline the human imagination. The issue becomes particularly pressing in view of the tendency of the imagination to get ahead of itself. What can rein it in? The nineteenth century had a short answer: *facts*.

In framing the investigation in terms of *facts* and *theories*, Cook's answer bears witness to a process that scientized police inquiries into criminal acts and that thereby eventually yielded the modern science of criminal forensics. The semantic aspect of this process becomes more apparent if we enlarge the vocabulary of *theory* and *fact* referenced by Cook in his statement by taking note of another concept frequently invoked in the newspaper articles reporting on the attack on Garfield. Prior to learning of Cook's disavowal of any fully formed theory, readers of the same newspaper, *The Boston Journal*, had been informed that Cook—in curious contrast to the caution that befell him on the subsequent day—"is certain there was a conspiracy and is devoting his whole time to tracing clues."[10] Reports in the same newspaper describe how support for this position crumbled in the following days: "The detectives and secret service men, who have chased down every clew and suspicious circumstance, have reported them all without foundation."[11] Meanwhile, *The St. Louis Globe-Democrat* informed its readers that "Every clew that was thought originally to tend to show that Guiteau had confederates had been followed up," and as a result it had been "proved that there is nothing on which to base the theory of the conspiracy."[12]

How does the clue (or clew) fit into the story of scientization? A promising place to start the search for an answer to this question is a famous essay by the Italian historian Carlo Ginzburg: "Clues: Roots of an Evidential Paradigm."[13] The evidential paradigm that Ginzburg references stands in a curious relationship of contrast and complementarity with what Ginzburg called the Galilean paradigm.[14] In this latter paradigm, observation is conducted with an eye to the higher unifying generality characterized by regularity and consistency. Examples for such a generality might be a law of nature or an ideal type. The search for a law of nature or the description of an ideal type proceeds by discarding all the anomalies and aberrations attendant upon an individual case. Thus, slight deviations from a planet's trajectory or peculiar idiosyncrasies exhibited by a zoological specimen can be ignored. This attitude is reversed within the evidential paradigm. Here anomalies and aberrations become the source of new knowledge.

As Ginzburg noted, the evidential paradigm has ancient antecedents. Hunters and trackers who learned to discern in the smallest detail—broken branches, footprints, a trace of fur or hair—the signs of their quarry were already operating within this mode. Long experience endowed the practitioners of this art with an almost preternatural ability to detect such clues. In the guise of one of its more modern—and admittedly fictional—practitioners, Sherlock Holmes's skills of observation and detection elicit frequent expressions of astonishment from his companion Dr. Watson. Yet regardless of how uniquely individual Holmes might seem in his combination of English eccentricity, opiate addiction, and confirmed bachelordom, the skills, methods, and perception he brings to bear upon the cases described by each story represent in fact a very general development at this time. This development affected modern nation-states who had discovered in the fight against crime a source of legitimacy germane to a society configured by the balance between public order and private freedoms—private freedoms that also extended to the engagement of private detectives to support public bodies in their effort to preserve public order. In the real world the skill set attributed to Holmes was, in fact, undergoing a process by which it was systematized, institutionalized, professionalized, and disseminated.[15] In fact, the Sherlock Holmes stories conform often to the logic of a conjuring trick: what at first seems to be the operation of a highly refined, intuitive ability to detect clues and divine motives is explicated in the denouement. Even if the audience is often made up of only the admiring Watson (and, of course, the reader), the mere fact that Holmes can give a reasoned account of the methods by which he solved the case suggests that there are lessons to be learned here—lessons, moreover, that can be both applied to future cases and passed on to other budding detectives.

Forensics belonged to a cohort of practices that were beholden to the evidential paradigm and that in the late nineteenth century—and, more precisely, in the decade 1870–1880—began to find a place as disciplines in the social and human sciences.[16] Ginzburg is not so forthcoming in explaining why this decade was so decisive. This prompts therefore a further question: What enabled the elevation of a very old technique to the status of a brand new science?

In lieu of a full answer to a big question, it suffices to point to out here how Ginzburg's essay on clues links up to the important inquiry undertaken by Lorraine Daston and Peter Galison into *Objectivity* (2007). As their work demonstrates, the aspiration of scientists to produce objective knowledge has been pursued under the auspices of varying "epistemic virtues." These virtues have normatively prescribed how scientists were to conduct their work and, in doing so, control, contain, or suppress their subjective biases. Thus, the natural philosophers of the eighteenth and early nineteenth century adhered to a creed of "truth-to-nature"; they strove to represent nature in accordance with its idealized forms, and in this manner to produce knowledge that would elicit broader recognition as valid.

However, in the late nineteenth and early twentieth century the legitimacy of this mode of representation was challenged. It now seemed to entail a projection of artificial aesthetic norms onto nature. The alternative lay in the attempt to capture nature in all its unadulterated messiness. The growing preference for this alternative ushered in a regime of what Daston and Galison describe as "mechanical objectivity." Scientists were exhorted to effectively recuse themselves from active participation in the representation of nature and to leave this to the more-or-less mechanical automation of recording devices. Science in this way became receptive to all those anomalies and aberrations that had previously represented the detritus of the observation process: "objects became specific, individual"; they were "no longer [merely] representative of a type."[17] This "shift from object-as-type to object-as-particular" was obviously germane to the scientization of the evidential paradigm, whose focus had always fallen on the irregularities and peculiarities of the particular case.[18] The *clue*, which had in the past been discerned on the basis of an almost tacit knowledge, was on the way to being objectified as a *fact*.

These thoughts intimate a context linking the rise of Daston and Galison's regime of mechanical objectivity with the scientization of Ginzburg's evidential paradigm. Both developments do indeed unfold more or less in parallel.[19] Moreover, they mutually reinforce each other and jointly effect profound changes in the late nineteenth-century production of knowledge. But it is tempting to push the inquiry even further by asking about the technical-material and institutional substrata that supported and promoted these developments. We restrict ourselves to one, admittedly negative comment: it was not—or, at least, not just—photography.[20]

The observation seems pertinent as photography's importance in the emergence of forensics has often been emphasized. The German literary critic and philosopher Walter Benjamin maintained that its "invention [...] was no less significant for criminology than the invention of the printing press was for literature."[21] After all, photography provided the means to capture those irregularities and peculiarities that a regime of mechanical objectivity willingly accepted as the assurance of scientific integrity and that the knowledge-generating practices of the evidential paradigm positively embraced as its raw material. Yet the neat technological determinism that posits photography as the driving force behind this change is belied by the chronology; curiously, we find that the adoption of a scientific vocabulary, encompassing terms such as *fact, clue,* and *theory*, predates the actual application of photography for identifying recidivist criminals and, subsequently, for preserving an image of the crime scene with all its morbid details.[22]

Theory in the Newspapers

The excerpt from the interview with the attorney general Cook begins with the journalist asking the question: "What is *your* theory of the assassination?" The possessive pronoun is important. If detectives and other practitioners of the nascent discipline of criminal forensics used *theory* to earmark certain explanations as provisional or speculative, the possessive pronoun points to a different—or rather, additional—function that *theory* fulfilled, this time for journalists. *Theory* served here as a shorthand for reported speech. It denoted an explanation that, at least at the moment the journalist was reporting, was not regarded as authoritative.

An example in the aftermath of a later assassination proves illuminating. On November 22, 1963, the Texan Governor John Connally sat in front of President Kennedy as the presidential motorcade made its way through Dallas. He was seriously wounded by one of the shots fired when the car reached Dealey Plaza. Three years later in *LIFE Magazine* he stated: "They talk about the 'one-bullet or two-bullet theory,' but as far as I am concerned, there is no 'theory.'"[23] Connally claimed to possess "absolute knowledge" that he had been wounded by a different bullet to the one that had first wounded Kennedy. Yet this knowledge was "absolute" only to Connally. The journalist from *LIFE Magazine* maintained a stance of neutrality by continuing to refer to Connally's account of events as a *theory* throughout the rest of the article. It existed on a par with all the other theories. One could perhaps differentiate between theories in terms of plausibility, but there was a basic equivalence in terms of their status as individual—and therefore quite possibly subjective—explanations.

Thus, *theory* had a role to play first in the practice and then in the creed of objectivity that journalists developed throughout the nineteenth century and into the twentieth century. Admittedly journalism in nineteenth-century America did not explicitly appeal to objectivity. But its attitude of "naïve empiricism," as it has been subsequently designated, entailed a devotion to facts that presaged and prepared the way for a fully articulated creed of journalistic objectivity.[24] Facts were nuggets of knowledge whose truth was guaranteed by a verifiable correspondence with the external reality. Journalists reported these facts. Their work was neither speculative nor subjective. And yet journalists were always encountering the fact of speculation or subjective viewpoints put forward by others. In this regard the words of the commentator Walter Lippmann are illuminating:

> The news does not tell you how the seed is germinating in the ground, but it may tell you when the first sprout breaks through the surface. It may even tell you what somebody says is happening to the seed underground. It may tell you that the sprout did not come up at the time it was expected.[25]

The first sentence affirms an obligation on the part of journalists to abstain from speculation about what they cannot see and hear—and therefore cannot verify—with their own eyes and ears. And yet, as Lippmann noted in the following sentences, there might be reasons to report on speculations and prognostications, so long as they came from others and were not submitted by the journalists themselves.

As a useful term for dealing with newsworthy speculation, *theory* had already established itself as part of the nomenclature of journalism over half a century earlier in the 1860s and 1870s. Some examples drawn from the mass of speculation on criminal cases prove illuminating. Page two of the *Cincinnati Daily Gazette* on April 26, 1867 informed its reader about a discovery of bones: "Some knowing person pronounced them the bones of a man, and speedily devised a *theory* to account for their being found where they were. They said that the man had evidently been murdered; that the hogs had eaten his flesh, with other horrible accomplishments. A closer investigation showed, however, that the remains were those of some animal; the inventors of the *murder theory* said they 'knew it would turn out so'; and the excitement subsided, with everybody feeling much more comfortable."[26] In the *Albany Evening Journal* on September 24, 1875, we read on page five: "The police think the child has been drowned but Mr. Sullivan firmly believes in the *abduction theory.*" In an article on page eight of the *New York Times* of July 16, 1881 with the headline "One of the Mysteries of Niagara Falls," we read of Olivet Rowell whose body had been found in the river; upon being retrieved, the body was seen to have "a rope around its neck and a bullet-hole in the head." A detective pays the widow a visit, which convinces him "that there was no conspiracy involving her or any of her family or friends." But the detective finds a motive involving inheritance and becomes suspicious: ". . . starting with this clue, he began to fortify his *theory of fraud* . . ." Finally "the *fraud theory*" is confirmed when Rowell is found alive. This leaves the journalist wondering whose body was found in the river: "It certainly is not that of Rowell."

In these examples we are witness not only to an uptake of *theory* as part of a scientific vocabulary adopted by forensics but also to a tendency to combine *theory* with a possible explanation of the crime. The last example in which the *fraud theory* was vindicated by the discovery of the living Rowell provides a case that could conceivably have induced a use of the term *conspiracy theory*, given that the detective at first suspected a "conspiracy" between the widow and her family and friends. Although *conspiracy theory* is not to be found in this particular article, a search of the relevant databases reveals other, earlier cases in which this term does indeed make an appearance. This is hardly surprising in view of the status of conspiracy as a crime in Anglo-American law.

Such considerations encourage a more systematic approach. By consulting databases that have digitized American newspapers from the nineteenth century, it is possible to gain an appreciation of how *theory* as a term made inroads into the discourse of crime. Thus, a search of the database *America's Historical Newspapers* identifies the following dates as the earliest mention for *conspiracy theory* and other terms built on the template (*crime x + theory*):[27]

murder theory (1867)
suicide theory (1871)
conspiracy theory (1874)
blackmail theory (1874)
abduction theory (1875)

The database *Nineteenth-Century U.S. Newspapers* yields the following results:[28]

suicide theory (1863)
murder theory (1871)
conspiracy theory (1873)
blackmail theory (1875)
abduction theory (1882)

And finally the same query was directed at the database *ProQuest*:[29]

suicide theory (1859)
murder theory (1870)
conspiracy theory (1875)
blackmail theory (1875)
abduction theory (1883)

Broadly these results align remarkably well with Ginzburg's claim that forensics, along with other disciplines informed by the evidential paradigm, came of age as a science in the decade 1870–1880. Yet they also indicate that the newspapers themselves had adopted *theory* in their own quest to report on ongoing investigations or trials in an impartial manner. This becomes obvious by noting that the first mention of *conspiracy theory* recorded by the databases *American Historical Newspapers* and *ProQuest* both refer to a specific case, the Beecher-Tilton scandal. The labyrinthine narrative of this scandal was initiated by an allegation of adultery leveled at Henry Ward Beecher, the famous Congregationalist preacher at the Plymouth Church in Brooklyn. The scandal engrossed the attention of the American public from 1872 onward and provoked the counter-charge from Beecher that he had been the victim of a conspiracy.[30] This line of defense generated numerous instances of the term *conspiracy theory*. Yet we are dealing here with a civil case that did not involve any appeal to forensic methods of fact finding; in this context, *theory* served as a simple device allowing reporters to indicate the speculative and subjective nature of the claims and explanations made by the protagonists in the case (Figure 4.1).

By contrast, a forensic dimension certainly did exist to the newspaper reports which in July 1881 enabled the American public to keep apace with the investigation into the Garfield assassination.[31] In the days after the shooting the term *conspiracy theory* appeared frequently to denote the suspicion of a wider complicity linking Guiteau to a circle of undiscovered and unidentified associates. Even the signs of Guiteau's obvious mental instability were not sufficient to dispel such a suspicion. Some speculated that "if Guiteau is insane there is 'method in his madness,' and that he was but a tool in the hands of others."[32] When—in a development that foreshadows the later shooting of Lee Harvey Oswald by Jack Ruby—Guiteau himself became the target of an attempt on his life a few days after his trial began in November 1881, speculation once more arose about a conspiracy. In the words of an article in the *St. Louis Daily Globe-Democrat*: "Mysterious hints have been thrown out from time to time since the beginning of the trial of the existence of a desperate band of conspirators who are bound by a terrible oath to risk their individual lives in turn until an end has been reached in Guiteau's death."[33] In the opinion of the reporter, it was, however, only the more "credulous and sensational who entertain the conspiracy theory . . ."

Commenting on the Term *Conspiracy Theory*

This disparaging attitude toward the "conspiracy theory" raises the possibility that this article was penned by the same journalist who, in the days after the original shooting, was responsible for a truly remarkable opinion piece in the same

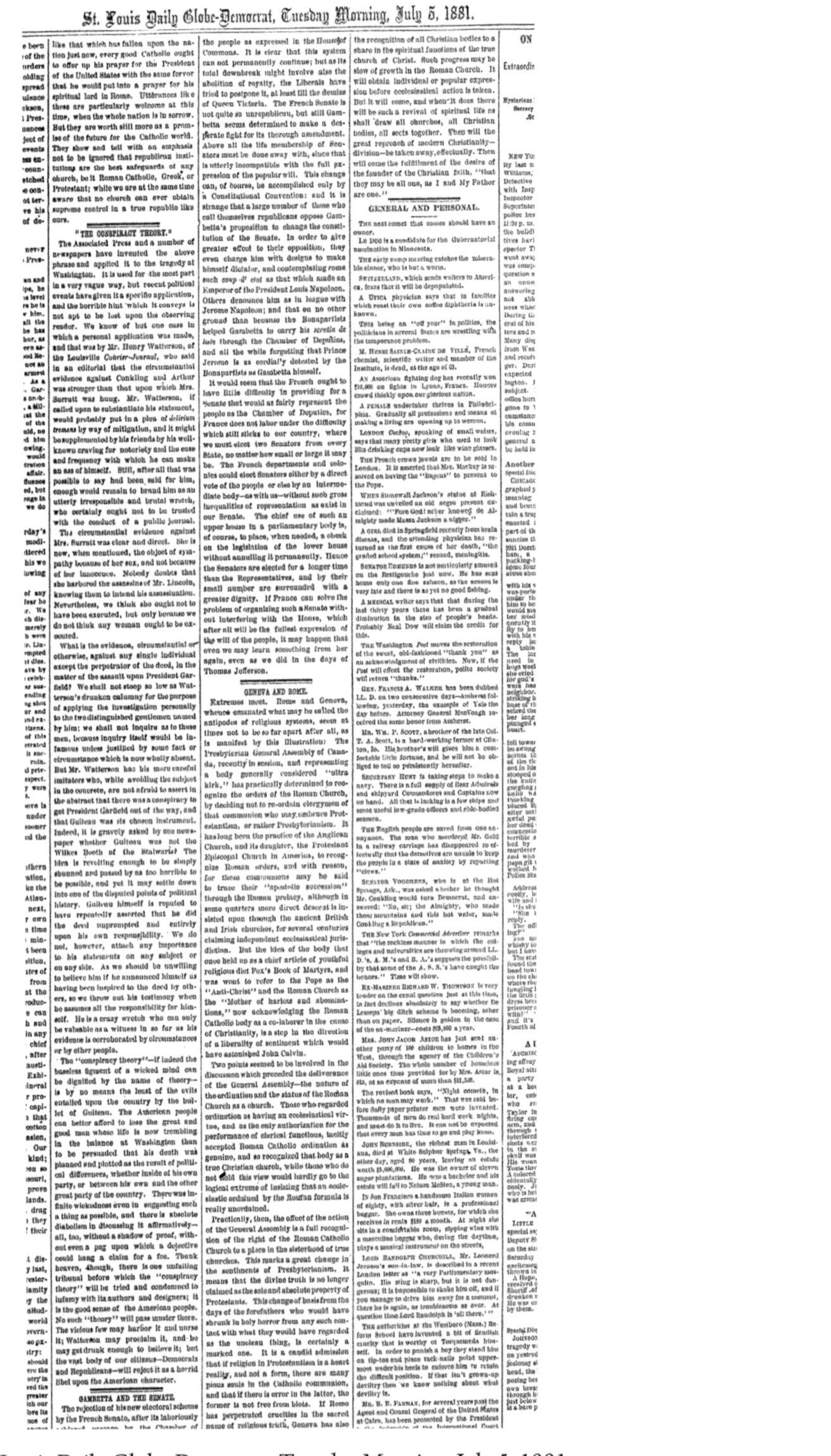

St. Louis Daily Globe-Democrat, Tuesday Morning, July 5, 1881.

like that which has fallen upon the nation just now, every good Catholic ought to offer up his prayer for the President of the United States with the same fervor that he would put into a prayer for his spiritual lord in Rome. Utterances like these are particularly welcome at this time, when the whole nation is in sorrow. But they are worth still more as a promise of the future for the Catholic world. They show and tell with an emphasis not to be ignored that republican institutions are the best safeguards of any church, be it Roman Catholic, Greek, or Protestant; while we are at the same time aware that no church can ever obtain supreme control in a true republic like ours.

"THE CONSPIRACY THEORY."

The Associated Press and a number of newspapers have invented the above phrase and applied it to the tragedy at Washington. It is used for the most part in a very vague way, but recent political events have given it a specific application, and the horrible hint which it conveys is not apt to be lost upon the observing reader. We know of but one case in which a personal application was made, and that was by Mr. Henry Watterson, of the Louisville *Courier-Journal*, who said in an editorial that the circumstantial evidence against Conkling and Arthur was stronger than that upon which Mrs. Surratt was hung. Mr. Watterson, if called upon to substantiate his statement, would probably put in a plea of *delirium tremens* by way of mitigation, and it might be supplemented by his friends by his well-known craving for notoriety and the ease and frequency with which he can make an ass of himself. Still, after all that was possible to say had been said for him, enough would remain to brand him as an utterly irresponsible and brutal wretch, who certainly ought not to be trusted with the conduct of a public journal.

The circumstantial evidence against Mrs. Surratt was clear and direct. She is now, when mentioned, the object of sympathy because of her sex, and not because of her innocence. Nobody doubts that she harbored the assassins of Mr. Lincoln, knowing them to intend his assassination. Nevertheless, we think she ought not to have been executed, but only because we do not think any woman ought to be executed.

What is the evidence, circumstantial or otherwise, against any single individual except the perpetrator of the deed, in the matter of the assault upon President Garfield? We shall not stoop so low as Watterson's drunken calumny for the purpose of applying the investigation personally to the two distinguished gentlemen named by him; we shall not inquire as to these men, because inquiry itself would be infamous unless justified by some fact or circumstance which is now wholly absent. But Mr. Watterson has his more careful imitators who, while avoiding the subject in the concrete, are not afraid to assert in the abstract that there was a conspiracy to get President Garfield out of the way, and that Guiteau was its chosen instrument. Indeed, it is gravely asked by one newspaper whether Guiteau was not the Wilkes Booth of the Stalwarts? The idea is revolting enough to be simply shunned and passed by as too horrible to be possible, and yet it may settle down into one of the disputed points of political history. Guiteau himself is reputed to have repeatedly asserted that he did the deed unprompted and entirely upon his own responsibility. We do not, however, attach any importance to his statements on any subject or on any side. As we should be unwilling to believe him if he announced himself as having been inspired to the deed by others, so we throw out his testimony when he assumes all the responsibility for himself. He is a crazy wretch who can only be valuable as a witness in so far as his evidence is corroborated by circumstances or by other people.

The "conspiracy theory"—if indeed the baseless figment of a wicked mind can be dignified by the name of theory—is by no means the least of the evils entailed upon the country by the bullet of Guiteau. The American people can better afford to lose the great and good man whose life is now trembling in the balance at Washington than to be persuaded that his death was planned and plotted as the result of political differences, whether inside of his own party, or between his own and the other great party of the country. There was infinite wickedness even in suggesting such a thing as possible, and there is absolute diabolism in discussing it affirmatively—all, too, without a shadow of proof, without even a peg upon which a detective could hang a claim for a fee. Thank heaven, though, there is one unfailing tribunal before which the "conspiracy theory" will be tried and condemned to infamy with its authors and designers; it is the good sense of the American people. No such "theory" will pass muster there. The vicious few may harbor it and nurse it; Watterson may proclaim it, and he may get drunk enough to believe it; but the vast body of our citizens—Democrats and Republicans—will reject it as a horrid libel upon the American character.

GAMBETTA AND THE SENATE.

The rejection of his new electoral scheme by the French Senate, after its laboriously [...] the people as expressed in the House of Commons. It is clear that this system can not permanently continue; but as its total downbreak might involve also the abolition of royalty, the Liberals have tried to postpone it, at least till the demise of Queen Victoria. The French Senate is not quite so unrepublican, but still Gambetta seems determined to make a desperate fight for its thorough amendment. Above all the life membership of Senators must be done away with, since that is utterly incompatible with the full expression of the popular will. This change can, of course, be accomplished only by a Constitutional Convention: and it is strange that a large number of those who call themselves republicans oppose Gambetta's proposition to change the constitution of the Senate. In order to give greater effect to their opposition, they even charge him with designs to make himself dictator, and contemplating some such *coup d' etat* as that which made an Emperor of the President Louis Napoleon. Others denounce him as in league with Jerome Napoleon; and that on no other ground than because the Bonapartists helped Gambetta to carry his *scrutin de liste* through the Chamber of Deputies, and all the while forgetting that Prince Jerome is as cordially detested by the Bonapartists as Gambetta himself.

It would seem that the French ought to have little difficulty in providing for a Senate that would as fairly represent the people as the Chamber of Deputies, for France does not labor under the difficulty which still sticks to our country, where we must elect two Senators from every State, no matter how small or large it may be. The French departments and colonies could elect Senators either by a direct vote of the people or else by an intermediate body—as with us—without such gross inequalities of representation as exist in our Senate. The chief use of such an upper house in a parliamentary body is, of course, to place, when needed, a check on the legislation of the lower house without annulling it permanently. Hence the Senators are elected for a longer time than the Representatives, and by their small number are surrounded with a greater dignity. If France can solve the problem of organizing such a Senate without interfering with the House, which after all will be the fullest expression of the will of the people, it may happen that even we may learn something from her again, even as we did in the days of Thomas Jefferson.

GENEVA AND ROME.

Extremes meet. Rome and Geneva, whence emanated what may be called the antipodes of religious systems, seem at times not to be so far apart after all, as is manifest by this illustration: The Presbyterian General Assembly of Canada, recently in session, and representing a body generally considered "ultra kirk," has practically determined to recognize the orders of the Roman Church, by deciding not to re-ordain clergymen of that communion who may embrace Protestantism, or rather Presbyterianism. It has long been the practice of the Anglican Church, and its daughter, the Protestant Episcopal Church in America, to recognize Roman orders, and with reason, for these communions may be said to trace their "apostolic succession" through the Roman prelacy, although in some quarters more direct descent is insisted upon through the ancient British and Irish churches, for several centuries claiming independent ecclesiastical jurisdiction. But the idea of the body that once held up as a chief article of youthful religious diet Fox's Book of Martyrs, and was wont to refer to the Pope as the "Anti-Christ" and the Roman Church as the "Mother of harlots and abominations," now acknowledging the Roman Catholic body as a co-laborer in the cause of Christianity, is a step in the direction of a liberality of sentiment which would have astonished John Calvin.

Two points seemed to be involved in the discussion which preceded the deliverance of the General Assembly—the nature of the ordination and the status of the Roman Church as a church. Those who regarded ordination as having an ecclesiastical virtue, and as the only authorization for the performance of clerical functions, tacitly accepted Roman Catholic ordination as genuine, and so recognized that body as a true Christian church, while those who do not hold this view would hardly go to the logical extreme of insisting that an ecclesiastic ordained by the Roman formula is really unordained.

Practically, then, the effect of the action of the General Assembly is a full recognition of the right of the Roman Catholic Church to a place in the sisterhood of true churches. This marks a great change in the sentiments of Presbyterianism. It means that the divine truth is no longer claimed as the sole and absolute property of Protestants. This change of basis from the days of the forefathers who would have shrunk in holy horror from any such contact with what they would have regarded as the unclean thing, is certainly a marked one. It is a candid admission that if religion in Protestantism is a heart reality, and not a form, there are many pious souls in the Catholic communion, and that if there is error in the latter, the former is not free from blots. If Rome has perpetrated cruelties in the sacred name of religious truth, Geneva has also [...] the recognition of all Christian bodies to a share in the spiritual functions of the true church of Christ. Such progress may be slow of growth in the Roman Church. It will obtain individual or popular expression before ecclesiastical action is taken. But it will come, and when it does there will be such a revival of spiritual life as shall draw all churches, all Christian bodies, all sects together. Then will the great reproach of modern Christianity—division—be taken away, effectually. Then will come the fulfillment of the desire of the founder of the Christian faith, "that they may be all one, as I and My Father are one."

GENERAL AND PERSONAL.

THE next comet that comes should have an owner.

LE DUC is a candidate for the Gubernatorial nomination in Minnesota.

THE early camp meeting catches the miserable sinner, who is but a worm.

SWITZERLAND, which sends waiters to America, fears that it will be depopulated.

A UTICA physician says that in families which roast their own coffee diphtheria is unknown.

THIS being an "off year" in politics, the politicians in several States are wrestling with the temperance problem.

M. HENRI SAINTE-CLAIRE DE VILLE, French chemist, scientific writer and member of the Institute, is dead, at the age of 63.

AN American fighting dog has recently won $10,000 on fights in Lyons, France. Honors crowd thickly upon our glorious nation.

A FEMALE undertaker thrives in Philadelphia. Gradually all professions and means of making a living are opening up to women.

LONDON *Cuckoo*, speaking of small waists, says that many pretty girls who used to look like drinking cups now look like wine glasses.

THE French crown jewels are to be sold in London. It is asserted that Mrs. Mackay is resolved on having the "Regent" to present to the Pope.

WHEN Stonewall Jackson's statue at Richmond was unveiled an old negro present exclaimed: "'Fore God! neber knowed de Almighty made Massa Jackson a nigger."

A GIRL died in Springfield recently from brain disease, and the attending physician has returned as the first cause of her death, "the graded school system;" second, meningitis.

SENATOR EDMUNDS is not particularly amused on the Restigouche just now. He has sent home only one fine salmon, as the season is very late and there is as yet no good fishing.

A MEDICAL writer says that that during the last thirty years there has been a gradual diminution in the size of people's heads. Probably Neal Dow will claim the credit for this.

THE Washington *Post* moves the restoration of the sweet, old-fashioned "thank you" as an acknowledgment of civilities. Now, if the *Post* will effect the restoration, polite society will return "thanks."

GEN. FRANCIS A. WALKER has been dubbed LL. D. on two consecutive days—Amherst following, yesterday, the example of Yale the day before. Attorney General MacVeagh received the same honor from Amherst.

MR. WM. P. SCOTT, a brother of the late Col. T. A. Scott, is a hard-working farmer at Clinton, Io. His brother's will gives him a comfortable little fortune, and he will not be obliged to toil so persistently hereafter.

SECRETARY HUNT is taking steps to make a navy. There is a full supply of Rear Admirals and shipyard Commodores and Captains now on hand. All that is lacking is a few ships and some useful low-grade officers and able-bodied seamen.

THE English people are saved from one annoyance. The man who murdered Mr. Gold in a railway carriage has disappeared so effectually that the detectives are unable to keep the people in a state of anxiety by reporting "clews."

SENATOR VOORHEES, who is at the Hot Springs, Ark., was asked whether he thought Mr. Conkling would turn Democrat, and answered: "No, sir; the Almighty, who made these mountains and this hot water, made Conkling a Republican."

THE New York *Commercial Advertiser* remarks that "the reckless manner in which the colleges and universities are throwing around LL. D.'s, A. M.'s and B. A.'s suggests the possibility that some of the A. S. S.'s have caught the honors." Time will show.

EX-MARINER RICHARD W. THOMPSON is very tender on the canal question just at this time, in fact declines absolutely to say whether De Lesseps' big ditch scheme is booming, other than on paper. Silence is golden in the case of the ex-mariner—costs $25,000 a year.

MRS. JOHN JACOB ASTOR has just sent another party of 100 children to homes in the West, through the agency of the Children's Aid Society. The whole number of homeless little ones thus provided for by Mrs. Astor is 815, at an expense of more than $11,535.

The revised book says, "Night cometh, in which no man may work." That was said before daily paper printer men were invented. Thousands of men do real hard work nights, and must do it to live. It can not be expected that every man has time to go and play keno.

JOHN BURNSIDE, the richest man in Louisiana, died at White Sulphur Springs, Va., the other day, aged 80 years, leaving an estate worth $3,000,000. He was the owner of eleven sugar plantations. He was a bachelor and his estate will fall to Nelson McStea, a young man.

IN San Francisco a handsome Italian woman of eighty, with silver hair, is a professional beggar. She owns three houses, for which she receives in rents $180 a month. At night she sits in a comfortable room, sipping wine with a masculine beggar who, during the daytime, plays a musical instrument on the streets.

LORD RANDOLPH CHURCHILL, Mr. Leonard Jerome's son-in-law, is described in a recent London letter as "a very Parliamentary mosquito. His sting is sharp, but it is not dangerous; it is impossible to shake him off, and if you manage to drive him away for a moment, there he is again, as troublesome as ever. At question time Lord Randolph is 'all there.'"

THE authorities at the Westboro (Mass.) Reform School have invented a bit of fiendish cruelty that is worthy of Torquemada himself. In order to punish a boy they stand him on tip-toe and place tack-nails point uppermost under his heels to enforce him to retain the difficult position. If that isn't grown-up deviltry then we know nothing about what deviltry is.

MR. E. E. FARMAN, for several years past the Agent and Consul General of the United States at Cairo, has been promoted by the President [...]

Figure 4.1 St. Louis Daily Globe Democrat, Tuesday Morning, July 5, 1881.

newspaper. It was headed " 'The Conspiracy Theory.' " The quotation marks are important; they indicate that the editorial was commenting upon the use of the term by other reporters. Obviously these reporters believed that "the conspiracy theory" merited serious consideration, although in the searches I have conducted the actual instances of such usage have proved frustratingly elusive.[34] Nevertheless, it can only be presumed that they existed, as they prompted the response printed on page four of the Tuesday morning edition of the *St. Louis Daily Globe-Democrat* on July 5, 1881. It represents a milestone of sorts, not because it elevated "conspiracy theory" from a term to a generic concept—"conspiracy theory" still retained a narrowly circumscribed applicability, referring only to a strand of speculation about Garfield's shooting—but because these four paragraphs represent in all likelihood the first time the term was exposed to any form of reflection or scrutiny. As significant as this is for the development of *conspiracy theory*, this piece, penned by an unknown journalist working for a daily newspaper in a Midwest-southern American city, was then consigned to the silent graveyard of yesterday's news. Most likely it would have remained buried there forever if the development of search algorithms and the digitization of old issues of nineteenth-century newspapers had not intervened. The happy convergence of these two developments has made its discovery and retrieval from obscurity possible.

The piece begins by referencing the editorial headline. It notes that the "Associated Press and a number of newspapers have invented the above phrase [i.e., *conspiracy theory*] and applied it to the tragedy at Washington. It is used for the most part in a very vague way, but recent political events have given it a specific application and the horrible hint which it conveys is not apt to be lost upon the observing reader." The author of the editorial was perturbed at the political point-scoring which seemed to motivate the speculation about the assassination. Indeed, according to this reading the "conspiracy theory" was not an intermediate stage in an honest attempt to ascertain the truth but rather a ploy used to cast aspersions and stir up unfounded suspicions.

The editorial rounded off its chastisement of those peddling claims of a conspiracy with the following words:

> The "conspiracy theory"—if indeed the baseless figment of a wicked mind can be dignified by the name of theory—is by no means the least of the evils entailed upon the country by the bullet of Guiteau [. . .] There was infinite wickedness even in suggesting such a thing as possible, and there is absolute diabolism in discussing it affirmatively—all, too, without a shadow of proof, without even a peg upon which a detective could hang a claim for a fee. Thank heaven, though, there is one unfailing tribunal before which the "conspiracy theory" will be tried and condemned to infamy with its authors and designers; it is the good sense of the American people. No such "theory" will pass muster there.

There are numerous aspects of this passage that invite comment, such as the reference to the relatively new job specification of the "detective" or the confidence in the judgment rendered by the tribunal of public opinion. Here we limit our commentary to two points.

1. Conspiracy Theory: From Neutral to Pejorative

As a mere term *conspiracy theory* did not, at this stage, carry any connotations, either negative or positive. For this reason, other journalists had presumably felt no inhibitions in submitting their suspicions of a conspiracy under this heading. It is nevertheless remarkable that, as soon as the transition is made for the first time from a mode in which the term is simply used to one in which it is commented upon, a decidedly disparaging tone asserts itself. In particular, the author expresses indignation at the way the word *theory* is traduced by its forced association with the postulate of a conspiracy. The disdain is justified by the absence of even a "shadow of proof"; a "shadow" that, if it did exist, would presumably legitimize the use of *theory* in the sense of a provisional or tentative explanation. And yet in the "wickedness [of] suggesting such a thing [i.e., a conspiracy] possible" one also senses an anticipation of the later animus that will be directed at conspiracy theories *a priori* once the concept exists to label them as such; it will then be possible to reject a conspiracy theory as soon as it has been identified and labeled as one. (To this point, see the chapters in this volume by Martin Orr and Ginna Husting, Matthew Dentith, Juha Räikkä and Lee Basham, and Steven Smallpage.) Over the long term, such an attitude, akin to a prejudice against explanations invoking conspiracy, runs a risk of compromising the open-minded neutrality that ideally should characterize the journalistic ethos.

2. Not Enough Evil to Instigate a Conspiracy, But Enough Evil to Insinuate One

Recent works in the field of conspiracy theory studies have drawn attention to the curious transition marking the development of many Western liberal societies: such societies in the course of the nineteenth and twentieth centuries went from fearing conspiracies to fearing the fear of conspiracies, as manifested most strikingly in the form of conspiracy theories.[35] In considering this reflexive form of fear, the words of Franklin D. Roosevelt at his 1933 inauguration speech inevitably come to mind: "the only thing we have to fear is. . . fear itself." And yet the editorial from the *St. Louis Daily Globe-Democrat* marks an earlier, far less prominent way station in this development. Its author obviously felt that there was no evidence suggesting that Garfield had fallen victim to a conspiracy: the "wickedness" infecting American politics was not so "infinite" nor the "diabolism" so "absolute" to justify considerations of such a possibility. At the same time the author harbored no doubt about a presence of evil adequate to the task of inspiring some opportunistic individuals to make such a claim. Conversely we might add that a conspiracy theory, proffered as an explanation for the assassination of an American president, contained nothing that was outrageous *per se* for those Americans who at later points in history felt that their society was indeed exposed to nefarious conspiratorial forces that could culminate in such an event.[36]

Conclusion

Some of the indignation expressed in the *St. Louis Daily Globe-Democrat* about the term *conspiracy theory* derived from a sense that the term *theory* had been coopted for the guise of impartiality it bestowed upon a biased version of events. In other words, the term was suspected of feigning an objectivity that belied the ulterior partisan motives that were the actual source of the suspicions of conspiracy voiced by some journalists and writers. (One thus can appreciate how deHaven-Smith's conspiratorial suspicions about the concept of conspiracy theory are, in fact, nothing new).

Objectivity itself, however, was not a term regularly used in this context at this time, either among journalists themselves or among those who critiqued journalism. Their embrace of the concept was one part of an effort undertaken by the profession's later intellectual overseers (such as Lippmann) to make it more scientific.[37] But what explains the sudden appearance of the concept *objectivity*, even if as a concept it did not feature in the newspaper articles themselves but instead played an ever more prominent role in the talk about the ideals and standards to be observed by those articles? The answer is interesting.

Objectivity began to be observed as a norm of journalism in response to the lack of objectivity that was felt to characterize other news sources. In particular the wartime experience with propaganda and the rising prominence of publicity agents in the postwar period had unsettled the old faith that the truth would shine through and automatically triumph over lies and deceit.[38] Lippmann pointed out that "the facts of modern life do not spontaneously take a shape in which they can be known."[39] One might still hold that "truth will out," but then, if so, it seemed that the truth would require the helping hand of objectivity.

It was as a result of a similar logic of contradistinction that a concept of conspiracy theory began to emerge in fits and starts in the twentieth century. Here the contrast was to social science. Social science was social science at least in part because it was not conspiracy theory. In fact, the discourse about journalistic objectivity and the discourse about conspiracy theories intersected—or at least bumped into each other—in a speech given in 1971 by the *New York Times* journalist Tom Wicker to the Massachusetts Historical Society. It bore the title: "The Tradition of Objectivity in the American Press: What's Wrong with It." His specific complaint? Either out of laziness or habit or as a result of limited resources, many journalists felt that they fulfilled their duty to be objective by relying on press releases, official statements, and interviews with delegated spokespersons. This gave rise to a tendency to conflate the official and the objective version. As the same time, Wicker was adamant about one thing: the tendency he lamented was not "the result of a conspiracy."[40] Other passages in the speech where Wicker dismisses "conspiracy theories" and where he appeals to a laymen's sociology grounded in a sense of "powerful currents at work in the world today" and "forces that affect the way every person in the world lives" pinpoint the challenge facing professional journalism, namely: how to steer a course between the rubber-stamped official version and the non-official yet sociologically unacceptable conspiracy theory.[41]

The challenge for all of us in dealing with conspiracy theories is slightly different and has to do with the fact that our perception of them has two points of origin. On the one hand the concept of the conspiracy theory emerged in the social sciences in the twentieth century—and carried with it from the very beginning a set of negative connotations simply because the social sciences defined themselves in opposition to the kind of explanation associated with the concept of *conspiracy theory*. Karl Popper represents only one figure within this tradition. On the other hand, as has become abundantly clear from this article, the term *conspiracy theory* was already to be found in newspapers in the nineteenth century.[42] Here it suggests a plausible postulate of a conspiracy (even if this postulate had, in specific circumstances, not been exempt from criticism, as the commentary on the term in the *St. Louis Daily Globe-Democrat* demonstrates). There is thus a polyvalence to *conspiracy theory*. Reconciling the need to dismiss conspiracy theories in the interest of social science with the need to entertain them in the interest of investigating crime has never been easy. Admittedly, historical semantics will not provide the answer. At the same time, this approach can contribute to a more precise understanding of the fundamental dilemma we face when dealing with conspiracy theories.

Notes

1. DeHaven-Smith, Lance. 2013. *Conspiracy Theory in America*. Austin: University of Texas Press: 25–32, 197–203.
2. The reference to Popper in the literature serves largely as a placeholder for a real answer to this question about the origins of the concept, and, as a result, few have noticed that "the conspiracy theory of society" actually was only integrated into the second edition (1952) of Popper's work after Popper launched the concept in two lectures he gave in 1948: "Towards a Rational Theory of Tradition" and "Prediction and Prophecy in the Social Sciences." Both lectures were printed in the volume Popper, Karl R. [1963] 2002. *Conjectures and Refutations*. London: Routledge: 161–182, 452–466. To deHaven-Smith's credit, he also points out that there are other usages of the term that predate Popper (2013, 91)
3. Ayto, John. 1999. *Twentieth Century Words. The Story of the New Words in the English Language over the Last Hundred Years*. Oxford: Oxford University Press: 18.
4. The concept seems to have been imported from the German, where the historian Lutz Raphael in 1996 identified the "Verwissenschaftlichung des Sozialen" (the scientiziation of the

social) as an important feature of twentieth-century social history (Raphael, Lutz. 1996. "Die Verwissenschaftlichung des Sozialen als methodische und konzeptionelle Herausforderung für eine Sozialgeschichte des 20. Jahrhunderts," *Geschichte und Gesellschaft* 22(2): 165–193). The contributors to the edited volume, *Engineering Society. The Role of the Human and Social Sciences in Modern Societies, 1880–1980*, have attempted to jump-start the discussion on this topic in English-speaking academia (Brückweh, Kerstin, Dirk Schumann, Richard F. Wetzell, and Benjamin Ziemann, eds. 2012. *Engineering Society. The Role of the Human and Social Sciences in Modern Societies, 1880–1980*. Basingstoke, UK: Palgrave Macmillan).

5. For a very lucid account of how the modern conceptual vocabulary of science emerged in the seventeenth century, with chapters on "fact" and "theory," see Wootton, David. 2016. *The Invention of Science. A New History of the Scientific Revolution*. London: Penguin, 2016: 251–399.

6. See James Clarke, who devises a typology of assassins and domestic terrorists throughout American history and then assigns Guiteau to type IV, comprising those cases where genuine mental derangement was in play (Clarke, James W. 2012. *Defining Danger: American Assassins and the New Domestic Terrorists*. New Brunswick: Transaction Publishers: 239–254).

7. For further details about the assassination, see Peskin, Allan. 1999. *Garfield*. Kent, OH: Kent State University Press: 582–614.

8. The statement was actually elicited from Cook by a journalist from the *Evening Star* newspaper, but it was quoted in Unknown. 1881. "The Assassin." *Boston Journal*, July 5, 1881, 4.

9. Schudson, Michael. 2001. "The Objectivity Norm in American Journalism." *Journalism* 2(2): 156.

10. Unknown, "The Assassin." *Boston Journal*, July 4, 1881, 4.

11. Unknown. 1881. "Guiteau: A Sensational Report Exploded—Complete Failure of the Conspiracy Theory," *Boston Journal*, July 6, 1881, Page [1].

12. Unknown. 1881. "Likely to Live," *St. Louis Globe-Democrat* (St. Louis, Missouri), Thursday, July 7, 1881; Issue 48.

13. See Ginzburg, Carlo. 1990. *Clues, Myths, and the Historical Record*. Translated by John Tedeschi and Anne C. Tedeschi. Baltimore: John Hopkins Press: 87–125.

14. The fact that the evidential paradigm relies on an appreciation of the regularities sought out by the Galilean paradigm has been pointed out by Caprettini, Gian Paolo. 1983. "Peirce, Holmes, Popper." In *Sign of Three. Dupin, Holmes, Peirce*, ed. Umberto Eco and Thomas A. Sebeok. Bloomington: Indiana University Press: 145.

15. Two works which contextualize crime fiction within the broader philosophical and scientific discussions of the nineteenth century are Thomas, Ronald R. 1999. *Detective Fiction and the Rise of Forensic Science*. Cambridge: Cambridge University Press; and Frank, Lawrence. 2003. *Victorian Detective Fiction and the Nature of Evidence: The Scientific Investigations of Poe, Dickens and Doyle*. Basingstoke, UK: Palgrave Macmillan. For the relationship between police and fiction in general, see Miller, D. A. 1989. *The Novel and the Police*. Berkeley: University of California Press.

16. Ginzburg, *Clues*, 102.

17. Daston, Lorraine, and Peter Galison. 2010. *Objectivity*. 2nd ed. New York: Zone Books: 148.

18. Ibid., 161.

19. See ibid., 124, for some indications of the time frame for the emergence of mechanical objectivity.

20. Daston and Galison (2010, 138) note this in discussing the rise of a regime of mechanical objective stating, ". . . the photographic and the mechanical were *not* coextensive, and the shift from depiction that celebrated intervention to one that disdained it did not come about *because* of photography."

21. Benjamin, Walter 2003. "The Paris of the Second Empire in Baudelaire." In *Walter Benjamin: Selected Writings. Volume 4: 1938–1949*, eds. Howard Eiland and Michael W. Jennings. Cambridge: Cambridge University Press: 27.

22. To appreciate the potential of photographic evidence, one can recall a well-known scene from the HBO series *The Wire* (Season 1, Episode 4) in which detectives Jimmy McNulty and Bunk

Moreland recreate a crime scene from the photos they have on file, all the while restricting their dialogue between each other to "fuck" and "motherfucker."

23. Hunt, George P. 1966. "A Matter of Reasonable Doubt." *LIFE Magazine*, November, 48.

24. The term *naïve empiricism* was introduced by Michael Schudson (1978. *Discovering the News: A Social History of American Newspapers*. New York: Basic Books: 6–7), and presented as a precursor to the veneration of objectivity, while David Mindich subsumed it under a journalistic ethos of "objectivity" (Mindich, David T.Z. 1998. *Just the Facts: How "Objectivity" Came to Define American Journalism*. New York: New York University Press: 95–112). On the links between science and journalism, see Peter Galison (2015. "The Journalist, the Scientist, and Objectivity." In *Objectivity in Science. New Perspectives from Science and Technology Studies*, ed. Flavia Padovani, Alan Richardson and Jonathan Y. Tsou. Cham: Springer, 57–75). However, Galison does not fully clarify the degree of independence and interdependence pertaining to the emergence of journalistic objectivity and scientific objectivity. Thus if Galison suggests that mechanical objectivity also was an epistemic virtue guiding journalists, it would seem hard to reconcile the observance of such a virtue with the emergence of the interview; journalists seeking interviews are not exactly acting in accordance with the "will-to-will-lessness" that one would associate with mechanical objectivity.

25. Lippmann, Walter. [1922] 1991. *Public Opinion*. New Brunswick: Transaction Publishers: 341.

26. In this and the following examples the italics are my own. Noteworthy is the fact that it is never really clear from these examples whether the adherents of these theories are themselves calling them theories because they acknowledge their provisional nature, or whether the journalists bring the term into play to acknowledge the limited support these explanations enjoyed.

27. *American Historical Newspapers* comprehends at the time of writing 1,050 newspapers extending from the 1690s and the publication of North America's first newspaper, Benjamin Harris's *Publick Occurrences*, until the present.

28. Admittedly I have taken a little liberty with the second entry, "murder theory," as the database actually records this term already in 1834. The context is, however, a religious-philosophical meditation on the right of an individual in self-defense to take another person's life.

29. The *ProQuest* database compiles the results of searches from *The New York Times*, *The Wall Street Journals*, the *Washington Post*, along with the British *Guardian* and *Observer*.

30. See Fox, Richard Wightman. 1999. *Trials of Intimacy. Love and Loss in the Beecher-Tilton Scandal*. Chicago: University of Chicago Press; Applegate, Debby. 2006. *The Most Famous Man in America. The Biography of Henry Ward Beecher*. New York: Doubleday.

31. It is interesting to ask why the searches of the databases reveal no occurrences of *conspiracy theory* for the assassination of Lincoln in April 1865. In large part this presumably has to do with the fact that, when it came to the question of conspiracy, there never was any need for the speculation that might be signaled by use of the term *theory*; the simultaneous attack upon Secretary of State William Seward on the night of April 14 left no doubt that John Wilkes Booth had been party to a genuine conspiracy. *Theory* was, however, used to denote other speculative elements in the reporting on the assassination, and one can imagine how competing accounts of the extent of the conspiracy might have inspired talk of different *conspiracy theories*. An article published on April 22, 1865, in *The Vermont Journal* under the heading "The Conspiracy" suggested that a possible use of the term was not out of the question, when it reports that the "most plausible motive yet suggested for the actor becoming an assassin, is in the theory that Booth has long been a member of a secret rebel association, formed for the purpose of killing Mr. Lincoln ... " And yet one has the feeling that the practice of building a compound phrase out of a type of crime (such as conspiracy) and *theory* had—as the database inquiries indicate—still not fully established itself in 1865.

32. "The Assassin." *Boston Journal*, July 4, 1881, page 4.

33. " 'The Conspiracy Theory.' " *St. Louis Globe-Democrat*, November 21, 1881; Issue 185.

34. This remains the case even though the article singles out for its special obloquy Henry Watterson, the editor of a rival Louisville newspaper, the *Louisville Courier-Journal*. Yet a

search of the archives of this newspaper failed to locate any usage of the term *conspiracy theory* in this period.

35. See, for example, Butter, Michael. 2014. *Plots, Designs, and Schemes: American Conspiracy Theories from the Puritans to the Present*. Berlin: Walter de Gruyter.

36. This speaks to the idea prevalent in contemporary social science suggesting that those who believe in conspiracy theories do so because that is the way they believe the world works. See Uscinski, Joseph E., and Joseph M. Parent. 2014. *American Conspiracy Theories*. Oxford: Oxford University Press.

37. See Streckfuss, Richard. 1990. "Objectivity in Journalism: A Search and a Reassessment," *Journalism & Mass Communication Quarterly* 67(4): 973–983. Of course, this raises familiar issues about how the naming of a phenomenon (in this case, journalistic objectivity) is to be integrated into the history of that phenomenon. Like Mindich, who is adamant that "objectivity" (N. B. the quotation marks) was "an issue at least since 1690 . . . " (1998, 11), Daniel Schiller in his earlier work (1981. *Objectivity and the News. The Public and the Rise of Commercial Journalism*. Philadelphia: University of Pennsylvania Press), had no difficulties in discerning objectivity in journalistic practices and norms before there was actual talk of objectivity.

38. See Streckfuss, "Objectivity in Journalism," 977–978, Schudson, "The Objectivity Norm in American Journalism," 162–163.

39. Lippmann, *Public Opinion*, 345.

40. Wicker, Tom. 1971. "The Tradition of Objectivity in the American Press: What's Wrong with It." *Proceedings of the Massachusetts Historical Society, Third Series* 84, 87.

41. Wicker, "Tradition of Objectivity," 87, 92–93.

42. Admittedly there is a need to extend the analysis beyond the purely American context that has provided the focus of this article.

5

Media Marginalization of Racial Minorities

"Conspiracy Theorists" in U.S. Ghettos and on the "Arab Street"

MARTIN ORR AND GINNA HUSTING

The epithet *conspiracy theorist* can be understood as what C. Wright Mills called a "vocabulary of motive." This vocabulary of motive is routinely used to dismiss scholars, journalists, and citizens who question, or worse yet document, the consolidation or abuse of political, economic, and cultural resources. The micropolitics of the term *conspiracy theory* have become so intense that grassy knoll (a term relating to belief in conspiracy theories about the assassination of President Kennedy) and other terms have become shorthand for those who on the one hand wear "tinfoil hats" to protect themselves from government mind-control rays and for those on the other hand who don't accept inside-the-Beltway wisdom.

Thus, pointing to Enron's conspiracy to manipulate the supply of electricity to inflate rates in California is akin to asserting the existence of little green men (for example, see the chapter in this volume by Jesse Walker). Concerned that the non-existence of weapons of mass destruction in Iraq might indicate broad crimes of state? Concerned that private contractors to the U.S. government are storing "metadata"—whatever that is—on U.S. citizens? Get off your grassy knoll and come back to reality.

The epithet *conspiracy theorist* is used to tarnish those who challenge authority and power. Often, it is tinged with racial undertones: it is used to demean whole groups of people in the news and to silence, stigmatize, or belittle foreign and minority voices. First, we show why it is important to understand the charge "conspiracy theory" as a vocabulary of motive. Then we show how the phrase works in news coverage to target two particular categories of people: African Americans and people in Muslim-majority nations. Our first case documents the trivializing of concerns of many African Americans about Central Intelligence Agency (CIA) involvement with drug trafficking. Our second case shows how mainstream news frames Muslim-majority nations as populated with irrational conspiracy theorists from primitive cultures, rather than by individuals with well-founded concerns regarding the "War on Terror." As a vocabulary of motive, the phrase contributes to the exclusion of oppressed peoples from the community of reasonable participants in democratic discourse.

A Vocabulary of Motive

C. Wright Mills' essay "Situated Actions and Vocabularies of Motive" provides an in-road to understanding the ways in which the charge of "conspiracy theorist" polices the boundaries of legitimate debate.[1] Mills argues that, whereas we typically treat motives as simply psychological phenomena—namely the product of the internal workings of individuals—motives are properly understood as social relations:

> Rather than fixed elements "in" an individual, motives are the terms with which interpretation of conduct *by social actors* proceeds. . . . [Rather than a biological or psychological account,] what we want is an analysis of the integrating, controlling, and specifying function a certain type of speech fulfils in socially-situated actions. . . . [Motives] themselves must be explained socially.[2]

When people talk about their own or others' motives, they do particular things with words—they justify, excuse, hide, impute blame, and avoid or change the subject. Talk about motives is a kind of micropolitical act that does particular kinds of work when invoked in interaction.

Conspiracy theorist is an example of motive talk; it imputes a motive to questions of power and dodges the content of the question in order to shift levels of analysis. The phrase allows an accuser to "go meta" on a speaker by impugning their character, intelligence, and often emotional maturity.[3] As a form of the social construction of reality, this discursive move reframes the ongoing definition of the situation, allowing an interactant to "claim the higher ground, or to displace attention from one issue to another, or to prevail in a battle over meanings of a key term."[4] In this way mainstream news constructs a form of cultural knowledge that does two kinds of work: maintaining inequalities across race, religion, and nationality, while simultaneously leaving economic, political, and military power unexamined.

The Characteristics of the Conspiracy Theorist

To demonstrate our points, we discuss an examination of 495 articles in the *New York Times* from 2005–2013 to highlight the typical ways *conspiracy theorist* is characterized. It is of course not a flattering portrayal. "Conspiracy theories" are, first and foremost, false. Conspiracy theories are "made up of whole cloth,"[5] and reason and evidence "debunks many unsubstantiated conspiracy theories."[6] They are "entirely specious and unjustified,"[7] "wildly counterintuitive,"[8] and in the end must always "confront the corroborating truth."[9] They are often conscious and out-rageous lies, amounting to the slander of victims:

> . . . the defense was asking jurors to believe a far-fetched conspiracy theory. In a case with such strong evidence, he said, "you always have to accuse the victims, and you always have to allege a conspiracy. . . ."[10]

In this case the victim of such slander, Goldman Sachs, is acknowledged to be "at the center of so many concentric circles of power," and yet concern about conspiracy and fraud exist only in "the grassy knoll realm of conspiracy theories."[11] This is oft-repeated in the news: "conspiracy theories [are] from the fringe."[12]

Why would anyone advance a conspiracy theory? The characteristics of the claim result from the characteristics of the claimant—"conspiracy theorists" are "wild-eyed."[13] It almost goes without saying that "frenzied paranoia . . . is tradi-tionally associated with conspiracy theory."[14] Although a bit tongue in cheek, Ginia Bellafante of the *New York Times* suggests that "conspiracy theorists" are insane, when in the course of her article on the television series *The Killing*, she offers parenthetically:

> (As a matter of due process it should be said that the series satisfies con-spiracy theorists with the .0009 percent chance that [he] is actually not guilty. The sane among us will run, as they say, with the facts on the ground.)[15]

Conspiracy theorists are seen as driven by emotion, anger, and vengeance. And they talk quickly. One such "rattled off personal grievances and a bizarre conspiracy theory."[16] They offer "[theories] tinged with anger."[17] They traffic in unreasonable and unsubstantiated rumors that encourage a breakdown of rational discourse: "Into that vacuum there were stories with conspiracy theories and other inaccuracies, and the situation became more dramatized."[18] Emotion takes over, and debate gives way to rumor: "Outrage and conspiracy theories ricocheted around local blogs, online mailing lists and newspapers."[19] Some conspiracy theorists can seem harmless— simply "accident buffs"[20] and "connoisseurs of conspiracy theories."[21] But since con-spiracy theories are "offensive on their face,"[22] there is of course the dark side:

> He had changed since high school: the shy, seemingly normal boy had experimented with drugs and, increasingly, with conspiracy theories that made sense to no one but himself.[23]

Here, experimentation with drugs is the gateway to conspiracy theorizing, where "[you've] drunk the . . .Kool-Aid"[24] and you've hit rock bottom.

Finally, "conspiracy theorists" are generally deemed guilty by association with other disreputable groups, and other groups are sometimes denigrated by associating them with "conspiracy theorists." In these stories on former Representative Ron Paul, these techniques are brought into play:

> "[He] fired up conspiracy theorists on the left as well as the right . . . ," [and] has animated a surprisingly diverse swath of political interests that includes mainstream civil liberties groups, Republican and Democratic lawmakers, conservative research groups, liberal activists and right-wing conspiracy theorists.[25]

The same tactic is used to describe participants in the Occupy Wall Street movement as a "dizzying assembly of libertarians and anarchists, Christian fundamentalists and Marxists, conspiracy theorists and individuals who appear mostly to be drawn by the daily camaraderie of camp life."[26] This tacitly acknowledges broad support for Occupy, apparently including people who like to go camping, but the participation of conspiracy theorists discredits the movement. In another characteristic article, Occupy "melded a variety of causes . . . , invoking socialism, police violence and Sept. 11 conspiracy theories, in addition to immigrant rights."[27] Here, the "Sept. 11 conspiracy theories" and "socialism" serve to discredit one another, and—given the weight of that—this becomes an attempt to bring perfectly mainstream concerns with police violence and immigrant rights into question.

The phrase, then, impugns the motives and value of anyone so labeled. We should next ask if there are patterns to who is so labeled and who is not. In the mainstream press, already marginalized groups, ethnic minorities, and indigenous peoples are often portrayed as a reified, undifferentiated group especially susceptible to the lure of the *conspiracy theory*.

Paranoia in the Ghetto

In August 1996, a series of articles by the late Gary Webb in *The San Jose Mercury-News* tied U.S.-supported troops seeking to topple the Nicaraguan Sandinista government in the 1980s to the crack cocaine distribution network in Los Angeles.[28] Webb's reporting led to outrage among members of black communities (as well as of course many others). The CIA was compelled to conduct an internal investigation of its connections to drug traffickers, ultimately acknowledging that, yes, the fundamentals of these "conspiracy theories" were true:

> . . . a senior member of [the] Sandino Revolutionary Front (FRS) agreed in late 1984 with [convicted drug trafficker Jorge] Morales that FRS pilots would aid in transporting narcotics in exchange for financial assistance . . . .

Morales agreed to provide financial support to the FRS, in addition to aircraft and training for FRS pilots. After undergoing flight training, the FRS pilots were to continue to work for the FRS, but would also fly narcotics shipments from South America to sites in Costa Rica and Nicaragua for later transport to the United States.[29]

More startling, perhaps, was the admission that these weren't simply "loose cannons" at the CIA. Although some secrets were kept from their superiors:

Allegations and information indicating drug trafficking by 25 Contra-related individuals was shared in a variety of ways with . . . Executive branch agencies. . . . CIA did inform the intelligence oversight committees in a timely manner of the 1984 allegations . . . .[30]

And President Reagan issued an Executive Order making CIA complicity in drug trafficking legal:

From August 15, 1979 to March 2, 1982, Attorney General Guidelines . . . required CIA to report to DoJ [Department of Justice] possible violations of "any" federal laws – thereby including narcotics laws – by persons who were employed by, assigned to, or acting for CIA. From March 2, 1982 [pursuant Executive order 12333] . . . , because of a change in the definition of "employee," agents, assets and independent contractors were moved to the non-employee category and thereby subject to the list of reportable offenses that did *not* include narcotics violations. . . . A February 8, 1985 internal DoJ memorandum stated explicitly that there was no requirement that CIA report potential narcotics violations.[31]

In sum, an order from the White House at the height of U.S. support of the Contras explicitly dropped the requirement that CIA report drug offenses committed by their paid associates. Subsequently, some members of the CIA were not only ignoring crimes but actively conspiring with drug traffickers. At least some of those drugs, possibly most, were destined for the United States (including the "inner cities").

But back in 1996, claims that the CIA was somehow involved in the cocaine trade were met with derision that singled out African Americans:

The *New York Times*, the *Los Angeles Times* and the *Washington Post* all ran lengthy stories . . . suggesting that the public – and particularly the African-American community – was unduly suspicious of government, if not downright gullible.[32]

Julian Beltrame reported that the charges against the CIA "[have] a whiff of a pre-posterous conspiracy theory . . . , [advanced, according to critics,] by American black leaders eager . . . to find a scapegoat for the crack tragedy."[33] One such critic was especially dismissive:

> So far, however, the CIA-L.A.-crack story is just another dubious chapter in the evolving myth of racial victimization, drawing force and credibility from the all too real history of racial mischief and oppression in America. This particular conspiracy theory implies that, but for foul plots hatched at CIA headquarters and elsewhere, possibly even the Reagan White House itself, the social pathologies so often associated with inner-city life would vanish.[34]

In these cases, the charges against the CIA (especially as laid out by Webb) are conflated with the more dubious claims (which few were making, but apparently "implying") that the CIA was solely responsible for the crack epidemic and that it was a deliberate plan to destroy black communities.

Another trend emerged, somewhat surprisingly, that—despite the collective dismissal of the concerns of African Americans—many were quick to put their alleged susceptibility to conspiracy theories in historical context.[35] As in the above passage—recognizing, while minimizing, the reality of "racial mischief"—there is a sense of patronizing forgiveness that conceded this reality. Donna Britt, an African-American journalist, was more specific on this "racial mischief," but much the same point is made: "What feels true to blacks has fueled numerous conspiracy theories. Some, such as the infamous Tuskegee Experiment, are true."[36] Despite the history and the contemporary inequities, the reason for conspiracy theories among blacks isn't grounded in these facts, but derives only from what "*feels* true" to *them*.

Under the dismissive title "Though Evidence is Thin, Tale of CIA and Drugs Has a Life of Its Own," Tim Golden is one of the few to allow the public a voice:

> "The established press ignored the story until they found out that black folks weren't going to just let this one be swept under the rug," said Don Middleton, 33, a jazz musician in Washington who read the series on the Internet. "The white press is pointing fingers at the black community, saying we're paranoid and quick to see conspiracy at every turn of the corner. Where have they been for the last 30 years? Can I just mention the Tuskegee syphilis study, Cointelpro, Watergate, Iran-Contra. Hello, America?"[37]

At all turns throughout this episode, African Americans were often portrayed as prone to a "conspiracy theory" that has, at least in general terms, been confirmed by the CIA itself. With Tuskegee, it is now part of the historical record. Despite recognition that the history of race in America might be a factor in black peoples' "gullibility," there is never the suggestion that their claims be given credence as a result. It is only part of the "evolving myth of racial victimization."[38]

Conspiracy Theories in the Muslim World

Coverage of Muslim voices in the mainstream press exhibits a similar pattern. Especially since the attacks of 9/11, Muslims have been vilified as a group and Islam painted as a uniquely and uniformly violent worldview. Islamophobia has led to the reification of a diverse religion with a diverse sets of adherents, and people in nations with Muslim majorities have been characterized as "rife" with unwarranted suspicion, especially, for some reason, of the motives of the West. Given this conflation of nations and ethnic groups, the attitudes of the "Arab Street"—whether Arab or not, and what in the "civilized world" would be characterized as "public opinion"—are often portrayed as grounded not in the facts of U.S. foreign policy but in unwarranted "conspiracy theory." Moreover, unlike the "conspiracy theories" among the black community being treated condescendingly as unfortunate but understandable given the long history of white supremacy, Muslims' attitudes are not put in the historical context of European colonialism and the ongoing War on Terror.

New York Times columnist Thomas Friedman sums up this reification of Islamic nations well: "The more these societies become monocultures, the less they spark new ideas and the more susceptible they are to diseased conspiracy theories and extreme ideologies."[39] Friedman's "Arab/Muslim world," "susceptible to diseased conspiracy theories," attributes conspiratorial thinking to a conflation of diverse peoples. In numerous articles on the nations and peoples that comprise the "Muslim world," this vocabulary of motive serves to discredit the very real concerns of entire populations.

As the first front in the "War on Terror," despite Afghanistan and Pakistan's ethnically diverse populations, the concerns of people in the "Af/Pak Theater" must be dismissed regularly:

> A tribal elder in Balkh Province, in the remote north, said the insurgency had disrupted life for farmers and herders, and he repeated one of a growing number of conspiracy theories about the Americans' intentions.[40]

This is no less true of those who support U.S. intervention, as "even among pro-government Afghans, conspiracy theories abound."[41] However, perhaps because the machinations and the chaos in the country are hard to paper over, attributions of conspiracy to Afghanis were relatively rare in the *New York Times* articles examined.

Not so with articles on Pakistan, a frequent target of the accusation. In Pakistan, "where conspiracy theories abound,"[42] "run rampant,"[43] "run rife,"[44] and are a "national sport,"[45] "conspiracy theories" are a part of their culture:

> [The] report was "larded with strange conspiracies," [he] said, adding that it was indicative of a broader culture of conspiracy theories. . . . "It's so untethered from rational discourse."[46]

The reasons why Pakistanis are so vulnerable to irrational conspiracy theories is not always clear, but Sabrina Tavernise proffers an explanation—it is the result of a collective psychological deficiency:

> Conspiracy theories are pervasive in Pakistan, and [she] offered an explanation. They are a projection, she said – a defense mechanism that protects one's psyche from something too difficult to accept. "It's not me, it's you," she said. "It's a denial of personal responsibility. . . ." (Tavernise, 2009b, p. 1). They turn to conspiracy theories to explain a reality that is otherwise too awful to face.[47]

Although he too emphasizes that "conspiracy theories" are part of the national character, Salman Masood, in a report on the son of a Chief Justice in Pakistan who had admitted to accepting bribes, has to dismiss his own reporting by blaming his profession:

> In a country where conspiracy theories seem to gain steam the more baroque they get, the case has riveted and confused much of the public, in part because the proceedings are based on news media speculation rather than any official complaint.[48]

(Unlike Pakistanis, we are fortunate indeed to enjoy a media system that avoids "speculation.") Also, still within the context of Pakistanis' inexplicable fascination with "conspiracy theories," and without saying it outright, there is sometimes a faint recognition that there just might be some basis to Pakistanis' concerns:

> To them, the affair sheds new light on a murky practice that they say should never take place: the recruitment of aid workers as intelligence operatives in a sensitive country like Pakistan, already awash in conspiracy theories about Western meddling.[49]

Still, for the most part, peoples' concerns are exaggerated, unfair, and overwrought: Despite that the United States has explicitly targeted infrastructure, "when the water stops running from the tap, people blame America."[50]

As the ultimate neocon project in the "War on Terror," Iraqis of all ethnic groups are frequently tarred with this broad brush. Iraq is "a country rife with conspiracy theories,"[51] they "are the currency of daily life,[52] and are "not uncommon on the streets of Iraq."[53] Indeed, Iraqis have "the conspiracy mindset."[54] This, apparently, makes it hard to focus: "As often happens these days in conversations with ordinary Iraqis, [he] first offered a reasonable explanation . . ., and then plunged into conspiracy theory."[55] As is typical when explaining the "conspiracy theory," Michael Schmidt psychologizes the problem:

> For some this has become too much, causing them to fall back into familiar ways of coping: concocting conspiracy theories, lashing out violently and stealing from their neighbors.[56]

Far from reasonable in the end, all that conspiracy theorizing (and violent thievery) is simply a coping mechanism.

Across North Africa, the Middle East, and South Asia, no Muslim nation appears untouched. Bangladesh, "where conspiracy theories are a national sport,"[57] "is rife with conspiracy theories [even] under normal circumstances."[58] In Africa, "far-fetched conspiracy theories . . . are now commonly heard in Egypt,"[59] where "they have a particular hold . . . , sowing confusion in order to avoid accountability."[60] To the north:

> [Turkish President Recep Erdoğan] "has conjured a dark conspiracy of secular subversives, bankers and Western media, but that is vintage Erdoğan, and vintage Turkey – a country of intrigues that exemplifies the old line: even paranoids have enemies."[61]

And several years before it became the target of the U.S.-backed Saudi assault, Yemen, perhaps presciently, was already a "land of conspiracy theories."[62]

Deflecting Critiques of Power

Conspiracy theorist is used to dismiss, denigrate, and to deflect critiques of power. It presents a "type" of argument as inherently false and absurd, illogical, and unreasonable, motivated by a delusional, angry and immoral mind—that of the "conspiracy theorist." They are the claims of those unworthy of participation in political debate. Then, the application of this term to two groups, African Americans and people in the Muslim-majority nations of North Africa, the Middle East, and South Asia was examined. A consistent pattern in the application of the label is its use to cordon off the often reasonable belief of populations that they have been subjected to and suffer from the domination of powerful groups. The origins of this use can be found in the chapter in this volume by Andrew McKenzie-McHargh.

To be sure, not only African Americans and Muslims have been tarred as "conspiracy theorists." They are indeed everywhere. They are "common in Russia,"[63] and of course "Bulgarians have a taste for conspiracy theories."[64] Not only is there "an Italian tendency to look for conspiracy theories,"[65] but, in "a country where [they] are often given more credence than news reports . . . , conspiracy theories . . . [come] naturally to Mexicans."[66] Even in "the gay community, conspiracy theories initially abounded" before they apparently came to their senses.[67]

It seems that everywhere one turns, marginalized groups share a concern with the abuse of power. That elites and their media would prefer to preempt these conversations should come as no surprise. This is not to suggest that memos from the executive offices of FOX News dictate media spin—the exercise of power is of course more complex. While media power is not, of course, the result of an overarching conspiracy to mask state power, in many ways it might as well be.

Notes

1. Mills, C. Wright. 1940. "Situated Actions and Vocabularies of Motive." *American Sociological Review* 5(6): 904–913.
2. Ibid., 904–906. Emphasis in the original text.
3. Simons, Herbert W. 1994. "'Going Meta': Definition and Political Applications." *Quarterly Journal of Speech* 80(4): 468–81.
4. Ibid., 469.
5. Moynihan, Colin. 2011. "Fight on Islamic Center Flares Anew as Ex-firefighter Takes Case to Court." *New York Times*, March 16, 2011.
6. Savage, Charlie. 2012. "Report by House Democrats Absolves Administration in Gun Trafficking Case." *New York Times*, January 31, 2012.
7. Cowell, Alan, and Burns, John F. 2012. "Cameron Dismisses Accusations of Deal with Murdoch Family." *New York Times*, June 15, 2012.
8. Kirkpatrick, David D., and Mayy el Sheikh. 2012. "Egypt's New President is Being Undercut by State-run Media." *New York Times*, July 14, 2012.
9. Warren, James. 2010. "Blagojevich Trial Shines a Light on Real Politics." *New York Times*, July 2, 2010.
10. Pérez-Peña, Richard. 2012. "Sandusky's Adopted Son, Claiming Abuse, Offered to Testify at Trial." *New York Times*, June 22, 2012.
11. Bowley, Graham. 2010. "At Brown, Spotlight on the President's Role at a Bank." *New York Times*, March 2, 2010.
12. Shear, Michael D. 2013. "A Sleeper Scandal Awakens, Post-election." *New York Times*, 22 May 2013.
13. Powell, Michael. 2013. "The Quashing of a Case against a Christie Ally." *New York Times*, October 11, 2013.
14. Kelly, C. 2013. "Thinking Beyond the Creationists and the Darwinists." *Texas Monthly*, February, 25B.
15. Bellafante, Ginia. 2011. "Murder and Melodrama: An Obsessive Killer is Revealed in a Stylish Whodunit." *New York Times*, June 20, 2011.
16. Goodman, J. David, and Vivian Yee. 2013. "'I was just sure they just wanted to kill this group of Persians.'" *New York Times*, November 15, 2013.
17. Lee, Trymaine. 2007. "Sorrow and Reflection in Killer's Housing Project." *New York Times*, January 25, 2007.

18. Pérez-Peña, Richard. 2012. "Ousted Head of University is Reinstated in Virginia." *New York Times*, June 27, 2012.

19. Miller, Stuart. 2012. "Brooklyn Pipeline Project Raises a Host of Worries." *New York Times*, August 30, 2012.

20. Wald, Matthew L. 2008. "Controversy Dogs Inquiry on Bridge Collapse." *New York Times*, January 30, 2008.

21. Hale, Mike. 2009. "The Week Ahead: March 8 – March 14: Film." *New York Times*, March 8, 2009.

22. Shane, Scott. 2009. "C.I.A. is Cagey about '63 Files Tied to Oswald." *New York Times*, October 17, 2009.

23. Carey, Benedict. 2001. "Red Flags at a College, but Tied Hands." *New York Times*, January 11, 2001.

24. Rohan, Tim. 2013. "Groups Want Bad Image of Penn State to Go Away." *New York Times*, September 17, 2013.

25. Shane, Scott, and Michael D. Shear. 2013. "Visions of Drones Swarming the Skies Touch Bipartisan Nerve." *New York Times*, March 9, 2013.

26. Burns, John F. 2011. "London Protesters Identify with New York Counterparts and Worry of Similar Fate." *New York Times*, November 16, 2011.

27. Archibold, Randal C. 2008. "In Smaller Numbers, Marchers Seek Immigrants' Rights." *New York Times*, May 2, 2008.

28. Webb, Gary. 1998. *Dark Alliance: The CIA, the Contras, and the Crack Cocaine Explosion.* New York: Seven Stories Press.

29. Office of the Inspector General, Central Intelligence Agency.1998. *Allegations of Connections between CIA and the Contras in Cocaine Trafficking to the United States, Volume II: "The Contra Story."* https://www.cia.gov/library/reports/general-reports-1/cocaine/contra-story/contents.html (Accessed February 5, 2015).

30. Ibid.

31. Ibid., emphasis added.

32. Salisbury, S. 1998. "Still on Trail of CIA Links to Drug-runners." *The Philadelphia Inquirer*, July 7, 1998.

33. Beltrame, J. 1996. "Did CIA Touch Off Epidemic of Crack?: Tie with Contras Claimed." *The Gazette* (Montreal, Quebec), September 21, 1996.

34. Yoder, E. 1996. "The CIA–Crack Scandal Myth." *Denver Post*, October 6, 1996.

35. For a discussion of this phenomenon, see Bratich, J. Z. 2008. *Conspiracy Panics: Political Rationality and Popular Culture*. New York: State University of New York Press.

36. Britt, Donna. 1996. "Finding the Truest Truth." *Washington Post*, November 16, 1996.

37. Golden, Tim. 1996. "Though Evidence is Thin, Tale of CIA and Drugs has a Life of its Own." *The New York Times*, October 21, 1996.

38. Yoder, "The CIA–Crack Scandal Myth."

39. Friedman, Thomas L. 2013. "From Beirut to Washington." *New York Times*, October 20, 2013.

40. Rubin, Alissa J. 2009. "Prospect of more U.S. Troops Worries a Wary Afghan Public." *New York Times*, November 7, 2009.

41. Ahmed, A. 2013. "The Haqqanis, Revered for Soviet Fight, Losing Favor among Countrymen." *International New York Times*, November 7, 2013.

42. Sirajuddin, S. 2010. "Quotation of the Day." *New York Times*, May 26, 2010.

43. Ellick, Adam B., and Huma Imtiaz. 2010. "Pakistani's Death in London sets off Unrest in Karachi." *New York Times*, September 18, 2010.

44. Walsh, Declan. 2013. "A Fiery Preacher's Arrival Shakes Pakistani Politics." *New York Times*, January 13, 2013.

45. Tavernise, Sabrina. 2010. "U.S. Heads a Cast of Villains in Pakistan's Conspiracy Talk." *New York Times*, May 6, 2010.

46. Walsh, Declan. 2012. "A Personal Quest to Clarify bin Laden's Last Days Yields Vexing Accounts." *New York Times*, March 8, 2012.

47. Tavernise, Sabrina. 2009. "Pakistanis View Market Blast with Disbelief, and Seek Places to Put Blame." *New York Times*, November 4, 2009.

48. Masood, Salman. 2012. "After Cabinet Officials, Next on the Docket for Pakistan's Chief Justice is His Son." *New York Times*, June 7, 2012.

49. Walsh, Declan. 2012. "Fallout of bin Laden Raid: Aid Groups in Pakistan are Suspect." *New York Times*, May 3, 2012.

50. Sirajuddin, S. "Quotation of the Day."

51. Nordland, Rod. 2009. "Sunnis and Shiites See an Omen for Reconciliation in Iraq." *New York Times*, August 23, 2009.

52. Healy, Jack. 2012. "Iraq Turns Justice into a Show, and Terror Confessions a Script." *New York Times*, January 8, 2012.

53. Santora, Marc. 2009. "7 Blasts around Baghdad kill at least 24." *New York Times*, June 23, 2009.

54. Farrell, Stephen. 2007. "From Iraq's Rumor Mill, a Conspiracy of Badgers." *New York Times*, July 31, 2007.

55. Filkins, Dexter. 2006. "Votes Counted. Deals Made. Chaos Wins." *New York Times*, April 30, 2006.

56. Schmidt, Michael S. 2011. "Heat Wave and Fasting Add to Woes of Iraqis." *New York Times*, August 3, 2011.

57. Sengupta, Somini. 2009. "Bangladeshi Premier Faces a Grim Crucible with Notes of Defiance." *New York Times*, March 14, 2009.

58. Yardley, Jim. 2013. "Grim Task Overwhelms Bangladeshi DNA Lab." *New York Times*, May 31, 2013.

59. Kirkpatrick, David D. 2013. "Secret Recordings Reveal Mubarak's Frank Views on a Range of Subjects." *New York Times*, September 23, 2013.

60. Lindsey, Ursula. 2013. "Tall Tales in Egypt." *New York Times*, September 1, 2013.

61. Keller, Bill. 2013. "The Revolt of the Rising Class." *New York Times*, July 1, 2013.

62. Kasinof, Laura. 2011. "As Yemen Teeters from Political Unrest, a Humanitarian Crisis May Not be Far Off." *New York Times*, June 28, 2011.

63. Levy, Clifford J. 2007. "Party's Triumph Raises Question of Putin's Plans." *New York Times*, January 15, 2007.

64. Higgins, Andrew. 2013. "Change Comes Slowly for Bulgaria, Even with EU Membership." *New York Times*, December 25, 2013.

65. Donadio, Rachel. 2013. "Vatican Bank Looks to Shed its Image as an Offshore Haven." *New York Times*, May 31, 2013.

66. Cave, Damien. 2011. "Mexico Crash Kills a Leader in Drug Fight." *New York Times*, November 12, 2011.

67. Becker, Jo. 2009. "The Road to Championing Same-sex Marriage." *New York Times*, August 19, 2009.

6

Conspiracy Theories and Philosophy

Bringing the Epistemology of a Freighted Term into the Social Sciences

M R. X. DENTITH

A notable feature about the study of things we call *conspiracy theories* is both how large and fragmented the literature is. This has led to the development of a number of different, often disparate research programs, largely as a result of scholars applying their own theoretical presuppositions to a largely interdisciplinary topic. [1]

However, many of these research programs are not easily reconcilable with each other, and this is a problem—I argue—which needs resolution. Just how we resolve the issue is, I think, simple, but the consequences may have repercussions for existing research programs which some scholars might find hard to stomach.

Now, despite the disparity in these existing research programs, most scholars agree that conspiracy theories are *theories* about *conspiracies*. Where we have tended to differ typically hinges on whether there is something more to a conspiracy theory than it *merely* being a theory about a conspiracy. These views fit the following (rough) classification:

> Conspiracy theories are prima facie false.
>
> Conspiracy theories are not prima facie false, but there is something about such theories which makes them suspicious
>
> Conspiracy theories are neither prima facie false nor typically suspicious. [2]

The first two options are what have been come to be known in philosophy as "generalist views" or *generalism*. [3] Generalists claim we have justification for a general, prima facie suspicion of conspiracy theories. That is, given that conspiracy theories are either false, or most of them are suspect, we have grounds to treat the class of *conspiracy theories* dismissively.

The third option is what we might term *particularism*;[4] when appraising any conspiracy theory we have to assess it on its particular (read: evidential) merits, rather than treat it dismissively just because it has been labeled a conspiracy theory.

Much of the *apparent* disagreement in the literature—I argue (and have argued elsewhere; see *The Problem of Conspiracism*[5])—hinges upon which option we choose. In this chapter I will demonstrate that our choices end up restricting our ability to analyze these things called conspiracy theories. Not just that, but they also prove to be problematic *generally*, restricting the kind of examples of what counts as a conspiracy theory, thus limiting our analyses from the outset. To illustrate this, let us look at each of these options in turn.

Option 1: Conspiracy Theories as Prima Facie False

Some scholars—admittedly not many—treat conspiracy theories as prima facie false and thus by extension irrational to believe.

For example, Viren Swami et al. define conspiracy theories as "a subset of **false beliefs** [emphasis mine] in which the ultimate cause of an event is believed to be due to a plot by multiple actors working together with a clear goal in mind, often unlawfully and in secret."[6] Or there is Daniel Pipes, who characterizes belief in conspiracy theories as a "fear of **nonexistent** [emphasis mine] conspiracies. *Conspiracy* refers to an act, *conspiracy theory* to a perception."[7]

Pipes here is aping the work of Richard Hofstadter who, in *The Paranoid Style in American Politics*, discusses how *certain* conspiracy theorists see conspiracies as *the* motive force in history, which is "set in motion by demonic forces of almost transcendent power[.]"[8] However, this mode of thinking is a paranoid *style,* not an actual clinical diagnosis of psychological paranoia; it is analogous to paranoid ideation but—crucially—not actual paranoia. Pipes, however, characterizes belief in conspiracy theories as fantastical, and so ends up treating the *paranoid style* as something akin to a clinical diagnosis of paranoid ideation on the part of the conspiracy theorist. Pipes is not alone in this; see also the work of Gordon Arnold[9] and Hannah Darwin et al.[10]

Numerous scholars have adopted Hofstadter's view explicitly. Joseph DiGrazia, for example, endorses Hofstadter's paranoid-style analysis of belief in conspiracy theories.[11] Michael Barkun also approvingly cites Hofstadter in his book *A Culture of Conspiracy: Apocalyptic Visions in Contemporary America.*[12] Meanwhile, Marvin Zonis and Craig T. Joseph—while not explicitly citing Hofstadter—also run a paranoid-style type of analysis in *Conspiracy Thinking in the Middle East,* claiming "[c]onspiracy thinking is isomorphic with, although not identical to, paranoia."[13]

Peter Knight, however, argues that treating the analogy that underpins the paranoid style *literally* is self-defeating, given that it rests upon claiming both belief in conspiracy theories is paranoid, and paranoid people believe conspiracy theories.[14] As I have argued in *The Problem of Conspiracism*, the problem with conflating cases of *putative* irrational conspiracy theorizing (often labeled as "conspiracist") with the wider array of conspiracy theorizing we find out in the world gets the scholarly analysis back-to-front. [15] We cannot infer anything interesting about the nature of belief in conspiracy theories if we only look at the class of people we have *predetermined* as believing such theories irrationally.

We should never operate with definitions that presume the answer to our research questions. Now, we could be charitable and say that scholars who operate with such definitions come to them as a *result* of their research: on examination, each and every conspiracy theory has been false (and thus by extension irrational to believe).

Now, aside from an inductive problem (how can we be sure the next conspiracy theory we research will turn out to be false?) there is no need to bake in any stipulation that conspiracy theories are *necessarily* false. After all, it is no threat to claim a conspiracy theory *could be true*, even if we lived in a world in which all investigated conspiracy theories have been false. After all, it is *logically possible* that some theory about a conspiracy *could* be true. Indeed, the fact we live in a world where at least one conspiracy theory has turned out to be true, the stipulation seems at best naïve, and at worst stupid.

After all, what do scholars like Pipes or Swami make of conspiracy theories that not only turned out to be true but were rational to believe *at the time*? Take, for example, the conspiracy theories about the Moscow Show Trials in the 1930s, or the Gulf of Tonkin incident in the 1960s. These are cases of cover-ups where members of influential institutions really did conspire to keep the truth of their actions secret from the public. Not just that, they unjustly and insincerely labeled their detractors as *conspiracy theorists*.[16]

Now, you could claim the conspiracy theorists in these cases were only accidentally right, or, more plausibly, the theory labeled "conspiracy" was never a conspiracy theory in the first place (a point we will return to later). But with respect to the possibility conspiracy theorists were only accidentally right, we can show, with respect to the Moscow Show Trials of the 1930s and the Gulf of Tonkin Incident of the 1960s, that said theorists offered plausible arguments and evidence for their conspiracy theories *at the time*, yet had their warranted conclusions dismissed *merely* because they were "conspiracy theorists" peddling "conspiracy theories." These examples are but the tip of an iceberg of warranted conspiracy theories that were dismissed because we were told conspiracy theorists and their theories should not be believed.

Given how implausible it is to argue that conspiracy theories are necessarily false, scholars of this persuasion—I argue—should shift their operating definition to one which *merely* claims said theories are suspicious. However, as we are about to see, this stipulation turns out to be just as problematic.

Suspicious Conspiracy Theories

Most scholars—to be fair—do not treat conspiracy theories as *necessarily* false. Rather, they work with a definition that on the whole stipulates there is something *suspicious* about such theories.

Gordon Wood, for example, argues that while belief in some *contemporary* conspiracy theories resembles paranoia (along the lines of Hofstadter), historically belief in such theories turned out to be understandable. As the providential view of politics—which saw the gods as being behind human affairs—was superseded with a more human-centric view of politics, it made sense to see the misfortunes of human affairs through the lens of conspiracies. Wood argues this view was just as mistaken, because it assumed the intentions of political agents were effectatious in a way that we, knowing more about politics *now*, should reject.[17] As such, one of the reasons why we might be tempted to think conspiracy theories are suspicious as a class of explanation is because conspiracies are unlikely, or that when they do occur they amount to little of note.

For example, Peter Lipton considers belief in conspiracy theories to be suspicious because conspiracy theorists overstate the probability of conspiracies as salient causes of events.[18] Preston Bost and Stephen Prunier talk about conspiracy theories with respect to their "**often** [emphasis mine] inherent-implausibility,"[19] while Daniel Jolley and Karen Douglas talk about conspiracy theories as "attempts to explain the ultimate causes of events as secret plots by powerful forces rather than as overt activities or accidents."[20]

Conspiracy theories under these views are suspicious because conspiracy theorists overplay the likelihood of conspiracies as salient causes of certain kinds of events, or because conspirators are typically convenient dupes rather than the real perpetrators.

The notion that conspiracies themselves are either unlikely, or unlikely to succeed, has been an influential position in the literature and dates back at least to the seminal work of Karl Popper. He argued that as most events in the world are not the result of successful conspiracies, belief in what he labeled the "conspiracy theory of society" was prima facie irrational.[21]

Yet, as Charles Pigden argues, Popper's argument rests upon a false dilemma; conspiracy theorists, it turns out, do not believe history to be *solely* the product of successful conspiracies. Rather, history is the result of some successful conspiracies, some unsuccessful conspiracies, and also the product of some non-conspiracies.[22] Not just that, but, as David Coady argues, many of the reasons we tend to think of conspiracies as unlikely or not noteworthy do not withstand scrutiny.[23] We *might* be tempted to think conspiracies rarely happen, tend to be insignificant, often fail, or that governments rarely conspire. Yet, a cursory glance at history (both contemporary and in antiquity) shows that conspiracies happen more often than many of us might think, and that they are often quite successful. Indeed, once we factor in past instances of conspiratorial activity—as I have argued elsewhere—the idea that we should not at least consider conspiracies as *potential* explanations for certain kinds of events means we are downplaying the role evidence plays in our reasoning.[24] Indeed, to borrow a term from Lee Basham, the idea that conspiracies are—at least in the West—uncommon and seldom successful is more an expression of political piety than the result of evidence-based reasoning.[25]

Crippled, Vice-Ridden Epistemologies

Some scholars find belief in conspiracy theories to be suspicious because conspiracy theorists suffer from some kind of pathology of reasoning. Take, for example, the work of Cass Sunstein and Adrian Vermeule; they posit that conspiracy theorists suffer from a *crippled epistemology*, locating the problem of belief in conspiracy theories in the epistemic practices of conspiracy theorists.[26] A similar argument is advanced by Quassim Cassam, who argues that conspiracy theorists suffer from the epistemic vice of gullibility.[27]

David Grimes takes an interesting perspective on this issue. The problem with belief in conspiracy theories, he argues, is that conspiracy theorists radically over-estimate the viability of conspiratorial activity. Grimes argues conspirators cannot help but leak evidence of their conspiracies the more time passes, which means not only that certain long-standing conspiracy theories are irrational to believe, but conspiracy theorists overstate the competence and ability of conspirators.[28] However, the problem with these kinds of arguments face a number of problems. For one thing, the kind of examples we typically use to show that conspiracies are unsuccessful are unsuccessful conspiracies; we use examples of failed conspiracies to infer that conspiracies typically fail. Yet we have inadequate grounds to make that inductive leap, for a multitude of reasons. The first is that part and parcel of many a successful conspiracy will be keeping that conspiracy out of public knowledge. As such, we are faced with the problem of not knowing how many successful conspiracies have occurred.

The second problem is that as long-term secrecy is only a function of some conspiracies, the revelation of a conspiracy tells us little about its viability; some conspiracies must be kept secret for a long time in order to keep up appearances (the Moscow Show Trials) while some conspiracies can be revealed almost immediately (the assassination of Julius Caesar).[29] The third issue is more prosaic: the kind of belief in conspiracy theories being referred to in these analyses are merely a *subset* of belief in conspiracy theories generally. The fact some conspiracy theorists may believe in ultimately unviable conspiracy theories tells us little about the viability or belief in the wide range of conspiracy theory beliefs. So for the Sunsteins, Vermueles, Cassams, and Grimes of the conspiracy theory world, the very basis of this argument is a pejorative understanding of what counts as a conspiracy theory. That is, they work with the subset of prima facie false theories to make claims about belief in those theories generally.[30] Yet, as I have argued extensively elsewhere, we should not generalize from a subset of these things called *conspiracy theories* in order to tarnish belief in such theories overall.[31]

The Social Consequences

Sometimes what is taken to be suspicious about conspiracy theories stems from the stipulation that because conspiracies are a sinister activity, belief in conspiracy theories *generally* has negative social consequences.

For example, Jan-Willem van Prooijen claims that there are "many detrimental implications of believing in conspiracy theories"[32] as do Michael Barkun[33] and Viren Swami.[34] Robert Brotherton and Christopher French claim that belief in conspiracy theories can have "detrimental consequences, both for individuals and for the wider community."[35] Sander van der Linden states that "potential exposure to conspiracy theories can have negative and undesirable societal consequences."[36] Karen Douglas, with Robbie Sutton, has argued that conspiracy theorists have a tendency to see conspiracies because they are the kind of person likely to conspire themselves.[37]

Looking specifically at anti-vaccine conspiracy theories, Karen Douglas and Daniel Jolley conclude their analysis by saying "Ongoing investigations are needed to further identify the social consequences of conspiracism, and to identify potential ways to combat the effects of an ever-growing culture of conspiracism."[38] Douglas and Robbie Sutton have also argued in a similar vein.[39]

Now, some of these scholars do pay lip service to the idea that belief in conspiracy theories can have positive social consequences (such as exposing government corruption, increasing watchfulness, etc.), but the negatives are taken to outweigh the positives.[40] The most charitable reading of such arguments stems from the claim that belief in conspiracy theories threatens something about the public order, and any belief that weakens social bonds and the like must be prima facie questionable.

Yet that argument can easily be subverted, or abused. Jack Bratich, for example, argues that much of the rhetoric against conspiracy theorizing comes out of a curious intolerance to views that challenge liberal democratic institutions.[41] Belief in conspiracy theories—under this kind of view—certainly could increase the public's distrust in influential institutions, but only as a consequence of our constantly being told that conspiracy theorizing is beyond the pale. That is, the prohibition of even talking about treating conspiracy theories seriously leads to the *othering* of political voices, the consequence of which has negative social consequences in a democratic society.

For example, Lee Basham has argued that there are certain facts that are too toxic to ever be widely admitted to, let alone disseminated by those in authority. That is, some truths are toxic, and so to prevent widespread alarm and resultant distrust in government and related institutions, these facts must be covered up.[42] As such, the prohibition against conspiracy theorizing—particularly because of its supposed negative consequences—is itself reason to be worried about what we might not be being told.

We might also think that some malign activities end up being politely ignored or downplayed by the public themselves. That is, sometimes we are *polite* about certain known sinister activities or injustices. For example—as evidenced by police corruption scandals of the 1970s, for example—the populace can be aware of systemic corruption and the like, but decide to *politely* ignore them. As I argue in "Conspiracy Theories on the Basis of Evidence," we do not necessarily need to think cover-ups take place from the top, flowing down to the populace.[43]

Whatever interpretation we take, the idea that we can justify our suspicion of conspiracy theories on the basis that belief in them has negative social consequences rests upon an assumption about the nature of our society, which is the very thing many conspiracy theorists question. Sometimes secretive behavior on the part of law enforcement might be necessary to uncover serious plots against the *polis*, and governments might have to negotiate with foreign powers behind closed doors in order to get the best deal for their citizens. However, just because belief in conspiracy theories might undermine our trust in the status quo, this is no reason to treat them as a suspicious class of theory. Indeed, treating conspiracy theories as inherently suspicious runs the risk of quashing necessary questions such as when secrecy is justified, and when such secrecy is actually conspiratorial.

Unofficial Stories

Conspiracy theories need not be considered sinister to be thought of as suspicious. Sometimes it is argued what makes belief in a conspiracy theory suspicious comes out of them being rivals to some other theory that has official status.

Perhaps the best example of this view is to be found in the work of Kathyrn Olmsted. She points out that talk of conspiracy theories is "often the story of the struggle over the power to control the public's perception of an event. . . .Conspiracy theorists challenge this *official story* [emphasis mine], proposing counternarratives to the government's history of an event."[44]

Olmsted's work goes to great lengths to show that such suspicions of conspiracy (to wit, conspiracy theories), given what we know of recent history and politicking, is not *epistemically* suspicious. However, other scholars of conspiracy theory take a harder line. For example, Michael Barkun,[45] Bessi et al.,[46] and Neil Levy[47] all posit that we have grounds for *preferring* official stories over rival conspiracy theories by virtue of official stories being official.

The chief problem here is in mistaking official status with epistemic authority (a point which I have critiqued elsewhere); the fact some theory has official status tells us nothing about its epistemic merits.[48] Sometimes we mistake officialness in a political sense with officialness in an expertise sense, and sometimes we mistake the *appearance of authority* (whether it be a fee-to-publish journal article or an astroturf organization's "documentary") with expertise. It turns out we are easily confused or fooled by the appellation *official*. This conflation, then, between officialness and epistemic merit has allowed some unwarranted conspiracy theories to flourish *merely* because they have the appearance of being official.

David Coady—taking a different tack—argues that conspiracy theories are *in some sense* unofficial stories. However, this simply marks out conspiracy theories as unofficial in the same way that rumors are unofficial; they are claims which have not been given some official imprimatur. Given that official theories can be conspiratorial, their officialness does not tell us they are epistemically superior. Rather, it just tells us that we typically refrain from calling official theories "conspiracy theories."[49]

Yet respect for common usage is still a problem. For one thing, it is not clear that the labels *conspiracy theory* and *conspiracy theorist* necessarily have much pejorative baggage. Indeed, many recent political scandals have been labeled as *conspiracy theories* yet been believed anyway. Take the claims of the Coalition of the Willing Back in 2003 members of the coalition tried to convince the public that the Iraqi regime was manufacturing Weapons of Mass Destruction (WMDs), and anyone who said that evidence was specious, fabricated, or disinformation were simply engaging in or promoting conspiracy theories. Then there is the case of then Prime Minister of New Zealand John Key's unsuccessful claim in 2014 that allegations of dirty politicking by his office was just a conspiracy theory; in both cases the label failed to have much effect. As recent work by Mike Wood shows, while there are many assumptions about the label "conspiracy theory" there has been little work to test whether the label has the pejorative implication some academics attribute to it.[50]

There are, I take it, two related problems here. The first is that so-called "official stories" (or "official theories") can, as Coady points out, be just as conspiratorial as some rival conspiracy theory. It is hard to not be a conspiracy theorist about the events of 9/11, because even the official theory advances a conspiracy; the hijackers worked in secret to carry out their terrorist attack. The other problem is both temporal and spatial: what gets called a *conspiracy theory* at one time or in one place can be labeled the *official story* at some other time or place. For example, Jolley, Douglas, and Sutton bake into their definition that conspiracy theories are largely rivals to some official explanation.[51] Yet the examples they cite as *true* conspiracy theories—Watergate, Iran–Contra, and Tuskegee syphilis scandals—are no longer rivals to official explanations (even if they were at the time). Relatedly, a theory which is the official, received wisdom in one polity can be considered a conspiracy theory in another culture; in Taliban-controlled Afghanistan the official theory that al-Qaeda was behind the 9/11 attacks was roundly condemned as a false conspiracy theory back in 2001.

Given, then, that the pejorative is not fixed, scholars who want to focus on the pejorative aspect of conspiracy theory at time x or place y should be clear that *generally* what the term refers to is agnostic; rather, what counts here as pejorative is socially constituted. See the chapters by Andrew McKenzie-McHargh, and Martin Orr and Gina Husting in this volume for more on this matter.

Indeed, the idea that the label *conspiracy theory* is a matter of rhetoric has long standing in the literature. As Orr and Husting have previously argued, *conspiracy theorist* is part of the "machinery of interaction," pointing out that "the label does conversational work no matter how true, false, or conspiracy-related your utterance is."[52]

Lance deHaven-Smith and Matthew Witt argue that treating the label as pejorative "risks weakening popular vigilance against abuses of power, election tampering, cover-ups, and other genuine threats to democratic governance."[53] Meanwhile, Jaron Harambam and Stef Aupers point out that the pejorative use of "conspiracy theorist" by academics effectively means said theorists' views are dismissed a priori, despite the boundary between conspiracy theories and non-conspiracy theories being contested ground.[54] Michael Butter and Peter Knight argue that the idea that we can produce *value-neutral* research on these things called conspiracy theories is misguided if we are working with *value-laden* definitions.[55]

The problem is this: Even if scholars claim that conspiracy theories can be warranted, by focusing their attention on the class of suspect theories, they often draw broad conclusions about the rationality of belief in conspiracy theories *generally*. Yet it is not clear this subset of suspect conspiracy theories is representative of the wider kind. Thus, such a focus has the effect of restricting our analysis. As such, should we not just work with a non-pejorative definition in the first place?

Conspiracy Theories as Theories about (Particular) Conspiracies

This, then, brings us to our third option. Once we rule out the utility of working with the first two kinds of definitions, then we are left with the option that all a conspiracy theory is, is *just* an explanation of an event which cites a conspiracy as a salient cause.

Indeed, if we are interested in the question of whether belief in conspiracy theories is rational or irrational, then this is the definition we *must* work with. After all, if we define belief in conspiracy theories as prima facie irrational or typically suspicious, then we end up assuming the very conclusion to our research questions.

The use of pejorative definitions—wittingly or unwittingly—artificially reduces the possibility that it might be rational to believe some conspiracy theory.

A non-pejorative definition of what counts as a conspiracy theory is to be found in the philosophical literature, where scholars have sought to distinguish what exactly are the epistemic features which make belief in conspiracy theories plausible or implausible. This work has focused on the character of conspiracy theories, treating them as theories and thus appraising them with respect to the kinds of arguments and evidence conspiracy theorists advance for them.

For example, Brian Keeley has argued that, on investigation, some *kinds* of conspiracy theories do turn out to be suspicious. Keeley's focus is on what he calls *mature* conspiracy theories, conspiracy theories which have persisted in our epistemic communities despite advancing no positive evidence. The lack of sufficient positive evidence over a significant period of time for the conspiracy is reason to be skeptical of these mature conspiracy theories. However, this skepticism for a particular class of conspiracy theory is not itself reason for a skepticism of the wider class of conspiracy theories generally. All it tells us is how epistemic agents should react to claims of mature conspiracy theories, not whether the conspiracy theories in question are false.[56]

Lee Basham (as previously noted) attacks the strategy that says evidence of conspiracies would be readily available by pointing out that there are certain incentives by those—journalists, the police, and the like—who ostensibly investigate or guard against conspiracies to *not* speak up or about them.[57]

David Coady has argued we have to radically rethink how we talk about conspiracy theorists, given both the rich history of conspiracies in our respective polities and the way in which some scholars are too reluctant to believe in conspiracies (and associated conspiracy theories).[58] As noted elsewhere in this chapter, Coady also argues that while we might think there is a common use distinction between a theory being official or conspiratorial, this is a social convention which does no epistemic work.[59]

Indeed, as I have argued in my book *The Philosophy of Conspiracy Theories*, the way in which we define what counts as either a conspiracy or a conspiracy theory effects our judgments about the prior probability or likeliness of conspiracies being in the pool of probable candidate explanations for particular kinds of events. Not just that, but once we are aware what work our definitions are doing, we come to realize that there is little hindrance to a conspiracy theory being the product of an inference to the best explanation.[60] I have also argued that scholars often characterize conspiracy theorists and their beliefs by reference to a subset of conspiracy theorists whose beliefs are not representative of conspiracy theorists generally, let alone the wide variety of theories believed or propounded by conspiracy theorists.[61]

Charles Pigden argues we should even expect segments of the population—investigative journalists, public prosecutors, and other officials who deal with the detection of corruption and malfeasance—to treat conspiracy theories seriously.

If conspiracies are occurring, we ought to investigate them. However, if we operate with a definition which bakes in that such theories are prima facie false or typically suspicious, then this has the unfortunate social consequence of making it easier for conspirators to get away with their conspiracies.[62]

Much of this philosophical work has focused on the question of whether our skepticism of these things called conspiracy theories holds any water. What is interesting about much of the scholarly work in our domain is the assumption that there *must* be something wrong with belief in conspiracy theories. Philosophers have interrogated the idea that we should hold conspiracy theories to a higher standard than other theories, and we have concluded that nothing about conspiracy theories per se justifies treating them differently.

This is not to say that we advocates of a general, non-pejorative definition think that belief in conspiracy theories is prima facie rational. Rather, we scholars of conspiracy theory must accept that we have to assess such beliefs on a case-by-case basis. That is, we ought to be particularists about conspiracy theories. The problem with generalist views that either bake in the idea that such theories are necessarily false, or that belief in such theories is typically problematic, is—as we have seen—that they get things back-to-front.

In the end, the worst that can be said about working with a non-pejorative definition of conspiracy theory is that it does not rule out the possibility that belief in conspiracy theories can be rational in a range of cases. That is, this definition entails the denial of a generalist thesis that there is something wrong with belief in conspiracy theories. If this is a problem for certain scholarly research programs, then this is not a problem with the definition. Rather, it is a problem that stems from working with definitions of conspiracy theory which bake in the irrationality or suspiciousness of such beliefs. The issue is not that conspiracy theories are epistemically suspect; the concern is we are working with suspect definitions of what counts as a conspiracy theory.

It is, after all, curious that as soon as we front *theory* with *conspiracy* some of us automatically treat such theories as prima facie suspicious. If certain scholars want to make a special case for conspiracy theories, then it is reasonable for the rest of us to ask whether we are playing fair with our terminology, or whether we have baked into our definitions the answers to our research programs.

Notes

1. I have, in earlier works, labeled such scholars as "conspiracy theory theorists," in order to distinguish the analysis of these things called *conspiracy theories* from conspiracy theorizing (the generation and propagation of conspiracy theories). Conspiracy theory theorists work in what I call the field of *conspiracy theory theories*, an interdisciplinary domain of research of which this book is undoubtedly a product.

2. We can also taxonomize conspiracy theories with respect to just how large or small we think conspiratorial groups need to be, whether conspiracy theories refer to inherently

sinister activities, and the like. For details, see chapter 4 of Dentith, Matthew R. X. 2014. *The Philosophy of Conspiracy Theories*. Basingstoke, U.K.: Palgrave Macmillan.

3. A term of art we owe to Joel Buenting and Jason Taylor's. See Buenting, Joel and Jason Taylor. 2010. "Conspiracy Theories and Fortuitous Data." *Philosophy of the Social Sciences* 40(4): 567–578.

4. Another term of art we owe to Buenting and Taylor (2010).

5. Matthew R. X. Dentith. 2017. "The Problem of Conspiracism" *Argumenta* 3(2): 327–343. DOI: 1023811/58.arg2017.den.

6. Swami, Viren, Martin Voracek, Stefan Stieger, Ulrich S. Tran, Adrian Furnham. 2014. "Analytic Thinking Reduces Belief in Conspiracy Theories" *Cognition*. 133(3): 572.
   Interestingly, in a 2010 paper, Viren Swami and his co-authors endorsed, a definition much more in keeping with the second taxonomic type described in this chapter, which simply marks out such beliefs as somehow suspicious. See Swami, Viren, Tomas Chamorro-Premuzic, and Adrian Furnham. 2010. "Unanswered Questions: A Preliminary Investigation of Personality and Individual Difference Predictors of 9/11 Conspiracist Beliefs." Applied Cognitive Psychology 24(6): 749–61.

7. Daniel Pipes. 1997. *Conspiracy: How the Paranoid Style Flourishes and Where It Comes From.* New York: Free Press: 2

8. Hofstadter, Richard. 1964. *The Paranoid Style in American Politics, and Other Essays*. 1st ed. New York: Knopf: 29

9. Arnold, Gordon B. 2008. *Conspiracy Theory in Film, Television and Politics*. Westport, CT: Praegar.

10. Darwin, Hannah, Nick Neave, and Joni Holmes. 2011. "Belief in Conspiracy Theories. The Role of Paranormal Belief, Paranoid Ideation and Schizotypy." *Personality and Individual Differences* 50(8): 1289–93.

11. DiGrazia, Joseph. 2017. "The Social Determinants of Conspiratorial Ideation" *Socius* 3 (February): 1–9.

12. Barkun, Michael. 2003. *A Culture of Conspiracy: Apocalyptic Visions in Contemporary America*. Berkeley: University of California Press.

13. Zonis, Marvin and Craig M. Joseph. 1994. "Conspiracy Thinking in the Middle East" *Political Psychology*. 15(3): 444.

14. Knight, Peter, ed. 2003. *Making Sense of Conspiracy Theories*. Santa Barbara, CA: ABC-CLIO.

15. Dentith, "The Problem of Conspiracism."

16. For further examples, see Olmsted, Kathryn S. 2009. *Real Enemies: Conspiracy Theories and American Democracy, World War I to 9/11*. Oxford: Oxford University Press.

17. Wood, Gordon S. 1982. "Conspiracy and the Paranoid Style: Causality and Deceit in the Eighteenth Century" *The William and Mary Quarterly* 39(3): 401–441. Wood's influence can be seen in Kaiser, eds. 2007. *Conspiracy in the French Revolution*. Manchester: Manchester University Press; Roisman, Joseph. 2006. *The Rhetoric of Conspiracy in Ancient Athens*. Los Angeles: University of California Press; Cubitt, Geoffrey. 1993. *The Jesuit Myth: Conspiracy Theory and Politics in Nineteenth Century France*. Oxford: Clarendon Press; and Pagán, Victoria Emma. 2012. *Conspiracy theory in Latin Literature*. Austin: University of Texas Press. Volker Heins argues (ala Gordon S. Wood) that while it is understandable to theorize about conspiracies, conspiracy theorists often go beyond the available evidence. See Heins, Volker. 2007. "Critical Theory and the Traps of Conspiracy Thinking." *Philosophy Social Criticism* 33(7): 787–801.

18. Lipton, Peter. 2004. *Inference to the Best Explanation*. 2nd ed. London: Routledge.
    This is a more modern gloss on Popper and is echoed by Franks, Bradley, Adrian Bangerter, and Martin W. Bauer. 2013. "Conspiracy Theories as Quasi-Religious Mentality: An Integrated Account from Cognitive Science, Social Representations Theory, and Frame Theory." *Frontiers in Psychology* 4(July). DOI: 10.3389/fpsyg.2013.00424.

19. Bost, Preston R. and Stephen G. Prunier. 2013. "Rationality in Conspiracy Beliefs: The Role of Perceived Motive." *Psychological Reports: Sociocultural Issues in Psychology*. 113 (1): 118–128.

20. Jolley, Daniel and Karen M. Douglas. 2014. "The Social Consequences of Conspiracism: Exposure to Conspiracy Theories Decreases Intentions to Engage in Politics and to Reduce One's Carbon Footprint." *British Journal of Psychology*. 105(1): 35–56.

21. Popper, Karl R. 1972. *Conjectures and Refutations*. 4th ed. London: Routledge and Kegan Paul. Interestingly, Lance deHaven-Smith, argues that Popper (along with the political writings of Leo Strauss) is the primary reason as to why conspiracy theories are treated so dismissively in contemporary discourse. We might think of this as a conspiracy theory within the field of the study of conspiracy theories (or conspiracy theory theories). See deHaven-Smith, Lance. 2010. "Beyond Conspiracy Theory: Patterns of High Crime in American Government." *American Behavioral Scientist* 53(6): 795–825.

22. Pigden, Charles. 1995. "Popper Revisited, or What Is Wrong With Conspiracy Theories?" *Philosophy of the Social Sciences* 25(1): 3–34.

23. Coady, David. 2012. *What to Believe Now: Applying Epistemology to Contemporary Issues*. Chichester, U.K.: Wiley-Blackwell.

24. Dentith, Matthew R. X. 2016. "When Inferring to a Conspiracy Might be the Best Explanation" *Social Epistemology*. 30(5–6): 572–591.

25. Basham, Lee. 2011. "Conspiracy Theory and Rationality." In *Beyond Rationality: Contemporary Issues*, eds. Carl Jensen and Rom Harré. Newcastle on Tyne, U.K.: Cambridge Scholars Publishing, 49–88.
    See also Dentith, "When Inferring to a Conspiracy Might be the Best Explanation."

26. Sunstein, Cass R. and Adrian Vermeule. 2009. "Conspiracy Theories: Causes and Cures." *Journal of Political Philosophy* 17(2): 202–227.
    Sunstein and Vermeule's crippled epistemology is approvingly cited by Lewandowsky, Stephan, Klaus Oberauer, and Gilles E. Gignac. 2013. "NASA Faked the Moon Landing––Therefore, (Climate) Science Is a Hoax : An Anatomy of the Motivated Rejection of Science." Psychological Science 24(5): 622–33; Swami, Voracek, Stieger, Tran, Furnham, "Analytic Thinking Reduces Belief in Conspiracy Theories."; Harambam, Jaron and Stef Aupers. 2014. "Contesting Epistemic Authority: Conspiracy Theories on the Boundaries of Science." Public Understanding of Science 24(4): 466–480; and Douglas, Karen M., Robbie M. Sutton, Mitchell J. Callan, Rael J. Dawtry, and Annelie J. Harvey. 2015. "Someone is Pulling the Strings: Hypersensitive Agency Detection and Belief in Conspiracy Theories." Thinking & Reasoning 22(1): 57–77.

27. Cassam, Quassim. *Bad thinkers*, Ed. Brigid Hains, vols., 2015, Available: http://aeon.co/magazine/philosophy/intellectual-character-of-conspiracy-theorists/; Quassim Cassam. 2016. "Vice Epistemology" *The Monist* 99(2): 159–180.

28. Grimes, David Robert. 2016. "On the Viability of Conspiratorial Beliefs." *PLoS ONE* 11(1): e0147905.

29. Dentith, Matthew R. X. and Martin Orr. 2017. "Secrecy and Conspiracy." *Episteme*: 1–18. DOI: 10.1017/epi.2017.9.

30. Coady has taken Sunstein to task in Coady, David. 2017. "Cass Sunstein and Adrian Vermeule on Conspiracy Theories." *Argumenta*. DOI: 10.23811/56.arg2017.coa.
    Charles Pigden has similarly critiqued Cassam's arguments in Pigden, Charles. 2016. "Are Conspiracy Theorists Epistemically Vicious?" In A Companion to Applied Philosophy, eds. Kasper Lippert-Rasmussen, Kimberley Brownlee, and David Coady. London: John Wiley & Sons, Ltd.

31. Dentith, "The Problem of Conspiracism."

32. Prooijen, Jan-Willem. 2016. "Why Education Predicts Decreased Belief in Conspiracy Theories." *Applied Cognitive Psychology* 31(1): 50–58.
    See also Prooijen, Jan-Willem and Michele Acker. 2015. "The Influence of Control on Belief in Conspiracy Theories: Conceptual and Applied Extensions." Applied Cognitive Psychology 29(5): 753–761.

33. Barkun, Michael. 2016. "Conspiracy Theories as Stigmatized Knowledge." *Diogenes* October. DOI: 10.1177/0392116669288.

34. Swami et al., "Analytic thinking reduces belief in conspiracy theories."

It is important to note that given Swami, et al. claim define belief in conspiracy theories as necessarily false, it would be weird if they did not in turn also claim that belief in such theories had negative social consequences.

35. Brotherton, Robert and Christopher C. French. 2014. "Belief in Conspiracy Theories and Susceptibility to the Conjunction Fallacy." *Applied Cognitive Psychology* 28(2): 238–248.

36. van der Linden, Sander. 2015. "The Conspiracy-effect: Exposure to Conspiracy Theories (About Global Warming) Decreases Pro-social Behavior and Science Acceptance." *Personality and Individual Differences* 87(December): 173.

37. Douglas, Karen M. and Robbie M. Sutton. 2011. "Does it Take One to Know One? Endorsement of Conspiracy Theories is Influenced by Personal Willingness to Conspire." *British Journal of Social Psychology.* 50(3): 544–552.

38. Douglas, Karen M. and Daniel Jolley. 2014. "The Effects of Anti-Vaccine Conspiracy Theories on Vaccination Intentions." *PLoS ONE* 9(2): e89177.

39. Douglas, Karen M. and Robbie M. Sutton. 2015. "Climate Change: Why the Conspiracy Theories are Dangerous." *Bulletin of the Atomic Scientists* 71(2): 98–106.

40. See, for example, Douglas, Sutton, Callan, Dawtry, and Harvey, "Someone is Pulling the Strings: Hypersensitive Agency Detection and Belief in Conspiracy Theories."; Brotherton, and French, "Belief in Conspiracy Theories and Susceptibility to the Conjunction Fallacy."; Jolley and Douglas, "The Social Consequences of Conspiracism: Exposure to Conspiracy Theories Decreases Intentions to Engage in Politics and to Reduce One's Carbon Footprint."; and Uscinski, Joseph E. and Joseph M. Parent. 2014. *American Conspiracy Theories.* Oxford: Oxford University Press; and van der Linden, "*The conspiracy-effect.*"

41. Jack Z. Bratich, *Conspiracy Panics: Political Rationality and Popular Culture*, (New, York: State University of New York Press, 2008).

42. Basham, "Joining the Conspiracy." See also: Basham, "Conspiracy Theory and Rationality."

43. Dentith, M. R. X. 2017. "Conspiracy Theories on the Basis of the Evidence." *Synthese* (August): 1–19.

44. Olmsted, *Real Enemies*, 6.

45. Barkun, "Conspiracy Theories as Stigmatized Knowledge."

46. Bessi, Alessandro, Mauro Coletto, George Alexandru Davidescu, Antonio Scala, Guido Caldarelli, and Walter Quattrociocchi. "Science vs Conspiracy: Collective Narratives in the Age of Misinformation." *PLoS One* 10(2): 1–17.

47. Levy, Neil. 2017. "Radically Socialized Knowledge and Conspiracy Theories." *Episteme* 4(2): 181–92.

48. Dentith, M. R. X. 2017. "Conspiracy Theories on the Basis of the Evidence." *Synthese* (August): 1–19; Dentith, *The Philosophy of Conspiracy Theories.*

49. Coady, David. 2012. *What to Believe Now: Applying Epistemology to Contemporary Issues.* Chichester, U.K.: Wiley-Blackwell, 2012.

   Coady's position has been glossed in the following works: Feldman, Susan. 2011. "Counterfact Conspiracy Theories." *International Journal of Applied Philosophy* 25(1): 15–24; Buenting and Taylor, "Conspiracy Theories and Fortuitous Data."; and Hagen, Kurtis. 2011. "Conspiracy theories and stylized facts." *The Journal for Peace and Justice Studies* 21(2): 3–22. For a similar analysis, see Robertson, David G. 2017. "The Hidden Hand: Why Religious Studies Need to Take Conspiracy Theories Seriously." *Religion Compass* 11(3–4): e12233.

50. Michael J. Wood, "Wood, Michael J. 2016. "Some Dare Call It Conspiracy: Labeling Something a Conspiracy Theory Does Not Reduce Belief in It." *Political Psychology* 37(5): 695–705." *Political Psychology.* 37 (2016): 695–705.

51. Jolley, Daniel, Karen M. Douglas, and Robbie M. Sutton. 2017. "Blaming a Few Bad Apples to Save a Threatened Barrel: The System-Justifying Function of Conspiracy Theories." *Political Psychology* (February). DOI: 10.1111/pops.12404.

52. Orr, Martin, and Ginna Husting. 2007. "Dangerous Machinery: 'Conspiracy Theorist' as a Transpersonal Strategy of Exclusion." *Symbolic Interaction* 30(2): 127.
    For similar arguments about the role the label 'conspiracy theory' plays in discourse, see Pelkmans, Mathijs, and Rhys Machold. 2011. "Conspiracy theories and their truth trajectories." Focaal — Journal of Global and Historical Anthropology 59(March): 66–80; Bjerg, Ole, and Thomas Presskorn-Thygesen. 2016. "Conspiracy Theory: Truth Claim or Language Game?" Theory, Culture & Society 34(1): 137–159; and McKenzie-McHarg, Andrew, and Rolf Fredheim. 2017. "Cock-ups and slap-downs: A quantitative analysis of conspiracy rhetoric in the British Parliament 1916–2015." Historical Methods: A Journal of Quantitative and Interdisciplinary History 50(3): 156–169.

53. deHaven-Smith, Lance, and Matthew T. Witt. 2013. "Conspiracy Theory Reconsidered Responding to Mass Suspicions of Political Criminality in High Office." *Administration & Society* 45(13): 267–295.

54. Harambam and Aupers, "Contesting Epistemic Authority: Conspiracy Theories on the Boundaries of Science."

55. Butter, Michael, and Peter Knight. 2016. "Bridging the Great Divide: Conspiracy Theory Research for the 21st Century." *Diogenes* (October). DOI: 10.1177/0392116669289.

56. Keeley, Brian L. 1999. "Of Conspiracy Theories." *The Journal of Philosophy* 96(3): 109–126.
    See also: Keeley, Brian L. 2007. "God as the Ultimate Conspiracy Theorist." Episteme 4(2): 135–49. See also: Dentith, Matthew R. X., and Brian L. Keeley. In press. "The applied epistemology of Conspiracy Theories." Ed. David Coady and James Chase. Routledge. Forthcoming.

57. Basham, "Conspiracy Theory and Rationality."

58. Coady, David. 2007. "Are Conspiracy Theorists Irrational?" *Episteme* 4(2): 193–204.

59. Coady, David. 2006. *Conspiracy Theories and Official Stories*. Ed. David Coady. Hampshire, U.K.: Ashgate.

60. Dentith, "When inferring to a conspiracy might be the best explanation."

61. Dentith, "The Problem of Conspiracism."

62. Pigden, "Popper Revisited, or What Is Wrong With Conspiracy Theories?"; Pigden, "Are Conspiracy Theorists Epistemically Vicious?"

HOW DO CONSPIRACY THEORISTS AND NON-CONSPIRACY THEORISTS INTERACT?

JOSEPH E. USCINSKI

Conspiracy theories are competitors in the marketplace of ideas. Their prime competition stems from the establishment: scientific consensuses, official findings, authoritative sources. For example, Kennedy assassination conspiracy theories conflict with the Warren Report. The establishment tends to win out over time, and very few conspiracy theories gain majority support. However, despite convincing only a few, conspiracy theories sometimes convince enough to do serious damage, whether that's small enclaves who forgo vaccination or lone wolfs who commit violence.

Establishments produce facts as well as the methods for ascertaining those facts. Conspiracy theories produce alternative facts and ways of knowing. This puts them at odds with the establishment. As such, conspiracy theorists and the establishment don't simply offer competing ideas; they must necessarily fight it out for supremacy. This battle for hearts and minds by the establishment seems at times like a conspiracy in and of itself, but it is what establishments must at times do when challenged. Or, they would not really have a claim to be "the establishment."

Conspiracy theories can upend how we think and talk about politics. Alfred Moore will show how even nonspecific accusations of conspiracy can have a corrosive effect on our politics, and Matthew Atkinson and Darin DeWitt will show how conspiracy theories are entrepreneurial, providing outsiders and losers with a way to change the rules of the game. Jay Cullen and Stephan Lewandowsky will provide their first-person accounting of how conspiracy theorists challenged sound science with terrible consequences. Juha Räikkä and Lee Basham in Chapter 11, and Steven Smallpage in Chapter 12 examine this tension between conspiracy theorists and the establishment.

Establishment institutions can be wrong, and conspiracy theories can sometimes help ferret out those mistakes. But, the establishment is right far more often than conspiracy theories, largely because their methods are reliable. When conspiracy theorists are right, it is by chance. Nonetheless, the battle of ideas will continue to play out in free societies, as it should. Unfortunately, this occasionally leads to disaster.

7

On the Democratic Problem
of Conspiracy Politics

ALFRED MOORE

The topic of conspiracy theory is often addressed—both in social science and in the wider public sphere—in the register of truth and falsehood.[1] Conspiracy theories are often defined as beliefs that are (among other things) untrue or unwarranted or unfalsifiable. The stereotypical examples are of claims that are not only unfounded but ludicrous, such as Donald Trump's claim that Barack Obama has been lying about his place of birth, or that "the concept of global warming was created by and for the Chinese in order to make U.S. manufacturing non-competitive."[2]

Research building on this basic framing of the problem has focused on identifying the "causes and cures" of belief in conspiracy theories. For instance, drawing on a wider research program on correcting political misinformation and misperceptions, Nyhan has argued that the media should stop reporting on conspiracy theories.[3] Others have experimented with different strategies for countering political rumors, including conspiracy theories about the attacks of 9/11.[4] And some have even proposed "cognitive infiltration" of extremist groups as a strategy for correcting their conspiratorial beliefs.[5] Rebuttals, debunking, fact checking, and attempts to correct misperceptions are surely valuable contributions to democratic citizenship. However, this framing of conspiracy theory draws attention to epistemic rather than directly political questions. It is for this reason that I focus in this essay not on conspiracy theory but rather on conspiracy politics.

By *conspiracy politics* I mean political discussion—including questions, statements, jokes, accusations, narratives, and so on—that is driven by insinuations of malign and hidden intentional agency in relation to some event or phenomenon. The agency could emanate from government, business, or some other organization, real or imagined. The rhetoric fueling conspiracy politics does not require direct reference to a specific conspiracy. This distinguishes it from most accounts of *conspiracy theory*, which insist (reasonably enough) on some reference to an actual suspected conspiracy in the sense of a coordinated, concealed plot being carried out by a specific set of villains who have clear malevolent goals and methods in mind. However, it remains close to the actual practice by which examples of "conspiracy theory" are identified. Consider, for instance, the episode in 2012 in which the US Bureau of Labor Statistics released a report declaring that the official unemployment rate had dropped to 7.8%, then the lowest level of Barack Obama's presidency, and in response, Jack Welch, former CEO of General Electric tweeted: "Unbelievable jobs numbers. . . these Chicago guys will do anything, . . can't debate so change numbers."[6] Donald Trump endorsed and repeated the message. The claim is vague. It clearly insinuates malign intent, but it does not describe a conspiracy or make any claim specific enough to be the basis of a formal accusation. One can of course construct a conspiracy theory from the claim, therefore it is often taken as an example of a conspiracy theory. Indeed, a team of political psychologists have gone so far as to use it as the experimental treatment in a study of the effect of belief in conspiracy theories on trust in government.[7] Yet the claim itself is little more than a vague gesture towards sinister actions by persons unknown.

This sort of pattern—in which the gesture of doubt is more important than the positive assertion or elaboration of a supposed conspiracy—has also been found among 9/11 conspiracy theorists on Internet discussion boards, who were more likely to argue against the official interpretation and less likely to argue in favor of their own interpretation. The authors of the study conclude that "conspiracy theorists" are defined less by their positive belief in a particular conspiracy theory than by their suspicion and "generalized rejection" of an official or conventional account.[8] I would simply describe these cases as examples of conspiracy politics.

Conspiracy politics is a matter of style and rhetoric,[9] and thus does not turn on the question of whether those propagating conspiracy claims actually *believe* them. This sidesteps a common problem with the interpretation of survey data, in which it is often not clear what people mean when they say they believe in a conspiracy theory, and it is possible that respondents are giving answers that express who they are rather than what they literally believe. For instance, research by Joanne Miller, Kyle Saunders, and Christina Farhart addresses affirmative responses to conspiracy theories as "endorsement" rather than as true belief. Adam Berinsky on the other hand, suggests that survey respondents are indeed sincere when they agree with conspiracy theories.[10]

One of the most widely publicized papers on conspiracy theory—by Mike Wood, Karen Douglas, and Robbie Sutton—in the last few years claimed that people who believe one conspiracy theory are more likely to believe another, even when those theories are contradictory. Subjects in the study seemed to believe that Princess Diana is actually still alive *as well as* believing that she was murdered.[11] This seems to show the severe irrationality of its subjects. But it is also possible that respondents are not assenting to the literal truth of a proposition, but rather are saying that they are "prepared to entertain the possibility" of X, or might "not rule out the hypothesis" that X, or simply "doubt the official account" of X, all of which would weaken the force of the supposed contradiction. In contrast to the notion of conspiracy *theory* (as used throughout this volume), the concept of conspiracy *politics* does not centrally focus on belief.

However, while conspiracy politics does not necessarily involve a *belief* in a *conspiracy*, it does invoke malign agency, and in this respect its central feature is deep distrust. Consider again the example of Jack Welch and Donald Trump's attempts to undermine the credibility of the Bureau of Labor Statistics. It is not at all clear that behind these tweets there is any clear conception of a plot or plan or any other paraphernalia of the genre of conspiracy theory. But it *is* clear that they were claiming that certain agents had both the capacity and the intention to act against what they considered to be the public good. Conspiracy politics is similar to distrust, in that they share an expectation that some other agent intends harm to you or your interests, yet they are not the same thing; one can hold an attitude of distrust, and undertake actions premised on distrust, without engaging in conspiracy politics. Yet it is hard to imagine conspiracy politics without distrust. Not only do statements such as that claiming manipulation of the unemployment figures *express* distrust; they clearly also have the potential—and are possibly even designed—to *generate* distrust. However, before I explore in more detail the relationship between conspiracy politics and distrust, I will first discuss the way in which trust, understood as a way of accepting some level of risk of potential harm in order to benefit from cooperation,[12] relates to distrust in democratic politics.

Democracy and the Dynamics of Trust and Distrust

Democracies need both trust and distrust: They require and demand trust, but they also depend on distrust and generate distrust. We find ourselves pulled into relations of trust with political representatives, and yet at the same time we are acutely aware of our vulnerability in the face of the temptations of power: "one entrusts government to those one distrusts."[13] Patti Tamara Lenard calls this "the paradox of trust and democracy": we need trust in order to enable effective democratic governance, but "we need to implement institutions that suggest a deep distrust of what our legislators [and other officials] will do when offered an opportunity to control the levers of power."[14] "Paradox" is the right word: it seems contradictory to say that democratic government needs both trust and distrust, yet it is probably true—or at least it would need to be true for the idea of democracy in its many of its current institutional forms to work. It is important to recognize that trust and distrust are always in a complex and dynamic relationship. What matters from this point of view is not the presence or absence of trust as such, but rather patterns of trust and distrust and the ways in which they are distributed and organized.

There are at least three general ways in which distrust can be organized into democratic politics. One is constitutional, in the form of the institutional *separation of powers.* Such separation was grounded in fears of the concentration of power, and expressed in ideas of "checks and balances" on the exercise of power.

Another takes the form of *popular vigilance.* This way of mobilizing distrust is most obviously associated with Jeremy Bentham.[15] However, practices of "contestatory vigilance," characterized by demands for publicity and empowerments to challenge and contest the decisions of political authorities, are also central to recent versions of republicanism and deliberative democracy.[16]

The third way of organizing distrust into democratic politics is through *partisan distrust.* Partisan distrust involves an expectation that political opponents intend to harm your interests; that is, it is an attitude of distrust framed by partisan identification. The organization of distrust through the institution of parties makes such distrust explicit and productive of the competition that is a core component of the modern conception of democracy.[17] Common to these various approaches is the idea that governmental conduct might be relatively uncorrupt and tolerably well aligned with public interests precisely *because* of the active exercise of distrust and suspicion by some.

These approaches suggest that trust can develop out of distrust.[18] Politics, although a uniquely unfavorable terrain for trust, can thus generate a positive dynamic, where an attitude of distrust motivates the creation of protective institutions that in turn generate the grounds for warranted trust.[19] Here the tension between trust and distrust is not decisively resolved, but rather organized and made productive.

An important part of this positive dynamic is the idea that *distrust motivates vigilance.* But is this true? Lenard, for instance, associates distrust with a form of closed-minded "cynicism and suspicion." She contrasts this with what she calls "mistrust," which involves "a cautious attitude that propels citizens to maintain a watchful eye on the political and social happenings within their communities."[20] Distrust, in her account, does not motivate scrutiny; rather, it promotes withdrawal from serious engagement, both cognitively and politically. Thus, she claims, "[v]igilance *does not require* an attitude of distrust towards our legislators and the vigilance we display in constraining our legislators *is not inconsistent* with trusting them."[21] Lenard grasps two important points. First, distrust is not the same as a mere absence of trust.[22] Trust involves a judgment to grant discretionary power to others over some good and to accept the vulnerability that comes with it.[23] Distrust involves a firm expectation that someone has both the will and the capacity to act against your interests. More than a mere absence of trust—that is, being simply agnostic or suspending judgment about whether to trust—distrust involves "an actor's assured expectation of intended harm from the other."[24] To distrust is to take a positive position on the question of the willingness of others to do you harm rather than merely being uncertain, cautious, and alert to the possibility.

It is not clear that distrust *must* lead to a sort of cynicism and apathetic disengagement. But, distrust can clearly also lead to intense—and perhaps even obsessive—scrutiny. This comes out most clearly in German sociologist Niklas Luhmann's account of distrust. He regards distrust as a "functional equivalent" of trust: they are both ways of reducing complexity. But while trust reduces complexity in a way that enables and supports cooperative action, distrust reduces complexity in a way that is personally exhausting and debilitating to action.

> A person who distrusts both needs more information and at the same time narrows down the information which he feels confident he can rely on. He becomes *more* dependent on *less* information. The possibility of his being deceived becomes once more something to be reckoned with. . . . In this way, strategies of distrust become correspondingly more difficult and more burdensome. They often absorb the strength of the person who distrusts to an extent which leaves him little energy to explore and adapt to his environment in an objective and unprejudiced manner, and hence allow him fewer opportunities for learning. Relatively, trust is the easier option, and for this reason there is a strong incentive to begin a relationship with trust.[25]

Distrust implies action to mitigate the threat or to protect oneself from it. Among other things, it implies actions directed to gathering information, making efforts to take care of the good independently, and engaging in active opposition. Distrust might—as Luhmann suggests—be exhausting and even unsustainable, but it is hard to see much motivation to vigilance without it. It is perhaps for this reason that political action itself—which is in part motivated by distrust of others and is manifest in oppositional action—is unpleasant and hard to sustain.[26] Distrust, in short, can lead to either scrutiny *or* withdrawal, to active opposition and popular vigilance *or* to defeatism and resentment.

In opposition to distrust, Lenard puts forward the term *mistrust*, by which she means cautious and watchful yet open-minded and fundamentally trusting attitude. She insists that mistrust is at the core of common observations about the democratic value of (what everybody else calls) distrust. This sort of distinction is attractive, and it is easy to think of cases in which we might neither trust *nor* distrust, not having enough information to justify either position, yet remain cautious and watchful. Yet there are at least two troublesome consequences of being suspended between trust and distrust.

One is that maintaining a position of undecided openness, skepticism, and caution, is not sustainable over any large number of issues or length of time. We often have sufficient reasons neither for trust nor for distrust, but we nonetheless need to act and "cannot afford to wait it out."[27] In such situations we may need to make a decision, and perhaps choose to act *as if* we trust, that is, act *as if* we had the appropriate beliefs about the competence and good intentions of another, even though we do not.

The second problem is to do with the motivation for vigilance. Mistrust, in the sense of a "careful and questioning mindset"[28] seems insufficient to motivate much action beyond the sort of light monitoring involved in "keeping an eye on the scene."[29] Lenard's claim, in essence, is that what motivates vigilance and scrutiny of political authorities is *uncertainty* about whether or not they are trustworthy. Yet mere uncertainty is surely not enough. Scrutiny is intensive and difficult work, requiring the investment of time and expertise, and the motivation to do it seems most likely to come either from strong distrust or from a professional role that involves a presumption of distrust (you might be hired to work for a newspaper or advocacy group, where you adopt a presumption of distrust in order to do your job).[30]

The idea of *as if* trust—that is, choosing to act as though you trust, even if you are in fact uncertain or even distrustful—may be a more useful way to think about the ambivalence of distrust than Lenard's distinction between "mistrust" and "distrust." In particular, *as if* trust helps make sense of power within relations of trust. In the circumstances of politics, we are automatically exposed to the exercise of power by others over the common good.[31] Since binding collective decisions will be made whether or not we take part, we have to participate in order to have any chance of influence, and we are thus pressured to extend trust while risking disappointment and betrayal. Citizens of modern democracies are not exactly *forced* to trust, but they are often forced to "choose between trust in their representatives or withdrawal."[32] We are supposed to act *as if* we trust even while we have misgivings, doubts, and suspicions if we are to have any hope of influence. Political relationships that have the structure of trust might thus be experienced as something more like resentful dependence.

Distrust out of Control

What, then, is the relationship between conspiracy politics and distrust? Conspiracy politics is both premised on and generative of distrust. In contrast to the positive dynamic in which distrust motivates scrutiny and institutional protections that in turn promote trustworthy government, there is also the possibility of a negative dynamic, in which distrust promotes further distrust. There are at least two ways in which this sort of negative dynamic can take place.

One is what we might call *partisan spirals of distrust*. Political parties have, through much of the twentieth century, been the main vehicles for the organization of distrust into democratic politics.[33] Parties realize and to some extent reconcile (at least in theory) the tension between trust and distrust: Particularized trust—the trust involved in group identities and defined against outsiders[34]—supports and promotes factionalism, oppositional relations, and party politics. Such partisan distrust can motivate vigilance and serve as a stimulus to actual engagement in political justification.[35] The danger for this view is that the outcome of partisan politics is often not a productive exchange of arguments underpinned by a common commitment to basic discursive norms, or what Rosenblum calls an ethos of "regulated rivalry."[36] Rather, partisanship can promote conspiracy politics.

Conspiracy politics can emerge from partisan politics through the very process of attempting to build and sustain the "particularized" trust on which representative relationships depend. The process of electoral representation depends on a "partisan connection"—"the bridge parties build between the people and the formal polity"—which involves listening to and responding to constituents, associations, supporters and various associations, and often entails "accommodating popular perceptions of conspiracy."[37] Representatives thus find themselves under pressure to "reason with" their constituents and, by extension, reason with their conspiratorial suspicions and fears. Trust is a fragile resource in the partisan relationship: On the one hand, representatives need the trust of their constituents in order to have sufficient credibility to challenge or rebut their conspiratorial fears; but on the other hand, their trust is won at least in part through a willingness to go along with those fears. This generates a characteristic tension between "maintaining a connection to the street" and "cynical deference to. . . arrant suspicions" or "pandering to and exploiting popular fears." [38]

Resolving the tension between maintaining a partisan connection and reinforcing popular fears depends on the judgment of particular representatives. The problem is that there is no clear line to tell us when conspiracy politics constitutes part of a robust practice of partisan political argument and political representation, and when it amounts to a degradation into a politics of fear that undermines the conditions of partisan politics itself. There may indeed (as Muirhead and Rosenblum argue) be a moral duty to oppose some expressions of conspiracy politics, such as when they demonize minorities or paint partisan opponents as enemies of the people. But not only is the line hard to draw, representatives themselves can find it difficult—and risky—to push back. Not only are partisan actors highly sensitized to suspect the intentions and capacities of their opponents;[39] they also have motives to respond to the distrust expressed by their constituents in ways that can generate a sort of negative feedback. Leaders might justify engaging in conspiracy politics with the need to appeal to constituents who distrust their opponents, in part because of earlier appeals to conspiracy politics. The chapter in this volume by Matthew Atkinson and Darin DeWitt speaks to this: Generally, mainstream parties do not engage in conspiracy theorizing but, if they are interested in building a coalition of conspiracy-minded supporters, then conspiracy-tinged rhetoric may succeed in gaining electoral support. In turn, there is some evidence that disrespectful and uncivil interactions between representatives (such as implying that they have fiddled the unemployment figures) can diminish political trust among citizens.[40] Such a negative dynamic means that conspiracy politics can emerge naturally, as it were, from the dynamics of electoral representation.

A second manifestation of the negative dynamic might be called the *self-fulfilling prophecy of distrust*. A self-fulfilling prophecy involves a situation in which a misleading belief creates the conditions for its own fulfilment, where the belief becomes, so to speak, the "father [to] the reality."[41] In our context, it refers to the idea that *unwarranted* distrust can itself generate behavior that would (in retrospect) give grounds for distrust. Consider the example of the so-called climategate[42] controversy, in which thousands of emails from researchers at the Climate Research Unit were hacked and leaked to the press in November 2009, shortly before the Copenhagen climate change summit. These emails were interpreted by climate sceptics as evidence that behind the apparent consensus on climate science lay a conspiracy of scientists suppressing uncomfortable data and attempting to manipulate the peer review process. U.S. Senator James Inhofe treated climategate as a central part of his conspiracy narrative in *The Greatest Hoax: How the Global Warming Conspiracy Threatens Your Future*.[43] Subsequent investigations found no scientific wrongdoing; however, some of their conduct was procedurally suspect. The point here is they were attempting to evade what they regarded as vexatious and manipulative FOIA requests. It seems plausible that it was because they did not trust that the requesters were acting in good faith, and because they felt themselves to be distrusted, they acted in ways that confirmed some of the critics' suspicions. As one of the emails put it: "Why should I make the data available to you, when your aim is to try and find something wrong with it"?

The self-fulfilling prophecy of distrust can be elaborated in terms of two contrasting models of accountability. In the "sanctions model" the interests of the principals and the agents are assumed to conflict. Alignment is achieved and maintained by costly and burdensome monitoring and retrospective sanctioning. In the "selection model" the "potential agent already has self-motivated, exogenous reasons for doing what the principal wants."[44] Here, "most of the congruence between the principals' desires and the agents' behavior is accomplished by the voters selecting a representative who is honest, competent, and already has policy goals much like the constituents."[45]

There are irreducible tensions and trade-offs between the types of accountability involved in the sanctions and selection models. One key trade-off concerns the motivation of agents. If the agents are self-motivated, then modes of monitoring and sanction premised on distrust can have the effect of undermining that self-motivation. Consider, for instance, research showing that introducing fines for late kindergarten pick-ups led more parents to pick their kids up late, the thought being that they shifted from thinking of themselves as having a moral obligation not to burden the teachers with staying late with the kids to thinking of themselves as effectively buying after-hours childcare.[46] Treating people as being incapable of acting morally can be a self-fulfilling treatment. Monitoring, too, can undermine intrinsic motivation, especially where those being monitored see it as an expression of distrust. As philosopher Onora O'Neill put it in a discussion of the way an "audit culture" can undermine professional bureaucracies: "Plants don't flourish when we pull them up too often to check how their roots are growing: political, institutional and professional life too may not flourish if we constantly uproot it to demonstrate that everything is transparent and trustworthy."[47] In this way, acting in ways that presume distrust can make authorities *less* trustworthy, and thus retrospectively justify the attitude of suspicion.

Exploring Distrust

The concept of conspiracy politics shifts our focus from questions of knowledge and ignorance to questions of trust and distrust. Focusing on distrust can be useful for thinking about the relationship between conspiracy politics and democracy. I have pointed to two broad sources of instability in the relation between distrust and trust in government: one focusing on partisan politics and the threat of spirals of distrust, and the other on popular vigilance and the threat of self-fulfilling prophecies of distrust.

This also suggests an empirical research agenda in which we distinguish distrust from the mere absence of trust, and focus specifically on distrust and its consequences.[48] Is the relationship between citizens and political authorities one of *mistrust* (in Lenard's sense) or *distrust*? To what extent is distrust endogenous to the process of political representation? And how might we imagine reforms that could limit the spiraling of distrust out of control?

Yet the pessimistic conclusion remains: For all that distrust is essential to democratic practice, and for all the attempts to distinguish its productive from its destructive manifestations, distrust is perhaps impossible to make safe for democracy. There is, and remains, an instability within the dynamics of trust and distrust, and we must therefore stay alert to the ways in which distrust can spiral out of control.

Notes

1. It is itself an interesting story how claims of conspiracy came to be framed specifically as conspiracy *theories*, and not as, for instance, conspiracy *myths*.
2. Trump, Donald. 2012. Twitter Post. November 6, 2012. 11:15am, https://twitter.com/realdonaldtrump/status/265895292191248385?lang=en.
3. Nyhan, Brendan. 2012. "Enabling the Jobs Report Conspiracy Theory." *Columbia Journalism Review.* http://www.cjr.org/united_states_project/enabling_the_jobs_report_conspiracy_theory.php?page=all#sthash.OLFq8PWf.dpuf (accessed October 30, 2014).
4. Berinsky, Adam. 2012. "Rumors, truths, and reality: A study of political misinformation." Massachusetts Institute of Technology. Manuscript.
5. Sunstein, Cass, and Adrian Vermeule. 2009. "Conspiracy Theories: Causes and Cures." *Journal of Political Philosophy*, 17(2): 202–227.
6. See Fores, Betsi. 2012. "Jack Welch: 'Chicago Guys Will Do Anything,' Including Cook Unemployment Rate." *The Daily Caller.* http://dailycaller.com/2012/10/05/jack-welch-chicago-guys-will-do-anything-including-cook-unemployment-rate/ (Accessed December 29, 2017).

7. Einstein, Katherine Levine, and David M. Glick. 2015. "Do I Think BLS Data are BS? The Consequences of Conspiracy Theories." *Political Behavior* 37(3): 679–701.

8. Wood, Michael J., and Karen M. Douglas. 2013. "'What About Building 7?' A Social Psychological Study of Online Discussion of 9/11 Conspiracy Theories." *Frontiers in Psychology* 4(July). DOI: 10.3389/fpysg.2013.00409.

9. In this respect I follow Hofstadter, Richard. 1964. "The Paranoid Style in American Politics." *Harpers Magazine*, April, 77–86.

10. Miller, Joanne, Kyle Saunders, and Christina Farhart. 2015. "Conspiracy Endorsement as Motivated Reasoning: The Moderating Roles of Political Knowledge and Trust." *American Journal of Political Science* 60(4): 824–844; Berinsky, Adam J. 2017. "Telling the Truth about Believing the Lies? Evidence for the Limited Prevalence of Expressive Survey Responding." *The Journal of Politics.* DOI: 10.1086/694258 (Accessed December 18, 2017).

11. Wood, Michael J., Karen M. Douglas, and Robbie M. Sutton. 2012. "Dead and Alive Beliefs in Contradictory Conspiracy Theories." *Social Psychological and Personality Science* 3(6): 767–773.

12. Dunn, John. 1988. "Trust and Political Agency." In *Trust: Making and Breaking Cooperative Relations*, ed. Diego Gambetta. Oxford: Basil Blackwell, 73–93.

13. Parry, Geraint. 1976. "Trust, Distrust and Consensus." *British Journal of Political Science* 6(2): 129–142.

14. Lenard, Patti Tamara. 2012. *Trust, Democracy, and Multicultural Challenges.* University Park: Pennsylvania State University Press: 67–68.

15. Bruno, Jonathan. 2017. "Vigilance and Confidence: Jeremy Bentham, Publicity, and the Dialectic of Trust and Distrust." *American Political Science Review* 111(2): 295–307.

16. Pettit, Philip. 2012. *On the People's Terms: A Republic Theory and Model of Democracy.* Cambridge: Cambridge University Press; Warren, Mark E. 1999. "Democratic Theory and Trust." *Democracy and Trust*, ed. Mark E. Warren. Cambridge: Cambridge University Press, 310–345.

17. Shapiro, Ian. 2017. "Collusion in Restraint of Democracy: Against Political Deliberation." *Daedalus* 146(3): 77–84.

18. In contrast to neoconservatives who treat trust as a non-renewable resource that emerges within society and is depleted by politics. See Fukuyama, Francis. 1995. *Trust: The Social Virtues and the Creation of Prosperity.* New York: Free Press.

19. Bruno, *Vigilance and Confidence*; Warren, *Democratic Theory and Trust.*

20. Lenard, Patti Tamara. 2008. "Trust Your Compatriots, but Count Your Change: The Roles of Trust, Mistrust, and Distrust in Democracy." *Political Studies*, 56(2) 2008: 312.

21. Ibid., 326. Italicized text in original.

22. Ullmann-Margalit, Edna. 2004. "Trust, Distrust, and In Between." In *Distrust*, ed. Russell Hardin, New York: Russell Sage Foundation, 60–82.

23. Warren, "Democratic Theory and Trust," 310.

24. Lewicki, R. J., McAllister, D. J., and Bies, R. J., 1998. "Trust and Distrust: New Relationships and Realities." *The Academy of Management Review* 23(3): 446.

25. Luhmann, Niklas. 1979. *Trust and Power.* Toronto: John Wiley and Sons: 72.

26. Indeed, this might be part of the reason people cycle in and out of political participation. See Hirschman, Albert. 1982. *Shifting Involvements: Private Interest and Public Action.* Princeton: Princeton University Press.

27. Ullmann-Margalit, "Trust, Distrust and in Between," 69.

28. Lenard, "Trust Your Compatriots," 313.

29. Schudson, Michael. 1998. *The Good Citizen: A History of Civic Life.* New York: Free Press, 311.

30. As British journalist Jeremy Paxman once said, the stance of the political interviewer should be: 'Why is this lying bastard lying to me?'

31. Nacol, Emily C. "The Risks of Political Authority: Trust, Knowledge and Political Agency in Locke's *Second Treatise.*" *Political Studies* 59(3): 580–595.

32. Warren, "Democratic Theory and Trust," 317.

33. Uscinski, Joseph E., and Joseph Parent. 2014. *Conspiracy Theories in America*. Oxford: Oxford University Press.

34. Uslaner, Eric. 1999. "Democracy and Social Capital." *Democracy and Trust*, ed. Mark E. Warren, Cambridge: Cambridge University Press, 121–150.

35. White, Jonathan, and Lea Ypi. 2011. "On Partisan Political Justification." *American Political Science Review* 105(2): 386.

36. Rosenblum, Nancy. 2008. *On the Side of the Angels. An Appreciation of Parties and Partisanship.* Princeton: Princeton University Press.

37. Muirhead, Russell, and Nancy L. Rosenblum. 2016. "Speaking Truth to Conspiracy: Partisanship and Trust." *Critical Review* 28(1): 63, 68.

38. Ibid., 69.

39. Uscinski and Parent, *Conspiracy Theories in America.*

40. Mutz, Diana, and Byron Reeves. 2005. "The New Videomalaise: The Effects of Televised Incivility on Political Trust." *American Political Science Review* 99(1) 2005: 1–15.

41. Merton, Robert. 1968. "The Self-Fulfilling Prophecy." *Social Theory and Social Structure. 1968 Enlarged Edition*. New York: Free Press, 478.

42. Delingpole, James. 2009. "Climategate: The Final Nail in the Coffin of 'Anthropogenic Global Warming?'" [Blog] *GlobalClimateScam.com*. Available at http://www.globalclimatescam. com/causeeffect/climategate-the-final-nail-in-the-coffin-of-anthropogenic-global-warming/ (Accessed December 30, 2017).

43. Inhofe, James. 2012. *The Greatest Hoax: How the Global Warming Conspiracy Threatens Your Future*. Washington, D.C.: WND Books.

44. Mansbridge, Jane. 2009. "A 'Selection Model' of Political Representation." *The Journal of Political Philosophy* 17(4): 369.

45. Ibid., 370.

46. Gneezy, Uri, and Aldo Rustichini. 2000. "A Fine is a Price." *The Journal of Legal Studies* 29(1): 1–17.

47. O'Neill, Onora. 2002. *A Question of Trust: The BBC Reith Lectures*. Cambridge: Cambridge University Press, 19.

48. Van De Walle, Steven, and Frédérique Six. 2014. "Trust and Distrust as Distinct Concepts: Why Studying Distrust in Institutions Is Important." *Journal of Comparative Policy Analysis: Research and Practice* 16(2): 158–174.

8

The Politics of Disruption

Social Choice Theory and Conspiracy Theory Politics

MATTHEW D. ATKINSON AND DARIN DEWITT

That conspiracy theories are for losers is the most significant empirical regularity social scientists have observed regarding the politics of conspiracy theories.[1] Conspiracy theories are a tool for the weak. When a conspiracy theory gains traction, power is redistributed from the powerful target to its weaker opponents. Conspiracy theories are a force of disruption.

Conspiracy theories instill fear in the powerful. For example, when Thomas Mann and Norman Ornstein asked incumbent members of the United States Senate what they fear most, they emphasized the power of conspiracy theories to undermine them: "all of them fear a stealth campaign . . . designed to portray the incumbent as a miscreant and scoundrel who should be behind bars."[2] When successful, conspiracy theories disrupt the existing order. And that makes crafting a theory of conspiracy theory politics extremely important and immensely challenging.

In political science, the field of political economy explains political order and shows that today's losers engage in entrepreneurial endeavors to change the way politics is played.[3] E. E. Schattschneider, in *The Semisovereign People*, and William Riker, in *Liberalism Against Populism*, focused scholarly attention on actors who reshape the constitutional order.[4] In these foundational texts and the subsequent literature they inspired, scholars focus on visionaries, actors who build a new political coalition to transform the governmental process, and neglect actors whose end goal is disruption. Conspiracy theories are a disruptive innovation, and we explain why they are incredibly effective game changers by situating conspiracy theory politics in the theory of social choice. For individuals who seek disruption, conspiracy theories are the most readily available means of game change. They are particularly effective in political environments such as mass democracies like the United States, which are characterized by widely dispersed power, incoherent individual-level preferences, and group-oriented mass politics.

Conspiracy theory politics involves political manipulations within a complex and unpredictable political landscape; it functions as just one tool in the political entrepreneur's toolbox, but for many political entrepreneurs it is the most useful tool. In this chapter we explain why, by describing how political scientists think about the dynamics of complex and unpredictable political environments and discussing how that style of thinking can be applied to conspiracy theories. We accomplish this by placing conspiracy theory politics within the social choice theory framework, where conspiracy theory politics is merely politics by other means.

Chaos and Instability: Why Conspiracy Theory Needs a System-Level Theory

Conspiracy theory politics, as we will show, develops in a context where power is widely dispersed and there are no strong rules or norms for organizing coalitions and resolving conflicts.[5] How do scholars begin to make sense of disruptive forces that evolve within unstructured and highly chaotic environments? Is it possible to develop a systematic theory of conspiracy theory politics, or are scholars of conspiracy theory confined to storytelling and post hoc description? In this section we explain why the disruptive nature of conspiracy theory politics confounds conventional political science theories, and, in the remainder of the essay, we look to the social choice literature's treatment of innovation and entrepreneurship to sketch a path forward.[6]

Political scientists have uncovered two rudimentary principles of how political systems work. First, disorder is the fundamental feature of the political world. Second, the art of governance is all about imposing order.

Social choice theory established the disorder principle by formally proving that political ideas evolve in a chaotic environment where anything can happen.[7] In a large and diverse society, even if problems and priorities are well-conceptualized by everyone, political outcomes do not follow directly from the will of the people. Public opinion imposes essentially no structure on the tactics and strategies employed by political actors. In practice, today's losers, with some political ingenuity, could be tomorrow's winners. For William Riker, the prevailing social outcome "is hardly the will of the people; it is just some choice that came out of the machine."[8]

To the extent that the dynamics of a political system are predictable and stable, we owe that predictability to the constraints that norms and institutions impose on what would otherwise be a chaotic system.[9] The literature on the new institutionalism shows that elaborate institutional environments vastly reduce the number of potential outcomes and produce stable social choices by restricting the range of ideas under consideration.[10] For example, in a game of checkers, orderly play is induced by rules that significantly constrain the range of choices players can make.

Analogously, Nobel laureate Douglass North conceives of institutions as similarly constraining the range of human behavior by providing a framework for human interaction composed "of formal written rules as well as typically unwritten codes of conduct that underlie and supplement formal rules."[11] We abide by these rules in both politics and checkers because even if they disadvantage us in the middle of today's game, we expect that we can win under the same rules in the near future, whereas we cannot predict how we would fare under a new system.[12]

Institutions comprise the rules and procedures that define the terms of political competition—who participates, who sets the agenda, and how choices are made. The great works of modern political science have focused on describing the institutional structures that impose order on a system lacking natural harmony. Prominent examples include John Aldrich on political parties, Kenneth Shepsle along with Gary Cox and Mathew McCubbins on Congress, John Zaller and Paul Sniderman on public opinion, Edward Carmines and James Stimson on partisan issue conflict, and Elinor Ostrom on managing common pool resources.[13] Each of these foundational studies has provided the organizing principles that have enabled future scholars to productively make sense of behavior and outcomes within the relevant domain.

Institutions reduce political disorder by entrenching the power of winners to control outcomes. Conventional political science explanations focus on distilling the rules of the game. Yet because political order—the rules of the game—concentrates power in the hands of a few winners, losers have strong incentives to disrupt the existing political arrangements by changing the game.

Losers are agents of change in politics, and they engage in innovative and unorthodox efforts to alter their situation. Therefore, leading scholars of political change such as E. E. Schattschneider, William Riker, John Kingdon, Norman Schofield, and Kenneth Shepsle suggest that the analytical focus should be on entrepreneurship— on the goals of political entrepreneurs, on the opportunities available to them, and on the choices they ultimately make.[14] Among the strategic choices available to rational political entrepreneurs is conspiracy theory politics. In spite of the general neglect of conspiracy theory politics in the social choice literature, conspiracy theories are typically the most readily available and lowest-cost method available for changing the game. What tools do political scientists have for understanding the dynamics of political disruption in general and of conspiracy theory politics in particular?

In their quest to disrupt the existing order, the choices of political entrepreneurs are entirely unconstrained by the political environment. This unconstrained behavior gives rise to a staggering level of complexity.[15] To understand the strategies and tactics of political entrepreneurs, we need a framework for coping with this complexity. The most widely referenced framework in the political science literature for making sense of behavior in a complex environment is John Kingdon's effort, in his book *Agendas, Alternatives, and Public Policies*, to explain "what makes an idea's time come?"[16] Kingdon finds that the Michael Cohen, James March, and Johan

Olsen garbage can model starts to sort out the complexity associated with widely dispersed and unconstrained power and helps explain the strategies and tactics underlying policy change.

We use the garbage can model of choice as an organizing framework to broadly address the competition of ideas in a political system, to explain how conspiracy theories evolve, and to understand why a select few conspiracy theories gain traction. We focus on how political entrepreneurs navigate this environment—the problems they face and the prospects for conspiracy theories to serve as solutions for their problems.

The Garbage Can Model of Choice

According to a long line of research in political science and political psychology, political losers do not become winners through the art of persuasion. Rather, in *The Art of Political Manipulation*, Riker famously argued that losers become winners by radically changing how people in the political system interact with one another— losers strive to activate new issues, reframe existing problems, and challenge existing norms.[17] In a word, their aim is to disrupt. Losers, according to Schattschneider, aim to draw new "people in the conflict until the balance of forces is changed."[18] Losers are the innovators. They are the source of political change.

We theorize the motives of political entrepreneurs by specifying three axioms regarding the environment, goals, and opportunities they face. First, the salient feature of the political environment is that power is widely dispersed such that entrepreneurial efforts—not entrenched power—can impact the flow of ideas. Second, the central ambition of the political entrepreneur is to galvanize collective action and attention, as these are the basis of power in mass politics.[19] Third, conspiracy theories are available as one class of solutions that might help entrepreneurs advance their ambition for power.

Given these assumptions, how will entrepreneurs behave, and what ideas will take hold? If conspiracy theories are for losers, then the analytical focus must be on the wider political environment. This decision-making arena is unstructured. Cohen, March, and Olsen label this environment an *organized anarchy* and have distilled its salient features:[20]

- *Politics Stream*: The set of ideas and participants in the process is highly variable, as individuals and groups filter in and out of the decision-making environment. At any point in time, latent participants can be drawn in and active participants can disengage. New ideas can evolve and old ideas can be reframed or displaced.
- *Problem Stream*: Participants (and potential participants) do not have elaborately defined and well-prioritized preferences, and the groups that exist within the system do not share well-defined common goals. Participants hold

nebulous conceptions of what the key problems are and how problems ought to be prioritized.[21]

- *Solution Stream*: With all the turbulence in the political system, reliably connecting problems and solutions is impossible. In Cohen, March, and Olsen's account, leaders have only a vague sense of how actions relate to outcomes and, therefore, "operate a lot by trial and error, by learning from experience, and by pragmatic intervention in crises."[22] As a result, problems and solutions tend to evolve independently of one another.

Cohen, March, and Olsen describe decision making in an organized anarchy as the *garbage can model of choice*. The garbage can consists of the three independent process streams—politics, problems, and solutions—circulating through the system, and each develops according to its own internal logic and dynamics. Interaction among these independently evolving streams shapes political outcomes. We discuss how each stream evolves and then discuss how they interact.

The problem stream is teeming with myriad social and economic conundrums that political debate might focus on. But only a small handful of problems gain prominence at any given time. Which problems are in the spotlight and which are relegated to darkness has profound implications for the dynamics of mass politics. Why? A problem, when paired with a compelling solution, proposes to animate a unique segment of mass opinion. In analyzing why conspiracy theories become activated, the first question to ask is this: Which groups are animated by the problem the conspiracy theory highlights? Then, to assess a conspiracy theory's prospects for spreading through society, the follow-up question is this: Does this set of groups comprise a broad base for disrupting the current distribution of political power?

In the solution stream, creative innovators develop ideas that might be applied to solve practical problems. In the garbage can model, solutions are not developed with specific problems in mind or in anticipation of forthcoming choices. However, once developed, solutions become answers looking for problems. As Cohen, March, and Olsen observe, often "you do not know what the question is in organizational problem solving until you know the answer."[23] For example, Kingdon shows how the highly abstract academic idea of deregulation came to be viewed a solution to the perceived economic problems of the 1980s.[24] In Kingdon's account, regardless of whether over-regulation was the cause of a specific economic problem, deregulation was almost always the proposed solution. Slow economic growth was a problem looking for a solution, and deregulation was a solution looking for a problem. Political entrepreneurs found it advantageous to pair the two. Similarly, on the left, there are often times when "soak the rich" is the proposed solution to any and all problems. Why these problem–solution pairings prove fruitful turns on the politics stream.

In the politics stream, political events provide opportunities for entrepreneurs to draw attention to problems, solutions, or a particular problem–solution pair. These opportunities include "swings of the national mood, vagaries of public opinion, election results, changes of administration, shifts in partisan or ideological distributions in Congress, and interest group pressure campaigns."[25] Owing to these events, the politics stream is highly volatile as the set of political actors and the issues that they care about are in constant flux. Schattschneider highlighted the fact that this volatility stems from the larger political system's lack of structure and its highly fluid set of participants:

> Political conflict is not like a football game, played on a measured field by a fixed number of players in the presence of an audience scrupulously excluded from the playing field. Politics is much more like the original primitive game of football in which everybody was free to join, a game in which the whole population of one town might play the entire population of another town moving freely back and forth across the countryside. Many conflicts are narrowly confined by a variety of devices, but the distinctive quality of political conflicts is that the relations between the players and the audience have not been well defined and there is usually nothing to keep the audience from getting into the game.[26]

Given this set-up, political entrepreneurs have the ability to reshape the political game depending on the problems and solutions that are paired together.

While prior conspiracy theory scholarship focuses on the controversy at stake in prominent conspiracy theories on an ad hoc basis, Joseph Uscinski and Joseph Parent show that the broader political landscape influences who will use conspiracy theories and which conspiracy theories will be successful at any given time.[27] In seeking to understand how this process works, we argue that the garbage can model of choice serves as the appropriate framework for explaining conspiracy theory politics.

In this untidy environment where problems, solutions, and political events are disconnected, political entrepreneurs influence when and why the three streams are coupled together. John Kingdon showed that the garbage can model explains how mainstream policy experts enact policy change. By contrast, in the next section we extend the garbage can model to accommodate a broader set of actors including those who push dubious ideas. This extended model helps account for why dubious ideas occasionally spread and endure as a function of rational choices.

Applying the Garbage Can Framework to Conspiracy Theory Politics

Newt Gingrich is the architect of the contemporary conservative coalition in Congress. In the 1980s and early 1990s, Gingrich, as a member of the United States

House of Representatives, remade the American political order using his skills of political disruption. In 1979, at the beginning of his tenure in the House, Gingrich is not only a member of the minority party—in fact, his party has not controlled the House since the 1950s—but he is also an insurgent within his own party.[28] As a political loser with very little prospect for advancement, Gingrich desperately searches for leverage to disrupt the established order. Initially he finds his leverage in conspiracy theories, using "themes of rampant corruption in Washington and a House rotten to the core."[29] He takes to the House floor accusing Democratic leaders of myriad conspiracies to advance communism and enrich themselves. Gingrich ultimately succeeds in drawing powerful leaders of the Democratic majority into a fight. Thomas Mann and Norman Ornstein quote the following account of Gingrich's insurgent strategy:

> "'The number one fact about the news media,' he told [journalists], "is they love fights." For months, he explained, he had been giving "organized, systematic, researched, one-hour lectures. Did CBS rush in and ask if they could tape one of my one-hour lectures? No. But the minute Tip O'Neill attacked me, he and I got 90 seconds at the close of all three network news shows. You have to give them confrontations. When you give them confrontations, you get attention."[30]

More generally, Mann and Ornstein observe that the Gingrich playbook centered on using "hyperbolic rhetoric to poke and agitate the Democratic leaders" and that Gingrich—as an outsider—succeeded when the Democratic leaders reacted to his antics.[31] These tactics come straight from the political science playbook of Schattschneider and Riker, where political losers are "continually poking and pushing the world to get the result they want" by drawing new participants into the conflict.[32]

In Mann and Ornstein's account, Gingrich was indifferent to the content of the ideas that he leveraged. He was not animated by concerns that the Democrats were promoting communism and enriching themselves at the public's expense, and he knew that the allegations he was promoting were beyond dubious. Yet those allegations served a useful purpose precisely because their disingenuousness reliably drew his powerful opponents into fights that made the otherwise marginalized Gingrich the center of political attention.

To account for the propagation of conspiracy theories like those proffered by Gingrich, we extend the basic description of the garbage can model of choice with two questions in mind. First, how could a fringe solution like a conspiracy theory become attached to the problem of a mainstream political entrepreneur? Second, if the political agenda or public attention can accommodate only a limited number of items, why would a conspiracy theory, a seemingly unworthy policy proposal, become a solution that rises to the top of the agenda?

Political entrepreneurs with varying concerns typically share an underlying problem of galvanizing collective action. This is the fundamental problem of politics. A half-century of social science research has shown that collective action problems are often exceedingly difficult to overcome and, as a result, most political entrepreneurs fail. As Kingdon convincingly demonstrates in *Agendas, Alternatives, and Public Policies*, successful entrepreneurs solve their problem by capturing attention for it and by coupling that problem with a salient solution.[33]

When facing a problem of collective action, political entrepreneurs look for pre-scripted solutions in the policy stream. Solutions in circulation might include organizing a protest, running for office, mobilizing constituent contact with members of Congress, or disseminating a conspiracy theory. For some political entrepreneurs, conspiracy theories are compelling solutions for the following two reasons.

First, psychologist Paul Bloom argues that narratives move people, not reason or evidence.[34] In fact, he finds that there are just a few archetypal narratives that command people's attention and spread throughout society. These include sex, corruption, and betrayal. Note that in classic garbage can style, nearly all the words Gingrich implored his protégés to haphazardly apply—bizarre, betray, anti-family, cheat, sick, traitors—invoke the archetypal themes Bloom highlights. A conspiracy theory will generally have some mix of these elements, and it is quite likely that other solutions will not. Bloom suggests that the elements available for engaging human interest comprise a surprisingly limited range.

Second, political entrepreneurs frequently solve collective action problems for unorganized groups.[35] Conspiracy theories are effective tools. To mobilize a group, an entrepreneur needs to get people thinking that they are a member of a particular group and to make decisions based on membership with that particular group— which is not an easy thing to do. Individuals are members of many groups. How do you make one particular group membership salient? Conspiracy theories help. Conspiracy theories often make the case that one group in society is benefiting at the expense of another group. In fact, by definition, conspiracy theories identify a virtuous group under threat from a nefarious enemy.[36] Since people systematically respond to the threat of loss much more than to some promised gain, conspiracy theories proposing that insiders are actively destroying your group are tailor made for stimulating a response.[37] In short, politics is about the division of resources, and conspiracy theories are couched in similar language. And while conspiracy theories are not the only explanation of how resources are divided, they are—relative to more mundane explanations—more likely to capture mass interest.

With our extension of the garbage can framework, it is now possible to explain and understand conspiracy theory dissemination as a rational choice. For political entrepreneurs seeking to solve their problem by appealing to the masses and engaging them with a talking point (or solution), a conspiracy theory looks quite promising. For instance, when Congresswoman Maxine Waters sought to build an electoral coalition in an impoverished South Los Angeles district, she chose to spread allegations based on a story printed in the *San Jose Mercury*.

> As someone who has seen how the crack cocaine trade has devastated the South-Central Los Angeles community, I cannot exaggerate my feelings of dismay that my own government may have played a part in the origins and history of this problem. Portions of this country may have been exposed, indeed introduced, to the horror of crack cocaine because certain U.S.-government paid or organized operatives smuggled, transported and sold it to American citizens.[38]

The garbage can framework helps us understand why the pre-scripted solution presented by the *San Jose Mercury*, which may seem irrational in isolation, is a perfectly rational and crafty solution for Congresswoman Waters's problem of building electoral support. This conspiracy theory, given Bloom's findings about human behavior, had better prospects of capturing attention in a congressional election than a conventional policy appeal.[39]

Political entrepreneurs with collective action problems have long used conspiracy theories to mobilize group support and disrupt the existing political order. For instance, in the Jacksonian era, political losers sought higher tariffs and public works. In an effort to build a base of support, these entrepreneurs donned the anti-Masonic label and propagated a conspiracy theory. They charged that the secret society of Freemasonry occupied "a disproportionate share of influential positions" (including the presidency under Andrew Jackson) and, as Olmsted argues elsewhere in this volume, practiced "'horrid oath-finding systems' that undermined republican government and thrust Americans into 'the very fangs of despotism.'"[40] This effort, which included many prominent leaders of the future Republican majority such as William Seward and Thaddeus Stevens, met with brief regional success.[41] Several decades later, at the end of the 1850s, political losers still strived for higher tariffs and public works. Now, under the Republican label, ambitious politicians argued that Chief Justice Roger Taney's *Dred Scott* decision portended a conspiracy to nationalize slavery.[42] The goal was to unite the Northeast and Northwest by emphasizing the common threat they faced from the South, because it was the division of the Northeast and the Northwest that had been the principal impediment to the loser's agenda. A conspiracy theory helped losers, who had wallowed in the minority for several decades, to disrupt the existing order.

To understand why some conspiracy theories successfully gain prominence in society, attention must also be paid to the politics stream, which provides opportunities for the coupling of problems and solutions and increasing their salience. In cases of successful propagation, we think it is useful to ask: What problem is the conspiracy theory solving, and how is it solving that problem?

Uscinski and Parent show that events in the political stream provide favorable opportunities for select political entrepreneurs and conspiracy theories.[43] Specifically, groups are more likely to engage in conspiracy talk when they lose political power or are persistently politically weak.[44] Furthermore, conspiracy theories gain traction when they attack the most powerful individuals and groups in society. It is these opportunities in the politics stream that a political entrepreneur will exploit. As such, the garbage can model helps extend Uscinski and Parent's "conspiracy theories are for losers" theory into a system-level environment. By integrating these two approaches, conspiracy theory scholars will begin to understand how entrepreneurs view the incentive structure of politics and what conspiracy theories do for individuals navigating this structure.

Why Politicians Disrupt

The Declaration of Independence is the greatest disruptive feat in American history, but it was also the "original American conspiracy theory."[45] To break from the existing order and declare a new country, the Founding Fathers marshaled 27 charges referring to a grand conspiracy by the King. But to successfully govern the new country, it took 13 years to agree on an effective framework. This historical case illustrates the challenge facing disruptors throughout American history: namely, the politics of disruption is different from the art of governance. While conspiracy theories disrupt by overturning the status quo, they do not establish new rules and procedures that entrench the power of the disruptors over society.

The political order created by the Constitution established a federal government that, up until the early 1900s, ordinary citizens rarely interacted with. Consequently, the federal government does not become an attractive target for conspiracy theories until its size and scope expands in the World War I era. The conspiracy theories are for losers theory posits that the Davids of the world disseminate conspiracy theories, and their targets are the Goliaths. In the pre–World War I era, the Goliaths were the social groups dominating the economy, as Olmsted details elsewhere in this volume, and the national government was included among the Davids, fighting to take down Wall Street's "money kings." In the World War I era, the national government shifts from being one the Davids to one of the Goliaths. In this new era, potential disruptors like Newt Gingrich target the federal government with their conspiracy theories.

In this chapter, we leveraged social choice theory and the garbage can model to explain conspiracy theory dissemination as a rational choice of strategic political actors. While psychologists have ably identified the irrational tendencies of the masses, these psychological theories do not account for how the political context shapes the evolution of conspiracy theories.[46]

Conspiracy theories are a political tool, and accounting for the dissemination of conspiracy theories requires an explanation rooted in political motives and context. Ambitious politicians seek political power, and out-of-power politicians practice the politics of disruption. Based on the findings of Bloom and Uscinski, we have explained why using conspiracy theories is often the most powerful and effective method of practicing the politics of disruption. A narrative where the subject is a set of social groups who have captured the public's imagination because of their power combined with Bloom's archetypal themes of sex, corruption, and betrayal will effectively galvanize attention and action. Conspiracy theories are a great mechanism for disruption, and they will crop up when ambitious out-of-power politicians have an incentive to use them. Going forward, to explain conspiracy theory dissemination, scholars must focus on the problems, incentives, and opportunities facing ambitious politicians.

Notes

1. Uscinski, Joseph E., and Joseph M. Parent. 2014. *American Conspiracy Theories*. Oxford: Oxford University Press; Edelson, Jack, Alexander Alduncin, Christopher Krewson, James A. Sieja, and Joseph Uscinski. 2017. "The Effect of Conspiratorial Thinking and Motivated Reasoning on Belief in Election Fraud." *Political Research Quarterly* 70(4). https://doi.org/10.1177/1065912917721061 (Accessed December 18, 2017).
2. Mann, Thomas E., and Norman J. Ornstein. 2016. *It's Even Worse Than It Looks: How the American Constitutional System Collided With the New Politics of Extremism*. New York: Basic Books.
3. Dixit, Avinash K., and Barry J. Nalebuff. 1993. *Thinking Strategically: The Competitive Edge in Business, Politics, and Everyday Life*. New York: W.W. Norton; McAdams, David. 2014. *Game-Changer: Game Theory and the Art of Transforming Strategic Situations*. New York. W.W. Norton.
4. Schattschneider, E. E. 1960. *The Semisovereign People: A Realist's View of Democracy*. New York: Holt, Rinehart and Winston; Riker, William H. 1982. *Liberalism Against Populism: A Confrontation Between the Theory of Democracy and the Theory of Social Choice*. Long Grove, IL: Waveland Press.
5. This is the vision of the pluralistic system that Dahl shows characterizes American politics. Dahl, Robert Alan. 1961. *Who Governs?: Democracy and Power in an American City*. New Haven: Yale University Press. In general, salient conspiracy theories develop in the setting of mass politics away from institutions and norms (as is consistent with Uscinski and Parent's [2014] finding that conspiracy theories are for losers) regardless of how concentrated political power is within a particular political system.
6. Uscinski and Parent were the first to sketch a path forward in *American Conspiracy Theories* (2014). We build on their efforts by placing the Uscinski and Parent model into the larger structure of the political system.
7. Arrow, Kenneth Joseph. 1963. *Social Choice and Individual Values*. New Haven: Yale University Press; Riker, *Liberalism Against Populism*.
8. Riker, William H. 1986. *The Art of Political Manipulation*. New Haven: Yale University Press.
9. Aldrich, John H. 1995. *Why parties?: The Origin and Transformation of Political Parties in America*. Chicago: University of Chicago Press; Azari, Julia R., and Jennifer K. Smith. 2012. "Unwritten Rules: Informal Institutions in Established Democracies." *Perspectives on Politics* 10(1): 37–55.

10. This is the theoretical argument of Arrow in *Social Choice and Individual Values* (1963) and Riker in *Liberalism Against Populism* (1982) when discussing decision making in majority-rule settings. The new institutionalist literature provided a broad range of support for these ideas across time and institutional settings. While the literature is too vast to cite here, seminal works include the following on agenda setting and legislative norms, respectively: Romer, Thomas, and Howard Rosenthal. 1978. "Political Resource Allocation, Controlled Agendas, and the Status Quo." *Public Choice* 33(4): 27–43; Weingast, Barry R. 1979. "A Rational Choice Perspective on Congressional Norms." *American Journal of Political Science* 23(2): 245–262.

11. North, Douglass C. 1990. *Institutions, Institutional Change, and Economic Performance.* Cambridge: Cambridge University Press.

12. Ostrom, Elinor. 2010. "Beyond Markets and States: Polycentric Governance of Complex Economic Systems." *American Economic Review* 100(3): 641–672; Shepsle, Kenneth A. 2017. *Rule Breaking and Political Imagination.* Chicago: University of Chicago Press.

13. Aldrich, *Why Parties?*; Shepsle, Kenneth A. 1979. "Institutional Arrangements and Equilibrium in Multidimensional Voting Models." *American Journal of Political Science* 23(1): 27–59; Cox, Gary W, and Mathew D. McCubbins. 2005. *Setting the Agenda: Responsible Party Government in the U.S. House of Representatives.* Cambridge: Cambridge University Press; Zaller, John. 1992. *The Nature and Origins of Mass Opinion.* Cambridge: Cambridge University Press; Sniderman, Paul M. 2000. "Taking Sides: A Fixed Choice Theory of Political Reasoning." In *Elements of Reason: Cognition, Choice, and the Bounds of Rationality*, eds. Samuel L. Popkin, Arthur Lupia, and Matthew D. McCubbins. Cambridge: Cambridge University Press, 67–84; Carmines, Edward G., and James A. Stimson. 1989. *Issue Evolution: Race and the Transformation of American Politics.* Princeton: Princeton University Press; Ostrom, Elinor. 1990. *Governing the Commons: The Evolution of Institutions for Collective Action.* Cambridge: Cambridge University Press.

14. Schattschneider, *The Semisovereign People*; Riker, *Liberalism Against Populism*; Kingdon, John W. 1984. *Agendas, Alternatives, and Public Policies.* Boston: Little, Brown; Schofield, Norman. 2006. *Architects of Political Change.* Cambridge: Cambridge University Press; Shepsle, *Rule Breaking and Political Imagination.*

15. Fiorina, Morris P., and Kenneth A. Shepsle. 1989. "Formal Theories of Leadership: Agents, Agenda Setters, and Entrepreneurs." In *Leadership and Politics: New Perspectives in Political Science*, ed. B.D. Jones. Kansas: University of Kansas Press, 17–40; Ostrom, *Governing the Commons.*

16. Kingdon, *Agendas, Alternatives, and Public Policies.*

17. Schattschneider, *The Semisovereign People*; Riker, *The Art of Political Manipulation*; McLean, Iain. 2001. *Rational Choice and British Politics: An Analysis of Rhetoric and Manipulation from Peel to Blair.* Oxford: Oxford University Press; Shepsle, Kenneth A. 2003. "Losers in Politics (and How They Sometimes Become Winners): William Riker's Heresthetic." *Perspectives on Politics* 1(2): 307–315.

18. Schattschneider, *The Semisovereign People*, 40.

19. Ibid.; Kingdon, *Agendas, Alternatives, and Public Policies*; Riker, *The Art of Political Manipulation*; Wagner, Richard E. 1996. "Pressure Groups and Political Entrepreneurs: A Review Article." *Public Choice* 1(1): 161–170.

20. Cohen, Michael D., James G. March, and Johan P. Olsen. 1972. "A Garbage Can Model of Organizational Choice." *Administrative Science Quarterly* 17(1): 1–25.

21. According to the social choice literature, when preferences are unclear, the problems of chaos and instability are magnified. In an organized anarchy, a conspiracy theory can easily disrupt the status quo, as it is exceedingly fragile.

22. Cohen, March, and Olsen, "A Garbage Can Model."

23. Ibid., 3.

24. Kingdon, *Agendas, Alternatives, and Public Policies.*

25. Ibid.

26. Schattschneider, *The Semisovereign People*.
27. Uscinski and Parent, *American Conspiracy Theories*, Chapter 6.
28. Theriault, Sean M. 2013. *The Gingrich Senators: The Roots of Partisan Warfare in Congress*. Oxford: Oxford University Press.
29. Mann and Ornstein, *It's Even Worse Than It Looks*, 39.
30. Ibid., 36.
31. Ibid., 34.
32. Riker, *The Art of Political Manipulation*; Schattschneider, *The Semisovereign People*.
33. Kingdon, *Agendas, Alternatives, and Public Policies*.
34. Bloom, Paul. 2010. *How Pleasure Works: The New Science of Why We Like What We Like*. New York: Random House.
35. Wagner, "Pressure Groups and Political Entrepreneurs."
36. Uscinski and Parent, *American Conspiracy Theories*.
37. Wilson, Rick K. 2011. "The Contribution of Behavioral Economics to Political Science." *Annual Review of Political Science* 14(June): 201–223.
38. Representative Maxine Waters to Attorney General Janet Reno, personal correspondence. August 30, 1996. https://www.narconews.com/darkalliance/drugs/library/32.htm (Accessed December 30, 2017).
39. While some authors have found evidence for Maxine Waters's claims, the argument was a conspiracy theory at the time it was initially promulgated.
40. Walker, Jesse. 2014. *The United States of Paranoia: A Conspiracy Theory*. New York: Harper Collins, 122; Olmsted, Chapter 17 in this book.
41. Walker, *The United States of Paranoia*, 122.
42. Donald, David Herbert. 1996. *Lincoln*. New York: Simon and Schuster.
43. Uscinski and Parent, *American Conspiracy Theories*.
44. Ibid., Chapters 1 and 6.
45. Uscinski and Parent, *American Conspiracy Theories*.
46. Douglas, Karen, Robbie M. Sutton, and Aleksandra Cichocka. 2017. "The Psychology of Conspiracy Theories." *Current Directions in Psychological Science* 26(6): 538–542.

9

Learning about Conspiracy Theories

Experiences in Science and Risk Communication with the Public about the Fukushima Daiichi Disaster

JAY T. CULLEN

On March 11, 2011, a 9.0 magnitude mega-thrust earthquake occurred under the Pacific Ocean roughly 130 km east of Sendai in eastern Japan and ~163 km northeast of the Fukushima Dai-ichi Nuclear Power Plant (FDNPP).[1] The massive amount of energy liberated by the earthquake generated devastating tsunami waves that reached heights of up to 40.5 m as they came ashore along eastern Japan, causing massive destruction along the coastline. Indeed, the tsunami traveled as much as 10 km inland[2] and caused 15,894 confirmed fatalities with 2,546 persons still reported missing according to the National Police Agency of Japan as of September 8, 2017.[3] In addition to this terrible loss of life and destruction of infrastructure, the earthquake and tsunami caused widespread damage to the FDNPP and subsequent releases of radioactive elements to the environment.

Through outreach and education efforts related to the environmental impact of the disaster, I have a firsthand understanding of the pitfalls of public science and risk communication. The purpose of this paper is to provide background about the nature of the disaster, scientifically sound monitoring information, and known risks resulting from the release of radioactive material from Fukushima. The paper is also an account of how conspiracy ideation and poor science literacy led to threats against my life and online harassment in response to my scientifically grounded monitoring program and evidence-based outreach efforts.

What Are the Dangers Associated with the FDNPP Disaster?

Radioisotopes are one source of ionizing radiation in the environment. When experienced by humans or other living organisms at high enough dose, ionizing radiation has measureable negative consequences including but not limited to cell death and cancer.[4] Certain of the artificial radioisotopes produced in the FDNPP reactors were released in large quantities and tend to concentrate in living organisms, and so could present a radiological health risk in the environment.

What was the amount of radionuclides released, what will be their fate in the environment, and what dose of ionizing radiation will be experienced by organisms are high-priority questions to answer when trying to understand the impact of the FDNPP disaster on environmental and public health. The amount of radioactivity released, or *source term*, is determined by both physical models and direct and in-direct observations of radionuclides in air, soil, water, and living organisms after a major nuclear disaster. All of these determinations carry uncertainties. The vast majority of releases to the environment from the FDNPP came in March–April 2011;[5] however, radionuclides continue to leak at much lower rates from the site to this day.[6] Best estimates of the Fukushima source term for radiologically signif-icant isotopes suggest that it is roughly a factor of 10 lower than releases from the Chernobyl disaster in 1986, and that the environmental impacts of Fukushima will be correspondingly much lower.[7] As of this writing the United Nations Scientific Committee on the Effects of Atomic Radiation (UNSCEAR) have determined that the doses of ionizing radiation experienced by the most exposed residents of Japan over their lifetime owing to Fukushima are low enough that there will be no discernable increased incidence of radiation-related illness in them or their descendants.[8] Similarly, the exposures of both terrestrial and aquatic (freshwater and marine) ecosystems were too low for acute effects to be expected. Based on the international scientific communities' monitoring efforts, we understand that any impacts on the ecosystem beyond the very localized areas most proximate to the FDNPP will likely be undetectable, and risks to human and environmental health will be insignificant.

How Will Fukushima Impact Ecosystem and Public Health in North America?

Based on the scientific consensus, the impact of the FDNPP disaster on the North Pacific ecosystem and the health of residents of North America from atmospheric fallout,[9] ocean current transport,[10] and consumption of seafood[11] are expected to be non-measurable.[12] Public access to the peer-reviewed scientific literature is some-times limited by expensive publisher paywalls or by the technical nature and scien-tific training expected by the readership of professional journals. As a consequence, there is considerable public demand for timely, accessible, quality information about expected and measured impacts.

In response to this demand, and in the absence of communication of quality in-formation from the scientific community, there has been a proliferation of pseudo and junk science on the Internet that misleads the public as to the risk to environmental and public health posed by Fukushima. Communicating risk associated with radiation in the environment to the public is a challenging task,[13] as the public has a mistrust of government and scientists stemming back to the Cold War and the nuclear arms race it spawned.[14] Therefore, the public perception of risk associated with radioactivity tends to be at odds with the actual risks. The contamination from the FDNPP has been detected worldwide, but the vast majority of the radioactivity was deposited in the North Pacific Ocean where prevailing currents will bring it to Canadian and U.S. territorial waters.[15] Monitoring by the international scientific community indicate that levels in seawater[16] and marine organisms,[17] now and expected when radioactivity levels peak in North American waters over the next two years, will not pose a danger to the public.

How I Became Involved With Science Knowledge Mobilization About the Fukushima Disaster

My area of expertise is marine chemistry, and my research seeks to understand how chemical elements are distributed in the ocean. Some of this research involves understanding how contaminants behave in seawater, and makes use of radioactive isotope tracers to understand present and past ocean processes. In response to questions from my family, friends, and members of the public in the aftermath of the FDNPP disaster, I began following the scientific research that was published in the peer-reviewed literature about the disaster. My family and I live in Victoria, British Columbia, Canada, which is downwind and downcurrent of Japan, and I was concerned about the potential threat the disaster represented to our health, the health of our community, and the health of the Pacific Ocean. We also belong to a Community Supported Fishery, and we consume more than average amounts of seafood harvested from the northeast Pacific Ocean.

My perception of the risk was shaped by the evidence garnered through the application of the scientific method, and I communicated the scientific consensus to those who asked. However, in late 2013 I began to receive email correspondence and hear from undergraduate students I teach about some of the poor-quality information being circulated online about the disaster. Pseudo-scientific writing and sensationalized and misleading reporting which exaggerates the environmental and human health impacts or attributes unrelated events to the disaster, are too common on the World Wide Web and reach large numbers of the public.[18]

In response to articles and reports in the same vein, I decided that I would conduct my own research and begin to speak and write publicly about what the international scientific community was learning about Fukushima, thus bringing published results out from behind publisher paywalls and translating the technical literature for the general public.

Conducting Research to Provide Quality Information about Fukushima to the Public: What We Have Found

Beginning in 2014, I spearheaded efforts to obtain grant monies and establish the Integrated Fukushima Ocean Radionuclide Monitoring (InFORM) project, which is a network involving academic, governmental, and nongovernmental organizations as well as citizen scientist volunteers. InFORM is acquiring data to support a thorough radiological impact assessment for Canada's west coast stemming from the FDNPP accident, and to effectively communicate these results to the public. InFORM is funded by the Marine Environmental Observation Prediction and Response network that was established at Dalhousie University in Nova Scotia in 2012, part of the Networks of Centres of Excellence of Canada.

InFORM's monitoring strategy is to make high quality measurements of Fukushima contamination in (1) seawater collected offshore using research vessels and at the coast collected by citizen scientist volunteers, and (2) marine biota collected in Canadian waters.[19] These measurements allow the team to track the arrival of the contamination in time and space and estimate risk to the health of the marine ecosystem. By monitoring marine organisms, predominantly Pacific salmon and shellfish, we are able to estimate health risks to members of the public who consume seafood.

The triple meltdowns at the FDNPP released many different radioisotopes to the environment, however only a very few of these were released in sufficient quantity to be measurable and unique to Fukushima. A reliable fingerprint radioisotope for Fukushima is Cesium-134 (^{134}Cs, half-life ~ 2 years). This is because ^{134}Cs is only produced in nuclear reactors, and it has a relatively short half-life, so that ^{134}Cs from other human sources, like the Chernobyl NPP disaster in 1986, are no longer present in the environment. Other isotopes such as Cesium-137 (^{137}Cs, half-life ~30 years) are not positive indicators of Fukushima since they were also products of atmospheric atomic weapons testing in the 20th century and Chernobyl and are still present in the environment from these legacy sources.

Seawater samples are collected monthly by dedicated citizen scientists in 16 of British Columbia's coastal communities. Oceanic contamination is monitored by bi-annual research expeditions up to ~1500 km out into the northeast Pacific, and annual expeditions to the Arctic Ocean. In addition, salmon from each of British Columbia's major salmon runs are sampled each summer to assess human and ecosystem health risks due to bioaccumulation of Fukushima-derived contamination. Thus far InFORM has collected and analyzed over 275 coastal and 450 oceanic seawater samples and over 300 Pacific salmon since the projects inception in August 2014. To date, seawater monitoring has shown levels of radionuclide activity (^{137}Cs ~10 Bq m^{-3} in the central NE Pacific) are well below Canadian safe drinking water standards (10,000 Bq m^{-3}). Similarly, radionuclide levels in the vast majority of salmon are well below the minimum detectable concentration for ^{134}Cs and on average contain ~0.2 Bq kg^{-1} ^{137}Cs, which is more than 5000-fold lower than Canadian food safety standards (1,000 Bq kg^{-1}). Through an active and multifaceted outreach campaign, these results are providing quality information to the public regarding the accident's environmental impact here in North America. Contamination levels continue to be below levels that are known to represent a significant threat to human or ecosystem health. Nothing we have found thus far, or have predicted by modeling studies, contradicts the international scientific consensus that Fukushima does not threaten the health of our marine environment or public health in North America.[20]

Public Outreach Related to Fukushima and the Consequences

What follows here is not meant to be a comprehensive account of my experiences with conspiracy theories, but to provide specific examples that characterize the general response of conspiracy theorists to my work on the Fukushima disaster. Most believe that some combination of the Government of Japan, Tokyo Electric Power Company (TEPCO), the United Nations including the World Health Organization (WHO), the International Atomic Energy Association (IAEA), the nuclear industry, and the international scientific community including Canadian universities, law enforcement, and the criminal justice system are coordinating and colluding to minimize public knowledge of the disaster's impact. This involves lying about emissions and covering up what are thought to be obvious indications of severe environmental impacts (e.g., death of the Pacific Ocean) globally resulting from the FDNPP disaster. Such an elaborate conspiracy is highly improbable, and I am not aware of any evidence to support such a conspiracy (but, of course, this is exactly what I would say if I were a part of the conspiracy).

Experiences Blogging about Research Related to the Disaster

In November 2013 I began maintaining a blog at the Daily Kos, an American political blog that publishes news and opinions from a liberal point of view.[21] I chose to post there only because I had found articles about science there to be well written and the community to be, overall, scientifically literate and dominated by evidenced-based discussion and by critical thinkers. However, in response to my posts on studies relating to Fukushima I experienced significant pushback and skepticism by a minority of the site readership. I was accused of pushing public relations and being a paid shill and apologist for the nuclear industry.[22]

My previous professional outreach experiences, mostly related to climate change, led me to believe that conspiracy ideation and rejection of scientific evidence was largely confined to those on the more far-right, conservative end of the political spectrum. I now recognize that this is not so.[23] Many of those reluctant to understand the implications of the scientific research I presented were self-identifying liberals who, for example, accept the science behind our understanding of climate and climate change. However, research into Fukushima funded by the same national governmental agencies that paid for climate research, and in certain cases by the same scientists, was rejected in cases where the segment of the populace, who are largely anti–nuclear power and anti-proliferation based on my experience, saw conspiracy to downplay the severity of the environmental and public health impacts of nuclear accidents. A clear case of ideology leading individuals to become blind to scientific evidence.

Online Misinformation and Pseudoscience

Where is misinformation about the impact of the Fukushima disaster on the marine environment coming from? The ENEnews.com (Energy News) site is one source of the misinformation that members of the public routinely cite as evidence that the scientific consensus regarding Fukushima is incorrect. One could also make a case that Energy News is more or less responsible for fueling the hatred and online attacks I have experienced and that led one individual to be charged and found guilty of criminal harassment against me. The owners and administrators of the website are unknown and anonymous, but they routinely report on the Fukushima disaster in ways that misrepresent or misunderstand the scientific literature such that readers of the site are misinformed on the topic. For example, the website reported on a public presentation I gave at the Feiro Marine Life Center in Port Angeles, Washington, in April of 2017. Rather than focusing on the take-home message that levels of Fukushima-derived contamination in the marine environment were much lower than those known to represent a significant risk to ecosystem or public health, they provide a headline stating "Peak of Fukushima radiation now moving to West Coast—Levels much higher than predicted—Huge red blob of nuclear waste near shore—San Francisco being hit hardest . . .". The website also routinely posts stories about changes in the marine ecosystem (e.g., sea star wasting syndrome, whale strandings) with the implication that Fukushima is the cause and painting scientific experts as "baffled" or "puzzled." By undermining public confidence in the scientific method and the expertise of the scientific community in this way, it is not surprising that the comment section of this website is populated by many references to conspiracy theories and attacks against the professional and personal integrity of scientists.

I have been accused of being paid by the "global nuclear cartel" to report the results of my independent research, and that my laboratory has been infiltrated by nuclear industry "embeds" that feed false results to me.

"I started out wanting to see Cullen as a tool more than a shill, but he keeps right on shilling."[24]

"What I challenged was a dumb data point . . . from his actual embedded radiological 'experts' who ran the samples for him. I literally thought when I first saw it that it was a sardonic 'joke' played on the oceanographers by the embeds, just because the oceanographers wouldn't know any better. Yeah, nuclear technicians can be real-clown funny sometimes, will no doubt hoot about it with their buds forevermore."[25]

An Energy News reader also thinks I was actively stalking them somewhere in the rural United States:

"So Cullen was trespassing on my property, stalking me, . . . So, how did he get my address, way out here on a dirt road, in the middle of nowhere? . . . Dozens of miles from town, dirt road, tiny rental car (not recommended), same shirt as in his vids, long, tan face, those hands, in a car trying to hide his face as I drove by in my big truck (recommended), sitting at our cemetery which hasn't been used for years, private property, placing his hands in his lap as if he was just waiting . . . in the middle of nowhere . . . But I saw his nervous face. I saw a man that looked exactly like Cullen. At first, I thought feds . . . who . . . huh? He looks familiar! Certainly out of place and an unusual event out here! I could see where one might assume one might not be noticed in plain clothes and car—if they had never been out to the hills. We don't dress like that or look like that 'round here. We just don't. And aint nobody gots no suntan. People notice those sorts of things in the boonies."[26]

Of course it wasn't me. But, it is both disturbing and somewhat entertaining to see that people think that I travel internationally to spy on them because of their online comments.

Online Attacks through YouTube: Dana R. Durnford and the Fukushima Hounds

The most unfortunate aspect of my experience was being subjected to online harassment,[27] which ultimately led to criminal charges being filed[28] and a guilty verdict delivered[29] against an individual who falsely believed I was part of a vast conspiracy to mislead the public about the Fukushima disaster. It started on January 16, 2014, when I was invited along with a colleague Dr. Ken Buesseler, a radiochemist from Woods Hole Oceanographic Institution, to do a radio interview about Fukushima on KALW 91.7 FM Local Public Radio, San Francisco.[30] The interview covered various aspects of the disaster and what the research community was learning about releases to the environment, and what the resulting impacts might be. On January 27 I received an email with the subject: You are the topic tonight! The email told me the "DANA" was going live in 5 minutes and that I should watch and defend myself. The link provided brought me to a YouTube stream called "Pt 2 Ken Buesseler & Dr. Jay Cullen Really Scientist or Wacko Nuclear Lobbyist" by a user named BeautifulGirlByDana, who I later came to know was Dana Ryan Durnford of Powell River, British Columbia. At that time I was not aware that members of the public streamed live video, using YouTube, to expound on various subjects. I watched the stream. The gentleman was not scientifically literate and was not capable of distinguishing between junk science and actual science, and stated many "facts" about Fukushima that had no basis in reality. Durnford became a very vocal critic of my expertise and outreach efforts and developed somewhat of a cult following.

A number of video streams by Durnford specifically attacking me, and hundreds more making negative comments or referencing me in a threatening way, were made over the next year and a half. As part of his bail conditions and subsequent conviction and probation, these videos were removed from YouTube and can no longer be accessed by the public. Durnford describes himself as a "truther," and an inspection of his other streams indicates that he subscribes to the belief that the September 11, 2001 attacks were conducted with the knowledge and/or participation of the U.S. federal government and that directed energy weapons were used to bring down the World Trade Center towers;[31] that fluoridation of toothpaste is child abuse;[32] and that the University of Victoria stole his idea to build fiberoptically cabled underwater observatories.[33] His attacks on me escalated, normally following my appearances in the media to discuss Fukushima, increasingly making use of dehumanizing rhetoric and inciting violence. Typical excerpts from his streams follow:

Shouldn't people take that $630,000 (referring to the funding of the InFORM project) away cuz he's actually truly is disgusting and disingenuous, he really truly is just a fake, hopeless, demented liar for apologists for nuclear industry. How can you do that Jay? Why would you do that man? What the hell is wrong with you? Don't you think we should deserve a chance Jay (yelling)?

—Dana R. Durnford, August 12, 2014

Every university, every academic, every nuclear scientist will be hunted down and fuckin' murdered in two weeks time when people find out what they done to the ocean. Every fuckin' one of them!

—Dana R. Durnford, August 24, 2014

No we need, we need a revolution, period. To take out the mouthpieces before it's too late. There's not going to be nothing left. And they're not gonna stop. They're not even gonna try. They got the homeless at Fukushima and they're not even

gonna try. And they're just gonna keep saying it Ken Buesseler [senior scientist with Woods Hole Oceanographic] and Jay Cullen and every other apologist out there it's like drinking water or it's like potatoes. And it really is now that everything is radiated and ionized. And I'm past the point of ever caring anymore about trying to have a debate. We're just gonna go out and get the evidence and hopefully the planet goes nuts and kills every single fucking one of them.
                                                    —*Dana R. Durnford, August 25, 2014*

Jay Cullen is murdering your loved ones, he's murdering everything on the coast line.
                                                    —*Dana R. Durnford, March 16, 2015*

. . . and Jay Cullen. . . let the whole planet wake up over the next year and everybody will start lynching these fuckers. Without me even being here – they're gonna do it. I just wouldn't mind accelerating it so I can get to enjoy it!
                                                    —*Dana R. Durnford, April 13, 2015*

Durnford concurrently raised money by soliciting donations online to conduct a photographic survey of the British Columbia coast, and maintains that radiation from low levels of Fukushima radionuclides has killed most of the plants and animals living in the intertidal zone. This view is at odds with what the professional scientists in the marine research community report along the coast and what is expected given levels of radioactivity present in our environment from Fukushima. After visiting Victoria and conducting a survey of the harbor here and finding clear evidence of life, he inferred that my employer, the University of Victoria, was actively seeding the harbor with organisms to maintain the illusion that everything was not dead:

A very odd day indeed I suspect local university propped up by the nuclear industries are seeding the harbor to trick people. Just like the nuclear industries apologist at those institutions have been doing to the local public for decades by insidiously equating Bananas potatoes potassium 40 and walking in sunshine with man made ionized radiation from melted reactors at Fukushima.
                                                    —*Dana R. Durnford, September 10, 2014*

In response to his threats and harassment, he was formally charged with two counts of criminal harassment between July 24, 2015, and October 1, 2015. The case resulted in a trial held September 20–22, 2016, in the Provincial Court of British Columbia, where I testified as a witness for the prosecution. Durnford was unable to secure a lawyer and represented himself. Based on the evidence presented, Durnford was found guilty on both counts and sentenced to three years probation where, among other conditions, he is prohibited from contacting me or conducting correspondence that references me directly or indirectly. Durnford is also prohibited from possessing weapons of any sort during the probation period. In his decision, the Honourable Judge R. Sutton specifically addressed Durnford's repeated attempts to introduce evidence of a conspiracy to justify his threats:

> *It is not about any conspiracy by the investigating officer. It is not about a conspiracy of the complainants. It is not about a conspiracy by the Crown or the nuclear industry, as Mr. Durnford seems to present to the court. This case is not much ado about nothing. This case is about criminal harassment charges against Mr. Durnford. . . . I conclude, on all of the evidence, that Mr. Durnford had the requisite mens rea and was reckless whether the complainants were harassed. I am satisfied that the Crown has proven the charges against him beyond a reasonable doubt. Mr. Durnford, would you please stand, sir, . . . I find you guilty of both charges as laid.*
>
> *—Honourable Judge R. Sutton*[34]

Durnford continues to make online videos nearly every day, demeaning the character of scientists and their professional work (which he clearly does not understand). He routinely refers to scientists as "demons" and "goblins" and categorically questions their humanity while he fantasizes about their gruesome deaths at his or some other hand. He believes strongly that the police, prosecuting crown attorney, and Judge Sutton were involved in the global conspiracy to hide the impact of the Fukushima disaster on the environment. Durnford is unrepentant and continues to believe, almost seven years since the meltdowns and despite all the scientific evidence, that Fukushima is an extinction-level event from which the planet will never recover. He has apparently refused to learn or is otherwise incapable of learning from his experience. Given the amount of anger he exudes, the number of tantrums and outbursts thrown and the dark images he invokes on YouTube, the act of holding on to this conspiracy theory appears to be highly detrimental to his well-being. Despite all of his hate toward me, I do hope he is able to find peace.

Overcoming Misinformation

Overall, the response of the public to my science knowledge mobilization efforts has been positive, with public presentations and writings being well received. My employer has recognized my efforts and commitment by recognizing me with prestigious awards for knowledge mobilization and engagement with the public. However, I am learning about risk communication, and learning how one can and cannot approach public misperceptions of risk or misunderstanding of complex environmental issues as simply the result of a lack of information that can be countered with appropriate science-based evidence.

Initially I was fascinated by the amount of hatred that people could feel and express online against someone they had never met. Eventually that fascination turned to concern and fear for my family and my own safety as the threats escalated. I have learned that there are people that because of their educational background, past experiences, and tendency to accept conspiracy theories will simply not accept scientifically derived information from experts. They reject scientific expertise a priori and cannot be brought to change their opinion with factual information when their opinion on a matter is not fact based. My efforts to engage, communicate scientific findings, mobilize knowledge gained through my research, and improve scientific literacy in the public continue unabated. I think these efforts are important and necessary in a time when many of the problems we face required evidence-based solutions and where scientifically derived knowledge overwhelmingly shapes how we live our lives. I have learned that a certain vocal minority of the public will not listen to expertise when it conflicts so strongly with their worldview. But, most people are truly fascinated with the natural world and want to learn more about it. I take comfort and encouragement from this fact.

Notes

1. Amano, Yukiua. 2015. *The Fukushima Daiichi Accident: Report by the Director Genearl.* Vienna: International Atomic Energy Agency; Povinec, Pavel P., Katsumi Hirose, and Michio Aoyama. 2013. *Fukushima Accident: Radioactivity Impact on the Environment.* Amsterdam: Elsevier; Steinhauser, George, Alexander Brandl, and Thomas E. Johnson. 2014. "Comparison of the Chernobyl and Fukushima Nuclear Accidents: A Review of the Environmental Impacts." *Science of the Total Environment* 470(February): 800–817. DOI: 10.1016/j.scitotenv.2013.10.029.
2. Hamada, Nobuyuki, and Haruyuki Ogino. 2012. "Food Safety Regulations: What we Learned From the Fukushima Nuclear Accident." *Journal of Environmental Radioactivity* 111(September): 83–99. DOI: 10.1016/j.jenvrad.2011.08.008.
3. Headquarters, Emergency Disaster Countermeasures. National Police Agency, Japan. 2015. "Damage Situation and Police Countermeasures Associated with 2011 Tohoku District – Off the Pacific Ocean Earthquake." http://www.npa.go.jp/news/other/earthquake2011/pdf/higaijokyo_e.pdf (Accessed December 29, 2017).
4. Brenner, David J., Richard Doll, Dudley T. Goodhead, Eric J. Hall, Charles E. Land, John B. Little, Jay H. Lunbin, Dale L. Preston, R. Julian Preston, Jerome S. Puskin, Elain Ron, Rainer K. Sachs, Jonathan M. Samet, Richard B. Setlow, and Marco Zaider. 2003. "Cancer Risks Attributable to Low Doses of Ionizing Radiation: Assessing What we Really Know." *Proceedings of the National Academy of Sciences* 100(24): 13761–13766. DOI: 10.1073/pnas.2235592100; Cooper, John R., Keith Randle, and Ranjeet S. Sokhi. 2003. *Radioactive Releases in the Environment: Impact and Assessment.* West Sussex, UK: John Wiley & Sons.
5. Povinec, Hirose, and Aoyama, *Fukushima Accident.*
6. Amano, *The Fukushima Daiichi Accident.*
7. Ibid.; Steinhauser, Brandl, and Johnson, "Comparison of the Chernobyl and Fukushima Nuclear Accidents."

8. United Nations Scientific Committee on the Effects of Atomic Radiation. 2013. *Levels and Effects of Radiation Exposure Due to the Nuclear Accident After the 2011 Great East Japan Earthquake and Tsunami.* https://reliefweb.int/sites/reliefweb.int/files/resources/13-85418_Report_2013_Annex_A.pdf (Accessed December 29, 2017).

9. Chester, A., K. Starosta, C. Andreoiu, R. Ashley, A. Barton, J.-C. Brodovitch, M. Brown, T. Domingo, C. Janusson, H. Kucera, K. Myrtle, D. Ridell, K. Scheel, A. Slomon, and P. Voss. 2013. "Monitoring Rainwater and Seaweed Reveals the Presence of 131I in Southwest and Central British Columbia, Canada Following the Fukushima Nuclear Accident in Japan." *Journal of Environmental Radioactivity* 124(October): 205–213. DOI: 10.1016/j.jenvrad.2013.05.013; Norman, Eric B., Christopher T. Angell, and Perry A. Chodash. 2011. "Observations of Fallout From the Fukushima Reactor Accident in San Francisco Bay Area Rainwater." *Plos One* 6(9). DOI: 10.1371/journal.pone.0024330; Smith, A. R, K. J. Thomas, E. B. Norman, D. L. Hurley, B. T. Lo, Y. D. Chan, P. V. Guillaumon, and B. G. Harvey. 2014. "Measurements of Fission Products From the Fukushima Daiichi Incident in San Francisco Bay Area Air Filters, Automobile Filters, Rainwater, and Food." *Journal of Environmental Protection* 5(3): 207–221. DOI: 10.4236/jep.2014.53025.

10. Behrens, Erik, Franziska U. Schwarzkopf, Joke F. Lübbecke, and Claus W. Böning. 2012. "Model Simulations on the Long-term Dispersal of 137 Cs Released into the Pacific Ocean off Fukushima." *Environmental Research Letters* 7(3): 034004; Rossi, Vincent, Erik Van Sebille, Alexander Sen Gupta, Véronique Garçon, and Matthew H. England. 2013. "Multi-decadal Projections of Surface and Interior Pathways of the Fukushima Cesium-137 Radioactive Plume." *Deep Sea Research Part I: Oceanographic Research Papers* 80(October): 37–46. DOI: 10.1016/j.dsr.2013.05.015; Smith, John N., Robin M. Brown, William J. Williams, Marie Robert, Richard Nelson, and S. Bradley Moran. 2015. "Arrival of the Fukushima Radioactivity Plume in North American Continental Waters." *Proceedings of the National Academy of Sciences* 112(5): 1310–1315. DOI: 10.1073/pnas.1412814112; Smith, John N., Vincent Rossi, Ken O. Buesseler, Jay T. Cullen, Jack Cornett, Richard Nelson, Alison M. Macdonald, Marie Robert, and Jonathan Kellogg. 2017. "Recent Transport History of Fukushima Radioactivity in the Northeast Pacific Ocean." *Environmental Science & Technology* 51(18): 10494–10502. DOI: 10.1021/acs.est.7b02712.

11. Chen, Jing. 2013. "Evaluation of Radioactivity Concentrations From the Fukushima Nuclear Accident in Fish Products and Associated Risk to Fish Consumers." *Radiation Protection Dosimetry* 157(1): 1–5. DOI: 10.1093/rpd/nct239; Chen, Jing, Michael W. Cooke, Jean-Francois Mercier, Brian Ahier, Marc Trudel, Greg Workman, Malcolm Wyeth, and Robin Brown. 2015. "A report on radioactivity measurements of fish samples from the west coast of Canada." *Radiation Protection Dosimetry* 163(2): 261–266. DOI: 10.1093/rpd/ncu150; Fisher, Nicholas S., Karine Beaugelin-Seiller, Thomas G. Hinton, Zofia Baumann, Daniel J. Madigan, and Jacqueline Garnier-Laplace. 2013. "Evaluation of Radiation Doses and Associated Risk From the Fukushima Nuclear Acccident to Marine Biota and Human Consumers of Seafood." *Proceedings of the National Academy of Sciences* 110(26): 10670–10675. DOI: 10.1073/pnas.1221834110.

12. Canadian Radiation Protection Bureau. 2015. *Special Environmental Radiation in Canada Report on Fukushima Accident Contaminants: Surveillance of Fukushima Emissions in Canada March 2011 to June 201.* http://www.hc-sc.gc.ca/ewh-semt/contaminants/radiation/impact/fukushima-eng.php (Accessed December 29, 2017).

13. Chen, Jing. (2015). "Issues and Challenges of Radiation Risk Communication to the Public." *Radiation Emergency Medicine* 4(1): 11–15.

14. Fisher, Nicholas S., Scott W. Fowler, and Daniel J. Madigan. 2015. "Perspectives and Reflections on the Public Reaction to Recent Fukushima-related Radionuclide Studies and a Call for Enhanced Training in Environmental Radioactivity." *Environmental Toxicology and Chemistry* 34(4): 707–709. DOI: 10.1002/etc.2860.

15. Behrens, Schwarzkopf, Lübbecke, and Böning, "Model Simulations on the Long-term Dispersal of 137 Cs Released into the Pacific Ocean off Fukushima"; Rossi, Van Sebille, Sen

Gupta, Garçon, and England, "Multi-decadal Projections of Surface and Interior Pathways of the Fukushima Cesium-137 Radioactive Plume."

16. Smith, Brown, Williams, Robert, Nelson, and Moran,"Arrival of the Fukushima Radioactivity Plume in North American Continental Waters"; Smith, Rossi, Buesseler, Cullen, Cornett, Nelson, Macdonald, Robert, and Kellogg, "Recent Transport History of Fukushima Radioactivity in the Northeast Pacific Ocean."

17. Chen, Cooke, Mercier, Ahier, Trudel, Workman, Wyeth, and Brown, "A report on radioactivity measurements of fish samples from the west coast of Canada"; Chester, Starosta, Andreoiu, Ashley, Barton, Brodovitch, Brown, Domingo, Janusson, Kucera, Myrtle, Ridell, Scheel, Slomon, and Voss, "Monitoring Rainwater and Seaweed Reveals the Presence of 131I in Southwest and Central British Columbia, Canada Following the Fukushima Nuclear Accident in Japan"; Fisher, Beaugelin-Seiller, Hinton, Baumann, Madigan, and Garnier-Laplace, "Evaluation of Radiation Doses and Associated Risk From the Fukushima Nuclear Acccident to Marine Biota and Human Consumers of Seafood"; Johansen, Mathew P., Elizabeth Ruedig, Keiko Tagami, Shigeo Uchida, Kathryn Higley, and Nicholas A. Beresford. 2015. "Radiological Dose Rates to Marine Fish From the Fukushima Daiichi Accident: The First Three Years Across the North Pacific." *Environmental Science & Technology* 49(3): 1277–1285. DOI: 10.1021/es505064d; Neville, Delvan R., A. Jason Phillips, Richard D. Brodeur, and Kathryn Higley. 2014. "Trace Levels of Fukushima Disaster Radionuclides in East Pacific Albacore." *Environmental Science & Technology* 48(9): 4739–4743. DOI: 10.1021/es500129b.

18. Snyder, Michael. 2013. "28 Signs That The West Coast Is Being Absolutely Fried With Nuclear Radiation From Fukushima." [Blog] *Activist Post*. Available at http://www.activistpost.com/ 2013/10/28-signs-that-west-coast-is-being.html (Accessed December 29, 2017).

19. Smith, Brown, Williams, Robert, Nelson, and Moran, "Arrival of the Fukushima Radioactivity Plume in North American Continental Waters"; Smith, Rossi, Buesseler, Cullen, Cornett, Nelson, Macdonald, Robert, and Kellogg, "Recent Transport History of Fukushima Radioactivity in the Northeast Pacific Ocean."

20. Behrens, Schwarzkopf, Lübbecke, and Böning, "Model Simulations on the Long-term Dispersal of 137 Cs Released into the Pacific Ocean off Fukushima"; Rossi, Van Sebille, Sen Gupta, Garçon, and England, "Multi-decadal Projections of Surface and Interior Pathways of the Fukushima Cesium-137 Radioactive Plume."

21. Cullen, Jay T. 2017. [Blog] *Marine Chemist*. Available at http://www.dailykos.com/user/ MarineChemist/history (Accessed December 29, 2017).

22. Ibid.

23. Lewandowsky, Stephan, Gilles E. Gignac, and Klaus Oberauer. 2013. "The Role of Conspiracist Ideation and Worldviews in Predicting Rejection of Science." *Plos One* 8(10). DOI: 10.1371/ journal.pone.0075637; Lewandowsky, Stephan, Klaus Oberauer, and Gilles E. Gignac. 2013. "NASA Faked the Moon Landing –Therefore, (Climate) Science Is a Hoax: An Anatomy of the Motivated Rejection of Science." *Psychological Science* 24(5): 622–633. DOI: 10.1177/ 0956797612457686; Uscinski, Joseph E. and Joseph M. Parent. 2014. *American Conspiracy Theories*. Oxford: Oxford University Press.

24. Energy News. 2014. "Newspaper: Strontium-90 From Fukushima Found Along West Coast of N. America—"Plutonium. . . Might be in the Plume"—Scientist: There Needs to be More Monitoring. . . No Sign radioactive Releases From Plant are Going to Stop." http://enenews. com/newspaper-strontium-90-from-fukushima-detected-along-west-coast-of-n-america-months-ago-plutonium-might-be-in-the-plume-scientist-no-sign-releases-from-plant-are-going-to-stop-there/ (Accessed December 29, 2017).

25. Ibid.

26. Energy News. 2015. "Man Arrested Over Fukushima-related YouTube videos — Charged with Criminal Harassment of University Scientists—Professor: I Certainly Don't Want to Jeopardize the Prosecution (VIDEO)." http://enenews.com/man-arrested-fukushima-re-lated-youtube-videos-charged-criminal-harassment-university-scientists-professor-dont-jeopardize-prosecution-video (Accessed December 29, 2017).

27. Daybreak North, CBC News. 2015. "Fukushima Nuclear Pollution Hasn't Hit B.C. Shore, Says Researcher Jay Cullen." http://www.cbc.ca/news/canada/british-columbia/fukushima-nuclear-pollution-hasn-t-hit-b-c-shore-says-researcher-jay-cullen-1.2990947 (Accessed December 29, 2017); Hume, Mark. 2015. "Canadian Researcher Targeted by Hate Campaign Over Fukushima Findings. *The Globe and Mail.* http://www.theglobeandmail.com/news/british-columbia/canadian-researcher-targeted-by-hate-campaign-over-fukushima-findings/article27060613/ (Accessed December 29, 2017).

28. Hume, Mark. 2015. "Charges Laid Against B.C. Man Who Called for Death of Fukushima Researcher." *The Globe and Mail.* http://www.theglobeandmail.com/news/british-columbia/charges-laid-against-bc-man-who-called-for-death-of-fukushima-researcher/article27136264/ (Accessed December 29, 2017); Wanklyn, Alastair. 2015. "Anti-nuclear Firebrand's Case Heads to Canadian Court Over Death Threats Against Fukushima Environmental Scientists." *The Japan Times.* November 17, 2015.

29. Regina V. 2016. "Dana Ryan Durnford: Reasons for Judgement of The Honourable Judge R. Sutton"; Wanklyn, Alastair. 2016. "Canada Activist Found Guilty of Harassing Scientists Over Fukushima Fallout." *The Japan Times.* https://www.japantimes.co.jp/news/2016/09/23/national/crime-legal/canada-activist-found-guilty-harassing-scientists-fukushima-fallout/ (Accessed December 29, 2017).

30. Cullen Jay T., and Ken Buesseler. 2014. *Today on Your Call.* By Rose Aguilar. 91.7 WKLAW FM, January 16, 2014.

31. Durnford, Dana R. 2013. "Proof Directed Energy Weapons Took Down the Twin Towers." YouTube, 24:11. BeautifulGirlByDana. Available at https://www.youtube.com/watch?v=0TtNJdXWkpo (Accessed December 29, 2017).

32. Durnford, Dana R. 2013. "Proof Directed Energy Weapons Took Down the Twin Towers." YouTube, 24:11. BeautifulGirlByDana. Available at https://www.youtube.com/watch?v=0TtNJdXWkpo (Accessed December 29, 2017).

33. Durnford, Dana R. 2010. NEPTUNE Canada Was my Business Model Stolen by University of Victoria B.C." YouTube, 6:53, BeautifulGirlByDana. Available at https://www.youtube.com/watch?v=iKCGsphnmhc (Accessed December 29, 2017).

34. Regina, "Dana Ryan Durnford: Reasons for Judgement of The Honourable Judge R. Sutton."

10

In Whose Hands the Future?

STEPHAN LEWANDOWSKY

"Lewandowsky, Jew, Psychologist! Shut the fuck up you Nazi Zionist Kike!"
—From the author's inbox

Some scientific propositions are so well established and supported by so much rigorous evidence that they are legitimately referred to as fact. The late Stephen Jay Gould defined a fact as being "confirmed to such a degree that it would be perverse to withhold provisional assent."[1] The U.S. National Academy of Science declared it a "fact" that greenhouse gas emissions from human economic activities are altering the world's climate, with potentially severe adverse consequences on our global community.[2]

And yet, even though the existence of climate change and its anthropogenic origins are no longer debated in the relevant scientific community,[3] a well-organized and well-funded political operation has vociferously opposed both policies to mitigate the risk from climate change and the science underpinning the need to act.[4]

I became interested in climate change in 2009, when public "skepticism" appeared to increase dramatically in the lead-up to the United Nations Climate Change Conference in Copenhagen. I had just completed research about how people processed information relating to the invasion of Iraq in 2003.[5] Our research identified skepticism about the motives underlying the war as a key predictor of accuracy of information processing. People who were skeptical of the U.S. government's official reason for the invasion, namely to rid Iraq of weapons of mass destruction (WMDs), were found to be better able to reject false information and accept true information than others who accepted WMDs as the *casus belli*.

I therefore approached "climate skepticism" with more than an open eye—on the contrary, I expected the "skeptics" to be incisive and trenchant in their critique. It took very little time for me to realize, however, that climate "skepticism" had nothing to do with skepticism and everything to do with politics. I was particularly struck by the conspiratorial content of much "skeptic" discourse on the

Internet, with its abundant references to the United Nations, a World Government, and scientists being "in it to get their grants renewed to line their pockets" and so on. Now, if there is one thing I know, it is that scientists do not line their pockets with grant money.

Intrigued by this distortion of public discourse, I entered the fray by publishing an opinion piece on the website of the Australian Broadcasting Corporation (ABC), in which I argued that in scientific matters such as climate change, "the only balance that matters is the balance of evidence rather than of opinion" and that "balance in media coverage does not arise from adding a falsehood to the truth and dividing by two. Balanced media coverage of science requires recognition of the balance of evidence."[6] This piece attracted more than 2,000 comments and triggered a personal and professional trajectory that took me from studying the basics of human cognition via computer modeling to the center of the public and scientific fray surrounding climate change and climate denial.

The most gratifying consequence of this first opinion piece, and the response to it from within the Australian climate science community, is that I became interested in basic climate science and climate modeling. Much to my surprise I discovered that computational and mathematical models of cognition are not altogether dissimilar from models of the climate system. Scientists explore the brain and the planet with surprisingly similar statistical and computational techniques. My newfound scientific interest stimulated a fruitful and ongoing collaboration with climate scientists.[7]

An even more instructive, though at times not always gratifying, consequence of this first public contribution to the climate debate involved my introduction to the netherworld of climate denial and its often brutish, thuggish, and toxic manifestations.

This chapter tells that story.

Encountering the Silencers

The public debate about climate change rarely highlights the positives, known as co-benefits, that can arise out of tackling climate change by cutting greenhouse gas emissions. Extending people's lifespans by cutting pollution might seem to be an attractive proposition to most people. I made those points in another opinion piece for the ABC that compared the potential risks of climate mitigation with those of business as usual.[8] To my surprise, this piece was followed by what would turn out to be the first of by now almost innumerable complaints to my host institution at the time, the University of Western Australia (UWA). The details of the complaint are not known to me, although I understand that the complainant demanded that the university take out full-page ads in national and regional papers with an apology for my opinion because, in the complainant's view, as a cognitive scientist I was not entitled to comment on the risk trade-offs between climate mitigation and continued business as usual (the issues in my opinion piece were eventually discussed in two peer-reviewed papers[9]). The complaint was dismissed, but it set the stage for what can only be described as a campaign to silence or embarrass me over the years to come.

Early in 2011, out of the blue, I received an email from a person who called herself Alene Composta, which opened thus:

> Dear Prof Lewandowsky, We have never met, although we do share a background in the field of psychology, so I feel emboldened to ask for your professional advice. You see we have something in common: a passionate concern for averting the looming catastrophe of runaway climate change.
>
> I recently began blogging, especially about climate change, and after a month my site was noticed. Noticed by the wrong people, sadly. Readers of Tim Blair and Andrew Bolt [two Australian tabloid personalities] have swamped my site with genuinely abusive comments, many relating to my disability, which I find very hurtful.
>
> So my question to you is this: How do you deal with monsters like this?
> I have read and savoured every column you have published . . .
> I'm a fragile woman and I thought my blog, Verdant Hopes, might be a force for good in the world. Instead it has made me a victim once again.
> Any advice you could share would be appreciated.

I am no fan of hyperbole such as the "looming catastrophe of runaway climate change," and a visit to Alene's blog left me with mixed feelings. Nonetheless, because I had by then become familiar with the effects of hate speech, I replied:

> Yes, I know all about those abusive comments and it is brave for you to reveal as much personal detail as you do on your blog. Alas, for some people that is an invitation to rip into you and get a laugh out of that—they are like the school bullies whom no one really liked and who didn't really have close friends, only followers.
>
> I deal with those comments and actions largely by ignoring them. . . .
>
> As far as your blog is concerned, bear in mind that it is yours and that you can shut down any comment and run any moderation policy that you want. That still doesn't make it easier to receive those hateful utterances in the first place, but at least it gives you some sense of control to shut them down. Bear in mind that a proportion of those comments is orchestrated and for all we know there are only a handful of people with multiple electronic "personas" each, who are paid to create disproportionate noise.

The final sentence turned out to be particularly prescient, because a short while later the entire exchange appeared on the Internet and it transpired that "Alene" did not exist. She was a "sock puppet"; that is, an Internet persona created by persons unknown whose motives appeared a little different from "Alene's" intent to "be a force for good in the world." The publication of my exchange with "Alene" stimulated much hilarity among blog commenters about how anyone could be gullible enough to believe that a seemingly troubled and challenged person was actually a troubled and challenged person. By a further leap of logic, my "gullibility," in turn, was taken to disprove the science underlying climate change.

Intrigued by my exposure to some of the discourse and actions of people involved in climate denial, I conducted a survey of visitors to climate blogs in late 2010 that polled their attitudes to various scientific propositions such as climate change, and that also probed their political attitudes and their belief in various conspiracy theories such as "A powerful and secretive group known as the New World Order are planning to eventually rule the world. . . ". The in-press paper and data for this study became available for download in July–August 2012.[10] I thus refer to this paper as *LOG12* from here on.

In replication of much existing research, the survey identified political ideology—in particular, the extent of endorsement of laissez-faire free-market economics—as being the principal driver of the rejection of climate science.[11] Another but quantitatively less pronounced factor associated with the rejection of climate science involved the belief in various conspiracy theories. The more people endorsed the threat of a New World Order, or other conspiracies such as Princess Diana being assassinated by members of the British royal family, the less they were willing to accept the findings from climate science. This observed association meshes well with related findings by Smith and Leiserowitz, who found that among people who deny climate change, up to 40% of affective imagery invoked conspiracy theories.[12] That is, when asked to provide the first word, thought, or image that came to mind in the climate context, up to 40% of responses would be "the biggest scam in the world to date," "hoax," or similar. The association in our survey also meshes well with a body of prior research that has linked conspiracist ideation to the rejection of science and the acceptance of pseudoscience.[13] Moreover, the link between conspiracist ideation and rejection of science in LOG12 was eventually replicated by our team with a nationally representative sample of Americans.[14]

Although the results of LOG12 were unsurprising to anyone familiar with research on science denial, the impending publication of the paper was met with intense behind-the-scenes efforts to suppress its publication and to have me sanctioned by my university. The editor of the journal that published LOG12 was almost immediately approached with numerous complaints about the paper that eventually escalated into requests to retract the article. An early summary of those events was reported elsewhere,[15] although attempts to effect a retraction of LOG12 continued at least until late 2014. As noted by Sleek (2013), the critics were invited to submit a commentary for publication in the same journal (*Psychological Science*), but none acted on that invitation. Eventually, a critique of LOG12 and its companion paper (Lewandowsky, Gignac, & Oberauer, 2013) was published (Dixon & Jones, 2015), together with a rebuttal (Lewandowsky, Gignac, & Oberauer, 2015b), but I am not aware of those authors being involved in approaches to the editor when LOG12 first appeared.[16]

In an ironic twist, accusations of ethical impropriety were launched against me vis-a-vis the journal when a Freedom of Information (FOI) request revealed that LOG12 was conducted *with* ethics approval. The allegation, made by a blogger operating outside any accountability mechanisms, rested on the fact that ethics approval was granted expeditiously via amendment (as is routine practice for low-risk research). Another ethical complaint, launched nearly two years after publication of LOG12, invoked the fact that our consent forms did not advise participants that their data would be disregarded during analysis if they only partially completed the survey. Complaints about LOG12 were also made to the publisher of the journal, the Association for Psychological Science. It is my understanding that further complaints were addressed to various national or international bodies, although I am not privy to those details.

Over time, those contrarian activities expanded further in scope. I was eventually contacted by several journalists who had reported on the findings of LOG12 when it first appeared, and who had been approached by an individual demanding the retraction of their news stories because of alleged flaws in LOG12.

As these events unfolded, I learned through colleagues among climate scientists that those tactics of approaching editors with repeated complaints—which can cross the threshold into intimidation—are quite common. I eventually learned of seven journals across a number of disciplines whose editors had been approached (or bullied) in this manner.

Little did I know at the time that these events were just mild precursors of things to come.

In parallel to those approaches to the journal and publisher, numerous similar or identical complaints were launched with the University of Western Australia. None of those complaints were upheld. One open question is the extent to which these complaints were coordinated. In the case of tobacco research there is clear evidence that complaints about academics to their institutions are not random but highly organized.[17] In my case, I have no direct evidence for coordination although it is possible that those complaints were encouraged or at least facilitated by a blogger's public posting of the name and email address of the executive at UWA responsible for research integrity.

When I moved to the United Kingdom in 2013, my new host institution, the University of Bristol, welcomed my move by announcing that I was the recipient of a Wolfson Research Merit Award from the Royal Society. This triggered several complaints to the university (for having hired me), including harassing phone calls to administrative staff in the School of Psychology that necessitated managerial counseling. Some blog commenters suggested that I was "fleeing" Australia as a consequence of (unspecified) investigations.

Encountering Conspiracist Discourse

In addition to those behind-the-scenes events, LOG12 engendered considerable discursive activity on "skeptical" Internet blogs when it first appeared in 2012. After a few days with growing reverberations in the blogosphere, it became apparent to me that the public response to LOG12 might be relevant to the scholarly question regarding the involvement of conspiracist discourse in the rejection of science. Our team thus commenced a research project that analyzed this public blogosphere discourse.

We monitored the content of a number of prominent "climate skeptic" blogs (from here on, we refer to that as the *blogosphere* for short) and catalogued the hypotheses about LOG12 that were advanced during that discussion. We then classified each of those hypotheses according to criteria for conspiracist ideation that we extracted from the existing literature. At least ten such hypotheses were identified. To illustrate, the most frequently cited hypothesis was that the LOG12 responses were "scammed" by participants who "faked" their responses to deliver a "desired" outcome. This hypothesis took on increasingly elaborate forms over time and identified an increasing number of "faked" responses in the data. Without rigorous a priori specification of what constitutes faked responses, the scamming hypothesis is in principle unfalsifiable: there exists no response pattern that could not be considered fake by an innovative theorist. This potentially self-sealing reasoning constitutes one known attribute of conspiracist cognition.[18] Elements of the "scamming" hypothesis also exhibited a possible incoherence that is characteristic of conspiracist discourse, for example by referring to the data from LOG12 simultaneously as being "badly collected" and "totally invented."[19]

The second illustrative hypothesis focused on the statement in the Method section of LOG12, that "links [to the survey] were posted on 8 blogs (with a pro-science stance but with a diverse audience); a further 5 'skeptic' (or 'skeptic'-leaning) blogs were approached but none posted the link."[20] Speculation in the blogosphere focused on the identity of those 5 "skeptic" bloggers. Within short order, 25 "skeptical" bloggers went on record that they had not been approached by the LOG12 team. Five of those individuals were invited to post links by the LOG12 team in 2010, and two of them had engaged in correspondence with the LOG12 research assistant. One individual airing the suspicion that "skeptic" bloggers had not been contacted also provided the email address to which allegations of research misconduct could be directed at UWA. This individual had been contacted twice by the research team.

After the identity of the five bloggers became publicly known, the specific hypothesis that no "skeptic" bloggers were contacted faded from prominence, although transformed variants persisted in the blogosphere discourse. For example, the hypothesis that LOG12 sought to exclude "skeptics" from the survey persisted in the discourse even though the original basis for that inference had been shown to be invalid. This "self-sealing" persistence of contrary-to-fact claims constitute an acknowledged symptom of conspiracist cognition.[21]

The analysis of the blog-centered public response to LOG12 was published as a thematic analysis in the online open-access journal, *Frontiers in Psychology*.[22] The thematic analysis was supported by citations, including links to the blogs on which the material had been published, thereby rendering the source of those public statements identifiable. This article, entitled *Recursive fury: Conspiracist ideation in the blogosphere in response to research on conspiracist ideation* (*Recursive Fury* from here on) appeared to be the most-read article in psychology in that journal in an analysis conducted in late 2014, with approximately 65,000 page views and 10,000 downloads.[23]

Recursive Fury also received some media attention, including in the *New York Times*.[24]

Recursive Fury: Overview of Events

By now, I was expecting the publication of *Recursive Fury* to elicit complaints to UWA and to the journal. What I did not expect at the time were the intensity and number of those complaints. Ultimately we had to respond to dozens of complaints by a relatively small number of individuals that were registered with the journal.[25]

As a result of those complaints, the journal first temporarily removed access to the article (shortly after its publication) and then instituted an academic, ethical, and legal review of its status. About a year after its publication, *Recursive Fury* was retracted (in March 2014) for legal, but not academic or ethical, reasons. The publisher deemed the legal risk under British libel laws that was posed by a non-anonymized thematic analysis to be too great.[26] The following retraction statement, agreed and signed by solicitors of both parties, replaced the copy of the article on the journal's website:

> In the light of a small number of complaints received following publication of the original research article cited above, Frontiers carried out a detailed investigation of the academic, ethical and legal aspects of the work. This investigation did not identify any issues with the academic and ethical aspects of the study. It did, however, determine that the legal context is insufficiently clear and therefore Frontiers wishes to retract the published article. The authors understand this decision, while they stand by their article and regret the limitations on academic freedom which can be caused by legal factors.

The University of Western Australia, where the work for *Recursive Fury* was conducted, came to a different risk assessment *under Australian law* and posted a copy of *Recursive Fury* at a dedicated URL (http://uwa.edu.au/recursivefury). The copy carried an affirmation of the University of Western Australia's commitment to academic freedom on its title page. In connection with the posting of the article, the University of Western Australia's General Counsel, Kimberley Heitman, stated publicly: "I'm entirely comfortable with you publishing the paper on the UWA web site. You and the University can easily be sued for hurt feelings or confected outrage, and I'd be quite comfortable processing such a phony legal action."[27]

Recursive Fury was viewed and/or downloaded on the UWA website a further 13,000 times between March 2014 and July 2015. The University received no complaints or legal action in response to its public posting of *Recursive Fury* for over a year. In July 2015, a revised and greatly expanded version of the article was published in another peer-reviewed journal, at which point *Recursive Fury* ceased to exist.

Those various events deserve to be unpacked and presented in more detail. Figure 10.1 provides an overview of the various papers involved in this story and explains their relationship.

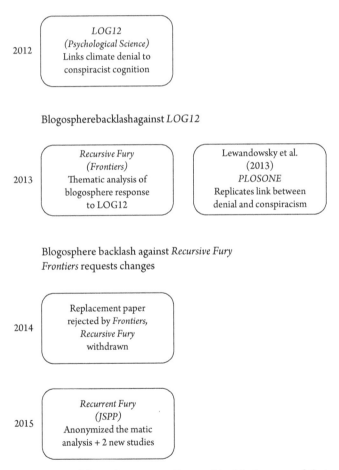

Figure 10.1. Overview of the various papers discussed in this chapter and their relationship, and an approximate timeline.

Because much of the affair involves confidential material, everything that follows is exclusively based on information that already entered the public record in 2014. This includes material that was obtained by illegal means (viz., a hacking attack on a website) but then became public through the actions of others. Because it is largely based on the existing public record, the story must remain incomplete, although I am confident that the following sections capture the essence of events.

The Complaints against *Recursive Fury*

The complaints were confidential, and I no longer have access to them as they were destroyed on legal instruction. However, it is a matter of public record that the complaints centered on the fact that our thematic analysis was supported by citation (via web links). This permitted identification of any individual who chose to make public statements using their own name and that were picked up by our search. Complainants considered this to constitute an ethical violation because we did not seek their consent before commenting on their public statement. Complainants also felt defamed by our analysis of their comments, arguing that this constituted "malice" on the part of the authors.

It is illustrative to examine how the case for "malice" on our part was constructed. This became possible because an investigative journalist used FOI to access some of the relevant documentation.[28] I explored the implications of this as follows:

> In the present context, it is most relevant that the accusations of malice against John Cook, one of the authors of Recursive Fury, were based on his apparent sanctioning of 'vile commentary' against the complainant and other bloggers.
>
> Indeed, the material cited in support contains irate statements that none of the authors of Recursive Fury would countenance.
>
> None of the authors made those statements.
>
> One will fail to find anything like those comments on Cook's blog, www.skepticalscience.com: None of the more than 88,000 public comments posted there to date contain anything that could be remotely construed as vitriolic or polemical—that's because 7000 comments were deleted by moderators owing to their inflammatory content.
>
> So where did the 'vile commentary' come from and how did John Cook 'sanction' it?
>
> The vile commentary was made by third parties unconnected to Recursive Fury on a private forum that was password-protected, and whose purpose was to permit open and completely uncensored discussion among a small group of collaborators. Those comments were posted in the

expectation of privacy, and they became public only through a criminal act—a hack attack on Skepticalscience . . . .

John Cook neither wrote those comments, nor could he be reasonably expected to moderate them. They were made in private and became public by an illegal act by parties unknown.

What John did was to host a private forum on which other people vented their anger. If that is malice, then so would be inopportune comments by your friends at an illegally wire-tapped dinner party. You better censor what your guests say in case your next party is bugged, lest you be accused of malice.

The complainant's conduct follows a common pattern in the Subterranean War on Science: Use of private correspondence obtained by an illegal act to construct allegations against scientists. Except that in this case, to allege malice against John Cook, hackers trolled through two years of his private conversations and found exactly nothing.

Zip. Zilch. Bupkis.

All the hackers and trolls could find were other parties expressing anger in the expectation of privacy. I cannot think of clearer evidence for the absence of malice in John Cook's conduct.

I nonetheless think there might be evidence of malice here.

Maybe some readers can spot it.[29]

My post concluded with the following question about the issue of privacy and public statements:

Are public statements by people who knowingly made them in public, subject to scholarly analysis? Or is it only stolen correspondence by third parties made in the expectation of privacy that can be used to allege malice on the part of someone who never said anything malicious himself?[30]

These questions continue to be worthy of exploration. It turns out that a panel of experts was able to shed some light on the question at the time.

The Expert Panel

In response to the complaints against *Recursive Fury*, the journal convened an independent panel of experts (I do not know their identity) to evaluate the scientific and ethical integrity of the article. This report was critical of our work but ultimately advised against a retraction of the article on academic or ethical grounds.

The report remains confidential, but one important excerpt concerning the issue of whether public statements can be used for scholarly analysis without anyone's consent became public under legal guidance:

> The question of participant status is an important and complex one. It turns on the question of whether an individual's (identifiable or not) postings to blogs comprise public information and therefore do not fall under the constraints typically imposed by ethics review boards. The issue is currently under debate among researchers and publishers dealing with textual material used in scientific research. Advice was sought from the leading researcher on web-based psychological studies and his response was that 'among psychological and linguistic researchers blog posts are regarded as public data and the individuals posting the data are not regarded as participants in the technical sense used by Research Ethics Committees or Institutional Review Boards. This further entails that no consent is required for the use of such data.' Although this view is held by many researchers and their ethics boards, it is by no means a unanimous judgment and it is to be expected that legitimate challenges, both on ethical and legal grounds, will be raised as web-based research expands in scope. But to the charges that Fury was unethical in using blog posts as data for psychological analysis, the consensus among experts in this area sides with the authors of Fury.[31]

My view on this issue is that scholarly analysis of public speech is an essential scientific and public good. The idea that it would not be permissible, say, to analyze the meaning and implications of President Trump's tweets without his consent is incompatible with democracy.[32] Indeed, if taken to an extreme, the complaints against using citations in *Recursive Fury* without the author's consent would imply that no citation in a peer-reviewed article could ever occur without seeking consent of the to-be-cited party, clearly an absurd proposition.[33] In my view, public speech by actors who seek publicity—and who could choose to remain anonymous by using a pseudonym—is a public good that must be open for scholarly analysis.

That said, there are legal implications associated with interpreting and commenting on public speech. As I already noted, those played a major role in the events surrounding *Recursive Fury*.

The Legal Angle and the Replacement Paper

Having been informed by the journal that on the basis of their expert panel *Recursive Fury* would not be retracted for ethical or academic reasons, the journal indicated that changes would have to be made to the paper in order to safeguard against the legal risk of defamation. I agreed to this process, based on our own legal advice based on U.K. law, which supported the journal's position even though no such risk had been identified by the General Counsel of UWA under Australian law. Events then unfolded as follows.

On August 28, 2013, I was informed by *Frontiers* that their analysis of the defamation risk—under English libel laws—had found the risk to be too great for the journal to carry the article, and that it would have to be retracted. This decision was accompanied by an invitation to submit a replacement article that dealt with the issues identified in the various reviews and assessments.

We submitted a replacement article on January 1, 2014, by which time English libel laws had changed significantly.[34]

This replacement article was prepared using a legal guidance document provided by the journal which requested that the thematic analysis be de-identified. We therefore anonymized the thematic analysis by paraphrasing verbatim public statements until they no longer yielded hits in Google. We also added two behavioral studies involving blind and naïve participants to buttress our thematic analysis. The new paper also included two additional authors, who were not associated with LOG12 and who independently confirmed the thematic analysis.

Frontiers rejected this replacement paper, arguing that it failed to deal adequately with the defamation issue. Our (English) legal advice at the time stated that defamation cannot arise if individuals cannot be identified in the minds of a "reasonable reader." My view, and that of my solicitor, was that if authors of public statements cannot be identified via Google on the basis of paraphrasing, then no "reasonable reader" could infer their identity.

The journal came to a different risk assessment and *Recursive Fury* was retracted.

The Fury after the Fury

The withdrawal of *Recursive Fury* engendered a number of notable and sometimes surprising events.

In response to the retraction, three editors of the journal publicly resigned in protest. A fourth editor provided a detailed critique of the journal's actions.[35]

The Australian Psychological Society issued a statement that expressed "dismay" at the withdrawal of *Recursive Fury*, stating that "this situation is greatly concerning on a number of fronts." The Australian Psychological Society also congratulated UWA for its decision to host *Recursive Fury* on their website. A similar public position was taken by the (American) Union of Concerned Scientists.[36] An NGO (*Forecast the Facts*) launched a petition calling for the reinstatement of *Recursive Fury* that attracted nearly 2,000 signatures.

At the other end of the spectrum, an anonymous team calling itself "NotStephan Lewandowsky" produced a YouTube parody of the events surrounding *Recursive Fury* by subtitling the "rant in the bunker" scene from the movie *Downfall* (starring Bruno Ganz as Hitler/subtitled as Lewandowsky).[37]

The retraction also found much echo in the global media.[38] To illustrate, one article cited *Frontiers*'s solicitor as stating that "Frontiers is concerned about solid science and it's obviously a regret when you have to retract an article that is scientifically and ethically sound." The tenor across many articles was one of the journal having "caved in" to climate deniers by retracting *Recursive Fury*. For example, one article that ran in the *Sydney Morning Herald* (one of Australia's largest broadsheets) quoted UWA's General Counsel:

> Kem Heitman, a lawyer for the UWA, said the university had done its own risk analysis before publishing the paper online. "There's no reason to take it down," Mr. Heitman said.
>
> The university had also received complaints from some groups. "It's quite relentless," he said.
>
> "There's always a close interest in everything that Steve (Lewandowsky) does," Mr. Heitman said. "We are conscious that we are going to be targeted by people opposed to his works."
>
> The university, though, had also received plaudits from around the world for its decision to publish the paper.
>
> "I couldn't list them," Mr. Heitman said. "And I wouldn't list them, having regard to the fact that anyone who issues a 'thanks UWA' will probably get their own enquiry."[39]

The same article went on to quote one of the reviewers of Recursive Fury, Elaine McKeown, as stating that the journal had been "spineless":

> "They caved in at the first pushback from the climate denial community," Ms. McKewon said. "To retract a paper is just the most extreme action that a journal can take, and it was thoroughly unwarranted in this decision," she said. "It was really quite breathtaking."

This reviewer also published an opinion piece in *Scientific American* that related her experiences:

> In any event, the journal's management and editors were clearly intimidated by climate deniers who threatened to sue. So Frontiers bowed to their demands, retracted the paper, damaged its own reputation, and ultimately gave a free kick to aggressive climate deniers.

I would have expected a scientific journal to have more backbone, certainly when it comes to the crucially important issue of academic freedom.[40]

The fury after the retraction might have ended there. Unfortunately it did not. Citing the intense media coverage, the journal issued a follow-up statement which, for the first time, alluded to ethical problems by stating: "Frontiers came to the conclusion that it could not continue to carry the paper, *which does not sufficiently protect the rights of the studied subjects*" [emphasis added].[41] This second statement also claimed that the journal had received no legal threats, and that our replacement paper had failed to conform to their instructions. I responded:

> Throughout the entire period . . . the only concern voiced by Frontiers related to the presumed defamation risk under English libel laws. While the University of Western Australia offered to host the retracted paper . . . because it did not share those legal concerns, Frontiers rejected an anonymized replacement paper on the basis that non-identifiable parties might feel defamed.
>
> No other cause was ever offered or discussed by Frontiers to justify the retraction of Recursive Fury. We are not aware of a single mention of the claim that our study "did not sufficiently protect the rights of the studied subjects" by Frontiers throughout the past year, although we are aware of their repeated explicit statements, in private and public, that the study was ethically sound.[42]

The journal's editor issued several further statements that expanded on the presumed ethical problems, culminating in the claim, "But there was no moral dilemma from the start—we do not support scientific publications where human subjects can be identified without their consent."[43] This claim appears to be irreconcilable with the initial retraction statement, signed by the solicitors of the journal and the authors, that the journal ". . . did not identify any issues with the academic and ethical aspects of the study." It also cannot be reconciled with the journal's own expert panel, cited earlier.

Those evolving discrepancies between the journal's various positions cannot be explained by outsiders. However, it can be noted that one of *Fury*'s reviewers wrote an opinion piece in direct response to the journal's increasingly divergent statements, which explained the issue in detail:

> As a reviewer, I was privy to some of the earliest threats sent to the journal following the paper's publication. Email exchanges between the journal's management, legal counsel and editors and reviewers clearly demonstrate that the journal received threats and responded to them as threats . . .

This email exchange culminated in a conference call to enable the journal's manager, legal counsel, editors and reviewers to discuss how the journal should proceed. Let me be perfectly clear: the very reason the journal convened the conference call was to deal with threats that had been received from climate denialists.[44]

The reviewer's public comments are consonant with testimony on Twitter and on blogs, in which some of the actors openly bragged about how much time and effort they expended talking to editors on the phone, and in which some other actors clarified that they *had* threatened the journal with legal action.

Restoring *Recurrent Fury*

In 2015, our team published an article entitled *Recurrent Fury: Conspiratorial Discourse in the Blogosphere Triggered by Research on the Role of Conspiracist Ideation in Climate Denial* (*Recurrent Fury* from here on).[45] Except for changes made in response to (double-blind) peer review, this article was materially identical to the intended replacement paper for *Recursive Fury* that was submitted to *Frontiers* in response to their guidance document.

This article reported three studies that, again, examined the discourse in the "climate skeptic" blogosphere in response to the publication of LOG12. The first study consisted of the thematic analysis that was the core component of *Recursive Fury*, albeit now anonymized and with paraphrasing of quotations to eliminate any legal risks. The second and third study were new and served the important purpose to provide independent and blind tests of our thematic analysis. The second study showed that when naïve judges (i.e., people who were not conversant with any of the issues and were blind to the purpose of the study) were asked to analyze the blogosphere content material, they reproduced the structure of hypotheses uncovered in our thematic analysis.

In the final study, naïve participants were presented with a sample of anonymized blogosphere content and rated it on various attributes that are typical of conspiracist discourse.[46] For each of several hundred such content items, participants were asked to respond to the following test items: "To what extent does the commenter believe that the scientists acted with questionable motives?" (Questionable Motives in Figure 10.2); "To what extent does the commenter express deep-seated suspicion?" (Suspicion); "To what extent does the commenter perceive himself/herself as a victim of scientists or research?" (Victim); "To what extent does the commenter firmly believe that there must be something wrong with the research?" (Something Must Be Wrong); "To what extent does the commenter offer a reasonable and well thought out criticism of the research?" (Reasonable Critique).

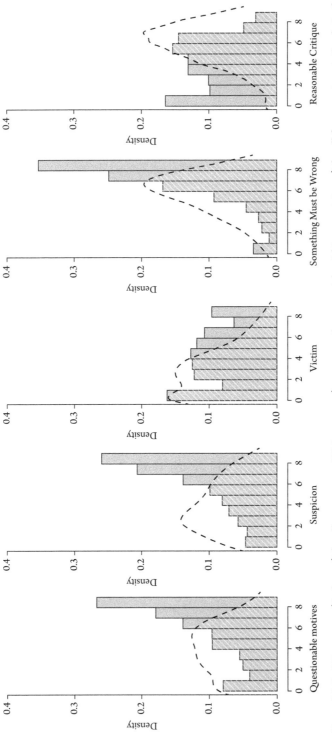

Figure 10.2. Histograms (dark gray) for all responses to Web content (not averaged across trials within a participant) for all five questions in Study 3 of Lewandowsky, Cook, et al., 2015. The dashed line that encloses the crosshatched area represents Gaussian kernel density estimates (using 1.5 times the standard bandwidth) of the equivalent responses to PhD-generated content. See text for details. (Figure reprinted with permission.)

For comparison, the study also included material written by junior scholars (PhD students) who were instructed to be as critical as possible of LOG12. The PhD-generated content was randomly interspersed with blogosphere content in the sequence of trials for each participant. The results of this study are shown in Figure 10.2.

It is apparent that the ratings for blogosphere content (histograms) were skewed toward the high end of the various conspiracist attributes. To illustrate, for "something must be wrong" and "suspicion" the *modal* response was a 10 on a 10-point scale. The only attribute of blogosphere discourse that deviated from this pattern was the "reasonable and well thought out criticism of the research" criterion, where the modal response instead was zero.

It is illuminating that the reverse pattern occurred with the PhD-generated material. In confirmation of their task to generate content that was as critical as possible of LOG12, the material generated by PhD scores was rated highly on the "reasonable and well thought out criticism" attribute. By contrast, it scored low or toward the center of the scale for the remaining conspiracist attributes.

Notably, these results (Figure 10.2) were obtained with anonymized material that was presented with no guiding context, to participants who knew nothing about the issue under consideration. The results clarify that the blogosphere's activities relating to LOG12 failed to contribute any discernible scholarship or identifiable reasonable critique.[47] The public stance of "skeptics" is that they contribute an important alternative perspective and significant scientific critique of actual climate science—and also LOG12. But the results of the third study (Figure 10.2) showed that their critiques were not considered, by blinded and naïve participants, to contribute anything to the scientific context or investigation.

This may be a good moment to invite the reader to guess about the likely course of events in response to publication of *Recurrent Fury*. At the institutional level, the paper triggered complaints and claims of ethical violations, this time to the University of Bristol rather than UWA. The complaints were not upheld.

In parallel, the journal was again approached by multiple parties with complaints and allegations. The nature of those approaches by one particularly persistent individual were characterized by the handling editor as follows:

> I received 4 e-mails from him recently (long and convoluted ones though, with many additional documents) . . . He called my department once or twice and told them to have me call him back, and he called my office number as well a few times . . .
>
> I felt somewhat bothered by this as I had stated a few times that we don't see any problems with the article and its ethics and referred him to submit his complaints or a critical review elsewhere (or as a scholarly commentary to the journal) but he continued to email more and more

detailed arguments. I haven't had any such reaction to articles before. And yes, I also *haven't experienced such persistence in reaction to my own work on contested issues including the Armenian genocide denial, Holocaust denial, the Israeli – Palestinian conflict, and the Rwandan genocide* [emphasis added]. I received a few individual emails by participants or readers, but never any follow up after that . . .

No commentary has been submitted by anyone to the journal for peer review. To the best of my knowledge, no efforts are currently underway to suppress LOG12 or *Recurrent Fury*. The reader is invited to speculate about what responses the present chapter might elicit.

Consequences of Conspiratorial Denial of Science

Because of the complexity of events, I briefly summarize the sequence of events that comprise the *Fury* affair (see Figure 10.1). *Recursive Fury* was published in the open-access journal *Frontiers* in 2013 and immediately became the target of complaints and legal threats, while also becoming one of the most widely read publications in the journal. Eventually, as clarified in an agreement signed by solicitors of all parties involved, *Recursive Fury* was retracted by *Frontiers* because of legal concerns but not for academic or ethical reasons. An exact copy of *Recursive Fury*, which differed from the originally published version only by an affirmation of the University of Western Australia's commitment to academic freedom, was then posted on the UWA website for approximately a year. During that time it received a further 13,000 downloads. An anonymized and expanded paper that *Frontiers* had also deemed to be unsuitable for publication appeared after double-blind peer review in the open-access *Journal of Social and Political Psychology* in 2015. This new paper, *Recurrent Fury*, has by now been downloaded nearly 17,000 times, and the journal's editor declined to indulge in attempts to suppress the paper. Throughout this three-year affair, UWA and the University of Bristol, my two host institutions during this period, received numerous complaints, none of which were upheld. At no time did anyone involved in the campaign against me and the two *Furies* submit anything for peer review to any journal. At no time was any legal action taken against a university or journal involved.

What are the consequences of the events just described? What are the effects of such insertions by external parties into the scientific process? I differentiate between the personal consequences I experienced, those that affect the scientific community in general, and the effects at an institutional level.

At a personal level, my initial feeling about the blogosphere response to LOG12, and the events leading up it, was a sense of puzzled bemusement. Engaging in a conversation with a non-existent "sock puppet" seemed bizarre (and creepy) at the time, but those feelings were tinged with the recognition that the event entailed a component of juvenile humor.[48] Similarly, receiving a Facebook friend invitation from an unknown person who tried to impersonate a well-known climate scientist was creepy but seemed harmless at the time. Thus, when 25 bloggers claimed not to have been contacted by the LOG12 team to post a link to a survey, although five of them had been contacted (including two who engaged in correspondence), I saw some humor in this situation. In consequence, some blog posts I wrote at the time reflected this bemusement because I infused them with what I considered to be a humorous touch. I now regret having taken that stance, because I soon realized that there was nothing funny about the toxicity of denial. I had underestimated the brutality and thuggishness with which some individuals were to try to silence me and discredit my work for several years to come. To illustrate, one individual alone issued nearly 400 tweets that defamed me or disparaged my work during the three years in question, or about one every 72 hours. This is not counting a further 150 or so tweets by the same individual that related to *Recursive Fury*.

I have nonetheless, until recently, continued to try and engage in conversation with adversaries when circumstances appeared benign. To date, none of those attempts have been successful. To illustrate, when I received an email some years ago from an avowed "skeptic" that suggested "we open a private dialogue with the intention of trying to better understand each other," I engaged by responding to the correspondent's specific question with hints to the relevant literature. This was initially appreciated ("thanks that does look relevant"), and I was prepared to continue the conversation, notwithstanding my original misgivings. However, this constructive turn was soon followed by another email that stated "I had hoped to work toward a better understanding between us . . . it is clear to me that you have not adhered to the proper ethics of academia and science." A few days later, the correspondent put this comment on his blog: "Lewandowsky is paid by big oil and conspires to make deniers fearful of suggesting that there is a conspiracy so we dare not mention this conspiracy to make us think there is an-other conspiracy to make us miss the real conspiracy that's absent" (paraphrased slightly). This type of exchange is no isolated incident. I have been involved in several such abortive conversations over the years, and many climate scientists have reported similar experiences. For example, Eric Steig ruefully noted that "many of my colleagues warned me many times not to trust the good intentions of . . . [names of individuals also involved in the attack on LOG12]. I have ignored them, evidently to my peril."[49]

Now, five years after LOG12 first became available, I believe that I have achieved a resolution between a number of conflicting emotions. On the negative side, I regret having been forced to revise my formerly rather unrefined views about human nature and political behaviors. I also find that it takes continued effort not to become cynical about the state of our societies, which to date have permitted a small number of political operatives and bloggers who are accountable to no one to prevent meaningful climate policies aimed at preserving civilization for future generations.

On the more positive side, I feel more resilient and determined than ever before to continue my work in cognitive science and climate science. There is now mounting evidence that climate denial involves a conspiratorial component that differs from conventional coherent cognition.[50] This is not only of scholarly relevance, but it is also crucial for the public to understand who is opposing the scientific consensus and why, and how that opposition is using misleading rhetoric.[51] Finally, above all, I feel a deep gratitude to the numerous colleagues who have experienced similar attacks on their work and who were thus able to provide support and understanding throughout. The vast majority of people in academia and beyond live their lives without being targeted by hate campaigns, and for them the effects of such campaigns are perhaps difficult to understand.

However, no one is safe from becoming a target of vilification and hatred. In the United Kingdom, a feminist journalist and blogger who (successfully) campaigned to have a woman featured on a new British banknote—with a picture of Jane Austen—became inundated with hateful messages on social media, including threats of mutilation, beatings, and worse. Two individuals ultimately faced criminal convictions over those threats.[52] Who would have thought, ahead of time, that the simple proposal to put a woman on a U.K. banknote would elicit this much abuse and hatred? The fact that no one is safe from hate campaigns renders the resilience of relevant institutions and communities all the more important. This resilience is, however, sometimes lacking or compromised.

At the level of the scientific community overall, there is little doubt that pressure from the tobacco industry has affected the course of medical research, if only by consuming massive amounts of scientists' time that could otherwise have been devoted to research.[53] The tobacco industry's activities also delayed the translation of medical research into interventions and policies that could have saved lives by reducing smoking rates.[54]

There is also a growing body of literature which suggests that the aggressive efforts by climate deniers have adversely affected the communication and direction of climate research.[55] To illustrate, I argued in a recent paper with colleagues that the public and subterranean activities of organized climate denial have "seeped" into the scientific community.[56] Climate scientists have done an admirable job pursuing their science under great political pressure, and they have tirelessly rebutted pseudoscientific arguments against their work. Nonetheless, being human, scientists operate with the same cognitive apparatus and limitations as every other person. In consequence, scientists may take public positions that they would be less likely to take in the absence of outspoken public opposition. Thus, when scientists are repeatedly stereotyped in public as "alarmists," a predicted response would be for them to try to avoid seeming alarmist by downplaying the degree of threat from climate change.

Finally, at the institutional and political level, the consequences of these contrarian activities were perhaps best summarized by Robert Manne, one of Australia's leading public intellectuals, as:

> trying to wound a supposed enemy by exploiting the rules governing liberal institutions, like universities and academic journals, with a blizzard of bewildering and remorseless distortions, pedantry and pettifoggery that is almost impossible for normal people to follow let alone judge fairly.

I encountered the effects of such pedantry and pettifoggery on institutions and journals throughout. The sheer volume of information generated online or in complaints, much of it banal or trivial, made it impossible for most of the people involved—including important decision makers—to keep track of events. To illustrate, one FOI request that I had to respond to at UWA was for "a printout of the web server log or the blog database showing the precise time (hours and minutes) and date of publishing; and the relevant time zone to which each time refers, in relation to each of the following posts [list of posts]." (It might be worth recalling that this FOI request was part of a campaign to discredit research that had identified conspiracist discourse as a component of climate denial.)

In addition to creating a blizzard of confusion that blurred the distinction between reality and accusation, and between substantive issues and pedantry, the constant drumbeat of accusations of "bias" and "activism" against me and my colleagues had subtle but pernicious consequences. It became apparent to me that for some decision makers in this affair, scientific expertise ultimately became conflated with "bias" or "activism." I recall conversations in which expert opinion was quickly dismissed with a phrase such as "but he is a climate scientist," and I experienced conversations in which my presumed antagonism toward climate denial was cited as a troubling issue. If such antagonism were a disqualifying attribute, then no law-abiding citizens could be criminologists because they would presumably have some sense of "antagonism" toward criminals. To my knowledge, no such scrutiny was applied by decision makers to the motivations of the (non-expert) complainants, some of whom have a long track record of politically motivated climate denial. I also do not recall too many mentions of academic freedom by anyone throughout this affair, even though the events described here go to the heart of academic freedom and freedom of expression.

I am not the only person to be concerned by those pernicious consequences of persistent politically motivated attacks on scientists. Climate scientist Eric Steig noted a similar problem:

> But you know what has given me the most pause? The fact that a number of my colleagues and many otherwise intelligent-seeming people

still seem to treat these guys [referring to individuals also involved in the attacks on LOG12 and *Recursive Fury*] as legitimate, honest commenters, . . . To those that still don't get this—and who continue to believe that these people can be trusted to present there scientific results honestly, and who continue to speculate that their may be truth in the allegations made over the years against [climate scientists] Mike Mann, Ben Santer, Phil Jones, Stephen Schneider, Andrew Weaver, Kevin Trenberth, Keith Briffa, Gavin Schmidt, Darrell Kaufmann, and many many others, just because they 'read it on a blog somewhere'—I'd be happy to share with you some of the more, err, 'colorful', emails I've gotten from [name] and his coauthors.

If you still don't get it, then I have a suggestion for a classic short story you should read. It's called, *The Lottery*, by Shirley Jackson.[57]

Likewise, owing to the same drumbeat of accusations and relentless approaches, it occasionally appeared to become difficult for decision makers to differentiate between offense and true injury. I was repeatedly admonished that I "offended a lot of people" (actually only a few dozen out of tens of thousands of readers), as if that by itself implied wrongdoing or cause for concern. The French satirical magazine *Charlie Hebdo* routinely causes offense, perhaps preferentially among Muslims, but their right to do so is a cornerstone of Western democracy. Evolutionary biologists routinely offend Christian fundamentalists, but that does not invalidate the fact that humans evolved. Likewise, if people are offended by my work on climate denial, this neither changes the results of my research (e.g., in Figure 10.2) nor its importance for the public who is being misled on what is arguably the most important issue facing civilization in the 21st century.[58]

The triage between confected outrage, pedantry, and vexatious complaints on the one hand, and legitimate grievances and public engagement in science on the other, currently consumes considerable public funds. The development of appropriate institutional procedures and recognition of the consequences of complaints must therefore continue to attract research attention.[59] Particularly relevant here is the small but growing scientific literature on querulous complainants.[60] More research on these issues is urgently needed, as are improved procedures to safeguard scientists from attacks while upholding the public's right to transparency.

Concluding Remarks

Science denial can kill. When denial becomes official government policy, the death toll can run in the hundreds of thousands, as in the case of South Africa under President Mbeki.[61] Mbeki's government refused to accept antiretroviral drugs to contain the AIDS epidemic, preferring instead to treat AIDS with garlic and beetroot. It has been estimated that more than 330,000 lives (or approximately 2.2 million person years) were needlessly lost because the South African government ignored consensus scientific opinion.[62] In the West, similar statistics can be cited in connection with depressed immunization rates arising from the activities of anti-vaccine movements.[63] And high-end estimates of the consequences of unmitigated climate change cite the possibility that 187 million people may be forcibly displaced globally, corresponding to more than 2% of the world's population.[64]

In light of the sometimes lethal track record of science denial, one might expect opprobrium to be reserved for those who deny or interfere with the public's right to be adequately informed about risks such as AIDS or climate change. Paradoxically, however, it appears to be scientists whose research aims to inform the public of such risks who have been targeted, in public and behind closed doors, in the manner just described. I know of numerous colleagues who have been subjected to similar treatment, but I know of no instance in which bloggers or political operatives who engage in such activities have been held accountable.

What are we to do? What can we do to render science more transparent while keeping it resilient?[65] On an earlier occasion I suggested:

> As in most cases of intimidation and bullying, we believe that daylight is the best disinfectant . . . Knowledge of the common techniques by which scientists are attacked, irrespective of their discipline and research area, is essential so that institutions can support their academics against attempts to thwart their academic freedom. This information is also essential to enable lawmakers to improve the balance between academic freedom and confidentiality of peer review on the one hand, and the public's right to access information on the other. Finally, this knowledge is particularly important for journal editors and professional organizations to muster the required resilience against illegitimate insertions into the scientific process.[66]

At the time of this writing, those recommendations stand, although they may have lost some of their impact in light of the current state of public discourse in the United States and United Kingdom. The words *post-truth* and *post-fact*, virtually unheard of before 2015, have exploded onto the media scene during the past 18 months. The concern that truth, evidence, and facts have lost traction in public discourse was amplified by independent fact checkers in 2016, who judged 70% of all statements made by Donald Trump on the campaign trail to be false or mostly false. Notably, Trump has referred to climate change as a "hoax" invented by the Chinese, and at the time of this writing, President Trump has announced the withdrawal of the United States from the Paris agreement on climate change. And his administration is suffused with people who deny climate change, to the point where Secretary of Energy Rick Perry's staff announced that he is "winning" his fight with climate scientists.[67] The "post-truth world" and the "politics of debasement," in which politicians celebrate their "win" over scientists rather than use science to design evidence-based policies, are in full swing at the time of this writing, to the point where scholars are expressing concern about the future of democracy in America.[68]

Daylight is still the best disinfectant, but at the time of this writing it must shine into increasingly darker places.[69]

Notes

1. Cited in Gregory, T. Ryan. 2008. "Evolution as Fact, Theory, and Path." *Evolution: Education and Outreach* 1(1): 46–52. DOI: 10.1007/s12052-007-0001-z.

2. National Academies of Science. 2010. *Advancing the Science of Climate Change*. Washington, D.C.: The National Academies Press.

3. Cook, John, Dana Nuccitelli, Sarah A. Green, Mark Richardson, Bärbel Winkler, Rob Painting, Robert Way, Peter Jacobs, and Andrew Skuce. 2013. "Quantifying the Consensus on Anthropogenic Global Warming in the Scientific Literature." *Environmental Research Letters* 8(2): 024024; Shwed, Uri and Peter S. Bearman. 2010. "The Temporal Structure of Scientific Consensus Formation." *American Sociological Review* 75(6): 817–840. DOI: 10.1177/0003122410388488.

4. Brulle, Robert J. 2014. "Institutionalizing Delay: Foundation Funding and the Creation of U.S. Climate Change Counter-Movement Organizations." *Climatic Change* 122(4): 681–694. DOI: 10.1007/s10584-013-1018-7; Oreskes, Naomi and Erik M Conway. 2010. *Merchants of Doubt*. London: Bloomsbury Publishing.

5. Lewandowsky, Stephan, Werner G. K. Stritzke, Klaus Oberauer, and Michael Morales. 2009. "Misinformation and the "War on Terror": When Memory Turns Fiction into Fact." In *Terrorism and Torture: An Interdisciplinary Perspective*, eds. Werner G. K. Stritzke, Stephan Lewandowsky, David Denemark, and Joseph Clare. Cambridge: Cambridge University Press, 179–203; Lewandowsky, Stephan, Werner G. K. Stritzke, Klaus Oberauer, and Michael Morales. 2005. "Memory for Fact, Fiction, and Misinformation: The Iraq War 2003." *Psychological Science* 16(3): 190–195. DOI:10.1111/j.0956-7976.2005.00802.x.

6. Lewandowsky, Stephan. 2010a. "Climate Debate: Opinion vs. Evidence." http://www.abc.net.au/news/2010-03-11/33178 (Accessed December 24, 2017).

7. Lewandowsky, Stephan, Mark C. Freeman, and Michael E. Mann. 2017. "Harnessing the Uncertainty Monster: Putting Quantitative Constraints on the Intergenerational Social Discount Rate." *Global and Planetary Change* 156(C): 155–166. DOI: 10.1016/j.gloplacha.2017.03.007; Lewandowsky, Stephan, Naomi Oreskes, James S. Risbey, Ben R. Newell, and Michael Smithson. 2015. "Seepage: Climate Change Denial and Its Effect on the Scientific Community." *Global Environmental Change* 33(July):1–13. DOI: 10.1016/j.gloenvcha.2015.02.013; Lewandowsky, Stephan, James S. Risbey, Michael Smithson, Ben R. Newell, and John Hunter. 2014. "Scientific Uncertainty and Climate Change: Part I. Uncertainty and Unabated Emissions." *Climatic Change* 124(1–2): 21–37. DOI: 10.1007/s10584-014-1082-7; Lewandowsky, Stephan, James S. Risbey, Michael Smithson, Ben R. Newell, and John Hunter. 2014. "Scientific Uncertainty and Climate Change: Part II. Uncertainty and Mitigation." *Climatic Change* 124(1–2): 39–52. DOI: 10.1007/s10584-014-1083-6; Lewandowsky, Stephan, James S. Risbey, and Naomi Oreskes. 2015. "On the Definition and Identifiability of the Alleged "Hiatus" in Global Warming." 5(November): 16784. DOI: 10.1038/srep16784; Lewandowsky, Stephan, James S. Risbey, and Naomi Oreskes 2016. "The "Pause" in Global Warming: Turning a Routine Fluctuation into a Problem for Science." *Bulletin of the American Meteorological Society* 97(5): 723–733. DOI: 10.1175/bams-d-14-00106.1; Risbey, James S., and Stephan Lewandowsky. 2017. "Climate Science: The

'Pause' Unpacked." *Nature* 545(7652): 37–39. DOI: 10.1038/545037a; Risbey, James S., Stephan Lewandowsky, John R. Hunter, and Didier P. Monselesan. 2015. "Betting Strategies on Fluctuations in the Transient Response of Greenhouse Warming." *Philosophical Transactions of the Royal Society A: Mathematical, Physical and Engineering Sciences* 373(2055). DOI:10.1098/rsta.2014.0463; Risbey, James S., Stephan Lewandowsky, Clothilde Langlais, Didier P. Monselesan, Terence J. O'Kane, and Naomi Oreskes. 2014. "Well-Estimated Global Surface Warming in Climate Projections Selected for Enso Phase." *Nature Climate Change* 4(9): 835–840. DOI:10.1038/nclimate2310.

8. Lewandowsky, Stephan. 2010b. "No Climate Change Alternatives." http://www.abc.net.au/news/2010-08-12/35848 (Accessed December 24, 2017).

9. Lewandowsky, Risbey, Smithson, Newell, and Hunter, "Scientific Uncertainty and Climate Change: Part I"; Lewandowsky, Risbey, Smithson, Newell, and Hunter, "Scientific Uncertainty and Climate Change: Part II."

10. Lewandowsky, Stephan, Klaus Oberauer, and Gilles E. Gignac. 2013. "NASA Faked the Moon Landing—Therefore (Climate) Science Is a Hoax: An Anatomy of the Motivated Rejection of Science." *Psychological Science* 24(5): 622–633.

11. For example, see Heath, Yuko, and Robert Gifford. 2006. "Free-Market Ideology and Environmental Degradation:The Case of Belief in Global Climate Change." *Environment and Behavior* 38(1): 48–71. DOI: 10.1177/0013916505277998; Kahan, Dan, Ellen Peters, Maggie Wittlin, Paul Slovic, Lisa Larrimore Ouellette, Donald Braman, and Gregory Mandel. 2012. "The Polarizing Impact of Science Literacy and Numeracy on Perceived Climate Change Risks." *Nature Climate Change* 2(10): 732–735.

12. Smith, Nicholas, and Anthony Leiserowitz. 2012. "The Rise of Global Warming Skepticism: Exploring Affective Image Associations in the United States over Time." *Risk Analysis* 32(6): 1021–1032.

13. Diethelm, Pascal, and Martin McKee. 2009. "Denialism: What Is It and How Should Scientists Respond?" *The European Journal of Public Health* 19(1): 2–4. DOI: 10.1093/eurpub/ckn139; Goertzel, Ted. 2010. "Conspiracy Theories in Science." *EMBO Reports* 11(7): 493–499; Kalichman, Seth. 2009. *Denying AIDS: Conspiracy Theories, Pseudoscience, and Human Tragedy.* New York: Springer Science & Business Media; Lobato, Emilio, Jorge Mendoza, Valerie Sims, and Matthew Chin. 2014. "Examining the Relationship between Conspiracy Theories, Paranormal Beliefs, and Pseudoscience Acceptance among a University Population." *Applied Cognitive Psychology* 28(5): 617–625. DOI: 10.1002/acp.3042; McKee, Martin, and Pascal Diethelm. 2010. "How the Growth of Denialism Undermines Public Health." *BMJ: British Medical Journal* 341(1): 1309–1311.

14. Lewandowsky, Stephan, Gilles E. Gignac, and Klaus Oberauer. 2013. "The Role of Conspiracist Ideation and Worldviews in Predicting Rejection of Science." *PLoS ONE* 8(10): e75637.

15. Lewandowsky, Stephan, Michael E. Mann, Linda Bauld, Gerard Hastings, and Elizabeth F. Loftus. 2013. "The Subterranean War on Science." *APS Observer* 26(9); Sleek, Scott. "Inconvenient Truth Tellers: What Happens When Research Yields Unpopular Findings." *APS Observer* 26(9).

16. Dixon, Ruth M., and Jonathan A. Jones. 2015. "Conspiracist Ideation as a Predictor of Climate-Science Rejection an Alternative Analysis." *Psychological Science* 26(5): 664–666; Lewandowsky, Stephan, Gilles E. Gignac, and Klaus Oberauer. 2015. "The Robust Relationship between Conspiracism and Denial of (Climate) Science." *Psychological Science* 26(5): 667–670; Lewandowsky, Gignac, and Oberauer, "The Role of Conspiracist Ideation."

17. Landman, Anne, and Stanton A. Glantz. 2009. "Tobacco Industry Efforts to Undermine Policy-Relevant Research." *American Journal of Public Health* 99(1): 45–58. DOI: 10.2105/ajph.2007.130740.

18. Lewandowsky, Stephan, John Cook, Klaus Oberauer, Scott Brophy, Elisabeth A. Lloyd, and Michael Marriott. 2015. "Recurrent Fury: Conspiratorial Discourse in the Blogosphere

Triggered by Research on the Role of Conspiracist Ideation in Climate Denial." *Journal of Social and Political Psychology* 3(1) 2015: 142–178. DOI: 10.5964/jspp.v3i1.443; Lewandowsky, Stephan, Elisabeth A. Lloyd, and Scott Brophy. 2017. "When Thuncing Trumps Thinking: What Distant Alternative Worlds Can Tell Us About the Real World." *Argumenta*. DOI: 10.23811/52.arg2017.lew.llo.bro.

19. Lewandowsky, Stephan, John Cook, and Elisabeth Lloyd. 2016. "The 'Alice in Wonderland' Mechanics of the Rejection of (Climate) Science: Simulating Coherence by Conspiracism." *Synthese* 195(1): 1–22. DOI: 10.1007/s11229-016-1198-1196; Wood, Michael, Karen M. Douglas, and Robbie M. Sutton. 2012. "Dead and Alive: Beliefs in Contradictory Conspiracy Theories." *Social Psychological and Personality Science* 3(6): 767–773. DOI: 10.1177/1948550611434786.

20. Lewandowsky, Oberauer, Gignac, "NASA Faked the Moon Landing."

21. Bale, Jeffrey M. 2007. "Political Paranoia V. Political Realism: On Distinguishing between Bogus Conspiracy Theories and Genuine Conspiratorial Politics." *Patterns of Prejudice* 41(1): 45–60; Keeley, Brian. 1999. "Of Conspiracy Theories." *Journal of Philosophy* 96(3): 109–126; Lewandowsky, Cook, Oberauer, Brophy, Lloyd, and Marriott. "Recurrent Fury"; Sunstein, Cass R., and Adrian Vermeule. 2009. "Conspiracy Theories: Causes and Cures." *Journal of Political Philosophy* 17(2): 202–227.

22. Lewandowsky, Stephan, John Cook, Klaus Oberauer, and Michael Marriott. 2013. "Recursive Fury: Conspiracist Ideation in the Blogosphere in Response to Research on Conspiracist Ideation." *Frontiers in Psychology* 4(73). DOI: 10.3389/fpsyg.2013.00073.

23. The journal's website has undergone a major redesign since then, and those figures were no longer accessible at the time of this writing. The analysis therefore could not be updated.

24. Gillis, Justin. 2013. "Unlocking the Conspiracy Mindset." *The New York Times*, February 21, 2013.

25. It appears that the same (or very similar) set of complaints was lodged with UWA, although I am not privy to those details. UWA did not uphold any of those complaints.

26. Our own legal advice concurred with this assessment under the British libel laws that had been in force *at the time of publication* of *Recursive Fury* (Lewandowsky, Cook, Oberauer, and Marriott 2013). Because of the adverse implications of those laws on freedom of expression, the U.S. Congress passed a law in 2010 that recognized the adverse impact of foreign libel laws on the "ability of scholars and journalists to publish their work" (PUBLIC LAW 111223) and which made judgments under U.K. libel laws not enforceable in the United States. Those U.K. laws were reformed with effect of 2014, and they now include a specific exemption for peer-reviewed scientific articles, but those did not retroactively apply to *Recursive Fury*.

27. Lewandowsky, Stephan. 2014. "Recursive Fury Goes Recurrent." [Blog] *Shaping Tomorrow's World*. Available at: http://www.shapingtomorrowsworld.org/rf1.html (Accessed December 24, 2017).

28. Readfearn, Graham. 2014. "Science Journal Set to Retract Paper Linking Climate Change Scepticism to Conspiracy Theorists after Sceptics Shout Libel." [Blog] *Desmogblog: Clearing the PR Pollution that Clouds Climate Science*. Available at: https://www.desmogblog.com/2014/03/20/science-journal-retracts-paper-showing-how-climate-change-sceptics-were-conspiracy-theorists-after-sceptics-shout (Accessed December 24, 2017).

29. Lewandowsky, Stephan. 2014. "The Analysis of Speech." [Blog] *Shaping Tomorrow's World*. Available at http://www.shapingtomorrowsworld.org/rfspeech.html (Accessed December 24, 2017).

30. Ibid.

31. Lewandowsky, Stephan. 2014. "The Frontiers Expert Panel." [Blog] *Shaping Tomorrow's World*. Available at http://www.shapingtomorrowsworld.org/xp.html (Accessed December 24, 2017).

32. Lewandowsky, Lloyd, and Brophy, "When Thuncing Trumps Thinking"; Ott, Brian L. 2017. "The Age of Twitter: Donald J. Trump and the Politics of Debasement." *Critical Studies in Media Communication* 34(1): 59–68. DOI: 10.1080/15295036.2016.1266686.

33. This problem has been noted by others. See Jones, Roger. 2014. "Froniers Retraction Controversy." [Blog] *Understanding Climate Risk*. Available at https://2risk.wordpress.com/2014/04/17/frontiers-retraction-controversy/ (Accessed December 24, 2017).

34. Lewandowsky, Stephan. "Revisiting a Retraction." [Blog] *Shaping Tomorrow's World*. Available at http://www.shapingtomorrowsworld.org/rf3.html (Accessed December 24, 2017).

35. Jones, "Froniers Retraction Controversy."

36. Halpern, Michael. "A Conspiracy Theory Researcher Falls Victim to Conspiracy Theories: Intimidated Journal to Retract Lewandowsky Paper." [Blog] *Union of Concerned Scientists: Science for a Healthy Planet and Safer World*. Available at https://blog.ucsusa.org/michael-halpern/a-conspiracy-theory-researcher-falls-victim-to-conspiracy-theories-intimidated-journal-to-retract-lewandowsky-paper-457 (Accessed December 24, 2017).

37. Lewandowsky, NotStephan. "Lewandowsky's Downfall." Video, 3:49. April 25, 2014. https://www.youtube.com/watch?v=bL_QWRgj_-k (Accessed November 9, 2017).

38. Lewandowsky, "Revisiting a Retraction."

39. Hannam, Peter. 2014. "'Conspiracist' Climate Change Study Withdrawn Amid Legal Threats." *The Sydney Morning Herald*. http://www.smh.com.au/environment/climate-change/conspiracist-climate-change-study-withdrawn-amid-legal-threats-20140401-35xao.html (Accessed December 24, 2017).

40. McKeown, Elaine. 2014. "Climate Deniers Intimidate Journal into Retracting Paper That Finds They Believe Conspiracy Theories." *Scientific American*. https://www.scientificamerican.com/article/climate-deniers-intimidate-journal-into-retracting-paper-that-finds-they-believe-conspiracy-theories/ (Accessed December 24, 2017).

41. Zucca, Constanza, and Fred Frenter. 2014. "Retraction of Recursive Fury: A Statement." [Blog] *Frontiers Blog*. Available at: https://www.frontiersin.org/blog/Retraction_of_Recursive_Fury_A_Statement/812/all_blogs (Accessed December 24, 2017).

42. Lewandowsky, "Revisiting a Retraction."

43. Markram, Henry. "Rights of Human Subjects in Scientific Papers." [Blog] *Frontiers Blog*. Available at https://www.frontiersin.org/blog/Rights_of_Human_Subjects_in_Scientific_Papers/830 (Accessed December 24, 2017).

44. McKeown, Elaine. 2014. "Editors Resign as Retraction Scandal Deepens at Science Journal That Caved in to Intimidation from Climate Deniers." [Blog] *Huffington Post Blog*. Available at https://www.huffingtonpost.com/elaine-mckewon/why-this-is-a-dark-time-for-the-field-of-climate-science_b_5174083.html (Accessed December 24, 2017).

45. Lewandowsky, Cook, Oberauer, Brophy, Lloyd, and Marriott. "Recurrent Fury."

46. For a derivation of those attributes, see ibid., and Lewandowsky, Lloyd, and Brophy, "When Thuncing Trumps Thinking."

47. After the events surrounding *Recursive Fury*, an unknown reader discovered an error in another publication: Lewandowsky, Stephan, Gilles E. Gignac, and Klaus Oberauer (2013). We re-analyzed the data and published a corrigendum; those errors did not affect any of the conclusions of the paper: Lewandowsky, Stephan, Gilles E. Gignac, and Klaus Oberauer. 2015. "Correction: The Role of Conspiracist Ideation and Worldviews in Predicting Rejection of Science." *PLoS ONE* 10(8). DOI: 10.1371/journal.pone.0134773. I support open access to data wherever possible: Lewandowsky, Stephan, and Dorothy Bishop. 2016. "Don't Let Transparency Damage Science." *Nature* 529(7587) 459; Morey, Richard D., Christopher D. Chambers, Peter J. Etchels, Christine R. Harris, Rink Hoekstra, Daniël Lakens, Stephan Lewandowsky, Candice Coker Morey, Daniel P. Newman, Felix D Schönbrodt, Wolf Vanpaemel, Eric-Jan Wagenmakers, and Rolf A. Zwann. 2016. "The Peer Reviewers' Openness Initiative: Incentivizing Open Research Practices through Peer Review." *Royal Society Open Science* 3(1). DOI: 10.1098/rsos.150547. The data for the core publications discussed in this chapter are all publicly available for re-analysis.

48. Lewandowsky, Stephan. 2011. "Bitten by a Sock Puppet, but the Climate Is Still Changing." *ABC News*. http://www.abc.net.au/news/2011-03-28/lewandowsky/45638 (Accessed December 24, 2017).

49. Steig, Eric. "O'Donnellgate." [Blog] *O'Donnellgate.* Available at http://www.realclimate.org/index.php/archives/2011/02/odonnellgate/ (Accessed December 24, 2017).

50. Lewandowsky, Cook, and Lloyd. "The 'Alice in Wonderland' Mechanics of the Rejection of (Climate) Science."

51. Lewandowsky, Stephan, Timothy Ballard, Klaus Oberauer, and Rasmus Benestad. 2016. "A Blind Expert Test of Contrarian Claims About Climate Data." *Global Environmental Change* 39(C): 91–97. DOI: 10.1016/j.gloenvcha.2016.04.013.

52. Topping, Alexandra. 2014. "Jane Austen Twitter Row: Two Plead Guilty to Abusive Tweets." *The Guardian.* https://www.theguardian.com/society/2014/jan/07/jane-austen-banknote-abusive-tweets-criado-perez (Accessed December 24, 2017).

53. Landman and Glantz. "Tobacco Industry Efforts to Undermine Policy-Relevant Research"; Proctor, Robert. 2011. *Golden Holocaust: Origins of the Cigarette Catastrophe and the Case for Abolition.* Berkeley and Los Angeles: University of California Press.

54. Oreskes and Conway, *Merchants of Doubt*; Proctor, *Golden Holocaust.*

55. Brysse, Keynyn, Naomi Oreskes, Jessica O'Reilly, and Michael Oppenheimer. 2013. "Climate Change Prediction: Erring on the Side of Least Drama?" *Global Environmental Change* 23(1): 327–337. DOI: 10.1016/j.gloenvcha.2012.10.008; Freudenburg, William R. and Violetta Muselli. 2010. "Global Warming Estimates, Media Expectations, and the Asymmetry of Scientific Challenge." *Global Environmental Change* 20(3): 483–491. DOI: 10.1016/j.gloenvcha.2010.04.003; Lewandowsky, Oreskes, Risbey, Newell, and Smithson, "Seepage."

56. Ibid.

57. Steig, "O'Donnellgate."

58. Lewandowsky, Ballard, Oberauer, and Benestad, "A Blind Expert Test of Contrarian Claims About Climate Data."

59. Bourne, Tom, Laure Wynants, Mike Peters, Chantal Van Audenhove, Dirk Timmerman, Ben Van Calster, and Maria Jalmbrant. 2015. "The Impact of Complaints Procedures on the Welfare, Health and Clinical Practise of 7926 Doctors in the UK: A Cross-Sectional Survey." *BMJ Open* 5(1): 1–13.

60. Lester, Grant, Beth Wilson, Lynn Griffin, and Paul E. Mullen. 2004. "Unusually Persistent Complainants." *The British Journal of Psychiatry* 184(4): 352–356. DOI: 10.1192/bjp.184.4.352; Mullen, Paul E., and Grant Lester. 2006. "Vexatious Litigants and Unusually Persistent Complainants and Petitioners: From Querulous Paranoia to Querulous Behaviour." *Behavioral Sciences & the Law* 24(3): 333–349. DOI: 10.1002/bsl.671.

61. Chigwedere, Pride, George R. Seage III, Sofia Grushkin, Tun-Hou Lee, and M. Essex. 2008. "Estimating the Lost Benefits of Antiretroviral Drug Use in South Africa." *JAIDS Journal of Acquired Immune Deficiency Syndromes* 49(4): 410–415. DOI: 10.1097/QAI.0b013e31818a6cd5.

62. Ibid.

63. Gangarosa, E. J., A. M. Galazka, C. R. Wolfe, L. M. Phillips, E. Miller, R. T. Chen, and R. E. Gangarosa. 1998. "Impact of Anti-Vaccine Movements on Pertussis Control: The Untold Story." *The Lancet* 351(9099): 356–361. DOI: 10.1016/S0140-6736(97)04334-1.

64. Nicholls, Robert J., et al. 2011. "Sea-Level Rise and Its Possible Impacts Given a 'Beyond 4 C World' in the Twenty-First Century." *Philosophical Transactions of the Royal Society of London A: Mathematical, Physical and Engineering Sciences* 369(1934): 161–181.

65. Lewandowsky and Bishop. "Don't Let Transparency Damage Science."

66. Lewandowsky, Mann, Bauld, Hastings, and Loftus. "The Subterranean War on Science."

67. Cribb, Esme. 2017. "Dept. Of Energy Boosts Perry: 'Winning' Fight against Climate Scientists." http://talkingpointsmemo.com/livewire/perry-energy-department-boost-climate-skeptic-column (Accessed December 24, 2017).

68. Lewandowsky, Stephan, Ulrich K. H. Ecker, and John Cook. 2017. "Beyond Misinformation: Understanding and Coping with the 'Post-Truth' Era.' *Journal of Applied*

Research in Memory and Cognition 6(4): 353–369. DOI: 10.1016/j.jarmac.2017.07.008; Mickey, Robert, Steven Levitsky, and Ahmad Way. 2017. "Is America Still Safe for Democracy: Why the United States Is in Danger of Backsliding." *Foreign Affairs* 96: 20–29; Ott, "The Age of Twitter: Donald J. Trump and the Politics of Debasement."

69. I want to extend my deep gratitude to my wife Annie, for her support and companionship throughout the events described in this chapter.

11

Conspiracy Theory Phobia

JUHA RÄIKKÄ AND LEE BASHAM

Many scholars and journalists have recently posed the question, "Why do people believe in conspiracy theories?" There is no consensus answer, but typical candidates include the suggestions that some people buy into conspiracy theories because they are cynical about politics and authorities, or because they commit epistemological fallacies, or because they believe in one conspiracy theory and are therefore likely to adopt a more encompassing set of conspiracy theories.[1] The question of why some people believe in conspiracy theories is commonly considered very important. The assumption is that if we know why some people tend to adopt conspiracy beliefs then we can develop effective measures to fight their spread. As many scholars have pointed out, some conspiracy theories are potentially dangerous (say, for religious minorities or political dissident communities), and it is important to adopt policy to make those theories less popular, rather than more.[2]

Bucking current scholarly trend, we will consider the reverse question and ask why some people do *not* explore or believe in conspiracy theories, and why they dismiss suspicions of conspiracy out of hand without appropriate consideration. This is a largely neglected question, and *conspiracy theory phobia* may be the answer.

A person suffers conspiracy theory phobia if (1) she rejects conspiracy theories without an appropriate evaluation of *evidence* that has been presented, or if (2) her reaction toward particular conspiracy theories is mockery, contempt, hostility, or a straw-person characterization of the argument presented.[3] There is no doubt that conspiracy theory phobia is irrational: Just as those who are a priori drawn to believe conspiracy theories over authoritative explanations exhibit a measure of irrationality when the evidence does not warrant it, a person who suffers from conspiracy theory phobia is also epistemically irresponsible.[4] While social scientists have recently built many research projects based on the idea that too many people believe conspiracy theories, we seek to push back against the current trend. We want to shed some light on why, in many instances, too many people *reject* conspiracy theories.

Characterizing Conspiracy Theories

Events and circumstances are often explained by referring to unintended side effects of intentional actions. When individuals decide to buy apartments in a certain area of a town, the prices of the apartments tend to rise in that area even if no one had a plan to raise them. The price rise can be explained by referring to the unintended effect of people's uncoordinated choices. Explaining data by pointing to unintended effects must be distinguished from explanations that refer to successful intentional actions. If the local government decides to close some public libraries in order to open more golf courses, then the fact that the town has fewer libraries than before can be explained by referring to successful but perhaps misguided intentional action.

Intentional explanations can be separated into two categories, for some of them refer to public actions (i.e., passing legislation) while others refer to covert actions (i.e., secret military operations). A subcategory of intentional explanations, *conspiracy explanations*, refers to covert actions consisting of conspiracies. These explanations are widely used by professional historians, journalists, and jurists, among others. The fact that a bomb exploded on the 20th of July 1944 at the Wolf's Lair conference room near Rastenburg, East Prussia, can be and has been explained by referring to a conspiracy carried out by a group of conspirators who attempted to assassinate Adolf Hitler. The fact that one of President Hamid Karzai's bodyguards was arrested in Afghanistan in October 2011 can be and has been explained by referring to a plot to kill Karzai. As these examples show, there is nothing exotic in conspiracy explanations. Like all other explanations of events and circumstances, conspiracy explanations are sometimes correct, sometimes not. All kinds of conspiracies have been rather common, not only in politics but also in the private sphere. There is no principled reason to dismiss all conspiracy explanations outright.

However, when it comes to *conspiracy theories*, many scholars and journalists say we should avoid them. For instance, we are told that we should not explain the death of Princess Diana, or the murder of Olof Palme, or the death of scientist David Kelly, by referring to a conspiracy. Conspiracy theories cannot be distinguished from other conspiracy explanations because conspiracy theories are always false while conspiracy explanations are not. Some conspiracy theories can be true. One reason why conspiracy theories are commonly distinguished from mainstream conspiracy explanations is simply that conspiracy theories tend to conflict with socially and politically recognized epistemic authorities—such as mainstream media, scientists, medical professionals, government officials, historians, and other experts.[5] (Sometimes the term appears to be a political tool of silencing, an attempt at "censoring" our larger epistemic resources.)

Usually, conspiracy theorists suspect two separate groups. On the one hand, they suspect a group of people who are claimed to be conspirators (say, representatives of Monsanto). On the other hand, they suspect the relevant, socially recognized epistemic authority that denies the alleged conspiracy (say, the health authorities). In certain specific cases, the epistemic authority is itself accused of engineering a conspiracy. Of course, to question the position of an epistemic authority *in a special case* does not mean that its position is questioned in general. Historically speaking, isolated individuals or at least investigative journalists have managed to show that "properly constituted epistemic authorities" can be wrong in specific instances.[6] It is reasonable to assume that our epistemic authorities can be wrong, at one time or another.[7]

In what follows, we focus on those explanations of events and circumstances that (1) cite an actual or alleged conspiracy, and (2) either conflict or conflicted with the authoritative account.[8] The conspiracy theories of interest here are those that challenge or have challenged what people take to be the existing truths.[9]

Why Conspiracy Theory Phobia?

So why do some people not evaluate conspiracy theories in the way they should, that is, by estimating the strengths and weaknesses of the evidence that is presented in support of a particular conspiracy theory? What makes them reject conspiracy theories at the outset, without rational reflection? What explains conspiracy theory phobia? We discuss four interrelated reasons.

Fly in the Ointment

Some conspiracy theories make claims so fantastical that they go beyond what most people can accept as true. For example, the claim that interdimensional lizard people secretly rule the planet is an extraordinary one, and therefore requires extraordinary evidence. While bizarre conspiracy theories like this are not representative of all or most conspiracy theories, they may spoil the whole, thereby driving people to reject, out of hand, more mundane and more evidenced claims of conspiracy.[10]

Preferring Conspiracy Theories to Be False

Conspiracy theories often include claims that many of us want to be *false*. We do not hope our food is poisoned, our cars damage the environment far more than the makers claim, political authorities spy on our texting, social media, and e-mails, politicians are ready to kill their own citizens to justify wars, or that vaccines have deadly or dangerous side effects that are intentionally hidden from public view. Conspiracy theorists frequently claim with their theories that *unpleasant*, even *infamous* states of affairs have prevailed, do prevail, or will prevail. This may well explain why some people tend to reject conspiracy theories and dismiss conspiracy theorists quickly and easily, without critical evaluation of the role of evidence in the theory or within the thinking of the theorists. Let us consider two psychological mechanisms.

Psychological Factors

Just as social psychologists have concentrated on people who have a disposition toward accepting conspiracy theories, we would like to focus on the people at the opposite end of that spectrum: people who are resistant to conspiracy theories. Both ends of the spectrum are irrational in the sense that they have a tendency to accept or reject conclusions based on predispositions rather than evidence.

Confirmation bias works to support existing dispositions by driving how people derive hypotheses and collect and evaluate evidence. When a person learns of a 9/11 conspiracy theory, for example, she might test the hypothesis that "It is *not true* that authorities knew in advance what would happen to the twin towers." After that, she will easily find evidence in support of this hypothesis and only little (if any) evidence against this hypothesis, as she searches for and interprets evidence in a selective way. This is a manifestation of confirmation bias—a very common psychological phenomenon. As a result, the person concludes that, fortunately, the conspiracy theory is clearly false—a "fanciful" or "absurd" story.[11] Her conclusion that the theory is false can be correct, of course, but her reasoning is faulty.

Pragmatic Hypothesis Testing

Suppose a person who suffers from a food allergy and cannot eat eggs is at the restaurant with her friend. She asks whether the portion she plans to order has eggs as an ingredient. The waiter replies that in his view it does not and that he remembers that someone else with similar allergy has eaten it. Her friend is convinced, but the allergic person wants more information, as she wants to avoid complications that eating egg would cause her. Her behavior is understandable—an error would be very costly for her—although she seems to have a very high *confidence threshold* for accepting the hypothesis that the food does not include egg. Imagine the waiter said, "I think it might have egg. I doubt it but I'm not really sure. I think I remember that someone got sick from it because of some allergy or something." She would immediately reject the hypothesis that the food does not have egg. This suggests that, because of pragmatic reasons, she accepts one conclusion much more readily than another.

When a person hears a disturbing conspiracy theory, she considers it, in her mind, as a hypothesis. Likely, she tests the hypothesis from a *pragmatic point of view*. If the conspiracy theory in question is one that asserts things people do not want to believe, the person wants plenty of evidence in support of the theory before she is ready to seriously suspect or believe in it. For her, it is important not to believe in a conspiracy theory if there is no conspiracy—much more important than to believe in a conspiracy theory when there *is* a conspiracy. The *error costs* for her can be considerable if it turns out that she believed and acted upon a false conspiracy theory.[12] The social price can be extensive. She might be seen as subversive and antisocial. Her rationality might be called into question by those with whom she shares important professional and personal relationships. Avoiding such strongly discomfiting situations can be of prime importance for her. The error costs for her would be minor if she did not believe in a conspiracy theory that was eventually revealed as true. Since most others (and the authorities) made the same mistake, the social price is minimal. If she did advocate it in the face of social rejection, accolades may follow if it turns out to be true, but the risks prior to public acceptance are severe. It follows that when a person evaluates a conspiracy theory, she accepts one conclusion much more easily than another. Her reasoning may be rational from a pragmatic point of view, but there is a considerable risk that she makes false conclusions.

Why Does Conspiracy Theory Phobia Matter?

Conspiracy theory phobia matters for at least three reasons: (1) it may allow some conspiracies to go undetected; (2) it may undermine vigilance and rational suspicion in functional democracies; and (3) it may distort social science concerning conspiracy theorizing.

In functional democracies, the salvation of the state lies in watchfulness of the citizen. A critical aspect of democracy is suspicion of societal powers, be they political, economic, or the entanglement of these. It is not just the emergence of extreme, overt tyranny citizens have to watch for. High-placed political conspiracies of lesser ambition are commonplace. In U.S. politics the evidence of spying by political opponents on each other is now known to be commonplace; the scandal of Watergate hardly abolished this tactic. Political enemies, like Anwar al-Awlaki, appear to have been executed by political authorities.[13] Historians have often confirmed that incidents are manufactured or falsely reported by political authorities to initiate wars that otherwise would not have been justifiable to the populace of a representational democracy. The false "Gulf of Tonkin incident," which led to the Vietnam war and the deaths of more than a million people, is now widely regarded by professional historians to be one instance.[14]

Just as proper empirical study of conspiracy theory and theorists must take rational and evidential elements seriously, serious accusations by citizens enabled with evidence must in that measure be taken as seriously. They should not be dismissed as evidencing pathology. That is the price of a functional democracy.

A proper understanding of the complexity of human cognition is important. If we want to understand humans—a social and highly organized, hierarchical, cooperative, and deceptive primate—we need to acknowledge all aspects of our practice of conspiracy theorizing. The point of departure should be historically literate. It should respect that many conspiracy theories have turned out to be true. If we are empirical researchers in the social sciences, this inevitably makes us appropriately situated theorists of conspiracy theory. Unfortunately, conspiracy theory phobia may distort these gifted research cultures. Both the factors of confirmation bias and pragmatic rejection can dispose researchers to neglect how rationality and evidence function in the cognitive practices of conspiracy theorists.

The result is a *pathologizing approach* to conspiracy theorizing. Conspiracy theorizing is reduced to a mysterious illness. Social science research often labels conspiracy theories as mere "ideation," "anomalous belief," "conspiracism," and other vague, dismissive terms.[15] Swept up by the pathologizing approach, many social science researchers deploy this de-rationalizing and dehumanizing language in their discussions of conspiracy theorizing and theorists.[16]

The distortion that may affect research in academia also tends to entwine our political life, undermining valuable political processes. It dissuades public intellectuals from raising legitimate questions and is used in attempts to silence popular dissent. This partial neglect of conspiracy theorists' reasoning seems unjustified. All of us routinely consider conspiracy theories as live options in the explanation of past and current events, and in the prediction of future ones. These events include personal and politically momentous ones. Recognizing the phobic blinders of the pathologizing approach in research and in our political sphere will produce a more balanced, honest, and accurate response to conspiracy theorizing and conspiracy theorists.

Let's Keep Our Eyes Open

People who suffer conspiracy phobia reject conspiracy theories without an appropriate evaluation of the evidence presented, and their reaction toward any particular conspiracy theory tends to be mockery, contempt, hostility, or a straw-person characterization of the arguments presented. We have argued that conspiracy theory phobia can be explained with non-rational psychological mechanisms.

Conspiracy theories challenge important truths. Our point here is not to say that, in general, it is irrational to trust in epistemic authorities. However, if it turns out that a particular explanation provided by the relevant epistemic authority looks problematic in the light of a conspiracy theorist's message, then there is a reason to be cautious. Although the burden of proof lies on the side of the conspiracy theorist, her arguments and the evidence she provides should be evaluated open-mindedly.[17] The fact that the conspiracy theorist offers an alternative account is not sufficient reason to reject her claims. Established epistemic authorities have made mistakes, and nothing guarantees that they won't make them again. If the issue looks scrappy and complicated, laypersons need not form any beliefs concerning the issue. Epistemic abstinence, a studied agnosticism, is often a virtue.[18]

Conspiracy theory phobia is closely related to ad hominem argumentation. A person who commits the ad hominem fallacy criticizes another person's character traits instead of trying to reply to the argument presented. Surely the defender of a conspiracy theory must believe in "demonic forces with transcendent powers" as suggested by some authors?[19] The question is about a silencing tactic. Conspiracy theory phobia is also associated with the idea that people should evaluate conspiracy theories as a group rather than on a case-by-case basis, and with the claim that the state should act against all or almost all conspiracy theories.[20] These are dangerous suggestions.

Understanding the logic of conspiracy theory phobia is a matter of great significance. A precondition of a successful fight against conspiracy theory phobia requires that the root causes behind the phenomenon are well known and empirically studied. It is imperative that we reveal conspiracies threatening justice, democracy, public safety, and human rights. Without an open and careful evaluation of conspiracy theories, some conspiracies may go unnoticed. When conspiracy theories get fair treatment and receive serious attention, the likelihood of successful conspiracies declines.

Notes

1. Goertzel, Ted. 1994. "Belief in Conspiracy Theories." *Political Psychology* 15(4): 731–742; Swami, Viren, and Rebecca Coles. 2010. "The Truth Is Out There." *The Psychologist* 23(7): 560–563; Wood, Michael J., Karen M. Douglas, and Robbie M. Sutton. 2012. "Dead and Alive: Beliefs in Contradictory Conspiracy Theories." *Social Psychological & Personality Science* 3(6): 767–773; Brotherton, Robert, and Christopher C. French. 2014. "Belief in Conspiracy Theories and Susceptibility to the Conjunction Fallacy." *Applied Cognitive Psychology* 28(2) 2014: 238–248; Sunstein, Cass R. 2014. *Conspiracy Theories and Other Dangerous Ideas*. New York: Simon & Schuster; Uscinski, Joseph E., and Joseph M. Parent, 2014. *American Conspiracy Theories*. Oxford: Oxford University Press.
2. Douglas, Karen, and Robbie Sutton. 2015. "Climate Change: Why the Conspiracy Theories Are Dangerous." *Bulletin of the Atomic Scientists* 71(2): 98–106. The anti-Semitic conspiracy theory that the Jewish people were responsible for the Black Death is a typical conspiracy theory that has been harmful for a religious group. See McConnachie, James, and Robin Tudge. 2005. *A Rough Guide to Conspiracy Theories*. New York: Rough Guides.
3. A parallel point applies to our reactions to those persons that report conspiracy theories to us and wish to explore these on the basis of evidence. Their evidence or lack of should guide our response. For a discussion see, e.g., Basham, Lee. 2017. "Pathologizing Open Societies: A Reply to the *Le Monde* Social Scientists." *Social Epistemology Review and Reply Collective* 6(2): 59–68.
4. Cf. deHaven-Smith, Lance. 2013. *Conspiracy Theory in America*. Austin: University of Texas Press, 84; Husting, Ginna, and Martin Orr. 2007. "Dangerous Machinery: 'Conspiracy

Theorist' as a Transpersonal Strategy of Exclusion." *Symbolic Interaction* 30(2): 131; Basham, Lee. 2016. "The Need for Accountable Witnesses: A Reply to Dentith." *Social Epistemology Review and Reply Collective* 5(7): 6–13.

5. David Coady argues that, in order to count as a "conspiracy theory," the "proposed explanation must conflict with an 'official' explanation of the same historical event." However, the official explanations should not be confused with the explanations supported by the relevant epistemic authorities. The official explanation, supported by political elite and administrative authorities, need not be supported by the relevant epistemic authorities. It is possible that state authorities support a conspiracy theory, i.e., an explanation which is not supported by the epistemic authority. Coady, David. 2003. "Conspiracy Theories and Official Stories." *International Journal of Applied Philosophy* 17(2): 199. Coady has withdrawn his "contrary to official stories" as a necessary condition for being a "conspiracy theory," taking the view that there is no clear definition of the phenomenon.

6. For a discussion, see Levy, Neil. 2007. "Radically Socialized Knowledge and Conspiracy Theories." *Episteme* 4(2): 181–192. Levy thinks, wrongly, that "[r]esponsible believers ought to accept explanations offered by *properly constituted epistemic authorities.*" For an engaging discussion and enumeration of conspiracy and its theory in world history, see Pigden, Charles. 2007. "Conspiracy Theories and Conventional Wisdom." *Episteme* 4(2): 219–232. For a compelling critique of Levy's epistemic authoritarianism see Coady, David. 2007. "Are Conspiracy Theorists Irrational." *Episteme* 4(2): 193–204.

7. Needless to say, what constitutes "properly constituted epistemic authorities" is a difficult question.

8. We might argue it is difficult to say in certain cases whether an explanation refers to a "conspiracy" or to some other sort of merely "confidential cooperation." However, secret cooperative activities whose aims and nature conflict with the so-called positive morality (that reflects our de facto moral commitments) or with specific prima facie duties are usually called "conspiracies," especially if the members of the cooperation have a certain position and if the goal of their activities differs from the goal they are authorized to pursue. Children may have morally questionable secret plans to influence events by secret means, but these incidents are seldom called conspiracies. Small children are not typically considered to be in a position to conspire. Perhaps they are correctly characterized as such, or not. Secret military operations may be morally rotten, but as far as they have authorized goals, they are not usually called conspiracies. (However, in some scenarios, like the 2003 U.S. invasion of Iraq, they appear to be.) The members of an "official" administrative meeting behind closed doors may secretly agree on issues they should not and start to pursue goals they should avoid. When this happens the participants can rightfully be accused of conspiracy, as they have unauthorized goals now. Conspiracies involve secret cooperation, but that does not mean that the conspirators must meet secretly so that outsiders do not know that they met in the first place.

9. Cf. Räikkä, Juha. 2018. "Conspiracies and Conspiracy Theories: An Introduction." *Argumenta* 3(2): 205–216; see also Räikkä, Juha. 2014. *Social Justice in Practice: Questions in Ethics and Political Philosophy.* New York: Springer, 61–64, 77–81.

10. Our working assumption here is that people do not think that *most* conspiracy theories are insane merely because *some* conspiracy theories—for instance theories that concern the alleged actions of the Antichrist—are insane.

11. Karen Douglas and Robbie Sutton have suggested that conspiracy theories are "fanciful." Douglas, Karen M., and Robbie M. Sutton. 2011. "Does It Take One to Know? Endorsement of Conspiracy Theories Is Influenced by Personal Willingness to Conspire." *British Journal of Social Psychology* 50(3): 544.

12. Cf. Trope, Yaacov, Benjamin Gervey, and Nira Liberman. 1997. "Wishful Thinking from a Pragmatic Hypothesis-Testing Perspective." In *The Mythomanias: The Nature of Deception and Self-Deception,* ed. M. Myslobodsky. Mahwah, NJ: Lawrence Erlbaum, 105–131. See also chapter 2 in Mele, Alfred. 2001. *Self-Deception Unmasked.* Princeton: Princeton University

Press. The point about costs also applies to *evidentially indeterminate* conspiracy theories that are taken by the persons around her, for pragmatic reasons, to be false.

13. Anwar al-Awlaki was the first U.S. citizen to be approved for targeted killing by the CIA. Awlaki was killed in September 2011.

14. Hanyok, Robert. 2001. "Skunks, Bogies, Silent Hounds, and the Flying Fish: The Gulf of Tonkin Mystery, 2 – 4 August 1964." *Cryptologic Quarterly* 19(1): 39. Hanyok's study, undertaken for internal use by the NSA, was officially released after a Freedom of Information Act (FOIA) lawsuit.

15. See, e.g., Brotherton and French, "Belief in Conspiracy Theories and Susceptibility to the Conjunction Fallacy," 238–248. There are many other instances.

16. Wood, Douglas, and Sutton. "Dead and Alive: Beliefs in Contradictory Conspiracy Theories," 767–773. The authors argue that some conspiracy theorists *literally believe* bin Laden is both dead and alive. Such persons would be the essence of insane. An examination of the paper reveals that its conclusion is based on a conflation of *suspicion* with *settled belief*. Suspicions do not generate contradictions. See Hagen, Kurtis. 2018. "Conspiracy Theorists and Monological Belief Systems." *Argumenta* 3(2): 303–326; Basham, "Pathologizing Open Societies," 64. We also witness dehumanizing allegations: Some allege most people who entertain conspiracy theories simultaneously *believe* obviously contradictory ones about the same momentous political event. This allegation is surprising, since all of us entertain conspiracy theories as live options. In the social sciences we can say the pathologizing approach is largely institutionalized. It merits reconsideration and correction.

17. See chapters one and two in Dentith, Matthew R. X. 2014. *The Philosophy of Conspiracy Theories.* New York: Palgrave MacMillan.

18. For a discussion of studied agnosticism see, e.g., Basham, Lee. 2003. "Malevolent Global Conspiracy." *Journal of Social Philosophy* 34(1): 91–103.

19. Hofstadter, Richard. 1964. *The Paranoid Style in American Politics and Other Essays.* London: Jonathan Cape, 29; Abalakina-Paap, Marina, Walter G. Stephan, Traci Craig, and W. Larry Gregory. 1999. "Beliefs in Conspiracies." *Political Psychology* 20(3): 637–647. Do people who believe in the Watergate conspiracy believe that demonic forces of almost transcendent powers control history? Forces like Richard Nixon?

20. See Sunstein, Cass R., and Andrian Vermuele. 2009. "Conspiracy Theories: Causes and Cures." *The Journal of Political Philosophy* 17(2): 202–227.

12

Conspiracy Thinking, Tolerance, and Democracy

STEVEN M. SMALLPAGE

When college and university professors research and teach conspiracy theories, the public is pushed to the limit in terms of what it will or will not tolerate. Indeed, professors that publicly hold conspiracy beliefs force the central question of political tolerance: What is the line between spirited debate and intellectual inquiry that allows for communities to flourish, on the one hand, and the expression of viewpoints that undermine that community's integrity altogether, on the other? The line is inherently blurry, as the assumption that all is not what it seems and careful skepticism seem to underlie both the best academic work *and* the psychology of conspiracy thinking. Similarly, common views of normatively good citizenship require free thinking, independent thought, and the right to dissent. To make matters more complicated, modern liberal education is premised on cultivating both intellectual curiosity and civic engagement in students.

Since conspiracy theorists often anger, provoke, and sometimes harass the public, we must decide as a community if we will tolerate professors who hold controversial conspiracy beliefs to remain in public life. But such decisions require thoughtful reflection on the similarities and differences between conspiracy thinking and its relationship to desirable traits of democratic citizens like tolerance, independent thinking, and academic freedom. Preemptively shutting out conspiracy thinking may actually harm our democracy.

Researchers should consciously grapple with the normative questions about the role of conspiracy thinking not only in the academy, but also in its larger role in a healthy democracy. In this chapter I outline briefly the recent high-profile American professors who have lost their positions largely due to their status as a "conspiracy theorist," that is, someone who publicly holds controversial conspiracy beliefs. The purpose of this section of the chapter is not to assess either the veracity of their various conspiracy beliefs nor to argue for their reinstatement. Instead, the purpose is to highlight the argument that many make about the close proximity between what academics do professionally and professors do vocationally: instill in their students a sense that "things are not what they seem," a "prudent paranoia," or a "political suspiciousness." The claim I make in this chapter is that conspiracy thinking and the virtues of civic engagement and independent thinking are more related than we would perhaps first notice or even like them to be.

In the second section of this chapter, I focus on American normative commitments to citizenship. Drawing on empirical data, I show that most Americans think that independent thought is the most important aspect of good citizenship. In the final section of this chapter, I highlight the importance of tolerating "conspiracy theorists" as a political group. Often we talk about political tolerance as the willingness to grant rights—freedom of speech, press, and to teach—to taboo groups like atheists and homosexuals. These groups have been largely "owned" by one of the two major political parties. This makes them fundamentally different from "conspiracy theorists." Conspiracy theorists are necessarily always on the outside looking in on the party establishments; this makes them an easy target for both of the major political parties. In this way, because both parties are united in opposing conspiracy theorists, I argue that a good measure of political tolerance is how we feel about conspiracy theorists.

Both of these points are placed within a larger discussion we should have more often: What good is conspiracy theorizing for a healthy democracy? To what extent is conspiracy thinking an important function of the American political environment? Put more forcefully, can we have democracy without conspiracy theorists of some kind? I think the answer is no.

Conspiracy Theorizing in the Academy
The Scholars for 9/11 Truth

The 9/11 Truth movement is a well-known collection of conspiracy theorists who argue against the official account of September 11th, 2001. Alternative explanations range from super-secret military laser canons to the less imaginative "inside job" by the Bush administration. While there is considerable disagreement among those within the "truther" camp, the common ground between them is straightforward: things are not what they seem. Though we will focus on only the most prominent professors who have pursued conspiracy theories about 9/11, it would be a mistake to not also illustrate the extent to which prominent politicians have supported or suggested suspicions about 9/11, like Independent ex-governor of Minnesota Jesse Ventura, Democratic Senators Cynthia McKinney, Mike Gravel, and Paul Wellstone, and prominent Republicans Ron and Rand Paul, to name only a few. The point is that when it comes to the 9/11 Truth conspiracy theories, these have entered the political mainstream—in fact, over 30% of Republicans and over 40% of Democrats are some kind of 9/11 truther. For an overview of such polling data, see the chapter by Adam Enders and me in this volume.

One segment of the 9/11 truther movement is the "Scholars for 9/11 Truth," and its splinter group "Scholars for 9/11 Truth and Justice." Scholars for 9/11 Truth was founded by retired University of Minnesota–Duluth philosophy Professor James H. Fetzer and Brigham Young University (BYU) physicist Steven E. Jones in 2005. Though Jones would later form the "Scholars for 9/11 Truth and Justice" after disagreements over which theories were viable alternatives to the official account, they pushed for a more "skeptical" investigation into the 9/11 attacks in response to the 2005 9/11 Commission Report, which codified the official story of planes crashing into the towers, causing the towers to eventually collapse.

When Jones gave a presentation on the controlled demolition of the World Trade Center towers, he was placed on paid academic leave by BYU. According to the BYU spokeswoman at the time, the concern was with what Jones may have said in the classroom: "We do believe professors must speak responsibly. Professors need to clarify when they are speaking for themselves on personal concerns." In response to his paid leave, Jones welcomed the investigation because it would bring needed attention: "My stewardship is to get people thinking and studying these things." Ultimately, he stood by his independent research and revealed his motivations for investigating the 9/11 attacks: "Because of my concern for college-age students I have taught and loved for decades, I am motivated to speak out emphatically against what I judge—after thorough study and reflection—to be terrible wars, wars of aggression, founded on deceptions." Six weeks later, Jones reached a retirement deal with BYU, closing any internal investigation.[1] BYU made it clear that they would not tolerate such ideas, particularly if expressed by their own faculty.

James Tracy and the Sandy Hook Conspiracy

On December 14th, 2012, Adam Lanza shot 20 children and six women staff members at Sandy Hook Elementary school in Newtown, Connecticut. Before opening fire on the school he murdered his mother at their home, and, after firing on the school, Adam Lanza shot himself. Finding that he acted alone, the authorities cited his mental health, disabilities, and ready access to weapons as the cause.

Soon after the official accounts were solidified in 2013, James Tracy, who was then a tenured Professor of Communication at Florida Atlantic University (FAU), claimed it was a hoax. In 2015, in a volume co-edited by Jim Fetzer, *Nobody Died at Sandy Hook*, Tracy concludes his chapter by saying:

> Regardless of where one stands on the Second Amendment and gun control, it is not unreasonable to suggest the Obama administration's complicity or direct oversight of an incident that has in very short order sparked a national debate on the very topic—and not coincidentally remains a key piece of Obama's political platform. . . . The move to railroad

this program through with the aid of major media and an irrefutable barrage of children's portraits, 'heartfelt' platitudes and ostensible tears neutralizes a quest for genuine evidence, reasoned observation and in the case of Newtown honest and responsible law enforcement. Moreover, to suggest that Obama is not capable of deploying such techniques to achieve political ends is to similarly place ones [sic] faith in image and interpretation above substance and established fact, the exact inclination that in sum has brought America to such an impasse.[2]

On December 10th, 2015, Lenny and Veronique Pozner, the parents of six-year-old Noah who was killed in the Sandy Hook shooting, wrote a letter to the editors of the *South Florida Sun Sentinel,* arguing that Tracy's consistent and mounting attacks on the official account of Sandy Hook—and, specifically, his publication of Noah's image—were causing significant emotional harm to the family. That Tracy was then tenured at FAU was unacceptable to the Pozners, who argued that Tracy had clearly crossed the line and FAU should terminate his employment. The Pozners asked: "When do the interests of the college and its students take precedence over the tenure of a professor . . .?" It was not enough for the Pozners that FAU ask Tracy not to mention the university among his credentials on his blog, but rather, they thought, the "civic responsibility" of FAU was to sever ties with Tracy completely.[3]

A few days later, Tracy responded in his own letter to the *Sun Sentinel.* At the end of his letter, Tracy largely reiterates the conclusion quoted above from his chapter in *Nobody Died at Sandy Hook:* "where imagery and emotion reign supreme, where fact is often replaced by unsubstantiated claims and hearsay, the eventual result will be a severe loss of our freedoms, perhaps outright tyranny, as de Tocqueville suggested following his tour of America almost two centuries ago." For Tracy, just as for Jones and his 9/11 Truth movement, the issue is civic responsibility. "Today, more than ever, citizens would be well-served to recognize that much of what they are left to witness via mass media requires serious interrogation, possible only through a consistent regimen of intellectual self-defense. If that is an outmoded ideal and a skill that can no longer be practiced or taught to young adults, I stand guilty as charged." For Tracy, his responsibility as a democratic citizen—and, further, as a professor in a democratic country—revolves around individual examination, evidence-based reasoning, and objective considerations of all alternatives as central virtues of engaged and meaningful citizenship. Even if, he would argue, one of those alternatives was that no one died at Sandy Hook.[4]

FAU terminated Tracy on January 8th, 2016. Tracy would later sue the FAU's Board of Trustees for wrongful termination. According to FAU, Tracy failed to disclose his outside work for multiple years—specifically, the money he received from his controversial conspiracy blog. Tracy's lawyers argued that he was fired because of the substance of his blog, which would constitute an infringement of free speech. As of this writing, Tracy's appeal went to a jury and, in December 2017, his termination was upheld: the jury did not find the motive behind his termination to be about the substance of his blog, but the failure to disclose required information.[5]

As would be expected, the American Association of University Professors (AAUP) was very vocal in opposition to the investigations into Jones' and Tracy's cases.[6] Shortly after Tracy's comments about Sandy Hook first gained national attention in 2013, the AAUP wrote a letter to the President of FAU. In the letter, the AAUP argued that even the sanction against Tracy for allegedly not distancing his controversial views on Sandy Hook from the institution's views was an unnecessary infringement on Tracy's freedom of speech and academic freedom as a tenured professor. For the AAUP, FAU's actions against Tracy "sets a precedent that potentially chills the spirited exchange of ideas—however unpopular, offensive, or controversial—that the academic community has a special responsibility to protect." The tension is between offending community sensibilities and defending precisely those offensive views: Is the responsibility of the university to assuage community outrage, or to defend academic freedom?[7]

Political Tolerance and Good Citizenship

Perhaps the most important modern political virtue is tolerance: the ability to allow or to endure something with which you disagree. Traditionally, political tolerance is measured by asking people if they would extend certain rights to certain groups.[8] The rights and liberties measured are the right to have a book in a library, the right to speak in your community, and the right to teach in a local college. The groups were often those perceived to be taboo or generally maligned: communists, militarists, racists, homosexuals, and atheists. So, social and political scientists, in order to better understand someone's tolerance, would ask: Would you allow someone who believes black people are biologically inferior to have a book in a local library? If an individual says no, we understand that person to have some degree of political intolerance.

Though systematic empirical evidence is lacking, the stories of Jones and Tracy tell us something about the American public's tolerance of conspiracy theorists: We do not want them teaching in our colleges and universities. Further, other professors seem split on whether conspiracy theorists should teach; as one put it: "I am not saying he doesn't have the right to speak, but ... when it comes from a professor, it makes me wonder: What did he teach his students?"[9] It is a struggle even for those in the same profession to accept conspiracy theorists among their ranks.

Yet, aside from committing a crime or breaking a law, if you ask the average American what the mark of a "good citizen" is, the overwhelmingly answer is "independent thinking": being able to do your own research, draw your own inferences,

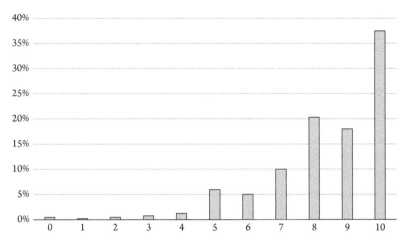

Figure 12.1. American Ratings of Importance of "Independent Thought" for Good Citizenship, Percent of Sample. *Source: United States Citizenship, Involvement, Democracy (CID) Survey, 2006 (n=43,360).*

and defend your own conclusions is paramount for meaningful, participatory citizenship.[10] Above in Figure 12.1 is data from the United States Citizenship, Involvement, Democracy (CID) Survey from 2006. Nearly 44,000 respondents were asked to rank from most important (10) to least important (0) the following statement: "To be a good citizen, how important would you say it is for a person to form his or her own opinion, independently from others?" Thirty-seven percent said that it was the most important (10); 75% of the sample ranked it between 8 and 10. Exercising independent thought is overwhelmingly what most Americans think of when they consider the norms of good citizenship.

Put simply, this is the "liberal" vision of citizenship, which has its roots in Enlightenment philosophy and politics.[11] This notion of citizenship is also at the center of what many Americans mean today by "liberal arts" education—the education necessary to exercise individual freedom in thought and meaningful action. Insofar as conspiracy thinking is related to independent thought and various types of citizen engagement, we should be careful to distinguish how conspiracy thinking is different from the vision of the good, active independent citizen. If we do not reflect on the differences (and similarities) between conspiracy theorizing on the one hand, and our normative understanding of engaged citizenship on the other, we run the great risk of throwing out both because we see one as far too dangerous to justify the other. In short, conspiracy thinking and theorizing has an intimate connection to our actual normative commitment to engaged, informative, and independent citizenship that needs to be further explored.

Tolerating Conspiracy Theorists

Before presenting preliminary data on tolerance and conspiracy theorists, I would like to simply demonstrate the typical political tolerance levels for partisans of other political groups: atheists, Christians, and homosexuals. At one point in time, equal rights and liberties were not extended to these groups, and, when it comes to teaching, many still harbor strong feelings about what they would teach their students.

Figure 12.2 shows the different ratings toward three groups: homosexuals, atheists, and Christians.[12] These three groups are often mentioned in discussions about tolerance. Respondents are separated according to partisanship. We can see a trend in the data: Some groups are more favorably rated than others, depending on the individual respondent's partisanship. More interesting, however, is that these groups' favorability ratings invert depending on political party. For example among Democrats, Christians are on average rated lower than either homosexuals or atheists. The reverse is true for Republicans, who rate both homosexuals and atheists well below Christians. In a way, then, given that different social or identity groups often make up one of the two major political parties in the United States, we should not be surprised to see partisan polarization.

Major political parties have adopted many of these groups as their own, thus tolerating these individuals is perhaps made easier because of partisanship and ideology. This is not the case with "conspiracy theorists," who, as a group, are not claimed by either party. In our current age of affective polarization, which makes people more prone to actively dislike the other political party (the "out-party"), that ratings of conspiracy theorists are almost identical to the ratings of the out-partisans

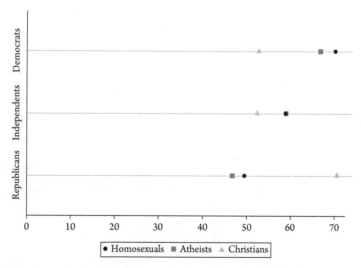

Figure 12.2. Mean Feeling Thermometer Ratings for Traditional Tolerance Groups, by Partisanship.

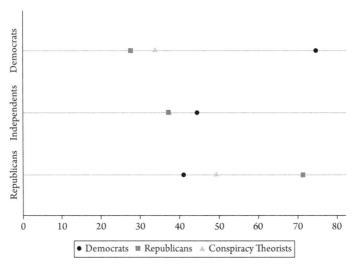

Figure 12.3. Mean Feeling Thermometer Ratings for Partisan Groups and Conspiracy Theorists, by Partisanship.

for both political parties, means tolerating conspiracy theorists is a very difficult thing to do.

Figure 12.3 shows the mean feeling thermometer rating for three groups: Democrats, Republicans, and "conspiracy theorists." The data is separated by respondent partisanship. So, for example, as one would expect, Democrats and Republicans routinely rate their own political party over the other. The telling result is that while all partisans rated on average the other party lowest, they all agreed that conspiracy theorists were near the bottom as well. In other words, no one ranks "conspiracy theorists" higher than both parties.

What explains why partisans dislike conspiracy theorists? While the trend of disliking conspiracy theorists almost as much as the out-party is true for either party, Republicans are more warm toward conspiracy theorists. What explains why Republicans have more warmth toward conspiracy theorists than Democrats? What explains why Independents rate conspiracy theorists higher than either of the two major parties? What explains tolerance of conspiracy theorists more generally? Are feelings toward conspiracy theorists a proxy for anti-establishment feelings and beliefs? These questions have not been answered by empirical political science. Hopefully, we will have some answers to these pressing questions soon.

Reflections

So, what do we do about conspiracy theorists inside and outside the academy? Tolerating conspiracy theorists will always be difficult. First, we do not like what they say: for example, that 9/11 was an inside job to gain public support for military intervention in the Middle East, or that the Sandy Hook mass shooting was a false flag operation by the Obama administration to take our guns. These theories, and others like them, often create more emotional distress for the victims of these tragedies. Yet, a clear majority of Americans not only have a (perhaps unconscious) knack for thinking like a conspiracy theorist, but what many consciously believe constitutes normatively good democratic citizenship empirically looks like what conspiracy theorists of all stripes do: raise questions, push for answers, and follow their own intuitions. But, as most research on conspiracy thinking has revealed, the most conspiratorial among us are actually *less* engaged with traditional politics, making their activity either profoundly (and potentially violently) anti-establishment and therefore quasi-revolutionary[13] or paradoxically quietist—busy with uncovering the secret plots, some conspiracy theorists ignore the traditional political means which are appropriate responses to their legitimate concerns.[14]

Since we hold on to this notion of engaged citizenship, we also defend everyone's First Amendment rights—particularly the freedom of speech. Especially on our college campuses, the value of free speech is incredibly important to defend—for both students and professors. But, even here we find it difficult to defend conspiracy theorists in our classrooms and in the ivory tower. Seemingly, people believe that a proper education is corroded the closer it gets to conspiracy theories. And, for professors, there is considerable legitimacy and authority lost when they publicly offer up conspiracy theories of their own.

So, not only is it difficult to tolerate conspiracy theories on intellectual grounds— be it as a matter of democratic citizenship or philosophical axiom—they are also tough to tolerate on political grounds. As we have seen, the two major political parties do not own the label *conspiracy theorist* or the groups of conspiracy theorists like they own the label *Christian* (Republican) or the actual groups of homosexuals (Democrat). Democrats and Republicans do, however, "own" particular conspiracy *theories*—like the "birther" conspiracy.[15] The major political powers in America do not own the label *conspiracy theorist*; instead, they often refer to those people they do not like as conspiracy theorists. Which, on some level, makes sense because partisan reasoning is, in fact, different from conspiracy thinking.[16] However, this makes it hard for us to tolerate conspiracy theorists even on political grounds, because they do not "belong" to any recognizable or legitimate group. Instead, they sit outside of the major political spectrum, making them uniquely the target of attacks on both the ideological and partisan left and right. In other words, just as much as it is Democratic to dislike Republicans, and just as much as it is Republican to dislike Democrats, it is equally *partisan* to dislike conspiracy theorists.

We have only scratched the surface of understanding conspiracy theorists as a political group. Though I have presented very preliminary findings here, further research will need to be done addressing how partisans understand and use the label *conspiracy theorist*, and the empirical consequences of owning or self-identifying as a conspiracy theorist. At a minimum, we have a new group of individuals who need to be included in many discussions of tolerance. We also need to reexamine our own normative commitments to the image of a good citizen within a democracy, since the virtues of the conspiracy theorist are nearly identical to it.

The Tension between Conspiracy Theorists and Political Power

This leads to the final point about tolerance and conspiracy theorists: the tension between conspiracy thinking and political power is central to democracy and civic education. Since the line between what is or not a conspiracy theory is often negotiated politically, and "conspiracy theorists" are not recognized as an important partisan subgroup, defending conspiracy theories is the quintessential test for political toleration. We often ask people if they would extend the right for a person with a controversial belief to teach at a local university. When it comes to conspiracy theorists, many Americans say no. The real challenge that conspiracy theorist professors like Steven E. Jones and James Tracy put before us is not that we are dupes who need to "wake up" to the larger conspiracies around us (or that we should ignore the emotional pleas of a victim's family), but that their defense of conspiracy theorizing as almost a natural corollary to a liberal arts or university education—and, following that chain of reasoning, to democracy itself. Many believe that conspiracy theorists have some natural deficiency that makes them unreasonable. Yet, as we have seen with recent scholarship, conspiracy thinking is a style of reasoning that is not only common but, some might say, is the core of our Enlightenment college curriculum. Could it be the case that, as a consequence of our political environment more than our natural proclivities, conspiracy thinking is not only common but indispensable for a healthy democracy?

Some scholars have raised this question, though I think it needs to be more central to the enterprise. As some say, democracy carries with it the price of conspiracy thinking, since "the fact is, we have pretty good reason to be prudently paranoid when it comes to many of the perpetrators of the most popular conspiracies, among them governments, intelligence agencies, corporations, and secret societies."[17] As Uscinski and Parent conclude in their book, *American Conspiracy Theories*: "Paradoxically, democracy is both a salve for, and a source of, conspiracy theories. . . . A skeptical eye toward power is therefore not only sensible but also desirable, and conspiracy theories are the culmination of this attitude."[18] These statements mirror Harvard political philosopher Judith Shklar's reading of the philosophical grandfather of the American political system, John Locke: "what the liberalism of fear owes to Locke is also obvious: that the governments of this world with their overwhelming power to kill, maim, indoctrinate, and make war are not to be trusted unconditionally, and that any confidence that we might develop in their agents must rest firmly on deep suspicion."[19] Maybe, just maybe, we must tolerate conspiracy theorists because we need them to remind us that "things are not what they seem." If this is the case, then tolerating conspiracy theorists among our ranks as colleagues and citizens is a price that we must always be ready—however difficult—to pay for our political system.

Most Americans do not like conspiracy theorists and their suspicions, and we think their conclusions are often wrong, but nevertheless we also recognize the importance for individuals to have those suspicions because, after all, we understand that not all suspicion is unwarranted. From an empirical perspective the problem, as with most things, is where we draw the line between healthy and unhealthy suspicion. We should try to find that line. From a political and educational perspective, we want to live in a place where the main problem is where to draw the line. We should never forget this lesson, because things are not always what they seem.

Notes

1. Walch, Tad. 2006. "BYU professor in dispute over 9/11 will retire." *Deseret News*, October 22. https://www.deseretnews.com/article/650200587/BYU-professor-in-dispute-over-911-will-retire.html.

2. Tracy, James. 2015. "Medical Examiner: More Questions than Answers." In *Nobody Died at Sandy Hook: It Was A FEMA Drill to Promote Gun Control*, eds. Jim Fetzer and Mike Palecek, 19–28. Moon Rocks Books, pg. 27.

3. Pozner, Lenny, and Veronique Pozner. 2015. "Sandy Hook Massacre 3rd Anniversary: Two parents target FAU conspiracy theorist." *Sun Sentinel*, December 10. http://www.sun-sentinel.com/opinion/commentary/sfl-on-sandy-hook-anniversary-two-parents-target-fau-professor-who-taunts-family-victims-20151210-story.html.

4. Tracy, James. 2015. "FAU professor questions whether Sandy Hook massacre was staged." *Sun Sentinel*, December 14. http://www.sun-sentinel.com/opinion/commentary/sfl-former-fau-professor-questions-whether-sandy-hook-massacre-was-staged-20151214-story.html.

5. McMahon, Paula. 2017. "Jury rules against fired FAU prof James Tracy in free speech case." *Sun Sentinel*, December 11. http://www.sun-sentinel.com/local/palm-beach/fl-reg-james-tracy-fau-closings-20171208-story.html.

6. Walch, Tad. 2006. "BYU action on Jones lamented." *Deseret News*, September 14. https://www.deseretnews.com/article/645200780/BYU-action-on-Jones-lamented.html.

7. American Association of University Professors. 2013. "AAUP Updates." AAUP.org. April 16. https://www.aaup.org/news/aaups-letter-faus-president-saunders#.WojEr66nEsg.

8. For a review of the literature on tolerance, see Gibson, James L. 2011. "Political Intolerance in the Context of Democratic Theory." In *Oxford Handbook of Political Science*, ed. Robert E. Goodin. Oxford: Oxford University Press, 323–341.

9. Pioneer Press. 2013. "Retired UMD professor theorizes that government behind Newtown massacre." *Twin Cities Pioneer Press*, January 4. https://www.twincities.com/2013/01/04/retired-umd-professor-theorizes-that-government-behind-newtown-massacre/.

10. van Deth, Jan W. 2007. "Norms of Citizenship." In *Oxford Handbook of Political Behavior*, eds. Russell J. Dalton and Hans-Dieter Klingerman. Oxford: Oxford University Press, 402–417.

11. Ibid.

12. The data is from an Amazon Mechanical Turk sample of 306 people. Descriptive statistics of the sample, along with replication materials, will be made available online.

13. Uscinski, Joseph E., and Joseph M. Parent. 2014. *American Conspiracy Theories*. Oxford: Oxford University Press.

14. Fenster, Mark. 2008. *Conspiracy Theories: Secrecy and Power in American Culture.* Minneapolis: University of Minnesota Press.

15. Smallpage, Steven M., Adam M. Enders, and Joseph E. Uscinski. 2017. "Partisan Contours of Conspiracy Theory Beliefs." *Research and Politics* 1–7.

16. Enders, Adam M., Steven M. Smallpage, and Robert N. Lupton. forthcoming. "Are All 'Birthers' Conspiracy Theorists? On the Relationship Between Conspiratorial Thinking and Political Orientations." *British Journal of Political Science.*

17. Brotherton, Robert. 2015. *Suspicious Minds: Why We Believe Conspiracy Theories.* New York: Bloomsbury/Sigma Press, pg. 113.

18. Uscinski and Parent, *American Conspiracy Theories,* 162.

19. Shklar, Judith. 1989. "Liberalism of Fear." In *Liberalism and the Moral Life,* ed. Nancy L. Rosenblum, 21–38. Cambridge, Massachusetts: Harvard University Press, pg. 30.

SECTION III

ARE CONSPIRACY THEORIES "ANTI-SCIENCE"?

JOSEPH E. USCINSKI

Conspiracy theorists are often accused of being anti-science. There is some-thing to this claim. Sizable portions of the public reject the science on vaccines, GM foods, fluoride, and climate change due to belief in conspiracy theories. Some conspiracy theories accuse scientists of being involved in a scam to defraud, injure, or kill the public. As Josh Pasek will show in Chapter 13, there exists a sizable distrust of science and scientists.

However, conspiracy theorists are fickle with their rejection of science. They tend to accept some findings and reject others. This selectivity is partially explained by their other worldviews. Those who believe that the theory of evolution is a fraud tend to be strongly religious. On the other hand, those who accept da Vinci Code conspiracy theories about Jesus' supposed progeny tend to be less Catholic and more New Age. Those who object to GM crops often do so because it is a backhanded way of attacking multinational corporations and expressing their objection to capitalism writ large. Those who object to climate change tend to do so because their views about free markets lead them to reject the collective solutions that solving climate change would necessarily entail. Morgan Marietta and David Barker will show in Chapter 14 that the rejection of many authoritative ac-counts is driven in varying degrees by two factors: conspiracy thinking and partisanship.

The majority of people accept vaccines as safe, but many within that lot denounce GM crops as unsafe. The people skeptical of adding fluoride to the water supply haven't raised an eyebrow about folic acid being added to breads and cereals. People are selective with the science they reject and the conspiracy theories they deploy.

There are a variety of factors that drive conspiracy theories about science—some findings butt directly into other deeply held views, such as creationist beliefs. In other instances political views drive the rejection of science. Sometimes stochastic events drive beliefs; for example, Andrew Wakefield's retracted paper linking autism to vaccines instigated a movement that continues despite its argument being completely discredited. Autism's causes are not fully understood, so people could attribute it to numerous un-verified causes, but people have chosen to blame it on vaccines because of a discredited paper. Conversely, there are numerous diseases we don't fully un-derstand, yet autism is one of a few that people have chosen to explain with conspiracy theories. Ted Goertzel in Chapter 15 looks at some scientists and other high-profile people who have advocated on behalf of anti-scientific conspiracy theories.

Conspiracy theorists are inconsistent with how they pick and choose evi-dence for their theories. 9/11 truthers base many of their arguments on bits and pieces gleaned from the same mainstream media and government reports that they believe are part of the conspiracy. This makes conspiracy theorists look inconsistent in some respects, but society functions on authoritative ac-counts, experts, and science. If people were to reject these things writ large, I shudder to think what their lives would be like. They would probably die of tooth decay in their twenties if starvation did not kill them first.

But just as conspiracy theorists pick and choose the science they reject, social scientists pick and choose, with ideological baggage of their own, which beliefs to label anti-scientific and which beliefs to study. Countless studies have examined climate change denial, no doubt because it's an issue of global importance but also because denialism is associated with those on the opposite side of the political spectrum from most scientists. Far fewer studies look at anti-scientific beliefs held by the left, and this is not because such beliefs are hard to find.[1]

Science has improved our existence in countless ways, mostly because its methods are reproducible and its findings reliable. If conspiracy theorists are going to reject its results, they should do so evenly and for good reason.

Note

1. Furnham, Adrian. 2013. "Commercial Conspiracy Theories: A Pilot Study." *Frontiers in Psychology* 4(June). DOI: 10.3389/fpsyg.2013.00379.

13

Don't Trust the Scientists! Rejecting the Scientific Consensus "Conspiracy"

JOSH PASEK

Papal Fallibility?

On June 18, 2015, Pope Francis released *Laudato Si'*, a papal encyclical stressing the "ecological crisis" of climate change and calling on Catholics worldwide to "come together to take charge of this home which has been entrusted to us."[1] The document outlined the current state of climate science and echoed the resounding consensus of researchers that large-scale warming is occurring and that this warming is being caused by humans (i.e., it is anthropogenic). In response to this evidence, the pope presented a moral case for action.

Even before the encyclical was public, Republicans vying for their party's 2016 U.S. presidential nomination expressed their concerns. In one radio interview, Catholic candidate Rick Santorum said, "The Church has gotten it wrong a few times on science, and I think we're probably better off leaving science to the scientists."[2] Another prominent Catholic candidate, Jeb Bush, similarly distanced himself from the papal statement, saying, "I don't get my economic policy from my bishops or my cardinals or my pope."[3] And James Inhofe, chair of the Senate environment and public works committee, echoed this sentiment saying, "The pope ought to stay with his job, and we'll stay with ours."[4]

The notion that the Vatican may not be as prescient about science as it is about morality is a reasonable one. After all, the Catholic Church did famously excommunicate the scientists of the Renaissance when their evidence challenged the dominant geocentric worldview. But the message could hardly come from a more hypocritical group. Both Bush and Santorum have contended that anthropogenic climate change is far from settled science,[5] thereby rejecting the conclusion of 97% of climate scientists.[6] Santorum and Inhofe have even gone so far as to deride the scientific evidence as "a hoax."[7] Yet despite an apparent unwillingness to listen to climate scientists and having no scientific training themselves, these politicians continued to debate and legislate on climate-related policies. And they were far from alone; in a search of Congressional Republicans' statements on the issue in 2014, fact-checker *PolitiFact*[8] found that only eight of 278 (2.9%) had made public statements asserting that anthropogenic climate change was happening. Most Congressional Republicans appeared to hold views contradicting the scientific evidence.

Questioning Climate Change

That Republican candidates have expressed skepticism over climate science should perhaps come as no surprise. In their perceptions, elites seemed very much in line with their constituents. A recent Pew survey found that less than half of self-identified Republicans (45%) thought that warming was occurring, only 22% asserted that it was anthropogenic, and a mere 21% regarded climate change as a very serious problem.[9] But unlike members of the public, who may not have heard anything about climate science, members of Congress and presidential candidates are regularly exposed to information about this salient political issue. It is thus hard to believe that their disbelief stems from sheer ignorance rather than some sort of willful process.

Elites who argue against the scientific consensus on climate change appear to take one of two tacks: They either state that the science is unsettled, or contend that the scientific consensus is itself a conspiratorial ploy. In his purported expose, *The Greatest Hoax: How the Global Warming Conspiracy Threatens Your Future*, Senator Inhofe argued for just such a ploy, laying out the motivations for scientists, liberals, and international bodies to collectively pedal "bad science."[10] Those who believe that the science is unsettled would presumably fail to recognize the presence of a scientific consensus. Yet Inhofe, Santorum, and others recognize the general consensus around climate change but do not trust the process that realized that consensus. Both sets of beliefs could presumably justify a policy agenda that does not recognize climate change as a threat.

These lines of reasoning have radically different implications for assessments of understanding of science, as well as attempts to improve scientific literacy and science policy. Elites and ordinary Americans who believe that climate science is unsettled presumably respect the scientific process but lack information, and providing them with additional information about the state of the science should improve awareness. Those who recognize the climate change consensus but regard it as a conspiracy or a hoax likely distrust the science and will be much harder to persuade. Hence, it is important to identify the extent to which disbelief for an issue like climate change is characterized by conspiratorial thinking rather than incomplete information.

A Larger Lack of Understanding

Climate change is far from the only policy issue where Americans fail to appreciate tenets of modern science even decades after they have been resolved. Since 1985, the National Science Foundation has collected data on Americans' acceptance of key scientific premises as part of the biennial *Science and Engineering Indicators* report. An analysis of these data from 1988 to 1999 revealed that knowledge of key science concepts improved only slightly over that period and led to the conclusion that "four out of five Americans cannot read and understand the science section of *The New York Times*."[11] And the 2014 edition of *Science and Engineering Indicators* reported that, across a series of questions about premises of physical and biological science, "the public's level of factual knowledge about science has not changed much over the past two decades."[12]

A number of scholars have recently questioned whether Americans' poor performance on science quiz questions highlights a lack of awareness about science—as has long been assumed—or instead might sometimes reflect a tendency to reject scientists' claims.[13] This distinction has significant implications for those hoping to influence public attitudes toward science and, by extension, science policy. As with climate change, if scientific illiteracy is largely due to a lack of awareness—the so-called deficit model—then refining the dissemination of scientific information should improve policy outcomes.[14] If this illiteracy is instead a product of rejectionism, persuasion is likely to be far more difficult.[15] And recent work provides evidence for rejectionism, revealing that more Americans can correctly state the scientific consensuses on evolution and the big bang than are willing to endorse these views themselves.[16]

Rejectionism and Distrust

One form that scientific rejectionism could take is that of a generalized distrust of scientists.[17] Individuals who distrust scientists may find the weight of scientific consensus less than compelling. They also might believe that the actions of scientists are self-interested or conspiratorial rather than altruistic.[18] And, if the scientific consensus is viewed as a conspiracy—a natural extension of these perceptions—then even citizens with lots of information may be unfazed by the scientific evidence. All of this could lead individuals who distrust scientists to reject their conclusions, and might thereby result in individuals who can simultaneously identify the scientific consensus while asserting contradictory claims. And the public discussion around scientific issues may sometimes reinforce scientific rejectionism, as Americans regularly encounter information from political elites like Inhofe, who publicly question scientific consensuses.[19]

To understand the nature of this sort of conspiratorial thinking about science, the rest of this chapter examines the extent to which individuals reject the scientific consensus about various matters and whether that rejection is associated with an explicit distrust of scientists. In 2014, using an online survey of a broad national sample of Americans, 2,737 respondents were asked a series of questions about their perceptions of what most scientists think and what they personally believed.[20] Responses to these questions provide a window into the extent to which individuals were aware of the science and actively rejected the scientific consensus. Because individuals could reject the consensus either due to conflicting beliefs or because they thought that the scientists were deceitful, I assess whether rejectionism tracked closely with distrust in scientists.

Do People Know the Scientific Consensus?

To measure knowledge of scientific consensuses, respondents were asked about a series of 10 scientific claims. These claims, designed to capture awareness of basic points of scientific agreement across a number of fields,[21] have been used extensively as part of the *Science and Engineering Indicators* reports by the National Science Foundation.[22] They include assertions such as, "the earliest humans lived at the same time as dinosaurs," "eating a genetically modified fruit could lead to a person's own genes being modified," and "plants produce the oxygen we breathe." The full list of items is presented in Table 13.1.[23] For each scientific claim, respondents were asked whether most scientists would make each particular claim. To determine whether respondents held views in line with the true scientific consensus, each of the questions about what scientists would say was followed by a question about respondents' personal beliefs.[24]

Responses to questions measuring awareness of the scientific consensus echoed the longstanding conclusion that Americans are not particularly knowledgeable about science (column 1 of Table 13.1). On average, respondents correctly answered 7.2 of the questions about scientific consensuses. If we were to assume that respondents either had correct knowledge or were guessing (i.e., that nobody was misinformed) and that guessing was completely at random, we would conclude that respondents knew the answers to 44.1% of these questions on average.[25] Awareness of the scientific consensus varied depending on which topic was queried; nearly 90% of respondents correctly identified the scientific consensus that plants produce oxygen, whereas only 53% recognized the consensus that humans share most of their DNA with mice (Table 13.1). The scope of awareness also varied considerably across respondents. Fourteen percent of respondents got all 10 questions correct, and 17.5% performed at or worse than chance.

When reporting on their own beliefs, respondents were even less likely to align with the true scientific consensus than this moderate level of awareness might

Table 13.1 **Scientific Knowledge Items and Distributions of Responses**

Full Wording of Items	True Consensus	Consensus Identified	Believe True Consensus	Average Difference	Scientific Literacy	Scientific Ignorance	Scientific Rejectionism
. . . that plants produce the oxygen that we breathe	TRUE	89.60%	88.60%	0.90%	86.20%	10.40%	3.30%
. . . that more than half of human genes are identical to those of mice	TRUE	53.10%	51.00%	2.10%	45.50%	46.90%	7.60%
. . . that electrons are smaller than atoms	TRUE	67.12%	66.93%	0.18%	59.44%	32.88%	7.67%
. . . that the continents on which we live have been moving their locations for millions of years	TRUE	85.20%	80.40%	4.90%	77.50%	14.80%	7.70%
. . . that sound travels faster than light	FALSE	64.30%	58.80%	5.60%	54.80%	35.70%	9.50%
. . . that the earth's climate has been warming in recent years [asked to half of respondents]	TRUE	82.80%	75.40%	7.40%	71.10%	17.20%	11.60%
. . . that the earliest humans lived at the same time as dinosaurs	FALSE	61.00%	56.30%	4.70%	49.30%	39.00%	11.80%
. . . that eating a genetically modified fruit could lead to a person's own genes being modified	FALSE	74.70%	69.10%	5.60%	62.70%	25.30%	12.00%

(continued)

Table 13.1 **Continued**

Full Wording of Items	True Consensus	Consensus Identified	Believe True Consensus	Average Difference	Scientific Literacy	Scientific Ignorance	Scientific Rejectionism
. . . that humans have been causing the earth's climate to warm in recent years [asked to half of respondents]	TRUE	77.50%	67.50%	10.00%	63.40%	22.50%	14.10%
. . . that the universe began with a huge explosion	TRUE	75.40%	54.90%	20.50%	51.60%	24.60%	23.90%
. . . that human beings, as we know them today, developed from earlier species of animals	TRUE	80.20%	56.90%	23.30%	53.90%	19.80%	26.30%
Average	—	73.07%	65.41%	7.66%	60.79%	26.92%	12.27%
Average by Number of Questions	—	7.31	6.54	0.77	6.08	2.69	1.23

Notes: Scientific Literacy is the proportion of responses for which respondents identified the true consensus and reported a matching personal belief. Scientific Ignorance is the proportion of responses for which the consensus was incorrectly identified. Scientific Rejectionism is the proportion of responses for which respondents identified the true consensus and reported a dissenting personal belief.

indicate (column 2 of Table 13.1). Personal beliefs matched the true consensus for 6.5 of the 10 questions on average, a difference of 0.8 questions from the awareness measure. This result is in line with the concern that measures of personal beliefs blend scientific awareness with rejectionism.[26] A closer question-by-question look at these measures reveals that the largest gaps occurred for questions about evolution, the big bang, and anthropogenic climate change, where religious and partisan factors might motivate additional distrust of the science (column 3).[27]

Do People Reject with the Consensus?

Identifying rejectionism required evidence that some individuals were aware of the scientific consensus but differed in their personal beliefs. In general, individuals who frequently recognized the scientific consensus and asserted similar personal beliefs could be considered scientifically literate. Individuals who frequently recognized the scientific consensus but often differed in their personal beliefs comprised rejectionists. And individuals who often misidentified the scientific consensus may have been either ignorant or misinformed, but clearly lacked scientific awareness.[28] Individuals who were frequently uninformed or misinformed about the scientific consensus but who asserted personal beliefs in line with the true consensus were also presumably unaware.

To assess the relative prevalence of scientific literacy, ignorance, and rejectionism, the proportion of responses that fell into each of these three categories was tallied for each respondent. These are plotted in the simplex shown in Figure 13.1, with each gray dot representing a single individual and the black triangle representing the average respondent. In it, individuals are arranged by the extent to which their beliefs reflect consistent literacy (closer to the top), consistent ignorance (closer to the bottom left) or consistent rejectionism (closer to the bottom right). In general, the dominant tradeoff was between those who were relatively unaware and those who both correctly identified and endorsed the scientific consensus (i.e. were relatively literate). For 60.8% of items, respondents correctly identified the scientific consensus and asserted concordant personal beliefs (Table 13.1, column 4). The consensus was wrongly identified for 26.9% of items (column 5). And 12.3% of items were answered in ways indicative of rejectionism (column 6). Hence, rejectionism does not appear to have been the dominant approach to scientific claims, but it was far from trivial; the average respondent was likely to answer 1.2 questions in ways that differed from a scientific consensus that they had properly identified.

The prevalence of rejectionism varied across both individuals and scientific claims. Fully 40.7% of respondents never expressed a rejectionist view; these individuals agreed with scientists every time they got the consensus question right (these individuals are on the line between least aware and most literate in the simplex in Figure 13.1). In contrast, 17.9% of respondents disagreed with a correctly identified consensus for three or more questions. Rejectionism was also heavily

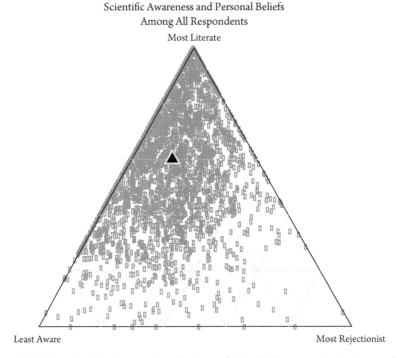

Scientific Awareness and Personal Beliefs
Among All Respondents

Most Literate

Least Aware   Most Rejectionist

Figure 13.1. Simplex plot showing distributions of scientific literacy, rejectionism, and ignorance across respondents.

concentrated around certain claims. Evolution and the big bang were the only items where more than 20% of respondents correctly identified the consensus and differed in their own views (26.3% and 23.9% respectively; Table 13.1). In contrast, very few respondents held rejectionist views about whether plants produce the oxygen we breathe or whether humans and mice share most of their DNA (3.3% and 7.6% respectively). For these questions, individuals who had incorrect personal beliefs were overwhelmingly either uninformed or misinformed about the scientific consensus. Evidence that rejectionism was much more common for some measures than others leads to the conclusion that a rejectionist pattern of responses was unlikely to simply be the product of respondents who were guessing on all of the questions. Instead, rejectionism seemed most likely to occur when individuals had some other reason to doubt scientists.

What Drives Rejection of the Consensus?

If the kind of conspiratorial thinking that dominates the climate change debate is behind why individuals adopt rejectionist perspectives, then rejectionism should be closely associated with a generalized distrust of scientists.[29] When individuals trust scientists, they would be expected to report that their personal beliefs mirror their perceptions of the science. Individuals who distrust scientists, on the other hand, might be expected to pick and choose from the science depending on whatever other motivations they might have. Thus, personal and scientific beliefs should be more concordant for those who trust scientists and less concordant for those who distrust scientists.

Indeed, rejectionism was closely associated with distrust in scientists. Compared to those who always trusted scientists and had complete confidence in their information, individuals who reported that they never trusted and had no confidence in scientists' information were far less likely to appear scientifically literate and far more likely to answer questions in ways indicative of both rejectionism and ignorance. For a typical respondent (Female, 50 years old, White, non-Hispanic, married, with some college education and an income of between $50,000 and $100,000), trust in scientists was strongly related to the prevalence of each of these categories (see Figure 13.2). At the lowest possible levels of trust, such a respondent would be

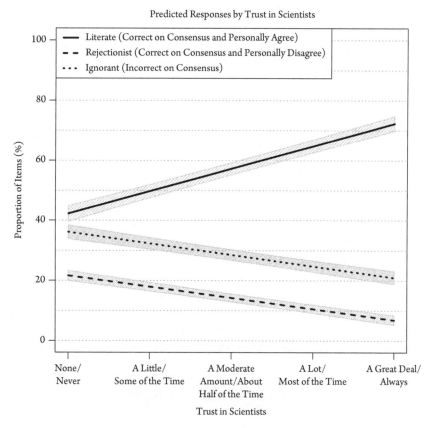

Figure 13.2. Predicted scientific literacy, rejectionism, and ignorance for an average respondent by trust in scientists.

expected to correctly identify the consensus and agree with it for 4.0 items on average, would be expected to misidentify the consensus for 4.1 items, and would be expected to know and reject the consensus for 0.9 items. At the highest possible levels of trust, the same respondent would be expected to correctly identify the consensus and agree with it for 7.3 items, to misidentify the consensus for 2.1 items and to know and reject the consensus on only 0.6 items on average.

The results thus suggest that trust in scientists provided strong insurance against rejectionism. For individuals who did not trust scientists at all, almost one-third of correct responses about the scientific consensus were associated with personal disagreement (31.6%). In contrast, only 6.2% of responses differed from a known scientific consensus for individuals who had the highest levels of scientific trust.[30]

Rejectionism and Perceptions of Scientific Conspiracy

Overall, scientific rejectionism behaves in the manner we might expect if rejectionists viewed scientific results as more or less conspiratorial. Rejectionism appears most prominently when scientists might be perceived to have alternate motivations from some members of the public, though it is present across many of the scientific issues examined. Further, it is most common when individuals distrust scientists. These findings lead to the conclusion that identifiable individuals, for certain issues, are more willing to deny the scientific evidence and accept an alternative claim.

Of course, believing that scientists are wrong about something and distrusting them is not sufficient to deduce that respondents think scientists are conspiring. Respondents may perceive scientists as wrong for some other systematic reason (e.g., they might think that the scientific process is broken). The fact that respondents appear to pick and choose which areas of science they should believe and which they should not is worrisome. The types of individuals who know and reject the scientific consensus are likely to be insensitive to additional scientific evidence,[31] and their continued presence is likely to keep these scientifically resolved issues as open political debates.

Further, coupled with results that indicate that the common thread in liberal and conservative rejection of science is the presence of conspiracist ideation, there are strong reasons to think that perceptions of conspiracy are a principal driver of both rejection of science and distrust in scientists.[32]

From Politicians to People

When American politicians and ordinary Catholics encountered a strong message from the pope that bolstered scientific evidence on climate change and framed the debate in moral terms,[33] they did not simply accept the new information. As has become increasingly apparent from theories of motivated reasoning and conspiracy belief, individuals took the pope's message and used it to reinforce their prior perceptions.[34] Republican and Democratic Catholics—those for whom the divide on climate is most salient [35]—were further balkanized in their perceptions.[36]

In an ideal world, political decisions about scientific matters would be informed by the best evidence research has made available. In practice, policies are often crafted by elites who have little or no specialized scientific expertise. This arrangement might be satisfactory if political actors deferred to scientists on questions about science and used their independent judgment solely to balance scientific conclusions with other policy goals. Yet public figures frequently question both the motivations and the conclusions reached by researchers in an effort to affect a particular policy agenda and to respond to their constituents.[37] This yields a contentious environment where scientific findings with political implications are often portrayed as unsettled long after scientists have reached agreement, and the scientific consensus itself is regarded as the product of conspiracy. It is perhaps unsurprising that, amid this cacophony, individuals in the public sometimes distrust scientists and reject scientific conclusions even when they are aware of what the majority of scientists say.

Notes

1. Francis. 2015. *Laudato Si' [Encyclical Letter]*. http://w2.vatican.va/content/francesco/en/encyclicals/documents/papa-francesco_20150524_enciclica-laudato-si.html (Accessed December 19, 2017).
2. Girodano, Dom. 2015, "Rick Santorum On Pope Francis' Letter On Climate Change: 'Leave The Science To The Scientist.'" http://philadelphia.cbslocal.com/2015/06/01/rick-santorum-on-pope-francis-letter-on-climate-change-leave-the-science-to-the-scientist/ (Accessed December 19, 2017).
3. Wolfgang, Ben. 2015. "Jeb Bush, Rick Santorum Say Pope Should Stay out of Climate Change Debate." *Washington Times*, June 17, 2015.
4. Goldenberg, Suzanne. 2015. "Republicans' Leading Climate Denier Tells the Pope to Butt out of Climate Debate." *The Guardian*, June 11, 2015.
5. Goldenberg, Suzanne. 2014. "Jeb Bush May be 'The Smart Brother' – But He's as Much of a Climate Denier as any Conservative." *The Guardian*, December 16, 2014.
6. Cook, John, Dana Nuccitelli, Sarah A. Green, Mark Richardson, Bärbel Winkler, Rob Painting, Robert Way, Peter Jacobs, and Andrew Skuce. 2013. Quantifying the Consensus on Anthropogenic Global Warming in the Scientific Literature. *Environmental Research Letters* 8(2): 024024. DOI: 10.1088/1748-9326/8/2/024024.
7. Inhofe, James. 2012. *The Greatest Hoax: How the Global Warming Conspiracy Threatens Your Future.* Washington, D.C.: WND Books; Schultheis, Emily. 2012. "Santorum: I never believed global warming 'hoax.'" https://www.politico.com/blogs/burns-haberman/2012/02/santorum-i-never-believed-global-warming-hoax-113739 (Accessed December 19, 2017).
8. Kliegman, Julie. 2014. "Jerry Brown Says 'Virtually No Republican' in Washington Accepts Climate Change Science." *Tampa Bay Times PolitiFact*, May 18, 2014.
9. Cooperman, Alan, Gregory Smith, Jessica Hamar Martinez, and Katherine Ritchey. 2015. *Catholics Divided Over Global Warming.* Washington, D.C.: Pew Research Center.

10. Inhofe, *The Greatest Hoax.*
11. Miller, Jon D. 2004. "Public Understanding of, and Attitudes toward, Scientific Research: What We Know and What We Need to Know." *Public Understanding of Science* 13(3): 273–294. DOI: 10.1177/0963662504044908.
12. National Science Board. 2014. *Science and Engineering Indicators 2014* (No. NSB 14-01) *National Science Foundation*. Arlington, VA: National Science Foundation.
13. Cf. Roos, J. Micah. 2014. "Measuring Science or Religion? A Measurement Analysis of the National Science Foundation Sponsored Science Literacy Scale 2006–2010." *Public Understanding of Science* 23(7): 797–813. DOI: 10.1177/0963662512464318.
14. Cf. Sturgis, Patrick, and Nick Allum. 2004. "Science in Society: Re-Evaluating the Deficit Model of Public Attitudes." *Public Understanding of Science* 13(1): 55–74. DOI: 10.1177/0963662504042690.
15. Lewandowsky, Stephan, Ulrich K. H. Ecker, Collen M. Seifert, Norbert Schwarz, and John Cook. 2012. "Misinformation and Its Correction: Continued Influence and Successful Debiasing." *Psychological Science in the Public Interest* 13(3): 106–131. DOI: 10.1177/1529100612451018.
16. Kahan, Dan M. 2015. "Climate-Science Communication and the Measurement Problem." *Advances in Political Psychology* 36(S1): 1–43. DOI: 10.1111/pops.12244; Pasek, Josh. 2017. "It's Not My Consensus: Motivated Reasoning and the Sources of Scientific Illiteracy." *Public Understanding of Science.* DOI: 10.1177/0963662517733681; Roos, "Measuring Science or Religion?"
17. Malka, Ariel, Jon A. Krosnick, and Gary Langer. 2009. "The Association of Knowledge with Concern About Global Warming: Trusted Information Sources Shape Public Thinking." *Risk Analysis* 29(5): 633–647. DOI: 10.1111/j.1539-6924.2009.01220.x.
18. Lewandowsky, Stephan, Klaus Oberauer, and Gilles E. Gignac. 2013. "NASA Faked the Moon Landing—Therefore, (Climate) Science Is a Hoax: An Anatomy of the Motivated Rejection of Science." *Psychological Science* 24(5): 622–633. DOI: 10.1177/0956797612457686.
19. Boykoff, Maxwell T., and Jules M. Boykoff. 2007. "Climate Change and Journalistic Norms: A Case-study of US Mass-media Coverage." *Geoforum* 38(6): 1190–1204. DOI: 10.1016/j.geoforum.2007.01.008.
20. Pasek, "It's Not My Consensus."
21. Cf. Miller, Jon D. 1998. "The Measurement of Civic Scientific Literacy." *Public Understanding of Science* 7(3): 203–223. DOI: 10.1088/0963-6625/7/3/001.
22. National Science Board, *Science and Engineering Indicators 2014.*
23. Readers may notice that there are 11 total questions presented, including two questions about climate change. This is the case because respondents who completed the battery were randomly asked to evaluate either claims about whether the climate was warming or whether humans were causing the climate to warm. To account for differences in these measures, a variable is included in all regressions to control for which of these two claims respondents were asked to evaluate.
24. See Pasek (2017) for a full description of study methods. Although the sample was national in scope, it was not designed to provide a window into the true distributions of beliefs among members of the public. Instead, the data should be viewed as suggestive of the types of beliefs among members of the public, the relative distributions of beliefs across measures, and the factors that relate to those beliefs.
25. These assumptions are almost certainly wrong. Some individuals likely hold objectively incorrect beliefs about science, and guessing is not truly random (see Pasek 2017). This can be calculated by solving the two equation system: *knowledge+guessing*=1 and *knowledge+*(*guessing**.5)=.7207.
26. Kahan, "Climate-Science Communication"; Roos, "Measuring Science or Religion?"
27. Pasek, "It's Not My Consensus."
28. Pasek, Josh, Gaurav Sood, and Jon A. Krosnick. 2015. "Misinformed About the Affordable Care Act? Leveraging Certainty to Assess the Prevalence of Misperceptions." *Journal of Communication* 65(4): 660–673. DOI: 10.1111/jcom.12165.

29. Lewandowsky, Oberauer, and Gignac, "NASA Faked the Moon Landing."

30. These numbers reflect the actual averages among the 169 respondents who reported the lowest levels of trust on both measures and 203 respondents who reported the highest levels of trust on both measures. The predicted values based on the regression results for the typical respondent described above were nearly identical, at 32.9% and 8.0% respectively.

31. Weber, Elke U., and Paul C. Stern. 2011. "Public Understanding of Climate Change in the United States." *American Psychologist* 66(4): 315–328. DOI: 10.1037/a0023253.

32. Dixon, Ruth M., and Jonathan A. Jones. 2015. "Conspiracist Ideation as a Predictor of Climate-Science Rejection: An Alternative Analysis." *Psychological Science* 26(5): 664–666. DOI: 10.1177/0956797614566469; Lewandowsky, Stephan, Gilles E. Gignac, and Klaus Oberauer. 2013. "The Role of Conspiracist Ideation and Worldviews in Predicting Rejection of Science." *PLoS ONE* 8(10). DOI: 10.1371/jounal.pone.0075637.

33. Landrum, Ashley R., Robert B. Lull, Heather Akin, and Kathleen Hall Jamieson. 2016. "Making It About Morals: Pope Francis Shifts the Climate Change Debate." https://ssrn.com/abstract=2997490.

34. Miller, Joanne M., Kyle L. Saunders, and Christina E. Farhart. 2015. "Conspiracy Endorsement as Motivated Reasoning: The Moderating Roles of Political Knowledge and Trust." *American Journal of Political Science* 60(4): 824–844. DOI: 10.1111/ajps.12234; Nyhan, Brendan, Jason Reifler, Sean Richey, and Gary L. Freed. 2014. "Effective Messages in Vaccine Promotion: A Randomized Trial." *Pediatrics* 133(4): e835–e842. DOI: 10.1542/peds.2013-2365.

35. Dunlap, Riley E., and Aaron M. McCright. 2008. "A Widening Gap: Republican and Democratic Views on Climate Change." *Environment: Science and Policy for Sustainable Development* 50(5): 26–35. DOI: 10.3200/ENVT.50.5.26-35.

36. Li, Nan, Joseph Hilgard, Dietram A. Scheufele, Kenneth M. Winneg, and Kathleen Hall Jamieson. 2016. "Cross-Pressuring Conservative Catholics? Effects of Pope Francis' Encyclical on the U.S. Public Opinion on Climate Change." *Climatic Change* 139(3–4): 367–380. DOI: 10.1007/s10584-016-1821-z.

37. McCright, Aaron M., and Riley E. Dunlap. 2010. "Anti-reflexivity: The American Conservative Movement's Success in Undermining Climate Science and Policy." *Theory, Culture & Society* 27(2–3): 100–133. DOI: 10.1177/0263276409356001.

Conspiratorial Thinking and Dueling Fact Perceptions

MORGAN MARIETTA AND DAVID C. BARKER

Conspiracy theories are about facts, and facts in America are no longer shared. Whether it is the existence of climate change, the prevalence of racism, the origins of sexual orientation, the likelihood of terrorism, or many other disputed realities from vaccines to marijuana we now hold dueling sets of facts, more connected to values and partisanship than to authority and evidence. Some scholars believe the primary driver is partisanship—polarized facts are partisan facts—while others argue that core values or social identities are the real foundation. But there is also an important connection to conspiratorial thinking. While most of this volume addresses literal conspiracies or conspiracy theories, this chapter addresses the connection of conspiratorial thinking to the ordinary facts that shape current political controversies. We offer several takeaway points:

1) Conspiratorial thinking is connected to perceptions of a range of politically influential facts, beyond conspiracy theories and actual conspiracies.
2) These include the more expected (vaccines, GMOs, the prevalence of false convictions) and the less expected (sexual orientation, national debt, climate change).
3) The connections between conspiratorial thinking and fact perceptions are equally strong within both political parties.
4) If current authority leans left, conspiratorial thinkers lean toward the factual perceptions of the right; if current authority leans right, conspiracy thinkers lean left.

Conspiratorial Thinking and Fact Perceptions

Conspiratorial thinking, like all forms of epistemology, is a matter of trust. Do we trust authority? Do we trust universities? Do we trust fact-checkers?[1] Do we trust our own instincts over the view of "experts"? Or do we *distrust* authority to the degree that official positions are evidence of the *opposite* reality? Given that so many of the influential facts of our current politics cannot be known to us personally—they are impersonal, unobservable by ordinary citizens, "invisible" as Walter Lippmann called them—we must rely on the reports of unknown experts, presented to us over news media.[2] Or we can replace that trust in authority with reliance on personal intuitions, village wisdom, and alternative news sources.

Perceptions of many mundane facts with political consequences are now deeply divided. Scholars have described this phenomenon as *contested facts, misinformation, cultural cognition, partisan facts,* and *dueling fact perceptions* (DFPs). By any name, Americans have become polarized around more than merely partisanship and ideology, broadening the scope of polarization to disputes over facts.[3] The prominence of DFPs seems to be connected to the cultural and ideological polarization of American politics.[4] Our divided ideologies and partisan loyalties are reinforcing the human tendency to project our preferred values onto our perceived facts.[5] In their recent book on this phenomenon (*Do Facts Matter?*), Jennifer Hochschild and Katherine Einstein argue that "the temptation to use misinformation can deeply damage the fragile system of democratic decision making."[6] With no agreement on basic realities, we have little chance of a consensus on which problems need to be solved, let alone how to address them. In other words, without agreement on *where we are,* deciding collectively *where we ought to go* is practically impossible.

Perhaps the most well-known disputed reality in contemporary politics is climate change. Undeniably, there is a mainstream scientific consensus that the Earth is warming at a faster pace than is attributable to natural causes.[7] However, a quick Internet search will reveal some scholars with elite-sounding titles who will confidently challenge the validity of the data and offer alternative theories of non-anthropogenic causes, opening the door to alternative interpretations.[8] Gallup data on perceptions of global warming reflect this problem. In response to the question, "Do you believe increases in the Earth's temperature over the last century are due more to the effects of pollution from human activities or natural changes in the environment that are not due to human activities?" 61% of Americans reported that human activities were to blame, while 33% thought natural causes were the more likely source as of 2001. In March of 2014, these numbers were 57% and 40%. Contrary to many expectations, perceptions of global warming have *not* moved closer to consensus over the last decade.

Another disputed reality that is highly polarized and politically relevant is the degree to which racism continues to shape the prospects of minority citizens in our society.[9] Gallup data on perceptions of racism show a remarkable division. In a 2008 national poll, 56% of Americans perceived racism to be widespread, while 42% disagreed. In 2016, the numbers were 61% to 38%, deeply divided even after widely publicized police shootings and the rise of the Black Lives Matter movement.

While scholarly authority may assert that there is a correct answer to this question, it would be challenging for an average citizen to verify it with confidence.

The same applies to whether the threat from Islamist terrorism is small or large, justifying government surveillance and military actions or not; whether the national debt is going to have tremendous negative consequences for the economy in the future or whether it is not something worry about, justifying restrictions on spending or not; whether sexual orientation is innate or experiential, which is a strong predictor of support for gay rights;[10] whether false convictions are common or rare, justifying police reforms or not; whether genetically modified foods (GMOs) are healthy or not; and perhaps most notoriously, whether vaccines cause autism or not, which has become a serious threat to public health.[11]

Why citizens fall on one side or the other of these divides is unclear. Most arguments about the origins of dueling facts have focused on partisanship and polarized values. But conspiratorial thinking also has a strong influence. Whom do you trust about the realities you can't easily observe for yourself? For conspiratorial thinkers, the answer is the opposite of contemporary authority.

Recent Evidence

Our evidence comes from a survey of 1,000 U.S. citizens conducted in June of 2017.[12] It focuses on California, which leans left but still contains many Republicans for comparison. More importantly, the state contains plenty of conspiracy thinkers.[13] Our question is how conspiracy thinking relates to perceptions of politically influential facts.[14] For some of these disputed facts, one perception is endorsed by the prevailing authorities of our society (academic consensus, government institutions, and mainstream media). For others, the authorities are divided in their messages. Our analysis allows us to see whether there is a connection between conspiratorial thinking and specific factual perceptions. Other factors influence those perceptions as well, such as partisanship, moral values, and demographics, but we control for those effects to isolate the independent connections to conspiracy thinking. The broad results are illustrated in Table 14.1.

Vaccines

The disputed fact with the strongest relationship to conspiratorial thought is the effect of vaccines. Citizens highest on the Conspiratorial Thinking Scale were over 40% more likely than those lowest on the scale to believe that vaccines cause autism. The belief that vaccines are harmful—counter to all of the legitimate scientific evidence—used to be more associated with the left (a belief more common among hippies and hipsters than churchgoers and red-meat eaters). No longer; this

Table 14.1 **The Influence of Conspiratorial Thinking**

Disputed Fact	Perception of Prevailing Authorities	Perception Associated With Conspiratorial Thinking	Probability	Marginal Change from Lowest to Highest in Conspiratorial Thinking *
Vaccines	Safe	Harmful	< .001	41.5%
GMOs	Safe	Harmful	< .001	35.9%
Sexual Orientation	Innate	Experiential	< .01	19.7%
False Convictions	(Mixed)	Prevalent	< .01	18.7%
National Debt	(Mixed)	Dangerous	< .02	15.5%
Climate Change	Real	Not Real	.14	9.3%
Racism	Influential	*No Effect*	.40	
Terrorism	Dangerous	*No Effect*	.99	

* Conspiratorial Thinking Scale (three question battery, see Uscinski & Parent 2014); Marginal probabilities were calculated through a logistic regression analysis of dichotomized fact perceptions (certainly true or probably true versus certainly false or probably false), controlling for party identification, moral values (Haidt), gender, race, age, education, and income; N = 862.

anti-empirical belief has been espoused more recently by pro-Trump populists. We found no relationship between partisan identity and perceptions of vaccines, but an extremely strong connection to conspiratorial thought. This relationship is demonstrated clearly in Figure 14.1, which illustrates the rising perception that vaccines cause autism as conspiratorial thinking moves from low to high.

Genetically Modified Foods

The next strongest relationship was with perceptions of GMOs. Republicans were more likely to believe GMOs are safe, in line with the scientific establishment. However, the effect of conspiratorial thinking is clear among both partisan groups. The perception that GMOs are safe is held by the majority of Democrats and Republicans who are low in conspiratorial thinking, but declines around 35% to a minority of citizens who are high on the conspiratorial spectrum.

Sexual Orientation

While vaccines and GMOs have frequently been the subject of conspiracy theories—with corporations and government regulators as the evil-doers—sexual

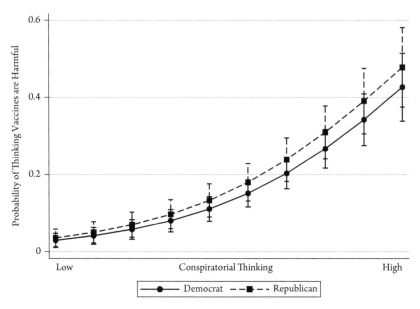

Figure 14.1 Conspiratorial Thinking and Vaccines.*
*Predicted probabilities with 95% confidence intervals.

orientation is less obviously connected to conspiratorial thinking. Nonetheless it bears the third strongest relationship. Beliefs about the origins of sexual orientation are divided between (1) perceptions that individuals feel a stable kind of attraction from the time they are relatively young, and (2) perceptions that socialization or life events influence whether someone is heterosexual or homosexual.[15] Perceptions of whether orientation is innate or experiential have been demonstrated to be one of the most powerful determinants of attitudes toward gay rights[16] and have been tracked by the Gallup poll since 1978 (as of 2014 the American public is split 42% to 37% on the question of innate versus experiential origins). Republicans start lower in perceptions that sexual orientation is innate (72% compared to 90%) and display a steeper slope as conspiratorial thinking rises (27% overall drop versus 17%). But the relationship is clear for both parties (see Figure 14.2): Higher levels of conspiracy thinking are associated with the view that sexuality is not innate.

False Convictions

The conflict over the prevalence of false convictions may reflect the popularity of *Making a Murder* and *Serial*, two cultural phenomena arguing that false convictions are prevalent, often due to police misconduct. It may also reflect the rise of the Innocence Project and the large number of exonerations in recent decades. One of

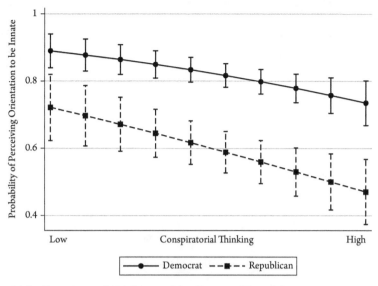

Figure 14.2. Conspiratorial Thinking and the Origins of Sexual Orientation.

the most well-known examples of a post-DNA test exoneration is the Central Park Five, who were convicted in 1990 of the rape of the Central Park jogger and freed in 2002 after the confession (and DNA match) of a convicted rapist currently in prison. Many citizens believe in their innocence, while others (famously including Donald Trump) believe they are guilty of the crime they confessed to (along with the other perpetrator). However, the effect among Democrats and Republicans is the same: as conspiratorial thinking rises, so does the perception of false convictions (Figure 14.3).

National Debt

The disputed reality of the national debt reflects a long-standing debate among economists and politicians about its long-term consequences.[17] If the debt chickens will one day come home to roost, we need to restrain the most expensive (and popular) federal spending (health care, other entitlements, and military expenditures). If these fears are unfounded, then concerns about spending are unfounded as well, and only serve to block attempts to provide greater social justice. Some see the debt as likely to have tremendous negative effects on the economy as well as on national security (or, as Admiral Mike Mullen, former Chairman of the Joint Chiefs of Staff, phrased it in 2010, "the most significant threat to our national security is our debt").[18] Others see the debt as essentially irrelevant as long as it is managed, especially when we consider the positive side of the ledger in terms of what the

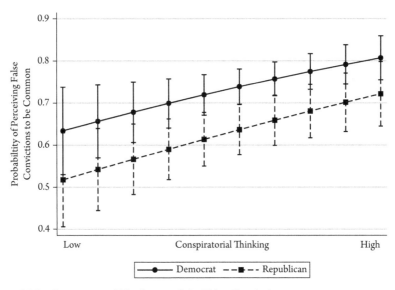

Figure 14.3. Conspiratorial Thinking and the False Convictions.

debt is buying: economic stimulus, infrastructure improvements, greater equality of access to health care, and education, all of which contribute to economic productivity. One of the clearest prominent voices on this side of the factual debate is Paul Krugman, Nobel Prize winning economist and columnist for *The New York Times*, who describes "the wrongheaded, ill-informed obsession with debt" as the "triumph of ideology over evidence," connected to "our postmodern, fact-free politics."[19] In this sense, one might think that only Republicans high in conspiratorial thought would be more likely to believe that the national debt has dangerous future consequences, but the relationship is actually stronger among Democrats. As illustrated in Figure 14.4, Republicans who are high in conspiratorial thinking are 12% more likely than those at the lower end of the scale to believe that the national debt is dangerous (moving from 76% to 88%). Democrats start lower (58%) but move up to 76%, an 18% gain as they move from low to high conspiratorial thought.

Climate Change

When it comes to climate change, the role of conspiracy thinking is less certain (*p*-value of .14) compared to the clear relationships for vaccines, GMOs, sexual orientation, false convictions, and the national debt. The connection is also weaker (around a 9% difference in perception from the lowest to highest range of conspiratorial thought). This extremely politicized fact perception is driven primarily by partisanship and core values, but nonetheless conspiratorial thought plays a small role for both Republicans and Democrats.[20]

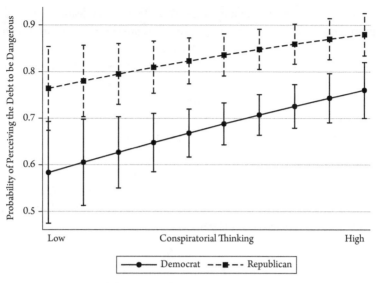

Figure 14.4. Conspiratorial Thinking and the National Debt.

Racism and Terrorism

It is important to note that conspiratorial thinking does not have a relationship with *all* DFPs in contemporary politics. One disputed fact that bears no relationship is the likelihood of terrorism. Another is the prevalence of racism. Neither Democrats nor Republicans see the role of racism to be stronger or weaker due to the influence of conspiracy. This may be because racism is neither secret nor controlled; it is the result of the attitudes and behavior of ordinary people. No conspiracy is necessary.

Authority and Partisanship

These examples illustrate that conspiratorial thought can lead to beliefs that are more liberal (false convictions are prevalent) or more conservative (sexual orientation is experiential, the national debt is dangerous). DFPs grounded in conspiracy thinking are neither left nor right as a rule, but instead reflect the rejection of current authority. In regard to vaccines, authorities from academia, government, and mainstream media all say they are safe, while conspiratorial thinkers tend to think the opposite. The same is true for GMOs, sexual orientation, and climate change: the authorities make one assertion, and conspiracy thinkers lean the other way. The messages from authorities regarding false convictions and the national debt can be more accurately described as mixed. Government authorities say false convictions are very low, while academic and media authorities say the reverse. Some academics and pundits say the national debt is dangerous, while others dismiss it as irrelevant. When presented with mixed messages from the prevailing authorities, conspiratorial thinkers seem to choose the side backed by shadowy power: a corrupt legal system creates false convictions, and a corrupt financial system creates a looming danger of debt. These trends hold among Democrats and Republicans alike. In our 2017 data, the conspiratorial predisposition is related to Democratic affiliation, as expected given that the Democrats are currently out of power.[21] However, within each domain, conspiracy thinking demonstrates the same relationship with fact perceptions for both Democrats and Republicans. Even for sexual orientation, Democrats who are also conspiratorial thinkers move toward the belief that orientation is not innate. Even for GMOs, Republicans who are conspiratorial thinkers are more likely to embrace the view that GMOs are harmful. The role of conspiracy thinking in fact perceptions is trans-partisan.

Conclusion

The Oxford English Dictionary declared *post-truth* to be its word of the year for 2016, defined as "circumstances in which objective facts are less influential in shaping public opinion than appeals to emotion and personal belief."[22] In a political environment characterized by polarized fact perceptions and struggles by elites and masses alike to grasp the implications of post-truth politics, it is not merely partisan leadership and conflicting values, but also conspiratorial thinking that leads to divided fact perceptions. Conspiracy thinking is related to perceptions of facts across a broad range, from vaccines to climate change. Perhaps most importantly, the connection is trans-partisan. Whichever dueling fact is supported by establishment authority, conspiratorial thinkers gravitate toward the opposing factual perception, regardless of their partisan affiliation. Conspiratorial thinkers distrust and reject prevailing wisdom. Truth relies on trust; as trust in authority fades, perceptions of truth fracture with it.

Notes

1. See Uscinski, Joseph, and Ryden Butler. 2013. "The Epistemology of Fact Checking." *Critical Review* 25(2): 162–180; and Marietta, Morgan, David Barker, and Todd Bowser. 2015. "Fact-Checking Polarized Politics: Does the Fact-Check Industry Provide Consistent Guidance on Disputed Realities?" *The Forum: A Journal of Applied Research in Contemporary Politics* 13(4): 577–596.
2. Lippmann, Walter. 1922. *Public Opinion.* New York: Free Press: 8, 17; Lippmann, Walter. 1927. *The Phantom Public.* New York: Macmillan: 3–4.
3. See Bartels, Larry. 2002. "Beyond the Running Tally: Partisan Bias in Political Perceptions" *Political Behavior* 24(2): 117–150; Bullock, John, Alan Gerber, Seth Hill, and George Huber. 2015. "Partisan Bias in Factual Beliefs About Politics." *Quarterly Journal of Political Science*

10(4):519–578; Barker, David C. 2002. *Rushed to Judgment: Talk Radio, Persuasion, and American Political Behavior.* New York: Columbia University Press; Gaines, Brian, James Kuklinski, Paul Quirk, Buddy Peyton, and Jay Verkuilen. 2007. "Same Facts, Different Interpretations: Partisan Motivation and Opinion on Iraq." *Journal of Politics* 69(4):957–974; Gerber, Alan, and Gregory Huber. 2010. "Partisanship, Political Control, and Economic Assessments." *American Journal of Political Science* 54(1):153–173; Jerit, Jennifer, and Jason Barabas. 2012. "Partisan Perceptual Bias and the Information Environment." *Journal of Politics* 74(3): 672–684; Joslyn, Mark, and Donald Haider-Markel. 2014. "Who Knows Best? Education, Partisanship, and Contested Facts." *Politics & Policy* 42(6): 919–947; Kahan, Dan. 2013. "Ideology, Motivated Reasoning, and Cognitive Reflection." *Judgment & Decision-Making* 8(4): 407; Kahan, Dan, and Donald Braman. 2006. "Cultural Cognition and Public Policy." *Yale Law & Policy Review* 24(1): 147–170; Kuklinski, James, Paul Quirk, Jennifer Jerit, David Schweider, and Robert Rich. 2000. "Misinformation and the Currency of Democratic Citizenship." *Journal of Politics* 62(3):790–815; Nyhan, Brendan, and Jason Reifler. 2010. "When Corrections Fail: The Persistence of Political Misperceptions." *Political Behavior* 32(2): 303–330; Reedy, Justin, Chris Wells, and John Gastil. 2014. "How Voters Become Misinformed: An Investigation of the Emergence and Consequences of False Factual Beliefs." *Social Science Quarterly* 95(5):1399–1418; Shapiro, Robert, and Yaeli Bloch-Elchon. 2008. "Do the Facts Speak for Themselves? Partisan Disagreement as a Challenge to Democratic Competence." *Critical Review* 20(1):115–139. For a summary of the current literature, see Flynn, D. J., Brendan Nyhan, and Jason Reifler. 2017. "The Nature and Origins of Misperceptions: Understanding False and Unsupported Beliefs About Politics." *Advances in Political Psychology* 38(1):127–150.

4. Scholars argue about whether we are polarized over partisanship, ideology, culture, religion, race, wealth, geography, media consumption, or several of these factors. See Abramowitz, Alan. 2013. *The Polarized Public: Why American Government is So Dysfunctional.* Boston: Pearson; Barker, David C., and Christopher Carman. 2012. *Representing Red and Blue: How the Culture Wars Change the Way Citizens Speak and Politicians Listen.* New York: Oxford University Press; Bishop, Bill. 2008. *The Big Sort.* New York: Houghton Mifflin; Brewer, Mark, and Jeffrey Stonecash. 2007. *Split: Class and Cultural Conflict in American Politics.* Washington, D.C.: CQ Press; Campbell, James. 2016. *Polarized: Making Sense of a Divided America.* Princeton: Princeton University Press; Hunter, James Davison. 1991. *Culture Wars: The Struggle to Define America.* New York: Basic Books; Layman, Geoffrey. 2001. *The Great Divide: Religious and Cultural Conflict in American Party Politics.* New York: Columbia University Press; Mann, Thomas E., and Norman J. Orenstein. 2012. *It's Even Worse Than it Looks.* New York: Basic Books; McCarty, Nolan, Keith T. Poole, and Howard Rosenthal. 2006. *Polarized America: The Dance of Ideology and Unequal Riches.* Cambridge: MIT. Press; Schier, Steven. 2016. *Polarized: The Rise of Ideology in American Politics.* Lanham, MD: Rowman & Littlefield; Theriault, Sean. 2008. *Party Polarization in Congress.* New York: Cambridge University Press; White, John Kenneth. 2002. *The Values Divide: American Politics and Culture in Transition.* Washington, D.C.: CQ Press.

5. On the fact/value distinction, see David Hume. 1739. *A Treatise of Human Nature;* and Weber, Max. 1946. "Science as a Vocation." in *From Max Weber: Essays in Sociology,* eds. H. H. Gerth and C. Wright Mills New York: Oxford University Press. More recently, Hillary Putnam has argued that the is/ought distinction is difficult for humans to disentangle: facts and values are so hopelessly intertwined that even scientists often make false claims of value-neutrality. See Putnam, Hillary. 2002. *The Collapse of the Fact/Value Dichotomy and Other Essays.* Cambridge: Harvard University Press. In many cases, the "facts" we believe may be little more than projections of our values. This expectation is supported by the psychological evidence of motivated reasoning, or the tendency to defend prior conclusions and maintain congruence among beliefs by applying a low burden of proof when an observation is in accord with our values and a high burden of proof when it is not. See Kunda, Ziva. 1990. "The Case for Motivated Reasoning." *Psychological Bulletin* 108(3): 480–498.

6. Hochschild, Jennifer, and Katherine Einstein. 2015. *Do Facts Matter? Information and Misinformation in American Politics*. Norman: University of Oklahoma Press, 6.

7. See Intergovernmental Panel on Climate Change (IPCC). 2014. *Climate Change 2014: Synthesis Report*, Fifth Assessment Report of the Intergovernmental Panel on Climate Change, Geneva.

8. See Hulme, Mike. 2009. *Why We Disagree About Climate Change: Understanding Controversy, Inaction and Opportunity*. Cambridge: Cambridge University Press.

9. See Peffley, Mark and Jon Hurwitz. 2010. *Justice in America: The Separate Realities of Blacks and Whites*. Cambridge: Cambridge University Press; Bonilla-Silva, Eduardo 2014. *Racism Without Racists: Color-Blind Racism and the Persistence of Racial Inequality in America* (4th ed.). Lanham, MD: Rowman and Littlefield; Norton, Michael, and Samuel Sommers. 2011. "Whites See Racism as a Zero-Sum Game That They Are Now Losing." *Perspectives on Psychological Science* 6(3): 215–218.

10. See Haider-Markel, Donald, and Mark Joslyn. 2008. "Beliefs About the Origins of Homosexuality and Support for Gay Rights: An Empirical Test of Attribution Theory." *Public Opinion Quarterly* 72(2): 291–310.

11. See Mele, Christopher. 2017. "Minnesota See Largest Outbreak of Measles in Almost 30 Years." *New York Times*, May 5, 2017; Sun, Lena H. 2017. "Anti-vaccine Activists Spark a State's Worst Measles Outbreak in Decades." *The Washington Post*, May 5, 2017; see also Kirkland, Anna. 2016. *Vaccine Court: The Law and Politics of Injury*. New York: NYU Press.

12. The CALSPEAKS panel is managed by the Institute for Social Research at California State University, Sacramento. It employs a combination of probability and quasi-probability sampling methods, and a detailed weighting procedure to achieve representativeness of the California population. Technical details regarding sampling, panel management, weighting, and sample characteristics can be observed at http://www.csus.edu/isr/calspeaks/methods%20and%20technical%20details.html.

13. 33% of the sample responded "Strongly Agree" to one or more of the three questions in the conspiratorial thinking battery ("Much of our lives are being controlled by plots hatched in secret places". . . "Even though we live in a democracy, a few people will always run things anyway". . . "The people who really 'run' the country are not known to the voters").

14. We cannot say for certain whether conspiratorial thinking leads to specific fact perceptions (which we believe is more likely), or the reverse (those fact perceptions lead to broader conspiratorial thinking). Statistical methods can only show the degree of relationship between conspiracy thinking and fact perceptions gauged with these questions: "Is this statement true or false?" [Certainly True, Probably True, Probably False, Certainly False] [random ½ sample for each version, combined to one variable] "The Earth is warming due to human activity" / "The Earth may or may not be warming but not due to human activity" "Racism often prevents minorities from being successful" / "Racism no longer has much influence over whether Americans are successful" / "Sexual orientation is something people are born with" / "Sexual orientation is based on choice or experience, not genetics" / "The national debt (the amount owed by the American government) is likely in the future to cripple economic growth and national security" / "The national debt (the amount owed by the American government) is manageable and will not cause large problems in the future" / "Terrorist attacks inspired by radical Islam are a substantial threat to Americans" / "Terrorist attacks inspired by radical Islam are not a substantial threat to Americans" / "Genetically modified foods (GMOs) are safe to eat" / "I don't trust that genetically modified foods (GMOs) are safe to eat" / "False convictions of innocent people are very rare" / "False convictions of innocent people occur frequently" / "Vaccines cause autism" / "Vaccines do not cause autism"

15. See Osmundson, Joseph. 2011. "'I Was Born This Way': Is Sexuality Innate and Should it Matter?" *LGBTQ Policy Journal at the Harvard Kennedy School* 1: 15–27; American Psychological Association, "Understanding Sexual Orientation and Gender Identity," 2013.

16. See Haider-Markel and Joslyn, "Beliefs About the Origins of Homosexuality."

17. See Reinhart, Carmen, and Kenneth Rogoff. 2010. "Growth in a Time of Debt." *American Economic Review* 100(2): 573–578; Reinhart, Carmen, Vincent Reinhart, and Kenneth Rogoff. 2012. "Public Debt Overhangs: Advanced Economy Episodes Since 1800." *Journal of Economic Perspectives* 26(3): 69–86. For a critique of Reinhart and Rogoff (2010) and Reinhart, Reinhart, and Rogoff, see Herndon, Thomas, Michael Ash, and Robert Pollin. 2013. "Does high public debt consistently stifle economic growth? A critique of Reinhart and Rogoff. *Cambridge Journal of Economics* 38(2): 257–279. Herndon takes issue over the economic influence of debt-to-GDP ratios above 90%. For a non-academic summary illustrating the difficulty in sorting out a definitive conclusion, see Cassidy, David. 2013. "The Reinhart and Rogoff controversy: A summing up." *The New Yorker,* April 26, 2013.

18. CNN Wire Staff. 2010. "Mullen: Debt is Top National Security Threat." http://www.cnn.com/2010/US/08/27/debt.security.mullen/index.html (Accessed December 30, 2017).

19. See Krugman, Paul. 2012. "Nobody Understands Debt." *New York Times,* January 1, 2012; Krugman, Paul. 2015. "Debt is Good." *New York Times,* August 21, 2015. Krugman emphasizes "the fact that federal debt isn't at all like a mortgage . . . First, families have to pay back their debt. Governments don't—all they need to do is ensure that debt grows more slowly than their tax base . . . Second, an over-borrowed family owes money to someone else; U.S. debt is, to a large extent, money we owe to ourselves." Hence, current concerns are a "wrong-headed, ill-informed obsession with debt" (Krugman 2012).

20. This finding comports with the evidence presented by Lewandowsky et al. regarding climate change as well as vaccines and GMOs. See Lewandowsky, Stephan, Gilles Gignac, Klaus Oberauer. 2013. "The Role of Conspiracist Ideation and Worldviews in Predicting Rejection of Science." *PLoS ONE* 10(8): e75637.

21. In a regression of conspiratorial thinking against PID, the *p*-value is .03 and the average Democratic identifier is .38 points higher on the Conspiratorial Thinking Scale than the average Republican identifier.

22. *Oxford English Dictionaries.* 2016. "Word of the Year: 2016." https://en.oxforddictionaries.com/word-of-the-year/word-of-the-year-2016 (Accessed December 30, 2017).

15

The Conspiracy Theory Pyramid Scheme

TED GOERTZEL

Seth Kalichman, a social psychologist who spent a year infiltrating HIV deni-alist groups, has described a three-tiered conspiracy theory pyramid scheme, the whole of which is more resilient than any of the components.[1] The top tier are writers and intellectuals who publish books and articles and give speeches that reinforce and legitimate conspiracy theories. The second tier are people who have a psychological propensity to believe in conspiracies and engage in conspiracy thinking.[2] The third tier are people worried about a specific issue that impacts their lives and potentially threatens them. Seeking a solution to their problem, they absorb ideas and arguments from first- and second-tier con-spiracy thinkers and learn a set of rhetorical devices which I have defined as the *conspiracy meme*.[3] When they become habituated to thinking in this way about one issue, they may apply it in other contexts and become second-tier conspiracy thinkers.

The conspiracy meme is a set of rhetorical devices used to defend strongly held beliefs that lack unambiguous empirical support. One device is to challenge those who disagree with a theory on speculative grounds, and then to demand that the opponents prove one's speculations to be wrong. Another is to selectively amass facts that support one's beliefs while ignoring or dismissing facts that do not. A third is to accuse one's opponents of hidden scheming and secret plotting. A fourth is to denounce the motivations of those who disagree, rather than grapple with the sub-stance of their arguments. A fifth is to exaggerate the power of the conspirators to conceal evidence of their perfidy. A sixth is to insist that there are two sides to every issue and to demand that "equal time" be given to conspiratorial arguments. Taken together, these rhetorical devices can be powerful tools that distort and bias discus-sion of important social and political issues.

Some first-tier intellectuals specialize in one of the rhetorical devices without ex-plicitly adopting the others. They deny that they are "conspiracy theorists" because their work does include explicit claims of secret plots. But they provide materials that second- and third-tier believers use as grist for their mills. Often their success in selling books and articles, and getting invitations to speak to large audiences, depends largely on second- and third-tier conspiracy thinkers.

This paper examines several influential writers and activists who have played important roles in conspiracy pyramid schemes: Andrew Wakefield, Robert F. Kennedy Jr., Frederick Seitz, James Inhofe, Vandana Shiva, Noam Chomsky, and Edward Herman. Our goal is to examine the interaction between their work and the activities of the other two tiers.

Andrew Wakefield

Andrew Wakefield is a physician who published a paper in *The Lancet,* a leading British medical journal, suggesting that an increase in autism diagnoses might be caused by measles, mumps, and rubella vaccines given to young children.[4] Wakefield's clinical sample was very small, and his results were suggestive at best. But it took time for medical researchers to test them, and media reports in the interim led to a panic among parents, some of whom did not vaccinate their children, exposing them and other children to infectious diseases.

In time, Wakefield's study was severely criticized in the medical literature. Journalists discovered that he had received funding from lawyers representing groups that wanted to sue vaccine manufacturers. *The Lancet* eventually retracted the study, and British medical authorities withdrew Wakefield's license to practice medicine for ethical violations.[5]

Wakefield moved to the United States, where he was welcomed by a third-tier movement of parents of autistic children who were eager to blame the medical establishment for their children's illness.[6] These parents seized on the presence of thimerosal, a preservative containing small amounts of ethylmercury, in some vaccines. Rigorous epidemiological studies failed to find an association between thimerosal in vaccines and autism, and when thimerosal was removed from most vaccines to reassure parents, the autism rate did not come down.[7] Rather than accept this result, many parents became persuaded of a conspiracy of public health officials and vaccine manufacturers to conceal the truth.

Andrew Wakefield was invited as keynote speaker at conferences, and published articles and books with fringe publishers.[8] He also headlined the 2016 Conspira-Sea Cruise in 2016, where he showed a film which alleged that the Centers for Disease Control had ironclad evidence that vaccines are linked to autism but had chosen not to release it.[9] A version of the film was later released as *Vaxxed: From Cover-Up to Catastrophe.*[10] Wakefield portrayed himself as a victim, told the cruise audience that "the story of my life is basically how to take a perfectly good career and flush it down the toilet" and asserted that the thimerosal issue was "a deliberate eugenics program, a deliberate population-control program."[11] While the mainstream press routinely described him as a discredited doctor who had lost his medical license,

Wakefield argues that he is the target of a "a ruthless, pragmatic attempt to crush any attempt to investigate valid vaccine safety concerns," and Wendy Fournier, president of the American Autism Association, defends him as "a man of integrity and honesty."[12]

Accepting engagements from anti-vaccine groups was the only way Wakefield could get support in view of the overwhelming scientific consensus against his claims. As reporter Susan Dominus observed, "The more he must defend his research, the more important he seems to consider it—so important that powerful forces have conspired and aligned against him. He said he believes that 'they'—public-health officials, pharmaceutical companies—pay bloggers to plant vicious comments about him on the Web."[13]

Robert F. Kennedy, Jr.

Robert F. Kennedy, Jr. became identified with the thimerosal issue by a different route, but also in response to advocacy from the third-tier anti-vaccine movement. A scion of America's most celebrated political family, traumatized as a child by the assassination of his father and his uncle, Kennedy struggled with heroin addiction and compulsive womanizing, leading to youthful criminal convictions and the suicide of his estranged wife.[14] These difficulties were widely publicized because of his family background, but the public and the criminal justice system were sympathetic and gave him a series of second chances.[15] Court-mandated public service led to a career as an environmental lawyer and activist. He used his training as a lawyer to found an environmental litigation clinic at Pace University, which filed successful suits against companies polluting New York rivers including one that forced Exxon Mobil to clean up millions of gallons of spilled oil on Newton Creek in Brooklyn.[16]

Kennedy reports that he was recruited into anti-vaccine activism by parents of autistic children: "I was drawn into the controversy only reluctantly. As an attorney and environmentalist who has spent years working on issues of mercury toxicity, I frequently met mothers of autistic children who were absolutely convinced that their kids had been injured by vaccines. Privately, I was skeptical."[17]

Kennedy has no training in research design or statistical data analysis, skills that are essential in evaluating epidemiological research. Instead of addressing the research directly, he focused on the motivations and behavior of the scientists. In 2005, he wrote an article for *Rolling Stone* and *Salon* in which he was outraged that scientists and public health officials have professional meetings that are not open to the public or the press. The article had several factual errors (such as claiming that the amount of thimerosal children received was 187 times the accepted limit when it was actually 187 micrograms, which is 40% over the limit) which led the magazines to issue corrections, and *Salon* withdrew it from its website in 2011.[18] Kennedy, however, republished it on his own website, claiming the errors were minor.

Despite his charisma, Kennedy has not been successful in convincing his mainstream political allies to join his crusade against thimerosal. Prominent political allies have urged him to drop the issue, telling him that it is a lost cause, but he insists that "the only way I can stop this is if someone shows me I'm wrong on the science."[19] He insists that his opponents prove to him that he is wrong, despite his lack of the quantitative skills needed to evaluate the epidemiological research. He says he finds the Center for Disease Control's refusal to agree with his recommendations "baffling" but fails to cite or respond to the arguments in any of the reports by respected scientific organizations that carefully explain the reasoning.[20] He denounces the CDC as a "cesspool of corruption" engaged in "scandalous conflicts with the $25 billion vaccine industry" and accuses it of publishing "fraudulent" studies.[21]

Kennedy's book *Thimerosal: Let the Science Speak* is a curious example of the use of conspiracy logic while avoiding explicit accusations of secret wrongdoing that might lead to lawsuits. Kennedy "compiled" the book and is listed as the editor. He claims to have "assembled a crack team of respected scientific researchers to review the voluminous peer-review literature related to thimerosal and human health."[22] This sounds promising until you notice that all the substantive articles in the book are anonymous. The names of the "respected scientific researchers" do not appear anywhere in the volume. This is not the norm for scientific publications; scientists are expected to take credit and responsibility for their published work and are normally eager to do so. The book was the result of a lengthy process whereby the more explicit claims were removed. This was described by Dan Burns in a review on the amazon.com website:

> Kennedy has, in his own word, "assembled" not one, but two books: a closely-held manuscript that exposes the conflicts of interest at the heart of the vaccine/autism cover-up. And a published book, this one, in which key revelations from the year-old draft—the so-called combustible chapters—have been dismembered, replaced, eviscerated, or buried.[23]

Despite its flaws, Kennedy's book has been cited enthusiastically by third-tier autism conspiracy believers on the Age of Autism website.[24] A reader review posted on the amazon.com web site stated that "Kennedy offers proof of a government conspiracy to shut down this debate."[25] Conspiracy theorists Richard Belzer and David Wayne cite Kennedy several times in their book on *Corporate Conspiracies,* arguing that he "establishes a clear case of Thimerosal being the toxin that is responsible for a health epidemic."[26] Kennedy, in return, praises *Corporate Conspiracies* as "a sobering chronicle of the world's model democracy's tragic devolution to corporate kleptocracy."[27] Both Kennedy's and Belzer and Wayne's books are published by *Skyhorse Publishing,* a publisher that lists 21 conspiracy books on its website.

Frederick Seitz

Frederick Seitz was a pioneer of solid-state physics and recipient of the National Medal of Science and many other honors. He served as president of Rockefeller University in New York City from 1968 to 1978, bringing to the university substantial support from the tobacco industry for health research. He was central in founding the George C. Marshal Institute, a think tank known for skepticism on the carcinogenic effects of tobacco smoke, the effects of acid rain, the effects of CFC on the ozone layer, and of human-caused global warming. His dissenting 1994 pamphlet on global warming and the ozone hole controversy was a carefully written and documented exposition of one side of the issue.[28]

Seitz was profoundly angered by the fact that most scientific specialists working on these issues were not persuaded by his arguments. Naomi Oreskes and Erik Conway observe that Seitz "harbored an enormous grudge against the scientific community that he once led."[29] In his memoir, Seitz observed that he was hesitant to accept the full-time presidency of the National Academy of Sciences because "I was keenly aware how quickly, and irrationally, the mood of the membership of an organization can change. I could become highly unpopular almost overnight because of some seemingly trivial issue."[30] When the global warming issue came to the forefront of public debate in 1996, he quickly sided with the "skeptics" movement that attacked climate scientists for conspiring to deceive the public. He published a letter titled "A Major Deception on `Global Warming'" in the *Wall Street Journal* on June 12, 1996. In the letter, which triggered a major controversy in the media, he accused a United Nations agency of "a major deception on global warming" because it had edited some comments in draft documents submitted by scientists.[31] Seitz interpreted routine editing as conspiratorial deceit. In a paper published by the Marshal Institute, he questioned the view that CFCs "are the greatest threat to the ozone layer" and asserted that "there is no good evidence that passive inhalation [of tobacco smoke] is truly dangerous under normal circumstances."[32]

James Inhofe

James Inhofe, United States Senator from Oklahoma, made a major splash on the national scene as a conspiracy theorist with a two-hour speech on the Senate floor on July 28, 2003, in which he stated "with all of the hysteria, all of the fear, all of the phony science, could it be that man-made global warming is the greatest hoax ever perpetrated on the American people? It sure sounds like it."[33] In the speech he attacked "the prophets of doom who peddle propaganda masquerading as science," arguing that they were seeking "an opportunity to tax the American people" and claimed to have "offered compelling evidence that catastrophic global warming is a hoax."[34]

Although he was not previously known as a writer and had no scientific training, Inhofe published the same arguments in a book, *The Greatest Hoax: How the Global Warming Conspiracy Threatens Your Future*.[35] It is very much a personal statement, describing his upbringing, his long marriage, his business experience, and his strong opposition to government regulations. He asserts that his 2003 speech was "the most thorough investigation of the science by any senator."[36] This is an odd claim, since senators are seldom trained in scientific methods and do not normally conduct scientific investigations. He also states that "I am not a scientist. But I do understand politics."[37] The endnotes to the book are references to speeches, news releases, and journalistic articles, not to articles in peer-reviewed scientific journals. He brags that "in more than twelve thousand words and several hours on the floor over two days, I brought numerous inconsistencies and gaps in the mainstream theory to light."[38] He attacked Al Gore and the "Hollywood elite" for "screaming about climate catastrophe and demanding that Americans use only one square of toilet paper, take cold showers or two-minute showers, not eat meat, and take public transportation, while clearly they were not willing to make these sacrifices themselves."[39]

Al Gore is excoriated for errors and alarmism in his documentary film *An Inconvenient Truth*. The United Nations is accused of scheming to redistribute wealth from America to poor countries. The release of purloined emails from British climate researchers is denounced as "Climategate." All these issues had been widely publicized. Inhofe's contribution was to frame them as a "hoax" rather than as an honest disagreement about the interpretation of complex and noisy scientific evidence.[40] This appealed to Inhofe's second- and third-tier audience of evangelical Christians, antigovernment conservatives, and people with economic interests in energy industries who felt threatened by the environmental movement. But it also offended people who saw Al Gore, who is also not a scientist, as possibly misguided in some ways but not as a devious hoaxer. The video "Not Evil, Just Wrong" was an effort by Gore's opponents to shift the debate to issues and evidence instead of attributions of conspiratorial motives.[41]

Vandana Shiva

Vandana Shiva earned a BS in physics in India and a PhD in philosophy of science from the University of Western Ontario. She is often introduced as a nuclear physicist, but she never pursued a career leading to publication in refereed journals in that or any other scientific field.[42] Instead, she used her credentials to launch a highly successful career as an environmental, feminist, and third world activist. The fact of her scientific training, along with her charismatic personality and her status as a third world woman, combined to make her a star of the movement against genetically modified seeds. She has accused Monsanto of "robbing Indian farmers of their lives" and "poisoning of the soil."[43] In one case after another, she portrays scientific and technological debates as struggles between the forces of good and evil, for example: "there are in Asia today two paradigms of forestry—one life-enhancing, the other life-destroying."[44] This has caused her to be showered with honors and awards including the Right Livelihood Award (known as the Alternative Nobel Prize), the Order of the Golden Ark, the Global 500 Roll of Honor, the Earth Day International Award, the LennonOno Grant for Peace Award, the Sydney Peace Prize, the Fukuoka Asian Culture Prize, and many others.[45] She has been called the "Gandhi of grain" and compared to Mother Teresa.[46] Bill Moyers called her "the rock star in the world-wide battle against genetically modified seeds."[47]

The problem for Shiva is that the overwhelming consensus of scientific research does not support her contention about genetically modified seeds.[48] Instead of balancing her criticisms by acknowledging the contribution of genetically modified crops in fighting hunger, Shiva rejects any studies that go against her thesis with conspiracy arguments, claiming, for example, that Monsanto has paid for these articles and that "they now control the scientific literature of the world," and that journals such as *Nature, Science,* and *Scientific American* "have just become extensions of their propaganda. There is no independent science left in the world."[49]

Noam Chomsky and Edward Herman

A distinguished linguist, Noam Chomsky is also very widely known for books, speeches, and political tracts bitterly hostile to the American and Israeli governing elites. He and frequent collaborator Edward S. Herman, a business school professor, adamantly deny being conspiracy theorists. In an essay on "The Propaganda Model Revisited," Herman says they realized that their work would be denounced as a conspiracy theory and devotes several pages to defining it instead as a "guided market system."[50] In a discussion of their work on *Manufacturing Consent,* Chomsky stated "There's nothing more remote from what we have been discussing than a conspiracy theory. If I give an analysis of, say, the economic system, and I point out that GM tries to maximize profit and market share—that's not a conspiracy theory; that's an institutional analysis. It has nothing to do with conspiracies."[51]

Chomsky and Herman say they are not conspiracy theorists because they do not make explicit claims about secret collusion. And they are correct that secret collusion is an important part of conspiracy theorizing.[52] But it is not essential that the word *conspiracy* be used to make this claim, and secret collusion can be implied rather than explicitly asserted. In an interview with journalist Scott Kaufman, Chomsky argues that "the whole drug war is designed, from policing to eventual release from prison, to make it impossible for black men and, increasingly, women to be part of [American] society."[53] Conspiracy theorists Richard Belzer and David Wayne highlight this statement in their book on *Corporate Conspiracies,* saying "that is the *design* of the system—to enslave minorities and limit their possibilities just as it was when Africans were brought to America and sold as slaves."[54] And they have a point; by arguing that the system was intentionally designed in this way, Chomsky is implying the existence of a conspiracy.

Chomsky and Herman generally focus on policies, not on the process by which they are made. A quote from Chomsky which has been posted on many websites is, "any dictator would admire the uniformity and obedience of the (U.S.) media."[55] They do not explain how this remarkable obedience is enforced, leaving it to their readers to infer that secret conspiring must have taken place. And the followers are often quick to make the inference. For example, one website relies on three quotes from Noam Chomsky to prove the argument that "neoliberalism is conspiracy instigated by the very rich, to favour the economic interests of the very rich against the interests of everyone else."[56]

Chomsky and Herman are not second-tier conspiracy advocates; they are narrowly focused on American and Israeli foreign and domestic policies and on their alleged domination of the mass media. Their primary audience includes second-tier conspiracy believers and third-tier leftists who share their political perspectives. This leads to disagreement with second-tier conspiracy junkies who resent their failure to accept that that the moon landing was faked or that the 9/11 attack on the World Trade Center was done by American or Israeli agents.[57] In his blog, truther Peter Zaza waxes indignant that "I've actually seen and read interviews where Noam Chomsky comes right out and says, 'It's not important who is behind 9/11, there are so many other things these people are guilty of . . . other things are more important' or 'it's just an Internet thing.'"[58] In an argument with a 9/11 truther, Chomsky rejected claims published on conspiracy websites and insisted that "there's a reason why there are graduate schools" in fields like civil engineering, and that reputable scientists "write articles in scientific journals" and submit their work to judgment by their professional peers.[59]

Chomsky has published extensively in professional journals on linguistics. But he does not submit his work on foreign policy to judgment by his professional peers in this way. He publishes popular books and articles in opinion journals aimed at the general public.

Chomsky and Herman can be characterized as conspiracy theorists because they allege consistent behavior on the part of American and Israeli elites that is difficult or impossible to explain without assuming that much must go on behind the scenes. Their Manichean world view ultimately depends on conspiracy logic to explain the extraordinary powers they ascribe to those they attack. Chomsky and Herman use concepts such as "thought control" and "manufactured consent" to explain how a small, selfish elite has somehow bamboozled most scholars and journalists, as well as members of the working class.[60] This argument has long been used by leftists frustrated by resistance to their ideas. As Karl Popper notes, their work on the media is an example of "conspiracy theory of ignorance," which is "well known in its Marxian form as the conspiracy of a capitalist press that perverts and suppresses truth and fills the workers' minds with false ideologies."[61]

This argument is viewed skeptically by scholars. As communication scholar Jeffrey Klaehn observes, "It is not a surprise, then, given the interrelations of the state and corporate capitalism and the `ideological network`, that the propaganda model has been dismissed as a `conspiracy theory` and condemned for its `overly deterministic` view of media behaviour. It is generally excluded from scholarly debates on patterns of media behaviour."[62]

How the Three Tiers Interact

The pyramid metaphor should not be taken to imply that the top tier is in control and dominates the second and third tiers of the pyramid. Interaction between the tiers is reciprocal, not hierarchial. First-tier writers, celebrities, and scientists are often recruited and proselytized by second- and third-tier believers, and they respond for a variety of reasons. They may have a psychological affinity for conspiracy theories for the same reasons other people do. They may be recruited when they are elderly and past their period of peak productivity. Their work may not have received the recognition they think it deserves from their professional peers. Or they may simply enjoy the larger audience their work receives when they appeal to the preconceptions of the first and second tiers.

First-tier conspiracy thinkers are heirs to a long tradition in American political rhetoric, one described by Richard Hofstadter in his classic essay, "The Paranoid Style in American Politics."[63] The paranoid style continues to play an important role in American politics, as illustrated by Donald Trump's use of the "hoax" argument about climate change and his claims about Barak Obama's birth certificate during his campaign for the presidency. Reports in the media say that he "continues to privately harbor a handful of conspiracy theories that have no grounding in fact."[64] But his staff are reported to strongly encourage him to keep these beliefs private because his political agenda would only be harmed by his being labeled a conspiracy theorist.

Criticism of conspiracy theories by Hofstadter and many others has stigmatized the term *conspiracy theory* so that sophisticated writers usually avoid the word. But if we look carefully at their logic, and at their interactions with their audiences, we can see that the paranoid style is still important. Indeed, it may be more pervasive than ever, thanks in part to the influence of postmodern philosophies that promote cynicism and subjectivity.[65] Conspiratorial thinking today has become a trope, a set of commonly recurring literary and rhetorical devices or memes. Use of this trope can bring fame and fortune to public intellectuals while reinforcing second- and third-tier movements. We can illustrate how this works with reference to several prominent first-tier intellectuals in addition to those already described.

Naomi Klein is a journalist with no academic qualifications in social science or economics, but her tremendously successful publications rival Vandana Shiva's and Noam Chomsky's in their angry indictment of corporate globalization.[66] Like Chomsky, her logic can be characterized as implicitly conspiratorial. Klein ascribes phenomenal powers to Milton Friedman's economic theories, blaming them for phenomena as varied as the American invasion of Iraq and the Chilean coup of 1973. As economist Joseph Stiglitz observes, "some readers may see Klein's findings as evidence of a giant conspiracy, a conclusion she explicitly denies."[67] Jonathan Chait of the *New Republic* observes that "with the pseudo-clarity of a conspiracy theorist, Klein dismisses out of hand the possibility of incompetence" and that "like every conspiracy theory, Klein's account of the world finally lacks internal logic."[68]

Much like Noam Chomsky, Klein is committed to a leftist political agenda and has frustrated second-tier conspiracy believers by her refusal to accept explicit conspiracy claims. Truther Peter Zaza complains,

> Sorry Naomi, I'm disappointed—I still think you are a great author with important, well presented information that everyone should be made aware of, but your inability to step over that line and deal with 9/11 is problematic to myself and others—this is precisely the difficulty we face when it comes to the wider population's suspension of disbelief regarding this issue. The reaction of that audience demonstrates so poignantly the struggle we face in bringing forth the truth about 9/11.[69]

The Nobel Prize winning chemist Linus Pauling was approached by health activists to endorse vitamin C as a cure for cancer and the common cold.[70] Pauling was 65 years old at the time and had never done medical research, but he quickly concluded that the consensus of specialists in the field was wrong. He never explicitly alleged a conspiracy, but his writings on vitamin C were widely cited by activists who view establishment medicine as a conspiracy. How else to explain why all the well-trained medical researchers were consistently wrong? Interestingly, it has recently come to light that Pauling had a broader interest in conspiracy theories—one commentator observes that "the world of conspiracy and intrigue held an allure for Pauling that he could not deny."[71] He had an interest in UFO conspiracy theories and in JFK assassination conspiracy theories and collected materials about them. But he never went public with his thoughts about these conspiracies, perhaps because he never found the evidence persuasive or because doing so would have sullied his reputation.

Peter Duesberg established a solid reputation as a molecular biologist early in his career with research on genetic aspects of cancer, specifically on the role of oncogenes. Later, however, he surprisingly came to doubt that oncogenes were important causes of cancer. Much more controversially, he also doubted that retroviruses were responsible for AIDS. In a book called *Inventing the AIDS*

Virus he argued that the human immunodeficiency virus is a harmless passenger virus and that AIDS is caused by drug use, sexual excesses, and the side effects of drugs used to treat AIDS. He explained the failure of most specialists to accept his arguments by arguing that there is a "wall of silence" suppressing the truth about AIDS, and insisting on equal time to debate with AIDS scientists. His work was cited by South African president Thabo Mbeki, who accused the Central Intelligence Agency of being part of a "conspiracy to promote the view that HIV causes AIDS."[72] Mbeki "came under the influence of maverick scientists known as AIDS-denialists, most prominent among whom was Peter Duesberg from Berkeley, California."[73]

Nancy MacLean is a historian whose books on race, gender, labor history, and the American south have won her numerous awards and prestigious professional positions.[74] Her early works had a clearly leftist perspective, and they were criticized by more conservative scholars for minimizing the role of religious belief and culture on human activity.[75] The controversies they generated made her increasingly prominent outside the world of academic historians, and as she began to write more for the general public she veered into conspiracy thinking. In 2017, she published a book accusing Charles Koch and the libertarian movement of "a stealth-bid to reverse-engineer all of America."[76] The book was well received by many reviewers and was nominated for a National Book Award, but one reviewer found that it "gets almost everything wrong, from the most basic of facts to the highest of theory."[77] Two bloggers criticized it as "conspiracy theory in the guise of intellectual history."[78] Even the leftist historian Rick Perlstein, who is a friend of MacLean's and shares her political views, says "it pains me deeply to say this . . . the foundation of the entire book is a conspiracy theory. . ."[79] Of course, MacLean has responded to these critics and the controversy continues, a controversy that has advanced her career as well as her political agenda.[80]

The motivations of the writers we have examined are varied. Peter Duesberg, Andrew Wakefield, and Frederick Seitz found themselves alienated from their professional communities and got support from third-tier activists, pushing them into conspiracy arguments. Robert F. Kennedy, Jr., was intensively recruited by the third tier of anti-vaccine activists. Vandana Shiva, Noam Chomsky, Naomi Klein, and Nancy MacLean have strong ideological convictions not always shared by the mainstream of their professional communities. They became celebrities and sold a great many books by appealing to second- and third-tier conspiracy believers.

We do not have much psychological information about most of our writers, but they are clearly very different personalities with different motivations. The ease with which Robert F. Kennedy, Jr. shifted from environmental to vaccine conspiracism suggests a generalized suspiciousness characteristic of a second-tier conspiracist. James Inhofe, also, seems to very readily find conspiracies wherever he looks. It may be that many intellectuals have a psychological affinity for conspiracy theories but are careful not to let this be known.

Noam Chomsky's intense hostility to the United States and Israel, the two countries to which he is personally related, has led some to characterize him as a self-hating Jew. His father was a religious school principal and taught at a Jewish college, and he was raised in an intensely Jewish environment. But he rejects inquiry into his or anyone else's psychological motivations, insisting that he is simply in pursuit of truth.

Like Chomsky, Ed Herman, James Inhofe, Vandana Silva, and Naomi Klein have strong ideological convictions and use the conspiracy meme to cover weak spots in their arguments. Andrew Wakefield and Peter Duesberg are researchers whose conclusions diverged from the mainstream of their disciplines and who use conspiracy arguments to explain why so many highly qualified colleagues disagree. Duesberg and Seitz and Linus Pauling may not be motivated so much by a generalized belief in conspiracies as by contrarianism and a strong sense of their own superiority as thinkers.

Detecting implicit conspiracism is more difficult than looking for explicit conspiracy arguments. An important clue is to ask whether the authors are honestly trying to understand a complex scientific or historical issue or whether they are using the conspiracy meme to defend a preestablished opinion. Are they trying to figure out what is driving global warming, or how to cure cancer, or the reasons for an increase in autism diagnoses, or to figure out how to best feed the hungry in the third world? Seth Kalichman, the social psychologist who spent a year studying AIDS denialists, says that:

> Having read a great deal of what the denialists have to say and having communicated at length with several of them myself, I am left to question how much any of these people actually care about AIDS and those affected by the disease. What denialists do apparently care about is the argument itself. It is the debate that seems to drive their interest in AIDS, not the other way around. None of the major figures in denialism has ever worked with HIV in the laboratory and none have worked with people infected with HIV.[81]

The same criticism could be made of our other authors. Naomi Klein does not try to learn from the economic and political successes of neoliberalism in Chile and Poland; she just tries to explain them away. Noam Chomsky endlessly criticized the United States and Israel while minimizing the flaws of communist regimes including the Pol Pot regime in Cambodia.[82] While the social sciences may not have reached the degree of consensus that one can find in the physical and environmental sciences, there is a body of scientific work on social issues that has made some real progress and that could be built upon. Klein, Shiva, Chomsky, and Herman are not about doing that; they seek to promote a fixed ideological idea with selective facts.

Our first-tier writers offer a worldview that is polarized between good and evil or between truth and falsehood. They bring scientific respectability and/or mountains of factual examples to large popular audiences that feel alienated from a political or scientific establishment. Theirs is a form of advocacy logic that begins with a firm, unshakable conviction and accepts sloppy evidence to support it while minimizing, disregarding, or distorting contradictory evidence. In many ways, their arguments are more dangerous than those of the second-tier conspiracy buffs because they are less blatantly flawed. They are part of a "post-truth" intellectual and political climate that values rhetoric and ideological correctness over honest inquiry.

Notes

1. Kalichman, Seth. 2009. *Denying AIDS: Conspiracy Theories, Pseudoscience, and Human Tragedy.* Göttingen, Germany: Copernicus, 150.
2. Goertzel, Ted. 1994. "Belief in Conspiracy Theories." *Political Psychology* 15(4): 733–744; Bost, Preston. 2015. "Crazy Beliefs, Sane Believers: Toward a Cognitive Psychology of Conspiracy Ideation," *Skeptical Inquirer* 39(1).
3. Goertzel, Ted. 2010. "Conspiracy Theories in Science," EMBO reports 11(7). http://www.nature.com/embor/journal/vaop/ncurrent/pdf/embor201084.pdf; Goertzel, Ted. 2011. "The Conspiracy Meme," *The Skeptical Inquirer* 35(1). https://www.csicop.org/SI/show/the_conspiracy_meme.
4. Wakefield, Andrew, S. H. Murch, A. Anthony, J. Linnell, D. M. Casson, M. Malik, M. Berelowitz, A. P. Dhillon, M. Thomson, P. Harvey, A. Valentine, S. E. Davies, and J. A. Walker-Smith. 1998. "RETRACTED: Ileal Lymphoid Nodular Hyperplasia, Non-specific Colitis, and Pervasive Developmental Disorder in Children." *Lancet* 351(9): 637–641.
5. Horton, Richard. 2004. "The Lessons of MMR." Lancet 363(9411): 747–749; Goodlee, Fiona, Jane Smith, and Harvey Macrovitch. 2011. "Wakefield's Article Linking MMR Vaccine and Autism was Fraudulent." editorial, *British Medical Journal* 342: c7452.
6. Baker, Jeffrey. 2008. "Mercury, Vaccines, and Autism: One Controversy, Three Histories." *American Journal of Public Health* 98(2): 144–153.
7. Wilson, Kuman, Ed Mills, and Dory Ross. 2003. "Association of Autistic Spectrum Disorder and the Measles, Mumps, and Rubella Vaccine: A Systematic Review of Current Epidemiological Evidence." *Archives and Adolescent and Pediatric Medicine* 157(7): 628–634; Hylid, Anders, Michael Stellfeld, and Jan Wohlfahrt. 2003. "Association Between Thimerosal-Containing Vaccine and Autism." *Journal of the American Medical Association* 290(13): 1763–1766.
8. Wakefield, Andrew ed. 2010. *Callous Disregard: Autism and Vaccines: The Truth Behind a Tragedy.* New York: Skyhorse Publishing.
9. Dickey, Brownen. 2017. "Climb Aboard, Ye Who Seek the Truth." http://www.popularmechanics.com/culture/a21919/conspiracy-theory-cruise/ (Accessed on December 1, 2017).
10. Available from http://vaxxedthemovie.com/stream/.
11. Dickey, "Climb Aboard."
12. CNN. 2011. "Medical Journal: Study Linking Autism, Vaccines is 'Elaborate Fraud.'" http://edition.cnn.com/2011/HEALTH/01/06/autism.vaccines/?hpt=T1 (Accessed on November 18, 2017).
13. Dominus, Susan. 2001. "The Crash and Burn of an Autism Guru." http://www.nytimes.com/2011/04/24/magazine/mag-24Autism-t.html?_r=1 (Accessed December 20, 2017).
14. Jacobson, Mark. 2007. "American Jeremiad: A harrowing ride up the proverbial creek and into the beating, bleeding heart of RFK Jr." http://nymag.com/news/politics/27340/ (Accessed December 20, 2017).

15. Oppenheimer, Jerry. 2015. *RFK Jr.: Robert F. Kennedy, Jr. and the Dark Side of the Dream.* New York: St. Martin's Press.

16. Brown, Kim. 2004. "ExxonMobil Sued Over 55-Acre Oil Spill in Newtown Creek." *Queens Chronicle,* July 8, 2004.

17. Kennedy, Jr, Robert F. 2005. "Deadly Immunity: Government Cover-up of a Mercury/Autism Scandal." http://robertfkennedyjr.com/articles/deadly_immunity.2005.html (Accessed December 20, 2017).

18. Lauerman. 2017. "Correcting Our Record." https://www.salon.com/2011/01/16/dangerous_immunity/ (Accessed November 30, 2017).

19. Kloor, Keith. 2014. "Robert Kennedy Jr.'s Belief in Autism-Vaccine Connection, and its Political Peril." *The Washington Post* July 18, 2014.

20. Kennedy, Jr. Robert F. 2014. *Thimerosal: Let the Science Speak,* New York: Skyhorse: xxiii. For example see Public Health Service, U.S. Dept. of Health and Human Services. 1999. "Thimerosal in vaccines: a joint statement of the American Academy of Pediatrics and the Public Health Service," *Morbidity and Mortality Weekly Report* 48(26): 563–565.

21. Kennedy, Jr., Robert F. 2015. "Letter to the Editor." *New York Times,* July 10, 2015; Kennedy, Jr. Robert F. 2015. Foreword to Kevin Barry. *Vaccine Whistleblower: Exposing Autism Research Fraud at the CDC.* New York: Skyhorse.

22. Kennedy, *Thimerosal.*

23. Burns, Dan. 2014. "Straddling the Vaccine Lines." http://www.ageofautism.com/2014/08/book-debut-thimerosal-let-the-science-speak-by-robert-f-kennedy-jr.html (Accessed on November 29, 2017); Keith Kloor (2014), of the *Washington Post,* also noted that "Some of the most controversial sections—the chapters connecting autism to thimerosal—Kennedy took out at the last minute."

24. For example, Dachel, Anne. 2014. "Thimerosal: Let the Science Speak by Robert F. Kennedy, Jr. & Drs. Martha Herbert and Mark Hyman Debuts August 4." http://www.ageofautism.com/2014/07/thimerosal-let-the-science-speak-by-robert-f-kennedy-jr-debuts-august-4.html (Accessed November 29, 2017).

25. Corbin, Clara. 2015. "No Issue More Important Than This." https://www.amazon.com/Thimerosal-Evidence-Supporting-Immediate-Neurotoxin-ebook/product-reviews/B0140EFEWK/ref=cm_cr_arp_d_viewopt_kywd?ie=UTF8&reviewerType=all_reviews&pageNumber=1&filterByKeyword=conspiracy (Accessed November 29, 2017).

26. Belzer, Richard, and David Wayne. 2017. *Corporate Conspiracies: How Wall Street Took Over Washington.* New York: Skyhorse: 8, 9, 61, 62, 135, 177.

27. Kennedy, Jr., Robert F. 2017. "Praise for *Corporate Conspiracies.*" https://www.amazon.com/Corporate-Conspiracies-Wall-Street-Washington-ebook/dp/B01HLN69K8/ref=sr_1_1?ie=UTF8&qid=1511971225&sr=8-1&keywords=Belzer+corporate+conspiracies (Accessed November 29, 2017).

28. Seitz, Frederick. 1994. *Global Warming and Ozone Hole Controversies: A Challenge to Scientific Judgment.* Washington, D.C.: George C. Marshall Institute.

29. Oreskes, Naomi, and Erik Conway. 2010. *Merchants of Doubt: How a Handful of Scientists Obscured the Truth on Issues from Tobacco Smoke to Global Warming.* London: Bloomsbury Press, 26.

30. Seitz, Frederick. 1994. *On the Frontier: My Life in Science.* College Park, MD: American Institute of Physics, 288.

31. Lahsen, Myanna. 1999. "The Detection and Attribution of Conspiracies: The Controversy Over Chapter 8." In *Paranoia within Reason: A Casebook on Conspiracy as Explanation,* ed. George Marcus. Chicago: University of Chicago Press, 111–136.

32. Hirschhorn, Norbert and Stella Aguinaga Bialous. 2001. "Second Hand Smoke and Risk Assessment: What Was In It for the Tobacco Industry?" *Tobacco Control* 10(4): 375–382. http://tobaccocontrol.bmj.com/content/10/4/375.full (Accessed December 30, 2017).

33. Revkin, Andrew. 2003. "Politics Reasserts Itself in the Debate Over Climate Change and Its Hazards." *New York Times,* August 5, 2003.

34. Inhofe, James. 2003. "Sen. Inhofe Delivers Major Speech on the Science of Climate Change." https://www.inhofe.senate.gov/epw-archive/press/bsen-inhofe-delivers-major-speech-on-the-science-of-climate-change/b-icatastrophic-global-warming-alarmism-not-based-on-objective-sciencei-ipart-2/i (Accessed December 20, 2017).

35. Inhofe, James. 2012. *The Greatest Hoax*. Washington D.C.: WND Books.

36. Inhofe, James. *Greatest Hoax* [Kindle Edition]. Washington D.C.: WND Books, 533.

37. Inhofe, *The Greatest Hoax,* 20–21.

38. Inhofe, *Greatest Hoax* [Kindle Edition], 539.

39. Ibid., 1550.

40. Tashman, Brian. 2012. "James Inhofe Says the Bible Refutes Climate Change." http://www.rightwingwatch.org/post/james-inhofe-says-the-bible-refutes-climate-change/ (Accessed December 20, 2017).

41. Wikipedia. "Not Evil, Just Wrong." https://en.wikipedia.org/wiki/Not_Evil_Just_Wrong (Accessed May 25, 2017).

42. Specter, Michael. 2014. "Seeds of Doubt: An Activist's Controversial Crusade Against Genetically Modified Crops." *The New Yorker*, August 25. A search of scholar.google.com finds no publications by Vandana Shiva in refereed journals.

43. Shiva, Vandana. 2017. "Peddling Poisons and Selling Seeds of Suicide." http://vandanashiva.com/?p=554 (Accessed November 30, 2017).

44. Shiva, Vandana. 1988. "Reductionist Science as Epistemological Violence." In *Science, Hegemony and Violence: A Requiem for Modernity,* ed. Ashis Nandy. Oxford: Oxford University Press: 232–256.

45. Vandana Shiva's awards are listed at http://vandanashiva.com/?page_id=19.

46. Howlett, Caitlin. 2015. "For the Love of Grain." [Blog] *Green Lifestyle*. Available at: http://www.greenlifestylemag.com.au/node/20438 (Accessed November 30, 2017). Also see Bharath, Deepa. 2016. "'Gandhi of Grain' Visits Soka University for Talk on Genetically Modified Crops, Globalization." http://www.ocregister.com/2016/04/28/gandhi-of-grain-visits-soka-university-for-talk-on-genetically-modified-crops-globalization/ (Accessed November 30, 2017).

47. Specter, "Seeds of Doubt."

48. Nicolia, Alessandro, Albert Manzo, Fabio Veronesi, and Daniele Rosellini. 2013. "An Overview of the Last 10 Years of Genetically Engineered Crop Safety Research." *Critical Reviews in Biotechnology* 34(1): 77–88. http://www.agrobio.org/bfiles/fckimg/Nicolia%202013.pdf (Accessed December 1, 2017); Domingo, José and Jordi Giné Bordonaba. 2011. "A Literature Review on the Safety Assessment of Genetically Modified Plants." *Environment International* 37(4): 734–742.

49. Specter, "Seeds of Doubt."

50. Herman, Ed. 1966. "The Propaganda Model Revisited." http://musictravel.free.fr/political/political7.htm (Accessed June 5, 2016).

51. IMDb. "Manufacturing Consent: Noam Chomsky and the Media." at http://www.imdb.com/title/tt0104810/quotes (Accessed December 1, 2017).

52. Uscinski, Joseph, and Joseph Parent. 2014. *American Conspiracy Theories*. Oxford: Oxford University Press, 32.

53. Kaufman, Scott. 2014. "Noam Chomsky: Reagan was an 'extreme racist' who re-enslaved African-Americans." [Blog] *Rawstory*. Available at: https://www.rawstory.com/2014/12/noam-chomsky-reagan-was-an-extreme-racist-who-re-enslaved-african-americans/ (Accessed December 12, 2017).

54. Belzer and Wayne, *Corporate Conspiracies,* 105.

55. Kawilarang, Harry. 2006. *Quotations on Terrorism*. Victoria, Canada: Trafford Publishing, 255.

56. Patricknelson750. 2015. "Neoliberalism is a conspiracy of the rich." [Blog] *patricknelson750*. Available at https://patricknelson750.wordpress.com/2015/01/06/neoliberalism-is-a-conspiracy-of-the-rich/ (Accessed May 26, 2017).

57. Chomsky's Philosophies. 2016. "Noam Chomsky – Conspiracy Theories," YouTube Video, 9:27. Posted May 8, 2016. At https://www.youtube.com/watch?v=JirrKIQfOmk&t=314s.

58. Zaza, Peter. 2017. "Naomi Klein – Female Chomsky and 9-11 Apologist." [Blog] *Rense.com*. Available at http://www.rense.com/general78/naom.htm (Accessed December 1, 2017).

59. Marshall, Colin. 2013. "Noam Chomsky Schools 9/11 Truther; Explains the Science of Making Credible Claims." [Blog] *Open Culture*. Available at http://www.openculture.com/2013/10/noam-chomsky-derides-911-truthers.html (Accessed December 1, 2017).

60. Chomsky, Noam. 1995. *Necessary Illusions: Thought Control in Democratic Societies*. Toronto: House of Anasi Press; Herman, Edward, and Noam Chomsky. 2011. *Manufacturing Consent*. New York: Pantheon.

61. Popper, Karl. 1963. *Conjectures and Refutations* [Kindle Edition]. London and New York: Routledge: 351.

62. Klaehn, Jeffrey. 2002. "A Critical Review and Assessment of Herman and Chomsky's 'Propaganda Model.'" *European Journal of Communication* 17(2): 147–182.

63. Hofstadter, Richard *The Paranoid Style in American Politics* [Kindle Edition]. New York: Vintage.

64. Haberman, Maggie, and Jonathan Martin. 2017. "Trump Once Said the 'Access Hollywood' Tape Was Real. Now He's Not Sure." *New York Times*. https://www.nytimes.com/2017/11/28/us/politics/trump-access-hollywood-tape.html (Accessed December 1, 2017).

65. Marcus, George, ed. 1999. *Paranoia within Reason*. Chicago: University of Chicago Press.

66. Klein, Naomi. 2007. *The Shock Doctrine: The Rise of Disaster Capitalism*. New York: Metropolitan Books.

67. Stiglitz, Joseph. "Bleakonomics." *New York Times*. http://www.nytimes.com/2007/09/30/books/review/Stiglitz-t.html?_r=1&oref=slogin (Accessed December 20, 2017).

68. Chait, Jonathan. 2008. "Dead Left." http://www.newrepublic.com/article/books/dead-left (Accessed December 20, 2017).

69. Zaza, "Naomi Klein."

70. Goertzel, Ted, and Ben Goertzel. 1995. *Linus Pauling: A Life in Science and Politics*. New York: Basic Books.

71. scarc. 2009. "Linus Pauling and the Search for UFOs." [Blog] *The Pauling Blog*. Available at https://paulingblog.wordpress.com/tag/conspiracy-theory/ (Accessed December 1, 2017).

72. United Press International. 2000. "Mbeki Says CIA had Role in HIV/AIDS Conspiracy." Reproduced at *Padraig O'Malley Blog*. Available at: https://www.nelsonmandela.org/omalley/index.php/site/q/03lv03445/04lv04206/05lv04302/06lv04303/07lv04308.htm (Accessed December 1, 2017).

73. Bosley, Sarah. "Mbeki AIDS Policy 'Led to 330,000 Deaths.'" *The Guardian*. https://www.theguardian.com/world/2008/nov/27/south-africa-aids-mbeki (Accessed December 1, 2017).

74. Wikipedia. "Nancy MacLean." https://en.wikipedia.org/wiki/Nancy_MacLean (Accessed December 7, 2017).

75. Jenkins, William. 1995. "Review of Behind the Mask of Chivalry: The Making of the Second Ku Klux Klan." *Journal of Social History* 29(1): 218–20.

76. MacLean, Nancy. 2017. *Democracy in Chains: The Deep History of the Radical Right's Stealth Plan for America*. New York: Viking, xv.

77. Horwitz, Steven. 2017. "Confirmation Bias Unchained." *Social Science Research Network*: 5. https://papers.ssrn.com/sol3/papers.cfm?abstract_id=3007751 (Accessed December 7, 2017).

78. Farrell, Henry, and Steven Teles. 2017. "Even the Intellectual Left is Drawn to Conspiracy Theories About the Right. Resist Them." [Blog] *Vox*. October 9, 2017. Available at https://www.vox.com/the-big-idea/2017/7/14/15967788/democracy-shackles-james-buchanan-intellectual-history-maclean (Accessed December 7, 2017).

79. Pearlstein, Rick. Facebook page. https://www.facebook.com/photo.php?fbid=10105442217265045&set=a.10101400332564385.1073741830.27435697&type=3&theater (Accessed December 7, 2017).

80. Adler, Jonathan. 2017. "Nancy MacLean Responds to Her Critics." *Washington Post*. https://www.washingtonpost.com/news/volokh-conspiracy/wp/2017/07/20/nancy-maclean-responds-to-her-critics/?utm_term=.aef727858117 (Accessed December 7, 2017).

81. Kalichman, *Denying AIDS,* 150.

82. Collier, Peter, and David Horowitz, eds. 2004. *The Anti-Chomsky Reader.* New York: Encounter Books.

SECTION IV

WHAT IS THE PSYCHOLOGY OF CONSPIRACY THEORIZING?

JOSEPH E. USCINSKI

Early studies, for example by Richard Hofstadter, treated conspiracy theorists as pathological: isolated, delusional, and paranoid. This led to a lingering perception that belief in conspiracy theories was a marker of psychopathology, and much of the research since the 1990s has been part of an effort to dismantle or at least contextualize that perception. Clearly, there are some people who believe conspiracy theories that are also mentally ill; but conspiracy beliefs are not likely the cause of their problems. Also, the sheer numbers of people who believe in conspiracy theories according to opinion polls suggests that either mental illness is not strongly correlated with conspiracy beliefs, or that everyone is mentally ill. The former is more likely than the latter, even though I sometimes have doubts.

Most of the studies published in the last decade come from the field of psychology and as such situate the locus of belief on the individual. Prior to 2007, psychologists largely ignored conspiracy theories: a handful of studies were published, but a significant research agenda did not take root.[1] A significant and rapidly growing body of research since then has attempted to understand the causes of conspiracy theorizing, discover the behavioral consequences of conspiracy beliefs, and discover tools for countering conspiracy theories.[2] Michael Wood and Karen Douglas in Chapter 16 will discuss the varied strands of inquiry and attempt to synthesize the prevailing findings.

Given the recent political ramifications, researchers have been more keen to study how conspiracy theories travel from person to person. In recent years, conspiracy theories have traversed rather quickly on social media, but the widespread transmission of conspiracy theories is nothing new. There is a long literature in psychology about rumor transmission, and in Chapter 17, Nick DiFonzo examines how that century-long literature can inform current studies into conspiracy theory transmission. In Chapter 18, Preston Bost looks forward to the next decade of psychology research into conspiracy theories by posing a series of introspective questions about what we know and what we don't.

Notes

1. Abalakina-Paap, Marina, Walter G. Stephan, Traci L. Craig, and W. Larry Gregory. 1999. "Beliefs in Conspiracies." *Political Psychology* 20(3): 637–647; Butler, Lisa D., Cheryl Koopman, and Philip G. Zimbardo. 1995. "The Psychological Impact of Viewing the Film "JFK": Emotions, Beliefs, and Political Behavioral Intentions." *Political Psychology* 16(2): 237–257; Goertzel, Ted. 1994. "Belief in Conspiracy Theories." *Political Psychology* 15(4): 733–744; McHoskey, John W. 1995. "Case Closed? On the John F. Kennedy Assassination: Biased Assimilation of Evidence and Attitude Polarization." *Basic and Applied Social Psychology* 17(3): 395–409.
2. Brotherton, Rob. 2015. *Suspicious Minds: Why We Believe Conspiracy Theories.* London: Bloomsbury Publishing; Brotherton, Rob, and Silan Eser. 2015. "Bored to Fears: Boredom Proneness, Paranoia, and Conspiracy Theories." *Personality and Individual Differences* 80(July): 1–5. DOI: 10.1016/j.paid.2015.02.011; Brotherton, Robert, Christopher C. French, and Alan D. Pickering. 2013. "Measuring Belief in Conspiracy Theories: The Generic Conspiracist Beliefs Scale." *Frontiers in Psychology* 4(May). DOI: 10.3389/fpsyg.2013.00279; Douglas, Karen M. and Robbie M. Sutton. 2015. "Climate Change: Why the Conspiracy Theories Are Dangerous." *Bulletin of the Atomic Scientists* 71(2): 98–106; Douglas, Karen M., and Daniel Jolley. 2017. "Prevention Is Better Than Cure: Addressing Anti-Vaccine Conspiracy Theories." *Journal of Applied Social Psychology* 47(8): 459–469. DOI: 10.1111/jasp.12453; Douglas, Karen M., Robbie M. Sutton, Mitchell J. Callan, Rael J. Dawtry, and Annelie J. Harvey. 2016. "Someone Is Pulling the Strings: Hypersensitive Agency Detection and Belief in Conspiracy Theories." *Thinking & Reasoning* 22(1): 57–77; Douglas, Karen, Robbie M. Sutton, and Aleksandra Cichocka. 2017. "The Psychology of Conspiracy Theories." *Current Directions in Psychological Science* 26(6): 538–542; Jolley, Daniel, and Karen Douglas. 2014. "The Effects of Anti-Vaccine Conspiracy Theories on Vaccination Intentions." *PLoS ONE* 9(2). DOI: 10.1371/journal.pone.0089177; Jolley, Daniel and Karen M. Douglas. 2014. "The Social Consequences of Conspiracism: Exposure to Conspiracy Theories Decreases Intentions to Engage in Politics and to Reduce One's Carbon Footprint." *British Journal of Psychology* 105(1): 35–56; Sutton, Robbie M., and Karen M. Douglas. 2014. "Examining the Monological Nature of Conspiracy Theories." In *Power, Politics, and Paranoia: Why People Are Suspicious of Their Leaders*, eds. Jan-Willem van Prooijen and Paul A. M. van Lange. Cambridge: Cambridge University Pess, 254–272; van Prooijen, Jan-Willem, Karen M. Douglas, and Clara De Inocencio. 2017. "Connecting the Dots: Illusory Pattern Perception Predicts Belief in Conspiracies and the Supernatural." *European Journal of Social Psychology*. DOI: 10.1002/ejsp.2331; Wood, Michael J., Karen M. Douglas, and Robbie M. Sutton. 2012. "Dead and Alive: Beliefs in Contradictory Conspiracy Theories." *Social Psychological and Personality Science* 3(6): 767–773. DOI: 10.1177/1948550611434786.

16

Conspiracy Theory Psychology

Individual Differences, Worldviews, and States of Mind

MICHAEL J. WOOD AND KAREN M. DOUGLAS

Conspiracy theories are a contentious subject. Beyond the already complex issue of what defines a conspiracy theory, people who disagree about conspiracy theories seem to be perennially confused by one another. People who generally reject conspiracy theories tend to deride people who believe them—how can these people take such ridiculous ideas seriously? On the other hand, people who take conspiracy theories more seriously wonder why everyone else seems so blind—how can these people buy into the obvious lies put out by the establishment? In a broader sense, these questions are asking the same thing: why do people differ in how much they believe conspiracy theories? This is an important question—as seen elsewhere in this volume, certain conspiracy theories can lead to serious consequences for vaccination rates, political engagement, pro-environmental behaviors, and even how people engage with their workplace.[1] On the other hand, if people really are routinely engaged in sinister conspiracies against the public good, being suspicious is probably a good idea.

Psychologists have been wondering about variation in conspiracy belief for a long time, at least since conspiracy theories about the John F. Kennedy assassination started to circulate in the 1960s. In the half-century since then, we have discovered a substantial amount about the psychology of conspiracy theories. Specifically, we have a basic picture of the personality factors that influence belief, the mindsets that are more likely to lead to conspiracy theorizing, the conditions under which conspiracy theories are likely to arise, and the effects of conspiracy theories on people's thoughts and attitudes.

Personality and Individual Differences

One of the strongest findings in social psychology over the past century has been the discovery of the Fundamental Attribution Error.[2] This is the tendency for people to think that others' behavior is mostly caused by the sort of person they are, rather than the situations they find themselves in. For example, if someone yells at another driver in a parking lot, they could be an average person having an unusually bad day. Maybe the other driver did something very dangerous or offensive. In other words, their reaction could come from something specific to provoke the situation. However, most people would generally jump to the conclusion that the angry person is just that—an *angry person*, someone with a naturally short temper and little patience for others.

Belief and disbelief in conspiracy theories is no exception to this way of thinking. A diehard skeptic might see conspiracy theories as the mark of someone who is paranoid and suspicious by nature. Likewise, for the more conspiracy-minded it is tempting to think that conspiracy skeptics are naïve and gullible. Because of the fundamental attribution error, these sorts of explanations are simply the first things that come to mind. It should be no surprise, then, that psychologists and other social scientists have spent a lot of time investigating exactly this kind of explanation for conspiracy theory belief—in other words, asking *what sort of person* believes (or rejects) a conspiracy theory. In psychology, this maps onto the general field of *individual differences*. The individual differences question drove much of the early research into conspiracy theories and continues to be highly influential today. If you want to know how seriously someone takes conspiracy theories, you should ask about how much they trust others, whether they are agreeable or open-minded, how much they think people are out to get them, and whether they routinely have unusual or paranormal experiences. Conspiracy theorizing may be driven in part by evidence, but is certainly driven by underlying psychological tendencies.

One of the earliest subjects investigated was interpersonal trust. Reasonably enough, people who believe more conspiracy theories tend to trust others less—not just the government, the media, or the institutions of society, but also other people in general, such as friends, neighbors, and co-workers.[3] This makes sense—people who are more suspicious of others are more likely to detect a conspiracy, genuine or otherwise. In line with this, some psychologists have speculated that conspiracy theories are a manifestation of healthy interpersonal suspicion.[4]

The research on trust is mostly correlational. We know that trust and conspiracy theories are correlated, but we do not exactly know why. Less trusting people might be suspicious in general and therefore more likely to detect a conspiracy, but it also makes sense that if you think others are conspiring a lot, you would probably end up trusting them less. Likewise, some third factor could influence both variables, or there could be a feedback loop between mistrust and conspiracy beliefs so that each one feeds the other. This is a limitation that is shared by much of the psychological research on conspiracy theories, particularly the individual differences research.

Other work has looked at predicting conspiracy theory belief from broad personality traits. These investigations have produced conflicting results. The two personality traits most often found to be connected to conspiracy belief are agreeableness and openness to experience—studies show that people who are more modest, compliant, and empathic are likely to reject conspiracy theories, as well as people who are less creative and open-minded.[5] However, there have also been studies showing no independent relationships between conspiracy beliefs and either openness to experience (Lobato et al.) or agreeableness.[6] Other studies have found that open-mindedness, a variable closely related to openness to experience, was *negatively* correlated with beliefs in conspiracy theories.[7] At the moment it is not completely clear how personality predicts conspiracy belief.

Research aside, popular fiction and news media very often characterize conspiracy theorists as paranoid and conspiracy theories as delusions.[8] Some research has looked into whether there really is a connection between conspiracy belief and paranoid delusion, but the relationship is not straightforward. The most common form of delusion in schizophrenia is the *persecutory delusion*, a paranoid belief that others are conspiring to persecute you—for example, harassing you on the street or deliberately making noise that prevents you from sleeping.[9] Persecutory delusions differ from what are usually called conspiracy theories in that delusions usually propose a conspiracy against the deluded person themselves ("they are out to get *me, specifically*"). However, conspiracy theories about 9/11, vaccines, or the moon landings tend to be much broader in scope. That is, someone who believes a standard conspiracy theory might be a member of a relatively large targeted group such as African Americans or the general public ("they are out to get *us*"), or they might be totally irrelevant to the conspirators' goals. This seems to be a key difference between everyday conspiracy theories and the delusions of conspiracy that stem from clinical paranoia.[10]

Still, there are enough similarities between conspiracy theories and the features of certain psychological disorders that there might be some kind of psychological connection. There is some evidence that nonclinical paranoia is correlated with beliefs in conspiracy theories, but most of the research in this area focuses on *schizotypy*, a theory that people fall on a broad spectrum of psychological experience ranging from complete normality to mild dissociative states to full-blown psychosis.[11] Mentally healthy individuals vary considerably in how schizotypal they are. Specifically, people who are higher in schizotypy tend to display higher creativity and artistic ability, impulsiveness, superstitious beliefs and magical thinking, disorganized thought patterns, introversion, and antisocial behavior.[12] Recently, psychologists have added conspiracy theories to this list—more schizotypal individuals, especially those more prone to magical thinking and unusual experiences, tend to take conspiracy theories more seriously.[13] The exact reason for this is unclear. Some researchers have theorized that more schizotypal individuals believe more conspiracy theories because they are simply more suspicious than others, but this has not been well supported by the available data.[14] Some evidence suggests that people high in schizotypy are more likely to detect intention or agency in ambiguous situations—that is, they are more likely to think that things happen intentionally rather than accidentally.[15] Because of this, they conclude that a conspiracy could be behind a set of events that others might dismiss as coincidence.[16] It is also possible that less schizotypal people simply come into contact with fewer unusual or unconventional beliefs, including conspiracy theories. As we will see in the next section, a person's other beliefs have a strong influence on what they think about a particular conspiracy theory.

Worldviews, Other Beliefs, and Politics

Next we review how conspiracy theories are made more or less credible by the other beliefs people hold. Naturally, whether someone agrees with a certain idea depends on more than just their personality, their level of schizotypy, or other general characteristics—it also depends on their broader belief system, ideology, religion, political leanings, and so on. A consistent finding running throughout the psychological research literature has been that beliefs in conspiracy theories, as well as the larger belief systems they are built on, are often better understood as *disbeliefs*. This can be seen in how people argue for conspiracy theories that they believe in. For example, in an analysis of online arguments about 9/11 we found that people advocating conspiracy theories more often argued *against* the mainstream explanation ("the official story is impossible") than *for* their own ("this is evidence that 9/11 was a conspiracy"). People arguing in favor of the mainstream account of 9/11 did the opposite.[17] This disbelief—a distrust of authority and officialdom, a perception of ulterior motives, and a conviction that things are not quite what they seem—is a feature of a great number of popular conspiracy theories. Maybe because of this common ground, one of the strongest predictors of someone's opinion of a conspiracy theory is their thoughts about other conspiracy theories. For instance, knowing what someone thinks of the JFK assassination, the moon landings, chemtrails, and the New World Order will allow you to predict fairly accurately what they think of water fluoridation or 9/11.[18]

Interestingly, the correlations between conspiracy beliefs also hold true for real historical conspiracies. Conspiracy skeptics also (incorrectly) apply their skepticism to things like the MKULTRA experiments (the CIA's Cold War mind control and brainwashing program) or various instances of government corruption, while conspiracy theorists will either be more aware of them or just think they sound more likely to be true.[19] It is not yet clear whether this connection stems from differences in historical knowledge, trust in government, or some combination of factors. However, beliefs in different conspiracy theories tend to be positively correlated even if the theories have nothing to do with one another, and even if they explicitly contradict one another.[20] This all points to a general tendency for people to accept or reject conspiratorial explanations, as well as general suspicions about particular topics. Individual conspiracy theories are an outward manifestation of these two forces.[21]

Of course, conspiracy theories are not the only way to embrace "fringe" knowledge and belief. Many other topics lie on the outer edges of what society considers to be acceptable knowledge or belief—like the paranormal, alternative medicine, urban legends, extreme politics, and pseudoscience. Other psychological research has looked at what makes people believe or disbelieve in these things as well, and the results are not totally dissimilar. Research has shown that people who are skeptical of conspiracy theories also tend to be skeptical of these topics.[22] Some of this comes down to a simple match in worldviews—if we are being lied to about 9/11, maybe we cannot trust mainstream medicine or archeology either. Beyond that, these correlations could be due to both conspiracy theories and other fringe beliefs being correlated with schizotypy, openness to experience, agency detection, an increased exposure to conspiracy theories in social circles where fringe topics are more openly discussed, a desire to find simple solutions to complex problems, or some other factor.[23]

More generally, a good deal of research points to a connection between beliefs in conspiracy theories and perceived "outsiderdom" or separation from mainstream society. This is especially evident when looking at work on the psychological concept of *anomie*. Anomie is a sense of social alienation or disconnection, a feeling that one's own values and beliefs are not represented in broader society.[24] Feelings of anomie have been shown to correlate significantly with beliefs in conspiracy theories in diverse samples.[25]

While conspiracy theories might be more popular on the fringes of society, of course that is not the only place they exist. Some conspiracy theories are fully mainstream: a clear majority of Americans believe that there was a conspiracy to assassinate John F. Kennedy, for instance. [26] Others are more or less popular because of their agreement with mainstream worldviews and ideologies. For example, Republicans were naturally more likely than Democrats to believe that Barack Obama was secretly born in Kenya, while Democrats take the idea that the Bush administration was involved with 9/11 more seriously.[27] People who follow a New Age spirituality are more likely than Christians to believe the conspiracy theories about Christianity popularized by *The Da Vinci Code*—these theories fit a New Age worldview just fine, but are a harder sell to a committed Christian.[28] Perhaps unsurprisingly, we find conspiracy theories about vote-rigging much more plausible when our favored candidate loses than when the election has the outcome we want.[29]

Some of it comes down to attitudes toward the group that is supposed to be behind the conspiracy. People who are high in the psychological variable of *right-wing authoritarianism*, which measures the tendency to submit to authority, to dislike outsiders, and to prefer convention and tradition to new ideas, are more likely to buy into conspiracy theories that accuse minorities and deviant groups of secretive plots to destroy society.[30] Stereotypes about particular groups are naturally influenced by attitudes toward those groups, as well—if someone sees a group of people, such as Jews, as more of a single-minded collective entity than simply a collection of individuals, conspiracy theories implicating that group will seem much more likely.[31] So, while belief in some conspiracy theories tends to predict belief in others, it is not that simple. Different theories appeal to different audiences, and many of the most successful conspiracy theories play on the anxieties and fears of particular social groups.

Psychological States, Specific Mindsets, and Social Context

Of course, personality and general beliefs about the world are not the whole story. After all, the fundamental attribution error is just that—an *error*. The ways we think and act are subject to more fleeting influences than our relatively consistent traits and worldviews—next, we will look at some fairly temporary psychological factors that influence how people think about conspiracies. A striking demonstration of this comes from a 2008 experiment where the researchers had participants write a short essay before completing a variety of tasks.[32] Half of the participants wrote about a time they lacked control over their lives, while the others described a time when they were in control. This task was meant to induce a feeling of having or lacking control—and a lack of control is thought to be a troubling psychological state that people are motivated to resolve. In follow-up tasks, the participants who had been manipulated to feel a lack of control were more likely to see patterns in noise, to make superstitious inferences about connections between events, and to perceive sinister conspiracies in ambiguous situations. Psychologists theorize that drawing connections and recognizing patterns in this way can help to restore a sense of control and certainty—to make sense of a world that, in that moment, seems difficult to predict or understand.[33] The world follows patterns; it is regular, knowable, and perhaps controllable, even if the wrong people (i.e., evil conspirators) are controlling it at the moment. Consistent with this experimental work, feelings of control have been found to correlate reliably with beliefs in conspiracy theories as well as with the related variables of mistrust and paranoia.[34]

The connection between pattern recognition and conspiracy theory belief makes some intuitive sense. Conspiracy literature often talks about connecting the dots, seeing the bigger picture based on the limited information that has slipped through the conspirators' fingers—they have covered their tracks well, so there is no single definitive piece of proof. Psychologists know this sort of thinking—seeing broad patterns and recognizing trends at the cost of ignoring some smaller details—as *holistic* or *intuitive* thinking. Its opposite—focusing on details and the interrelationships between parts of a system at the expense of looking at the whole—is called *analytic*

or *rational* thinking.[35] While everyone uses both modes of thinking, it is possible to induce someone to rely more heavily on one system or the other at a given time. When someone is thinking more analytically, conspiracy theories seem much less plausible than otherwise. People with a more generally analytic thinking style tend to be more skeptical of conspiracy theories as explanations for events than those with a more holistic/intuitive style.[36]

When measuring people's opinions of conspiracy theories, psychologists generally employ questionnaire methods. They present survey participants with a statement, such as "The government is covering up alien visitations," and ask them to rate their agreement with it on a scale. Most of these scales do not contain the words "conspiracy theory" at all, because of a concern that the term has negative connotations and it would influence people's views. Instead, they tend to ask about plots, intrigue, covert orchestration, and so on. This matches a general concern that "conspiracy theory" has such baggage that it works as a kind of rhetorical weapon, and poisons people against anything that it's applied to. However, some research has shown that people are no less likely to agree with something when it is labeled a conspiracy theory than when given a more neutral label, suggesting that the presence or absence of the term may not be as important as once thought.[37]

What Makes Particular Theories More Appealing?

Finally, some more recent research has moved beyond looking at what makes people reject or accept conspiracy theories in general. This line of research focuses more on the theories themselves—in other words, what makes a good conspiracy theory? This research is in its early days, but we are starting to get a general picture.[38] A successful conspiracy theory explains important events or social conditions, implicates a group seen as both powerful and immoral, and provides a coherent motivation for the conspirators. 9/11 conspiracy theories are a good example. The conspirators are said to be powerful politicians and financiers, the event itself was a major historical moment, and the motivation, a war for oil in the Middle East and a crackdown on civil liberties at home, is easily understandable. These elements help to engage people in the search for a hidden truth, and motivate them to find patterns that point to the possibility of conspiracy.

Conspiracy theories about a particular group seem particularly likely when someone holds unfavorable social stereotypes about them, or when the less powerful party in a hierarchical social relationship has little control over matters but depends on the more powerful party for a vital resource.[39] It should be no surprise that feelings of power are relevant to beliefs in conspiracy theories. On a very basic level, conspiracy theories are basically stories about power—the secret power of a particular group, and the new power of the people who have come to see through their deception.[40] People who feel relatively powerless are more likely to agree with

conspiracy theories, and general conspiracy mentality predicts prejudice against high-power but not low-power groups.[41]

Groups that are implicated as conspirators are generally seen as being fairly powerful. They tend to have a lot of resources at their disposal—at least enough to carry out their plot, create a cover story of some sort, and maintain a cover-up more or less indefinitely. In general, people see conspiracies as much more competent than individuals are. In extreme examples, the conspirators are seen as having a sort of superhuman power and near infallibility in executing their plans. Research has shown that people are more likely to perceive a conspiracy when a disastrous event occurs than when a disaster was narrowly averted, possibly because of this idea that conspiracies of powerful people usually manage to do what they set out to do. Unlikely or unusual events are more likely to give rise to conspiracy theories than likely or normal ones are.[42] Critics of conspiracy theories point out that the more elements there are in a conspiracy the more likely it is that at least one would fail, and that conspiracy theorists overestimate how likely it is that large conspiracies could be successfully carried out.[43]

Even assuming a very high level of competence among the perpetrators, conspiracies are still risky.[44] On a very basic level, a plausible conspiracy theory must have a good reason for the conspirators to risk being caught committing some terrible crime or another. Motive is everything. In fact, a fairly strong predictor of conspiracy theorizing is not just someone's understanding of the conspirators' motives, but also their *own* willingness to conspire in a specific situation. For example, some research has shown that those who are most convinced that Princess Diana was secretly killed by the British royal family believe so because they are also more likely than others to say that they themselves would have had her assassinated, had they been in the royal family's position.[45] This finding also occurs for several other conspiracy theories, and the immorality of the suspected conspirators also plays an important role. For example, conspiracy theories are easier to believe when the conspirators are seen as immoral.[46] People are especially sensitive to immoral behavior by authorities when they are feeling uncertain. Perceptions of immorality and of the existence of ulterior motives can prompt suspicion, which social psychologists see as a state of ambiguity. When we are suspicious, we are not sure what to think, so we entertain several hypotheses for why others are acting the way they are.[47] Suspicious people do not always come to uncharitable conclusions about others—instead, they suspend judgment and look for further information.[48] This matches the nonspecificity and vagueness of conspiracy theory beliefs highlighted above.

Conclusion

Despite all that we know about the psychological factors associated with conspiracy theories, we know much less about their social consequences. In part, this might be

due to the incorrect assumption that conspiracy theories are trivial notions believed only by disenfranchised, paranoid, or distrustful people.[49] However, dismissing all conspiracy theories as either trivial or ridiculous risks overlooking some of the potential consequences of the theories that many members of society find at least plausible, such as those associated with vaccination, climate change, or the sinister motives of particular social groups.[50] In such cases, conspiracy theories may be harmful if they are used to discredit information for which there is clear legal, scientific, or historical evidence.[51]

Too often, the question of *why* people believe (or refuse to believe) conspiracy theories becomes a question of *who* believes conspiracy theories. While psychologists have made some strides in identifying people who are most likely to take conspiracy theories seriously, perhaps more importantly we have started to move beyond the *who*. We also know something about *when* conspiracy theories are most plausible, *how* they fit into larger systems of belief, and *what* the effects (and, perhaps, functions) of conspiracy theories are. The "why" is a much broader question that encompasses all of these areas, and the next few years of research will develop our understanding of it even further.

Notes

1. Jolley, Daniel, and Karen M. Douglas. 2014. "The Effects of Anti-Vaccine Conspiracy Theories on Vaccination Intentions." *PLoS ONE* 9(2). DOI: 10.371/journal.pone.0089177; Jolley, Daniel, and Karen M. Douglas. 2014. "The Social Consequences of Conspiracism: Exposure to Conspiracy Theories Decreases Intentions to Engage in Politics and to Reduce One's Carbon Footprint." *British Journal of Psychology* 105(1): 35–56; Douglas, Karen M., and Ana C. Leite. 2017. "Suspicion in the Workplace: Organizational Conspiracy Theories and Work-Related Outcomes." *British Journal of Psychology* 108(3): 486–506.
2. Ross, Lee. 1977. "The Intuitive Psychologist and His Shortcomings: Distortions in the Attribution Process." *Advances in Experimental Social Psychology* 10(C): 173–220.
3. Abalakina-Paap, Marina, Walter G. Stephan, Traci Craig, and W. Larry Gregory. 1999. "Beliefs in Conspiracies." *Political Psychology* 20(3): 637–647; Goertzel, Ted. "Belief in Conspiracy Theories." *Political Psychology* 15(4): 731–742; Hamsher, J. Herbert, Jesse D. Geller, and Julian B. Rotter. 1968. "Interpersonal Trust, Internal-External Control, and the Warren Commission Report." *Journal of Personality and Social Psychology* 9(3): 210–215; Simmons, William Paul, and Sharon Parsons. 2005. "Beliefs in Conspiracy Theories among African Americans: A Comparison of Elites and Masses." *Social Science Quarterly* 86(3): 582–598; Wright, Thomas L., and Jack Arbuthnot. 1974. "Interpersonal Trust, Political Preference, and Perceptions of the Watergate Affair." *Personality and Social Psychology Bulletin* 1(1): 168–170; Yelland, Linda M., and William F Stone. 1996. "Belief in the Holocaust: Effects of Personality and Propaganda." *Source: Political Psychology Political Psychology* 17(3): 551–562.
4. Darwin, Hannah, Nick Neave, and Joni Holmes. 2011. "Belief in Conspiracy Theories. The Role of Paranormal Belief, Paranoid Ideation and Schizotypy." *Personality and Individual Differences* 50(8): 1289–1293.
5. Swami, Viren, Tomas Chamorro-Premuzic, and Adrian Furnham. 2010. "Unanswered Questions: A Preliminary Investigation of Personality and Individual Difference Predictors of 9/11 Conspiracist Beliefs." *Applied Cognitive Psychology* 24(6): 749–761; Swami, Viren,

Rebecca Coles, Stefan Stieger, Jakob Pietschnig, Adrian Furnham, Sherry Rehim, and Martin Voracek. 2011. "Conspiracist Ideation in Britain and Austria: Evidence of a Monological Belief System and Associations between Individual Psychological Differences and Real-World and Fictitious Conspiracy Theories." *British Journal of Psychology* 102(3): 443–463.

6. Lobato, Emilio, Jorge Mendoza, Valerie Sims, and Matthew Chin. 2014. "Examining the Relationship between Conspiracy Theories, Paranormal Beliefs, and Pseudoscience Acceptance among a University Population." *Applied Cognitive Psychology* 28(5): 617–625; Swami, Viren, Jakob Pietschnig, Ulrich S. Tran, Ingo W. Nader, Stefan Stieger, and Martin Voracek. 2013. "Lunar Lies: The Impact of Informational Framing and Individual Differences in Shaping Conspiracist Beliefs About the Moon Landings." *Applied Cognitive Psychology* 27(1): 71–80.

7. Swami, Viren, Martin Voracek, Stefan Stieger, Ulrich S. Tran, and Adrian Furnham. 2014. "Analytic Thinking Reduces Belief in Conspiracy Theories." *Cognition* 133(3): 572–585.

8. Wood, Michael J. 2016. "Some Dare Call It Conspiracy: Labeling Something a Conspiracy Theory Does Not Reduce Belief in It." *Political Psychology* 37(5): 695–705.

9. American Psychiatric Association. 2013. *Diagnostic and Statistical Manual of Mental Disorders: DSM-5.* 5th ed. Arlington: American Psychiatric Association.

10. Hofstadter, Richard. 1964. "The Paranoid Style in American Politics and Other Essays." *Harper's Magazine.* https://harpers.org/archive/1964/11/the-paranoid-style-in-american-politics/ (Accessed December 29, 2017).

11. Brotherton, Robert, and Silan Eser. 2015. "Bored to Fears: Boredom Proneness, Paranoia, and Conspiracy Theories." *Personality and Individual Differences* 80(July): 1–5.

12. Batey, Mark, and Adrian Furnham. 2008. "The Relationship between Measures of Creativity and Schizotypy." *Personality and Individual Differences* 45(8): 816–821; Siever, Larry, J. 2002. "Schizotypy: Implications for Illness and Health." *American Journal of Psychiatry* 159(4): 683–684.

13. Barron, David, Kevin Morgan, Tony Towell, Boris Altemeyer, and Viren Swami. 2014. "Associations between Schizotypy and Belief in Conspiracist Ideation." *Personality and Individual Differences* 70(November): 156–159; Dagnall, Neil, Kenneth Drinkwater, Andrew Parker, Andrew Donovan, and Megan Parton. 2015. "Conspiracy Theory and Cognitive Style: A Worldview." *Frontiers in Psychology* 6(February): 206; Darwin, Neave, and Holmes, "Belief in Conspiracy Theories"; Swami, Pietschnig, Tran, Nader, Stieger, and Voracek, "Lunar Lies."

14. Barron, Morgan, Towell, Altemeyer, and Swami, "Associations between Schizotypy and Belief in Conspiracist Ideation."

15. van der Tempel, Jan, and James E. Alcock. 2015. "Relationships between Conspiracy Mentality, Hyperactive Agency Detection, and Schizotypy: Supernatural Forces at Work?" *Personality and Individual Differences* 82(August): 136–141.

16. Brotherton, Robert, and Christopher C. French. 2015. "Intention Seekers: Conspiracist Ideation and Biased Attributions of Intentionality." *PLoS ONE* 10(5). DOI: 10.1371/journal.pone.0124125; Douglas, Karen M., Robbie M. Sutton, Mitchell J. Callan, Rael J. Dawtry, and Annelie J. Harvey. 2015. "Someone Is Pulling the Strings: Hypersensitive Agency Detection and Belief in Conspiracy Theories." *Thinking & Reasoning* 22(1): 1–21.

17. Wood, Michael J., and Karen M. Douglas. 2013. "What about Building 7?" A Social Psychological Study of Online Discussion of 9/11 Conspiracy Theories." *Frontiers in Psychology* 4(July):407; Wood, Michael J. and Karen M. Douglas. 2015. "Online Communication as a Window to Conspiracist Worldviews." *Frontiers in Psychology* 6(June): 836.

18. Brotherton, Robert, Christopher C. French, and Alan D. Pickering. 2013. "Measuring Belief in Conspiracy Theories: The Generic Conspiracist Beliefs Scale." *Frontiers in Psychology* 4(May): 279; Goertzel, "Belief in Conspiracy Theories."; Swami, Coles, Stieger, Pietschnig, Furnham, Rehim, and Voracek, "Conspiracist Ideation in Britain and Austria"; Wood, Michael J., Karen M. Douglas, and Robbie M. Sutton. 2012. "Dead and Alive: Beliefs in Contradictory

Conspiracy Theories." *Social Psychological and Personality Science* 3(6): 767–773; Wood and Douglas, "'What about Building 7?'"; Sutton, Robbie M., and Karen M. Douglas. 2014. "Examining the Monological Nature of Conspiracy Theories." In *Power, Politics, and Paranoia: Why People Are Suspicious of Their Leaders*, eds. Jan-Willem van Prooijen and Paul A. M. van Lange. Cambridge: Cambridge University Press, 254–272.

19. Wood, "Some Dare Call It Conspiracy."

20. Wood, Douglas, and Sutton, "Dead and Alive."

21. Wood, Michael J. 2016. "Conspiracy Suspicions as a Proxy for Beliefs in Conspiracy Theories: Implications for Theory and Measurement." *British Journal of Psychology* 108(3): 507–527.

22. Bruder, Martin, Peter Haffke, Nick Neave, Nina Nouripanah, and Roland Imhoff. 2013. "Measuring Individual Differences in Generic Beliefs in Conspiracy Theories across Cultures: Conspiracy Mentality Questionnaire." *Frontiers in Psychology* 4(April): 225; Darwin, Neave, and Holmes, "Belief in Conspiracy Theories"; Dagnall, Drinkwater, Parker, Donovan, and Parton, "Conspiracy Theory and Cognitive Style"; Stieger, Stefan, Nora Gumhalter, Ulrich S. Tran, Martin Voracek, and Viren Swami. 2013. "Girl in the Cellar: A Repeated Cross-Sectional Investigation of Belief in Conspiracy Theories about the Kidnapping of Natascha Kampusch." *Frontiers in Psychology* 4(May): 297; Swami, Coles, Stieger, Pietschnig, Furnham, Rehim, and Voracek, "Conspiracist Ideation in Britain and Austria"; van der Tempel and Alcock, "Relationships between Conspiracy Mentality, Hyperactive Agency Detection, and Schizotypy"; van Prooijen, Jan-Willem., André P. M. Krouwel, and Thomas V. Pollet. 2015. "Political Extremism Predicts Belief in Conspiracy Theories." *Social Psychological and Personality Science* 6(5): 570–578.

23. Barkun, Michael. 2003. *A Culture of Conspiracy: Apocalyptic Visions in Contemporary America.* Berkeley: University of California Press.

24. Durkheim, Emile. [1897] 1951. *Suicide: A Study in Sociology*. Trans. John A. Spaulding and George Simpson. Glencoe, IL: Free Press, 405.

25. Abalakina-Paap, Stephan, Craig, and Gregory, "Beliefs in Conspiracies"; Goertzel, "Belief in Conspiracy Theories"; Leman, Patrick J, and Marco Cinnirella. 2013. "Beliefs in Conspiracy Theories and the Need for Cognitive Closure." *Frontiers in Psychology* 4 (June): 378.

26. Enten, Harry. 2017. "Most People Believe in JFK Conspiracy Theories." https://fivethirtyeight.com/features/the-one-thing-in-politics-most-americans-believe-in-jfk-conspiracies/ (Accessed December 27, 2017).

27. Oliver, J. Eric, and Thomas J. Wood. 2014. "Conspiracy Theories and the Paranoid Style(s) of Mass Opinion." *American Journal of Political Science* 58(4): 952–966.

28. Newheiser, Anna Kaisa, Miguel Farias, and Nicole Tausch. 2011. "The Functional Nature of Conspiracy Beliefs: Examining the Underpinnings of Belief in the Da Vinci Code Conspiracy." *Personality and Individual Differences* 51(8): 1007–1011. DOI: 10.1016/j.paid.2011.08.011.

29. Uscinski, Joseph E., and Joseph M. Parent. 2014. *American Conspiracy Theories*. Oxford: Oxford University Press.

30. Grzesiak-Feldman, Monika, and Monika Irzycka. 2009. "Right-Wing Authoritarianism and Conspiracy Thinking in a Polish Sample." *Psychological Reports* 105(2): 389–93; Swami, Viren. 2012. "Social Psychological Origins of Conspiracy Theories: The Case of the Jewish Conspiracy Theory in Malaysia." *Frontiers in Psychology* 3(August): 280.

31. Grzesiak-Feldman, Monika, and Hubert Suszek. 2008. "Conspiracy Stereotyping and Perceptions of Group Entitativity of Jews, Germans, Arabs, and Homosexuals by Polish Students." *Psychological Reports* 102(3): 755–758.

32. Whitson, Jennifer A., and Adam D. Galinsky. 2008. "Lacking Control Increases Illusory Pattern Perception." *Science* 322(3): 115–117.

33. Kay, Aaron C., Jennifer A. Whitson, Danielle Gaucher, and Adam D. Galinsky. 2009. "Compensatory Control: Achieving Order through the Mind, Our Institutions, and the Heavens." *Current Directions in Psychological Science* 18(5): 264–268.

34. Abalakina-Paap, Stephan, Craig, and Gregory, "Beliefs in Conspiracies"; Mirowsky, J., and C. E. Ross. 1983. "Paranoia and the Structure of Powerlessness." *American Sociological Review* 48(2): 228–239; Hamsher, Geller, Rotter. "Interpersonal Trust, Internal-External Control, and the Warren Commission Report."

35. Stanovich, K. E., and R. F. West. 2000. "Individual Differences in Reasoning: Implications for the Rationality Debate?" *Behavioral and Brain Sciences* 23(5): 645–665.

36. Swami, Voracek, Stieger, Tran, and Furnham, "Analytic Thinking Reduces Belief in Conspiracy Theories."

37. Wood, "Some Dare Call It Conspiracy."

38. Miller, Joanne M., Kyle L. Saunders, and Christina E. Farhart. 2016. "Conspiracy Endorsement as Motivated Reasoning: The Moderating Roles of Political Knowledge and Trust." *American Journal of Political Science* 60(4): 824–844; Oliver and Wood, "Conspiracy Theories and the Paranoid Style(s) of Mass Opinion"; Munro, Geoffrey D., Carrie Weih, and Jeffrey Tsai. 2010. "Motivated Suspicion: Asymmetrical Attributions of the Behavior of Political Ingroup and Outgroup Members." *Basic and Applied Social Psychology* 32(2): 173–184; Van Prooijen, Jan-Willem, and Eric Van Dijk. 2014. "When Consequence Size Predicts Belief in Conspiracy Theories: The Moderating Role of Perspective Taking." *Journal of Experimental Social Psychology* 55(November): 63–73.

39. Kramer, Roderick M. 1998. "Paranoid Cognition in Social Systems: Thinking and Acting in the Shadow of Doubt." *Personality and Social Psychology Review* 2(4): 251–275.

40. Sapountzis, Antonis, and Susan Condor. 2013. "Conspiracy Accounts as Intergroup Theories: Challenging Dominant Understandings of Social Power and Political Legitimacy." *Political Psychology* 34(5): 731–752.

41. Abalakina-Paap, Stephan, Craig, and Gregory, "Beliefs in Conspiracies"; Dagnall, Drinkwater, Parker, Donovan, and Parton, "Conspiracy Theory and Cognitive Style."

42. Grimes, David Robert. 2016. "On the Viability of Conspiratorial Beliefs." *PLoS ONE* 11(1). DOI: 10.1371/journal.pone.0147905.

43. Ibid.

44. Uscinski and Parent, *American Conspiracy Theories.*

45. Douglas, Karen M., and Robbie M. Sutton. 2011. "Does It Take One to Know One? Endorsement of Conspiracy Theories Is Influenced by Personal Willingness to Conspire." *British Journal of Social Psychology* 50(3): 544–552.

46. van Prooijen, Jan-Willem, and Nils B. Jostmann. 2013. "Belief in Conspiracy Theories: The Influence of Uncertainty and Perceived Morality." *European Journal of Social Psychology* 43(1): 109–115.

47. Kramer; Fein, Steven. 1996. "Effects of Suspicion on Attributional Thinking and the Correspondence Bias." *Journal of Personality and Social Psychology* 70(6): 1164–1184.

48. Sinaceur, Marwan. 2010. "Suspending Judgment to Create Value: Suspicion and Trust in Negotiation." *Journal of Experimental Social Psychology* 46(3): 543–550.

49. Bratich, Jack Z. 2008. *Conspiracy Panics.* New York: State University of New York Press; Husting, Ginna, and Martin Orr. 2007 "Dangerous Machinery: 'Conspiracy Theorist' as a Transpersonal Strategy of Exclusion." *Symbolic Interaction* 30(2): 127–150.

50. Douglas, Karen M., and Robbie M. Sutton. 2015. "Climate Change: Why the Conspiracy Theories Are Dangerous." *Bulletin of the Atomic Scientists* 71(2): 98–106.

51. Goertzel, Ted. 2010. "Conspiracy Theories in Science." *EMBO Reports* 11(7): 493–499; Lewandowsky, Stephan, Gilles E. Gignac, and Klaus Oberauer. 2013. "The Role of Conspiracist Ideation and Worldviews in Predicting Rejection of Science." *PLoS ONE* 10(8). DOI: 10.1371/journal.pone.0075637.

17

Conspiracy Rumor Psychology

NICHOLAS DIFONZO

Rumor psychology can shed light on conspiracy theories. Rumor, which is un-confirmed information in circulation, has tantalized social psychologists and sociologists on several continents for eight decades.[1] Indian psychologist Jamuna Prasad analyzed rumors after the Great Indian Earthquake of 1934, American psychologists Gordon Allport and Leo Postman explored *The Psychology of Rumor* in 1947, and Japanese sociologist Tomotsu Shibutani argued for thinking of rumor as *Improvised News* in 1966.[2] We know a lot about rumors.

Examining conspiracy theories using the lens of rumor psychology leads to interesting questions that might not otherwise be raised. This is because when trying to understand conspiracy theories, the typical focus has been on the indi-vidual: Why do *individuals* believe such outlandish, unlikely, and paranoid tales? And often this question becomes: What *individual* personality traits or personal characteristics predispose such gullibility? But using the rumor framework leads us to see conspiracy theories as part of a social system of interacting persons. We begin to think of conspiracy theories as stories that are communicated between people *in relationships* and as stories that grow out of the hubbub of the *group*. Thinking of it this way makes a great deal of sense because, after all, the vast majority of conspiracy theorists didn't theorize their conspiracies. Conspiracy theories are *heard and told*; hearing and telling are things done with other people and in groups.

If we do this, the focus then shifts to the social relationships and group dynamics involved in communicating conspiracy theories. Several intriguing questions are then spotlighted: In what sorts of situations do groups start telling and hearing con-spiracy theories? What do they *do* for groups in such situations? Why do people communicate them to one another? What is it about the groups or the relationships that spawns and sustains such wildly false stories (and every once in a while a true one)? Let's apply what we know from 80 years of research on rumor to our under-standing of conspiracy theories.

Are Conspiracy Theories a Type of Rumor?

Rumors can be thought of as unproven information claims in circulation that may be true or false.[3] The statement "Tropical Fantasy Fruit Punch contains a substance that makes black men sterile," for example, made a specific claim about the ingredients of a popular soft drink sold in Brooklyn during the early 1990s that could have been true but turned out to be false.[4] The dubious nature of the rumor claim is often signaled with the preface "I don't know if this is true, but I heard that . . . ," or the teller may pass it along as fact. Rumor claims are often smaller stories that are part of larger narratives; for example, rumors in 2004 that the U.S. military was poisoning Iraqi cows fit neatly into larger narratives about the Crusades and colonialism that everyone in that culture knew.[5] This fit with narratives that are well known to the teller's club, clan, or culture makes many rumors—even the fantastic ones—seem quite plausible to the teller.[6]

Conspiracy theories can also be thought of as unproven information claims in circulation that may be true or false. The Watergate conspiracy tale about a U.S. presidential plot to bug Democratic National Committee headquarters, for example, proved true. In addition, conspiracy theories have a common story line: a powerful and secret group is engaging in covert, malevolent, and organized activities against vulnerable groups.[7] One popular conspiracy theory claims that world events such as political revolutions and economic recessions are clandestinely orchestrated by the Illuminati, a secret organization of powerful world leaders.[8] Like rumors, which draw on narratives in general, conspiracy theories draw on *exclusionary* narratives, which are stories about how the powerful oppress the weak.[9]

And so, conspiracy theories are really a type of rumor. Indeed, we might just as well call them *conspiracy rumors*: rumors characterized by stories about the covert and malevolent activities of powerful and secretive groups (and so I'll use the terms conspiracy theory and conspiracy rumor interchangeably). It makes sense therefore to think about conspiracy theories in light of what we know about the psychology of rumor, that is, to develop a *conspiracy rumor psychology*. In the remainder of this chapter, I'll do just that by posing some of the main questions that social psychologists have asked about rumor, summarizing what they have found and posing the same questions about conspiracy theories.

When Do Conspiracy Rumors Flourish?

This question gets at the *circumstances* that breed conspiracy rumor activity, and what they *do* for groups in these circumstances. Rumors arise in situations that groups have trouble interpreting. When important events happen without explanation, or the meaning of a situation seems unclear, it is unpleasant. We then interact to fill in the gaps with rumors. In other words, when reliable news is in short supply, groups "improvise" by crafting their own explanations, which are rumors.[10] This sort of circumstance is especially plentiful during times of change, instability, conflict, when information is contradictory, or communication is poor. If confronted with bad events that do not make sense to us, explanations also make us feel less uncertain and more in control. Simply understanding why bad things happen is a way of emotionally coping with those bad things. Similarly, the explanations that conspiracy theories offer for a wide range of distressing, chaotic, and unfair events help people cope by fulfilling psychological needs for certainty and a sense of control.[11] (A later chapter in this volume by Jan-Willem van Prooijen furthers this point.)

Rumors also arise in situations that groups interpret as threatening. The urge to protect ourselves immediately is indeed strong, can overpower ordinarily slower and cooler thinking, and can lead us to act hastily on dubious information claims. Better safe than sorry. Threats may be physical, having the potential to harm our health, wealth, or well-being, and rumors then help groups prepare for or avoid danger. But the threats that conspiracy rumors help groups cope with seem to be psychological.

Psychological threats are when we feel our identity, values, community, party, ideology, or anything else we happen to cherish is ridiculed, criticized, derogated, blamed, or otherwise humbled.[12] This too is unpleasant. Groups may then use rumors in psychological self-defense.[13] One of the most common ways that rumors defend us is when the rumors we spread about our group are positive, and those about rival groups are negative. This seems to be what now routinely happens in U.S. Presidential elections. In 2008, for example, rumors about then-Senator Barack Obama that he was secretly a Muslim bent on U.S. collapse, and about Governor Sarah Palin that she tried to ban books in a public library and had posed in a bikini while holding an assault rifle, were born and gained momentum in very active conservative and liberal political blogospheres[14]. Where there is conflict, telling stories about our own virtues and the other's villainy is quite useful in discrediting the other side and distracting us from our own peccadillos.

And so, in circumstances that are unclear and threatening, conspiracy rumors explain matters and help groups defend themselves psychologically. Consider the conspiracy theory that President Obama was purposely overwhelming the U.S. economy with government spending and weakening the military in order to destroy the United States, this time because he was a socialist.[15] Or that 9/11 and subsequent U.S. military campaigns were orchestrated by George W. Bush in order to further his family's oil interests.[16] Both conspiracy theories enabled ideological partisans to "see" a unifying purpose behind the actions of each president and to neutralize ever-present psychological threats by casting aspersions on him.

What Psychological States Lead to Transmission?

Conspiracy rumors would cease altogether if people didn't *communicate* them. So why *do* people communicate them?

Rumor researchers have asked this question in a couple of ways. The first way asks: What are the *psychological conditions* or *states* that lead people to transmit rumors? This is of course the flip side of circumstances, because psychological states come in part from how we interpret our circumstances. Circumstances lay outside of us; our experience of those circumstances lives inside of us.

Researchers have found that *anxiety, believing* the rumor to be true, and having a sense of *uncertainty*, which is a lack of sureness about current or future events, all predict rumor transmission.[17] These states are a natural response to circumstances that groups have difficulty interpreting or that they interpret as threatening. Research also points to *distrust*, especially distrust of official news sources or statements.[18] Before the fall of the "iron curtain," for example, Russians did not trust the state-controlled news and relied heavily on rumors.[19] And in one workplace undergoing radical downsizing, employees who distrusted management spread negative rumors *regardless* of how anxious or uncertain they were.[20]

Do anxiety, uncertainty, belief, and distrust lead people to transmit conspiracy theories?

Though not investigated directly, there is some indirect evidence on these questions. For example, research connecting anxiety and *belief* implies a link between anxiety and *transmission*: Since Hofstadter's seminal work in 1965, paranoia, a psychological state riddled with anxiety, has long been thought to promote belief in conspiracy theories.[21] Researchers think that conspiracy theories are believed as a way of coping with "feelings of powerlessness sparked by complex economic, social, and political phenomena" or with perceived in-group threat from powerful and secretive out-groups.[22] Well, "feelings of powerlessness" and "perceived threat" sound a lot like anxiety.

And recent research found that abnormal levels of anxiety, having an anxious personality, and feeling anxious due to one's situation were all correlated with belief in conspiracy theories.[23] This picture is mixed, though, because belief in one study was *not* correlated with anxiety but rather with feeling *stressed*, that is, feeling that life's situations are "unpredictable, uncontrollable and overloaded."[24] But anxiety may still play a key role: The researchers in that study suggested that highly anxious individuals may react more strongly to stressful events.

Similarly, research connecting the psychological state of uncertainty and *belief* implies a link between uncertainty and *transmission*.[25] In one experiment, university students in Amsterdam read a bogus report that oil companies "frequently violate international environmental policies in developing countries" and were then asked if oil companies ordered the start the (2003–2011) U.S. war with Iraq for financial gain.[26] Students were more likely to believe this conspiracy theory if they had first been asked to write about their emotions and physical reactions when they felt uncertain, as compared to when they were watching TV. In other words, just thinking about uncertainty increased belief in a well-known conspiracy theory!

Anecdotal evidence also suggests that conspiracy theories, like rumors, may be transmitted as a way of reducing uncertainty. For example, a plethora of conspiracy theories arose in response to the mysterious March 8, 2014, disappearance of Malaysian Airlines 370.[27] In this puzzling situation—in which proposed explanations included alien abduction, jihadist terror, and government cover-up—uncertainty abounded, no doubt amplified by nonstop news coverage. Even uncertainty that is raised by the conspiracy theory itself seems to lead to transmission. For example, the conspiracy theory that the Apollo moon landings were a hoax draws attention to supposed inconsistencies in the lunar images of that event, such as the absence of stars[28] (lest I promote uncertainty in the reader, stars couldn't be seen because of glare caused by the sun and because shutter speeds necessitated by the blinding rays of the sun were too fast to detect dim starlight).

What about the role of belief in conspiracy theory transmission? Ironically, there is little evidence either way on this question. Ironic because while belief is what researchers have been most interested in, they have focused on the question what *leads* to belief, rather than the question, what does belief lead *to*. Or doesn't: A tantalizing and plausible possibility is that belief has little to do with transmission of conspiracy theories, despite conversational norms to tell what one believes to be true.[29] The motives inherent in a conspiracy theory interchange (see below) may override tell-the-truth conversational norms. In a later chapter in this volume, Matthew Atkinson and colleagues examine this as *costly signaling*.

Finally, there is indirect evidence that a posture of *distrust*, especially of powerful out-groups, leads to conspiracy theory transmission. For example, conspiracy theories circulating on the Internet that vaccines cause autism express strong themes of distrust of the medical establishment and expertise.[30] And given that attitudes that go hand in hand with distrust—such as political cynicism, anomie, and negative attitudes toward authority—predict conspiracy theory belief, it seems likely that distrust also predicts conspiracy theory transmission.[31] Folklorists in the African-American community have documented persistent and widespread conspiracy rumors born out of decades of racial conflict and distrust, for example, "the KKK did it," "the powers that be want to keep us down," "they want to sterilize us," "they want us to take all of those drugs."[32]

Conspiracy theory researchers say that distrust born of perceptions of oppression is central to conspiracy thinking.[33] For example, the death toll from AIDS has been especially high in Africa, several times higher than on any other continent. Why? One well-known conspiracy theory "explains" it: AIDS is a secret Western government plot to wipe out Africans.[34] Indeed, feeling a strong sense of solidarity with a *vulnerable* group that you believe is being victimized by a *powerful* group is a good recipe for conspiratorial beliefs.[35] This is likely behind the AIDs in Africa story just mentioned. The story meshes well with narratives of white oppression circulating actively in black communities.[36] In one study, black persons believed black-targeted conspiracy theories more strongly than white persons believed them (of course, given slavery and segregation, narratives like this seem justifiable).[37] This recipe for conspiratorial thinking becomes especially potent in times of political polarization, civil unrest, or racial tension.[38]

What Psychological Motives Lead to Transmission?

"Why do people communicate conspiracy rumors?" can be asked a second way: What are the *psychological motives* or *aims* that lead people to transmit rumors?[39]

Rumor researchers point to three general motives or aims for spreading rumors: *fact finding* to get at the truth, *relationship enhancement* to increase liking between teller and hearer, and *self-enhancement* to boost self-esteem.[40] Other motives include *revenge*, *propaganda* to achieve a strategic goal, *entertainment*, *emotional coping* to feel better about a negative outcome, and *altruism* to help others.[41]

What aims do people intend when they spread conspiracy rumors?

Conspiracy theorists might be motivated by fact finding, especially given a general distrust of official information sources. Indeed, according to Coady, such distrust is warranted.[42] Whether or not this is so, the persistence and atypicality of conspiracy thinking has often baffled scientists and frustrated laypeople. Other motives seem to be at work.

Conspiracy theory researchers recently pointed to the role of social identity in conspiracy theory belief, and social identity implies relationship-enhancement and self-enhancement motives. [43] My *social identity* is my sense of who I am, that is, my values, beliefs and attitudes, based on the group that I think of myself as being part of.[44] Believing the false conspiracy theory that an inexpensive and popular fruit drink contains a substance that will sterilize black men may seem bizarre, but I may suspend my skepticism if this theory fits a deeply held group narrative of white oppression, and I may share this theory with others in the community as a way of communicating and affirming my group membership.[45] In other words, the exchange: "Hey man, did you hear that Tropical Fantasy can make you sterile?—*What?* Damn! Thank you brother" may be more of a social greeting than a fact-finding discussion. And as a social greeting, it is relationship-enhancing ("we are part of the same group") and self-enhancing ("you think as I do").

Similarly, sharing conspiracy theories with others who believe them is likely motivated by a desire to affirm a common worldview.[46] This too is aimed at relationship enhancement and self-enhancement. For example, a stranger once described a rumor to me of how, during the Clinton years, he had witnessed planes crisscrossing Washington, DC that were leaving trails of white smoke—or so he thought at the time. He then heard that the planes were spraying contraceptive "dust" as part of a secret government plan to reduce the population. (This is a variant of long-standing "chemtrails" conspiracy theories).[47] He professed not to believe these conspiracy rumors at first, but conveyed how he gradually became convinced of their truth. It was clear that he shared this conspiracy theory with me at least partly in order to assess whether or not I possessed the same general outlook of deep suspicion of powerful secret groups. My assent would have simultaneously formed a bond of common identity between us (relationship-enhancement motive) and affirmed his deeply held "opposition to officialdom" (self-enhancement motive).[48] Indeed, when conspiracy theorists discuss such beliefs as "AIDS is a plot to wipe out minority groups," "the government is storing information in its files to use against its citizens," and "fluoridating drinking water will hurt people," they may be more strongly driven by social bonding and in-group identity affirmation aims than by their individual personality or cognitive style.

Why are Conspiracy Rumors (Mostly) False?

To apply the label "conspiracy theory" to a story is not just to say that it is in doubt, but that it is false, and wildly so. Although some conspiracy theories turn out to be true, these are the exception. Why are conspiracy rumors almost always false?

To answer this question, rumor researchers suggest a mix of motive and ability.[49] When the primary motive is fact finding, accurate rumors seem more likely to emerge over time. But any *other* primary motive, such as revenge, strategic gain, relationship enhancement or self-enhancement, is likely to yield less accurate rumors.[50] Groups, after all, may or may not be primarily interested in the facts. For example, in long-standing workplace grapevines, rumors about potential layoffs are often 100% true; employees truly want facts about these matters. But the situation is quite different in settings where groups are competing or in conflict. When I transmit a rumor to a fellow group member that praises our group or warns against dangers from the rival group, regardless of how true it is I get a nice boost to my popularity ("Nolan is in the know!") and self-esteem ("I'm associated with a good group"). And I am easily forgiven if it turns out to be false or exaggerated.

Rumor researchers also point to the capability of the group to ferret out the facts.[51] Information can become distorted and riddled with error simply because there are limits to human attention and memory. And perceptions are frequently biased. Add to this that it is sometimes difficult for any community to check the truth of a rumor: Often nothing is known, time pressure is extreme, information sources are distrusted, strong conformity is expected, and communication networks function like echo chambers.

For conspiracy theories, once again it appears that two key ingredients are social identity and distrust. Relationship-enhancement and self-enhancement motivations stemming from social identity needs are likely to trump accuracy motivation. Plus, conspiracy theory communities are probably less able to check the conspiracy rumor's truth because they distrust formal information sources. Both factors compromise a group's desire and ability to ferret out the facts. For example, after the mass murders at Sandy Hook Elementary School in Newtown, Connecticut, in 2012, conspiracy theories that they were an elaborate hoax to promote gun control and confiscation were propagated by fearful gun rights advocates getting their information from *InfoWars*.[52] Alternately, a false rumor that *InfoWars* host Alex Jones had been named Trump White House Press Secretary was disseminated by fearful left-wing partisans getting their information from *The Babylon Bee*.[53]

If we add in a third ingredient, *in-group echo chambers*, to this mix of social identification and distrust, then we cook up a super-recipe for false conspiracy theory birth, growth, and resilience. In-group echo chambers are communication networks where people from the same group are densely connected with one another but isolated from people outside their group.[54] We find, for example, two vast ideological in-group echo chambers thriving on the Internet, one consisting of liberal blogs and the other of conservative blogs.[55] We can represent this visually with blogs as circles and hyperlink connections as lines. If we do, what emerges is two enormous clusters of circles, one red and the other blue, with a dense web of lines connecting the circles within each cluster but very few lines connecting circles across the clusters. Birds of a feather *talk* together, not with birds from a different flock. Political discussions on Twitter also follow this *polarized crowd* pattern where two distinct discussion groups do not interact and do not share news media sources.[56] Because one rarely or never hears a dissenting opinion, in-group echo chambers polarize opinions and beliefs, yield a crop of incredible conspiracy rumors, resist hoax-busting efforts, and magnify distrust of the other crowd's news sources.[57] It is no wonder then that Democrats are equally likely to believe "truther" conspiracy theories that George W. Bush knew beforehand about the events of 9/11, as Republicans are to believe "birther" conspiracy theories that Barack Obama was not born in the United States.[58]

Looking Forward: Conspiracy Rumors as Social Interaction

We know a lot about conspiracy theories, but I think we can learn more. The great strength of rumor research is that it has approached rumor as social and group interaction. This means that rumor moves between people and within groups; it is not stationary inside of a person. With this approach, the focus is on relationships and group dynamics. With some exceptions, conspiracy theory research has instead focused on individuals, and in particular why individuals *believe* such incredible and improbable tales.[59] This is an important question, and fascinating work has explored individual conspiracy theorists' characteristics, such as personality, attitudes, judgmental biases, and thinking style.[60] But there is a yawning gap in this work. Conspiracy theory research has rarely, if ever, investigated questions about why people *transmit* conspiracy theories. This question is at least as important because conspiracy theories, like rumors, are a social and group interaction. Conspiracy theorists almost never theorize their conspiracies, *they hear them and tell them to one another.* Conspiracy theory researchers have learned a lot about "conspiracy theories and the people who believe them," but they can learn even more about "conspiracy theories and the group members that communicate them."

Notes

1. Bordia, Prashant, and Nicholas DiFonzo. 2002. "When Social Psychology Became Less Social: Prasad and the History of Rumor Research." *Asian Journal of Social Psychology* 5(1): 49–61.
2. Prasad, Jamuna. 1935. "The Psychology of Rumour: A Study Relating to the Great Indian Earthquake of 1934." *British Journal of Psychology* 26(1): 1–15; Allport, Gordon W., and Leo Joseph Postman. 1947. *The Psychology of Rumor.* New York: H. Holt; Shibutani, Tamotsu. 1966. *Improvised News: A Sociological Study of Rumor.* Indianapolis: Bobbs-Merrill.
3. DiFonzo, Nicholas, and Prashant Bordia. 2007. "Rumor, Gossip and Urban Legends." *Diogenes* 54(1): 19–35.
4. Freedman, Alix M. 1991. "Rumor Turns Fantasy into Bad Dream." *The Wall Street Journal,* May 10, 1991.
5. Bernardi, Daniel Leonard, and Pauline Hope Cheong. 2012. *Narrative Landmines: Rumors, Islamist Extremism, and the Struggle for Strategic Influence.* Piscataway, NJ: Rutgers University Press.
6. Fine, Gary Alan, and Nicholas DiFonzo. "Uncertain Knowledge." *Contexts* 10(3): 16–21.
7. Bale, Jeffrey M. 2007. "Political Paranoia V. Political Realism: On Distinguishing between Bogus Conspiracy Theories and Genuine Conspiratorial Politics." *Patterns of Prejudice* 41(1): 45–60.
8. Byford, Jovan. 2001. *Conspiracy Theories: A Critical Introduction* [Proquest ebook]. New York, Basingstoke, Hampshire [England]: Palgrave Macmillan.
9. Swami, Viren, and Adrian Furnham. 2014. "Political Paranoia and Conspiracy Theories." In *Power, Politics, & Paranoia: Why People Are Suspicious of Their Leaders,* eds. Jan-Willem van Prooijen and Paul A. M. Lange. Cambridge: Cambridge University Press, 218–236.
10. DiFonzo, Nicholas, and Prashant Bordia. 1998. "A Tale of Two Corporations: Managing Uncertainty During Organizational Change." *Human Resource Management (1986–1998)* 37(3–4): 295.
11. Ibid.; van Prooijen, Jan-Willem, and Nils B. Jostmann. 2013. "Belief in Conspiracy Theories: The Influence of Uncertainty and Perceived Morality." *European Journal of Social Psychology* 43(1): 109–15; van Prooijen, Jan-Willem, and Paul A. M. van Lange. 2014. "The Social Dimensions of Belief in Conspiracy Theories." In *Power, Politics, and Paranoia: Why People Are Suspicious of Their Leaders,* eds. Jan-Willem van Prooijen and Paul A. M. van Lange. Cambridge: Cambridge University Press, 237–253.
12. DiFonzo, Nicholas, Jerry Suls, Jason W. Beckstead, Martin J. Bourgeois, Christopher M. Homan, Samuel Brougher, Andrew J. Younge, and Nicolas Terpstra-Schwab. 2014. "Network

Structure Moderates Intergroup Differentiation of Stereotyped Rumors." *Social Cognition* 32(5): 409.

13. Ibid.

14. Bacon Jr., Perry. 2007. "Foes Use Obama's Muslim Ties to Fuel Rumors About Him." *Washington Post*, November 29, 2007; Smith, Ben. 2008. "E-Mails, Conspiracy Rumors Plague Palin." https://www.politico.com/story/2008/09/e-mails-conspiracy-rumors-plague-palin-013307 (Accessed October 14, 2009).

15. Root, Wayne Allyn. 2010. "Obama's Agenda: Overwhelm the System." *Las Vegas Review Journal.* https://www.reviewjournal.com/opinion/obamas-agenda-overwhelm-the-system/ (Accessed December 20, 2017).

16. Meacher, Michael. 2003. "This War on Terrorism Is Bogus." *The Guardian.* https://www.theguardian.com/politics/2003/sep/06/september11.iraq (Accessed December 20, 2017).

17. Rosnow, Ralph L. 1991. "Inside Rumor: A Personal Journey." *American Psychologist* 46(5): 484.

18. DiFonzo, Nicholas, and Prashant Bordia. "How Top PR Professionals Handle Hearsay: Corporate Rumors, Their Effects, and Strategies to Manage Them." *Public Relations Review* 26(2): 173–190.

19. Bauer, Raymond A., and David B. Gleicher. 1953. "Word-of-Mouth Communication in the Soviet Union." *Public Opinion Quarterly* 17(3): 297–310.

20. DiFonzo, Nicholas, and Prashant Bordia. 2007. *Rumor Psychology: Social and Organizational Approaches.* Washington, D.C.: American Psychological Association, Chapter 8.

21. Hofstadter, Richard. 1964. *The Paranoid Style in American Politics and Other Essays.* Vol.1. New York: Knopf; Brotherton, Robert, and Silan Eser. 2015. "Bored to Fears: Boredom Proneness, Paranoia, and Conspiracy Theories." *Personality and Individual Differences* 80: 1–5.

22. Swami and Furnham, "Political Paranoia," 224.

23. Swami, Viren, Laura Weis, Alixe Lay, David Barron, and Adrian Furnham. 2016. "Associations Between Belief in Conspiracy Theories and the Maladaptive Personality Traits of the Personality Inventory for DSM-5." *Psychiatry Research* 236(28): 86–90; Grzesiak-Feldman, Monika. 2013. "The Effect of High-Anxiety Situations on Conspiracy Thinking." *Current Psychology: A Journal for Diverse Perspectives on Diverse Psychological Issues* 32(1): 100–118.

24. Swami, Viren, Adrian Furnham, Nina Smyth, Laura Weis, Alixe Lay, Angela Clow. 2016. "Putting the Stress on Conspiracy Theories: Examining Associations between Psychological Stress, Anxiety, and Belief in Conspiracy Theories." *Personality and Individual Differences* 99(September): 73.

25. van Prooijen, Jan-Willem. 2012. "Suspicions of Injustice: The Sense-Making Function of Belief in Conspiracy Theories." In *Justice and Conflicts*, eds. Elisabeth Kals and Jürgen Maes. Berlin, Heidelberg: Springer-Verlag Berlin Heidelberg, 121–132.

26. van Prooijen and Jostmann, "Belief in Conspiracy Theories," 111.

27. Miller, Nick. 2015. "Crash Conspiracy Theories Alive and Well Organised: Mh17: One Year On." *The Age* 2015: 12. Web.

28. Perlmutter, David D., and Nicole Smith Dahmen. 2008. "(In)Visible Evidence: Pictorially Enhanced Disbelief in the Apollo Moon Landings." *Visual Communication* 7(2): 229–251.

29. Grice, H. Paul. 1975. "Logic and Conversation. the William James Lectures." In *Syntax and Semantics* Vol. 3, eds. P. Cole and J. L. Morgan. New York: Academic Press, 41–58.

30. Kata, Anna. 2010. "A Postmodern Pandora's Box: Anti-Vaccination Misinformation on the Internet." *Vaccine* 28(7): 1709–1716.

31. Abalakina-Paap, Marina, Walter G. Stephan, Traci Craig, and W. Larry Gregory. 1999. "Beliefs in Conspiracies." *Political Psychology* 20(3): 637–647; van Prooijen and van Lange, The Social Dimensions of Belief."

32. Turner, Patricia A. 1993. *I Heard It through the Grapevine: Rumor in African-American Culture.* Berkely and Los Angeles: University of California Press.

33. Swami and Furnham, "Political Paranoia"; van Prooijen and Jostmann, "Belief in Conspiracy Theories."

34. Turner, *I Heard it Through the Grapevine.*

35. van Prooijen and van Lange, "The Social Dimensions of Belief."

36. Fine, Gary Alan, and Patricia A. Turner. 2001. *Whispers on the Color Line: Rumor and Race in America.* Berkeley and Los Angeles: University of California Press.

37. Crocker, Jennifer, Riia Luhtanen, Stephanie Broadnax, and Bruce Evan Blaine. 1999. "Belief in U.S. Government Conspiracies against Blacks among Black and White College Students: Powerlessness or System Blame?" *Personality and Social Psychology Bulletin* 25(8): 941–953.

38. Knopf, Terry Ann. 1975. *Rumors, Race, and Riots.* New York: Transaction Publishers.

39. Bordia, Prashant, and Nicholas DiFonzo. 2005. "Psychological Motivations in Rumor Spread." In *Rumor Mills: The Social Impact of Rumor and Legend,* eds. Gary Alan Fine, Véronique Campion-Vincent, and Chip Heath. New York: Transaction Publishers, 87–101.

40. Bordia and DiFonzo, "Psychological Motivations in Rumor Spread."

41. Bordia, Prashant, Kohyar Kiazad, Simon Lloyd D. Restubog, Nicholas DiFonzo, Nicholas Stenson, and Robert L. Tang. 2014. "Rumor as Revenge in the Workplace." *Group & Organization Management* 39(4): 363–88; DiFonzo, Nicholas, and Prashant Bordia. 2007. "Rumors Influence: Toward a Dynamic Social Impact Theory of Rumor." In *The Science of Social Influence: Advances and Future Progress,* ed. Anthony R. Pratkanis. Philadelphia: Psychology Press, 271–296; DiFonzo, Nicholas. 2008. *The Watercooler Effect: A Psychologist Explores the Extraordinary Power of Rumors.* New York: Avery.

42. Coady, David. 2006. "Rumour Has It." *International Journal of Applied Philosophy* 20(1): 41–53.

43. van Prooijen and van Lange, The Social Dimensions of Belief"; Mashuri, Ali, and Esti Zaduqisti. 2015. "The Effect of Intergroup Threat and Social Identity Salience on the Belief in Conspiracy Theories over Terrorism in Indonesia: Collective Angst as a Mediator." *International Journal of Psychological Research* 8(1): 24–35.

44. Hogg, Michael, and Dominic Abrams. 1990. *Social Identifications: A Social Psychology of Intergroup Relations and Group Processes.* Florence, KY: Routledge.

45. Freedman, "Rumor Turns Fantasy into Bad Dream"; Fine and Turner, *Whispers on the Color Line.*

46. Bessi, Alessandro, Mauro Coletto, George Alexandru Davidescue, Antonio Scala, Guido Caldarelli, and Walter Quattrociocchi. 2015. "Science Vs Conspiracy: Collective Narratives in the Age of Misinformation." *PloS one* 10(2). DOI: 10.1371/journal.pone.0118093.

47. Watson, Traci. 2001. "Conspiracy Theories Find Menace in Contrails." *USA Today.* https://usatoday30.usatoday.com/weather/science/2001-03-07-contrails.htm (Accessed December 20, 2017).

48. Warner, Benjamin R., and Ryan Neville-Shepard. 2014. "Echoes of a Conspiracy: Birthers, Truthers, and the Cultivation of Extremism." *Communication Quarterly* 62(1): 7.

49. DiFonzo, Nicholas. 2010. "Ferreting Facts or Fashioning Fallacies? Factors in Rumor Accuracy." *Social and Personality Psychology Compass* 4(11): 1124–1137.

50. Bordia, Kiazad, Restubog, DiFonzio, Stenson, and Tang, "Rumor as Revenge in the Workplace"; DiFonzo and Bordia, "Rumors Influence."

51. DiFonzo, "Ferreting Facts or Fashioning Fallacies."

52. Mikkelson, David. 2015. "Sandy Hook Exposed." https://www.snopes.com/politics/guns/newtown.asp (Accessed December 20, 2017).

53. Truth-or-Fiction.com. 2017. "Alex Jones Appointed White House Press Secretary—Fiction!" https://www.truthorfiction.com/alex-jones-white-house-press-secretary/ (Accessed December 20, 2017).

54. DiFonzo, Suls, Beckstead, Bourgeois, Homan, Brougher, Younge, and Terpstra-Schwab, "Network Structure Moderates Intergroup Differentiation."

55. Adamic, Lada, and Natalie Glance. 2005. *The Political Blogosphere and the 2004 US Election: Divided They Blog.* In Proceedings of the 3rd International Workshop on Link Discovery. New York: ACM. DOI: 10.1145/1134271.1134277.
56. Smith, Marc A., Lee Rainie, Ben Shneiderman, and Itai Himelboim. 2014. *Mapping Twitter Topic Networks: From Polarized Crowds to Community Clusters. Pew Center Research* 20. http://www.pewinternet.org/2014/02/20/part-2-conversational-archetypes-six-conversation-and-group-network-structures-in-twitter/ (Accessed December 20, 2017).
57. McCarthy, Justin. 2014. "Trust in Mass Media Returns to All-Time Low." http://news.gallup.com/poll/176042/trust-mass-media-returns-time-low.aspx (Accessed December 20, 2017).
58. Nyhan, Brendan. 2009. "9/11 and Birther Misperceptions Compared." [Blog] *The Blog.* Available at https://www.huffingtonpost.com/brendan-nyhan/911_and_birther_misperceptions_b_726561.html (Accessed December 20, 2017).
59. Swami, Viren. 2012. "Social Psychological Origins of Conspiracy Theories: The Case of the Jewish Conspiracy Theory in Malaysia." *Frontiers in Psychology* 3:1–9. DOI: 10.3389/fpsyg.2012.00280; Byford, Jovan. 2014. "Beyond Belief: The Social Psychology of Conspiracy Theories and the Study of Ideology." In *Rhetoric, Ideology and Social Psychology: Essays in Honour of Michael Billig,* eds. Charles Antaki and Susan Condor. New York: Routledge/Taylor & Francis Group, 83–93.
60. Swami, Viren, Tomas Chamorro-Premuzic, and Adrian Furnham. 2010. "Unanswered Questions: A Preliminary Investigation of Personality and Individual Difference Predictors of 9/11 Conspiracist Beliefs." *Applied Cognitive Psychology* 24(6): 749–61.

18

The Truth Is Around Here Somewhere

Integrating the Research on Conspiracy Beliefs

PRESTON R. BOST

On the evening of the 2016 Indiana Republican primary, veteran political correspondent and *Meet the Press* host Chuck Todd gave a television interview with Brian
Williams and Rachel Maddow on MSNBC. One topic of discussion, as with most
political coverage at the time, was the presidential candidacy of Donald Trump.
And Todd, like most political analysts at the time, expressed some skepticism about
Trump's chances—chiefly, in this case, on the grounds of his attraction to conspiracy theories. Commenting on Trump's suggestion that a political rival's father
had been involved in the assassination of President John F. Kennedy, Todd said the
following:

> [Trump's] got a lot of bad tics that he's got to deal with before going into
> a general election. This is one of them—that he seems to not be able to
> pass up a conspiracy theory. He cannot let a conspiracy theory go without
> trying to find a way to believe it, or pass it on even if he doesn't . . . It's
> Trump's undoing if he's not careful. . . at some point, his fetish for con-
> spiracy theories is going to . . . cost him with people that have been looking
> for a reason to vote for him.[1]

Todd's cogent analysis reflected both the conventional wisdom of the moment and
the fervent hopes of public intellectuals. But a scholar of conspiracy beliefs would
have observed that it was also almost certainly wrong. Whatever the threats to his
campaign may have been, Mr. Trump's public espousal of conspiracy theories was
not among them.

Why not? For all that we do not yet know about conspiracy theories and those
who believe them, we do know this: that Mr. Trump has lots of company, and this
company is not confined to the fringes of society. Though there is no commonly
accepted base rate of conspiracy belief in the United States population, a good

starting point is Oliver and Wood's study of 2011 public opinion data. Examining responses to a set of seven conspiracy theories ranging from the highly familiar (the United States government planned the attacks of September 11, 2001; President Barack Obama was not born in the United States) to the less familiar (aircraft vapor trails are chemicals being released as part of a government program) to one that the researchers created themselves (compact fluorescent light bulbs facilitate mind control) the researchers found that 55% of respondents agreed with at least one of the claims.[2]

If "conspiracy theorist" includes anyone who endorses at least one conspiracy theory, then 55% is surely a conservative estimate. The menu of conspiracy theories includes hundreds that dot the political, medical, technological, and athletic landscapes; there is something for everyone. Unconvinced that the Illuminati control worldwide political and financial affairs?[3] Perhaps NBA star Kyrie Irving's flat-earth claim is more tempting.[4] Too preposterous to claim that the U.S. government is hiding alien artifacts in Area 51?[5] Perhaps then an earthbound alternative—that the government is hiding evidence that vaccines cause autism.[6] Don't believe that Hitler survived? Maybe Osama bin Laden did.[7] If the definition of "conspiracy theory" expands to include not only the fantastic examples attached to noteworthy events, people, and institutions but also similar beliefs about one's local environment (for example, Dilbert-style management cabals), then we might even consider the capacity for conspiracy beliefs to be an unremarkable, if not universal, feature of human cognition. There seemingly aren't enough foil hats to go around.

The dawning recognition that conspiracy beliefs cut across history, geographical boundaries, and demographic characteristics has gradually recast the scholarly narrative.[8] Over the last decade, researchers who once regarded conspiracy theories as a vexing mystery—a manifestation of intractable human irrationality—have approached them with studied curiosity, trading glib dismissals for an increasingly vigorous campaign of scholarship aimed at unpacking the psychological underpinnings of conspiracy beliefs and the sociocultural contexts in which they occur. Reviews of the burgeoning literature, including the one by Karen Douglas and Michael Wood in this volume, draw an impressive picture of the methodological and theoretical scope of the psychological work.[9] This research has also begun to connect with emerging scholarship in other disciplines—particularly political science, which explores the mechanisms of belief as they operate within the negotiation and flow of power.[10]

How far have scholars come? Judging by the pace of publication, the field has made substantial progress. Just within the field of psychology, a PsychINFO search for published work with "conspiracy theories" or "conspiracy beliefs" in the title or subject listing yielded 35 hits from 1998–2007, and 145 hits from 2008–2017. In a way, however, the excitement of discovery camouflages another reality: that we have many silos of information but relatively few meaningful patterns. Accumulation has outpaced synthesis. Though there are doubtless novel trails to blaze, and though there may not be a grand unified theory of conspiracy beliefs for us to discover, the time is ripe to investigate the ways in which the disparate findings align—or don't—into a coherent account.

In doing so, researchers will push toward answering the questions that we really want the answers to. It's one thing to ask, for example, how closely conspiracy beliefs are correlated with personality traits, or how they respond to falsifying information. Such necessary and interesting questions, however, ultimately serve a deeper one: where do conspiracy beliefs fit into the functional machinery of human cognition—which, after all, ultimately evolved for human survival?

Locating this theoretical grounding will help with the most pressing question that comes up: what can we *do* about conspiracy theories in the marketplace of ideas, where citizens, consumers, and patients make consequential choices? There are no clear, convincing, or consensus answers to that question. Connecting findings into a functional understanding of conspiracy beliefs should help us craft something more satisfactory. The purpose of this chapter is to explore just a few of the areas in which such thematically driven quilting efforts may be profitable, working within the following questions: (1) What is a conspiracy theory? (2) What are the causes of conspiracy beliefs? (3) What are the effects of conspiracy beliefs?

What Is a Conspiracy Theory?

Consider two people with competing explanations of the events of September 11, 2001: one who attributes those events to secret, coordinated action among members of a terrorist organization, and another who attributes the same events to secret, coordinated action among members of the United States government. Both believe that a conspiracy has occurred, but only the second is a "conspiracy theorist" whose belief is subject to public ridicule as well as scrutiny by research psychologists. The point is obvious but important: Until we establish the boundaries that distinguish conspiracy theories from other types of beliefs, it is unclear what beliefs and believers researchers should be studying.

As chapters by Jesse Walker and Joseph Uscinski in this volume point out, the term *conspiracy theory* is particularly fuzzy in public discourse. But the operational definition isn't crystal clear among researchers, who still operate more from common understanding than from consistent, explicit definition. We may not be able to tell you exactly what a conspiracy theory is, but we know one when we see it. Some scholars have pointed out the resulting variance in definitions of "conspiracy theory."[11] But seldom do they identify the primary dividing lines in those definitions explicitly, or drill deeply into the implications for the research agenda.

Published definitions find common ground on two components: that the machinery behind a conspiracy consists of *multiple coordinated actors* operating in *secret*. Sources vary on the particulars, such as whether the number of actors is typically small or vast, or whether "secrecy" includes not only hiding in the shadows but also actively propagating deceptive messages[12] Nevertheless, this pair of propositions constitutes an adequate "bare bones" definition.[13]

So far, so good. But other definitions include add-ons that narrow the category and shape how we perceive and study those who believe conspiracy theories. For example, some definitions propose that conspirators *abuse power* from a position of institutional and/or socioeconomic influence.[14] Other definitions assert *nefarious intent* on the part of the conspirators, who undermine the law and/or the common good by their actions.[15] In other words, conspiracy theorists believe in mustache-twirling villains. These propositions certainly account nicely for the most famous conspiracy theories, in which government officials and captains of industry lie, cheat, steal, and cover up their ill-gotten gains. To accept them as definitional, however, is to define conspiracy theorists as abnormally suspicious and cynical.[16] Matters that ought properly to be empirical questions—such as whether conspiracy theories are a departure from or a manifestation of adaptive social cognition, or whether conspiracy theories are diagnostic of cognitive pathology—instead become assumptions.

Other ways of narrowing the bare-bones definition raise similar concerns. First, some define conspiracy theories by their place in public discourse, pointing out that they *oppose received or official accounts* of the event in question.[17] Making the implication more explicit, some scholars, predominantly social scientists, assert that conspiracy theories are *epistemologically broken*—by nature implausible, lacking in logical or empirical grounding, and unfalsifiable.[18] To put a fine point on it, conspiracy theorists believe things that are untrue. These definitions starkly divide our two 9/11 theorists, placing them on opposite sides of the rules of rationality. They also rescue those who, at the earliest stages of the Watergate investigation, might well have been labeled conspiracy theorists for obsessing over President Nixon's alleged wrongdoings but eventually were vindicated by the evidence. And so the research runs into this complication: being a conspiracy theorist isn't about what you believe per se, but rather about your belief in relation to "epistemic authorities" who decide which beliefs are valid and which ones aren't.[19] Philosophers have pointed out the difficulty in establishing *a priori* criteria that would clearly delineate between valid conspiracy claims and anomalous, invalid "conspiracy theories"—meaning that the pejorative term *conspiracy theorist* could apply equally to a person who is steeped in cognitive error or to an early adopter of a conspiracy belief waiting to be confirmed.[20] If the Watergate conspiracy theorist merited psychological study before the Oval Office tapes emerged but not after, even as their beliefs stayed constant, what phenomenon are researchers studying exactly?

What makes this discussion anything more than academic? Different definitions of the phenomenon invite different strategies for inquiry. Most attempts to narrow the definition place conspiracy believers on the margins and lead naturally to research grounded in the language of pathology. If such beliefs are distinctive or even aberrant, so must be the believers and/or their thought processes. The task is therefore to understand the characteristics of those who commit this strange cognitive sin, and the specific errors they make. Indeed, this approach has dominated the psychological literature to date.[21] The more inclusive bare-bones definition lends itself to research grounded in the language of adaptation: what are the conditions of social living that make this type of belief readily accessible? What specific conditions activate this software, regardless of whether the resulting belief is true or false?

The second of these options is more radical than it may initially sound. It opens the possibility that all types of conspiracy beliefs, valid and not, may have a common origin point, and that understanding the invalid beliefs that attract our attention may require adopting a two-pronged research model: How do conspiracy beliefs originate, and what factors lead to their resilience among competing ideas in the marketplace? These questions, only the second of which establishes a category of invalid beliefs, map well onto Uscinski and Parent's two-stage account of conspiracy theory development—activation, followed by resistance to disconfirmation.[22] And they lead to this follow-up question: If conspiracy theories are defined not simply by believing in a conspiracy but rather by their immunity to the rules of evidence, in what way are they truly distinct from other types of erroneous beliefs? Studies that catalog the well-understood cognitive errors present in conspiracy beliefs and those who believe them—for example, innumeracy, inattention to the rules of inference, misapplication of rule-of-thumb cognitive strategies, confirmation bias, motivated reasoning—may not be "discovering" diagnostic properties of conspiracy thinking so much as simply revealing that the mental gymnastics of protecting a deeply held conspiracy belief, examined closely, look pretty much the same as the mental gymnastics of protecting deeply held non-conspiratorial beliefs.

Under the more inclusive definition of "conspiracy theory," one that does not attempt a categorical distinction between valid and invalid beliefs, the best potential for a truly explanatory account of conspiracy belief per se lies in the *first* stage of Uscinski and Parent's account, where conspiratorial explanations of events germinate. The common ground of all such beliefs—valid and invalid, small and large scale—is the application of suspicion, the perception that somebody is getting away with something. A general account of such a phenomenon would attend carefully to the rules of social cognition, where both the universal, innate capacity for suspicion and the situational triggers that activate it may be informative.[23] Such an approach treats conspiracy beliefs not as exotic, but as a manifestation of underlying adaptive machinery.[24]

So researchers need to decide on the boundaries of what they are studying, which requires a more thorough taxonomy of conspiracy beliefs than is currently available. Alleged conspiracies vary considerably in their particulars—familiarity, duration, number and type of alleged actors, potential victims, and even terrestrial origin. Are you a conspiracy theorist if you believe...

that the Priory of Sion has concealed the lineage of Jesus for the past 2000 years?[25]
that Taylor Swift publicized a fake dating relationship with Tom Hiddleston?[26]
that a multinational corporation has concealed evidence of extravagant gifts to influential politicians?
that a multinational corporation has concealed evidence of extravagant gifts to charitable organizations?
that the referees in a football game worked against your team?
that the National Football League office ordered the referees in a football game to work against your team?
(on Sept 12, **2001**)...that the attacks of 9/11 were coordinated by members of a terrorist group?
(on Sept 12, **2001**)...that the attacks of 9/11 were coordinated by members of the United States government?
(on Sept 12, **2017**)...that the attacks of 9/11 were coordinated by members of the United States government?

Not all beliefs are equally at odds with available evidence; not all evoke precisely the same type of reasoning strategies in the audience; and not all touch equally on the primary concerns within a given person's mind.[27] A careful consideration of the dimensions on which conspiracy theories vary, and how these characteristics relate to antecedent conditions and behavioral effects, would therefore appear to be in order.[28]

Where Do Conspiracy Theories Come From?

The common ancestor for much conspiracy theory research is a study by Goertzel, in which participants read statements describing a set of 10 conspiracy theories and rated how true they believed each statement to be.[29] Observing that those who believed any conspiracy were likely to believe others, Goertzel concluded that conspiracy beliefs constitute a "monological belief system," a network of correlated, self-reinforcing cognitions that we could call a worldview. Numerous subsequent findings have suggested that conspiracy beliefs tend to be general rather than discrete; believing in a particular conspiracy theory is a good predictor of believing in other specific conspiracy theories, and of the inclination to see world events as driven by conspiracies.[30] Observing stability over time in individual differences in conspiracy thinking, some researchers have concluded that conspiracy thinking is a generalized political attitude in the same fashion as right-wing authoritarianism or social dominance.[31]

These findings invite the suspicion that the precondition for believing in conspiracies is simply being the type of person who believes such things. But despite years of research into the psychological profile of conspiracy theorists, the forensic sketch is maddeningly indistinct. The conspiracy believer tends to be suspicious and alienated, but lacks a clearly defined personality, educational background, or demographic profile.[32] Besides undermining stereotypes about conspiracy believers, this picture creates apparent tension with the observation of stable individual differences in conspiracy thinking. Confronting this tension is vital for theoretical progress, because settled conclusions about *conspiracy theorists* with overarching worldviews tend to set them apart as a class, and foreclose on research into one possibility raised in the previous section: that conspiracy beliefs sit logically within adaptive social cognitive processes. How then can we reconcile the apparently global, stable patterns of belief with the marked variability in who is doing the believing?

An obvious possibility is that we haven't yet located the distinguishing feature(s) and just need to keep up the hunt. For instance, Brotherton and French have observed that conspiracy believers tended also to overuse heuristic reasoning—a rule-of-thumb judgment process that bypasses evidence-based probabilities—and over-attribute intentionality to events.[33] The authors noted, however, that the results did not lock down causality; do conspiracy beliefs derive from a particular cognitive style, or vice-versa? Or do they both derive from some other ultimate cause(s), as yet unknown? These questions point out a larger issue with many investigations into the psychological characteristics of conspiracy believers: they are correlational, so we don't know how much those characteristics actually lead to conspiracy beliefs. Except as our methods address this problem, even a high-resolution picture of the conspiracy believer will leave us wondering whether these characteristics truly create a conspiracy mindset, or whether they are simply along for the ride.

What if we shift our gaze less toward the *person* and more toward the *circumstances*—life events or emotional states that cut across demographic and personality characteristics? Investigations along this line have been relatively few but tantalizing. Whitson and colleagues have found that experimentally inducing a loss of perceived control or emotional uncertainty—for instance, by having participants read a passage about a chaotic stock market—increases the tendency to assign conspiratorial explanations to events.[34] These findings dovetail with the observation that participants recover some sense of control after appealing to conspiracy-like explanations of threatening events, but that their inclination to do so is reduced by first restoring their sense of control by other means.[35] Although the strength and stability of these effects outside of the laboratory is uncertain, it is easy to imagine real-life externalities—labor/management relations in the workplace, grinding economic stress—that could create a perpetual sense of uncertainty or loss of control, with a resulting inclination to perceive conspiracies. Potential situational contributors such as these remain a relatively untapped area of research, but the initial work at least teases the possibility that even an overarching worldview is a tailored response to environmental conditions—a kind of strategic hypervigilance—rather than a sign of pathology or other defects in the person.

Pushing one step further, how generalized is the conspiracy mindset really? We know that conspiracy believers can't seem to stop at one, but we know little of the logic governing their selections. To what extent do conspiracy beliefs congregate around particular themes or concerns? Because the research agenda has largely emphasized the stable internal characteristics of the person, it has tended to bypass historical or situational variables that could predispose someone to believe one conspiracy and reject another—an oversight compounded by the absence of a taxonomy of conspiracy beliefs. The growing consensus that conspiracy thinking is tied to threat perception, however, should prompt some investigation into whether and how the type of threat filters one's choice of conspiracy theories. There is at least some preliminary evidence of this kind of selectivity in conspiracy thinking; in the United States, for instance, the minority political party tends to propagate more government-related conspiracy theories.[36] To the extent that conspiracy thinking is intended as self-protective, as some have suggested, further pursuing this line of inquiry would help determine the extent to which conspiracy beliefs are efficiently targeted, or instead reflect a more general cognitive bias.[37]

What Are the Effects of Conspiracy Beliefs?

The conspiracy theories researchers typically study are an example of misdirected suspicion, an activation of normal social cognitions in the absence of verifiable malfeasance. Some have argued that a bias toward such false alarms is understandable given the potential costs of exploitation; better to be hypervigilant than to leave oneself exposed to malevolent forces.[38] Casting a suspicious eye toward people in power is not per se irrational or harmful, and perhaps believing that the moon landing was faked is an acceptable excess cost of that particular business. But the energy and rhetoric in the research community indicates a deep concern about the potential tradeoffs, and there is some reason to believe that this concern is well placed (for example, see the chapters in this volume by Alfred Moore, Stephan Lewandowsky, and Jay Cullen). Much early work in this area was correlational, simply demonstrating associations between conspiracy beliefs and, for example, suboptimal personal health choices.[39] But some research employing the experimental method has shown conspiracy beliefs to be a true antecedent of potentially undesirable outcomes. For example, exposure to government-related conspiracies decreases intentions to vote, and exposure to climate change conspiracy theories decreases intentions to reduce one's carbon footprint.[40]

In general, observed behavioral correlates are domain-specific. For example, African-American participants who endorse the belief that the human immunodeficiency virus is a plot against the African-American population—a belief with roots tracing back to the very real conspiracy enacted in the notorious Tuskegee syphilis study—are also less likely to report protecting themselves against sexually transmitted diseases.[41] People who believe that the medical establishment is suppressing evidence of harmful vaccine side effects are less likely to seek vaccinations.[42] Exposure to government-related conspiracies generally affect measures of civic disengagement.[43] These observations suggest broadly that if there is any self-protective function to conspiracy beliefs, it comes with a price tag. They also invite further examination of whether conspiracy theorizing truly reflects a worldview or whether there are clearer connections to be found among the content of conspiracy beliefs, the precipitating conditions, and the consequent behavior. If conspiracy theorizing truly constitutes a worldview, we should observe that some effects cross over domains. One example of which I am aware is Jolley and Douglas's demonstration that climate change conspiracy theories reduce intentions not only toward "green" behavior but also toward civic engagement.[44] If conspiracy beliefs are more discrete, we should be able to catalog additional domain-specific effects; for example, common conspiracy theories about economic manipulation and control by powerful institutions should lead to measurable effects in financial decision making.

And what of the other side of the equation? Are all the correlates of conspiracy beliefs negative? If loss of perceived control contributes to conspiracy thinking, do the resulting beliefs restore a sense of control? Scapegoating, a cousin of conspiracy thinking, has precisely this effect.[45] That outcome doesn't sound so bad; in fact, perceiving control over one's circumstances is known to have desirable mental and physical outcomes.[46] Because current research into the effects of conspiracy theories is asymmetric, focusing on the consequences of false alarms, some additional investigation into the brighter side of conspiracy thinking is probably warranted.[47] For example, is there evidence that the defensive stance of the conspiracy believer actually reduces exposure to exploitation? Do conspiracy theorists encourage good behavior on the part of the powerful?

Further broadening our angle of view, what accumulated impact do conspiracy beliefs have on our collective welfare? How do they affect the scales of power, the distribution of resources, and public safety? Again, our knowledge is piecemeal and preliminary. Some investigators have certainly sounded the alarm on public safety, suggesting that the proliferation of conspiracy theories could be a threat to the environment or to vaccination efforts.[48] But we are a long way from settled conclusions about the practical consequences; as Jolly points out, some studies of "outcomes" are correlational, making it difficult to know if the conspiracy beliefs preceded or followed the behavior.[49] And investigations using the experimental method have understandably tended to measure expressed intentions rather than behavioral choices.[50] So we know relatively little about how conspiracy beliefs translate into actions with public consequences.

Returning to Chuck Todd's analysis of Donald Trump's campaign, whether and how conspiracy theories influence United States elections is also up for debate.

Uscinski and Parent observed roughly symmetrical distribution of conspiracy thinking across the political spectrum, and found that those with greater conspiratorial tendencies were also less likely to report having voted—suggesting that in the aggregate, conspiracy theories likely do not tip the scales in favor of either major political party.[51] But what of isolated elections? Election cycles are certainly thick with conspiracy allegations of the same basic type. The question begs for additional quantitative analysis, perhaps tracking the propagation of conspiracy theories in media stories in relation to the movement of polling data.

In studying the societal-level effects of conspiracy beliefs, it will again be important to consider both the potential positive as well as negative consequences. In this volume, Räikkä and Basham, Matthew Dentith, and Alfred Moore suggest that conspiracy theories are an important counterweight to institutional power, and indeed there is evidence to suggest that conspiracy beliefs predict intentions to challenge the status quo; for example, see the chapter in this volume by Matthew Atkinson, Darin DeWitt, and Drew Wegner. Any student of United States history would be able to identify cases in which this impulse has paid off for the collective good, which begs an additional question: Who pays the higher price, those who make accusations of conspiracy or those who are accused? And, under what conditions do these costs vary?

What Do We Do with Conspiracy Theories?

The research community has a fraught dual relationship with conspiracy theories, acting as dispassionate investigator while at the same time counting itself among the epistemic authorities who may judge that conspiracy beliefs are invalid. Much of the published work embodies both roles, often explicitly treating conspiracy theories as a blight on public discourse, a problem that persistent research might someday solve. The dawning realization that conspiracy belief is not a clinical disorder, and that believers are not sharply distinguishable from nonbelievers in their psychological profiles, has reined in some of the more strident language. For example, see the detailed literature review in this volume by Michael Butter and Peter Knight. So too has the possibility that conspiracy beliefs are intertwined with broader social cognitive processes that we could consider adaptive. The deeper we look, the more difficult it becomes to treat conspiracy thinking as alien to rationality, or even alien to ourselves.

And yet . . . there *are* conspiracy theories that are demonstrably at odds with settled evidence and which *do* persist in ways that are unhelpful. Efforts to maintain desirable rates of vaccination compete with not only misinformation about vaccines causing autism, but also the allegation that public health authorities have engaged in a cover-up of the misinformation. Initiatives to combat climate change compete with not only the misinformation that climate change is not occurring, but also with the allegation that the scientific community has suppressed the truth and lined its coffers with the resulting grant money. And there is some evidence that conspiracy beliefs undermine public discourse about science more broadly.[52] Whether the underlying machinery of conspiracy beliefs is truly different from that of other types of erroneous, unhelpful beliefs is yet to be settled. But the question of how to engage these beliefs in the public sphere is before us now. These conversations are fraught with pitfalls; as some researchers have pointed out, attempts to correct misinformation can backfire, particularly among the population that is most committed to the misinformation.[53]

A full review of the literature on confronting misinformation is beyond the scope of this chapter. Fortunately, some have already been provided by scholars, most prominently by Stephan Lewandowsky and colleagues, who explored the cognitive reasons behind the persistence of misinformation and suggested some corresponding strategies for countering it.[54] The suggestions include some that are likely to come naturally to the research community (frame the debate around facts), and some that will require more practice (keep arguments simple and brief). Embedded in the list is the biggest stretch of all: affirm the worldview of the audience. When we arrive at the point where a conspiracy theory investigator can affirm the worldview of a conspiracy believer, we will know that the field has matured indeed.

Notes

1. Maddow, Rachel. 2016. "Trump Can't Resist a Conspiracy Theory: Todd." Video, 3:44, 2016. http://www.watchable.com/shows/12164-rachel-maddow/videos/85601-trump-can-t-resist-a-conspiracy-theory-todd (Accessed December 27, 2017).
2. Oliver, J. Eric, and Thomas J. Wood. 2014. "Conspiracy Theories and the Paranoid Style(s) of Mass Opinion." *American Journal of Political Science* 58(4): 952–966.
3. Galer, Sophia S. 2017. "The Accidental Invention of the Illuminati Conspiracy." http://www.bbc.com/future/story/20170809-the-accidental-invention-of-the-illuminati-conspiracy (Accessed December 27, 2017).
4. Taylor, Jon. 2017. "Kyrie Irving is Back on His Flat-Earth Theory Nonsense." *Sports* https://www.si.com/nba/2017/11/01/kyrie-irving-celtics-flat-earth-theory (Accessed December 27, 2017).
5. Blitz, Matt. 2017. "The Real Story Behind the Myth of Area 51." http://www.popularmechanics.com/military/research/a24152/area-51-history/ (Accessed December 27, 2017).
6. Kaplan, Sarah. 2017. "The Truth About Vaccines, Autism, and Robert F. Kennedy Jr.'s Conspiracy Theory." *The Washington Post.* https://www.washingtonpost.com/news/speaking-of-science/wp/2017/01/10/the-facts-about-vaccines-autism-and-robert-f-kennedy-jr-s-conspiracy-theory/?utm_term=.d877704de0d1 (Accessed December 27, 2017).
7. Kingsley, Patrick, and Sam Jones. 2011. "Osama Bin Laden Death: The Conspiracy Theories." https://www.theguardian.com/world/2011/may/05/osama-bin-laden-conspiracy-theories (Accessed December 27, 2017).
8. Uscinski, Joseph E., and Joseph M. Parent. 2014. *American Conspiracy Theories.* Oxford: Oxford University Press.
9. See also Bost, Preston R. 2015. "Crazy Beliefs, Sane Believers: Toward a Cognitive Psychology of Conspiracy Ideation." *Skeptical Inquirer* 39(1): 44–49.

10. Uscinski and Parent, *American Conspiracy Theories.*

11. For example, see Jolley, Daniel. 2013. "Are Conspiracy Theories just Harmless Fun?" *The Psychologist* 26(1): 60–62.

12. For a definition postulating a number of actors, see Keeley, Brian L. 1999. "Of Conspiracy Theories." *The Journal of Philosophy* 96(3): 116. For a definition postulating wider scope, see Swami, Viren, and Rebecca Coles. 2010. "The Truth is Out there: Belief in Conspiracy Theories." *The Psychologist* 23(7): 560–563. For a definition that includes the active propagation of deceptive message, see Einstein, Katherine Levine, and David M. Glick. 2015. "Do I Think BLS Data are BS? the Consequences of Conspiracy Theories." *Political Behavior* 37(3): 679–701.

13. Keeley, "Of Conspiracy Theories"; Leman, Patrick John, and Marco Cinnirella. 2013. "Beliefs in Conspiracy Theories and the Need for Cognitive Closure." *Frontiers in Psychology* 4(378). DOI: 10.3389/fpsyg.2013.00378.

14. Douglas, Karen M., and Robbie M. Sutton. 2015. "Climate Change: Why the Conspiracy Theories are Dangerous." *Bulletin of the Atomic Scientists* 71(2): 98–106; Imhoff, Roland, and Martin Bruder. 2014. "Speaking (Un-) Truth to Power: Conspiracy Mentality as a Generalised Political Attitude." *European Journal of Personality* 28(1): 25–43; Jolley, Daniel, and Karen M. Douglas. 2014. "The Social Consequences of Conspiracism: Exposure to Conspiracy Theories Decreases Intentions to Engage in Politics and to Reduce One's Carbon Footprint." *British Journal of Psychology* 105(1): 35–56; Sunstein, Cass R., and Adrian Vermeule. 2009. "Conspiracy Theories: Causes and Cures." *Journal of Political Philosophy* 17(2): 202–227.

15. Darwin, Hannah, Nick Neave, and Joni Holmes. 2011. "Belief in Conspiracy Theories: The Role of Paranormal Belief, Paranoid Ideation and Schizotypy." *Personality and Individual Differences* 50(8): 1289–1293; Oliver and Wood, "Conspiracy Theories and the Paranoid Style(s) of Mass Opinion"; Swami, Viren, Tomas Chamorro-Premuzic, and Adrian Furnham. 2010. "Unanswered Questions: A Preliminary Investigation of Personality and Individual Difference Predictors of 9/11 Conspiracist Beliefs." *Applied Cognitive Psychology* 24(6): 749–761; van Prooijen, Jan-Willem, and Eric van Dijk. 2014. "When Consequence Size Predicts Belief in Conspiracy Theories: The Moderating Role of Perspective Taking." *Journal of Experimental Social Psychology* 55(November): 63–73.

16. Uscinski and Parent, *American Conspiracy Theories.*

17. Einstein and Glick. "Do I Think BLS Data are BS? The Consequences of Conspiracy Theories"; Keeley, "Of Conspiracy Theories."

18. Brotherton, Robert, and Silan Eser. 2015. "Bored to Fears: Boredom Proneness, Paranoia, and Conspiracy Theories." *Personality and Individual Differences* 80(July):1–5.

19. Uscinski and Parent, *American Conspiracy Theories*; see also Levy, Neil. 2007. "Radically Socialized Knowledge and Conspiracy Theories." *Episteme* 4(2): 181–192. DOI: 10.3366/epi.2007.4.2.181.

20. Keeley, "Of Conspiracy Theories."

21. For a relevant review, see Bost,"Crazy Beliefs, Sane Believers."

22. See Uscinski and Parent, *American Conspiracy Theories*, especially chapter 2.

23. On the innate capacity for suspicion, see Bost, Preston R., and Stephen G. Prunier. 2013. "Rationality in Conspiracy Beliefs: The Role of Perceived Motive." *Psychological Reports* 113(1): 118–128; Uscinski, Joseph E. 2013. "Placing Conspiratorial Motives in Context: The Role of Predispositions and Threat, a Comment on Bost and Prunier (2013)." *Psychological Reports* 115(2):612–617. On situational triggers, see Bost and Prunier, "Rationality in Conspiracy Beliefs"; Whitson, Jennifer A., and Adam D. Galinsky. 2008. "Lacking Control Increases Illusory Pattern Perception." *Science* 322(5898): 115–117.

24. Kramer, Roderick M., and Dana Gavrieli. 2005. "The Perception of Conspiracy: Leader Paranoia as Adaptive Cognition." In *The Psychology of Leadership: New Perspectives and Research,* eds. David M. Messick and Roderick M. Kramer. Mahwah, NJ and London: Taylor & Francis, 241–274.

25. Schorn, Daniel. 2006. "The Priory of Sion: Is the 'Secret Organization' Fact or Fiction?" https://www.cbsnews.com/news/the-priory-of-sion/ (Accessed December 27, 2017).
26. Bryant, Kenzie. 2016. "Taylor Swift, Tom Hiddleston, and the Arrival of the Celebrity Conspiracy Economy." https://www.vanityfair.com/style/2016/09/taylor-swift-tom-hiddleston-celebrity-conspiracy-theories (Accessed December 27, 2017).
27. Bost, Preston R., Stephen G. Prunier, and Allen J. Piper. 2010. "Relations of Familiarity with Reasoning Strategies in Conspiracy Beliefs." *Psychological Reports* 107(2): 593–602.
28. Brotherton and his coauthors takes a step in this direction. Brotherton, Robert, Christopher C. French, and Alan D. Pickering. 2013. "Measuring Belief in Conspiracy Theories: The Generic Conspiracist Beliefs Scale." *Frontiers in Psychology* 4(May). DOI: 10.3389/fpsyg.2013.00279.
29. Goertzel, Ted. 1994. "Belief in Conspiracy Theories." *Political Psychology* 15(4): 731–742.
30. For a summary of relevant findings see Bost,"Crazy Beliefs, Sane Believers."
31. Imhoff and Bruder, "Speaking (Un-) Truth to Power."
32. On suspicion and alienation, see Abalakina-Paap, Marina, Walter G. Stephan, Traci Craig, and W. Larry Gregory. 1999. "Beliefs in Conspiracies." *Political Psychology* 20(3): 637–647. On personality, see Brotherton, French, and Pickering, "Measuring Belief in Conspiracy Theories." On educational background, see Goertzel, "Belief in Conspiracy Theories" and Simmons, William Paul, and Sharon Parsons. 2005. "Beliefs in Conspiracy Theories among African Americans: A Comparison of Elites and Masses." *Social Science Quarterly*, 86(3): 582–598. On demographics, see Bost, "Crazy Beliefs, Sane Believers."
33. Brotherton, Robert, and Christopher C. French. 2014. "Belief in Conspiracy Theories and Susceptibility to the Conjunction Fallacy." *Applied Cognitive Psychology* 28(2): 238–248; Brotherton, Robert, and Christopher C. French. 2015. "Intention Seekers: Conspiracist Ideation and Biased Attributions of Intentionality." *PLoS ONE* 10(5). DOI: 10.1371/journal.pone.0124125. For an investigation of the relationship between conspiracy beliefs and the perception of intentionality see Douglas, Karen M., Robbie M. Sutton, Mitchell J. Callan, Rael J. Dawtry, and Annelie J. Harvey. 2016. "Someone Is Pulling the Strings: Hypersensitive Agency Detection and Belief in Conspiracy Theories." *Thinking & Reasoning* 22(1): 57–77.
34. Whitson and Galinsky, "Lacking Control Increases Illusory Pattern Perception." See also Whitson, Jennifer A., Adam D. Galinsky, and Aaron Kay. 2015. "The Emotional Roots of Conspiratorial Perceptions, System Justification, and Belief in the Paranormal." *Journal of Experimental Social Psychology* 56(January): 89–95.
35. Rothschild, Zachary K., Mark J. Landau, Daniel Sullivan, and Lucas A. Keefer. 2012. "A Dual-Motive Model of Scapegoating: Displacing Blame to Reduce Guilt or Increase Control." *Journal of Personality and Social Psychology* 102(6): 1148–1163.
36. Uscinski and Parent, *American Conspiracy Theories*, chapter 6.
37. Shermer, Michael. 2011. *The Believing Brain*. New York: Times Books, chapter 4.
38. Ibid.
39. For a summary of some relevant findings, see Jolley, "Are Conspiracy Theories Just Harmless Fun?"
40. On voting behavior, see Butler, Lisa D., Cheryl Koopman, and Philip G. Zimbardo. 1995. "The Psychological Impact of Viewing the Film 'JFK': Emotions, Beliefs, and Political Behavioral Intentions." *Political Psychology* 16(2): 237–257. On carbon footprint, see Jolley and Douglas, "The Social Consequences of Conspiracism."
41. For more on the enduring effects of the Tuskegee study on current perceptions of the medical establishment, see Thomas, Stephen B., and Sandra C. Quinn. 1991. "The Tuskegee Syphilis Study, 1932 to 1972: Implications for HIV Education and AIDS Risk Education Programs in the Black Community." *American Journal of Public Health* 81(11): 1498–1505. On the consequences for HIV protection, see Bogart, Laura M., and Sheryl Thorburn. 2005. "Are HIV/AIDS Conspiracy Beliefs a Barrier to HIV Prevention among African Americans?" *JAIDS Journal of Acquired Immune Deficiency Syndromes* 38(2): 213–218.

42. Jolley, Daniel, and Karen M. Douglas. 2014. "The Effects of Anti-Vaccine Conspiracy Theories on Vaccination Intentions." *PloS ONE* 9(2). DOI: 10.1371/journal.pone.0089177.
43. Butler, Koopman, and Zimbardo, "The Psychological Impact of Viewing the Film 'JFK.'"
44. Jolley and Douglas, "The Social Consequences of Conspiracism."
45. Rothschild, Landau, Sullivan, and Keefer, "A Dual-Motive Model of Scapegoating."
46. Ryon, Holly S., and Marci E. J. Gleason. 2014. "The Role of Locus of Control in Daily Life." *Personality and Social Psychology Bulletin* 40(1): 121–131.
47. For one example of testing for negative outcomes see Douglas and Sutton, "Climate Change: Why the Conspiracy Theories are Dangerous."
48. Ibid. See also Jolley and Douglas, "The Effects of Anti-Vaccine Conspiracy Theories on Vaccination Intentions."
49. Jolley, "Are Conspiracy Theories Just Harmless Fun?"
50. Butler, Koopman, and Zimbardo, "The Psychological Impact of Viewing the Film 'JFK'"; Jolley and Douglas, "The Social Consequences of Conspiracism"; Jolley and Douglas, "The Effects of Anti-Vaccine Conspiracy Theories on Vaccination Intentions."
51. Uscinski and Parent, *American Conspiracy Theories*.
52. Lewandowsky, Stephan, Gilles E. Gignac, and Klaus Oberauer. 2013. "The Role of Conspiracist Ideation and Worldviews in Predicting Rejection of Science." *PLoS ONE* 8(10): 1–11. DOI: 10.1371/journal.pone.0075637.
53. Nyhan, Brendan, and Jason Reifler. 2015. "Does Correcting Myths about the Flu Vaccine Work? An Experimental Evaluation of the Effects of Corrective Information." *Vaccine* 33(3): 459–464.
54. Lewandowsky, Stephan, Ullrich K. H. Ecker, Colleen M. Seifert, Norbert Schwarz, and John Cook. 2012. "Misinformation and its Correction: Continued Influence and Successful Debiasing." *Psychological Science in the Public Interest* 13(3): 106–131. For a meta-analysis of research on techniques for correcting misinformation, see Chan, Man-pui Sally, Christopher R. Jones, Kathleen Hall Jamieson, and Dolores Albarracín. 2017. "Debunking: A Meta-Analysis of the Psychological Efficacy of Messages Countering Misinformation." *Psychological Science* 28(11): 1531–1546.

WHAT DO CONSPIRACY THEORIES LOOK LIKE IN THE UNITED STATES?

JOSEPH E. USCINSKI

Conspiracy theories have been part of the United States since before the states united. Colonists—based upon spectral evidence—believed witches were conspiring with Satan; so they burned them. Colonists later believed King George III was conspiring to instill tyranny over the colonies, so they rebelled. As Kathryn Olmsted details in Chapter 19, conspiracy theories involving numerous groups have continued what the colonists began.

As Steven Smallpage and Adam Enders will show in Chapter 20, all Americans believe in one conspiracy theory or another. About 60 percent of U.S. citizens believe in one form of JFK assassination theory. About 25 percent believe in each of the birther and truther theories. Even conspiracy theories that pollsters invent garner the support of about 20 percent of the public. Americans are happy to endorse conspiracy theories.

In Chapter 21, Darin DeWitt, Matthew Atkinson, and Drew Wegner seek to uncover the ways that conspiracy theories spread from person to person. Many researchers and commentators have blamed the Internet for allowing the spread of conspiracy theories, but few have been able to provide a theory to explain how conspiracy theories spread. DeWitt and colleagues show that the herd model usually discussed in most accounts is lacking, and that other models may have more explanatory power.

19

Conspiracy Theories in U.S. History

KATHRYN S. OLMSTED

Surrounded by hostile empires, the British colonists in Virginia and Massachusetts feared conspiracies against them from the moment they landed in America. They worried that Catholic immigrants were plotting to undermine their governments and turn them over to French or Spanish control. They fretted that enslaved Africans planned to organize and inflict upon their masters the same violence that their masters perpetrated against them. After the creation of the American republic, the list of Americans' internal enemies grew even longer. Mormons, Masons, anarchists, Wall Street financiers, and many more, all threatened American freedom, they believed.[1]

In the early twentieth century, American conspiracy theories underwent a fundamental transformation. Though white Protestant Americans continued to fear those of different races or religions, and though fears of the Illuminati and international bankers persisted, the number of believers in ethnic and fraternal conspiracy theories began to dwindle, and these theories moved to the margins of American political life. Instead, Americans began to identify a new, powerful threat to their experiment: the U.S. government itself. The political views of those who believed in conspiracy theories about the U.S. government would shift with administrations; Democrats were more inclined to see government conspiracies during Republican administrations, and vice versa. But the overall trend—Americans' increasing distrust of government—transcended partisan identification.

It's important to remember that American conspiracy theories have always existed. Though the villains in these theories may change over time, the theories themselves are in fact a normal part of American history and politics.

A Fragile Experiment

Many scholars have tried to explain why Americans seem particularly eager to embrace conspiracy theories. Most agree that American conspiricism stems from the difficulty of defining a national identity. In a land of immigrants, some Americans have resorted to demonizing outsiders as a way of bolstering their own sense of self. As the historian David Bennett has argued, anti-alien movements have helped many Americans find "closeness, community, and authority."[2] In the most influential interpretation of American conspiracy theories, historian Richard Hofstadter discerned a "paranoid style in American politics" that distinguished U.S. political rhetoric from the 1790s to the 1960s. In part, he attributed this paranoia to the fluidity and diversity of American life, which led Americans to have "status anxieties" that they assuaged by striking out against hidden enemies. He also noticed a kind of hyper-patriotic defensiveness among immigrants and children of immigrants who worried, deep down, that they were not "really and truly and fully American."[3] Hofstadter and other historians noted another common characteristic of American conspiracy theories: that their country was simultaneously the chosen land—John Winthrop's "city on a hill"—and yet uniquely vulnerable to assaults by its enemies. As the noted historian David Brion Davis has said, "Many Americans have been curiously obsessed with the contingency of their experiment with freedom."[4]

The obsession with finding and casting out the "un-Americans" has been a constant in American conspiracy theories. The earliest conspiracy theory in British America came over with the first immigrants. Back in England, Protestants had banished, burned, and beheaded the people they called "papists" for nearly a century before the first English colonists set out for American shores. In the new world, British colonists found themselves surrounded by two rival Catholic empires, France to the north and Spain to the south. Early American leaders believed that the pope, "the most detestable Monster the Earth ever had upon it," was sending swarms of priests to aid these foreign empires and ruin the English colonies.[5]

Early Americans also worried about conspiracies emanating from other oppressed groups. The fear of slave revolts exploded periodically in most of the British colonies, even those with relatively few slaves. In New York in 1741, the colonial government hanged 17 African Americans and burned another 13 alive because they had allegedly participated in an "unparallel'd Hellish plot" to kill all the white men and rape the women.[6] The colonists were also terrified of plots by native peoples. Even though many tribes distrusted and warred against each other, the settlers worried, as one Rhode Island colonist nervously reported in 1675, that "all the Indians were in combination and confederacie to exterpate and root out the English."[7]

Conspiracy played a crucial role in the ideology of American Revolution. Rebellious colonists believed that a cabal in London conspired against colonists' liberties—that the British wanted to impose a kind of slavery on their white settlers. The Declaration of Independence recited a long list of King George III's "repeated injuries and usurpations, all having in direct object the establishment of an absolute Tyranny over these States." Indeed, in their influential book on American conspiracism, Joseph E. Uscinski and Joseph M. Parent have called the Declaration the "original American conspiracy theory."[8]

As soon as the founders created the republic, they feared that it would collapse. In the 1790s, some Americans eagerly read Scotsman John Robison's *Proofs of a Conspiracy*, which alleged that secret members of the Illuminati were trying "to insinuate their Brethren into all offices which gave them influence on the public mind."[9] The Illuminati hysteria quickly died down, but the fear of conspiracy did not. Americans fought the War of 1812 at least in part because they believed that the republic was "in peril" and needed to prove to internal and external enemies that the American experiment could survive and prosper.[10]

In the Civil War, too, both sides charged that their opponents were part of a conspiracy to take over the government. Slaveholders were terrified that abolitionists, "envenomed by hate, and impelled by lust of power and dominion," were trying to eliminate slavery by subverting the republic.[11] At the same time, their enemies in the North also feared a secret conspiracy, but their nightmare featured the rapacious expansion of the "Slave Power Conspiracy." In the view of some abolitionists, the "slaveocracy" aimed to unite with northern industrialists, take over the U.S. government, and reduce free white men to slavery throughout the land. It was the duty of the abolitionists to expose this conspiracy of the "Lords of the Lash and the Lords of the Loom," in the words of anti-slavery activist Wendell Phillips.[12]

After the Civil War, the "lords of the lash" lost their human property, but the lords of the loom had more power than ever before. Some Americans worried that the great gap between rich and poor that accompanied industrialization would undermine American independence and opportunity. The Populist revolt of the 1890s was inspired by the real difficulties of small farmers in an era of falling prices, but also by their conviction that a few individuals were to blame. The chief demons were the "money kings" of Wall Street, particularly J. P. Morgan, the personification of the money trust. British bankers, who owned a lot of the loans taken out by American farmers, and Jews, who were the perpetual villains in the morality tales told by Protestant debtors, were also favorite targets.

The nineteenth century witnessed periodic waves of conspiracy theories about religious minorities and fraternal societies. Anti-Catholic movements continued to grow as millions of immigrants from European countries, particularly Ireland and Germany, fled persecution or poverty in their home nations and came to America. Some Protestant Americans believed that these newcomers put duty to the pope over loyalty to country, and they worried that the U.S. culture of openness would prove its undoing. One leader of the anti-Catholic movement, inventor Samuel F. B. Morse, wrote in the 1830s: "We are the dupes of our hospitality. The evil of immigration brings to these shores illiterate Roman Catholics, the tools of reckless and unprincipled politicians, the obedient instruments of their more knowing priestly leaders."[13]

Much like the Catholics, Masons and Mormons also aroused the suspicion of nineteenth-century Americans. Anti-Masons organized into a political party in the 1830s after the murder of an ex-Mason who had vowed to divulge the order's secrets. Advocating for higher tariffs and more roads as well as the end of Freemasonry, the Anti-Masonic Party elected two governors and dozens of state legislators and U.S. congressmen during its brief heyday. Anti-Masons frequently equated Catholicism and Freemasonry as "horrid oath-finding systems" that undermined republican government and thrust Americans into "the very fangs of despotism."[14] One anti-Masonic handbook declared that Freemasonry was "an engine of Satan . . . dark, unfruitful, selfish, demoralizing, blasphemous, murderous, anti-republican and anti-Christian."[15]

Anti-Mormon propaganda borrowed many tropes from anti-Catholicism and anti-Masonry. Conspiracy theorists yoked Mormons with Masons because they practiced secret rituals in temples closed to outsiders. Like Catholics, Mormons were accused of all kinds of sexual depravity, including rape, incest, and sadism. In particular, the Latter Day Saints' early practice of polygamy struck anti-Mormons as a "deep humiliation and outrageous wrong" committed against women.[16] The accusations of sexual cruelty tapped into anxieties about changing roles of women, while titillating the Protestant faithful and thus bringing anti-Mormonism and anti-Catholicism to a wider audience.

World War I and the Dawn of a New Era

These anti-alien movements began to recede in the early twentieth century as American conspiracy theories shifted their focus. Before the 1910s, the most popular American conspiracy theories targeted ethnic or religious minorities, or small groups like the "Slave Power" that allegedly set out to control the government. But as the federal government grew during and after World War I, many conspiracy theorists came to believe that the American state represented the greatest danger to their freedom.

World War I was a watershed in the development of the U.S. federal government. During the war, the government drafted soldiers, took over key sectors of the economy, and monitored and imprisoned critics of the war. It also criminalized opposition to the war. Under the Espionage and Sedition Acts, more than a thousand people went to prison for using "disloyal, profane, scurrilous or abusive language" about the government. After the war, the Bureau of Investigation continued to watch and collect information on suspected dissidents. The new head of the Bureau, J. Edgar Hoover, developed a filing system that listed the activities of hundreds of thousands of people who allegedly threatened the government.[17]

Members of Congress charged that new, powerful executive agencies were conspiring to thwart the will of the people. In the 1930s through the 1950s, several extensive and well-funded congressional committees investigated charges of conspiracies within the executive branch. Senator Gerald Nye (R-ND) led a multi-year inquiry into allegations that arms dealers and bankers ("merchants of death") had worked with executive branch officials to manipulate or coerce the United States into entering World War I. After the end of World War II, a joint congressional committee investigated charges that President Franklin Roosevelt had known in advance about the Japanese attack on Pearl Harbor and deliberately withheld this information from the local commanders. In the 1950s, Senator Joseph McCarthy (R-WI) charged that employees in federal agencies were conspiring with the Soviet Union to weaken America. The senator alleged that U.S. foreign policy reverses were the result of "a conspiracy on a scale so immense as to dwarf any previous such venture in the history of man. A conspiracy of infamy so black that, when it is finally exposed, its principals shall be forever deserving of the maledictions of all honest men."[18]

The congressional investigators were correct on one point: With the growth of executive power in the twentieth century, the federal government could threaten Americans' civil liberties. This was particularly true at the nation's internal security agency, the Federal Bureau of Investigation (FBI). President Franklin Roosevelt added the word "Federal" to the Bureau's title in 1935 and soon expanded its duties, budget, and power. Throughout the 1940s and early 1950s, the FBI spied on the U.S. Communist Party and then watched with satisfaction as prosecutors sent its members to jail. But then the Supreme Court began issuing a series of decisions that made it harder for the government to put communists in prison. In response, J. Edgar Hoover started a massive domestic covert action program, known by the code name COINTELPRO, to infiltrate communist groups and try to "expose, disrupt, misdirect, discredit, or otherwise neutralize" their members.[19] Hoover soon moved to spy on other dissident and reformist groups, including the Southern Christian Leadership Conference under Martin Luther King, Jr. The FBI agents did not just monitor these dissidents, but tried to provoke them to commit crimes so that they could be arrested.[20]

As the Cold War continued, Congress created more secret agencies—and thus more targets for conspiracy theorists. When Congress set up the Central Intelligence Agency (CIA) in 1947, many lawmakers feared that the president would use it like a "Gestapo" or Soviet-style secret police to spy on and punish his political enemies. To allay these concerns, drafters of National Security Act of 1947 specifically stated that the CIA would "have no police, subpoena, law enforcement powers, or internal security functions." But the National Security Act also contained an "elastic clause," which charged the CIA with performing "such other functions and duties related to intelligence affecting the national security as the National Security Council may from time to time direct."[21]

In the years to come, CIA officials would stretch this elastic clause to include programs that would inspire many conspiracy theories. In the 1950s and 1960s, as part of an operation code-named MK-ULTRA, U.S. spies dropped LSD into the drinks of unsuspecting bar patrons in hopes of discovering how Americans would react if the communists spiked the country's water supply with hallucinogenic drugs.[22] The agency learned little, and the Soviets never tried to drug the American water supply. But the innocent American victims of this U.S. government program were convinced that they were losing their minds. Since the agency failed to track those who ingested the drugs, no one knows what happened to them. In another Cold War plot, the U.S. Joint Chiefs of Staff recommended that President John Kennedy agree to stage fake terrorist attacks—including the shoot-down of an airliner—that could be blamed on the Cuban government.[23]

The Cuban communists inspired some of the most bizarre secret U.S. government plots in the early 1960s. In another, later infamous CIA operation, the U.S. government contracted with Mafia leaders to try to discredit, and ultimately to kill, Cuban leader Fidel Castro. First, American spies tried to dust Castro's boots with a depilatory so that his beard would fall out, and then, in an effort to make him sound crazy, tried to lace his cigars with a hallucinogen. As they moved to more lethal plots, the U.S. agents used exploding seashells, deadly fungus, and a syringe of poison disguised as a ballpoint pen in their numerous attempts to assassinate the Cuban leader.[24] Their efforts failed, and Castro died of old age in 2016, having outlived all the men who had plotted his murder.

Though the Castro plots failed, and Kennedy nixed the fake terrorist attacks, the later revelation of these secret government conspiracies would cause Americans to question whether they could trust their government. Many citizens wondered: If government officials could engage in these ludicrous plots, then what other crazy things had they done—and were they continuing to do?

Six Seconds in Dallas

Most Americans did not know about these secret FBI and CIA programs at the time. The media did not look too closely at the classified programs of agencies that were fighting the communists, while the congressional committees charged with overseeing the CIA and FBI deliberately refrained from asking tough questions. As one overseer, Senator Leverett Saltonstall (R-MA), explained: "The difficulty in connection with asking questions and obtaining information is that we might obtain information which I personally would rather not have."[25]

But this unqualified support for the nation's internal security agencies began to ebb in the 1960s. In part, the unpopularity of the Vietnam War caused many Americans to ask tougher questions of their government's secretive bureaucracies. At the same time, the murder of the president prompted some to question the truthfulness and honor of the nation's leaders.

From the moment that the television networks announced the death of John F. Kennedy on November 22, 1963, some Americans began to suggest that the president had been the victim of a conspiracy. The suspected gunman, Lee Harvey

Oswald, had a mysterious past. He had served as a U.S. Marine, then defected to the Soviet Union, then re-defected back to the United States. He had consorted with American communists, anti-Communist Russians, and anti-Castro Cubans. Oswald's rifle, with his fingerprints, was found in a sniper's nest in a building near where Kennedy was killed. But he claimed that he was merely a "patsy" who had been framed by other conspirators.[26]

The conspiracy theory gained traction when a local strip club owner, Jack Ruby, shot and killed the alleged assassin two days after Oswald's arrest. Ruby claimed that he acted because of his own rage and grief over the president's murder. But the execution caused many Americans to wonder if Oswald had been a patsy after all.

To quiet these doubts, President Lyndon Johnson appointed an investigatory commission headed by Earl Warren, chief justice of the U.S. Supreme Court. The Warren Commission issued a comprehensive report in 1964 that declared Oswald to be the lone assassin. Polls showed that the number of Americans believing in a conspiracy did decline—at first.[27]

But in 1967, JFK conspiracy theories gained a prominent adherent when New Orleans District Attorney Jim Garrison joined the cause. Known for his fearless (some would say irresponsible) prosecutions, Garrison charged that former CIA agents decided to kill the president to stop him from withdrawing American troops from Vietnam. In New Orleans, he argued, these agents had ensnared Oswald in their plot and then trapped him into taking the blame. Afterwards, the FBI and CIA had conspired to hide the truth. To prove his charges, he put a New Orleans businessman on trial for Kennedy's murder.

Garrison's crusade ended when a jury found the businessman not guilty. However, the colorful prosecutor succeeded in raising doubts about the Warren Commission Report. Soon dozens, and then hundreds of books backed Garrison's theory or proposed new ones. By the mid-1970s, 81 percent of Americans believed that Kennedy was the victim of a conspiracy. The Warren Commission lone-gunman theory was left "almost totally without adherents," according to pollsters.[28]

Watergate and Its Legacies

Americans' distrust of their government continued to climb in the 1970s with the revelation of more real government conspiracies. The investigation of the Watergate break-in and subsequent cover-up led to the downfall of a president—and inspired a new generation of conspiracy theorists.

On June 17, 1972, five burglars with sophisticated surveillance equipment broke into the Democratic Party national headquarters in the Watergate building in Washington, D.C. Police caught them in the act and put them under arrest. Most of the burglars had once worked for the CIA, and one was the chief of security for the Committee to Re-elect the President.

During the subsequent investigation, Americans learned that the Watergate burglary was only one of many committed by President Nixon's aides, and that his re-election campaign had been systematically spying on his rivals for years. They discovered that the Nixon campaign had paid for these surveillance activities with a multimillion-dollar slush fund that it had accumulated through bribery and extortion. Finally, they found out that the president had personally tried to obstruct the FBI's investigation of the crime by paying off the burglars and attempting to blackmail the CIA.[29]

Nixon's efforts to obstruct justice were recorded on his Oval Office taping system. In one conversation, which took place six days after the Watergate break-in, the president met with his chief of staff, Bob Haldeman, and discussed how they might stop the FBI's investigation of the burglary. This tape later became known as the "smoking gun." On the tape, Nixon can be heard telling Haldeman how to force CIA director Richard Helms to derail the FBI's investigation. "We protected Helms from one hell of a lot of things," Nixon says mysteriously. If the true story of Watergate got out, Nixon tells his aide, it would blow "the whole Bay of Pigs thing," which would be "detrimental" to the CIA.[30]

Nixon's resignation in August 1974 did not resolve all the Watergate mysteries. Many journalists, congressmen, and ordinary citizens continued to raise questions about the CIA's role in the break-in and cover-up. What had Nixon meant by protecting the CIA from "one hell of a lot of things"? Was he referring to the Kennedy assassination? Did the CIA have more secrets that the nation should know?

In a series of revelations dubbed "Son of Watergate," the press began to discover and publicize other CIA abuses and crimes. In the *New York Times*, investigative reporter Seymour Hersh revealed that the CIA had been spying on Americans in the United States for several years. The story was explosive because the CIA was prohibited by law from spying on Americans at home. Despite this ban, President Lyndon Johnson had pressed the agency to spy on protesters against the Vietnam War. President Nixon had continued and expanded the domestic surveillance program, called Operation CHAOS, to include several domestic dissident groups, such as the women's liberation movement. Subsequent newspaper stories revealed other questionable practices of the CIA and the FBI, including the FBI's COINTELPRO spying, its wiretapping of Martin Luther King, Jr., and the CIA's deals with the Mafia to kill Castro.

These post-Watergate media exposés of secret agencies prompted Congress to launch several simultaneous investigations. After years of raising questions about secret government activities, skeptics now leaped at the opportunity to learn all about them. "All the tensions and suspicions and hostilities that had been building about the CIA since the Bay of Pigs and had risen to a combustible level during the Vietnam and Watergate years, now exploded," wrote the CIA's director, William Colby.[31]

The most important inquiry was led by Frank Church (D-Idaho). During 15 months of investigation, Church's special Senate committee served as a kind of truth commission for Cold War America. The Church committee compelled testimony from dozens of secret agents, including FBI informants, Mafia dons, and angry and defensive CIA officials. Among other sensational discoveries, the senators revealed a "suicide letter" that had been written by an FBI official and sent to Martin Luther King, Jr., with the intent of trying to blackmail him into taking his own life.

In the end, the Church committee issued 14 volumes of reports on secret government programs at the height of the Cold War. The assassinations report, which documented the CIA's often bizarre plots against Castro's life, received the most attention, but the rest contained bombshells of their own. Illegal mail-opening, extensive infiltration of peaceful protest groups, covert actions against democratically elected governments: all were documented by this official U.S. government investigation.

Senator Church had hoped that the investigation would help restore faith in a government that possessed the courage to confront its past crimes. But the revelations had the opposite effect. The process persuaded a lot of Americans that public officials routinely committed crimes, hid evidence, and escaped without consequences. Transparency did not create trust. Indeed, more Americans distrusted their government after Senator Church ended his investigation than before he began it.[32]

The Church committee was only one of several public investigations of secret government abuses in the 1970s. One congressional committee revealed extensive U.S. Army spying on ordinary citizens. Yet another examined the soon-to-be-infamous Tuskegee experiment, in which public health officials had denied potentially life-saving treatment to African-American men for decades. Investigators also discovered that the CIA had tested drugs on unsuspecting Americans as part of an ill-conceived experiment in mind control. The most expensive and extensive congressional investigation looked at the assassinations of John Kennedy and of Martin Luther King, Jr. The House Assassinations Committee concluded that there was probably a broad conspiracy behind Kennedy's murder (but not King's). After it released its final report, 95 percent of Americans believed in conspiracy theories about either the King or the Kennedy assassinations—and sometimes both.[33]

The post-Watergate investigations of secret government activities created a crisis of faith in American institutions.[34] Now the most outrageous conspiracy theories seemed plausible—especially when a new government scandal broke that many called worse than Watergate.

Trust No One

When Ronald Reagan became president in 1981, he proclaimed that the CIA had been shackled by the post-Watergate investigations and vowed to release it. He appointed a new, aggressive CIA director, William Casey, who would soon involve the agency in a momentous scandal. In the Iran–Contra affair, as in Watergate, real government conspiracies prompted more conspiracy theories about the government.

Casey and Reagan decided to launch a covert war in Central America that quickly grew unpopular with the Democratic majority in Congress. Under Casey's direction, the CIA funded and trained a counterrevolutionary army that opposed the communist government in Nicaragua. When the army, known as the Contras, began assassinating local government officials and committing acts of terrorism, Congress cut off funding and prohibited the CIA from aiding the Contras.

Angry at the congressional action, Casey decided to find a way around the law. He ordered a staff member in the National Security Council, Oliver North, to find money for the Contras and help them purchase arms. At the same time, North was coordinating an effort to ransom American hostages in the Middle East by secretly violating an arms export law and selling missiles to the government of Iran. North eventually got the "neat idea" to combine the illegal Contra war with the Iranian arms sales: he took the profits from the secret missile deals and diverted them to the CIA's army in Nicaragua.[35]

The Iran–Contra conspiracy began to unravel in October 1986 when one of North's planes was shot down by the Nicaraguan army. Two weeks later, the Iranian government decided to leak the story of its secret missile deals with the Reagan administration.

After an 11-month investigation, a joint House–Senate committee denounced the president's aides as a "cabal of zealots" who had broken laws and subverted the Constitution.[36] Because there was no written evidence that Reagan had known about the most serious element of the affair—the diversion of profits from the hostage deals to the Contra army—the president was able to stay in office. A special prosecutor brought charges against North and other government officials. But all the accused avoided jail time, either because their convictions were overturned on technicalities or because they were pardoned by Reagan's successor, George H. W. Bush.

The principals in the Iran–Contra affair may have evaded prison, but they did not escape the accusations of conspiracy theorists. The scandal had revealed that unelected staff members in the White House could create, as Senator Daniel Inouye said, "a shadowy government with its own air force, its own navy, its own fundraising mechanism, and the ability to pursue its own ideas of the national interest, free from all checks and balances and free from the law itself."[37]

Those on the far left and the far right of American politics saw great danger in the Iran–Contra affair. Militia sympathizers and anarchists alike believed that the scandal showed that the "insiders" had truly taken over the American government. In a 1995 article in the New Yorker, journalist Michael Kelly coined the term "fusion paranoia" to describe the conspiracy theories embraced by these strange political bedfellows.[38]

The implosion of the Soviet Union and the end of the Cold War in 1991 did not help Americans feel more secure. In the absence of the Red threat, more skeptics transferred their fears to their own government. Some African-American activists charged that the U.S. government had deliberately created the AIDS virus in a laboratory as part of a diabolical plot to decimate the black community.[39] Others said that the CIA had helped the Contras to sell crack cocaine in America's ghettoes to raise money for the secret war and destroy the black community. Some mainstream media sources attributed these theories to "black paranoia," but many African-American leaders contended that "paranoia" was a reasonable position given their history. As novelist Richard Wright said, "I know I am paranoid. But you know, any black man who is not paranoid is in serious shape. He should be in an asylum and kept under cover."[40]

By the 1990s, even the head of government shared this suspicion of secret government conspiracies. When Bill Clinton entered the White House in 1993, he asked an old friend, Webster Hubbell, to use his new position at the Justice Department to find the answers to two questions: "One: Who killed JFK? And two: Are there UFOs?"[41]

American popular culture reflected the mainstreaming of conspiracism. The TV show *The X-Files* captured the mood of the country with its catchphrases "Trust No One" and "The Truth is Out There." Some TV executives doubted at first whether viewers would believe the show's premise of a government-within-a-government in league with aliens, but it became a cult hit.[42] To the large majority of Americans who thought that the government was hiding information about UFOs, the *X-Files* theories seemed plausible.

After the terrorist attacks of September 11, 2001, suspicion of government continued to climb. The George W. Bush administration proposed its own, official conspiracy theory of the attacks that posited collusion between Iraq's secular dictator, Saddam Hussein, and the religious fundamentalists in al-Qaeda. Meanwhile, some skeptics began devising their own, alternative conspiracy theories, especially after the United States invaded Iraq in 2003. The most popular 9/11 theories differed on whether the Bush administration executed the attacks, or merely failed to stop them (MIHOP, or made it happen on purpose, versus LIHOP, or let it happen on purpose). But all shared a common core belief: that the U.S. government had murdered thousands of its citizens in a false flag operation to rally support for an unpopular war.

Conclusion

The prominence of conspiracy theories in the 2016 U.S. presidential election has led some Americans to believe that we are living in a new age of conspiracism. But as we've seen, conspiracy theories are a normal feature of U.S. political history. That doesn't mean that all Americans in all eras believe the same conspiracy theories. What Richard Hofstadter identified as a "paranoid style in American politics" has evolved over the years. The earliest American settlers worried about outsiders who owed allegiances to supposedly un-American authorities: the pope, native chiefs, fellow slaves, Freemasonry, the Mormon Church, or simple greed. As the nation modernized, these conspiracy theories based on ethnicity, religion, or class were replaced by those focusing on federal government plots. This transition occurred at the same time as government agencies gained the power to conspire against Americans—and indeed, sometimes *did*.

Once, when Richard Nixon was devising one of his many plots, he explained to his aides that he needed to respond to schemes by un-American forces. "We're up against an enemy, a conspiracy," he said.[43] As long as U.S. leaders continue to create and to justify their own conspiracies, American citizens will have rich material from which to form new conspiracy theories.

Notes

1. See Olmsted, Kathryn S. 2009. *Real Enemies: Conspiracy Theories and American Democracy, World War I to 9/11.* New York: Oxford University Press.
2. Bennett, David H. 1995: *The Party of Fear: From Nativist Movements to the New Right in American History.* New York: Vintage Books, 11.
3. Hofstadter, Richard. 1994. *The Paranoid Style in American Politics and Other Essays.* Cambridge, MA: Harvard University Press, 58.
4. Davis, David Brion, ed. 1971. *The Fear of Conspiracy: Images of Un-American Subversion from the Revolution to the* Present. Ithaca: Cornell University Press, xiii.
5. Bennett, *Party of Fear*, 20.
6. Lepore, Jill. *New York Burning: Liberty, Slavery, and Conspiracy in Eighteenth-century* Manhattan. New York: Vintage, 13.
7. Walker, Jesse. *The United States of Paranoia: A Conspiracy* Theory. New York: Harper Perennial, 27.
8. Uscinski, Joseph E., and Joseph M. Parent. 2014. *American Conspiracy Theories.* New York: Oxford University Press, 1.
9. Davis, *Fear of Conspiracy*, 41.
10. Brown, Roger H. 1971. *The Republic in Peril: 1812.* New York: Norton.
11. Davis, *Fear of Conspiracy*, 148.
12. Nye, Russel B. 1972. "The Slave Power Conspiracy: 1830–1860," In *Conspiracy: The Fear of Subversion in American History*, eds. Richard O. Curry and Thomas M. Brown. New York: Holt, Rinehart, and Winston, 80.
13. Quoted in Bennett, *Party of Fear*, 40.
14. McCarthy, Charles. 1903. "The Antimasonic Party, A Study of Political Antimasonry in the United States, 1827–1840." In *Annual Report . . . for the Year 1902, 1.* Washington, D.C.: American Historical Association: 544.
15. Hofstadter, *Paranoid Style*, 17.
16. Davis, *Fear of Conspiracy*, 159.
17. Gentry, Curt. 1992. *J. Edgar Hoover: The Man and the Secrets.* New York: Plume, 79.
18. Hofstadter, *Paranoid Style*, 7.

19. U.S. Congress. Senate Select Committee to Study Governmental Operations with Respect to Intelligence Activities. 1976. 94th Cong., 2nd sess., *Final Report*, Part II. Washington, D.C.: Government Printing Office, 20.

20. U.S. Congress. Senate Select Committee to Study Governmental Operations with Respect to Intelligence Activities. 1976. 94th Cong., 2nd sess., *Final Report*, Part III. Washington, D.C.: Government Printing Office, 34.

21. Donovan, Robert J. 1996. *Conflict and Crisis: The Presidency of Harry S. Truman, 1945–1948.* Columbia, MO: University of Missouri Press, 308.

22. See U.S. Congress. Senate, Select Committee on Intelligence and the Subcommittee on Health and Scientific Research of the Committee on Human Resources. 1977. *Joint Hearings on Project MKULTRA, the CIA's Program of Research in Behavioral Modification*, 95th Cong., 1st sess. Washington, D.C.: Government Printing Office; Marks, John. 1979. *The Search for the 'Manchurian Candidate': The CIA and Mind Control.* New York: Times Books.

23. Olmsted, *Real Enemies*, 2.

24. The Castro plots are laid out in U.S. Congress. Senate. Senate Select Committee to Study Governmental Operations with Respect to Intelligence Activities. 1974. 94th Cong., 2nd sess., *Interim Report: Alleged Assassination Plots Involving Foreign Leaders.* New York: W.W. Norton: 71–180.

25. Quoted in Johnson, Loch K. *A Season of Inquiry: Congress and Intelligence.* Chicago: Dorsey Press, 7.

26. Olmsted, *Real Enemies*, 117.

27. Appleton, Sheldon. 2000. "Trends: Assassinations," *Public Opinion Quarterly* 64(4): 514.

28. Olmsted, Kathryn S. 1996. *Challenging the Secret Government: The Post-Watergate Investigations of the CIA and FBI.* Chapel Hill: University of North Carolina Press, 99.

29. On Watergate, see Kutler, Stanley. 1999. *Abuse of Power: The New Nixon Tapes.* New York: Free Press; Schell, Jonathan. 1976. *The Time of Illusion: An Historical and Reflective Account of the Nixon Era.* New York: Vintage; Lukas, J. Anthony. 1988. *Nightmare: The Underside of the Nixon Years.* New York: Penguin.

30. Kutler, *Abuse of Power*, 69, 68.

31. Colby, William Colby, and Peter Forbath. 1978. *Honorable Men: My Life in the CIA* New York: Simon & Schuster, 391.

32. See Pew Research Center. 2017. "Public Trust in Government, 1958–2017." http://www.people-press.org/2017/05/03/public-trust-in-government-1958-2017/ (Accessed December 20, 2017).

33. Olmsted, *Challenging*, 100.

34. Ibid.

35. Draper, Theodore. 1991. *A Very Thin Line: The Iran-Contra Affairs.* New York: Hill and Wang.

36. Inouye Daniel K., and Lee H. Hamilton. 1988. *Report of the Congressional Committees Investigating the Iran-Contra Affair* [Abridged ed.]. New York: Times Books, 34.

37. Quoted in Olmsted, *Real Enemies*, 179.

38. Kelly, Michael. "The Road to Paranoia." *New Yorker*, June, 60–75.

39. Turner Patricia A. 1993. *I Heard It Through the Grapevine: Rumor in African American Culture.* Berkeley and Los Angeles: University of California Press.

40. Quoted in Rowley, Hazel. 2001. *Richard Wright: The Life and Times.* New York: Henry Holt, 491.

41. Hubbell, Webb. 1997. *Friends in High Places: Our Journey from Little Rock to Washington, D.C.* New York: William Morrow, 282.

42. Delasara, Jan. 2000. *PopLit, Popcult and 'The X-Files': A Critical Exploration.* Jefferson, NC: McFarland, 2000, 16.

43. Kutler, *Abuse of Power*, 8.

20

Polls, Plots, and Party Politics

Conspiracy Theories in Contemporary America

ADAM M. ENDERS AND STEVEN M. SMALLPAGE

In the aftermath of the 2016 American presidential election, mainstream media outlets proclaimed that America entered a new "age of conspiracy."[1] Coincidently, the new age of conspiracy has a new "conspiracy theory President," Donald Trump.[2] For some, the age of conspiracy *is* the age of Trump: "This represents a historical milestone of sorts. Trump's administration has fully erased the boundary between legitimate conservatism and the most disreputable paranoid discourse on the far right."[3] The blurred line between conspiracy thinking and traditional politics marks a new era of American political life.

While conspiracy theories and theorists have gained considerable publicity in the media, we should be clearer on the role recent conspiracy theories play in contemporary American culture. Conspiracy thinking *does* play a significant role in American politics, but not because we have entered a "new age of conspiracy" or because prominent political elites promote conspiracy theories.[4] Rather, in light of the new ambiguity between traditional ideology and conspiracy theorizing, the recent focus on conspiracy thinking by social scientists provides us with an opportunity to explore a phenomenon that many have long ignored: political suspicion or skepticism, which drives conspiracy thinking and other non-ideological disruptive political attitudes. In this way, conspiracy thinking is more than merely believing in conspiracy theories—it is a common, significant feature of American public opinion that reaches far beyond any one conspiracy theory.

What is the role of conspiracy thinking in America? We highlight some of the answers to this question from recent academic studies on conspiracy thinking. Current research demonstrates:

1. Conspiracy theories and conspiracy theorists are pervasive.
2. Democrats and Republicans both hold conspiracy beliefs.
3. Measurement matters.

4. Conspiracy thinking is an ideology.
5. Conspiracy thinking is disruptive politics.

Conspiracy Theories and Conspiracy Theorists Are Pervasive

Who believes conspiracy theories? *Most* Americans! Rather than musings of a few tinfoil-hatted loons, conspiracy beliefs are quite prevalent among even "ordinary" individuals. Consider Figure 20.1. Over 55% of Americans believe in at least one conspiracy theory about the Iraq War, 9/11, Barack Obama's birthplace, the 2008 financial crisis, "chemtrails," George Soros, or energy-efficient lightbulbs.[5] Even among this small sample of conspiracy theories, many Americans believe in more than one. Approximately 27% of Americans believe two conspiracy theories, and 12% believe three or more.

Beliefs in some conspiracy theories also tend to persist over time, Figure 20.2 shows the average percentage of Americans who believe that Lee Harvey Oswald did not act alone in assassinating JFK. According to a host of polling houses, in 1963 about half of Americans believed that more than one person was involved in the assassination. That number climbs to 81% in 1976, remains stable through the early 2000s, and only begins to decline to about 60% in 2013, 50 years after the assassination. This means that more people today believe Lee Harvey Oswald did not act alone than did people in the weeks and years immediately following the assassination. In other words, looking at simply one salient conspiracy theory, we have evidence that somewhere between 50% and 80% of Americans believed in just this one conspiracy theory at any given time. Adding more conspiracy theories may well cover the entirety of the American population. Contrary to

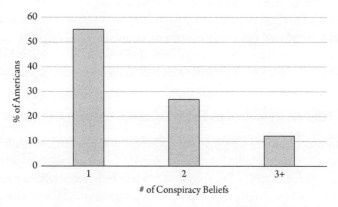

Figure 20.1. Percentage of Americans Who Believe in 1, 2, or 3 or More Conspiracy Theories. Source: Oliver and Wood, 2014.

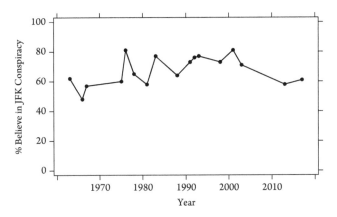

Figure 20.2. Average Belief that Lee Harvey Oswald Had Co-Conspirators in Assassinating JFK Over Time. Sources: ABC News, ABC/Washington Post, CBS News, CBS News/New York Times Poll, Gallup, Harris, Time/CNN/Yankelovich, Clancy Shulman.

narratives common in popular cultural and even journalistic circles, belief in conspiracy theories is common.

Democrats and Republicans Both Hold Conspiracy Beliefs

While most Americans may believe in at least one conspiracy theory, not all conspiracy theories are the same. People will accept or reject different conspiracy theories for reasons having to do with the content of the theory. Conspiracy theories cover myriad topics. The characteristics of a given conspiracy are presumably reflective of the motivations of its creator, and these characteristics increase the appeal and salience of the conspiracy theory for others who encounter it, assuming that motivations are shared between creator and endorser. The key point here is that motivation matters. We outline two general, and related, motivations below: ideological and partisan motivated reasoning, and feelings of political powerlessness.

Political Orientations Drive Belief in Conspiracy Theories

Certain factors do amplify, or at least publicize, the otherwise constant, low hum of American conspiracy talk. The most important factor driving conspiracy talk is political socialization and political context.[6] While conspiracy talk may respond to particularly shocking events (e.g., a presidential assassination), it is also driven by elites: If elites are saying it, chances are many others will, too.[7] Conspiracy talk is further driven by partisanship—an individual's psychological attachment to a political party.[8] Combined, levels of conspiracy theorizing can be substantially increased through political socialization (thinking in terms of Democrat and Republican).

Why would partisanship *increase* conspiracy beliefs? As many conspiracy theories are about salient partisan figures and groups, they are often adopted by partisans to discredit or otherwise impugn the integrity of their political opponents. Conspiracy theories implicating Democrats—regarding Barack Obama's birthplace and religious affiliation, for example—find higher levels of support among individuals identified with the Republican Party.[9] The opposite is true of conspiracy theories that implicate Republicans, such as those about ties between Donald Trump's 2016 U.S. presidential campaign and the Russian government, the role of the Bush administration in planning 9/11, or the levee breaches in 2005 after Hurricane Katrina ravaged New Orleans.

From this perspective, belief in some prominent American political conspiracy theories is not indicative of unique innate psychological processes, but rather familiar political gamesmanship. Partisans hold, for instance, that the out-party and members of the out-party's electoral coalition are more likely to conspire against the rest of us, regardless of any specific conspiratorial act. For example, Figure 20.3 presents differences in the groups that Republicans and Democrats are most likely to view as potential "conspirators." The black dots represent the proportion of Republicans who see the associated group along the vertical axis as a conspirator minus the proportion of Democrats who believe as much. Democrats are more likely to view Republicans and corporations as potential conspirators, while Republicans are more likely to view

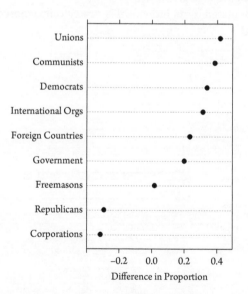

Figure 20.3. Difference in the Proportion of Republicans and Democrats Who Believe that the Following Groups are Likely to "Conspire against the Rest of Us." Source: 2012 Cooperation Congressional Election Study.

Democrats, communists, and labor unions as potential conspirators.[10] The difference between partisans is not *whether* someone is out there plotting against the rest of us, but rather *who* those conspirators are.

Partisan political conspiracy theories function more like typical partisan attitudes than beliefs in other conspiracy theories do because partisan dividing lines are rigid. Figure 20.4 presents several different conspiracy theories by partisanship. For example, the idea that global warming is a hoax, a belief many more Republicans hold than Democrats, stems from strategic partisan considerations rather than the tendency to view the world in conspiratorial terms. That is, partisans hold these beliefs because they are motivated to intentionally discredit opponents or to further their own partisan interests, not because they are "conspiratorial."

Thus, partisan motivations can help explain why people believe in conspiracy theories: Believing that corporations are evil and secretly control the world is what it means to be a Democrat; believing that the communists are around every corner is what it means to be a Republican. In this way, the partisan content of a conspiracy theory—especially the central partisan figure or group impugned by the conspiracy theory or harmed by the conspirators—may trigger a set of subconscious psychological mechanisms: *cognitive dissonance* and *motivated reasoning*.[11] When individuals are confronted with new information incongruent with previously held beliefs (e.g., a Democrat coming across positive information about a corporation's recent attempts to go "green"), they experience mental discomfort called cognitive dissonance.[12] One method of reducing this mental discomfort is through motivated reasoning, a subconscious psychological process whereby the information encountered by an individual is strategically ignored, avoided, or otherwise discredited.

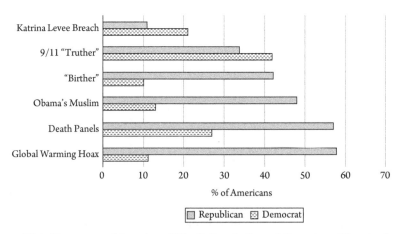

Figure 20.4. Percentage of Americans Who Believe in Several Conspiracy Theories, by Partisanship. Sources: 2012/2016 American National Election Study, Public Policy.

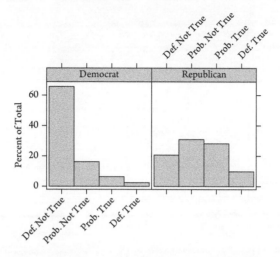

Figure 20.5. Distribution of Beliefs in "Birther" Conspiracy by Partisanship. Source: 2012 American National Election Study.

In short, where other predispositions, orientations, and attitudes—such as authoritarianism, paranormal beliefs, anomie, or distrust—may *correlate* with beliefs in particular conspiracy theories, they do not *determine* those beliefs. This is not the case with partisanship. When clear, salient partisan groups or figures lie at the center of a conspiracy theory, partisanship causes belief in a conspiracy theory.

This is easily demonstrated by noticing that belief in particular conspiracy theories are largely restricted to members of only one party. Looking at Figure 20.5, which is a breakdown of the birther conspiracy beliefs by partisanship, Democrats, for instance, simply do not believe in the birther conspiracy theory. Over 60% of Democrats say that the idea that Barack Obama was born outside the United States is "definitely not true." Republicans, however, are much more supportive of the conspiracy theory. Indeed, nearly half of Republicans think that Obama was "probably" or "definitely" born outside of the United States. Simply put: partisanship drives belief in many conspiracy theories.

We can obtain additional nuance in the relationship between partisanship and conspiracy belief by considering the *strength* of partisan attachments. In Figure 20.6, we plot the distribution of "birther" beliefs by partisanship and strength of attachments. As the strength of partisan attachments increases among Republicans, the distribution of birther beliefs shifts from exhibiting a positive skew (for "leaners" and "weak" Republican identifiers) to exhibiting a negative skew (for "strong" identifiers). Indeed, more than 50% of "strong" Republicans believe the birther conspiracy theory is probably or definitely true, whereas less than 40% of Republican "leaners" believe the same. Thus, not only does the "direction" of partisan orientations matter, but so too does the strength of individual attachments

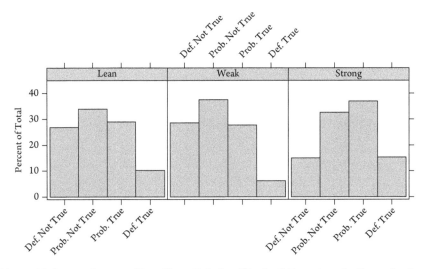

Figure 20.6. Distribution of Republican Beliefs in "Birther" Conspiracy by Strength of Attachment to the Republican Party. Source: 2012 American National Election Study.

to the political parties. The stronger the attachments to the major political parties, the more likely individuals are to receive strategic elite communications about conspiracy theories, and the more likely individuals are able to make sense of partisan cues at the center of conspiracy theories.[13] In other words, the more partisan one is, the more likely they will be to engage in the partisan motivated reasoning that promotes conspiracy belief.

Conspiracy Theories Are for Losers

Feelings of powerlessness and marginalization can also explain individuals' predispositions toward conspiracy thinking. Partisans, often committed to winning an election, can also display feelings of powerlessness. In this way, partisanship itself may be a leading cause for a sense of powerlessness: when a party loses an election, members of that party are more susceptible to conspiracy theorizing as a rationale for that loss.[14]

In the 2016 presidential election, Republican Donald J. Trump won the Electoral College yet failed to win the popular vote by almost three million votes. Figure 20.7 shows the difference in conspiracy thinking between Democrats and Republicans before and after the election. Before the election, Democrats and Republicans were indistinguishable from one another. After the election, however, Republicans became *less* conspiratorial, while Democrats became more conspiratorial. As Nyhan notes, "Just as Republicans disproportionately endorsed prominent misperceptions during the Obama years (like the birther and death panel myths), Democrats are

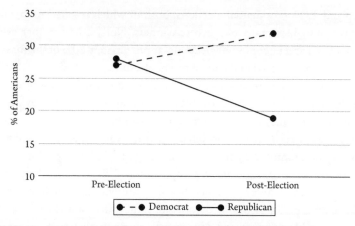

Figure 20.7. Percentage of Americans Agreeing to General Conspiratorial Predisposition Survey Items Before and After 2016 U.S. Presidential Election, by Partisanship. Source: *New York Times.*

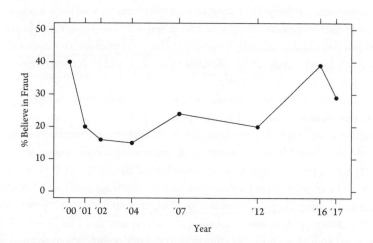

Figure 20.8. Average Belief that the Most Recent Election Was Stolen, or that Fraud Was Involved. Sources: ABC News, CNN/Opinion Research Corporation, Farleigh Dickinson University, Gallup/CNN/USA Today, Quinnipiac University.

now the opposition partisans especially likely to fall victim to dubious claims about the Trump administration."[15] Now that Democrats are out of power, their feelings of powerlessness—being the "loser"—have increased. In other words, one factor driving conspiracy beliefs in America is American democracy: Elections have winners and losers, and the losers tend to endorse conspiracy theories.

In Figure 20.8 we plot the proportion of individuals who believe that the most recent election (restricted to national elections) was stolen or that fraud was involved. We observe sharp increases in the proportion of fraud beliefs following the 2000 and 2016 presidential elections, both of which resulted in incongruent popular vote and Electoral College vote winners. Note, however, that even after non-presidential and uncontested elections, approximately 20% of the mass public believes fraud was involved in the most recent election.

What do accusations or beliefs about electoral fraud tell us about conspiracy thinking in America? Whereas motivated reasoning is a *subconscious* psychological mechanism that may drive belief in some conspiracy theories, partisans can be *consciously* motivated to assert conspiracy theories, too. Indeed, some conspiracy theories may be promoted by partisan elites as part of a "strategic logic" to make the out-party look bad or shore up allied opposition.[16] The fact that partisans "own" particular conspiracy theories—much like they are willing to cede ownership of particular public policy issues in theories of issue ownership (e.g., Republicans and the military, Democrats and education)—suggests that partisan conspiracy theories are partisan messages or communication strategies rather than markers of psychopathology or a predisposition to view the world in conspiratorial terms.[17] Furthermore, partisans recognize which parties are the frequent promulgators of a given conspiracy theory. For example, approximately 86% of Republicans recognize the birther conspiracy theory as associated with the Republican Party, even though few Republicans actually believe it.[18] The same goes for a conspiracy theory about "death panels" in the 2010 Affordable Care Act, and global warming as a hoax perpetrated by nefarious scientists.

Even the influence of partisanship on specific conspiracy beliefs can be partially explained by power dynamics. The "conspiracy theories are for losers" theory holds that partisans will support conspiracy theories that malign members of the out-party, and that these kinds of conspiracy theories will pervade among members of the party not in power.[19] That is to say, members of the party not in power (admittedly an issue of perception) are more likely to construct and spread conspiracy theories impugning the party in power as an attempt to both regain power and explain their losses. But, nonpartisan individuals can also feel like "losers." Indeed, Edelson and colleagues find that conspiratorial thinking predicts individual beliefs that fraud has affected election outcomes, even controlling for partisanship.[20] Perceptions of loser status can stem from predispositions, orientations, and characteristics beyond partisan affiliations. Yet, in America, partisanship is a particularly salient identity regardless of other sociodemographic characteristics, which also has intuitive connections with politics and implications for political outcomes.

Measurement Matters

As with all matters of scientific inquiry, measurement matters. When it comes to conspiracy beliefs, the most practical and popular method of assessment is survey questions about specific conspiracy theories. Academics, pundits, pollsters, and members of the media often conduct surveys to measure beliefs in conspiracy theories. The goal, of course, is to draw generalizable, reliable, and valid inferences about American public opinion. When it comes to sensitive topics like conspiracy theories, at least three elements of survey questions can influence the substantive inferences about the nature and level of conspiracy beliefs that we might make using such survey questions: (1) the conspiracy theory queried; (2) the question wording, especially the presence (absence) of partisan or political stimuli; and (3) the response options.

Specific Conspiracy Theories

While conspiracy theories surround all types of major sociopolitical events (e.g., wars, mass shootings, terror attacks, policy changes), sectors of society (e.g., pharmaceutical companies, political regimes, corporations, international organizations), and topics (e.g., vaccinations, GMOs, public policies, plane crashes), not all conspiracy theories are created alike. Conspiracy theories about the moon landing, for instance, are quite different than conspiracy theories about so-called death panels in the Affordable Care Act of 2010. While the former is well known and exists to explain a major cultural event, it does not receive much support by the mass public. Only approximately 6% of Americans believe that the moon landing was faked. In contrast, approximately 40% of Americans believe a "death panels" provision definitely or probably exists in Obamacare. On the one hand, choosing simply the most salient or popular conspiracy theories might further diminish the reliability of the estimates, since theories like a faked moon landing or a flat earth are not widely believed. Yet, on the other hand, choosing popular political conspiracy theories may drastically inflate the estimate of conspiracy thinking because it is tapping into partisan motivations and ideological reasoning—not conspiracy thinking. The question of which conspiracy beliefs to measure is a difficult one that does not have an easy answer.

Question Wording

Not only does choosing the specific conspiracy theory potentially influence our findings, but so too does question wording. First, questions may have partisan political cues in questions about conspiracy theories, which play a particularly large and measurable role in altering our estimation of conspiracy beliefs. Though the moon landing was associated with the Kennedy administration and was certainly a major political event, major partisan or ideological divisions are not cued by moon landing conspiracy theories like they are with regard to death panel conspiracy theories, for instance. Survey questions about death panel beliefs mention the Affordable Care Act (or, "Obamacare"), cueing partisan affect toward Obama and Democrats. It is precisely stimuli in the form of various political actors (Barack Obama vs. George W. Bush), political regimes (Republican vs. Democratic control), and economic conditions (good vs. bad economy) that can alter conspiracy theory beliefs on surveys. Indeed, questions designed this way—employing partisan stimuli—elicit something approaching a standard partisan attitude rather than a belief in an elaborate plot on the part of a few powerful individuals toward the end of self-gain or mass oppression.

We provide an example of the power of partisan stimuli in Figure 20.9. In a survey experiment fielded in 2016 on Amazon's Mechanical Turk crowdsourcing platform, we randomly assigned respondents to an experimental condition with one of two possible partisan stimuli embedded in a question about the Jade Helm 15 conspiracy theory.[21] Each respondent was confronted with the same base question:

Some people believe that Jade Helm 15, a U.S. military training exercise which was ordered by President [Obama/Bush], was a scheme to

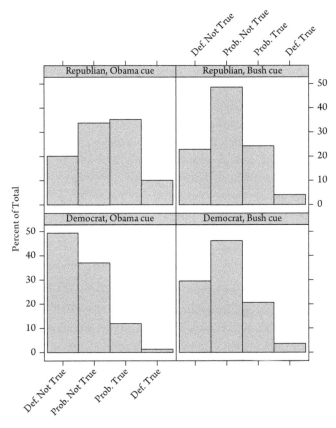

Figure 20.9. Distribution of Beliefs in Jade Helm Conspiracy Theory for Those Told that Bush Was Perpetrator and Those Told that Obama was the Perpetrator, by Partisanship. Source: 2016 Amazon MTurk data collected by authors.

confiscate firearms from law-abiding citizens. Others do not believe this. What do you think?

Some respondents received the version of the question where George W. Bush was the Jade Helm 15 perpetrator, an externally invalid question since this conspiracy theory was developed in 2015 with respect to Barack Obama. Other respondents received the version of the question implicating Obama.

In Figure 20.9, the distribution of responses to the Jade Helm 15 questions are broken down by the partisanship of the respondent and experimental partisan cue (Obama, Bush). Considering the top row first, we can see that Republicans who received the Obama cue were more likely than Republicans who received the Bush cue to respond that the Jade Helm 15 conspiracy theory was definitely or probably true. Conversely, Democrats who received the Obama cue were less likely than those Democrats who received the Bush cue to respond that Jade Helm 15 was definitely or probably true. Put another way, Democrats were more likely to endorse the Jade Helm 15 conspiracy theory when Bush was the perpetrator than when Obama was the perpetrator, and vice versa for Republicans.

This example neatly underscores the power of partisan cues in questions about conspiracy beliefs. Even when a conspiracy theory is not, in reality, associated with a particular figure or group, just as Jade Helm 15 has nothing to do with George W. Bush, such stimuli are still capable of manipulating stated conspiracy beliefs on surveys. The details of a conspiracy theory *in reality* are, then, not as important as the details of a conspiracy theory *as presented* to survey respondents.

Second, the cues about the motivations behind a perceived conspiracy may affect survey responses. Consider, for example, Figure 20.10, which presents two questions about the Sandy Hook conspiracy theory. The first question references a more open-ended "political agenda" as a potential motivation, while the second question explicitly references "gun control." This is similar to the differences in asking about "Area 51" and general belief in extraterrestrial life.[22] The differences in recorded belief could be due to the difference in question wording, particularly the types of considerations that certain words cue respondents to make in considering their beliefs about a given conspiracy theory. Thus, the particular words in questions about conspiracy beliefs have the potential to complicate our understanding about the distribution of conspiracy beliefs and our ability to make valid inferences about the greater population.

Response Sets

Finally, observed conspiracy beliefs are highly sensitive to the responses available to survey respondents. In most of the conspiracy belief questions we have considered in detail thus far, respondents are provided with four response options: "definitely true," "probably true," "probably not true," and "definitely not true." The important

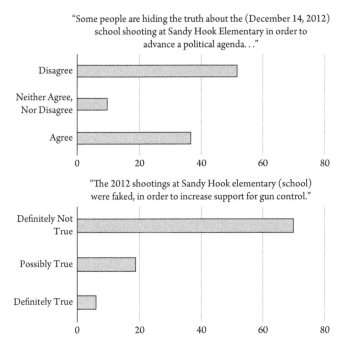

Figure 20.10. Distribution of Beliefs in Sandy Hook Conspiracy Theory by Different Question Wording and Response Options. Sources: 2013, 2016 Farleigh Dickinson University's Public Mind Poll.

feature of this measurement strategy is that it allows for varying levels of certainty. One must neither be completely tethered to a conspiracy theory nor forced to wholeheartedly reject it. Rather, respondents are allowed to express direction-ality (belief vs. nonbelief) and uncertainty (probably vs. definitely). Hence, this strategy has the potential to elicit more information from respondents than simpler strategies.

Consider the significant differences in the two poll results in Figure 20.11. Conspiracy theory questions on less scientific polls—the kinds of polls conducted by major news outlets or other commercial polling houses—oftentimes provide respondents with fewer choices. With many of these questions, respondents must simply choose whether they believe or don't believe a given conspiracy theory. There are a number of undesirable consequences of this type of measurement strategy. First, most people are simply not completely sure about many attitudes about main-stream political objects, let alone about conspiracy theories. Forcing respondents to choose belief or disbelief will result, for some individuals, in responses that do not accurately reflect their true attitudes, or cause other individuals to fail to answer the survey question (i.e., by refusing to provide a response, or saying "don't know/ unsure"). Notice in Figure 20.11 the differences in conspiratorial beliefs about the

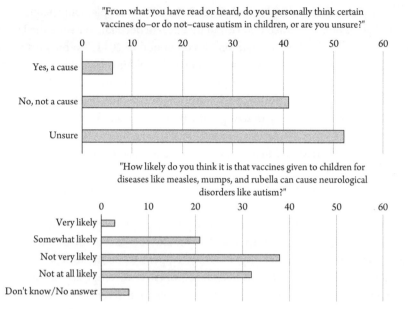

Figure 20.11. Distribution of Beliefs in the Conspiracy Theory about the Link between Vaccines and Autism by Different Response Options. Source: Gallup Poll, CBS News Poll.

link between childhood vaccines and autism across the two surveys. The dichotomous choices present respondents with a stark choice between affirming and denying a conspiracy theory, while the other survey presents degrees of (dis)belief. The former method overstates the difference significantly.

Second, the former measurement strategy is incongruent with scholarly consensus on the nature of conspiratorial thinking—the latent predisposition that (partially) causes specific conspiracy beliefs. As we will discuss below, conspiracy thinking is continuous, not dichotomous. We are all prone to conspiracy thinking to some extent; conspiracy thinking is a matter of degree. Since we know that conspiracy thinking is not as simple as "true" or "false," it follows that we should not treat specific conspiracy theories in such a dichotomous, black and white manner.

Conspiratorial Thinking Is an Ideology

One might believe that conspiracy theories about governmental malfeasance and control of information are unrelated, since one could assume that people believe in conspiracy theories based on the content of those conspiracy theories.[23] However, recent research shows that, aside from partisan motivations, the strongest predictor for believing a conspiracy theory is believing in another conspiracy theory—even if the conspiracy theories are logically inconsistent. For example, some people believe both that Osama bin Laden is alive and that he had been killed before the U.S. military shot and killed him in a raid on his compound in 2011.[24] While to some this contradiction may demonstrate that people often hold incoherent beliefs, to others it suggests that an underlying predisposition toward conspiracy thinking drives conspiracy beliefs. As the prevalence of conspiracy beliefs among the American mass public suggests, conspiracy thinking—the predisposition to see the world in conspiratorial terms—is a widely shared individual characteristic that leads individuals to impose conspiratorial intent, action, or general structure on the major political phenomena they observe.

According to the tradition started by the *American Voter*, an "ideology" is a cognitive structure with abstract ideas that help order otherwise unordered objects.[25] The most salient ideological dimension in American politics is the familiar liberal–conservative or left–right dimension. We should note that an ideology is the cognitive structure, and the left–right variety happens to be the most parsimonious variant. Party identification and liberal–conservative ideology are classic and empirically validated mechanisms by which people filter information about politics and integrate that information into a psychological structure of beliefs that guide future reasoning in making political decisions, and future motivations in engaging in political behaviors.[26]

Conspiracy thinking, too, is an "ideology."[27] Though core ideas about the nature and role of government in society are most frequently thought to be guided by one's partisan and ideological orientations, this might not be the case for some highly conspiratorial Americans. Rather, such fundamental ideas about government are likely guided more by a heated suspicion toward authority and a desire to distance oneself from the potentially oppressive powers of that authority. Just as liberal and conservative principles do, conspiratorial thinking provides structure to the political world. Some even liken it to narrative reasoning about unfolding events—a method for constructing a reality where clandestine, nefarious groups are exerting power over others for their own benefit or amusement.[28]

More than a new substantive type of belief system that many individuals possess, however, conspiracy thinking is at odds with traditional forms of political constraint in the American political context. Though specific conspiracy beliefs—especially about salient partisan groups and objects—are the joint product of conspiratorial thinking and partisan motivations, these psychological antecedents of conspiracy beliefs are, themselves, unrelated.[29] In other words, Democrats are no more predisposed to view the world in conspiratorial terms than are Republicans, even though partisanship may drive them to believe in different conspiracy theories.

Though we do not wish to claim that everyone is a conspiracy theorist, we suggest that most individuals evince some of the characteristics that ultimately promote specific conspiracy beliefs. In this way, those who believe conspiracy theories are not necessarily psychotic, alienated "nut jobs." Rather, they are individuals who submit to the same psychological biases and possess the same orientations toward government and authority that many people do. Moreover, being a "conspiracy theorist" should be thought of as a continuous rather than a dichotomous trait: it not the case that some are and others are not conspiratorial; rather, everyone is more or less conspiratorial.[30] This makes defining who is a conspiracy theorist difficult, though it should be clear that Americans believe conspiracy theories for many reasons, few of which are inherently unreasonable.

Conspiracy Thinking Is Disruptive Politics

With recent major elections across the world characterized by heavily populist sentiments, a seeming infiltration of conspiracy theories into mainstream political rhetoric, and record low trust in government, times seem ripe for fuller investigations of how people think about politics and how these ideas translate into political action. The picture of the effects of conspiracy thinking on American political behavior is not pretty: conspiracy theorists are likely to be more politically extreme, more supportive of violence, participate less in electoral politics, and shy away from supporting mainstream candidates.[31] In other words, conspiracy thinking clearly has the potential to be very disruptive to the status quo and traditional, normative beliefs.

Figure 20.12 shows the probability that someone wants to overturn gun control laws by level of conspiracy thinking, controlling for other traditional political predispositions like partisanship and ideology. The story from this figure

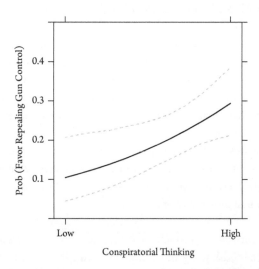

Figure 20.12. Predicted Probability of Favoring the Repeal of Gun Control Laws as Conspiratorial Thinking Increases. Source: 2014 Cooperative Congressional Election Study.

is clear: People high in conspiracy thinking are more likely to resist gun control laws, showing that conspiracy thinking is not simply about believing in conspiracy theories but has significant other effects on other political attitudes and behaviors.

Theoretically, how does conspiracy thinking relate to disruptive politics? Typically, Americans orient their political thinking through their partisanship and ideology, which implies that individuals have two independent but related considerations possible at any time: commitment to the group, but also a potential withdrawal of that commitment. As the authors of the *American Voter* note, "This is not to say that [the average American voter] could never be jarred from these loyalties. Quite to the contrary, we must suppose that he remains a perceiving, evaluating individual with a healthy suspicion."[32] At the core of the average American voter's ideology is not necessarily the familiar left–right abstract concepts (which they get only by proxy of their group attachments), but a "healthy suspicion" that may at times lead the individual to actually suspend their psychological commitment to that group altogether. In other words, Americans often have two simultaneous psychological processes unfolding at the same time: partisan or ideological reasoning and political suspicion, or what we have called *conspiracy thinking*.

While being high on the conspiracy scales is often correlated with extreme behaviors that can be considered disruptive, the real issue moving forward is this: Political suspicion or conspiracy thinking is a matter of degree—while there are bad consequences at either end of the spectrum (too much and too little suspicion), there is seemingly a "healthy suspicion" in the middle somewhere. The line between healthy and unhealthy suspicion is constantly being negotiated in political life, making it very difficult to empirically trace. Yet, political suspicion of some kind is necessary, especially in American politics. As Samuel Huntington argued, American political life is best understood in light of an "antipower ethic":

> In the United States, however, awareness of power induces suspicion, hostility, and outrage. Because of the prevalence of the antipower ethic, awareness of power breeds its own reduction and hidden power is more effective. Because power is less legitimate in the United States than in other cultures, greater efforts have to be made to obscure it. It becomes necessary to deny the facts of power in order to preserve those facts. Yet the opportunities and the pressures to expose and publicize power pervade American public life. Consequently, because its visibility is its greatest vulnerability, the most effective exercise of power is the concealment of power; to cover up power is the first imperative of power.[33]

Upon observing the extent to which most Americans were preoccupied with "moralistic themes like mudslinging and chicanery" and a thorough political "cynicism" that politicians are "slick," the authors of *The American Voter* concluded that the mass public generally lacks a sophisticated understanding of politics. However, for

Huntington, these attitudes are not evidence for a lack of understanding of American politics, but (albeit crude) expressions of the "antipower ethic."[34] For Huntington, there is a recognition—a healthy suspicion—in the American public that things are not what they seem, and that most of us must be ready to evaluate the world on our own terms. This is why in the American political environment "in which secrecy is salvationary, conspiracy theories are heuristically indispensable."[35] Far from being a product of a diseased psychopathology, conspiracy thinking plays a functional role in our everyday American political lives.

As Barack Obama, himself the victim of numerous conspiracy theories, noted: "This notion of a conspiracy out there, it gets wrapped up in concerns about the federal government. Now, there's a long history of that. That's in our DNA. The United States was born suspicious of some distant authority."[36] On this point Obama is right: Americans are a suspicious lot. Conspiracy thinking and political suspicion are not accidental or new to American politics, but rather among its essential ingredients.

Conclusion

Conspiracy thinking is a common political ideology in American politics. It helps individuals sort through information, make sense of the world around them. In American politics there are two traditional ways individuals sort political information: liberal–conservative ideology and Democratic–Republican partisanship. Conspiracy theories and partisanship may seem to go hand in hand at times: Republicans believe the birther conspiracy theory, Democrats believe that 9/11 was an inside job. But while we know that conspiracy theories may be adopted and deployed for political purposes, the precise relationship between conspiracy thinking on the one hand, and these more traditional political modes of thinking on the other, has only recently been investigated.

There are many promising and normatively important tracks for future research on American conspiracy theories to take. First, the concept of conspiratorial thinking as an ideology or a distinct political orientation should be considered more fully. Conspiracy thinking is not simply about believing in conspiracy theories. Instead, as a more comprehensive worldview, we should understand conspiracy thinking to be a distinct mode of thought—a belief system that stands in contrast to liberal–conservative principles or Democratic–Republican partisanship. Political scientists and psychologists have spent too much time examining traditional political modes of thinking and not enough time on the exceptional modes of thinking that nevertheless exist among the American mass public. This narrow view on establishing the (admittedly substantial) role of traditional left–right ideology and partisanship in explaining and understanding American political behavior is undoubtedly important, until it is not, like in 2016. Scholars should guard against complacency in the age of polarization by studying where partisanship and ideology fail, and not dismiss this failure as ignorance.

Second, the deployment of conspiracy theories by elites in political communications should receive more attention. Regardless of the sincerity of, or motivations behind, elite propagation of conspiracy theories, it appears that conspiracy theories are at least capable of being used to send signals to electoral bases and mobilize support.[37] The media by which these signals are sent, characteristics of those who receive and fail to receive such messages, and the precise electoral effects of such messages all require investigation.

Finally, the future research should more carefully consider the broader role of conspiracy thinking in American political culture, particularly with respect to related constructs such as (dis)trust and polarization. While elite polarization has been steadily increasing since the 1960s and trust in government has been declining, some attempts at estimating conspiracy thinking over time reveal a relatively stable time series, despite recent popular attention to conspiracy theories. Both the indirect nature of the data employed for estimating conspiracy thinking and the theoretical opacity regarding the structural relationships between conspiracism, trust, and polarization may be the culprit. Thus, researchers should think more clearly about their choices during the design of their research, so that their data collection efforts comport with their theory and to the cultural component of conspiracy thinking.

Notes

1. Freeman, Daniel, and Jason Freeman. 2017. "Are We Entering a Golden Age of the Conspiracy Theory?" *The Guardian*. https://www.theguardian.com/science/blog/2017/mar/28/are-we-entering-a-golden-age-of-the-conspiracy-theory (Accessed December 18, 2017).
2. Cillizza, Chris. 2017. "Donald Trump Was a Conspiracy-Theory Candidate. Now He's on the Edge of Being a Conspiracy-Theory President." *The Washington Post*. https://www.washingtonpost.com/news/the-fix/wp/2017/03/04/donald-trump-was-a-conspiracy-theory-candidate-now-hes-on-the-verge-of-being-a-conspiracy-theory-president/?utm_term=.bb2c4993027e (Accessed December 18, 2017); Uscinski, Joseph E. 2016. "Will Trump Become Conspiracy Theorist in Chief?" *Newsweek*. http://www.newsweek.com/trump-become-conspiracy-theorist-chief-442847 (Accessed December 18, 2017).
3. Chait, Jonathan. 2017. "Donald Trump Has Finally Erased the Line Between Conservatism and Conspiracy Theories." *New York Magazine*. http://nymag.com/daily/intelligencer/2017/08/trump-erases-the-line-between-conservatism-and-conspiracy.html (Accessed December 18, 2017).
4. Uscinski, Joseph E., and Joseph M. Parent. 2014. *American Conspiracy Theories*. Oxford: Oxford University Press.
5. Oliver, J. Eric, and Thomas J. Wood. 2014. "Conspiracy Theories and the Paranoid Styles(s) of Mass Opinion." *American Journal of Political Science* 58(4): 952–966.
6. Uscinski and Parent, *American Conspiracy Theories*.
7. Smallpage, Steven M., Adam M. Enders, and Joseph E. Uscinski. 2017. "The Partisan Contours of Conspiracy Theory Beliefs." *Research and Politics* 4(4): 1–7. DOI: 10.1177/2053168017746554.

8. Enders, Adam M., Steven M. Smallpage, and Robert N. Lupton. Forthcoming. "Are All 'Birthers' Conspiracy Theorists? On the Relationship Between Conspiratorial Thinking and Political Orientations." *British Journal of Political Science*; Miller, Joanne M., Kyle L. Saunders, and Christina E. Farhart. 2016. "Conspiracy Endorsement as Motivated Reasoning: The Moderating Roles of Political Knowledge and Trust." *American Journal of Political Science* 60(4): 824–844.

9. Miller, Saunders, and Farhart, "Conspiracy Endorsement as Motivated Reasoning."

10. Smallpage, Enders, and Uscinski, "The Partisan Contours of Conspiracy Theory Beliefs."

11. Taber, Charles S., and Milton Lodge. 2006. "Motivated Skepticism in the Evaluation of Political Beliefs." *American Journal of Political Science* 50(3): 755–769.

12. Festinger, Leon. 1957. *A Theory of Cognitive Dissonance*. Stanford: Stanford University Press.

13. Smallpage, Enders, and Uscinski, "The Partisan Contours of Conspiracy Theory Beliefs."

14. Uscinski and Parent, *American Conspiracy Theories*.

15. Nyhan, Brendan. 2017. "Why More Democrats Are Now Embracing Conspiracy Theories." *New York Times*. https://www.nytimes.com/2017/02/15/upshot/why-more-democrats-are-now-embracing-conspiracy-theories.html (Accessed December 29, 2017).

16. Uscinski and Parent, *American Conspiracy Theories*.

17. Petrocik, John R. 1996. "Issue Ownership in Presidential Elections, with a 1980 Case Study." *American Journal of Political Science* 40(3): 825–850.

18. Smallpage, Enders, and Uscinski, "The Partisan Contours of Conspiracy Theory Beliefs."

19. Uscinski and Parent, *American Conspiracy Theories*.

20. Edelson, Jack, Alexander Alduncin, Christopher Krewson, James A. Sieja, and Joseph E. Uscinski. 2017. "The Effect of Conspiratorial Thinking and Motivated Reasoning on Belief in Election Fraud." *Political Research Quarterly* 70(4): 933–946.

21. For details, see Enders, Adam M., and Steven M. Smallpage. 2018. "On the Measurement of Conspiracy Beliefs." *Research and Politics* January-March: 1–4.

22. Brotherton, Robert, Christopher C. French, and Alan D. Pickering. 2013. "Measuring Belief in Conspiracy Theories: The Generic Conspiracist Beliefs Scale." *Frontiers in Psychology* 4(May): 279. DOI: 10.3389/fpsyg.2013.00279.

23. Ibid.

24. Wood, Michael J., Karen M. Douglas, and Robbie M. Sutton. 2012. "Dead and Alive: Beliefs in Contradictory Conspiracy Theories." *Social Psychological and Personality Science* 3(6): 767–773.

25. Campbell, Angus, Philip E. Converse, Warren E. Miller, and Donald E. Stokes. 1960. *The American Voter*. New York: Wiley.

26. Ibid.

27. Oliver and Wood, "Conspiracy Theories and the Paranoid Styles(s) of Mass Opinion."

28. Hofstadter, Richard. 2008. *The Paranoid Style in American Politics*. Vintage Books; Raab, Marius Hans, Nikolas Auer, Stefan A. Ortlieb, and Claus-Christian Carbon. 2013. "The Sarrazin Effect: The Presence of Absurd Statements in Conspiracy Theories Makes Canonical Information Less Plausible." *Frontiers in Psychology* 4(July): 453. DOI: 10.3389/fpsyg.2013.00453.

29. Enders, Smallpage, and Lupton, "Are All 'Birthers' Conspiracy Theorists?"; Uscinski, Joseph E., Casey Klofstad, and Matthew D. Atkinson. 2016. "What Drives Conspiratorial Beliefs? The Role of Informational Cues and Predispositions." *Political Research Quarterly* 69(1): 57–71; Uscinski and Parent, *American Conspiracy Theories*.

30. Brotherton, French, and Pickering, "Measuring Belief in Conspiracy Theories: The Generic Conspiracist Beliefs Scale"; Bruder, Martin, Peter Haffke, Nina Nouripanah, and Roland Imhoff. 2013. "Measuring Individual Differences in Generic Beliefs in Conspiracy Theories across Cultures: The Conspiracy Mentality Questionnaire." *Frontiers in Psychology* 4(April). DOI: 10.3389/fpsyg.2013.00225; Uscinski and Parent, *American Conspiracy Theories*.

31. Jolley, Daniel, and Karen M. Douglas. 2014. "The Social Consequences of Conspiracism: Exposure to Conspiracy Theories Decreases Intentions to Engage in Politics and to Reduce One's Carbon Footprint." *British Journal of Psychology* 105(1): 35–56; Uscinski and Parent, *American Conspiracy Theories*; van Prooijen, Jan-Willem, Andre P. M. Krouwel, and Thomas V. Pollet. 2015. "Political Extremism Predicts Belief in Conspiracy Theories." *Social Psychological and Personality* Science 6(5): 570–578.

32. Campbell, Converse, Miller, and Stokes. 1960. *The American Voter*.

33. Huntington, Samuel P. 1983. *American Politics: The Promise of Disharmony.* Cambridge: Harvard University Press, 78.

34. Ibid., 242–244, 437.

35. Ibid., 79.

36. Enders, Adam M., and Steven M. Smallpage. 2016. "Obama was Right: Conspiracy Theorists are More Likely to Oppose Gun Control." [Blog] Monkey Cage. Available at https://www.washingtonpost.com/news/monkey-cage/wp/2016/01/19/obama-was-right-conspiracy-theorists-are-more-likely-to-oppose-gun-control/?utm_term=.ea822330d0aa   (Accessed December 29, 2017).

37. Smallpage, Enders, and Uscinski, "The Partisan Contours of Conspiracy Theory Beliefs."

21

How Conspiracy Theories Spread

DARIN DEWITT, MATTHEW D. ATKINSON, AND DREW WEGNER

Conspiracy theories are pervasive.[1] But only a few gain currency among a wide swath of the population. As Cass R. Sunstein argues, in *Conspiracy Theories and Other Dangerous Ideas*, "the key question is why some [conspiracy] theories take hold, while many more vanish into obscurity," and the answer to that question requires scholars to identify the "mechanisms that produce, sustain, and spread conspiracy theories."[2] Sunstein notes that this is a pressing issue as conspiracy theories "have become ubiquitous" and "easy to spread" in the Internet era.[3]

We respond to Sunstein's charge and propose four theoretical models from the social sciences that plausibly account for how conspiracy theories spread through society. At present, research into conspiracy theories tends to either gloss over the issue of theoretical mechanisms or uncritically assert that a particular mechanism explains propagation. In the latter case, scholars advance the herd behavior model, without presenting much justification, to explain how ideas of uncertain merit spread as a function of rational choices.[4] Herding is a convenient mechanism because it can account for the outcomes conspiracy theory scholars are trying to explain. However, just because a theory *can* explain a particular outcome does not mean that it *does*. As we will show, the process posited by the herd behavior mechanism does not accurately explain the spread of many widely studied conspiracy theories.[5] Thus, scholars must evaluate a wider range of models when considering the question of why particular conspiracies theories do or do not travel.

Social scientists have been criticized for being all too willing to endorse elegant theories that purport to explain significant outcomes of interest without scrutinizing whether the circumstances driving the outcome are consistent with the theoretical mechanism.[6] Nascent literature on conspiracy and the Internet is a case in point. While scholars document the diversity of information that people seek out and share, this information is not evaluated in light of theoretical models.[7] We seek to address this shortcoming by helping conspiracy theory researchers think more rigorously about empirically observable processes and the theoretical mechanisms through which they propagate. D. J. Flynn, Brendan

Nyhan, and Jason Reifler point out that we know far more about the individual psychology of conspiracy theory beliefs than the political communications structure through which these ideas spread.[8] We present four models that account for opinion formation and behavior. Our goal is not to render a verdict but to demonstrate the alternative processes that could be in play. For each model, we describe the underlying mechanism and discuss its empirically observable implications. Then, we introduce the logic of each model by presenting a simple, illustrative example. And, lastly, we argue why each model might plausibly account for how conspiracy theories spread.

Herd Behavior

Mechanism. Rational individuals with limited information will sometimes defer to crowd behavior and ignore private knowledge.

Illustrative Example

Imagine you are in line at the multiplex. You read a positive review for a family comedy, which suggests that watching this movie will be worthwhile. But you notice that everyone in front of you purchases a ticket for a brand-new action film. In turn, you might also buy a ticket for the action film, choosing to imitate others under the presumption that each person is making an independent judgment about which film to see on the basis of private information—newspaper review, word-of-mouth, prior screening, and so on. Since the wisdom of the crowd is that the action film is the best movie, it is rational to ignore your private information and follow the crowd.

But what if the people in front of you were not making choices based on their own independent information? In this case, while it still may be rational to follow the crowd, the wise crowd you intend to follow might, in fact, be a herd. For example, suppose the first two people in line see the action film because they won free tickets. This situation highlights three core features of herds. First, the collective wisdom of the crowd may rest on scant information. If subsequent ticket buyers disregard their private information and make decisions based on the actions of others, the sold out screening will be the result of no actual information regarding the film's quality. Second, herd-like behavior can lead people to make suboptimal choices. The choices of the first few people in line may lead others to ignore their private information and forego watching a movie they would likely enjoy. Finally, herds are fragile. Since herding rests on limited information, an individual later in the decision-making sequence can easily disperse the herd by publicly revealing new information (e.g., by announcing that early ticket buyers won free tickets).

Application to Conspiracy Theory

In both *Conspiracy Theories and Other Dangerous Ideas* and *On Rumors: How Falsehoods Spread, Why We Believe Them, and What Can Be Done*, Cass R. Sunstein posits that the herd behavior mechanism is the principal means by which conspiracy theories spread.[9] When applied to conspiracy theories, the herd behavior mechanism is driven by an effort to tap into the wisdom of crowds. You encounter a conspiracy theory and must decide if it is a good or bad idea. Your private information tells you to be skeptical, but you observe that many other people are talking about the conspiracy theory.[10] The prevalence of the idea and the willingness of so many people to express it in public suggests that there might be high-quality information out there supporting the conspiracy theory. As a result, you may abandon your private information—your innate skepticism of conspiracy theories—and begin to espouse the idea in public, too, and in turn your behavior may lead others to abandon their private information and adopt the conspiracy theory. As each person's adoption of the conspiracy theory is cumulatively viewed by others, the herd will continue to grow.

For example, the herd behavior model helps explain the evolution of attitudes toward genetically modified food. As Uscinski and Parent show, fringe leftists with anti-corporate inclinations believe that the need for and safety of genetically modified crops was fabricated by agricultural behemoths such as Monsanto and that GMO foods are unsafe.[11] In spite of broad scientific consensus to the contrary, the general idea that GMOs pose health risks spread to mainstream development and environmental organizations as well as approximately half of all Americans, including equal numbers of Democrats and Republicans.[12] This idea gained traction without any new scientific evidence to fuel the flames of GMO conspiracy theorists and without mainstream political elites picking sides.

As with any good theory, the herd behavior model of conspiracy theory dissemination posits a precise and falsifiable dynamic. Conspiracy theory dissemination based on herding follows a well-defined and specific process. Some conspiracy theories spread in a way that is consistent with the herding process (e.g., GMO skepticism), while others do not. Thus, the conditions under which herds are the appropriate explanation for conspiracy theory dissemination are explicit.

Herds form when individuals make decisions based on the actions of others. And in order for herd behavior to work with conspiracy theories in the same way it works for a stock market bubble or the opening-weekend box office success for a terrible action film, it would have to be the case that people knew nothing about the depth of the private information and beliefs of the collective. Individuals considering whether to accept or reject a conspiracy would need to have no contextual information about the individuals spreading conspiracy theories. When you observe both the actions of others as well as their private information, herds no longer develop. Once private information about conspiracy entrepreneurs is made public (for example, via Megyn Kelly's interview of Alex Jones), you do not ignore your private information. If the herd behavior mechanism is at play, we would expect that conspiracy theory dissemination should halt once contextual information is revealed.

According to the herd behavior dynamic, conspiracy theories should spread like wildfire when information is limited. For instance, Sunstein argues that conspiracy theories are more likely to travel in authoritarian regimes because, in the absence of a free press, citizens "have good reason to distrust all or most of the official denials they hear."[13] In such regimes, there is often no credible information to disperse the herd.

By contrast, consistent with the herd behavior model, Sunstein argues that "in an open society with a well-functioning marketplace of ideas and a free flow of information," individuals "are unlikely to distrust all knowledge-creating institutions" and, as a result, an infusion of new information will disperse the herd.[14] In fact, open societies should encourage the infusion of such information. The more a conspiracy theory attracts attention and the larger the herd becomes, the more incentive rival actors have to put forth disconfirming evidence. For example, President George W. Bush and the United States Congress created the 9/11 Commission, in part, to marshal evidence against truther conspiracies. This new public information disperses the herd—just like the release of Enron's financial information burst the stock market bubble.

Is it necessary to examine additional mechanisms? Yes. In reviewing the extant literature, Sunstein notices that, not infrequently, individuals ignore new information and continue subscribing to a dubious idea. In response, Sunstein heavily qualifies the herd behavior model and presents three additional conditions that must be met for new information to disperse the herd: "If those hearing the false rumor do not have strong motivations for accepting it, if they do not have a lot of prior knowledge, and if they trust those who are providing the correction, then corrections will dissipate false rumors."[15] Perhaps these qualifications are sufficient, but it is just as plausible that alternative models explain the dissemination of many conspiracy theories. It is a virtue of Sunstein's herding model that it is falsifiable. It works in some cases, such as the spread of anti-GMO conspiracy theories, but not in others such as the spread of the birther thesis.[16] We aspire to follow the same spirit of offering additional falsifiable mechanisms. And we implore conspiracy theory scholars to keep the full range of mechanisms in mind when exploring the dynamics of any particular conspiracy theory.

Follow-the-Leader

Mechanism. Individuals take cues from ideologically like-minded opinion leaders.

Illustrative Example

People use shortcuts to make sense of the larger world. According to political scientist John Zaller's follow-the-leader model of opinion formation, ordinary citizens do not evaluate the logic and evidence associated with political messages; rather, they evaluate a message's source and other contextual cues.[17] Therefore, perceived ideological compatibility and source credibility matter more than anything else when people evaluate new information. If a citizen perceives a source to be both credible and ideologically compatible, then messages encountered from that source are accepted and retained in memory for use in opinion formation. In contrast, if a source is judged to be either not credible or ideologically incompatible, then its messages will be rejected and not retained for use in opinion formation.

A simple example illustrates the intuition behind the follow-the-leader model. Suppose you follow a dining blog with a small but loyal readership. Each time the blog endorses a new restaurant, you are eager to try it. The blog tends to cover hot new restaurants that many people are keen to try and, as a result, it is often hard to reserve a table. However, in one instance something exceptional happens: you find it easy to book a table. While the Offal House restaurant opened with a rave review from your favorite blog, the buzz about town from early patrons is negative. Rumor has it that the food is slimy and funny looking. And when you arrive at the Offal House, you find that the restaurant is empty. But you notice that the pizza joint next door, which your favorite restaurant blog gave a lukewarm review, is packed. What do you do? Do you follow-the-leader by eating at Offal House and deferring to the blog's judgment? Or do you follow-the-herd and eat at the pizza joint, under the assumption that no one seems to like the Offal House and you will be no exception? The follow-the-leader model makes an unambiguous prediction: your dominant consideration about Offal House is the food blog's unqualified endorsement and, as such, you will dine at Offal House.

Application to Conspiracy Theory

The follow-the-leader dynamic makes two key assumptions. First, people passively process political information—that is, they do not think critically for themselves. Second, when people passively process information, source credibility drives opinion formation.

While political scientist Arthur Lupia has shown that follow-the-leader decision making can help citizens efficiently arrive at informed opinions, this approach to opinion formation lacks an inherent mechanism for neutralizing inaccurate information when dubious sources gain stature.[18] As a result, followers are led into a situation in which they lose touch with reality and access to objective points of reference—the informational equivalent of a house of carnival mirrors. Political science research has shown that many partisans prefer the funhouse mirror to reality—even when followers have ready access to accurate information, they will-fully choose to ignore it in deference to the leaders and political symbols with which they have formed an attachment.[19]

In the era of decentralized media, false information has better prospects for spreading through the follow-the-leader dynamic. For instance, in the concentrated media system of the late twentieth century, media outlets had an economic incentive to appeal to a mainstream audience and, therefore, they chose to proactively weed out fringe sources of all stripes.[20] In those days, citizens susceptible to fringe belief systems were deprived of ready access to purveyors of those belief systems unless they actively sought them out, which few citizens are inclined to do. Today's decentralized media landscape, by contrast, presents media organizations with a different incentive: pander to audiences and their prejudices.[21] While the media once functioned as a robust gatekeeper ensuring that only ideas compatible with the ideological establishment were transmitted, contemporary media no longer performs this gatekeeping role.

Although contemporary political communication is highly decentralized, the follow-the-leader dynamic anticipates that communication will nevertheless flow through a hub and spoke system. To gain substantial traction, a conspiracy theory must be endorsed by a major hub or it will not propagate. Some leaders serve as large hubs with enormous numbers of followers (e.g., Donald Trump and Barack Obama). When these types of leaders advocate an idea, no matter how dubious, millions of followers readily adapt their beliefs in response. Other leaders have smaller numbers of followers (e.g., Alex Jones), but these less prominent leaders may influence the messages coming out of larger hubs. For instance, when Fox News host Sean Hannity or President Donald Trump repeats one of Alex Jones's ideas, that idea gains widespread traction.

The mechanisms presented so far can be distinguished as follows: In the follow-the-leader dynamic, citizens look to specific leaders and parrot their beliefs, whereas citizens engaging in herd behavior look to see what other people in the larger crowd are doing. Consider the conspiracy theory that President Obama wiretapped Trump Tower. In that case, several informed experts came forward to dispel the rumor, but the rumor persisted. This persistence cannot be explained by efforts to follow crowd wisdom. Rather, it persisted because some individuals accepted Trump's argument that the dispelling authorities were in on the conspiracy—in other words, they followed the leader. In the real world, evidence of which mechanism is at play is usually confounded at any given point in time. In this way, conspiracy theories are like crowded restaurants—it is hard to determine whether a restaurant's success is due to its perceived popularity (herd behavior) or its strong reviews (follow-the-leader). Fortunately, by taking propagation mechanisms seriously, conspiracy theory researchers can begin to disentangle confounding evidence by looking at the spread of conspiracy theories over time. Opinion driven by the follow-the-leader and herd behavior mechanisms may look the same at one snapshot in time; but the patterns of growth will be different over time, with herd behavior exhibiting a reinforcing dynamic of exponential growth, and follow-the-leader exhibiting more punctuated jumps that coincide with the timing of messages disseminating from major communication hubs.[22] For instance, when President Lyndon Johnson's Commission on the Assassination of President Kennedy issued its verdict that Lee Harvey Oswald, acting alone, assassinated the president, Gallup found that aggregate support for that idea jumped from 29 to 87 percent.[23]

Preference Falsification

Mechanism. Individuals will hide their support for an unpopular belief until a critical mass of like-minded people creates a sense of safety in numbers by publicly advocating the idea.

Illustrative Model

Timur Kuran's preference falsification model explains why individuals publicly endorse unpopular ideas and how such ideas snowball.[24] In the canonical example, an individual is deciding whether to publicly support or oppose her country's dictatorial regime. Suppose that an individual's private preference is to oppose the regime. In choosing a public preference, she looks to public opinion. If public opinion is uniformly in favor of the dictatorship, she will be reluctant to express her opposition because she expects social disapproval. In such cases, she will likely engage in preference falsification and misrepresent her private preference. However, as public opinion moves against the dictatorship, the danger associated with expressing opposition views decline. Each person has a political threshold—a level of public support where she feels safety in numbers and switches her public preference from rejecting to accepting the unorthodox idea. A political event that leads one new person to express the unpopular idea may provide enough safety for others with low thresholds to follow, which in turn may inspire those with moderate thresholds. The resulting bandwagon will surprise, because while each individual knows their own private preference and threshold, the distribution of private preferences and thresholds in society are unknown.

Preference falsification helps explain communist and Arab revolutions. For instance, in Egypt, a bandwagon occurred in 2011, ousting President Mubarak after 29 years in office. In 2011, anti-regime beliefs propagated because protestors concentrated their activities in Tahrir Square, a famous public landmark.[25] Other Egyptians, through media and personal visits, could accurately assess the size of public opposition and determine when their political threshold was met. In short, "millions were prepared to stand up in defiance if they ever sensed that this was sufficiently safe."[26]

Application to Conspiracy Theories

The preference falsification dynamic is relevant to conspiracy theory politics if two conditions are met: individuals privately hold conspiratorial beliefs and social pressure prevents public expression of these conspiratorial beliefs. The masses view politics through their group attachments, organizing social groups into the categories of friend and foe.[27] This maps onto a conspiratorial mindset: According to political psychologists Donald Kinder and Nathan Kalmoe, antagonism toward out-groups is "the most powerful force" shaping public opinion and is activated when out-groups benefit at the expense in-groups.[28] Social norms inhibit the expression of out-group hostility in the form of conspiracy theories.[29] Yet, when people perceive the possibility of safety in numbers, they are more willing to reveal their private preferences, and conspiracy theories can spread. Of course, as Joseph Uscinski, Casey Klofstad, and Matthew Atkinson show, individuals vary in their political threshold for expressing conspiratorial beliefs.[30] In short, it is highly plausible that conspiratorial beliefs bubble below the surface of American politics and have prospects for rapidly breaking out.

Mark Fenster's account of the 9/11 truth movement, which informs our discussion below, is consistent with a preference falsification dynamic.[31] In 2004, the 9/11 Commission, created by President George W. Bush and the United States Congress, issued its report arguing that Osama bin Laden's al-Qaeda organization coordinated the terrorist attacks targeting the World Trade Center and the Pentagon. Individuals skeptical of the official government report began to coalesce around an alternative conspiracy narrative that the Bush administration played an active role in these attacks.

In order for an unorthodox idea to spread (here, the truther conspiracy theory), you need some people who privately harbor great skepticism of the government report. Members of the 9/11 truth movement were convinced that they had latent support, but, as Mark Fenster argues, it was "virtually impossible to evaluate with any authority the size of the conspiracy community or the extent to which the public accepts, or even knows much about, 9/11 conspiracy claims."[32] Prospects for a bandwagon were unknown because, as in the Kuran model of falsified public preferences, private preferences and political thresholds are hidden from public view.

It was reasonable for the truthers to suspect that some portion of the public believes their conspiracy theory but engages in preference falsification by parroting the findings of the 9/11 Commission report. There is a reputational cost to expressing an unpopular idea. In Kuran's model, the decision to falsify preferences depends on the distribution of public opinion. For most conspiracy theories, the initial state of public support is either weak or unknown. Thus, individuals predisposed to a particular conspiracy theory will lack the safety in numbers that they need to publicly express a dubious idea and, instead, falsify their preferences.

To create a sense of safety in numbers and help propagate their conspiracy theory, members of the truth movement began to publicly advocate the idea that 9/11 was an inside job. Fenster finds that truther websites included "how-to guides for creating local 'community hubs' of truth activists" and national conferences "encouraged local groups to form, either by rallying and increasing the member-ship of organizations that hosted the events, or by enabling people from the same locations to travel together to the conference or meet for the first time during the conference."[33] And *Loose Change,* a truther documentary, implored viewers to "Share this information with friends, family, total strangers. Hold screenings, con-ferences, whatever you have to do to get the word out."[34]

If safety in numbers encouraged those who privately believed in the truther con-spiracy theory to publicly express their support, then a large bandwagon could be engineered. Large swaths of Americans have a strongly realized preference of dis-trust when it comes to the media and government.[35] Even if these individuals do not initially believe the truther conspiracy theory, they are by nature distrustful of official reports. As they encounter more and more people rejecting the 9/11 Commission report, they now feel safe in sharing their general distrust by endorsing the truther conspiracy theory. This reveals that an even larger number of individuals hold the underlying preference of the truther conspiracy theory, making it accept-able for even more people to express that idea.

In general, people may be wary of revealing conspiratorial tendencies or beliefs in public. They may think that the conspiracy belief is unpopular. So, an individual's true preference is to believe the conspiracy theory, but this is not public informa-tion. Owing to this suppression, we are unaware of how many people believe an idea. When the preferences of individuals are revealed, that may lead to a decline in preference falsification and the spread of a conspiracy theory.[36]

To the extent that preference falsification explains conspiracy theory propaga-tion, social scientists should think critically about the meaning of straightforward survey responses. American elite rhetoric has an anti-conspiracy bias and this will encourage preference falsification among respondents to mainstream survey organizations.[37] Most surveys, except for the very crafty, will likely underreport inclinations toward conspiracy theories. Kuran illustrates this tendency with a story about Nicaragua's 1990 presidential election.[38] While a *Washington Post–ABC News* poll gave the Sandinista candidate a 16-point lead over his UNO opponent, the UNO candidate beat the Sandinista by 14 points on election day. An experiment by Katherine Bischoping and Howard Shuman showed that the discrepancy was a result of preference falsification: in a pre-election poll where respondents filled out a survey with a pen labeled "UNO" the actual presidential election outcome was predicted with great accuracy, but surveys filled out with an unmarked or "Sandinista" pen replicated the *Washington Post–ABC News* result.[39] When polling surprises such as these occur, it might not be due to flawed sampling but, instead, preference falsification. In any case, preference falsification is difficult to test in the field; but the prevalence of recent polling errors suggests that members of the public falsify their preferences on important issues in a way that could lay the groundwork for an opinion cascade.[40]

Costly Signaling

Mechanism. You need an efficient way of signaling your iconoclastic beliefs to strangers so that you can find like-minded individuals and mobilize politically.[41]

Illustrative Example

Costly signals help individuals credibly communicate hidden information. In the classic signaling model, a job candidate would like to convince a prospective employer of her aptitude.[42] But pronouncing her capability is insufficient. All candidates, irrespective of skill level, will profess competency. High-quality candidates must credibly communicate their underlying aptitude through a costly signal that less qualified candidates cannot mimic. One such signal is a bachelor's degree. Educational attainment requires skills that also make for good employees and, furthermore, individuals with lower levels of talent will find it near impossible to gain admission and pass college-level classes. Thus, the costly signal of educational attainment allows an employer to hire a competent employee.

While costly signals can transmit information that is hard to observe, they are also used to convey beliefs or actions that must remain hidden because they exist outside the bounds of polite society. There are myriad reasons why individuals with unorthodox preferences need to signal to one another in order to undertake collective action. Consider the face tattoos many gang members have. Just as a bachelor's degree credibly conveys underlying aptitude, a gang tattoo on the face communicates the individual's unbreakable commitment to the gang.

Gang members find that the face tattoo is an effective costly signal for two reasons. First, it effectively discriminates committed criminals from upstanding citizens, police, informants, and individuals with weak ties to the criminal enterprise. As the economist Raymond Fisman argues with respect to gang tattoos, "the uncommitted might consider the future cost of finding legal employment, how he'll be perceived in 'polite' society, or the financial and physical pain involved in removing the words 'F*** the LAPD.'"[43] This means that individuals without a strong commitment to criminal life are unable to mimic this signal. Fellow gang members can trust that such people are not undercover police officers and are unlikely to snitch. Second, when a costly signal communicates information that is illegal or violates social norms, the sociologist Diego Gambetta argues that it must do so under conditions of plausible deniability.[44] Here, the face tattoo conveys criminality without providing incriminating evidence that could send its bearer to jail. In short, face tattoos are costly signals that allow hardened criminals to find one another while avoiding the punishment that would follow from transparently discussing prior illegal activities.

Application to Conspiracy Theories: Seth Rich and WikiLeaks

Societal norms constrain individuals harboring extreme political ideas from expressing their beliefs. Fringe conspiracy theories might serve as a costly signal whereby individuals who hold extreme ideologies advertise their beliefs under the cover of plausible deniability and find like-minded individuals who they can open up to behind closed doors. By fringe conspiracy theories, we refer to highly implausible conspiracy theories including whether Ted Cruz's father assassinated President John F. Kennedy, Hillary Clinton campaign staffers conducted a pedophilia ring in the back of a Washington, D.C., pizza parlor, and members of the Democratic National Committee orchestrated the murder of employee Seth Rich, which we will focus on in this subsection.

On July 10, 2016, Seth Rich, a Democratic National Committee staffer, was shot to death in the District of Columbia. Shortly thereafter, on July 22, 2016, WikiLeaks published approximately 20,000 leaked emails from prominent members of the Democratic National Committee. On niche conservative social media sites, rumors began to spread that Seth Rich was a source of these leaked emails and that individuals affiliated with the Democratic National Committee orchestrated Rich's murder. As of December 2016, local police insisted that Rich's death occurred during a failed robbery attempt, and American intelligence agencies concluded that Russian military hackers provided WikiLeaks with the emails.[45] Yet, this conspiracy theory continued to circulate and began to receive wider coverage, including on Fox News in January 2017.[46] Then, in May, Fox News reported new evidence that Seth Rich leaked Democratic National Committee emails to WikiLeaks. The story was swiftly debunked, Fox News retracted its story, and conservative journalists at a broad array of outlets—including the *National Review* and even Fox News— forcefully argued that the Seth Rich conspiracy was a "fake story."[47] Nonetheless, conservative media personalities such as Sean Hannity continued to press the conspiracy, leading it to gain even more currency.[48]

The Seth Rich conspiracy theory is puzzling from the perspectives of herd behavior and follow-the-leader. It spreads after intelligence experts cast doubt on the key claims animating the conspiracy, and it spreads even further after reliably conservative journalists forcefully reject the conspiracy as wholly inconceivable. The spread of this conspiracy theory is also puzzling from the preference falsification perspective: if someone dies in D.C., there cannot be too many people who immediately lean toward the idea that a political committee orchestrated the killing. We are left with a puzzle: Why would a rational person propagate such a conspiracy theory? The costly signaling mechanism provides an answer.

Imagine a barber with extreme right-wing views who serves a clientele with preferences for limited government conservatism. Our extremist would like to find fellow hardliners. To maintain his clientele, he cannot endorse white nationalist politics, but he can repeat a nascent conspiracy theory that Democratic National Committee staffers murdered one of the DNC's own employees. The very dubiousness of the Seth Rich conspiracy theory serves two purposes. First, espousing it is costly—it's not the most agreeable topic of conversation—and, as such, it will discriminate between types. Customers who are not extremists and simply harbor traditional limited government views can easily find like-minded individuals and receive no benefit from repeating a conspiracy theory condemned by the *National Review*. Second, espousing this conspiracy theory will not tarnish an individual's reputation. An undercover extremist who espouses the Seth Rich conspiracy theory comes off as wacky to nonbelievers, whereas his true views—in favor of white nationalist ideology—would come off as dangerous. In summary, when an extremist shares a fringe conspiracy theory and finds a receptive audience, he has likely found a like-minded person who will talk in private about extreme political views.

Why the Seth Rich conspiracy theory? Well, there are a limited number of conspiracy theories that one can repeat before people question your sanity. To signal that you are a hardliner, you need a conspiracy theory that sends the right signal to fellow compatriots. The Seth Rich conspiracy theory—even if you find it implausible—communicates a lot of information about who you are, who you listen to, and who you are in a coalition with—you prefer Sean Hannity and extreme conservative Reddit groups over the *National Review*. Sending these signals accounts for why some people endorse dubious conspiracy theories: dubious ideas are might be advocated not because their proponents believe them to be true but because advocating dubious ideas is an efficient way to distinguish between people with conventional and extreme ideologies—just as an unattractive face tattoo discriminates committed criminals from everyone else. In short, conspiracy theories can represent symbolic beliefs. Or, to use the terminology of Trump followers, they are messages to be taken seriously but not literally.

The costly signal mechanism predicts that members of the ideological fringe actively seek symbolically meaningful signals. Because the conspiracy theories that travel are imbued with the most salient appeals to identity and emotions, it is no surprise that dubious conspiracy theories often evolve as reliable signals of ideological beliefs.

Theory Development for Conspiracy Theories

In recent years, conspiracy theory politics has gained a prominent place in American politics. A relatively new conspiracy theory literature has evolved to grapple with the causes and consequences. In any new field of research, scholars must start with description before they can move on to explanation. For conspiracy theory researchers, the time has come for theory building. This process involves identifying general patterns in the case studies.

Cass Sunstein broke theoretical ground for conspiracy theory scholars by advancing the herd behavior mechanism as an explanation of why some conspiracy theories take hold. Conspiracy theory propagation is complex and, even in careful experiments, the mechanisms at work are hard to untangle. For example, in a study of a rumor confounding palliative care with health care rationing, Adam Berinsky explores the psychology of rumor acceptance advanced by Flynn, Nyhan, and Reifler. Berinsky finds that the more the communications environment repeats a rumor, the more likely an individual is to believe it. Berinsky's finding is consistent with all four of our mechanisms.[49] Going forward, researchers should evaluate the political environment in which rumors propagate by designing studies that distinguish between the competing mechanisms.

Notes

1. In a study of 39 conspiracy-minded Facebook pages in Italy, scholars collected 208,591 conspiracy posts over a four-year period. Bessi, Alessandro, Mauro Coletto, Goerge Alxeandru Davidescu, Antonio Scala, Guido Caldarelli, Walter Quatrociocchi. 2015. "Science vs Conspiracy: Collective Narratives in the Age of Misinformation." *PloS ONE* 10(2). DOI: 10.1371/journal.pone.0118093.
2. Sunstein, Cass R. 2014. *Conspiracy Theories and Other Dangerous Ideas*. Simon and Schuster, 2, 13.
3. Sunstein, Cass R. 2014. *On Rumors: How Falsehoods Spread, Why We Believe Them, and What Can Be Done*. Princeton University Press, 1–2.
4. This model was first advanced in economics. See Banerjee, Abhijit V. 1992. "A Simple Model of Herd Behavior." *The Quarterly Journal of Economics* 107(3): 797–817.
5. The canonical finding is that efforts to correct misinformation often backfire. See Nyhan, Brendan, and Jason Reifler. 2010. "When Corrections Fail: The Persistence of Political Misperceptions." *Political Behavior* 32(2): 303–330.
6. Watts, Duncan J. 2017. "Should Social Science be More Solution-Oriented?" *Nature Human Behaviour* 1: 0015.
7. Bessi, Coletto, Davidescu, Scala, Caldarelli, Quatrociocchi, "Science vs Conspiracy"; Starbird, Kate. 2017. "Examining the Alternative Media Ecosystem through the Production of Alternative Narratives of Mass Shooting Events on Twitter." In *ICWSM*, 230–239.
8. Flynn, D. J., Brendan Nyhan, and Jason Reifler. 2017. "The Nature and Origins of Misperceptions: Understanding False and Unsupported Beliefs about Politics." *Political Psychology* 38(S1): 127–150.
9. Sunstein, *Conspiracy Theories and Other Dangerous Ideas*, 15–16; Sunstein, *On Rumors*, 19–27. The terms *herd behavior* and *information cascade* are used interchangeably in the academic literature. Economists tend to use the term *herd behavior* while sociologists tend to use the term *cascade*. In his work on conspiracy theories, Sunstein uses the term *cascade*, but explains the mechanism with frequent reference to the herd behavior models developed and tested in economics. We prefer the term *herd behavior* because that term is more intuitive for the novice reader.
10. Underlying skepticism will vary across individuals. See Uscinski, Joseph E., Casey Klofstad, and Matthew D. Atkinson. 2016. "What drives conspiratorial beliefs? The role of informational

cues and predispositions." *Political Research Quarterly* 69(1): 57–71; Uscinski, Joseph E., and Joseph M. Parent. 2014. *American Conspiracy Theories.* Oxford University Press.

11. Ibid.

12. American Association for the Advancement of Science. 2012. "Statement by the AAAS board of directors on labeling of genetically modified foods." http://www.aaas.org/sites/default/files/AAAS GM statement.pdf (Accessed December 9, 2015); Funk, Cary, and Brian Kennedy. 2016. "The New Food Fights: U.S. Public Divides Over Food Science." http://www.pewinternet.org/2016/12/01/the-new-food-fights (Accessed December 21, 2017).

13. Sunstein, *Conspiracy Theories*, 8, 12.

14. Ibid., 8 and 23. See also pages 9 and 29, which show that such informational diffusion may require the "cognitive infiltration" of isolated social networks.

15. Sunstein, *On Rumors*, 56.

16. While anti-GMO conspiracy theories have been confined to a minority of the U.S. public, fears about the safety of GM foods have increased drastically due to the GM movement. For an evaluation of the herd behavior mechanism in the context of the birther conspiracy theory, see Uscinski, Joseph E., Darin DeWitt, and Matthew D. Atkinson. 2018. "Conspiracy Theories and the Internet." In *The Brill Handbook of Conspiracy Theory and Contemporary Religion.* Leiden, Netherlands: Brill.

17. Zaller, John. 1992. *The Nature and Origins of Mass Opinion.* Cambridge: Cambridge University Press; Lenz, Gabriel S. 2013. *Follow the Leader? How Voters Respond to Politicians' Policies and Performance.* Chicago: University of Chicago Press.

18. Lupia, Arthur. 1994. "Shortcuts Versus Encyclopedias: Information and Voting Behavior in California Insurance Reform Elections." *American Political Science Review* 88(1): 63–76.

19. Bartels, Larry M. 2002. "Beyond the Running Tally: Partisan Bias in Political Perceptions." *Political Behavior* 24(2): 117–150; Bullock, John G., Alan S. Gerber, Seth J. Hill, and Gregory A. Huber. 2015. "Partisan Bias in Factual Beliefs About Politics." *Quarterly Journal of Political Science* 10(4): 519–578; Caplan, Bryan. 2011. *The Myth of the Rational Voter: Why Democracies Choose Bad Policies.* Princeton: Princeton University Press; Nyhan and Reifler, "When Corrections Fail."

20. Uscinski, Joseph E. 2014. *The People's News: Media, Politics, and the Demands of Capitalism.* New York: New York University Press.

21. Bennett, W. Lance, and Shanto Iyengar. 2008. "A New Era of Minimal Effects? The Changing Foundations of Political Communication." *Journal of Communication* 58(4): 707–731.

22. See Uscinski, Atkinson, and DeWitt (2018) for one attempt to evaluate these competing mechanisms for conspiracy theories, for example the birther thesis as well as other ideas of uncertain merit, such as mindfulness.

23. Gillon, Steven. 2017. "Why the Public Stopped Believing the Government about JFK's Murder." www.history.com/news/why-the-public-stopped-believing-the-government-about-jfks-murder (Accessed December 21, 2017).

24. Kuran, Timur. 1997. *Private Truths, Public Lies: The Social Consequences of Preference Falsification.* Cambridge: Harvard University Press. For an accessible introduction to the ideas presented in these articles, see Clark, William Roberts, Matt Golder, and Sona Nadenichek Golder. 2017. *Principles of Comparative Politics.* Washington, D.C.: CQ Press.

25. Patel, David. 2013. "Preference Falsification, Revolutionary Coordination, and the Tahrir Square Model." *Annual Proceedings of the Wealth and Well-Being of Nations* 4: 61–71.

26. Kuran, Timur. 1991. "Now Out of Never: The Element of Surprise in the East European Revolution of 1989." *World Politics* 44(1): 33.

27. Kinder, Donald R., and Cindy D. Kam. 2010. *Us Against Them: Ethnocentric Foundations of American Opinion.* Chicago: University of Chicago Press; Green, Donald P., Bradley Palmquist, and Eric Schickler. 2004. *Partisan Hearts and Minds: Political Parties and the Social Identities of Voters.* New Haven: Yale University Press.

28. Kinder, Donald R., and Nathan P. Kalmoe. 2017. *Neither Liberal nor Conservative: Ideological Innocence in the American Public*. Chicago: University of Chicago Press.

29. Bratich, Jack Zeljko. 2004. "Trust No One (on the Internet): The CIA-Crack-Contra Conspiracy Theory and Professional Journalism." *Television & New Media* 5(2): 109–139.

30. Uscinski, Klofstad, and Atkinson, "What Drives Conspiratorial Beliefs?"

31. Fenster, Mark. 2008. *Conspiracy Theories: Secrecy and Power in American Culture*. Minneapolis: University of Minnesota Press.

32. Ibid., 243. In this discussion, Fenster argues that even if we assume honest responses, opinion polls measuring public trust in the Bush administration or beliefs about what the Bush administration knew in advance do not properly convey the breadth of support for the idea that the Bush administration was actively involved in terrorist attacks.

33. Ibid., 247–248.

34. Quoted in Ibid., 278.

35. Ladd, Jonathan M. 2011. *Why Americans Hate the Media and How It Matters*. Princeton: Princeton University Press; Hetherington, Marc J., and Thomas J. Rudolph. 2015. *Why Washington Won't Work: Polarization, Political Trust, and the Governing Crisis*. Chicago: University of Chicago Press.

36. How far the conspiracy theory spreads depends on the distribution of individual political thresholds. As Uscinski, Klofstad, and Atkinson (2016) show, the partisan nature of many conspiracy theories, combined with the disinclination of some to publicly espouse conspiracy theories of any sort, means that most conspiracy theories will not gain the support of more than 25 percent of the population.

37. Bratich, "Trust No One."

38. Kuran, *Private Truths*, 340–341.

39. Bischoping, Katherine, and Howard Schuman. 1992. "Pens and Polls in Nicaragua: An Analysis of the 1990 Preelection Surveys." *American Journal of Political Science* 36(2): 331–350.

40. With growing political distrust and polarization, citizens are more cautious about publicly revealing their true attitudes. See Klar, Samara, and Yanna Krupnikov. 2016. *Independent Politics*. Cambridge: Cambridge University Press.

41. For a more in-depth analysis of this mechanism and its application to conspiracy theories, see Atkinson, Matthew, Darin DeWitt, and Joseph E. Uscinski. 2017. "Conspiracy Theories in the 2016 Election." In *Conventional Wisdom, Parties, and Broken Barriers in the 2016 Election*, eds. Jennifer C. Lucas, Christopher J. Galdieri, and Tauna S. Sisco. Lanham, MD: Lexington Books, 163–180.

42. Spence, Andrew Michael. 1974. *Market Signaling: Informational transfer in hiring and related screening processes*. Cambridge: Harvard University Press.

43. Fisman, Ray, and Tim Sullivan. 2016. *The Inner Lives of Markets: How People Shape Them— And They Shape Us*. New York: PublicAffairs, 67.

44. Gambetta, Diego. 2009. *Codes of the Underworld: How Criminals Communicate*. Princeton: Princeton University Press.

45. Sanger, David E. 2017. "Putin Ordered 'Influence Campaign' Aimed at U.S. Election, Report Says." *New York Times*. https://www.nytimes.com/2017/01/06/us/politics/russia-hack-report.html (Accessed December 21, 2017).

46. Zimmerman, Malia. 2017. "Slain DNC Staffer's Father Doubts WikiLeaks Link as Cops Seek Answers." *Fox News*. http://www.foxnews.com/politics/2017/01/10/slain-dnc-staffers-father-doubts-wikileaks-link-as-cops-seek-answers.html (Accessed December 21, 2017).

47. L.A. Times staff and Associated Press. 2017. "Fox News Retracts Story Alleging DNC Staffer Seth Rich Leaked Information to WikiLeaks Before Death." *Los Angeles Times*. http://www.latimes.com/politics/washington/la-na-essential-washington-updates-fox-news-retracts-story-alleging-dnc-1495565128-htmlstory.html (Accessed December 21, 2017); French, David. 2017. "The Seth Rich Conspiracy Theory Is Shameful Nonsense." *National Review*.

http://www.nationalreview.com/article/447903/sean-hannity-seth-rich-conspiracy-theory-disgrace (Accessed December 21, 2017).

48. Bromwich, Jonah Engel. 2017. "How the Murder of a D.N.C. Staff Member Fueled Conspiracy Theories." *New York Times*. https://www.nytimes.com/2017/05/17/us/seth-rich-dnc-wikileaks.html (Accessed December 21, 2017).

49. Berinsky, Adam J. 2017. "Rumors and Health Care Reform: Experiments in Political Misinformation." *British Journal of Political Science* 47(2): 260.

SECTION VI

WHAT DO CONSPIRACY THEORIES LOOK LIKE AROUND THE WORLD?

JOSEPH E. USCINSKI

Most accounts of conspiracy theorizing focus on a single place, and usually suggest that the people in that place are the most conspiracy-minded in the world. As Martin Orr and Ginna Husting point out in Chapter 5 of this volume, it seems as though every account suggests the people under study are particularly prone, whether it is Mexicans, Pakistanis, Africans, or Americans; everyone seems to be the most taken with conspiracy theories. Of course, this can't be true.

Researchers need to provide more cross-cultural studies so that we can understand which groups are the most conspiracy minded and why. Also, because most research focuses on one country, the national factors that could affect conspiracy theorizing are largely constant, therefore researchers can't discern their effects. Without more cross-national surveys, for example, the literature will not be able to make claims about the types of national culture or politics that drive conspiracy theorizing. Hugo Drochon provides a strong step forward in Chapter 22 by providing a cross-national survey including several countries in Europe as well as Argentina. His data shows which countries believe in particular conspiracy theories the most. He also find that people who are on the outside of mainstream politics tend to believe in conspiracy theories the most. In Chapter 25 Wiktor Soral, Aleksandra Cichocka, Michał Bilewicz, and Marta Marchlewska tie national politics in Poland to conspiracy theorizing, suggesting that conspiracy theorizing in Poland is not so much the result of individual traits but rather the result of a collective conspiracy mentality.

Chapters 23 and 24 by Scott Radnitz and Ilya Yablokov, respectively, examine how post-Soviet states engage in conspiracy theorizing, in particular by focusing on the varied levels of government in these states. Chapters 26 and 27 by Turkay Nefes and Tanya Filer, respectively, examine how political elites use conspriacy theories for rational purposes. Nefes shows how Turkish legislators selectively use accusations of "deep state" interference to further their political goals. Tanya Filer details how former Argentine President Cristina Fernández de Kirchner used conspiracy theories to urge supporters to see circumstances her way. Kirchner has been charged in the cover-up of a bombing, and a trial date is soon to be set.

Moving forward, researchers need to provide more cross-national research, particularly surveys. Which countries have the most conspiracy minded people and why? What forms of government drive conspiracy theorizing? We also need more research into how elites across different countries use conspiracy theories. What purposes are they used for, and what makes those uses successful? Conspiracy theorizing is a worldwide phenomenon, and researchers need to study more countries than just those in the West.

22

Who Believes in Conspiracy Theories in Great Britain and Europe?

HUGO DROCHON

From the assassination of JFK to Donald Trump, who launched his political career with the "birther" movement that challenged Barack Obama's U.S. citizenship, not to mention Roswell, the moon landings and Sandy Hook, are conspiracy theories the preserve of the United States? Two conspiracy theory surveys—the first of their kind—conducted with YouGov in Great Britain in February 2015 (England, Scotland, and Wales excluding Northern Ireland) and across Europe in March 2016 (Great Britain, Germany, Italy, Poland, Portugal, and Sweden), show that they are not. The British and Europeans are as likely—in some cases even more likely—to believe in at least one conspiracy theory as are the Americans. After all, the British can claim as their own David Icke, who believes the royal family are in fact extrater-restrial "archonic" reptilian beings (lizards); the Holocaust denier-in-chief David Irving; and indeed theories about how—and why—Lady Diana came to pass. On the Continent, Holocaust denial remains rife: we found that 25% of young Polish men believe that "the official account of the Nazi Holocaust is a lie and the number of Jews killed by the Nazis during World War II has been exaggerated on purpose," while we were not allowed to ask that question in Germany where Holocaust de-nial is illegal.

These initial findings suggest that the strongest explanatory factor for belief in conspiracy theories is *complete exclusion*. By this is meant *political exclusion*, a deep distrust of political institutions and a rejection of the political system as a whole, married to *economic exclusion*, being poorer financially and in terms of education. *Complete exclusion* is valid both domestically in Great Britain and in Europe interna-tionally. Poorer and less democratic countries, as measured by indices such as GDP, the Democracy Index, Transparency International, and the Gini coefficient (which measures inequality within a country) return higher levels of conspiracy thinking than those that do better. For example Portugal, which fares worse on these indices, experiences much higher levels of conspiracy thinking than does Sweden, which does better. So countries in which inequality is higher and democracy is considered not to be functioning as well as it should—that is, where citizens feel excluded *politically* and *economically*—will exhibit higher levels of conspiracy thinking.

More research needs to be done to confirm these preliminary findings—the discussion here is not meant to be conclusive so much as to motivate future analysis. The study does reveal, however, a deep malaise at the heart of Western liberal democracies. Conspiracy theories here appear to be more the symptom than the cause of disenchantment with democracy. It is not conspiracy theories that lead to the disenchantment with democracy, rather it is disenchantment with democracy that leads to conspiracy theories. This implies that policies that aim at better political and economic integration will help reduce conspiracy thinking.

American Conspiracy Theories

In 2014 Uscinski and Parent, in *American Conspiracy Theories,* set about dispelling a number of myths, most prominent among these the notion that there is a rising tide of conspiracy theories in the United States. Their work shows that, apart from peaks in the 1890s and the 1950s, conspiracy thinking has actually remained quite stable over the last century and, the *X-Files* notwithstanding, has even started to tail off since the 1960s. Other myths they challenge include the idea that American men are more likely than woman to speculate (they are not), or that those who engage in conspiracy thinking tend to live on the political extremes of society (independents are as likely, in their findings, to be prone to catch the bug).

Certain stereotypes, however, seem confirmed: Conspiracy theorists are more likely to be poor, both financially and in terms of education; are more likely to have a narrower group of friends (isolation); and are more likely to see violence as a solution to their problems and those of society. Perhaps one of the most interesting conclusions of their study is that Republicans and Democrats are as likely as one another to be conspiracy theorists. Which one is more prone to start speculating at any given time depends on who is in power. If the Democrats are in power, expect theories from the right (communist takeover plots à la Manchurian candidate), while when it's the Republicans' turn, expect the left to cast the allegations (big business in cahoots with the government). In any case, on Uscinski and Parent's account, conspiracy theories track power: when one is out of it, one is more likely to theorize. Conspiracy theories are therefore a reaction to being away or out of power and fearing the consequences. The link to perceived menace is reproduced on the international stage—foreign threats are a strong trigger for conspiracy thinking.

Uscinski and Parent close their book with a few suggestions for future research. The first and most obvious issue that arises is that their study concentrates solely on the United States. What would our findings be if we ran the same or similar, adapted to their contexts, opinion surveys in Europe? What kind of answers would we get across western, eastern, southern and northern Europe? Are conspiracy theories as rife across the European political spectrum? Are European men and women as likely to dip into the well?

British Conspiracy Theories

On the 3rd and 4th of February 2015, YouGov polled a representative sample of 1,759 adults across Great Britain (England, Scotland, and Wales, but excluding Northern Ireland). We asked our respondents to agree or disagree with a series of statements about conspiracy theories involving AIDS, aliens, Sharia law, 9/11, and global warming. Overall, only a minority of the British public believe in individual conspiracy theories: 8% percent agreed with the statement "The AIDS virus was created and spread around the world on purpose by a secret group or organization"; 14% believe that "Humans have made contact with aliens but this fact has been deliberately hidden from the public"; 11% that "The U.S. government played a deliberate role in making the 9/11 terrorist attacks happen in America on the 11th September, 2001"; 18% think that "Some courts in the U.K. legal system are choosing to adopt Islamic 'Sharia' law";, and 18% hold that "The idea of man-made global warming is a hoax that was deliberately invented to deceive people."

How does this compare with the United States? Working with a different set of conspiracy beliefs, Eric Oliver and Thomas Wood found that 52% of Americans believed in at least one of seven conspiracy theories surrounding the Iraq War, 9/11, Obama's birthplace, Wall Street, chemtrails, George Soros, and light bulbs.[1] In our case, we found that 55% of respondents agreed with at least one of the statements about the secret group, AIDS, aliens, Sharia law, or climate change. Conspiracy theories are thus not a U.S. speciality: the British are as likely, if not marginally more, to believe in at least one conspiracy theory as are the Americans. Whereas Oliver and Wood found that 19% of Americans believe that 9/11 was an inside job, we found that 11% of British thought it too; and 18% of British believe that climate change is a hoax compared to 13% in the United States.

Two questions we asked, however, returned significantly higher results. Fifty-five percent of respondents agreed with the statement, "The Government is deliberately hiding the truth about how many immigrants really live in this country," and 52% concurred with the view that "Officials of the European Union are gradually seeking to take over all law-making powers in this country." Conducted one year before the Brexit referendum in the United Kingdom (June 23, 2016), these strongly held views about immigration and the European Union's encroachment into U.K. sovereignty—the two main arguments made in favor of leaving the European Union—was to presage what was to come. In fact, these numbers mirrored exactly the final Brexit vote. A note of caution here nonetheless: these two questions are not simply tapping into conspiracy thinking in the same manner as questions on aliens do, but are contained an overarching ideological element and reference to political context, to which we shall return.

For Uscinski and Parent, the essence of conspiratorial thinking revolves around the notion that "powerful groups covertly control events against the common good." As such, the key question we asked in our survey was, "Regardless of who is officially in charge of governments, media organizations, and companies, there is a secret group of powerful people who really control world events like wars and economic crises." Whoever answered yes to that question (secret cabal) we took to be a conspiracy theorist.

Uscinski and Parent found that 27% of American respondents agreed with this statement, and in Great Britain that figure was 34%.[2] If we take into account the fact that a greater proportion of American respondents chose the intermediate "neither agree nor disagree" option, any disparity vanishes. Among those polled who had a firm opinion, 47% of British respondents agreed, compared to 46% of the American respondents.

Again, not much separates the Americans from their cousins across the pond, and our survey reproduced a number of their main findings. Notably, we found that women (35%) are as likely as men (33%) to answer in the affirmative the question concerning the secret cabal. On that same question, those of a lower socioeconomic grade responded positively 41% of the time while only 29% of the higher grade did.

This aligns with Uscinski and Parent's findings that individuals with lower financial status and levels of education are more prone to speculate. In this regard, far-right UKIP voters—considered to be more on the "extremes" of the political spectrum—were only marginally more likely to agree with the statement than were left-wing Labour voters (considered more mainstream, at least before Jeremy Corbyn took over in September 2015), at 46% and 43% respectively. Indeed, Labour and Conservative voters are almost exactly as likely to believe in at least one conspiracy theory. The percentage for Labour voters stands at 54%, while Conservatives are at 53%. So conspiracy thinking is rife across the political spectrum, and not just limited to its extremes.

But are they more prevalent at the extremes? On questions concerning conspiracy theories surrounding AIDS, aliens, and 9/11, often considered to appeal more to the left side of the political spectrum, UKIP voters find themselves in good company with Labour voters. So to questions such as "The AIDS virus was created and spread around the world on purpose by a secret group or organization," 'Humans have made contact with aliens but this fact has been deliberately hidden from the public," and "The U.S. Government played a deliberate role in making the 9/11 terrorist attacks happen in American on 11th September, 2001," UKIP voters (18% of respondents) align well with Labour voters (14%).

On questions such as "Some courts in the U.K. legal system are choosing to adopt Islamic 'Sharia' law," "The government is deliberately hiding the truth about how many immigrants really live in this country," "Officials of the European Union are gradually seeking to take over all law-making powers in this country," and "The idea of man-made global warming is a hoax that was deliberately invented to deceive people"—this time thought to be more right-wing—here, UKIP voters find themselves closer to Conservatives, although they feel much more intensely about them. Thus 87% of UKIP voters believe the government is deliberately misleading the public as to the true number of immigrants in the United Kingdom compared to 52% for Conservatives and 57% for Labour (only 37% for the centrist Liberal-Democrats). Regarding the question of an E.U. takeover, 87% of UKIP voters agree with our statement compared to 67% for the Conservatives and 42% and 38% for Labour and Lib-Dem voters respectively.

So, right-wing voters have been against the European Union for some time, which is why Theresa May seems to have no option but to pursue a hard Brexit. Labour has its difficulties, too: a significant number, although not a majority, of its voters are opposed to the European Union, but immigration is a real concern, which is why Jeremy Corbyn and Keir Starmer are trying to square single-market membership with control over immigration.

Caveats surrounding the more highly politicized nature of these questions notwithstanding, these findings tend to suggest that while Uscinski and Parent are correct in underlining how conspiracy theorists exist across the political spectrum, some are nonetheless felt more commonly at the extremes, at least in terms of the far right, and certainly less forcefully at the center. The conspiracy theories backed by UKIP voters are usually thought of as right-wing ones—although they are as inclined as left-wing voters to believe what are usually thought of as left-wing conspiracy theories, and this cross-cutting again suggests that more extreme voters are more receptive to conspiratorial accounts.

As it happens, at the time of the survey both the parties to the left and furthest to the right of the political spectrum—Labour and UKIP—were out of power. At first glance, this thus seemed to confirm Uscinski and Parent's central claim that conspiracy theories negatively track power: if you're out of it, you are more likely to speculate. While 43% of Labour voters and 43% of UKIP voters agreed with the key "secret cabal controling all world events" statement, only 27% did for Conservatives and 17% for the Lib-Dems, the coalition at the time. What is the main explanatory factor here? Being on the political fringes, or being out of power? More research must be undertaken to answer this question.

Our survey found that physical distance from power does not increase one's propensity to speculation. Levels of conspiracy thinking were relatively stable across the regions of London, Rest of South, Midlands/Wales, and the North. In fact, the area with the lowest returns in terms of conspiracy theorizing was actually Scotland, the furthest from Westminster (although Scotland does have its own parliament). On the question of secret groups running things, the Scottish sample thought it true for 25% of respondents, compared to 34% for London and the Rest of South and 36% for Midlands/Wales and the North. Scotland, of course, has its own parliament—but given that the survey was conducted less than half a year after the Scottish independence referendum (September 18, 2014), a higher degree of political turmoil might have been expected (our relatively low sampling size—160 out of 1,749—means we are unable to confirm our findings more broadly).

The Scottish results, however, do give rise to the question of whether we should be concerning ourselves less with physical distance than with perceived distance from power. One could live in London and feel more distant, in a very direct and personal way, from power than someone living further away (on questions of AIDS and 9/11, London actually leads the way). It is perhaps more the experience of feeling closer or excluded from power that is central here. It is this sense of exclusion, this chapter suggests, that is key in understanding conspiracy theories.

European Conspiracy Theories

In March 2016 we extended our survey to six European countries: again in Great Britain, but also in Germany, Italy, Poland, Portugal and Sweden. Our aim was to compare European democracy East/West and North/South. All Continental countries use proportional representation: Germany uses a "mixed-member proportional representation," where you vote both for a candidate and for a list; and Italy, Poland, Portugal, and Sweden all use the "party list" system, some with minimum thresholds. This would then allow us to test Uscinski and Parent's hypothesis that countries with proportional representation might return lower levels of conspiracy thinking, because citizens would feel more represented. However, if *political exclusion*, as suggested in the introduction, is a key factor in conspiracy theorizing, we would expect to find that proportional representation will have no measurable impact on the level of conspiracy thinking, as it only addresses representation *within* the political system itself. Conspiracy theorists reject the political system *as a whole*. Indeed, our preliminary pilot findings show that the feeling of being represented has little bearing on whether one is likely to be a conspiracy theorist, which suggests that whether the political system is representative or not will have no impact whatsoever on the prevalence of conspiracy thinking.

Political disenfranchisement is a complicated matter, but there are socioeconomic factors associated with it, too. We might thus expect to find that countries— namely Sweden, in this case—that are richer in terms of GDP and have lower levels of inequality as measured by the Gini coefficient, alongside generally high rankings in Transparency International and Democracy Index and to whom we might impart a higher level of sociopolitical integration, might return lower levels of conspiracy thinking. This addresses the second key factor we identified in the introduction, namely *economic exclusion*, which might then translate into feelings of higher political integration. Conversely, we would expect to find that countries that are poorer and have higher Gini coefficients, in particular Portugal, which also ranks lower on the Transparency and Democracy Index scales, would return higher instances of conspiracy thinking than, for example, Sweden, even though it uses almost exactly the same proportional list system (Sweden has minimum thresholds). For comparison: worldwide Sweden is ranked 15th on GDP, 8th on Gini coefficient, 4th by Transparency International, and 3rd on the Democracy Index, whereas Portugal is 42nd, 29th, 29th, and 28th respectively.

And that is indeed what we did find. On the key question of the secret cabal running the world, a whopping 47% of Portuguese agreed, compared to only 10% of Swedes. Indeed, Sweden was the only country in which the answer "None of these [statements concerning conspiracy theories] are true" came out on top, at 49%, whereas in all the other countries the statement "Even though we live in what's called a democracy, a few people will always run things in this country anyway" came first (70%) in Portugal. Moreover, whereas we found that among all countries at least half of the population believes in at least one conspiracy theory—thus making the Europeans as likely to do so as the Americans—Sweden was the only country in our sample in which a plurality said that none of the statements about conspiracy theories were true (35%), whereas in Portugal 24% of respondents thought that three of the statements were true.

The question "The government is deliberately hiding the truth about how many immigrants really live in this country" yielded some interesting results, too. The view that that is the case remained stubbornly high in Great Britain at 41%[3]— remember, three months later the U.K. would vote to leave the European Union. It was even higher in Germany, at 42%, most probably in reaction to Merkel's decision the summer before, in 2015, to allow in Syrian refugees. This would lead to the rise of the far-right anti-immigration party "Alternative for Germany," which for the first time in its history broke into the Bundestag in the general election of September 2017. It was also relatively high in Sweden, at 31%, and we will see whether that has an impact on Swedish elections due in September 2018 and whether such a view will help the nationalist and anti-immigration Swedish Democrats. The level is lower in Italy (29%) where the vast majority of immigrants first land (over 80% for the first half of 2017), and it is the lowest in Portugal at 16%. The difference between place of first arrival and final destination may account for this difference.

Another interesting result was to the question, "Secret plots that harm the nation are more common in this country than in other countries," which came out high in Poland (31%) and Portugal (29%) whereas in Great Britain, Germany, and Sweden it was all under 10%. Might this continued fear of a foreign enemy interfering in the affairs of the country find its source in the countries' authoritarian past? Or being beside a bigger and domineering neighbor?

So what are we to conclude from this survey? Do conspiracy theories track power, as Uscinski and Parent argue? At the time of the survey Great Britain, Germany, and Poland had center-right (or in Poland's case right-wing) governments, while in Italy, Portugal, and Sweden the governments were center-left. In our survey we found that across Europe, right-wing respondents more readily accepted conspiracy theory statements. Whether conspiracy theories are to be located more to the left or to the right of the political scale is a highly subjective matter, but in asking about conspiracy theories surrounding immigration, global warming, secret plots, AIDS, aliens, and Holocaust denial, we had hoped to have covered the entire spectrum.

In any case, as we saw above, conspiracy theories about the government concealing the number of immigrants there are in the country—one we might clearly identify as being right-wing—are widely believed in countries that have both left-wing governments (Sweden, Italy at 29%) and right-wing ones (Germany, Great Britain); and countries where they are less widely believed—Poland (20%), Portugal—have either a right-wing (Poland) or a left-wing (Portugal) government. So conspiracy theories about immigrants are believed regardless of which party is in power. Indeed, the two countries that have the highest belief in conspiracy theories surrounding immigrants (Germany and Great Britain) both have right-wing governments, which confirms the view that these beliefs are held by right-wing respondents even though their party is in power (and in fact, in Germany many shifted even more to the right—to the AfD—because of immigration).

Like in our pilot, we found that physical distance from power played little to no role in conspiracy theorising. While there seems to be a level of resentment toward Berlin in Germany, a more decentralized regime, we again found no devolution effect for Wales or Scotland in Great Britain.

What about religion? The U.S. example suggested religion might play a role, and we found evidence of it here, too, although not in the manner one might have expected. It won't have been lost on the reader that the countries that turned out higher degrees of conspiracy thinking are Catholic countries, but it would be a mistake to associate conspiracy theories directly with Catholicism. Instead, religion played a role if it was a minority position within the country. So if one is highly religious in Sweden, Great Britain, Poland, or Germany, then one is more likely to be a conspiracy theorist, thus cutting across confessional lines of Protestant (Sweden, Great Britain, Germany) or Catholic (Poland). Indeed, it is in Sweden where religion is most strongly linked to conspiracy theorizing, such that if you are highly religious in a country that is highly secularized—43% of respondents concurred with the statement that "none of what happens in my life is caused by a 'higher force' such as God, fate, or destiny"—then you are more likely to be a conspiracy theorist. Inversely, if you are highly religious in Portugal or Italy, countries somewhat less secular—in these two countries respondents were more likely to believe that "some of what happens in my life is caused by a 'higher force' such as God, fate, or destiny"—then you are in fact *less* likely to be a conspiracy theorist.

Being in a minority brings us back to the issue of exclusion. And indeed the stereotype of the white, working class, middle-aged man as the prototypical conspiracy theorist held true here again—with the sole caveat that it is not only lacking tertiary education that is a strong predictor, but being out of work, that is, being *economically* excluded. That was even stronger. Social integration—we asked about membership of church or religious organizations; art, music or cultural organizations; political parties; environmental organizations; organizations providing assistance to people; sports clubs or hobby groups—had, in fact, little impact on conspiracy thinking. Yes, Sweden had the highest participation and Portugal the lowest, but Great Britain, which came second lowest on the cabal question at 13% behind Sweden at 10%, has almost as many people who are not part of any type of organization (60%) as Portugal (64%—in Sweden that figure is 48%). After all, one might be very well integrated into one's group, but that doesn't mean that group isn't excluded from power (think of African Americans in the United States). Nor can we add that being optimistic about the economy, or whether one wanted more or less intervention in the economy, have much predictive power when it came to conspiracy thinking.

Conclusion

Attempts to address conspiracy theories have often been made at the individual level, trying to draw conspiracy theorists away from their beliefs by rationally and psychologically pointing out the pitfalls of their theoretical constructs. This has met with some success but has often butted up against the "self-sealing" character of conspiracy theories: if you are trying to convince them otherwise, you must be part of the plot. Our research suggests that conspiracy theories might be addressed at a more structural level too. Policies supporting political and economic integration—policies that address questions of inequality, integration, and political participation—might help in reducing the degree of conspiracy thinking within a country. Education is also a promising route to explore. Sweden ranks higher in the OECD's PISA test than does Portugal, and within individual countries those with higher education are less likely to believe in conspiracy theories than those with lower educational achievements.

As such, conspiracy theories appear not to be the cause of disenchantment with democracy but rather its symptom, which has to do with political and economic disenfranchisement. Addressing those would surely reduce the number of conspiracy theorists living within our midst. However—and however tempting it might be in the age of Trump, where conspiracy theories and "fake news" played a key role in his election—it would be a mistake to want to eradicate them completely, even if that were possible. As Cass Sunstein and Adrian Vermeule have argued, conspiracy theorists suffer from "crippled epistemologies" in the sense that "they know very few things, and what they know is wrong," as they put it.[4] But conspiracy theories, once they do not come to dominate entirely the public sphere, are in fact the price to pay for the existence of a critical public sphere. Christopher Hitchens has spoken of conspiracy theories as the "exhaust fumes" of democracy. Yes, conspiracy theorists tend to get it wrong, but the skeptical mindset they participate in, when used correctly, is essential to the proper functioning of modern democracies. To want to eradicate that completely would be to want to eradicate all dissent.

Of course our survey has focused on relatively stable European liberal democracies, but who believes in conspiracy theories in unstable, authoritarian, or semi-authoritarian regimes? Clearly more research is needed.

We have already extended our survey to Argentina, one of the most unequal societies in the world, where conspiracy theories are rife: 31% believe a secret cabal rules the world; 25% that there are secret plots against it (a legacy of CIA involvement?); 25% that humans have made contact with aliens but this has been covered up; and 21% that the AIDS virus was created on purpose. These last two by far the highest, more than double what one finds in Europe.[5] A recent study of Greece, which is currently going through a difficult period, suggests that up to 80% of the population thinks that "there are secret organizations working behind the scenes and pulling strings"—no doubt linked to the presence of the Troika in the country (European Commission, European Central Bank, and International Monetary Fund)—and 27% believe in chemtrails.[6] In the Middle East, 78% of respondents think 9/11 was the work either of the CIA or Mossad.[7] If conspiracy theories shift from being a minority to a majority sport, how are we to understand them and the role they play in their societies? That will be for future research to explore.

Notes

1. Oliver, Eric, and Thomas Wood. 2014. "Conspiracy Theories and the Paranoid Style(s) of Mass Opinion." *American Journal of Political Science* 58(4): 952–966.
2. Uscinski and Parent's wording was slightly different: "Big events like wars, the current recession, and the outcomes of elections are controlled by small groups of people who are working in secret against the rest of us."
3. The nature of our revised survey, which only allowed for binary yes/no answers, instead of the pilot, which allow for a range from "Definitely true, Probably true, Don't know, Probably not true, Definitely not True," where the trues and not trues were tallied up, gave us slightly different results.
4. Sunstein, Cass, and Adrian Vermeule. 2009. "Conspiracy Theories: Causes and Cures." *The Journal of Political Philosophy* 17(2): 202–227.
5. See Tanya Filer's chapter in this collection.
6. Georgakopoulos, Thordoris. 2017. "What Greeks Believe in 2017." https://www.dianeosis.org/en/2017/04/greeks-believe-in-2017/ (Accessed January 9, 2017). Thanks to Christos Aliprantis for bringing this to our attention.
7. Sunstein and Vermeule, "Conspiracy Theories," 2002–2003.

23

Why the Powerful (in Weak States) Prefer Conspiracy Theories

SCOTT RADNITZ

As research in several fields has demonstrated, conspiracy theories have arisen countless times in history and continue to prosper. Whatever our normative views, conspiracy belief can no longer be viewed as deviant or abnormal, but must be considered a normal part of social life. Today, the collusion between politics and business and the growth of the national security apparatus in contemporary democracies give rise to (often well founded) fears about unbridled power or secretive plots. Chapters in this volume by Martin Orr and Gina Husting and by Lee Basham and Juha Räikkä underscore this point.

Conspiracy theories have gained large numbers of adherents in the United States and Western Europe.[1] Yet even while they thrive at the popular level, conspiracy theories are rarely central to the *political discourse* of institutionalized democracies (prior to 2016, anyway). It is taken for granted that politicians should not publicly espouse conspiracy theories lest they be derided and mocked in the media. The fact that elected officials have typically not publicly promoted conspiracy theories—with some notable exceptions[2]—testifies to the relatively constrained temperament of politics where consolidated democracy and strong institutions prevail.

By contrast, even a cursory glimpse at the public discourse outside of established democracies in strong states—that is, in most of the world—reveals how pervasive conspiracy theories are. Substantial percentages of the population of many countries take the existence of conspiracies for granted.[3] Furthermore, political elites of all stripes, including democratically elected heads of state, representatives of populist, right-wing, and left-wing political parties, demagogic dictators, run-of-the-mill authoritarian leaders, and the occasional technocrat are all prone to making conspiracy claims for one reason or another. The upshot, in many countries, is that conspiracy theories become a normal part of the political discourse. As opposed to news stories that agonize about why so many people seem to believe in conspiracy theories,[4] one is likely to see straightforward and unapologetic endorsements of conspiracy claims by intellectuals, legislators, and newspaper columnists.

This chapter lays out some propositions on how conspiracy becomes a favored tactic of politicians in weak and developing states. It argues that national narratives about global power and the nature of domestic politics provide a repertoire of material from which conspiracy theories can be constructed, but they typically circulate informally and are not politically salient. It is when open political intrigue or jarring and unexpected events occur that politicians are likely to make a decisive turn to conspiratorial rhetoric. The exaggeration and personification of threats enable politicians to justify their rule when it might be called into question. While not sufficient to explain conspiracy theories in politics everywhere, these factors represent an initial attempt to link structural and institutional factors to the deployment of conspiracy claims in an effort to advance theory building.

I show how these factors operate with examples from Russia, Turkey, and Afghanistan. Although distinct in history and culture, politicians in these three countries have long promoted a suspicion of outsiders—often with good reason—and portrayed their countries as victims. They are also prone to secrecy, infighting, and intrigue as a style of practice politics. This combination makes conspiracy an attractive—and often effective—rhetorical strategy.

The Historical Roots of Conspiracy in Weak States

Conspiracy theories tell a compelling story that we can all relate to: there is a misdeed, a perpetrator, a victim, and usually a motive. The world conspiracy theories describe is one in which powerful actors cause harm to society in order to advance their interests. Their simple yet captivating logic enables people to self-identify as the conspiracy's victims, and to imagine solidarity with others presumed to share the same misfortune. Politicians can both promote this solidarity and harness it for political purposes.

Instead of viewing conspiracy theories as a type of *knowledge*, which leads to the puzzle of *belief*, they can also be seen as a form of *narrative*, which opens up questions about their social and political *uses*. The chapters in this volume by Matthew Atkinson and Darin DeWit and by Nick DiFonzo further this idea of *uses* as well. Politics is about the authority to set the terms of debate and build coalitions. In political settings where institutions fail to guide behavior and politicians cannot rely on established parties to generate public support, actors fall back on focal points or cues that can help their group coordinate.[5] This often involves forming "negative coalitions" that are first and foremost defined by their opposition to common adversaries rather than fidelity to an affirmative set of goals.[6] Common rhetorical tropes include invoking threats, claiming victim status, and delegitimizing one's opponents by linking them to feared or disliked others, all of which conform to the logic of conspiracy. Thus, conspiracy theories have characteristics that make them useful for politicians, especially at times of heightened risk.

In much of the world, politicians need not labor too hard to convince people that malevolent forces are the cause of their misfortune. Highly suspicious beliefs about the world may be fully justified. Personal experiences shape people's expectations of the risks and benefits of trusting others. Where people have placed faith in others and found their gestures reciprocated, they can reasonably trust others in future encounters; where they have been cheated, they are justified in avoiding interaction, even if that means they forgo future benefits.[7] The cost of getting spurned again may be too high.

Subjective impressions of power follow along similar lines. The experience of abuse by the state generates justified fears about the everyday likelihood of being exploited again. When generalized to whole societies, fear of exploitation can lead to widespread habits of distrust and non-cooperation.[8] Surveys of Russia since the breakup of the USSR consistently show low trust in other people and suspicion of elites.[9] Ilya Yablokov provides multiple of examples of this later in this volume. This has translated into low levels of compliance with the law and is reflected in outcomes like tax avoidance and resistance to military conscription. In Afghanistan, strong local identities and traditional governance institutions have led to suspicion of the central government and stoked resistance.[10]

The history of a nation—and the translation of that history into narratives disseminated in the media, written into textbooks, and internalized by the mass public—are instrumental in shaping the way that people relate to the powerful and the possibility of succeeding in one's own endeavors. National narratives in states that were the victims of colonialism or the object of invasions tend to embody tropes about the unjust distribution of global power.[11] For Turkey, the formative events of the republic involve an (actual) plot by European powers to dismantle the Ottoman empire for their own gain. Official histories glorify Turkey's successful resistance to Western interference and insinuate ongoing international efforts to hinder Turkey's progress.[12] In Russia, long-standing insecurity and ambivalent European and Asian identity are reflected in the insular and suspicious worldview of the ruling elite. Claims about encirclement were common in the Soviet Union's rhetoric, and informed its foreign policy during the Cold War.[13]

Explanations for perceived global injustices tend to favor personalized rather than structural factors, and lend themselves to conspiracy theories. For example, in Russia, citizens overwhelmingly fault Mikhail Gorbachev for deliberately weakening and then dismantling the Soviet Union—an explanation that ignores the global and domestic explanations.[14] As the USSR's primary competitor, the United States is blamed not only for the state's collapse—in which it reluctantly played a part—but also for Russia's later miseries. The West's later involvement is viewed in Russia not as a well-meaning but misguided effort to shepherd Russia's transition to a market economy, but as a deliberate plot to punish its longtime adversary and impoverish its citizens.[15] The enlargement of NATO is viewed not as a gradual and haphazard process driven by U.S. domestic politics and lack of foresight, but as a premeditated and calculated policy intended to take advantage of Russia at a time of weakness.[16]

Short-Term Triggers for Conspiracy Theory

If the historical narratives predispose politicians to think about the world in conspiratorial terms, their actual experience may confirm that worldview. The domestic political scene in many transitional and developing countries can make conspiracies seem all too real, for three reasons.

First is the pall of uncertainty, which can have major effects on political life. Where power holders cannot be confident that they will serve to the end of their term in office, they have an incentive to selfishly avail themselves of their position and strike deals that will pay off quickly. Just as important, they will anticipate that other politicians will act in equally mercenary ways. An atmosphere of distrust can prevail merely out of the precautionary principle of avoiding future exploitation. In conditions of high uncertainty, leaders risk over-interpreting information, leading them to favor malevolent explanations over accidents or complex causes in their accounting of events.

Second is intrigue, which can make politics look more like a John le Carré novel than an American politics textbook. Politicians amass power through the use of coercion, corruption, backstabbing, deception, character assassination, and various other ruses, rather than the mundane work of crafting policy and building coalitions through persuasion familiar in established democracies. Incumbents can rig elections by stuffing ballot boxes, compelling state employees to vote, or using their resource advantage to dominate the media. When politics is a blood sport, its combatants must learn to play by its rules or they are eliminated from the game.

A third reason conspiracy takes root is the presence of factions in politics. In some states, the historical struggle over power led to the creation of self-contained groups that continue to exercise influence behind the scenes. Sometimes labeled the "deep state," the phenomenon is presumed to exist and is the object of speculation and insinuation in many states; claims tend to appear where the military has long played a leading role, as in Pakistan and Turkey,[17] yet oddly surfaced in the early months of the Trump administration on the political right in the United States.[18] Deep state factions often have a stranglehold over national economies, enabling them to block, or benefit from, privatizing reforms. They often control the means of coercion, either directly through their organizational mission or indirectly through control over appointments to security agencies. Their economic interests and hold on power are mutually self-reinforcing—or are at least reputed to be.

The combination of uncertainty, intrigue, and secretive factions makes it difficult to ascertain truth and falsehood, and the imagination runs wild. The political environment is such that small groups can act in secret to benefit themselves at the expense of others and get away with it, the very definition of a conspiracy. Or at least it *appears* that they may do so, which is precisely the point. Where publics are constantly informed of corruption, malfeasance, and backstabbing in politics, but there are no trusted arbiters to help distinguish rumor from reality, why not believe in conspiracies?

Leaders who are socialized in such a political milieu can never be certain of the intentions of their subordinates, much less their rivals, and live with the fear that they may suddenly lose their claim to rule. Fortunately for those in power, most intrigue takes place behind the scenes, even if some episodes leak out to the public in the form of rumors. For example, people may hear of a corrupt deal that goes bad, an official who falls out of favor, or elites jockeying for position. These rumors may or may not merit commentary by those in power, as they are not very consequential and do not undermine the leader's authority. However, visible breaks with the status quo—public allegations of malfeasance, open and large-scale demonstrations of opposition, or violence and instability—demand a public response. Failure to persuasively account for these missteps can lead to a loss of confidence and erosion in the leader's support. It is when events visibly target incumbents or call into question their command of power that politicians actively deploy conspiracy claims.

The case studies below show how conspiracy theories can become a central preoccupation of politicians. Even in states where conspiracy theories lie below the surface—and real conspiracies probably occur on a fairly regular basis—politicians are selective in their deployment of conspiracy claims, lest they prematurely exhaust their credibility. Conspiracy theories emerge as a useful tool for them to maintain power and legitimacy when they are perceived to be under threat.

Institutional Weakness, Intrigue, and the Advent of Conspiracy Rhetoric

Russia has suffered its share of trauma over the years, and the events of the Gorbachev and Yeltsin years did little to reassure its inhabitants that the world was fundamentally just. On the surface, Russia was transitioning to democracy, but the state was being hollowed out. New capitalists sought to protect their property in the absence of a functioning legal system, resulting in private protection rackets and competition over market share that sometimes resulted in violence. One of the few parts of the state that was not dismantled during the transition was the security services, agents of which took advantage of their near-monopoly of violence and penetrating networks to secure a share of privatized property.[19] In the 1990s, casual readers of Russian newspapers were faced with reports of multifaceted intrigue and conspiracy on a daily basis: clashes between rival organized crime groups over market share; among oligarchs over deals gone bad; within Boris Yeltsin's *family*[20]; between the *family* and the oligarchs; between the state security services and private violent organizations; among politicians in competitive but legally unconstrained elections; and between politicians, businessmen, and organized criminal groups.

Given the freewheeling nature of politics in this period, conspiracy claims proliferated, as actors vying for power or property sought to undermine their adversaries by tying them to invidious plots. Analyses of politics in this period note the proliferation of scandals, as accusations of corruption became routine (Wilson, 2005).[21] What is often missed is that these scandals took on a Russian-hued leap from mundane malfeasance to grand and global linkages, for example, *the war in Chechnya was a bid by the security services to weaken Yeltsin and reinstate authoritarian rule.*[22] *Oligarchs deliberately crashed the Russian economy. Yeltsin and the Americans are destroying the political system in order to plunder Russia.*

When Vladimir Putin came to power, the source of conspiracy claims shifted to the state itself. The KGB networks that Yeltsin neglected to break up benefited when one of its own took the reins, and further entrenched themselves to become something akin to a deep state. In the course of reestablishing the state as the locus of power, the Putin regime both used conspiracy claims and engaged in conspiracies. For example, in the Yukos Affair, the government accused the CEO of the largest oil company in Russia of tax evasion, which most experts agree was a pretext to take over its assets. Putin, in his drive to consolidate power, would often insinuate foreign influence over oligarchs or imply a lack of patriotism (especially of oligarchs who were Jewish or held dual nationalities). As the state regained control over assets that had been privatized under Yeltsin, especially natural resources, Putin's close allies were appointed to head the major state corporations that now managed them. To a casual observer, this appeared a conspiracy perpetrated by the so-called *siloviki*, a shadowy network of Putin's allies from Russia's power ministries.[23]

In the middle of the decade, due to worsening relations with the United States and unanticipated and visible events that challenged Putin's narrative of restored control—mass protests in former Soviet republics—the regime projected its conspiracy claims outward. The so-called color revolutions in Georgia (2003), Ukraine (2004), and Kyrgyzstan (2005) were the result of disenchanted publics and partially authoritarian regimes. Just as Putin had seemingly stabilized Russia—at least according to the official narrative—these challenges to authoritarian leaders on Russia's periphery could not simply be dismissed. The fact that the successor governments in Georgia and Ukraine established strong pro-Western foreign policies made the so-called color revolutions appear even more ominous.[24]

By early 2005, Russian politicians and the state-controlled media were engaged in a campaign to convince their citizens and foreign audiences that the revolutions on Russia's periphery had been encouraged, planned, or even orchestrated by some permutation of President Bush, the CIA, the State Department, and George Soros. One of the vehicles for mass mobilization in Georgia and Ukraine was nongovernmental

organizations (NGOs), many of which had received American funding through democracy assistance programs and the U.S. Agency for International Development.
Ostensibly intended to strengthen civil society and enhance the quality of governance, their role in challenging election fraud, raising money, organizing protests,
and ultimately overthrowing (Russia-friendly) autocrats made them look like
instruments of U.S. foreign policy. As a result, the Russian government began to put
pressure on Western-funded NGOs.[25]

The Russian campaign against externally driven "velvet revolutions" borrowed
heavily from Soviet tropes about encirclement, espionage, and fifth columns,
creating a coherent and powerful narrative of Russian insecurity and Western duplicity. Putin, for example, warned ominously about fifth columns in Russia secretly working with the United States: "There are those inside our country who act
like jackals at foreign embassies, foreign diplomatic missions, counting on foreign
funds and governments, and not on the support of their own people."[26] The head
of Russia's national security service warned that "[f]oreign secret services are ever
more actively using non-traditional methods for their work and with the help of different NGOs' educational programs are propagandizing their interests, particularly
in the former Soviet Union."[27]

These events, and the anti-Western conspiracy discourse that continued to
evolve in Russia over the ensuing years, laid the groundwork for complete embrace
of conspiracy by the Russian political establishment and media following the overthrow of Ukrainian President Victor Yanukovych by pro-European activists in 2014.
Fusing long-standing tropes about Western encroachment and the uncertainty inherent in mass protest, Putin invoked a sinister but unnamed actor "who stood behind the . . . events in Ukraine."[28] Referring to Russia itself, he said that the "Western
special services continue their attempts at using public, non-governmental and
politicised organisations to pursue their own objectives, primarily to discredit the
authorities and destabilise the internal situation in Russia."[29] In other contexts,
his proxies fleshed out other parts of a grand conspiracy against Russia involving
NATO, the CIA, Russian liberals, Ukrainian "fascists," and even ISIS.[30]

By the end of Putin's third term, the notion of conspiracy was the coin of the
realm for the government. It was not inevitable that it would become so central
in discourse, but the character of post-Soviet politics and the availability of tropes
from Russia's recent history provided the people in power with a useful tool kit—
and, what is more, they may actually believe many of their claims.

Turkey followed a different path to political conspiracy discourse. Whereas
Putin's rise coincided with the consolidation of the state with the assistance of
loyal networks, Prime Minister Recep Tayyip Erdoğan's political success belied his
ongoing struggles against a "deep state," producing a steady drumbeat of political
intrigue. The guardian of Turkish politics since Ataturk, the military, sustained itself through authoritarian rule or pliant democratic leaders, all while maintaining
a dominant role in the economy.[31] Erdoğan, enjoying an overwhelming electoral

mandate and ideologically at odds with the military, sought to weaken it over his successive terms. He used both his power over appointments and his influence over the legal system to prosecute generals. They were charged with several plots over the years, with varying levels of plausibility, including false flag attacks against civilians as a pretext to justify a coup. As is often the case, a semblance of truth could be found.[32] As often happens, conspiracy allegations were flung in both directions; if the charges were fictitious, then it was Erdoğan who was behind a conspiracy.

As Erdoğan turned more authoritarian and sought to gain a wider margin of victory for his party in parliament, he became more sensitive to challenges to his authority. The Gezi Part protests of 2013, opposing an urban development project in Istanbul, was therefore a visible and threatening setback to Erdoğan. As in Russia, mass protests were seen by the government as threatening both to the dominant narrative of progress through development and the pretense of broad support for his policies. The extended duration of the protests and the diversity of participants—especially those with liberal and Western orientations—were inviting for intimations of conspiracy. While endorsing heavy-handed dispersal tactics against demonstrators, Erdoğan alleged a plot brought on by "internal traitors and external collaborators."[33] (Turkay Nefes addresses these sorts of accusations elsewhere in this volume.) Members of the government also accused Jews, both directly and as a thinly veiled "interest rate lobby," of seeking to harm Turkey.[34]

Later in his term, having neutralized Turkey's military as a threat, Erdoğan was confronted with another "deep state." Fetullah Gülen, a wealthy spiritual leader with a network of schools across Turkey, had been allied with Erdoğan against the nationalist old guard, but they parted ways as Erdoğan sought greater power. While their disagreement had been an object of rumors for several years, Erdoğan only turned to embrace conspiracy theory when the intrigue broke out into the open in 2014, after Erdoğan became the target of corruption allegations and members of his inner circle were arrested. An audio recording surfaced purportedly of Erdoğan instructing his son to move large amounts of cash in advance of a police raid. He claimed that he was the victim of a conspiracy by Gülen supporters, who were reputed to populate the police and legal systems and owe their primary allegiance to Gülen. Erdoğan retaliated by firing dozens of law enforcement officials and indicting Gülen.[35] Given the magnitude of the challenge, the conspiratorial claim had to be grand as well. So it was that Erdoğan accused his adversary of launching the July 2016 coup attempt, which resulted in over 300 deaths. Calling the plotters the "Gülenist Terrorist Organization," Erdoğan arrested or purged tens of thousands of people with purported Gülenist ties, however tenuous, and used the coup as a pretext to secure greater presidential powers.[36]

Was it possible that an old man living in exile in Pennsylvania was able to work through hundreds of acolytes that had infiltrated the highest echelons of the Turkish state to nearly overthrow the president? Yes, agreed most Turks.[37] This view makes sense given what Turks know about their own politics, and what they believe about the exercise of power in Turkish history. They might also be forgiven for believing the opposite: that Erdoğan contrived the coup as a false flag operation to increase his own power.[38] As is often the case, people had little to fall back on to determine what to believe, a fact that the government used to its advantage when increasing its control over the mass media. This example illustrates the affinity between conspiracy and authoritarianism, but both were facilitated by the prior reality of factional intrigue and national insecurities.

Afghanistan's history is a series of episodes of geopolitical intrigue, and Afghans alive today can recall two great power invasions bookending a civil war. In addition, the continual meddling by Pakistan, subtly or overtly, in Afghan politics means that conspiracies are often either likely real or sufficiently plausible to be invoked. Hamid Karzai ascended to the presidency in part thanks to his masterful ability to engage in intrigue, balancing between his American patrons, a meddling Pakistan, an Islamist opposition, warlords pursuing their local interests, and rival ethnic groups. As much as anywhere, actual and imagined conspiracies are a normal and predictable part of the lives of ordinary Afghans. Yet it was only in the latter part of Karzai's presidency that he began openly and frequently promoting conspiracy claims.[39]

While the first several years of Karzai's rule involved stabilizing the country and consolidating power, beginning in 2006 the Taliban reconstituted and launched an insurgency in Pashtun areas of the country. As the head of a weak state and an army unable to project power far out of Kabul, it was essential for Karzai to project the *impression* of control in order to convince people to support him. Yet attacks continued, and the International Security Assistance Force's (ISAF) counterinsurgency campaign not only failed to dampen such attacks but in some instances led to unnecessary civilian deaths. These visible manifestations of failure, albeit largely outside Karzai's control, constituted a threat to his rule. (If not for massive election fraud in 2009, he probably would have lost the presidency.)[40] To add insult to injury, Karzai's Western backers began to advocate negotiating with the Taliban.

In the course of a weakening hold on power and visible challenges to stability in the form of terrorist attacks in Kabul, Karzai began to assert that Afghanistan (and he personally) were the victims of a conspiracy between ISAF forces and the Taliban. In numerous speeches in both Pashto and English, along with accusations made in private, Karzai claimed that the United States had abandoned him and was collaborating with the Taliban to reach a deal behind his back.[41] As ridiculous as this may appear on its face, it provided an accounting for the failure of the world's most powerful army to squelch a rebellion of ragtag peasants, while absolving Karzai of blame for the slippage of greater amounts of territory outside the government's control. It also invoked a trope from Afghan history, of outsiders working through local proxies to spread their control. As in previous cases, Karzai may have believed his own claims, but that is not sufficient to explain why he promoted them. Ultimately, politicians decide to vocalize their allegations when they regard them as politically useful, and in the decaying institutional environment of late-Karzai Afghanistan, conspiracy was as compelling an explanation as any at hand.

Conspiracy Theories Are Not Only for the Masses

Where institutions are weak, much of what passes for politics takes place in the shadows, and the lack of transparency—or transparent falsehoods—in politics naturally engenders alternative narratives about power. Coupled with this, a geopolitical dimension lurks in the national narratives in the parts of the globe that are former imperial cores or were once victims of colonialism. Narratives of victimization and predatory politics give rise to a jaundiced view of how power is exercised. Politicians, though often the object of conspiracy theories themselves, have a ready arsenal of tropes they can deploy to account for contemporary setbacks and misfortunes by claiming conspiracies from both within and without.

Contrary to popular portrayals of leaders who endorse conspiracy theories as powerful demagogues using conspiracy to keep the populace docile and enthralled, the use of conspiracy theories was reactive. The leaders in question, though at times exhibiting authoritarian tendencies, had all won democratic elections and earned popular support in conventional ways such as supplying economic growth and security. It was only later in their tenures, when visibly destabilizing incidents occurred that undermined their claim to rule, that they turned to conspiracy theories. The new narratives identified and named known malefactors to account for sometimes complex phenomena, such as protests or violence, that social scientists typically ascribe to structural or institutional forces. Yet in the local milieu, where prejudices against those agents long preceded the events, the claims carried surface plausibility. None of these leaders risked the mocking and disapproval that meet conspiracy theorizing in established democracies.[42] In societies used to official malfeasance and politics that is governed by intrigue, that conspiracies take place is common sense; the only question is when and by whom.

How do we move forward? First, it is assumed that conspiracy is less prominent in democracies than authoritarian systems, and indeed, conspiracy theories emerged as leaders took their countries in authoritarian directions. But the causality is unclear. The fact that all three systems remained competitive in fact may have contributed to the need for politicians to deploy conspiracy theories to gain the upper hand. While dictators may enjoy unrivaled control over the political agenda, competition in politics invites other players to participate by offering their own theories, claims, and counterclaims.

Second, access to the media is a critical component of the conspiracy game. State control limits what messages can be disseminated, relegating subversive conspiracy theories to the margins, whereas media pluralism and a free market for ideas should be associated with both a greater amount and diversity of conspiracy claims. Social media can now be used to break through where the regime otherwise monopolizes the public sphere.

Finally, this explanation begs the question of how historical trauma, such as a history of civil violence or war, affects elites' propensity to perceive conspiracies or promote such claims. Many people in Russia and Afghanistan have lived through wrenching changes and been subjected to intense stress—a psychological state associated with a need to restore a sense of control over one's life. Why wouldn't politicians with the same experiences view the world in similar ways? As this essay has shown, caution is in order before assuming that politicians simply reflect their cultural surroundings. Taking political institutions into account suggests that when they publicly privilege conspiratorial explanations, there is probably a strategic element to the decision, but they are more likely responding to events outside their control than they are shaping reality to their whims.

Notes

1. Hence, descriptions of the United States as "conspiracy nation" or "conspiracy culture" refer to mass beliefs.

2. Inhofe, James M. 2012. *The Greatest Hoax: How the Global Warming Conspiracy Threatens Your Future.* Washington, D.C.: WND Books; Musgrave, Paul. 2017. "Donald Trump is Normalizing Paranoia and Conspiracy Thinking in U.S. Politics." *Washington Post.* https://www.washingtonpost.com/posteverything/wp/2017/01/12/donald-trump-has-brought-us-the-american-style-in-paranoid-politics/?utm_term=.1f1f6c9963e5 (Accessed December 21, 2017).

3. For example, Bortin, Meg. 2006. "Muslims 'Still in Denial' About 9/11, Pew Survey Finds." *International Herald Tribune.* http://www.nytimes.com/2006/06/22/world/europe/22cnd-pew.html (Accessed December 21, 2017).

4. Eichenwald, Kurt. 2014. "The Plots to Destroy America." *Newsweek.* http://www.newsweek.com/2014/05/23/plots-destroy-america-251123.html (Accessed December 21, 2017).

5. Chwe, Michael Suk-Young. 2013. *Rational Ritual: Culture, Coordination, and Common Knowledge.* Princeton: Princeton University Press.

6. Beissinger, Mark R. 2013. "The Semblance of Democratic Revolution: Coalitions in Ukraine's Orange Revolution." *American Political Science Review* 107(3): 574–592; Radnitz, Scott. 2016. "Paranoia with a Purpose: Conspiracy Theory and Political Coalitions in Kyrgyzstan." *Post-Soviet Affairs* 32(5): 474–489.

7. Hardin, Russell. 1993. "The Street-level Epistemology of Trust." *Politics & Society* 21(4): 505–529.

8. Putnam, Robert D., Robert Leonardi, and Raffaella Y. Nanetti. 1994. *Making Democracy Work: Civic Traditions in Modern Italy.* Princeton: Princeton University Press; Hedlund, Stefan. 2005. *Russian Path Dependence: A People with a Troubled History.* London and New York: Routledge.

9. Mishler, William, and Richard Rose. 2005. "What are the Political Consequences of Trust? A Test of Cultural and Institutional Theories in Russia." *Comparative Political Studies* 38(9): 1050–1078.

10. Goodson, Larry P. 2001. *Afghanistan's Endless War: State Failure, Regional Politics, and the Rise of the Taliban.* Seattle: University of Washington Press.

11. Miller, Manjari Chatterjee. 2013. *Wronged by Empire: Post-Imperial Ideology and Foreign Policy in India and China.* Palo Alto: Stanford University Press.

12. Guida, Michelangelo. 2008. "The Sèvres Syndrome and "Komplo" Theories in the Islamist and Secular Press." *Turkish Studies* 9(1): 37–52.

13. Tsygankov, Andrei P. "Finding a Civilisational Idea: 'West,' 'Eurasia,' and 'Euro-East' in Russia's Foreign Policy." *Geopolitics* 12(3): 375–399.

14. Shlapentokh, Vladimir. 1991. "A Glut of Conspiracy Theories." *Los Angeles Times.* http://articles.latimes.com/1991-04-16/local/me-17_1_conspiracy-theorie (Accessed December 21, 2017).

15. Cohen, Stephen F. 2001. *Failed Crusade: America and the Tragedy of Post-communist Russia.* London: W.W. Norton: 144–147.

16. Carpenter, Ted Galen, and Barbara Conry, eds. 1998. *NATO Enlargement: Illusions and Reality.* Washington, D.C.: Cato Institute.

17. Trofimov, Dmitri. 2014. "Pakistan Leader's Predicament Shows Power of 'Deep State.'" *Wall Street Journal.* https://www.wsj.com/articles/pakistan-leaders-predicament-shows-power-of-deep-state-1410282028 (Accessed December 21, 2017).

18. Manchester, Julia. 2017. "Trump Promotes Hannity's 'Deep State' Monologue." *The Hill.* http://thehill.com/media/338241-trump-shares-hannity-tweet-on-monologue-calling-for-leakers-to-be-jailed (Accessed December 21, 2017).

19. Volkov, Vadim. 2016. *Violent Entrepreneurs: The Use of Force in the Making of Russian Capitalism.* Ithaca: Cornell University Press.

20. This refers to his close network of associates including both kin and non-kin. See Kryshtanovskaya, Olga, and Stephen White. 2005. "The Rise of the Russian Business Elite." *Communist and Post-Communist Studies* 38(3): 293–307.

21. Wilson, Andrew. 2005. *Virtual Politics: Faking Democracy in the Post-Soviet World.* New Haven: Yale University Press.

22. Sakwa, Richard, ed. 2005. *Chechnya: From Past to Future.* London: Anthem Press.

23. Dawisha, Karen. 2015. *Putin's Kleptocracy: Who Owns Russia?* New York: Simon and Schuster.

24. Ukraine's Orange Revolution was especially painful for Putin, who had openly endorsed and sent political consultants to advise the ultimate loser from the events, Viktor Yanukovych.

25. Horvath, Robert. 2013. *Putin's Preventive Counter-Revolution: Post-Soviet Authoritarianism and the Spectre of Velvet* Revolution. London and New York: Routledge.

26. BBC Russian. 2007. "Putin sravnil opponentov s shakalami." *BBC Russian.* http://news.bbc.co.uk/hi/russian/russia/newsid_7105000/7105258.stm (Accessed December 21, 2017).

27. Walsh, Nick Paton. 2005. "Russia Says Spies Work in Foreign NGOs." *The Guardian*, May 13, 2005.

28. Putin Vladimir. 2014. "Address by President of the Russian Federation, Official Internet Resources of the President of Russia, March 18, 2004.' http://en.kremlin.ru/events/president/news/20603 (Accessed December 30, 2017).

29. Putin, Vladimir. 2015. "Federal Security Service Board Meeting." http://en.kremlin.ru/events/president/news/49006 (Accessed December 21, 2017).

30. Ennis, Stephen. 2014. "Russian TV sees US Plot behind Ukraine and IS Militants." *BBC News.* http://www.bbc.com/news/world-europe-29368707 (Accessed December 21, 2017).

31. Cook, Steven A. 2007. *Ruling but Not Governing: The Military and Political Development in Egypt, Algeria, and Turkey.* Baltimore: Johns Hopkins University Press.

32. Anonymous. 2013. "Turkish politics: Justice or revenge?" *The Economist.* https://www.economist.com/news/europe/21583312-harsh-verdicts-are-handed-down-ergenekon-trial-justice-or-revenge (Accessed December 21, 2017).

33. Hurriyet. 2013. "Turkish Prime Minister Vows to Increase Police Force." *Hurriyet.* http://www.hurriyetdailynews.com/turkish-prime-minister-vows-to-increase-police-force.aspx?pageID=238&nID=49006&NewsCatID=338 (Accessed December 21, 2017).

34. Winer, Stuart. 2013. "Turkish Deputy PM Blames Jews for Gezi Protests." *Times of Israel.* http://www.timesofisrael.com/turkish-deputy-pm-blames-jews-for-gezi-protests/ (Accessed December 21, 2017).

35. Williams, Carol J. 2014. "Turkish Government Sacks 350 Police Carrying Out Corruption Probe." *Los Angeles Times.* http://articles.latimes.com/2014/jan/07/world/la-fg-wn-turkey-corruption-police-sacked-20140107 (Accessed December 21, 2017).

36. Kingsley, Patrick 2017. "Erdogan Claims Vast Powers in Turkey After Narrow Victory in Referendum." *New York Times.* https://www.nytimes.com/2017/04/16/world/europe/turkey-referendum-polls-erdogan.html (Accessed December 21, 2017).

37. Reuters Staff. "Turks Believe Cleric Gulen was Behind Coup Attempt: Survey." *Reuters.com.* http://www.reuters.com/article/us-turkey-security-survey-idUSKCN1060P1 (Accessed December 21, 2017).

38. Fontanella-Khan, Amana. 2016. "Fethullah Gülen: Turkey Coup May Have Been 'Staged' by Erdoğan Regime." *The Guardian.* https://www.theguardian.com/world/2016/jul/16/fethullah-gulen-turkey-coup-erdogan (Accessed December 21, 2017).

39. Searches of both Lexis Nexis and Wikileaks for mentions of Karzai along with conspiracy and related words confirm this.

40. Tavernise, Sabrina, and Abdul Waheed Wafa. 2009. "UN Official Acknowledges 'Widespread Fraud' in Afghan Election." *New York Times.* http://www.nytimes.com/2009/10/12/world/asia/12afghan.html (Accessed December 21, 2017).

41. Rubin, Elizabeth. 2009. "Karzai in his Labyrinth." *New York Times Magazine.* http://www.nytimes.com/2009/08/09/magazine/09Karzai-t.html?pagewanted=all (Accessed December 21, 2017); Inskeep, Steve. 2013. "Hamid Karzai Lives in a 'World of Paranoia and Conspiracy.'" *NPR.org.* http://www.npr.org/2013/11/21/246492072/hamid-karzai-lives-in-a-world-of-paranoia-and-conspiracy (Accessed December 21, 2017).

42. See other chapters in this volume on the normative connotations of conspiracy theories in the West.

24

Conspiracy Theories in Post-Soviet Russia

ILYA YABLOKOV

"Why does the West hate us?" asked the famous post-Soviet conspiracy theorist Nikolaĭ Starikov in the title of his popular book.[1] In his view all Russian revolutions, liberal reforms, and political turbulence that have taken place in the last 300 years can be closely linked to a conspiring minority of West-leaning activists who used financial resources provided by the West, primarily the United Kingdom and the United States, to destroy Russia from within. Indeed, most post-Soviet Russian authors of conspiracy theories base their ideas on the notion that the West—perceived as a single, undifferentiated entity—has a devilish plan to destroy their great country, divide its massive territory into a number of puppet states, and plunder its gas, oil, and other natural resources.[2] Conspiratorial ideas about the West permeate the language of the post-Soviet media and politics, and some particularly notorious conspiracy theorists joined the ranks of high-profile politicians and public intellectuals in the late 2000s.

Since 1991, conspiracy theories have been gradually moving from the margins of political discourse into its center. This process reached its highest point in 2014–2016 during the Ukraine crisis, when anti-Western and anti-U.S. conspiracy theories became a feature of daily life for millions of Russians and their political leaders. In 2015 we learned from Vladimir Putin that the Internet was the invention of the CIA and therefore part of the anti-Russian conspiracy.[3] From First Deputy Prime Minister Arkadiĭ Dvorkovich, we got to know that the drop in the price of oil was brought about by foreign plotters who were trying to destroy Russia.[4] In 2016 we learned from Putin's economic advisor Sergeĭ Glaz'ev that the Russian government had been infiltrated by foreign agents who were determined to undermine the country's economic stability by means of international sanctions.[5] Influenced by their leaders, Russians started to believe that the United States and the European Union were Russia's worst enemies and that Ukraine was a puppet state whose leaders were appointed in Washington, D.C. to assist in Russia's downfall.[6]

In order to understand how conspiracy theories have developed and functioned in Russian society post-1991, it is important to bear in mind that they can serve as an effective tool for interpreting power relationships in the modern world, analyzing complex issues that affect people's daily lives, and explaining why a particular community (or, indeed, an entire nation) undergoes traumatic experiences. Turbulent times often produce talented leaders who successfully mobilize the public by spreading conspiracy theories which gain them popularity and political success. As Mark Fenster noted, conspiracy theories can be seen as populist theories of power.[7] They possess an important communicative function by helping to unite their audience as "the people" against an imagined "other," a secret "power bloc." These populist calls help leaders to polarize society and undermine their opponents by ruining their reputations and in some cases even justifying repression against them. This is what we can observe in post-Soviet Russia, where anti-Western conspiracy theories have become part of daily life and cannot be treated, as is often the case, as part of a paranoiac's worldview. They have been a very effective and powerful weapon in the power battles that helped the Kremlin justify its move toward authoritarianism and its introduction of new antidemocratic laws in the 2000s.

Conspiracy theories in Russia can be analyzed in two ways. First, they can be seen as a tool of national and social cohesion. Second, they can be treated as a powerful instrument in the battle between political opponents. With the emergence of nation-states out of the former Soviet Union and their attempts to establish a sovereign people and a path toward democracy, the conditions were created for the emergence of populism. The populist rhetoric, in turn, enabled politicians to discursively divide the social into two camps, with "the other" acting in opposition to "the people." In the case of Russian national identity, the "other" has historically been the West, regarded either as a positive model for Russia to emulate or a negative example to be rejected. This has helped to determine the idea of Russia's national identity and its place in world history.[8] In this context, fears about anti-Western conspiracy arise as part of the so-called *ressentiment* that came from the recognition of the discrepancy between Russia and the West, and which demonstrated either Russia's equality with or its superiority over the West.[9] In the mind of a typical Russian nationalist with anti-Western views, the West appears as the ultimate and insidious other that seeks to undermine the progress of the Russian nation toward its glorious future.

Virtually all of the main actors in political life in post-Soviet Russia have employed the rhetoric of conspiracy: it enables them to strengthen their legitimacy in the competition for public support and power resources. For example, the Kremlin regularly uses conspiracy ideas to explain the authoritarian measures it takes against its opponents, which include foreign NGOs, opposition politicians, and diplomats. This provides it with an opportunity to shape the image of the dangerous other and convince the population of the need to continue to support the government. At the same time, the liberal opposition also uses conspiracy theories about the Kremlin, insisting it is run by the KGB clan, which will stop at nothing to protect its power. One example is the theory that Putin was responsible for the explosions in apartment houses across Russia in 1999; this effectively justified the war in Chechnya in the 2000s, which in turn enabled Putin's popularity to skyrocket within months of his appointment as prime minister and even attracted a reasonable amount of support from the oppositionist communities.[10]

In analyzing post-Soviet Russian conspiracy theories, it is worth considering the following aspects of the phenomenon:

1. While there are several alternative theories—for example, it could be the Jews or the Russian government conspiring against the Russian people—the most popular theory is that there is a Western conspiracy against Russia. This originated in a particular reading of the Soviet collapse in December 1991. The speed of the collapse, and the confusion it produced both in the population as a whole and among the country's elites, resulted in the spread of the idea that the United States and the internal agents of "Western influence" were behind it. Thus, the Soviet collapse and the events which followed it—the economic reforms and the decrease in Russia's influence in the world—were seen as the highest point in the West's bid to destroy Russia.

2. Russian politicians and intellectuals often actively exploit conspiracy theories to help them carry out their domestic policies and nation-building agenda, as well as achieve their goals in international relations.[11] Conspiracy theories are a powerful tool in popular mobilization, and they can also help to destroy the reputations and legitimacy of political opponents by connecting their names to the U.S. government or intelligence services. Therefore, the conspiratorial reading of the Soviet collapse helps to define as "us" the Russian public which is loyal to the country, and "them" as those who welcomed the destruction of the USSR, benefited from it, and worked for the West. This division within Russian society helps the Russian authorities to demonize their opponents and delegitimize their positions on the political stage. Since these notions are actively exploited to challenge the Kremlin's political rivals, conspiracy has become a crucial element in political discourse.

3. Russian political leaders are very careful in how they spread conspiracy theories themselves. This role is given to either public intellectuals or low-ranking politicians who have access to the state-affiliated media. Yet the Russian political leadership also, at times, refers to or hints at conspiratorial ideas, which turns them into a valid part of political discourse. This careful and instrumental application of anti-Western conspiracy theories is used by the Kremlin to confuse observers and polarize the Russian population.

4. Unlike in the United States, where conspiracy theories spread from grassroots to the upper level of society, in Russia this has been a top-down process, with Kremlin-loyal intellectuals, book publishers, and the media helping to spread these theories among the population. However, it is important to note that although this discourse is important for the stability of Putin's political regime, the

Kremlin does not allow genuine conspiracy theorists—that is, true believers in conspiracy theories—to fill powerful positions. Accordingly, these people have limited capacity to define the political agenda of the country.

1991: The Triumph of Russia's Enemies

"The Soviet Union collapsed not as a result of natural processes . . . , but as a result of political conspiracy on the part of the 'fifth column' . . . as a result of conspiracy headed by B. Yeltsin."[12] In 1999 the MP and former general prosecutor Viktor Iliukhin accused the then Russian president, Boris Yeltsin, of destroying the USSR and letting a small "cabal" of 200 rich families loot the economy and destroy those remnants of the population who still remembered living a relatively prosperous life in the Soviet Union. This speech and the attack on Yeltsin was an important moment; it marked the point at which anti-Western conspiracy theories appeared in parliament as a political instrument which could undermine Yeltsin's legitimacy during the 1998–1999 impeachment procedure. A determined focus on the 1991 collapse led to Yeltsin being presented as the "other," a puppet of the West who stood against the Russian nation. The attempt to impeach Yeltsin also coincided with a rise in anti-Western sentiment in Russia which was related to the NATO operation in Serbia in 1999; this too was used by the opposition to win voters' support.

Iliukhin's arguments benefited immensely from an already elaborated corpus of ideas about the Soviet collapse which appeared in Russia post-1991. The anti-Western ideas that circulated during the Cold War in the USSR had informed the first generation of conspiracy theorists, who claimed that the destruction of the USSR was the United States' top-priority goal, while Mikhail Gorbachev's Perestroika—a set of reforms that liberalized the country's politics and economy in the late 1980s—was part of a malicious plan aimed at the destruction of the Soviet Union.[13]

A number of articles, which were actually based on forgeries, explained to the Russian readers how Soviet and Russian political leaders, in collaboration with the West, destroyed the Soviet Union. The most popular forged text in this collection— the so-called *Plan Dallesa (The Plan of Dulles)*—was purported to be a U.S. National Security Council directive about a strategy for the moral and cultural corruption of the Soviet people.[14] Another claimed that Mikhail Gorbachev actually confessed that he destroyed the Soviet Union, with the support of the United States, out of hate for the country.[15] Russian nationalists actively shared and discussed the supposed revelations made by President Bill Clinton in his speech at a Joint Chiefs of Staff meeting in 1995 about a Western plot against Russia.[16] Each of these texts encapsulates popular conspiracy ideas about American (or British) involvement in the destruction of the USSR and depicts Gorbachev and Yeltsin as key destructive individuals following the plan of their "American masters." In the 1990s, Yeltsin's opponents, together with some Russian nationalists, used these negative images of the Russian political elite to delegitimize their policies and gain the support of both the national patriotic and communist electorate.[17]

The opening up of Russia to Western European cultural influence resulted in the transfer of some conspiracy theories from abroad with a view to understanding what happened to the USSR in 1991. An ex-KGB officer, Igor Panarin, claimed that in 1943 the United States and the United Kingdom started the "first information war" against the Soviet Union.[18] The Committee of 300, the Trilateral Commission, and the Council on Foreign Relations reputedly waged this war by organizing subversive campaigns against the USSR. It is likely that Panarin's concept absorbed and was shaped by notions of global conspiracy that were popular in Western Europe and the United States at that time; he then went on to reinterpret these conspiracies as exclusively anti-Russian. For example, Panarin identified American banker David Rockefeller as the mastermind behind the Soviet collapse. Panarin also depicted The Committee of 300, the Council on Foreign Relations, and the Trilateral Commission as the main centers of anti-Russian conspiracy in the West. Indeed, these organizations do play major roles in the New World Order conspiracy theory, but they do not mention Russia specifically.[19]

Starting from the mid-2000s, the Soviet collapse became an important component of the Kremlin-endorsed nation-building narrative. Rueful feelings about this once-great country having lost its greatness because of its attempt at democratization, supported by the notion of a conspiracy on the part of "Western enemies," cemented national cohesion and represented the political leadership as being in tune with the people. The dramatic picture drawn by Putin and his aides from the mid-2000s focused on the socioeconomic and political inequities faced by Russian society in the 1990s. The famous Putin argument, that the Soviet collapse was "the major geopolitical disaster of the century," signified the start of this process.[20] Therefore, a positive attitude toward a lost past, connected with the Soviet experience, offered an alternative image of the post-Soviet changes; it served as an important tool with which to identify "the people" as a pan-national "community of loss" and contrast them with the collective "other" represented by a group of people who had no such nostalgia for the Soviet past. This is a model of nation-building which Serguei Oushakine described as "the patriotism of despair."[21] The actors included in this collective other usually consisted of the most westernized part of Russian society. This, in principle, made it possible for them to be represented in the emerging official discourse as agents of foreign and subversive influence.

The official narrative of the Soviet collapse in 1991, which was disseminated through the media and public speeches of pro-Kremlin intellectuals and politicians, merged nostalgia about the lost Soviet Union with the conviction that Russia, as an important player in world politics, was under attack by countries wanting to acquire its vast territory and its abundant natural resources. The Soviet collapse was closely linked to a loss of national identity and was seen as a tragic event caused solely by a conspiracy on the part of Western enemies.

Conspiracy Theories and Conspiracy Practices

The first attempts to use anti-Western conspiracy theories on the Russian political stage were made in 2003–2004 when the Kremlin faced several challenges from its political rivals. Putin's close aide Vladislav Surkov expressed the belief that anti-national conspiracy existed within Russia as well as outside its borders:

> We should all recognize that the enemy is at the gates. The frontline goes through every city, every street, every house . . . in a besieged country the fifth column of left- and right-wing radicals has emerged . . . Fake liberals and real Nazis have a lot in common. [They have] common sponsors from abroad. [They have] common hatred toward Putin's Russia, as they describe it. In reality [it is a hatred toward] Russia as such.[22]

The active employment of anti-Western conspiracy theories since then has turned these theories into a crucial element in domestic politics.

In 2003 the richest man in the country, Mikhail Khodorkovsky, was arrested, largely because of his political ambitions and lack of loyalty to the Kremlin.[23] The case against Khodorkovsky was made by conservative groups of pro-Kremlin elites in the context of a "creeping conspiracy of oligarchs" who saw Putin as a weak leader who should be replaced. Khodorkovsky's enemies unabashedly claimed that Khodorkovsky was preparing to overthrow the regime and pass power to a small cabal of financial tycoons who profited from extracting fossil fuels, and who would protect their power by appealing to the West for support. It was also rumored that documents had appeared on Putin's desk which provided evidence that Khodorkovsky had struck a deal with U.S. Secretary of State Condoleezza Rice that included the assurance that when he was president of Russia, he would abandon nuclear weapons.[24] This alleged deal with the United States was instrumental in sealing Khodorkovsky's fate. His openness to the world, political ambitions, and willingness to become part of the global financial elite were seen as indicative of just how alien he was to Russia. During the second trial against him in 2009–2010, a famous Russian conspiracy theorist, Alexander Dugin, suggested that Khodorkovsky was an agent of the New World Order which aimed to destroy Russia's sovereignty and place it in the hands of the United States.[25] As a result, Khodorkovsky spent 10 years in prison, and Putin was rid of his competitor.

Fighting Against Revolutions

The next challenge to the regime came in 2004 when the "color revolutions" in the post-Soviet states demonstrated to the Kremlin that its power could be challenged by alternative forces. Russia's power brokers had a very important task: to ensure that the transfer of power in 2007–2008 from Putin to his successor would be smooth and secure, especially given the events in Ukraine in 2005 where crowds in the center of Kyiv prevented the election of the pro-Kremlin candidate. Again, the threat was linked to the West—specifically, to the United States—which, according to pro-Kremlin sources, planned to overthrow the Russian regime as soon as Putin, after serving two consecutive terms as president, was required by the constitution to leave the Kremlin. Supposed threats to the regime were said to emanate both from the political opposition and from the nongovernmental organizations that monitor elections and violations of human rights and which were said to be linked to the United States. They have been constantly demonized in the Kremlin-loyal media as conspirators and internal enemies who destroyed the USSR in 1991. Authoritarian changes in legislation were justified by the Kremlin as an attempt to protect the country from foreign invasion brought about by the subversive actions of NGOs.

Both the parliamentary and presidential campaigns of 2007–2008 and 2011–2012—both of which were seen as crucial elements in preserving the legitimacy of the regime—have revolved around the notion of a Western plot to overthrow Putin. This has helped the Kremlin to ensure a sufficient level of public support, has strengthened Putin's power, and has justified repression against the opposition. Putin is represented by the state-aligned media as the key figure defending the country from Western conspiracy. Moreover, Putin's public image has been constructed in such a way that he seemingly represents not only the Russian nation but all of the nations that are trying to resist the United States and other forces of globalization, which are sometimes referred to as the New Order.

The Kremlin's reaction to the Ukraine crisis in 2014 is a clear illustration of how essential anti-Western conspiracy theories have become for the political establishment in Russia, and how conspiracy theories have been used as an apparently legitimate part of political discourse. Putin's appeal to the Council of the Federation on March 1, 2014, for permission to deploy military force in Ukraine was explained by the senators of the Federal Council as a response to the threat of a U.S. invasion of Ukraine and was supported unanimously.[26]

The media campaign to persuade the population to interpret Russia's policies in Ukraine in an anti-Western light is seen by pro-Kremlin politicians and media as payback for the collapse of the Soviet Union in 1991, which was supposedly organized by the West. By means of the press and television talk shows, public intellectuals and politicians loyal to the Kremlin interpreted the Euromaidan movement—civil resistance to the corrupt regime in Ukraine—as a result of subversive Western action which brainwashed Ukrainian citizens and turned them against Russia. The opposition in Ukraine and the new president Poroshenko have been described as a "fascist government" under the auspices of the CIA. At the same time, the intervention in the Crimea was justified by the need to protect "compatriots" from extreme Ukrainian nationalists backed by the West and the NATO fleet. The Crimea's annexation was described in the state-aligned press as the end of the New World Order's rule in Russia and a key step in the construction of the Russian nation.[27]

Conspiracy Theorists at the Kremlin Throne

Public intellectuals loyal to the Kremlin have been the key element in spreading conspiracy theories in post-Soviet Russia. It was they who explained that the dramatic domestic changes experienced by Russian citizens in the 1990s, during the economic reform and political transition from socialism to democracy, were the result of subversive actions by the "conspiring West." Public intellectuals' criticism of the West, as expressed in conspiracy theories, also provided both the population and the authorities with an idealized image of Russia: despite the country's socioeconomic upheavals, they managed to present it as a great multi-ethnic state, which managed even after the 1991 shock to resist attempts of the West to control its territory and resources.

What distinguishes Russian conspiracy culture from, for example, that of the United States, is the engagement of public intellectuals on the side of the ruling elites. The anti-elitism of conspiracy theorists in the United States suggests that they belong to "the people" and strengthens the populist nature of their rhetoric. It is likely that U.S. conspiracy theorists would like to become a part of the political elite and influence the political agenda in the country.[28] However, in contrast to Russia, public consensus in the United States regarding the boundaries and rules of acceptable forms of political rhetoric significantly lessens the chances of American conspiracy theorists acquiring high social and academic standing.

Unlike their American counterparts, Russian authors of anti-Western conspiracy theories are often seen as particularly influential public intellectuals who have published well-received books and have access to the media, particularly those controlled by the state.[29] Conspiracy theorists are employed to delegitimize political opponents and, in some cases, justify major changes to legislation. Natalia Narochnitskaia, a pro-government historian, and Alexander Dugin, a prominent philosopher, are two good examples. They both blame the West for waging a war against Russia which, they argue, is aimed at destroying Russia's greatness and military potential.[30] All the same, they depict Russia as a great state which is managing to resist occupation by the New World Order. In her speeches Narochnitskaia has often described pro-Western liberal opponents to the Kremlin as a group of internal conspirators in collaboration with the West who have nothing in common with the Russian nation and who are doing untold harm to Russians' memory of their great past.[31]

Even the most bizarre conspiratorial ideas are not excluded from mainstream Russian politics. Public intellectuals provide the grounds for the popularization of conspiracy theories which top-ranking officials can use later for various domestic and international purposes. For example Nikolaï Patrushev, head of the major counterintelligence agency from 1999 to 2008 and now secretary of the Security Council, openly claimed that the United States was the main instigator of the Ukrainian conflict in 2014. According to Patrushev, the motive behind the Ukraine crisis was not the people's desire to have a more democratic country; rather, it was the United States' desire to create a new generation of Ukrainians who despised Russia and would ensure that Ukraine was removed from Russia's sphere of influence.[32]

How Paranoid Is the Kremlin?

At the high point of the Ukraine crisis in March 2014, German Chancellor Angela Merkel observed, in a telephone conversation with then U.S. president Barack Obama, that Vladimir Putin had "lost touch with reality."[33] She hinted that Putin had lost his mind and that his actions were not rational. However, for Russian elites, conspiracy theories are not a way of perceiving reality but a crude and powerful mechanism of popular mobilization. Few people in Europe and the United States are aware of this.

Some of the leading Russian conspiracy theorists' criticism of Kremlin policies— which is primarily concerned with what they see as a lack of active engagement in eastern Ukraine—reveals an interesting interaction between the Kremlin and the ardent supporters of conspiracy theories.[34] It also shows how Kremlin policies, wrapped in conspiratorial rhetoric, can be misunderstood by Europeans and Americans. The limited and largely covert involvement of Russian forces in eastern Ukraine was not enough for those who advocated the immediate annexation of the region. The regions of eastern and southern Ukraine, which had been part both of the Russian Empire and the Soviet Union, were seen by anti-Western Russian philosophers as the crucial focal point for the restoration of the empire. This was the linchpin of many Russian nation-building projects as well as a major battleground with the West.[35] The Kremlin used this historical heritage when bargaining with the European Union and the United States to justify both the federalization of Ukraine and Russia's resistance to the Ukrainian authorities in the Donbass region. Yet these issues disappeared from the mainstream media and political discourse as soon as the Kremlin achieved certain goals.[36]

Some Russian conspiracy theorists saw the conflict as the beginning of a conservative revolution in Russia and the end of the Western domination.[37] Some went even further. For the most prolific anti-Westerner, Alexander Dugin, this was the start of the long-awaited "war of the continents"; for others it was the start of a new cold war.[38] Neither of these plans was on the Kremlin's agenda at the time, and their supporters suffered minor repercussions. This case proves that those at the top of the Russian political elite are generally circumspect in their use of conspiracy theories; they keep genuine theorists at a distance from the decision-making process on important matters, unless their actions benefit the Kremlin's plans.

Conclusion

The case of post-Soviet Russian conspiracy culture sheds light on how conspiracy theories can help to keep an authoritarian regime in power. In Putin's Russia, theories about a malign and dangerous West have helped to maintain social cohesion and have formed the basis of many political campaigns aimed at legitimizing the regime. The constant juxtaposition of "the people" of Russia, whose concern (unlike in 1991) is the preservation of the state and the maintenance of the status quo, and the "other," which seeks to undermine the integrity of the nation, is a tool that has been used to deal with ever-emerging conflicts in the country. The West is presented as the embodiment of a powerful external foe that bolsters the nation's internal enemies. Social mobilization is carried out through aggressive campaigns in the state-aligned media to detect and destroy enemies and allows the Kremlin to meet social, political, and inter-ethnic challenges.

Many of the conspiracy theories popular in Russia today originated in Europe and the United States, but by the mid-2010s they found a place in the rhetoric of Russia's mainstream intellectuals and politicians. The importation of conspiracy theories, their application to the domestic situation, and even their subsequent exportation by means of international broadcasting (for example, the television channel Russia Today, now known as RT) is a curious case of how global conspiracy theories work in this new, "post-truth" world.[39]

The events of the last decade have demonstrated that Russia can swiftly evolve from the position of decaying post-imperial state located on the outskirts of the growing European Union to that of an important player in international affairs, capable of undertaking a significant role in the domestic politics of the United States, the United Kingdom, and other European countries. Conspiracy theories have been the key element in this process. On the one hand, they have become the driving force in popular mobilization, creating space for the authorities to implement their ideas about how the country should be run. On the other hand, active disinformation campaigns abroad questioned the quality of democracy in many European countries, not to mention the United States. The success of these disinformation campaigns, which are based on conspiracy theories, depends on independent actors working tactically for their own benefit.[40] Therefore, a deeper analysis of Russia's conspiracy theories will help us to comprehend what strategies Russia's elite can design to protect and increase its power.

Notes

1. Starikov, Nikolaï. 2009. *Zapad protiv Rossii: Za chto nas nenavidiat?* Moscow: Éksmo.
2. Etkind, Alexander, and Ilya Yablokov. 2017. "Global Crises as Western Conspiracies: Russian Theories of Oil Prices and the Ruble Exchange Rate." *Journal of Soviet and Post-Soviet Politics and Society* 3(2): 47–87.
3. MacAskill, Ewan. 2014. "Putin Calls Internet a 'CIA project' Renewing Fears of Web Breakup." *Guardian.* https://www.theguardian.com/world/2014/apr/24/vladimir-putin-web-breakup-internet-cia (Accessed November 26, 2017).
4. Kuvakin, Ilya. 2015. "Dvorkovich dopustil zagovor protiv Rossii kak prichinu padeniia tsen na neft'. *RBC.* http://www.rbc.ru/economics/17/02/2015/54e2760b9a7947ea2a641f0a (Accessed November 26, 2017).
5. Adrianova, Anna. 2016. "Putin's Maverick Adviser Defies Nabiullina With $64 Billion Plan." *Bloomberg.* https://www.bloomberg.com/news/articles/2016-10-30/putin-s-maverick-adviser-defies-nabiullina-with-64-billion-plan (Accessed November 26, 2017).
6. Levada-Center. 2017. "Druz'ia' i 'vragi' Rossii." *Levada-tsentr.* https://www.levada.ru/2017/06/05/druzya-i-vragi-rossii-2/ (Accessed November 26, 2017).
7. Fenster, Mark. 2008. *Conspiracy Theories: Secrecy and Power in American Culture.* Minneapolis: University of Minnesota Press, 89.
8. Tolz, Vera. 2001. *Russia.* London: Arnold.
9. Greenfield, Leah. 1992. *Nationalism: Five Roads to Modernity.* Cambridge: Harvard University Press.
10. Litvinenko, Alexander, and Yuri Felshtinsky. 2007. *Blowing Up Russia: The Return of the KGB.* London: Gibson Square Books.
11. Yablokov, Ilya. 2014. "Pussy Riot as Agent Provocateur: Conspiracy Theories and the Media Construction of Nation in Putin's Russia." *Nationalities Papers: The Journal of Nationalism and Ethnicity* 42(4): 622–636.
12. Iliukhin, Viktor. 2017. "Obviniaetsia El'tsin." http://www.viktor-iluhin.ru/node/328 (Accessed November 26, 2017).
13. Shironin, Valerii. 2010. *Agenty perestroïki.* Moscow: Éksmo.
14. Dulles, Allen. "Plan Dallesa po unichtozheniiu SSSR (Rossii)." http://www.russkoedelo.org/mysl/miscellaneous/dulles_plan.php (Accessed November 26, 2017).
15. Gorbachev, Mikhail. 2010. "Tsel'iu moeï zhizni bylo unichtozhenie kommunizma." *Newsland.* https://newsland.com/user/4297656659/content/gorbachiov-tseliu-moei-zhizni-bylo-unichtozhenie-kommunizma/4074611 (Accessed November 26, 2017).
16. Unknown. n.d. "*Rech' prezidenta SShA B. Klintona.*" http://militera.lib.ru/science/kapitanetz/08.html (Accessed November 26, 2017).
17. March, Luke. 2002. *The Communist Party in Post-Soviet Russia.* Manchester, UK: Manchester University Press.
18. Igor', Panarin. 2010. *Pervaia Informatsionnaia Voïna: Razval SSSR.* St. Petersburg, Russia: Piter.
19. Cooper, Milton William. 1991. *Behold a Pale Horse.* Flagstaff, AZ: Light Technology Publications.
20. Putin, Vladimir. 2005. "Annual Address to the Federal Assembly of the Russian Federation." http://archive.kremlin.ru/eng/speeches/2005/04/25/2031_type70029type82912_87086.shtml (Accessed November 26, 2017).
21. Oushakine, Seguei. 2009. *The Patriotism of Despair: Nation, War and Loss in Russia.* Ithaca: Cornell University Press.

22. Kaftan, Liudmila. 2004. "Zamestitel' glavy administratsii Prezidenta RF Vladislav Surkov: Putin ukrepliaet gosudarstvo, a ne sebia." *Komsomol'skaia Pravda*, http://www.kp.ru/daily/23370/32473/. (Accessed November 26, 2017).

23. Sakwa, Richard. 2014. *Putin and the Oligarch: The Khodorkovsky-Yukos Affair*. New York: I.B. Tauris.

24. Zygar, Mikhail. 2016. *All the Kremlin's Men*. New York: PublicAffairs.

25. Onlooker1001. 2009. *"Podlye plany Khodorkovskogo i YuKOSa v otnoshenii Rossii."* YouTube video, 10:05. Posted December 12, 2009. https://www.youtube.com/watch?v=jlv-aaiOaHw (Accessed November 26, 2017).

26. The Council of the Federation. 2014. "Stenogramma trista sorok sed'mogo (vneocherednogo) zasedaniia Soveta Federatsii. Moscow." *The Council of the Federation*. http://council.gov.ru/media/files/41d4c8b9772e9df14056.pdf (Accessed November 26, 2017).

27. Remizov, Mikhail. 2014. "Zhertva krymskoï kampanii." *Izvestiia*. http://iz.ru/news/567486 (Accessed November 26, 2017).

28. Kay, Jonathan. 2011. *Among the Truthers: A Journey through America's Growing Conspiracist Underground*. New York: HarperCollins.

29. Clover, Charles. 2016. *Black Wind, White Snow. The Rise of Russia's New Nationalism*. New Haven: Yale University Press.

30. Dugin, A. 2000. *Osnovy geopolitiki*. Moscow: Arktogeia-tsentr.

31. Narochnitskaia, Nataliia. 2007. *"Nataliia Narochnitskaia: 'My dolzhny stat' natsiei.'"* http://www.narochnitskaia.ru/in-archive/nataliya-narochnitskaya-quot-myi-dolzhnyi-stat-natsiey-quot.html?view=full (Accessed November 26, 2017).

32. Rostovskii, Mikhail. 2016. "Nikolai Patrushev: 'Mirovoe soobshchestvo dolzhno skazat' nam spasibo za Krym'." *Moskovskii Komsomolets*. http://www.mk.ru/politics/2016/01/26/nikolay-patrushev-mirovoe-soobshhestvo-dolzhno-skazat-nam-spasibo-za-krym.html (Accessed November 26, 2017).

33. Paterson, Tony. 2014. "Ukraine Crisis: Angry Angela Merkel Questions Whether Putin is in 'Touch with Reality." *Telegraph*. http://www.telegraph.co.uk/news/worldnews/europe/ukraine/10673235/Ukraine-crisis-Angry-Angela-Merkel-questions-whether-Putin-is-in-touch-with-reality.html (Accessed November 26, 2017).

34. Rosbalt.RU. 2014. "Strelkov: Surkov vedet Rossiiu k pozornoi kapituliatsii v Novorossii i Krymu." *Rosbalt*. http://www.rosbalt.ru/ukraina/2014/12/23/1351475.html (Accessed November 26, 2017).

35. Laruelle, Marlene. 2016. "The Three Colours of Novorossiya, or the Russian Nationalist Mythmaking of the Ukrainian Crisis." *Post-Soviet Affairs* 32(1): 55–74.

36. O'Loughlin, John, Gerard Toal, and Vladimir Kolosov. 2017. "The Rise and Fall of 'Novorossiya': Examining Support for a Separatist Geopolitical Imaginary in Southeast Ukraine." *Post-Soviet Affairs* 33(2) 2017: 124–144.

37. Laruelle, Marlene. 2016. "The Izborsky Club, or the New Conservative Avant-Garde in Russia." *Russian Review* 75(4): 626–644.

38. Balmforth, Tom. 2014. "From the Fringes toward Mainstream: Russian Nationalist Broadsheet Basks in Ukraine Conflict." *Radio Free Europe/Radio Liberty*. https://www.rferl.org/a/26534846.html (Accessed November 26, 2017).

39. Yablokov, Ilya. 2015. "Conspiracy Theories as Russia's Public Diplomacy Tool: The Case of 'Russia Today' (RT)." *Politics* 35(3-4): 301–315.

40. Cull, Nicholas J., Vasily Gatov, Peter Pomerantsev, Anne Applebaum, and Alistair Showcross. 2017. "Soviet Subversion, Disinformation and Propaganda: How the West Fought Against It." London: LSE Consulting, 68.

25

The Collective Conspiracy
Mentality in Poland

WIKTOR SORAL, ALEKSANDRA CICHOCKA, MICHAŁ BILEWICZ,
AND MARTA MARCHLEWSKA

Poland is a country in which conspiracy beliefs seem ubiquitous in social and political life.[1] Major political debates surround issues of potential foreign involvement in the death of the former president, liberal powers threatening the Catholic Church, or the Jewish conspiracy. One common thread is that they usually touch on how people perceive members of other groups. They are at the heart of one particular type of Polish national identity and are strongly related to the perceived role of Poles both in history and on the contemporary international stage. Therefore, work on conspiracy theories in Poland sheds light on the inter-group dimensions of conspiracy theories.

Introduction

Although past research does not necessarily neglect the importance of group identification in forming support for conspiracy theories, its specific role in driving conspiracy beliefs requires more in-depth theoretical understanding. Conspiracy theories are an inseparable part of political and inter-group conflicts. Group members are often involved in clandestine actions directed against enemy groups, and expect that the enemy groups will act the same way. Thus, group members may cast unjustified accusations of alleged hostile plots, and detect real conspiracies as well. Whether justified or not, conspiracy theories are one of the main determinants of inter-group relations, peaceful or violent, especially in countries driven by the irresistible winds of history. Conspiracy theories influence not only how the out-group image is shaped but also how the collective self is construed.

Poland is a country with a long history of fights against foreign powers and struggles for sovereignty, a country whose fate was determined by agreements of neighboring empires and global superpowers: in Petersburg in 1772, in Paris in

1919, in Moscow in 1939, and in Yalta in 1945.[2] A brief look at Polish history and literature shows that many famous Poles were personally involved in some sort of clandestine plot of Polish patriots aimed at fighting the occupying forces. Yet, the majority of Poles tend to ascribe conspiratorial intrigues to members of disliked out-groups: Jews, Germans, or Russians.[3] This tendency seems relatively stable over time. Such a form of *collective conspiracy mentality* can be considered a typical instance of siege mentality, a more general collective mental state in which other nations are viewed as hostile and negatively intended toward one's own nation.[4]

In this chapter we will cover different factors that can add up to forming a collective conspiracy mentality. Classical and recent studies conducted in Poland establish the contextual and personality-related factors triggering conspiracy theories popular among Poles. Particularly, belief in conspiracy theories can be regarded as a kind of defensive response to threats, which is observed especially at the level of relations between the in-group and the out-group. Conspiracy theories and in-group image are mutually related, and endorsement of conspiracy theories can affect attitudes toward others: out-group members, foreign institutions and authorities, and internal political actors and decisions they take.

Threat, Uncertainty, and Belief in Conspiracy Theories

Belief in conspiracy theories is frequently linked to perception that the social world is a dangerous, uncontrollable, and unpredictable place. General state anxiety—evoked simply by waiting for an examination—can lead to greater endorsement of conspiracy theories.[5] Moreover, endorsement of conspiracy theories correlates positively with symptoms of paranoia, such as self-centered thought, suspiciousness, and assumptions of ill will and hostility.[6] Given these findings, belief in conspiracies can be understood as one of the ways individuals use to manage their everyday fears and restore feelings of control and certainty.[7] In line with this reasoning, Marchlewska, Cichocka, and Kossowska found in two studies conducted among Polish participants that people who are motivated to reduce feelings of uncertainty (i.e., those high in need for cognitive closure) rely on temporarily salient conspiracy theories, especially when they refer to mysterious events with unknown official explanations.[8] This is probably an attempt to retain a sense of safety and predictability.

However, reducing perceptions of threats or dangers via the endorsement of conspiracy theories seems to be ineffective in the long run.[9] Rather than restoring a sense of control, the individual's feelings of (political) powerlessness seem to increase after exposure to conspiracy theories.[10] This reveals the paradoxical nature of conspiracy theories: On the one hand they can provide individuals with a sense of meaning and predictability, but on the other hand, conspiracy theories point to causal factors that by nature are unpredictable, uncontrollable, and hostile. Thus, exposure to conspiracy theories can actually increase perceptions of threats and dangers. For example, exposure to anti-vaccine conspiracy theories increases the belief that vaccines are dangerous to children.[11] All this by no means indicates that individuals who endorse conspiracy theories inevitably end up in a state of hopelessness and alienation. Rather, they seem to be pushed toward extremist views, radical authoritarian leaders, and fundamentalist groups.[12]

The link between the belief in a dangerous world and the endorsement of conspiracy theories is particularly evident among individuals with high levels of right-wing authoritarianism (RWA). According to recent reformulations of the classical concept of authoritarianism, the belief in a dangerous world is one of the main characteristics of individuals with high RWA.[13] Driven by this belief, individuals scoring high on RWA tend to adopt positive attitudes toward coercive social control, obedience and respect for existing authorities, and conforming to traditional and religious norms and values. These solutions allow for establishing and maintaining collective security, order, cohesion, and stability. Presumably, a conviction about the ubiquity of conspiracies is a part of a worldview maintained by individuals high in RWA. Indeed, studies by Grzesiak-Feldman and colleagues conducted in the Polish context consistently demonstrated positive correlations between RWA and beliefs in conspiratorial intentions of out-groups that tend to be considered threatening by Poles: Jews, Arabs, Germans, and Russians.[14]

Therefore, the role of conspiracy theories in restoring feelings of certainty, predictability, and personal control seems to be palliative at best.[15] These negative feelings seem to trigger belief in conspiratorial intentions of out-groups, but the mechanism does not provide the ultimate solution to everyday fears.

Conspiracy Theories and In-Group Image

While the individual has no chance in confrontation with hidden plots, there is a chance that powerful and united *collective* can effectively face its enemies. This means that ultimately conspiracy theories should be regarded as collective phenomena, and more attention should be devoted to the relation between conspiracy theories and how in-group and out-group representations are construed. Particularly, historical representations of Poles as victims versus dissidents, as well as a defensive type of national identification, are known to be related to the belief in conspiracy theories.

In-Group as a Shield against Conspiracies: The Role of In-Group Victimhood

On April 10, 2010, a plane crashed in Smoleńsk (Russia) a kilometer short of the runway in foggy weather conditions, killing all passengers including Polish president

Lech Kaczynski and 95 other important political figures. Since then, Polish society has been regularly confronted with a multitude of conspiracy explanations for the catastrophe.[16] Among numerous theories the most prominent were those of artificial fog supposedly cast by Russians around the Smoleńsk airport, but also unconfirmed reports of possible use of a fuel-air bomb on the deck of the airplane.[17] According to these conspiracy theories both Polish and Russian authorities were responsible for the Smoleńsk crash—which, according to official explanations, resulted from bad planning and pure coincidence.

In 2013, 25% of Poles believed that the catastrophe was a result of a conspiracy of Polish and Russian authorities, and nearly 50% believed that Polish and Russian authorities are trying to conceal the true cause of the catastrophe. According to a very recent survey conducted by the Center for Research on Prejudice, the percent of Poles endorsing Smoleńsk conspiracy in 2017 is almost unchanged, with 28% of Poles believing in it.[18] Soral and Grzesiak-Feldman pointed that even those individuals that do not believe in the assassination attempt are distrustful toward the authorities with respect to the official explanations of the catastrophe.[19] Interestingly, conspiracy theories of the Smoleńsk catastrophe seem to be endorsed especially by those at the conservative end of political spectrum, but also by those with liberal views, albeit to smaller degree. In general, the conspiracy theories of Smoleńsk are endorsed by those at the extremes of the political spectrum rather by those with centrist views.[20]

In popular discourse, the Smoleńsk catastrophe is often viewed as a breaking point that was followed by a significant change in the Polish society. The Smoleńsk catastrophe and related conspiracy theories have raised questions about who controls world events. They have diminished trust in the efficacy of the ruling party and highlighted the possibility of hidden, hostile out-groups lurking nearby. Such challenges were likely to increase strivings to obtain information that would allow people to see the in-group as a "shield" protecting them from threats. Studies by Soral and Kofta provide initial support for this hypothesis, suggesting that perception of collective threats increases cognitive accessibility of traits related to in-group agency.[21]

Hence, the conservative shift observed—especially among Polish youths—after the rise of conspiracy theories of the Smoleńsk catastrophe is likely a result of a more basic striving to restore safety and control through collective means.[22] A recent small study by Soral traced the Internet popularity of topics that would present Poles as actively resisting enemy forces, prior to and after the Smoleńsk catastrophe.[23] Two such topics were selected: the "cursed soldiers" and the Warsaw Uprising of 1944. The term *cursed soldiers* refers commonly to guerrilla movements that operated in Poland right after World War II, and actively resisted the communist authorities supported by the Soviet Union. These partisan movements are nowadays one of the most controversial symbols of a Polish fight for sovereignty and against the oppressing forces. In turn, the Warsaw Uprising was a major WWII operation of Polish resistance to liberate the Polish capital from German occupation. Figure 25.1 depicts annual trends of the popularity of these topics on Polish Wikipedia.[24] The trends clearly depict the date of April 10, 2010 as a tipping point, followed by an exponential growth of popularity of both topics on the Wikipedia website.

This rapid increase in popularity of these topics is not solely an aftermath of the Smoleńsk catastrophe, depicted frequently as an example of collective trauma. Rather, we would argue, it is strictly related to growing levels of distrust and anxiety driven by ubiquitous conspiracy theories surrounding the Smoleńsk catastrophe. Conspiracy theories, presented as threatening narratives, deprive the individual of very basic needs for security and control. In such instances individuals are more prone to look for agentic groups and leaders who might promise to act as a buffer against the overwhelming threat and fight fire with fire.[25]

The Smoleńsk catastrophe took place on the exact anniversary of another well-known national trauma, the assassination of Polish military officers in the Katyń forest in 1940. Passengers of 2010 flight were traveling to attend anniversary commemorations in the Katyń forest. This context stresses another important component of Polish in-group image: perception of in-group victimization. Studies

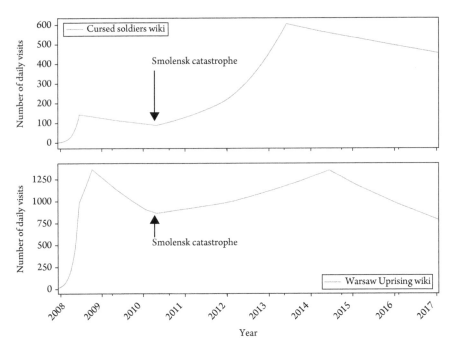

Figure 25.1. Number of Daily Visits to Polish Wikipedia Sites on Cursed Soldiers and Warsaw Uprising. Only annual trend is presented, with seasonal, weekly, and random variations removed. Date of Smolensk catastrophe (April 10th, 2010) is marked.

conducted in Poland after the Smoleńsk catastrophe found that a focus on the in-group's victimhood (either measured or experimentally induced) increased Poles' support for conspiracy explanation of the Smoleńsk catastrophe, and this was particularly true among participants highly identified as Poles.[26] This suggests that the narratives of past group victimhood create a propensity for interpreting current events in a conspiratorial way. Hence, the need to interpret political events in conspiratorial way might be especially strong for those with chronic beliefs that the in-group is threatened or victimized.

In-Group Positivity and Conspiracy Beliefs

A threatened sense of Polish national identity predicts belief in conspiracy theories about out-group members. One line of research focuses on the associations between the endorsement of conspiracy theories and collective narcissism—an unrealistic belief in the greatness of an in-group, associated with the need to validate the in-group image in the eyes of others.[27] Collective narcissism is a defensive type of in-group identification, linked to an increased sensitivity to inter-group threats.[28]

Cichocka et al. examined the links between national collective narcissism and beliefs that other groups are purposefully conspiring against the Polish people.[29] In one study, Polish collective narcissism was associated with the endorsement of conspiracy theories about the Smoleńsk crash. This relationship was driven by the perception that the fate of the Polish nation was threatened. Another study examined people's reactions to the celebration of the fall of the Berlin Wall in Germany on November 9, 1989. Although for other nations the demolition of the Berlin Wall often serves as the symbol of the fall of the Iron Curtain, Polish people tend to take pride in the role played by the Solidarity movement and the partially free elections of June 4, 1989 in fighting the communist regime. Indeed, some people seem to believe there is an international conspiracy aimed at undermining Polish achievements in combating communism, and this belief was stronger for those high in national collective narcissism.

The links between national collective narcissism and beliefs in out-group conspiracies were originally derived from the observation of Polish political rhetoric. However, further research demonstrated that they extend beyond the Polish context. For example, another study by Cichocka et al. was conducted in the United States and examined beliefs about conspiratorial actions of foreign (out-group) versus one's own (in-group) governments.[30] While American collective narcissism was associated with a belief that foreign governments were involved in conspiratorial actions, it was unrelated to the endorsement of conspiracy theories that assumed involvement of the American government.[31]

Overall, research shows that conspiratorial explanations of inter-group events are linked to the need to defend the undermined or victimized in-group image. However, not all forms of in-group identity are necessarily threatened or defensive.

In all three studies by Cichocka et al., national identification without the defensive, narcissistic component was associated with lower endorsement of out-group conspiracy theories.[32] This effect was especially clear once the variance shared between collective narcissism and in-group identification was accounted for. Such non-narcissistic national in-group positivity was a negative predictor of out-group conspiracy beliefs, due to lower perceptions of threat to the in-group.

In general, research conducted in the Polish context and beyond indicates that conspiracy theories are linked to the way the in-group image is construed. This is probably not surprising if we consider that conspiracy theories are often defined as beliefs about hostile actions of out-group members that plot to harm the in-group.[33] In the next section we review work examining ways in which the conspiring out-groups are portrayed and what kind of action against the conspiring out-group the threatened in-group is ready to take.

Conspiracy Theories and Out-Group Image

Although conspiracy theories are certainly driven by in-group-based motivations and image concerns, their content is mostly devoted to ill-intended out-group members. Kofta and Sędek coined the term *conspiracy stereotypes* to denote perceptions of conspiring out-groups.[34] Conspiracies attributed to out-groups have detrimental consequences for inter-group relations, leading to prejudice, animosity, and conflict. Two such conspiracy stereotypes play a crucial role in Polish discourse: Jewish conspiracy theories and the gender conspiracy theory.

Jewish Conspiracy Theories

Although Jewish conspiracy theories date back to the beginning of the nineteenth century, they are still endorsed by almost half of Polish society. Figure 25.2 shows the results of a survey conducted on a representative sample of Polish adults in 2017 by the Center for Research on Prejudice.[35] Among other topics, participants in the survey were asked about their attitudes toward different claims related to Jewish conspiracy theories. Almost half of the sample (a plurality) agreed with such statements (see Figure 25.2).

Beliefs in Jewish conspiracy are rooted in the same identity structures as other forms of conspiracy beliefs. They are more often observed among people high in national collective narcissism, with a strong sense of victimhood and group deprivation.[36] Additionally, there are clear situational triggers of such beliefs. The effects on prejudice of conspiracy stereotypes about Jews are stronger in times of parliamentary elections—that is, when feelings of uncertainty and lack of control seem to be on the rise—an effect found both in longitudinal studies using student samples and in nationwide representative sample studies.[37]

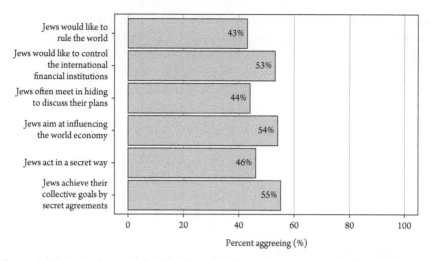

Figure 25.2. Attitudes of Adult Poles Toward Different Statements Related to Belief in Jewish Conspiracy.

The effects of conspiracy stereotypes on hostile intentions, prejudice, and discrimination are particularly evident if we look at those who believe in the Jewish conspiracy theory. For example, Golec de Zavala and Cichocka conducted a survey examining the psychological concomitants of anti-Semitism in Poland.[38] They found that endorsing the conspiracy stereotype of Jews was associated with higher anti-Semitic prejudice (expressed for example in higher social distance toward Jews). Furthermore, both the conspiracy stereotype and anti-Semitic beliefs were predicted by national collective narcissism. In a more detailed study of prejudicial consequences of such beliefs, Bilewicz et al. found that belief in Jewish conspiracy theory predicts support for the enforcement of discriminatory laws against Jews, an unwillingness to accept Jews as neighbors or co-workers, and biases in donations to Jews.[39] Further studies showed that even in a behavioral decision-making task, participants who believed in Jewish conspiracy theory distributed less money to Jewish organizations. The belief in Jewish conspiracy theory has clearly the strongest discriminatory consequence.

The Gender Conspiracy

Belief in the "gender conspiracy" is a relatively recent phenomenon in Polish public discourse, visible mostly in the Catholic media and among far-right-wing political movements.[40] According to this belief, gender theory or gender studies—officially presented as transdisciplinary areas of research that engage critically with gender norms, relations, or identities—are not what they seem to be.[41] This "is a classic example of an ideology, it is a tool in a ruthless fight for benefits for the atheistic gender and homo-lobby," said Catholic priest Dariusz Oko, the leading proponent of this conspiracy theory, in one of his interviews. He also claimed that gender studies will destroy the Catholic Church and introduce a totalitarian regime controling all aspects of human life and promoting "sex mania, genocide, destruction of the family and brutal sexualization of children."[42] In line with this theory, Catholics are under threat and should prepare themselves to fight against the ruthless representatives of gender studies.

Slogans proclaimed by gender conspiracy believers, such as ". . . gender is supported by all enemies of God and religion" or "defend the homeland against totalitarian genderism," were endorsed by many Poles.[43] Research conducted by Marchlewska et al. showed that the likelihood of endorsing the "gender conspiracy" theory was positively predicted by Catholic collective narcissism but not religiosity per se, replicating the pattern of results obtained in the previous studies on defensive (narcissistic) in-group positivity as a positive predictor of belief in out-group conspiracies.[44] Furthermore, Marchlewska et al. showed that adopting gender conspiracy beliefs was positively related to hostile intentions toward non-Catholics. For example, people high in gender conspiracy beliefs declared that "they would not hesitate to fight against those who undermine the positive image of Catholicism," indicating that conspiracy theories lead not only to individual maladaptiveness but also to inter-group aggression.

Conspiracy theories about out-groups—conspiracy stereotypes—are not merely beliefs about ill-intended out-group members, but rather they are perceptions of *other groups* understood as ontologically separate, agentic forces.[45] The Jewish and gender conspiracy theories not only target out-group members but also artificial social constructs. Both refer to some sinister powers whose sole purpose is bringing chaos and harm to the in-group, whether it is through destroying traditional Catholic values or controling the world's economy.

The overarching concept of collective conspiracy mentality helps to explain why group members tend to endorse various logically unrelated conspiracy beliefs. Their primary role is to point to other groups, nations, or institutions as ill-intended and willing to conspire against the in-group. This urge stems from a threatened or victimized sense of national identity and may be motivated by group defensive mechanisms.

How to Overcome the Collective Conspiracy Mentality?

In this chapter we aimed to describe the most popular contemporary conspiracy theories in Poland: the Smoleńsk catastrophe conspiracy theories and the "gender conspiracy" theories, as well as the historical (yet still endorsed by the majority of the Polish society) Jewish conspiracy theory. The common basis of Polish conspiracy beliefs seems to be the presence of a strong collective component. The conspiracy theories can be viewed as a manifestation of more general collective mentality in which other nations are viewed as hostile toward one's own nation. Inspired by works on siege mentality, we name such a mental state *collective conspiracy mentality*.[46]

Future work should focus on further examining these processes both from the theoretical and applied perspective. A key theoretical challenge is to investigate the causal mechanisms linking identity, conspiracy theories, and inter-group relations as well as the long-term consequences of the collective conspiracy mentality. The collective conspiracy mentality involves intra-group motivations instigated by feelings of existential threats and (realistic or fictitious) beliefs about in-group victimization. These motivations are likely to occur among those vigilant to social or inter-group threats. Driven by the threats, some individuals tend to construct the social world, and out-groups more specifically, as hostile and untrustworthy. At the same time, these individuals might construct their in-group as a shield protecting them from external threats and dangers. It is easy to see, however, that the role of such social representations seems to be palliative at best. In fact, the process resembles a sort of vicious circle resulting in (often transgenerational) maintenance of conspiracy beliefs, inter-group suspicion, and conflict. Future work should then also focus on identifying ways in which these processes can be attenuated. Developing interventions that could decrease the defensiveness associated with collective conspiracy mentality would likely contribute to more constructive inter-group relations both within the Polish society and in other contexts where suspicion and threat drive inter-group attitudes.

Notes

1. Wiktor Soral's contribution to the project was financed with a Preludium grant by the National Science Center (no 2014/13/N/HS6/03766). Marta Marchlewska's contribution to the project was financed with an ETIUDA scholarship from the National Science Center (no 2016/20/T/HS6/00039).
2. Davies, Norman. 2005. *God's Playground. A History of Poland: Volume II: 1795 to the Present.* Oxford: Oxford University Press.
3. Winiewski, Mikołaj, and Michał Bilewicz. 2015. "Antysemityzm: Dynamika i psychologiczne uwarunkowania [Anti-semitism: Dynamics and psychological antecedents]." In *Uprzedzenia w Polsce [Prejudice in Poland]*, eds. Anna Stefaniak, Michal Bilewicz, and Mikolaj Winiewski. Warsaw: Liberi Libri, 15–40.
4. The term *conspiracy mentality* used here was borrowed from works of Moscovici, who used it to refer to a certain mode of collective thought. See Moscovici, Serge. 1987. "The Conspiracy Mentality." In *Changing Conceptions of Conspiracy*, ed. Carl F. Graumann, and Serge Moscovici. New York: Springer-Verlag, 151–169. Conspiracy mentality was recently reformulated by Imhoff and Bruder as a generalized political attitude. Here, however, by drawing greater attention to similarities with siege mentality we would like to emphasize collective components of conspiracy mentality and its relations to images of in-group vs. out-groups. See also Bar-Tal, Daniel, and Dikla Antebi. 1992. "Siege Mentality in Israel." *International Journal of Intercultural Relations* 16(3): 251–275.

5. Grzesiak-Feldman, Monika. 2013. "The Effect of High-Anxiety Situations on Conspiracy Thinking." *Current Psychology* 32(1):100–118.

6. Grzesiak-Feldman, Monika, and Anna Ejsmont. 2008. "Paranoia and Conspiracy Thinking of Jews, Arabs, Germans, and Russians in a Polish Sample." *Psychological Reports* 102(3): 884–886. See also Cichocka, Aleksandra, Marta Marchlewska, and Agnieszka Golec de Zavala. 2016. "Does Self-love or Self-hate Predict Conspiracy Beliefs? Narcissism, Self-esteem and the Endorsement of Conspiracy Theories." *Social Psychological and Personality Science* 7(2): 157–166.

7. Kossowska, Małgorzata, and Marcin Bukowski. 2015. "Motivated Roots of Conspiracies: The Role of Certainty and Control Motivation in Conspiracy Thinking." In *The Psychology of Conspiracy*, eds. Michał Bilewicz, Aleksandra Cichocka, and Wiktor Soral. London and New York: Routledge, 145–161; Whitson, Jennifer A., and Adam D. Galinsky. 2008. "Lacking Control Increases Illusory Pattern Perception." *Science* 322(5898): 115–117.

8. Marchlewska, Marta, Aleksandra Cichocka, Malgorzata Kossowska. 2017. "Addicted to Answers: Need for Cognitive Closure and the Endorsement of Conspiracy Beliefs." *European Journal of Social Psychology*. DOI: 10.1002/ejsp.2308/full (Accessed December 22, 2017). For the need for cognitive closure see Kruglanski, Arie W., and Donna M. Webster. 1996. "Motivated Closing of the Mind: 'Seizing' and 'freezing.'" *Psychological Review* 103(2): 263–283.

9. Douglas, Karen M., Robbie M. Sutton, and Aleksandra Cichocka. 2017. "The Psychology of Conspiracy Theories." *Current Directions in Psychological Science* 26(6): 538–542. DOI: 10.1177/0963721417718261.

10. Jolley, Daniel, and Karen M. Douglas. 2014. "The Social Consequences of Conspiracism: Exposure to Conspiracy Theories Decreases the Intention to Engage in Politics and to Reduce One's Carbon Footprint." *British Journal of Psychology* 105(1):435–456; Kofta, Mirosław, et al. n.d. "What Breeds Conspiracy Beliefs? The Role of Political Powerlessness and Meaninglessness in the Belief in Jewish Conspiracy." Forthcoming.

11. Jolley, Daniel, and Karen M. Douglas. 2014. "The Effects of Anti-Vaccine Conspiracy Theories on Vaccination Intentions." *PloS ONE* 9(2). DOI: 10.1371/journal.pone.0089177.

12. Bartlett, Jamie, and Carl Miller. 2010. *The Power of Uunreason: Conspiracy Theories, Extremism and Counter-terrorism*. New York: Demos; van Prooijen, Jan-Willem, and Andre P. M. Krouwel. 2015. "Mutual Suspicion at the Political Extremes: How Ideology Predicts Belief in Conspiracy Theories." In *The Psychology of Conspiracy*, eds. Michał Bilewicz, Aleksandra Cichocka, and Wiktor Soral. London and New York: Routledge, 79–98.

13. Duckitt, John, and Chris G. Sibley. "Personality, Ideology, Prejudice, and Politics: A Dual-Process Motivational Model." *Journal of Personality* 78(6): 1861–1894.

14. Grzesiak-Feldman, Monika, and Monika Irzycka. 2009. "Right-Wing Authoritarianism and Conspiracy Thinking in a Polish Sample." *Psychological Reports* 105(2): 389–393; Grzesiak-Feldman, Monika. 2015. "Are the High Authoritarians More Prone to Adopt Conspiracy Theories? The Role of Right-Wing Authoritarianism in Conspiratorial Thinking." In *The Psychology of Conspiracy*, eds. Michał Bilewicz, Aleksandra Cichocka, and Wiktor Soral. London and New York: Routledge, 99–121.

15. Jost, John T., and Orsolya Hunyady. 2003. "The Psychology of System Justification and the Palliative Function of Ideology." *European Review of Social Psychology* 13(1): 111–153.

16. Soral, Wiktor, and Monika Grzesiak-Feldman. 2015. "Socjo-psychologiczne wyznaczniki wiary w spisek smoleński [Socio-psychological antecedents of belief in Smoleńsk conspiracy]." In *Uprzedzenia w Polsce [Prejudice in Poland]*, eds. Anna Stefaniak, Michal Bilewicz, and Mikolaj Winiewski. Warsaw: Liberi Libri: 285–304; Grzesiak-Feldman, Monika, and Agnieszka Haska. 2012. "Conspiracy Theories Surrounding the Polish Presidential Plane Crash Near Smolensk, Russia." http://deconspirator. com/2012/11/22/conspiracy-theories-surrounding-the-polish-presidentialplane-crash-near-smolensk-russia (Accessed December 22, 2017).

17. Koziński, Agaton. 2014. "Wybuch w salonce, sztuczna mgła, bomba termobaryczna. . . Smoleńskie teorie spiskowe [Explosion, artificial mist, fuel-air bomb. . . Smoleńsk conspiracy

theories]." *Polska / The Times.* http://www.polskatimes.pl/artykul/3399133,wybuch-w-salonce-sztuczna-mgla-bomba-termobaryczna-smolenskie-teorie-spiskowe-galeria,id,t.html. (Accessed June 15, 2017).

18. Winiewski, Mikołaj, et al. n.d. *Prejudice in Poland in 2017.* Forthcoming.
19. Soral and Grzesiak-Feldman, "Socjo-psychologiczne wyznaczniki."
20. For potential explanation of this curvilinear relation, see van Prooijen and Krouwel, "Mutual Suspicion at the Political Extremes."
21. Soral, Wiktor, and Mirosław Kofta. n.d. "In-Group as a Shield: Existential Threat to the In-Group Increases Accessibility of Group Agency-Related Traits." Forthcoming.
22. CBOS. 2015. *Zainteresowanie polityką i poglądy polityczne w latach 1989–2015. Deklaracje ludzi młodych na tle ogółu badanych.* http://www.cbos.pl/SPISKOM.POL/2015/K_135_15.PDF (Accessed December 22, 2017).
23. Soral and Kofta, "In-Group as a Shield."
24. The entries date back to 2003, but due to technical constraints of Wikipedia only data after December 1, 2007 were available.
25. See also Stollberg, Janine, Immo Fritsche, and Anna Bäcker. 2015. "Striving for Group Agency: Threat to Personal Control Increases the Attractiveness of Agentic Groups." *Frontiers in Psychology* 6(649): 1–13.
26. Bilewicz, Michał, et al. n.d. "Conspiracy Divide. How Endorsement of Conspiracy Theories Affects Social Distance between Conspiracy Believers and Non-Believers After Societal Trauma." Forthcoming; Witkowska, Marta, et al. n.d. "Historia est Magistra Vitae? The Impact of Historical Victimhood on Current Conspiracy Beliefs." Forthcoming.
27. Golec de Zavala, Agnieszka, Aleksandra Cichocka, Roy Eidelson, Nuwan Jayawickreme. 2009. "Collective Narcissism and its Social Consequences." *Journal of Personality and Social Psychology* 97(6): 1074–1096.
28. Golec de Zavala, Agnieszka, Aleksandra Cichocka, and Irena Iskra-Golec. 2013. "Collective Narcissism Moderates the Effect of In-group Image Threat on Intergroup Hostility." *Journal of Personality and Social Psychology* 104(6): 1019–1039. See also Cichocka, Aleksandra. 2016. "Understanding Defensive and Secure In-Group Positivity: The Role of Collective Narcissism." *European Review of Social Psychology* 27(1): 283–317.
29. Cichocka, Aleksandra, Marta Marchlewska, Agnieszka Golec de Zavala, and Mateusz Olechowski. 2016. "'They Will Not Control Us': In-Group Positivity and Belief in Intergroup Conspiracies." *British Journal of Psychology* 107(3): 556–576.
30. Ibid.
31. For a similar pattern see Cichocka, Marchlewska, and Golec de Zavala, "Does Self-love or Self-hate Predict Conspiracy Beliefs," Study 2.
32. Cichocka, Marchlewska, Golec de Zavala, and Olechowski, " "They Will Not Control Us."
33. van Prooijen, Jan-Willem, and Paul A. M. van Lange. 2014. "The Social Dimension of Belief in Conspiracy Theories." In *Power, Politics, and Paranoia. Why People are Suspicious of Their Leaders*, eds. Jan-Willem van Prooijen and Paul A. M. van Lange. Cambridge: Cambridge University Press, 237–253.
34. Kofta, Mirosław, and Grzegorz Sędek. 2005. "Conspiracy Stereotypes of Jews during Systemic Transformation in Poland." *International Journal of Sociology* 35(1): 40–64.
35. Winiewski, Mikołaj, et al. *Prejudice in Poland 2012.*
36. Golec de Zavala, Agnieszka, and Aleksandra Cichocka. 2012. "Collective Narcissism and Anti-Semitism in Poland." *Group Processes and Intergroup Relations* 15(2): 213–229; Bilewicz, Michał, and Anna Stefaniak. 2013. "Can a Victim Be Responsible? Antisemitic Consequences of Victimhood-Based Identity and Competitive Victimhood in Poland." In *Responsibility: An Interdisciplinary Perspective*, ed. Barbara Bokus. Warsaw: Matrix; Bilewicz, Michał, Mikolaj Winiewski, Miroslaw Kofta, and Adrian Wojcik. 2013. "Harmful Ideas: The Structure and Consequences of Anti-Semitic Beliefs in Poland." *Political Psychology* 34(6): 821–839; Bilewicz, Michał, and Ireneusz Krzemiński. 2010. "Anti-Semitism in Poland and Ukraine: The

Belief in Jewish Control as a Mechanism of Scapegoating." *International Journal of Conflict and Violence* 4(2): 234–243.

37. Bilewicz, Michał, and Grzegorz Sędek. 2015. "Conspiracy Stereotypes. Their Sociopsychological Antecedents and Consequences." In *The Psychology of Conspiracy,* eds. Michał Bilewicz, Aleksandra Cichocka, and Wiktor Soral. London and New York: Routledge, 3–22; Kofta, Mirosław, and Grzegorz Sędek, "Conspiracy Stereotypes . . . "

38. Golec de Zavala and Cichocka, "Collective Narcissism and Anti-Semitism in Poland."

39. Bilewicz, Winiewski, Kofta, and Wojcik, "Harmful Ideas."

40. Campoy, Ana. 2016. "A Conspiracy Theory about Sex and Gender Is Being Peddled Around the World by the Far Right." *Quartz.* https://qz.com/807743/conservatives-have-created-a-fake-ideology-to-combat-the-global-movement-for-lgbti-rights/   (Accessed June 15, 2017).

41. Marchlewska, Marta, et al. n.d. "In Search of an Imaginary Enemy: Catholic Collective Narcissism and the Endorsement of Gender Conspiracy Beliefs." Forthcoming.

42. Cichobłazińska, Anna. 2013. "Gender Ideology Destroys a Cradle of Humankind—A Family. Interview with Dariusz Oko." *Sunday Catholic Weekly.* http://sunday.niedziela.pl/artykul.php?lg=gb&nr=&dz=spoleczenstwo&id_art=00672 (Accessed June 15, 2017).

43. Luxmoore, J. 2014. "Polish Church Declares War on Gender Ideology. A Pastoral Letter by Polish Bishops Has Caused Backlash from Some Who See Attack as a 'Witch Hunt." https://www.osv.com/ (Accessed December 22, 2017).

44. Marchlewska, Marta, et al., "In Search of an Imaginary Enemy."

45. Kofta, Mirosław, and Grzegorz Sędek. "Conspiracy Stereotypes of Jews."

46. Krekó, Péter. 2015. "Conspiracy Theory as Collective Motivated Cognition." In *The Psychology of Conspiracy,* eds. Michał Bilewicz, Aleksandra Cichocka, and Wiktor Soral. London and New York: Routledge, 62–75. See also Kramer, Roderick M., and Jennifer Schaffer. 2014. "Misconnecting the Dots: Origins and Dynamics of Outgroup Paranoia." In *Power, Politics, and Paranoia. Why People are Suspicious of Their leaders,* eds. Jan-Willem van Prooijen and Paul A. M. van Lange. Cambridge: Cambridge University Press, 199–217.

26

The Conspiratorial Style in Turkish Politics

Discussing the Deep State in the Parliament

TÜRKAY SALIM NEFES

Turkey is an ideal context to study conspiracy theories, as there is a plethora of conspiratorial accounts shaping mainstream politics. In the last decade, the Turkish government put on trial 275 prominent intellectuals, journalists, statesmen, and military personnel on the suspicion that they formed a secret group, Ergenekon, conspiring to overthrow the regime. This did not mark the end of conspiracy rhetoric. The current government claims that a secret clique, a parallel state, is responsible for various conspiracies that hinder Turkish democracy and security.

This chapter focuses on an amorphous but significant conspiracy theory, the deep state, which argues that a clandestine elite group is determined to defend the Turkish state ideology and the political stability by legal, and often illegal, means. In order to delineate the different uses and significance of this theory, I look at the parliamentary proceedings between 1996 and 2010. These show that political parties use deep state rhetoric in line with their interests. While they all agree on the existence of the deep state, they have proposed different and incompatible accounts because of their contradictory political interests. This is reminiscent of the blind men and elephant joke in which each blind man touches one part of the animal and comes to a different conclusion about the shape of an elephant. All in all, the conflicting interests of the Turkish political parties ensure the continuity of this rhetoric.

Historical Background of Conspiracy
Theories in Turkey

Turkish politics is replete with conspiratorial rhetoric on various topics ranging from minorities to the plots of secret state institutions.[1] To understand the prevalence of the conspiratorial rhetoric in Turkey, one needs to go back to the nineteenth century, the period of collapse of the Ottoman empire, the predecessor of the Turkish Republic.[2] The Ottoman empire, spread from the Balkans to North Africa and composed of various ethnic and religious groups, collapsed mainly due to wars against colonial powers and the independence movements of its minorities in the nineteenth and early twentieth centuries. In response, the majority of these political movements endeavored to avoid complete dismemberment. Three ideological directions that attempted to save the empire were Ottomanism, Islamism, and Turkism. Ottomanism aimed at the unity of all minorities under the Ottoman identity as a solution; Islamism proposed that the Ottoman identity was Muslim, and the unity among Muslim populations could save the empire; and Turkism attempted to create an ethnic unity among Turks.

Despite all efforts, the Ottoman empire was completely dysfunctional at the end of the First World War. The Sèvres Treaty in 1920 between the empire and the allied countries left only a very small portion of the country to the Ottomans. The remaining Ottoman forces waged a successful Independence War (1919–1923) under the leadership of Mustafa Kemal Atatürk. Consequently the Lausanne Treaty, signed in 1923, secured the current borders of Turkey. This gave way to the establishment of the Turkish Republic in the same year. The breakup of the Ottoman Empire by foreign powers and ethnic/religious minorities created a conspiratorial style which suggested that foreign powers could manipulate local minorities as pawns to undermine the Turkish Republic. Scholarship called this conspiratorial perspective Sèvres syndrome, as the Sèvres Treaty represented a point in which the conspiracies of foreign powers were successful and therefore a point to avoid at any expense. Initially the republican elite perceived the Sèvres Treaty as proof of existential threats in the early twentieth century.[3] Subsequently, various powerful political actors such as the military helped the continuity of the conspiratorial vision. Studies suggest that this conspiratorial rhetoric influenced the school curriculum, isolationist state policies, foreign policy, and Turkish intellectuals' understanding of politics. [4]

A renowned Turkish journalist, Mehmet Barlas, talks about the prevalence of this conspiratorial vision of foreign powers.[5] In Urfa, a Turkish city famous for the Lake of Abraham, people did not fish in the lake because of an ancient belief that Abraham's ashes were transformed into fishes. During the Second World War, a German painter came to spend long hours in the area. Locals became suspicious of this foreigner and thought that he was a Nazi spy, who had come to copy the shapes of these "holy fishes to improve German submarine design." They secretly watched him only to discover his real motive: the painter spent long hours around the lake to catch and barbeque those holy fishes at night.[6]

Another example of this wary and conspiratorial vision of the possible dismemberment of the country can be found in the first line of the Turkish national anthem, which begins with the assurance that the Turkish Republic will not disperse: "No Fear! For the crimson flag that proudly ripples in this glorious twilight shall not fade." In parallel, the discussion about the deep state resonates with the conspiracy rhetoric surrounding the Sèvres syndrome. Indeed, Mehmet Ağar, a right-wing former politician who served for the special forces in the southeastern Turkey and is identified with the deep state, defined the deep state as the determination to not to retreat one more step after losing Kirkuk, the last province lost by the Ottoman empire in the First World War. That is to say, Ağar justified the possible existence of the deep state as a protective measure against the threat of losing land, which characterizes the Sèvres syndrome.

The Deep State in Turkey

The deep state discussion is an important part of the conspiratorial rhetoric in Turkish politics, particularly in the post-1980s. Freely describes the deep state as a faceless clique that is alleged to have held power in Turkey since the establishment of the republic in the early twentieth century.[7] It is believed to consist of high-level officials from the national intelligence service, military, academy, judiciary branch, and bureaucracy, who hold an ultra-statist and nationalist ideology. Kavakci notes that the members of the deep state are alleged to come from various institutions ranging from universities to media, from army generals to former Kurdish separatists.[8] The former prime minister Bülent Ecevit and former president Kenan Evren both referred to the existence of the deep state.[9] Süleyman Demirel, seven-time prime minister and a former president, implied the existence of the deep state in the following manner: "It is a fundamental principle that there is one state. In our country there are two."[10]

The deep state is alleged to curb the marginal elements in Turkish politics and has been related to many events including the assassinations of leftists in the 1970s and Kurdish insurgents in the 1990s. Three events from the recent past were seen as evidence for the existence of the deep state. In 1996, a road accident in Susurluk unveiled the secret relationship between Huseyin Kocadağ, a high-ranking police officer; Abdullah Catli, former leader of Turkey's far- right; and Sedat Bucak, a Kurdish tribal leader and a member of the parliament at that time. The parliamentary report on the Susurluk incident pointed to close ties between state authorities and criminal gangs.[11]

In 2005, three men bombed a bookstore the southeastern city of Semdinli, which was allegedly linked to the Kurdish separatist insurgent group The Kurdistan Workers' Party (PKK). Two of them were members of the Turkish army, and the other was a police informer. The sentences for the bombers were overturned a year later on the grounds that they should have been tried by a military court.[12] Moreover, Hrant Dink, a Turkish Armenian who had challenged the Turkish state's stance on the Armenian deportation, was assassinated by a right-wing militant, Ogun Samast. The current president, Recep Tayyip Erdoğan, claimed that the dark forces of the deep state might be at work in this event.[13] After his capture, two policemen took a photo with Samast in front of a Turkish flag on which was a statement of the founding father of Turkey, Atatürk: "The soil of the motherland is sacred; it cannot be left on its [own] destiny."[14]

In the last decade, the AKP government endeavored to tackle the allegations about the deep state in the Ergenekon trials.[15] Although the trials mostly resulted in imprisonment, this did not mark the end of conspiracy rhetoric about the deep state, because the verdicts were seen as biased and based on thin evidence. Indeed, the AKP government in 2017 accuses some of the public prosecutors who were involved in the Ergenekon case of forming another conspiratorial clique, the parallel state.

Method, Context, and Actors

The article analyzes the mentions of the deep state in the Turkish parliamentary proceedings between 1996 and 2010. It should be noted that the political parties in the parliament are not representative of all political views in Turkey, as the country follows a D'Hondt elections system with a 10% threshold rule. Hence only a minority of political parties that pass the threshold enter the parliament. These mentions span between the 20th and 23rd periods of the parliament. Each period comprises different political actors.

Members of the political parties represented in the 20th period mentioned the deep state in ways shown in Table 26.1. Center-left political parties (DSP and CHP)

Table 26.1 **Mentions of the Deep State in the 20th Period**

Party	Date	Associating the deep state with
CHP	14/12/1996	the murders of left-wingers and liberals
DSP	27/05/1997	the murders of left-wingers and liberals
DYP	10/07/1997	the February 28 coup
RP	19/11/1997	the February 28 coup
RP	26/11/1997	human rights violations in the Southeast Turkey
DYP	17/12/1997	the February 28 coup
RP	17/12/1997	the February 28 coup
DSP	13/01/1998	The mafia
FP	24/03/1998	human rights violations in southeast Turkey
FP	30/07/1998	repression of religious and ethnic identities; the February 28 coup
ANAP	20/03/1999	the mafia related to Susurluk scandal

described the deep state as an extralegal group responsible for the murders of left-wingers and liberals. Sema Piskinsut (DSP) stated that "many scientists, journalists, lawyers and students were assassinated before the coup in 1980, e.g. the massacre of the 1 May demonstrations in 1978. . . many countries have shady cliques such as deep state. . . counter-guerilla." The center-right ANAP underlined that the deep state was a mafia, which became apparent in the Susurluk scandal. They underlined that the ANAP coalition government had no relation to that entity. Right-wing political Islamists (RP and FP) associated the deep state with human rights violations in southeast Turkey and the February 28 "postmodern" coup in 1997, in which army pressure led to overthrow of the government formed by Islamists and liberals. Mehmet Emin Aydinbas (RP) expressed his disappointment with the president of the time (1997), Süleyman Demirel, for not challenging the coup: ". . . Demirel used to be a hope against the deep state, which overshadows our democracy." In short, the Susurluk scandal in 1996 and the postmodern coup triggered the communication of deep state conspiracy theories.

As seen in Table 26.2 below, during the 21st period the deep state has been mentioned seven times. The majority of these came from FP members. They continued to argue that the February 28 coup was carried out by the deep state, and associated the existence of the deep state with lack of democracy and equality. Halil Cin (FP) quoted a newspaper article which claimed that the deep state wanted to have another national election: " . . . this means that the elections will take place because of the will of the deep state, not the parliament. If politicians see democracy only as a tool for their own interests, the system will cease to be a democracy." A DSP member from the center-left talked about the deep state on two occasions with regard to political assassinations of two left-wing secularist intellectuals, Ahmet Taner Kışlalı and Ugur Mumcu. He argued that the deep state discussion confuses everyone by creating an imaginary enemy and therefore functions as a distraction to investigating the murders: "the deep state descriptions puzzle everyone by obscuring who the members of this clique really are."

Table 26.2 **Mentions of the Deep State in the 21st Period**

Party	Date	Associating the deep state with
FP	25/08/1999	the February 28 coup
DSP	26/10/1999	a distraction to investigating political murders
DSP	20/01/2000	a distraction to investigating political murders
FP	15/06/2000	the February 28 coup
FP	27/06/2000	the February 28 coup
SP	29/11/2000	seeing migrants in cities as a potential danger
AKP	27/09/2001	political murders, torture, and lack of democracy

Table 26.3 **Mentions of the Deep State in the 22nd Period**

Party	Date	Associating the deep state with
CHP	10/11/2004	corruption in governance
ANAP	22/11/2005	harming the state's reputation among the public
AKP	15/12/2005	an imaginary concept harming the state's reputation among the public

As seen in Table 26.3 below, in the 22nd period, a center-left MP mentioned the deep state to argue that there was widespread corruption in state institutions. While talking about an alleged corruption in the Ministry of Education, Muharrem Ince (CHP) claimed that " . . . the letter ends with deep regards. . . would that be related to the deep state? I do not think so. . . but I do not know what deep regards mean." Another mention was from the center-right, Erkan Mumcu (ANAP). Reflecting on the Semdinli bombing, Mumcu linked the deep state with the alleged lawlessness in the southeast and concluded that this was damaging the public perception of the Turkish state in the region: "this event [Semdinli bombing] created a perception that the state officers could commit crime in that region and started a discussion on the deep state and the visible state." Two weeks later, an AKP representative repeated this argument and added that the deep state was an imaginary concept, not a real entity.

The 23rd period saw an increase in the mentions of the deep state as outlined in Table 26.4 below. This is partly due to the entry of the pro-Kurdish HDP members to the parliament, as they referred to the rhetoric most often. HDP associated the deep state with the conflict in the southeast region, particularly referring to the Semdinli bombing and the Susurluk scandal: "after the cases of Susurluk and Yuksekova, now we find the Semdinli gang. These criminals were seen as the good guys and promoted [by the deep state]. . . Hence, the deep state continues to exist in Turkey." HDP MPs accused the deep state of political murders and saw it as an obstacle against peace and democracy. In addition, they inquired whether the deep state was involved in the fall of the Ecevit government in 2002. HDP also criticized some popular television shows, such as *The Valley of the Wolves* series, for promoting hate speech against Kurds and justifying the deep state violence. CHP linked the deep state with the killing of protesters on the celebrations of May 1 in 1977, namely the Taksim Square massacre. Kemal Anadol (CHP) stated that "instead of focusing on meaningless cases, look at the 1 May 1977 to find the deep state. . ." Along with the HDP, they accused the AKP government of not searching for the real deep state in the Ergenekon trial and of establishing its own deep state. A MHP representative also blamed the government for creating its own deep state. Representatives of the governing party, AKP, referred to the deep state rhetoric to reject these accusations.

Table 26.4 **Mentions of the Deep State in the 23rd Period**

Party	Date	Associating the deep state with
HDP	23/01/2008	counter guerrilla and Semdinli bombing
CHP	13/05/2008	the Taksim Square massacre
AKP	03/06/2008	rejecting the deep state accusations toward the AKP
CHP	08/07/2008	political murders
HDP	15/01/2009	crime and Turkish nationalism
HDP	27/01/2009	Semdinli bombing, Susurluk scandal, anti-Kurdish murders
HDP	13/11/2009	oppression of Kurdish identity via crime
CHP	09/02/2010	Gulen movement's increasing power in police
HDP	10/02/2010	unresolved political murders
HDP	10/02/2010	political murders in the Kurdish region, obstacle to democracy
MHP	11/02/2010	the AKP
CHP	11/02/2010	the AKP
AKP	11/02/2010	rejecting deep state accusations toward the AKP
HDP	11/02/2010	the AKP
CHP	20/04/2010	the Taksim Square massacre
HDP	05/10/2010	the fall of the Ecevit government in 2002
HDP	07/12/2010	*The Valley of the Wolves,* a popular TV series

Conspiracy Rhetoric in the Zero-Sum Game of Turkish Politics

The zero-sum game of Turkish parliamentary politics ensures the continuity of the deep state conspiracy theory: political parties' conflicting interests thwart them from coming to an agreement about who the deep state is, and taking action against this alleged group. As a result, the deep state is a known unknown in Turkish politics. All political actors talk about it, but there is little agreement as to what it is.

To start with, the conspiratorial rhetoric about the deep state builds on the historical legacy of the Sèvres syndrome, an anxiety about the dismemberment of the country, as it is believed to be a disguised official clique that uses illegal means to avoid collapse. Accordingly, the deep state was discussed by politicians as an example of lawlessness and an obstacle to democratic governance and human rights. Unresolved political murders in southeast Turkey and the February 28 coup were argued to be the work of this secret clique. Moreover, the deep state seems to function as an alternative explanation to significant events that are not convincingly explained by the official narrative. Assassinations of prominent intellectuals, the Semdinli bombing, the Susurluk scandal and the Taksim Square massacre were all attributed to the deep state because the official verdicts were not viewed to be just. Indeed, in most cases no one was imprisoned.

Moreover, the political parties interpreted the conspiratorial rhetoric about the deep state in line with their ideological perspectives and interests. After the February 28 coup, which ended the RP–DYP coalition government, members of both political parties underlined that this was plotted by the deep state. Left-wing political parties, CHP and DSP, did not associate the deep state with the coup but linked this alleged secret clique to the violence against left-wingers and liberals. The pro-Kurdish HDP linked the deep state to the assassinations and bombings in southeast Turkey. In parallel, it seems that the conspiratorial rhetoric is likely to be used by opposition parties pragmatically: the RP accused the government that came to power after the February 28 coup of serving the interests of the deep state. The governments, in contrast, tend not to use deep state accusations and deny those against them. For example, an ANAP representative denied allegations by the RP that ANAP was collaborating with the deep state; during the AKP government, an AKP representative also denied the existence of the deep state. This is in line with Uscinski and Parent's study claiming that conspiracy theories are likely to be used by political groups that are not in power.[16]

An instrumental rationale is apparent in the communication of the deep state conspiracy theory in the Turkish parliament. This resonates with some previous studies about the use of the rhetoric pragmatically among Taiwanese online users and Turkish conspiracy readers.[17] The conclusion also hints at a solution for preventing the continuity of the spread of the deep state debate. If mainstream political parties could create an agreed definition of the deep state regardless of their political interests, then we might see a decrease in the use of the rhetoric. To that end, they could create a commission to investigate the deep state. This, however, is not likely to end this rhetoric completely, as unconvincing official explanations and the legacy of the Sèvres syndrome also seem to be important factors triggering the deep state discussion. As Jan-Willem van Prooijen suggests later in this volume, more transparency and openness in government could provide a way to move forward from these conspiracy theories.

The current AKP government is attempting to clamp down on the supposed parallel state, which they associate with the failed coup attempt in July 2016. In this endeavor the Turkish state declared a state of emergency. Despite supporting the state's attempt to cull the parallel state, various political groups have already called the AKP government's actions a politically motivated "witch hunt" against opposing political parties. For example, Kemal Kilicdaroglu, the leader of the main opposition party (CHP), has been walking between Ankara and Istanbul to protest against the injustice practiced against all political groups in this process. This 250-mile protest is named the Justice March.[18] This political situation is foreseeable from the findings of the deep state discussion. Turkish politics is locked in a zero-sum game between political parties that keeps them from agreeing on who the true conspirators really are. This political context facilitates the continuity of conspiracy theories about the parallel state as well. If power changes hands or becomes more evenly distributed, then these conspiracy theories may have less of an opportunity to flourish.

Notes

1. Baer, Marc David. 2013. "An Enemy Old and New: The Dönme, Anti-Semitism, and Conspiracy Theories in the Ottoman Empire and Turkish Republic." *Jewish Quarterly Review* 103(4): 523–555; Kavakci, Merve. 2009. "Turkey's Test with Its Deep State." *Mediterranean Quarterly* 20(4): 83–97.
2. Nefes, Türkay Salim. 2012. "The History of the Social Constructions of Dönmes (Converts)." *Journal of Historical Sociology* 25(3): 413–439; Nefes, Türkay Salim. 2013. "Ziya Gökalp's Adaptation of Emile Durkheim's Sociology in his Formulation of the Modern Turkish Nation." *International Sociology* 28(3): 335–350; Nefes, Türkay Salim. 2013. "Political Parties' Perceptions and Uses of Anti-Semitic Conspiracy Theories in Turkey." *The Sociological Review* 61(2): 247–264; Nefes, Türkay Salim. 2015. "Scrutinizing Impacts of Conspiracy Theories on Readers' Political Views: A Rational Choice Perspective on Anti-Semitic Rhetoric in Turkey." *The British Journal of Sociology* 66(3): 557–575; Nefes, Türkay Salim. 2017. "The Impacts of the Turkish Government's Conspiratorial Framing about the Gezi Park Protests." *Social Movement Studies* 16(5): 610–622. DOI: 10.1080/14742837.2017.1319269.
3. Göçek, Fatma Muge. 2011. *The Transformation of Turkey: Redefining State and Society from the Ottoman Empire to the Modern Era.* New York: IB Tauris.
4. Aras, Bülent. 2009. "Turkey's Rise in the Greater Middle East: Peace-Building in the Periphery." *Journal of Balkan and Near Eastern Studies* 11(1): 29–41; Webb, Edward. 2011. "Resisting Anamnesis: A Nietzschean Analysis of Turkey's National History Education." *Journal of Contemporary European Studies* 19(4): 489–500; Yılmaz, Hakan. 2011. "Euroscepticism in Turkey: Parties, Elites, and Public Opinion." *South European Society and Politics* 16(01): 185–208; Guida, Michalengelo. 2008. "The Sèvres Syndrome and 'Komplo' Theories in the Islamist and Secular Press." *Turkish Studies* 9(1): 37–52.
5. Ibid.
6. Ibid., 46–50.
7. Freely, Maureen. 2007. "Why They Killed Hrant Dink." *Index on Censorship* 36(2): 15–29.
8. Kavakci, "Turkey's Test with Its Deep State."
9. BIA News Center. 2005. "Doğrudur, Derin Devlet Vardır." http://bianet.org/bianet/siyaset/58067-dogrudur-derin-devlet-vardir (Accessed December 22, 2017); Hurriyet. 2005. "Ecevit: Türkiye'de Bir Derin Devlet Olayi Var." http://www.hurriyet.com.tr/ecevit-turkiyede-bir-derin-devlet-olayi-var-3544213 (Accessed December 22, 2017).
10. Gorvett, Jon. 2006. "Talking Turkey: Turkey's 'Deep State' Surfaces in Former President's Words, Deeds in Kurdish Town." *Washington Report on Middle East Affairs* 25(1): 37–41.
11. Park, Bill. 2008. "Turkey's Deep State: Ergenekon and the Threat to Democratisation in the Republic." *The RUSI Journal* 153(5): 54–59.
12. Ibid.
13. Rainsford, Sarah. 2008. "'Deep State Plot' Grips Turkey." *BBC.* http://news.bbc.co.uk/1/hi/world/europe/7225889.stm (Accessed December 22, 2017).
14. Kavakci, "Turkey's Test with Its Deep State," 89.
15. Rainsford, "'Deep State Plot' Grips Turkey."

16. Uscinski, Joseph E., and Joseph M. Parent. 2014. *American Conspiracy Theories*. Oxford: Oxford University Press.

17. Nefes, Türkay Salim. 2014. "Rationale of Conspiracy Theorizing: Who Shot the President Chen Shui-bian?" *Rationality and Society* 26(3): 373–394.

18. Shaheen, Kareem. 2017. "Turkey's Opposition Begins 250-Mile Protest March over MP's Imprisonment." *The Guardian*. https://www.theguardian.com/world/2017/jun/15/turkeys-opposition-begins-protest-march-over-mps-imprisonment-enis-berberoglu   (Accessed December 22, 2017).

27

The Hidden and the Revealed

Styles of Political Conspiracy Theory in Kirchnerism

TANYA FILER

Democracy officially returned to Argentina on December 10, 1983, following eight years of brutal military authoritarianism (1976–1983). Thirty years later, on December 10, 2013, a jubilant celebration took place to mark the longest period of uninterrupted democracy in Argentine history. President Cristina Fernández de Kirchner (2007–2015) of the center-left Peronist Victory Front (FpV), encouraged a mood of festivity, dancing, and beating a saucepan to the tune of a triumphant song.[1] Her face beamed across screens in the the Plaza de Mayo, the historic square outside the presidential palace where thousands of Argentines had gathered. The appearance of societal cohesion and contentment that the mass attendance suggested could not, however, mask a more fragmented reality. Just a few days earlier a wave of antigovernment police strikes and lootings had swept the country.[2] They signaled that though Argentine democracy had proved to be robust over the past three decades, a politics of anger was unsettling official claims to widespread political satisfaction.

Fernández alluded to the protests and violence in her speech at the museum, engaging a language pregnant with metaphor:

> I am not naïve. I don't believe in coincidences, nor do I believe in events that are produced through contagion [. . .] some things that occur in Argentina and some things that happen on specific dates and with specific leaders are not a matter of contagion, they are produced through planning and execution with surgical precision [. . .] we all know that there's no such thing as a contagious effect, we know that there is political incitement.[3]

The most recent authoritarian regime had spoken of the need to "operate" on the nation in order to remove the "disease" of communism that was apparently riddling it.[4] In her mobilization of this familiar discourse of national malady and military cure,

Fernández evocatively tarred the protestors as heirs to the authoritarian imaginary.[5] She portrayed herself, by contrast, as the symbolic incarnation of the democracy that had vanquished their ideology from power. The language of premeditation— "planning" and "execution"—not only bolstered the accusation of conspiracy, which was now framed as a distinctly dictatorial behavior but also evoked memories of the authoritarian murder of thousands of so-called subversives. Amid the joyousness of the democratic anniversary, Fernández turned to the language of conspiracy to emphasize that the authoritarian past had not fully passed, its violence and quiet machinations threatening to re-emerge and disrupt Argentine democracy at any hint of disunion within the *pueblo*.[6]

Almost every president in the post-authoritarian period has turned to conspiracy theory as a mechanism for shoring up their authority, often evoking the specter of the recent past and stoking fears of its return. Yet Fernández was among the most conspiracy-minded. This chapter considers how and why Fernández engaged conspiracy discourse. It begins by suggesting an intimate relationship between conspiracy theory and Kirchnerism, the populist movement led by Fernández and her late husband President Néstor Kirchner (2003–2007) (this chapter concentrates on the period when Fernández was president). It then puts forward a thesis on two specific *styles* of conspiracy theory that Fernández engaged, suggesting that together they provided an efficient and emotive method for bolstering the central tenets of her populist authority: vertical leadership and the illusion of direct contact with "the people." The chapter concludes in advancing a broader argument about the study of conspiracy theory as a valuable mechanism for understanding populism.

Kirchnerism, Conspiracy Theory, and Evidence

The message that Fernández issued at the museum, and on many other occasions, was clear. Citizens needed to remain alert and follow her lead if they were to spot the signs of conspiracy and avoid being duped into the kind of moral panic that had helped to empower the authoritarians whose demise the festivities marked. Yet as she issued this warning, Fernández also subtly intimated its superfluity: her seemingly organic shift from a claim to individual knowledge ("I am not naïve") to a claim to collective knowledge ("we all know") hinted that she was telling the people what they already knew. This seemingly strange pronominal shift spoke directly to the logics of Kirchnerism.

Populism had emerged to mass support in Argentina the mid 1940s when Juan Perón, a charismatic labor leader, rose to power. Amid popular dissatisfaction with liberal elites, Peronism provided working-class Argentines with a revised mechanism for imagining democracy. It kept alive a sense of popular sovereignty through maintaining elections and democratic forms of representation.[7] Crucially, however, Peronism also took on a vertical structure, promoting "the figure of the leader, who was then fully presented as the best interpreter of the will of people."[8] This heroization was fused with a constructed sense of "direct contact" between the leader and citizenry.[9] In this Peronist logic, the "I" of the leader and the "we" of the *pueblo* (people) become synthesized into one: the government *is* the expression of the people, who are subsumed into a pure and univocal mass. Any appearance of opposition, it follows, can only be the construct of exogenous and anti-national forces. The idea of such opposition plays a critical role in shoring up the power of the populist leader, who frames their rule as requisite to resisting the threat presented by an apparently perilous and duplicitous "other." Kirchnerism drew on the Peronist legacy of populism in Argentina but skillfully updated it for the specific conditions of the post-authoritarian and post–financial crisis context.[10] The Kirchnerist "other" was an apparent power bloc committed to neoliberal economic interests, globalization, and excessive cosmopolitanism (as opposed to regional solidarity), and either disinterested in human rights or actively opposed to their safeguarding.[11]

On a global scale, populist leaders and parties often turn to conspiracy theory to suggest the presence of a threatening "other." Conspiracy theory is a useful narrative form for this work, its structure well suited to pitting the interests of an elite minority against the well-being of the majority. It is improbable, though, that the populist use of conspiracy theory is always a deliberate and strategically engaged choice. It may have more to do with underlying parities in structure and intentionality between conspiracy theory and the populist worldview than with meticulous discursive planning. Populism and conspiracy theory try to "explain and narrate a world of unequal power."[12] They also both derive their authority from an apparent interpretive superiority, their proponents *seeing* the enemy before or better than the people who they magnanimously inform and save from dupery. Populists have long held a reputation for misinforming, but, in common with conspiracy theorists, their arguments are often premised upon at least an element of truth. Left-wing populists, for example, typically do not invent the inequalities that they decry; no such ingenuity is needed. They emphasize (and sometimes exaggerate) real inequities and minoritarian power, and often win support by promising to abolish the socioeconomic marginalization that touches the lives of many.[13] Given these overlaps in structure and intention, conspiracy theory appears a natural fit for populist political communications.

Despite the propensity for conspiracy theorizing exhibited by populist leaders and others, we typically view conspiracy theory as a relatively homogenous genre. We acknowledge thematic variation, from birtherism to climate change. We also note the varied discursive spheres in which conspiracy theories proliferate, from journalism to political speech and novels.[14] Yet we tend not to categorize according to stylistic characteristics.[15] This investigatory lack is cause and effect of the tendency to understand conspiracy theory as a relatively formulaic discursive category, with little formal variety within: conspiracy stories are "simple, understandable, and attractive to people seeking an explanation for their woes," and their interpretive logic is "marked by broad structural similarities across time and space."[16] Yet subgenres exist, and reflecting on their usage helps to elucidate with granularity and precision the specific affordances of conspiracy theory to populist authority.

As a leader, Fernández moved between two contrasting categories of conspiracy theory. This duality was expedient to her cause but not necessarily the purposive product of an orchestrated communications campaign. In the first subgenre, which I term "the hidden," "the people" were guided to have a quasi-religious faith in her knowledge that nullified the need for evidence of her claims. This evidentiary absence both produced an abbreviated narrative form and bolstered the vertical authority associated with populist rule. In the second, "the revealed," Fernández sought to construct a sense of intimate connection with "the people" through enabling them to "see" through her eyes. In contrast to "the hidden" style, this protracted form of conspiracy theory depended upon presenting to her audience an overabundance of apparent evidence. She thus constructed a sense of "common knowledge" with them through the intimacy of shared vision. Alternating between the hidden and the revealed provided Fernández with a powerful rhetorical mechanism for maintaining both the hierarchical structure upon which populist leadership depends *and* the sense of direct contact with the people through which her authority was derived. Examining the official narratives that initially emerged to account for the suspicious fatality of special prosecutor Alberto Nisman (a "hidden" conspiracy theory) and then to downplay and deprecate the antigovernment protests that followed his death (a "revealed" conspiracy theory) helps to illuminate this broader discursive tendency within Kirchnerism and to understand its power.

The Hidden: The Death of Alberto Nisman, or Knowledge Beyond Evidence

In the early hours of January 18, 2015, Nisman was found dead of a gunshot to the head in his apartment in the exclusive Puerto Madero district of Buenos Aires. Nisman, a 51-year-old special prosecutor, had risen to public prominence in Argentina during his decade-long investigation into the bomb attack on July 18, 1994 on the headquarters of the Asociación Mutual Israelita de Argentina (AMIA), a Jewish community center in downtown Buenos Aires. The attack killed 85 people and injured a further 300. Nisman was due to present evidence before Congress on January 19 that would implicate Fernández in covering up the role of Iran in the bombing. He intended to show that she had sought the withdrawal of Interpol arrest warrants for Iranian officials suspected of involvement in the attack in exchange for an agricultural trade deal with the Islamic Republic (Figure 27.1).

After her initial silence following the death—all the more notable given her normal loquaciousness and (by then) quick-paced social media output—Fernández

Figure 27.1. Cristina Fernández de Kirchner greeting an audience in Buenos Aires, Argentina, in 2014.

intimated that Nisman had committed suicide. But a few days later she backtracked, in a letter posted to her website and Facebook page under the subtitle "the suicide (that I am convinced) was not a suicide."[17] Fernández explained in the epistle that she had "no evidence" but "no doubts" either that Nisman had been the victim of a political murder plot: "they used him alive," the President declared, "and then they needed him dead." In this provocative statement, Fernández did not suggest that she was privy to evidence that she could not share, but that her analysis was based instead on an innate understanding. Her accusation, moreover, unambiguously presented the death as a conspiracy whose primary motivation was not to silence the prosecutor but to weaken her government: "The true operation against the Government was the Prosecutor's death after accusing the President, the Foreign Minister, and the Secretary General of La Cámpora [the Kirchnerist youth] of being accessories to the Iranians accused of the terrorist bombing of AMIA."[18] This framing encouraged readers to view the fatality as an attack on the nation, not because the judicial independence so vital to democracy was at risk but because the death apparently targeted the leader—the ultimate representative of the *pueblo*. In the days that followed, Fernández pointed the finger directly at SIDE (the Secretariat for State Intelligence) agents. She claimed that parts of the secret service were corrupt and unaccountable, despite her having previously empowered the service and lauded its work. "You cannot lay siege to democracy with fear and extortion," she explained in an hour-long broadcast in which she announced her decision to dissolve SIDE and replace it with a new federal intelligence agency.[19] In engaging the metaphor of ex-tortion, Fernández once again evoked the specter of authoritarian practice. Lacking her protection, she intimated, Argentina risked falling victim once again to covert and nondemocratic power mechanisms.

Besides SIDE, the media also featured heavily in the presidential critique. Damian Pachter, a journalist, had broken the story of the discovery of the corpse on Twitter. Fernández interpreted his publicizing of the death as a means of bolstering antigov-ernment sentiment and stoking political scandal. A few days after breaking the story, Pachter fled to Israel, claiming that he was being followed and feared for his life. In response, Fernández baited the journalist and his defenders, tweeting an image of his supposed return flight ticket (a flecked photograph that appeared to be a screen-shot from an internal airline computer system) in an effort to intimate that he had not fled and that his claim of being pursued was yet another strategy to besmirch her image. If her story were true, the scheme appeared to be working: 24 hours after Pachter broke the story, the hashtag #CFKAsesina ('CFKMurderer') had appeared in more than 50,000 tweets, as distressed citizens drew a direct link between the increasingly unpopular president and the corpse.[20] Visual memes that implicated Fernández circulated across social media platforms, drawing on references from popular culture, from the U.S. television series *House of Cards* to *Chronicle of a Death Foretold* by Gabriel García Márquez. But this macabre jocularity was coupled with forcefully articulated demands by the media and citizens for evidence, prompt in-vestigation, and, ultimately, a "justice" for Nisman that they now equated with the seemingly ever-deferred "justice" for the victims of the AMIA attack.

The demand for evidence spoke to a pervasive culture of distrust surrounding the veracity and accessibility of political information in the 2010s. Deep-seated animosities between the state and media industry dated back to at least the 1940s, but their relationship hit a low point in the post-authoritarian context under Fernández. The president stopped holding press conferences, and state *and* media discourse often appeared to take the form of *relatos*, or stories, rather than fact-based journalism or political communications. Few citizens perceived politicians or the media to be credible sources of factually accurate information.[21] Yet the clamor for evidence-based justice also pointed toward a particular characteristic of the Kirchnerist narrative surrounding the fatality, one also evident in official discourse surrounding other political events: In her claim to "know" the truth despite having "no evidence," Fernández did not just disregard pieces of evidence as false but seem-ingly negated the very need for this category of information at all.

Indifference to evidence is a curious standpoint in this context: conspiracy theory typically functions through drawing multiple strands of supposed evidence, all ap-parently connected to one another, into a grand narrative. Many of the most well-known conspiracy theories, from climate change denialism to birtherism, display this characteristic. Far from denying a need for evidence, conspiracy theorists sug-gest that the "correct" interpretation of an abundance of evidence—an interpretation that they apparently supply—enables knowledge of a conspiracy. Within the logic of populism, however, the knowledge of the leader does not always depend upon proofs. Populism, the historian Federico Finchelstein observes, rests "on a form of leadership that might be best described as religious" because it tends to "deify its causes and leaders."[22] If we consider the mechanics of this deification, it becomes clear that it depends upon a dual visibility and hiddenness. On the one hand the leader is imagined to be in unmediated contact with the people: visible, knowable, a tangible presence in their lives. But this apparent visibility works in tandem with the image of an epistemological hiddenness: the belief that the leader has "an innate and better knowledge than the people of what they really want."[23] Citizens outsource their judgment to the populist leader on the basis of this belief, legitimizing the leader's acting even beyond the mandate of political representation.[24]

The mystery-knowledge of the leader, always already beyond the access the people, neatly eliminates the need for evidentiary processes in political decision making.[25] The leader cannot admit to nescience because the admission of not knowing puts at stake the very legitimacy of their claim to power; having "no doubts" regarding the death of Nisman was, then, the only response available to Fernández. The claim to have "no evidence," moreover, did not signify ignorance but instead intimated to her followers an innate knowledge beyond the proofs required by democratic process, or earthly courts and their jurisprudential proceedings. The type of conspiracy narrative that this epistemological claim produces is necessarily condensed, a "hidden style" free from the adornment of an effluence of apparent evidence. The anti-Kirchnerist cultural historian Beatriz Sarlo wrote in 2012 that Fernández had two discursive strategies: "silence and monopoly."[26] She argued that Fernández typically opted for discursive monopolization, seeking dominance over the public narrative. In contrast, Fernández treated with silence circumstances for which she did not "have an argument prepared." Although her analysis has an element of anti-Kirchnerist caricature, many critics suggested that the death took Fernández by surprise, leaving her unrehearsed and quieted. Yet silence—whatever its cause—can be powerful. On the basis of such apparently instinctive yet "silent" inarticulable knowledge, citizens were guided not only to accept the interpretation of the death that Fernández proposed but also to view any actions that she premised upon it—the disbandment of the secret service included—as in their best interests.

The Revealed: 18F, or Aesthetic Manipulation

Public prosecutors, long embattled with the ruling party over judicial independence, publicly pleaded with Fernández not to interfere into the investigation into the death of Nisman. Many predicted judicial stalling from soon after the story of the death broke.[27] A month after the fatality, on February 18, 2015, members of the Argentine judiciary organized a multiparty silent rally, breaking with the sonic overload of the pot banging that has punctuated most Argentine protests since the financial crisis of 2001. The official demands of the organizers included investigatory independence and justice in the Nisman and AMIA cases. Fernández did not take these claims at face value, instead identifying a "hidden and implicit objective" in the rally. 18F, as the march was known, was not "a tribute to a person who died tragically" or "even an unusual demand for justice," she determined, but "purely and simply an opposition rally" (partisan slogans were banned by the protest organizers, though they were not completely absent).[28] The rally represented "the baptism of fire of the Judicial Party," the politicization of the courts apparently evident in every footstep that trod the streets. This agenda could be discerned, Fernández asserted, "in gestures and in words and quite visibly."[29] The true objective was only really hidden, then, to those who looked with insufficient care or chose not to see. Just as she had argued at the thirtieth anniversary celebrations, citizens could *choose* not to be duped by forces external to the *pueblo* if they only opened their eyes to the "true" interpretation of the event—the reading that she provided to them (Figure 27.2).

The most salient features of the rally included its duration and social media tail. Political protests in Argentina typically take place over one evening, but 18F extended across time zones as people congregated outside embassies and consulates abroad, from England to Australia.[30] Photographs and videos from every location were shared widely online, over several hours, including umbrella-filled scenes of a stormy Buenos Aires. Digital media seemingly fuses instantaneity (through a constant updating that renders obsolete any event that occurred a moment prior) and

Figure 27.2. 18F Silent Rally, 18 February 2015, Buenos Aires, Argentina.

permanence (through the affordances of archiving and search). Yet the extended "real time" of the rally appeared to evade the instantaneous element, refusing to vanish from public international sight. In its mass turnout and online visual endurance, the rally posed a direct challenge to the idea of the *pueblo* united behind Fernández. A popular antigovernment protest is oxymoronic within the populist rationale: if the government represents an apparently homogenous popular will, to protest against it is to protest against the collective self. Popular protest *must*, then, be a counterfeit production. Fernández could only declare the rally a fake. The way in which Fernández unveiled the apparent duplicity spoke of her attentiveness to the power of visuality. She declared the rally the object of aesthetic manipulation by wily anti-Kirchnerist media, in partnership with the judiciary, bent on "institutionally destructive and predatory work." The president even instructed her audience in how to spot the signs of the deceit. The event was apparently a deception across media, involving an arsenal of online and offline techniques. The evidence of this duplicity was to be found in "the photographs and their use of perspective, the texts, the occupied common physical space and their capacity," which together produced a falsehood through inflating real levels of support. The dense compilation of visual evidence reflected, Fernández suggested, the lack of subtlety in this amplification. The "lie" was "far too blatant," the truth of the event revealed through the very visibility of its artifice.[31]

In entering into this detailed and didactic visual analysis, Fernández invited her audience to see through her eyes, collapsing the sensorial gap between her and them. This discursive strategy served as a mechanism for producing the sense of direct contact with the people that populism demands and that Peronism, in its various iterations, has long cultivated. Her content analysis emphasized the point: drawing attention to the constructedness of the visual forms that she denigrated, the apparently unmediated vision that she "shared" with the *pueblo*—from her eyes to theirs—was brought into still sharper relief. This expository technique, beyond constructing sensory intimacy, also provided a replicable schematic for visual interpretation of anti-Kirchnerist protest. It made clear that at least one kind of antigovernment conspiracy consisted of a multitude filling public space, posing as—or made to look like—the *pueblo* that they could not possibly be. In common with the aesthetics of the crowd that other populist leaders have identified as conspiratorial, an *excess* of visibility rather than its denial appeared to represent conspiracy.[32] The supposed plotters may have attempted to hide their true identities (the judiciary as party), but the events that they planned were intended to reach the public limelight and remain there: to sap power from the state through an unflinching physical and visual endurance.

The image of the mass contrasts starkly with the ocular appearance that we typically associate with conspiracy in liberal democracies: "hidden hands" that pull strings from covert nooks; businessmen in sealed off, smoky rooms; a lone corpse found stashed away; a spectacular yet momentary explosion; or a heist conducted with utmost furtiveness, its agile perpetrators gone in a flash. These images of private plotting and fleeting public sights do not present the same type of affront to populist leadership as do scenes of publicness and longevity. To be sure, the image of a roomful of elite businessmen plotting their financial self-gain may illuminate the societal inequities that the left-wing populist leader promises to eradicate. It can stoke the resentments that make catnip of a leader who promises to fight a system that has alienated many citizens and failed to provide the conditions in which they may prosper. But it is the appearance of an oppositional mass that poses the more direct challenge to the leader because it risks giving lie to their legitimacy: their constructed identity as desired by and representative of *every* loyal citizen. In its expansiveness, 18F seemed not to be a mere fragmentation of "the people"—a dissensus from within the body politic—but, more threateningly, simply to *be* them. The citizenry needed urgently, then, to see the event through the shrewd perception of presidential eyes. The act of sharing vision was at once intimate and pedagogical, deriving its affect through the imbrication of these dual registers.

Conspiracy Theory, Populism and Emotions

Understanding conspiracy theory not as homogenous genre of political narrative but as constituted of different stylistic and epistemological subtypes helps to reveal its multilayered uses within strategic and political communications. The movement between the "hidden" and "revealed" styles of conspiracy narrative may be singularly efficacious to a populist regime, the two subgenres working complementarily with one another to bolster the qualities of populism that have given this style of political leadership its longevity in Argentina.[33] The narrative combination mirrors the fusing of verticality and directness that are critical to populist authority and appeal, reinforcing the powerful image of the leader as at once deific—possessed of an epistemological authority beyond standard human reach—and an everyman who not only "sees things our way" but also offers to show us things "their way." Conspiracy theory is clearly not, then, simply a fixed discursive category whose only utility to the populist leader is in producing or drawing attention to an "other." In its varying epistemological claims, and through the stylistic variation that necessarily results, conspiracy narratives play a more multidimensional role in constructing the leader and maintaining their authority than the production of a threatening outsider alone.

Viewing conspiracy theory from a stylistic perspective also helps us to think with specificity about the emotional sway that this discourse can exercise. Populist conspiracy theory has long been associated with the stirring of a narrow repertoire of "negative" political emotions. There can little debate that individual conspiracy theories foment (and draw upon) fear, anger, resentment, and envy by focusing attention on acts of apparent wrongdoing and their covert planning.

Fernández clearly sought to mobilize such negative sentiments at the thirtieth anniversary of redemocratization, producing this emotional appeal through stirring historical memory. Yet her constant movement between the hidden and revealed styles during her presidential career enabled Fernández to make a broader range of emotive bids than fear alone. Her apparent epistemological superiority and interpretive capacities, suggested in her usage of the hidden and revealed styles respectively, may have worked together to induce a sense of awe and veneration, promoting fervent followership. The invitation to shared vision implicit in the "revealed" style may also have promoted a sense of intimate connection between leader and citizen—the promise of not being alone in this fragile world. Subgenres of conspiracy theory can evidently be used, then, to make a variety of emotional appeals to the people who believe in them. Given their popularity as a discursive form among populist leaders globally, understanding these subgenres is crucial to the work of identifying the complex emotional and psychological dynamics at play within populism.

Notes

1. Pot banging is a feature of popular protest in Argentina. This type of protest is known as a *cacerolazo*, and rose to prominence during the protests surrounding the financial crisis of 2001–2002.
2. Associated Press. 2013. "Argentinian Looting Spreads amid Police Strikes." *The Guardian*. https://www.theguardian.com/world/2013/dec/10/argentinian-looting-spreads-police-strikes (Accessed April 8, 2017).
3. Fernández de Kirchner, Cristina. "Todo lo que falta lograr, sólo se puede hacer en democracia." December 10, 2013. https://www.casarosada.gob.ar/informacion/archivo/26950-todo-lo-que-falta-lograr-solo-se-puede-hacer-en-democracia-afirmo-la-presidenta. (Accessed April 8, 2017).
4. Rock, David. 1992. *Authoritarian Argentina: The Nationalist Movement, Its History and Its Impact*. Berkeley: University of California Press, xx.
5. Peronists have also used the cancer metaphor to speak of a need to root out their adversaries. See for example, Puiggrós, Rodolfo. 1974. "El nuevo peronismo en la universidad. Declaraciones a *Confirmado*, 12 de Junio 1973." *La Universidad Del Pueblo*. Buenos Aires: Crisis.
6. On patterns of continuity and repetition in police brutality since the authoritarian years (albeit to a much reduced extent) see Bonner, Michelle D. 2014. "'Never Again': Transitional Justice and Persistent Police Violence in Argentina." *International Journal of Transitional Justice* 8(2): 235–255.
7. Finchelstein, Federico. 2014. "Returning Populism to History." *Constellations* 21(4): 477.
8. Ibid.
9. Plotkin, Mariano Ben. 2002. *Mañana es San Perón: A Cultural History of Perón's Argentina*. Wilmington, DE: Scholarly Resources, 82.
10. In late 2001, the Argentine economy reached crisis point when the peso was devalued and there was a rush on the banks to convert pesos to dollars. To avert an aggravation of the bank run, the Minister of Economy Domingo Cavallo announced a freeze on bank deposits.
11. By April 2015, Fernández had linked many of these disparate groups to one another, arguing that she was the target of a conspiracy involving U.S. hedge funds, acquaintances of Nisman,

and Jewish organizations. Goñi, Uki, and Jonathan Watts. 2015. "Argentina President: US 'Vulture Funds' Backed Nisman before His Death." *The Guardian.* https://www.theguardian.com/world/2015/apr/21/argentina-president-fernandez-alberto-nisman (April 19, 2017).

12. Fenster, Mark. 2009. "On His Book *Conspiracy Theories: Secrecy and Power in American Culture (Revised and Updated Edition).*" http://rorotoko.com/interview/20090120_fenster_mark_on_conspiracy_theories_secrecy_power_american_culture/ (Accessed December 22, 2017).

13. On the "truths" of populists in a contemporary European context see Lausen, Lukas, and Nicolas Stuehlinger. 2017. "The Populists Can Be Beaten. Here's How." *The New Statesman.* https://www.newstatesman.com/2017/03/populists-can-be-beaten-heres-how (April 11, 2017).

14. Studies attentive to genres of conspiracy theory include Fenster, Mark. 2008. *Conspiracy Theories: Secrecy and Power in American Culture.* Minneapolis: University of Minnesota Press; Kelman, David. 2015. *Counterfeit Politics: Secret Plots and Conspiracy Narratives in the Americas.* Lewisburg, PA: Bucknell University Press.

15. To be sure, the critical literature on conspiracy theory is no stranger to the idea of "style." Since Richard Hofstadter conceptualized conspiracy theory as an expression of the "paranoid style in American politics," scholars have devoted many pages to the claim. Yet conspiracy theories are narratives: they not only articulate a political style but *have* a style also. Hofstadter, Richard. 1964. "The Paranoid Style in American Politics." *Harper's Magazine,* November, 77–86.

16. Fenster, *Conspiracy Theories,* 8, 87.

17. Fernández de Kirchner, Cristina. 2015. "AMIA y la denuncia del fiscal Nisman." http://www.cfkargentina.com/amia-y-la-denuncia-del-fiscal-nisman/ (Accessed May 15, 2015).

18. This translation appeared on the presidential website.

19. Cristina Fernández de Kirchner. 2015. "Cristina Kirchner Anunció La Creación de La Agencia Federal de Inteligencia (Ex Side)." YouTube video, 1:00. Posted January 26, 2015. https://www.youtube.com/watch?v=OBYn8W8uupA (Accessed December 22, 2017).

20. On the Twitter discourse that emerged in the aftermath of the fatality see Filer, Tanya, and Rolf Fredheim. 2016. "Sparking Debate? Political Deaths and Twitter Discourses in Argentina and Russia." *Information, Communication & Society* 19(11): 1539–1555.

21. According to survey results from early 2016—a few weeks after the FpV government had left office and been replaced by the center-right PRO government of Mauricio Macri—this culture of distrust continued into early 2016. YouGov, and Leverhulme Trust Conspiracy and Democracy Project. *Conspiracy (Argentina).* YouGov, 2016.

22. Finchelstein, "Returning Populism to History," 469.

23. Ibid., 477.

24. Ibid.

25. The idea of the populist conspiracy theorist as possessing deific qualities sits in provocative juxtaposition with the vision that Karl Popper put forward of *conspirators* as secular "gods" with hidden intentions. Popper, Karl. [1945] 1957. *The Open Society and Its Enemies, Vol 2.* London: Routledge and Keagan Paul, 306.

26. Sarlo, Beatriz. 2012. "La 'filosofía del lenguaje' K." *La Nación.* http://www.lanacion.com.ar/1456937-la-filosofia-del-lenguaje-k (Accessed December 22, 2017).

27. Their concerns proved warranted. Viviana Fein, the first judged charged with the investigation, was dismissed following disputes with the ex-wife of Nisman, and it took a year for a judge to determine that the fatality was probably the result of a homicide.

28. Fernández de Kirchner, Cristina. 2015. "18F The Baptism of Fire of the Judicial Party." http://www.cfkargentina.com/18f-the-baptism-of-fire-of-the-judicial-party/2/ (Accessed July 4, 2016).

29. Ibid.

30. 18F was not the first or only rally to include participants outside Argentina, but the numbers involved and social media activity from abroad were reportedly more extensive than previously.

31. Fernández de Kirchner, 2016.

32. Ibid. For a brief comparative case study, illuminating how the populist government of Nicolás Maduro in Venezuela also interpreted mass gathering as conspiracy, see Filer, Tanya. 2015. "The Conspiratorial Queue? Perceptions of 'anti-Government' Aesthetics." *Conspiracy and Democracy.* http://www.conspiracyanddemocracy.org/blog/the-conspiratorial-queue-perceptions-of-anti-government-aesthetics/ (Accessed May 20, 2015).

33. To a more limited extent, non-Peronist governments in Argentina have also exhibited populist tendencies. Post-authoritarian examples include the Radical government led by Raúl Alfonsín (1983—1989).

HOW SHOULD WE LIVE WITH CONSPIRACY THEORIES?

JOSEPH E. USCINSKI

How can we live with conspiracy theories? How *should* we live with conspiracy theories? Conspiracy theories do not exist out on the fringes; they are not ideas that affect someone else. They affect our everyday lives and reach not just close to home, but into our homes.

As an example, consider conspiracy theories about religion. The debate over teaching creationism in schools is rarely an issue in Europe, but in the United States it has been a contentious issue for nearly a century. As the evidence for evolution has solidified, and courts have increasingly scrutinized the use of religious ideas in schools, creationists have turned to conspiracy theories to explain away the lack of evidence supporting their beliefs. Creationists contend that there exists a conspiracy to keep "creation scientists" out of scientific journals, to keep God out of public schools and colleges, and to lead the public astray with false ideas. Some creationists assert a "Satanic conspiracy." As Michael Shermer notes, "creationists do not publish in scientific journals because they do not do science. . . creationism is not taught in public school science courses because there is nothing to teach—'God did it' makes for a short semester."[1]

But, others see more earthly conspirators: *Expelled*, a documentary film about the lack of God in schools and universities "asserts that people in academia who see evidence of a supernatural intelligence in biological processes have unfairly lost their jobs, been denied tenure or suffered other penalties as part of a scientific conspiracy to keep God out of the nation's laboratories and classrooms."[2] This is par for the course according to

Ben Stein, economist, game show host, and narrator of *Expelled* who blames science for the Holocaust and claimed that "love of God and compassion and empathy leads you to a very glorious place," while "science leads you to killing people."[3]

Conspiracy theories about religion, however, are not confined to the religious. Among many conspiracy-laden accounts of religion, the popular conspiracy documentary *Zeitgeist* argues that modern religions are based on ancient mythologies about the sun, the earth's orbit around the sun, and the earth's rotation. The major claim is that Jesus never existed on this earth, and Christianity is a contrived religion designed to control the masses. Respected historians, even those like Richard Carrier who argue that Jesus is myth rather than man or god, denounce the conspiracy accounts because they contain factual errors and poor interpretations of the available evidence. *The DaVinci Code* by author Dan Brown is based upon semi-historical accounts arguing that Jesus did exist but, rather than being divine, fathered a child with a prostitute, Mary Magdalene, and that this child escaped to France. According to this account, secretive groups aware of Jesus's progeny (the Knight's Templar and the Priory of Zion) have held this over the head of the Catholic Church, and also provided clues in their artwork so that the world can learn of this deception.

Our culture is awash in conspiracy theories. They affect our spiritual life, our education, our jobs, and our politics. Chapter 28 by Asbjørn Dyrendal and David Robertson examines the intersection of religion and conspiracy theorizing. Chapter 29 by Brian Keeley compares different forms of explanation— scientific, religious and conspiracy-minded. Chapter 30 by Jan-Willem van Prooijen suggests that better, more inclusive and transparent government would lessen the sting of many conspiracy theories. Chapter 31 provides guidance, particularly for journalists, for how to discuss conspiracy theories.

Notes

1. Shermer, Michael. 2004. "Then a Miracle Occurs." https://michaelshermer.com/2004/05/then-a-miracle-occurs/ (Accessed December 28, 2017).
2. Dean, Cornelia. 2008. "No Admission for Evolutionary Biologist at Creationist Film." *The New York Times*. http://www.nytimes.com/2008/03/21/science/21expelledw.html?mtrref=www.google.com&gwh=C729F9A07E34EEBE2DC2567F684FC52B&gwt=pay (Accessed December 28, 2017).
3. Linkins, Jason. 2009. "Ben Stein Dropped as University of Vermont Commencement Speaker." *Huffington Post*. https://www.huffingtonpost.com/2009/02/03/ben-stein-dropped-as-univ_n_163586.html (Accessed December 28, 2017).

28

Conspiracy Theories and Religion

Superstition, Seekership, and Salvation

DAVID G. ROBERTSON AND ASBJØRN DYRENDAL

In the second volume of *The Open Society and its Enemies*, philosopher of science Karl Popper described conspiracy theories as "the secularization of religious super-stition" and the abandoned gods replaced with "the Learned Elders of Zion, or the monopolists, or the capitalists."[1] So since the academic inception of the term *con-spiracy theory*, the connection with religion has been there, and in the popular im-agination, conspiracy theories and religion (or at least, *certain* kinds of religion) are seen as the antithesis of the Enlightenment ideals of reason, science, and secularism.

There are some similarities and connections between religious beliefs and conspiracy beliefs, and between religious people and conspiracists. In Western democratic societies, religious beliefs vary in their relation to conspiracy beliefs: con-ventional, socially accepted religious beliefs seem to barely correlate with conspiracy beliefs.[2] Paranormal and apocalyptic beliefs, on the other hand, clearly do so. There are multiple reasons why.

In this chapter we set out to outline some of these correlations and connections, focusing particularly on what a perspective from Religious Studies brings to the table.

Belief

To start with, we should deal with the matter of *belief*. Especially in the context of religion, where it tends to be given pride of place, this is a concept we need to ap-proach with some care.

A simple definition of belief might be something like "the state of a cognitive system holding information . . . as true in the generation of further thought and behavior."[3] Yet, actions may be motivated by multiple factors, the paradigmatic example being my desire for self-preservation trumping my belief in pacifism.

Mundane factors like egotism, sexual desire, even hunger may play a part. Nor is it the case that the propositional belief remains constant even when not in action. Martin Stringer presents several examples of conflicting or contradictory beliefs being held by modern Britons: devoted Christians who nonetheless talk to the spirits of their deceased husbands, young parents at a church play group who switch from mocking spiritual healing to taking it seriously when in a precarious health situation.[4] This leads him to theorize that belief is not *propositional* but *situational*, with beliefs as dispositions toward action in different contexts. At times of illness or stress, for example, some may find it more relevant to "believe in," say, homeopathy or conspiracy, whereas this "believing" is not activated under other circumstances. In this model, belief is not a pristine inner statement that is *expressed by language* but rather is *a function of language*, as the individual negotiates the various behaviors potentially available to him or her in a given situation. People have different, and some have more, beliefs, a larger repertoire of possible (re)actions, to draw on than others.

Propositional belief statements such as "I believe x" or even "I believe *in* x" may also be an act of active *commitment*. Such belief statements *do* something; they perform the act of committing. These are also statements of perceived importance; to believe in somebody or something is to invest them with special significance, perhaps even to grant sacred status.

These arguments have come to the fore in Religious Studies in recent years, on two fronts. First, in interpreting data from national censuses and attempting to understand that data within the framework of secularization, it has become clear that ticking the box next to a particular religion means different things to different people, and often to the same person in different contexts. For some (such as Glasgow Catholics or secular Jews) it is an act of cultural identity, and little can be implied about any beliefs at all. For others, this will be a conscious act of religious identification and commitment, and for still others an act of rebellion against religious belief, as in the case of the campaign to answer "Jediism" in the 2001 U.K. census. Many, perhaps most, are simply indifferent.

Second, the growth of research into so-called Invented Religions—that is, religions who *openly and self-consciously* use fictional works as source material[5]— has led to further reflection on the nature of belief. For one thing, it underlines that religious identification and belief in any sort of supernatural agency are not contingent upon one another. Indeed, statistics have shown that belief in supernatural phenomena like UFOs or ghosts remains high, even in places where religious identification is declining. Another thing highlighted by Invented Religion is that *entertainment* is also a factor, particularly satire and anarchic countercultural humor. The Church of the Flying Spaghetti Monster, for example, uses a satirical deity to challenge the hegemony of Christianity in state institutions like schools and courts, ironically revealing a clear "belief in" the Enlightenment ideals of science, reason, and secularism.

We are thereby reminded that reported beliefs vary with time and circumstance, and that they vary in meaning. People may report that they "believe in" conspiracy theories to the extent that they deny counter-evidence, but these "theories" may also be situational beliefs driven by a perceived threat from, for instance, unemployment (the government is bringing in immigrants to wipe out white Christians; Jews are stealing all the wealth) or ill health (autism is caused by vaccination; the government is suppressing natural therapies). Equally they may be driven by a desire to satirize the *realpolitik* machinations of post–World War II nations. In many cases we will find a complex mixture. For many of the novelists for whom conspiracy was an important theme, including Umberto Eco, Thomas Pynchon, and Robert Anton Wilson, such ideas were simultaneously a playful exercise in narrative uncertainty and a genuine threat in contemporary societies.

Our focus below will be mostly on the *situational* aspect of belief. While we recognize and make use of the research from psychology, our interest will primarily be in locating the beliefs within religion as social phenomena with a cultural history.

Paranormal Beliefs, Conspiracy Theory, and the Cultic Milieu

Analyzing their findings connecting subscales of schizotypy to conspiracy beliefs, Barron et al. note, first, that the most relevant subscale, "odd beliefs or magical thinking," is closely related to the paranormal beliefs of paranormal beliefs scales. Second, they note that "both conspiracist ideation and paranormal beliefs require a rejection of official mechanisms of information generation and expert opinion," and they tie this to differential personality traits such as the need for control.[6]

These specific rejections of "official mechanisms of information generation" are however also tied to larger societal phenomena. The items most often used in measuring paranormal beliefs range in content from cryptozoology and parapsychology on the one hand to a variety of mostly, but not wholly, unorthodox and explicitly "religious" beliefs on the other. From a sociological interest in religion, the items stand out as being very much a catalogue of beliefs related to the Western "cultic milieu," a shared sociocultural environment giving rise to new religious experiments.

The concept of a *cultic milieu* was constructed by British sociologist Colin Campbell in 1972 as part of an explanation of the continued rise and demise of new religious groups.[7] They often had similar ideas, and many of the same people would, over time, show up in different groups. The social milieu includes but is not limited to practitioners of "deviant sciences" (self-proclaimed psychics, healers, astrologers) and so-called alternative medicine, and their customers. It also includes a variety of identifiable religious currents, such as spiritualism and "New Age." One of the challenges facing nascent groups in this wider milieu was that the ground from which they sprung had *seekership* as a shared, basic ethos.[8] This meant that the audience at which the nascent groups directed themselves were skeptical toward organization and toward established authority in general.

Historically springing from a mystical form of religion negatively inclined toward orthodoxy-oriented religion, the milieu's skepticism of orthodoxy and authority also more and more included the sciences, as the latter took over the role of epistemic gatekeepers. The milieu has thus become characterized by a network-based circulation of "rejected knowledge," with a shared identity based on deviance and opposition to perceived orthodoxies. It defines itself through what it opposes— mainstream science and religion—while also drawing on esoteric heritage.

Conspiracy theories are belief-consonant with other ideas circulating in the milieu; notions of hidden conspiracy fit well into the register. The stress on secret knowledge held by a secret cabal, for instance, resonates with established ideas about "secret chiefs," Emic historiography is full of (alternative) histories about secret societies with hidden sources of power. All that is needed to make them relevant conspiracy theories is to invert them, so the wise chiefs seeking to serve, enlighten, and save are presented as having dark intent. In struggles over moral capital, such inversion has long been a commonplace.[9] Both this and other popular items of conspiracy culture have a long history in the precursors to the cultic milieu.[10] Similarly, some of the methods—symbol interpretation, numerology—used to connect events and actors in conspiracy theories are gathered from practices in the cultic milieu and its forebears.[11]

Conspiracy theories also come in handy in explaining why the milieu's "special knowledge" and related practices do not achieve wide acceptance. It is also useful to enhance a feeling of collective solidarity. With the cultic milieu characterized by rudimentary organization, soft boundaries, unclear rules of membership, and being low on doctrine, its "groupiness" is weak and inherently unstable. Theorizing evil conspiracy (and confronting it in discursive conflict) as threatening opposition on the outside is one way to confer a stronger sense of in-group identity.

This does not mean that personality traits at the individual level are unimportant. In an open religious economy, the pull of practices and beliefs shared with people of similar profiles may, for example, account for a differential representation of attitudes between religious scenes and groups. People higher in the above-mentioned dimensions of schizotypy seem to be differentially attracted to current manifestations of the cultic milieu.[12] The milieu may also attract people who are more prone to having special, "delusion-like" experiences, the milieu giving meaning to the experiences.[13]

There will also be push factors. The cultic milieu by definition is skeptical toward epistemic authority, which should lower the participation of authoritarians. The ethos tends toward the highly egalitarian, which would predict less social dominance orientation among participants. Those scoring higher along those dimensions should then be more likely to be attracted to other forms of religion.

Millennialism/Apocalypticism

Another notable feature of the cultic milieu shared by both religious and conspiratorial thinking is *millennialism*, or *apocalypticism*. For brevity, we are using these terms essentially interchangeably here, as both posit the immanent end of the world as we know it; whether the outcome is positive (millennial) or negative (apocalyptic) depends on whether your position is in-group or out-group.

Conspiracy thinking seems almost to posit the future by necessity; for there to be a conspiracy, the conspirators must have an aim, and that aim must have some endpoint. Indeed, Fran Mason presents the conspiracy theorist as a "subject-outside-history," with the individual both at the center of time and outside of time, seeing visions of not only the future but also of the past.[14] The *spokesperson* for conspiracy worldviews indeed often acts as a kind of prophet, albeit typically one of the type Michael Barkun described as finding "divine messages concealed or encoded in events or attributes of society."[15] In some cases however, such as David Icke, the conspiracy spokesperson is a prophet of the classic type, communicating messages directly from a supernatural source or even the godhead.[16]

In either case—religious or conspiratorial—the prophet must establish his/her authority through successful prophecy. One way in which a prophet may amplify prophetic success is through "rolling prophecy"; small prophecies are made on a regular and ongoing basis, with those which can be interpreted as successes being amplified through repetition while the majority that cannot be are quietly dropped.[17] This system works particularly well for leaders of relatively small religious groups who can speak to the congregation on a regular basis, updating their material and thereby presenting their interpretation and commentary upon ongoing events. However, this technique is also seen very clearly in conspiracist spokespeople who present their material on radio or YouTube rather than publishing in books, such as Alex Jones. Indeed, as observed by Damian Thompson, this helps us to see how much prophesying may be more about the present than about the future. Essentially the prophet offers a vision of the future almost as satire, or *reductio ad absurdum* of the present. Such "explanatory millennialism" may help to explain why the apparent failure of many (if not all) of these prophecies does not appear to have a significant impact on the capital of the prophet.[18]

The modern study of millennialism begins with Leon Festinger's classic study of one group in the United States led by Marion Keech, *When Prophecy Fails* (1956), which was concerned particularly with the behavior of the group following failed prophecy.[19] Festinger and his coauthors were particularly interested in what he saw as the anomaly that many of the members of the group were not put off when Keech's prophecy seemed to fail, but in fact became more active proselytizers than before. Although methodologically and theoretically questionable,[20] Festinger's work is nevertheless important in introducing the idea of *cognitive dissonance* into the argument. Festinger et al. described the various strategies that were mobilized by the group to counteract the cognitive dissonance between their belief in the efficacy of his prophecy and its apparent disconfirmation. Some argued that the prophecy did not fail, but happened on the spiritual rather than physical plane. For others, the prophecy was true but only for the group, and not mankind as a whole. Others argued that there has been some garbling of information during its transmission and reception, and therefore the date was misinterpreted. Finally, some argued that due to the efforts of the group to spread the prophetic message, they had managed to change the course of events so that the predicted outcome was no longer necessary.

However, a further strategy not mentioned by Festinger is to argue that the prophecy did not fail but rather was prevented from happening by a hitherto unsuspected counteragency. Such a move not only absolves the group of responsibility for said failure, it may also heighten group identification by identifying a common enemy and further underlining the urgency of the group's mission. In fact, we see this turn to explanatory conspiracy narratives in a number of cases where new religions have faced failure of prophecy, a failure of mission, or societal resistance more generally. This can be seen clearly in the case of Heaven's Gate, where, as the group became more isolated and failed to attract new membership, there was an increasing tendency to explain this as the result of a concerted but concealed campaign against them by government agencies.[21] This trajectory can also be seen in the case of Aum Shinrikyo and Scientology, as well as more generally in the New Age milieu. [22]

Grand Explanatory Narratives

As noted above, apocalypticism is not tied merely to "the end of the world," Narratives of *apokalypsis*—revelation—are much more. They reveal secrets, and the secrets revealed may range from the creation of world and its true moral order, through history to explain what was meant to be, what has (instead) become, and what that means for tomorrow. Apocalypticism employs this kind of master narrative to connect events to conceptions of a moral universe, thus making sense of what is happening and why.

In the process of fitting what happens into stories, some elements are highlighted, others are distorted, some may be completely invented, some are left out—and a pattern is constructed. Apocalyptic beliefs—and paranormal ideation—give meaning to events by making them part of a pattern. They are, more particularly, ways of making meaning not only out of the random and the peculiar but specifically also to the troublesome. This is where narratives of conspiracy enter the picture. Conspiracy beliefs often fill the function of theodicy, explaining in particular "why bad things happen to good people" and doing so in a way that calls in the explanation for personal agency, intention, and plan. Explaining problematic events with reference to personal agency and intent as explanation gives the narrative its villains, but more importantly it invokes an idea of underlying moral order.

This complex of elements made Karl Popper argue[23] that the "conspiracy theory of society" could be seen as a secular continuation of religious mythology. While those guiding the course of the world and planning its conflicts were no longer gods, they were still impossibly powerful in how perfectly outcomes matched plans. Conspiracy theories of society, in making a holistic pattern that explains what is, do not take into account the inevitable side effects of even the most perfectly executed plan, and thus match more the idea of providence than a real social science.

Conspiracy theories, when totalizing tales, are by necessity gross simplifications. They are not merely grand explanatory narratives; they are grand simplifying narratives that summarize and connect holistically in a way that can be made consistent with ideology—what Frederic Jameson called "the poor person's cognitive mapping."[24] For apocalypticism, conspiracy theory ties actors and events to the grand scheme; for conspiracy theory, as noted by Michael Barkun, the revealed order of an apocalypse promises hope for the future. When crisis has passed and the secret knowledge has played its role in rooting out evil, a better world may take its place.

This brings us to why mainstream religion tends to be less susceptible to both grand and lesser conspiracy theorizing. Mainstream religions tend toward what sociologist David Bromley calls a priestly mode, where there is continuity between God's plan for the world and the way it is developing.[25] The order of the social world may be lacking and in need of refinement, but it is not, unlike religion in a prophetic mode, wholly depraved and in need of revolution. The grand narrative of the world may be consonant with lesser conspiracies taking place, but these conspiracy narratives basically serve as system justifications. The grand conspiracy theories, on the other hand, sever the ties between society-as-it-is and true moral order. Moreover, mainstream religion tends to be better represented in the middle to upper layers of society. Since, as Uscinski and Parent succinctly put it, "conspiracy theories are for losers"[26]—that is, those who feel outside of power and influence—adherents may feel less attracted to them.

Paranormal beliefs will, to a certain extent, overlap with apocalypticism. As styles of thought, they are , both "semiotically aroused," meaning that they make things and events into symbols that fit a pattern. But paranormal beliefs on their own lack the dualistic element of apocalypticism that makes it so consonant with conspiracism. However, paranormal beliefs tend to share the social fate of apocalypticism in that they are dismissed and judged unworthy of serious consideration. They are, with respect to the knowledge elites, "losing" propositions in the social games of knowledge. Thus, even when they are not subject of actual suppression they may be defended by partisan, motivated reasoning that readily invokes conspiracy against believers.

Epistemic Capital/Special Knowledge

It is not only the particular contents of stigmatized knowledge that is shared by religious and conspiratorial worldviews, but the sources of knowledge that are drawn upon to support such claims. Ironically, given their dismissal by socially mandated knowledge elites, these groups see themselves as possessors of elite knowledge not accessible to the unenlightened. While such knowledge elites invoke reason, supported by the scientific method, to support their claims, tradition is also a significant source of epistemic authority—most of our systems of government and society are built upon and adapted from earlier systems, and religions we are very familiar with, such as Christianity, certainly seem to get a pass regarding irrationality where new religions do not. The religious or conspiratorial authority will invoke both scientific rationality and tradition, but will also make appeals to experience, channeled communications with spiritual or extraterrestrial beings, as well as synthetic knowledge, that is, the diachronic connection of different pieces of data to reveal the underlying structure (or, typically, expose some plot).

Conspiracist spokespersons are adept at strategically mobilizing these different forms of epistemic capital. Often we will see scientific papers held up as authoritative when they agree with the spokesperson's thesis, but at other times rejected for being too scientific, with academia part of the control system that suppresses the truth of these different kinds of knowledge. But these are by no means only the domain of the spokesperson; conspiracist literature, like the New Age "spiritual biography," is replete with accounts of how the individual "woke up" or "became Woke." This conspiracist enlightenment is often portrayed as a kind of gnosis, transforming the world and the place of the individual in it, and indeed Gnostic language is encountered frequently in the more spiritualized parts of the conspiracist milieu.[27] The special knowledge both elicits the transformation and is the transformation in itself; the individual has the (reptilian) scales fall from their eyes, and finds himself/ herself part of an elite fighting an ancient battle with the fate of humanity at stake. The apocalyptic import is obvious, and for some it is this gnosis that will decide the outcome. For Alex Jones, to take one topical example, the Infowar ("there's a war on—for your minds") will only be won when a tipping point is reached in the global awakening of people seeing through the illusory reality perpetuated by the controlling elites.

Concluding Remarks

Organized, mainstream religion may of course also partake in disseminating conspiracy theories. When conspiracy theories count as established knowledge within a country's mainstream, there is no general reason why adherents of mainstream religion would not adopt them. When conspiracy theories are used to bolster power, the "belief" aspect may be irrelevant, while any power that mainstream religion has to legitimate official policies will be all the more important. And in cases where mainstream religion is engaged in power struggles or adherents feel their position threatened, such as during American anti-Catholic nativist episodes, conspiracy beliefs about "the other" may be easily awakened and used in identity politics.[28]

None of this is specific to religion. "It" is not a separate dimension of human existence, but a set of (sub)scenes where human cognition and sociality takes place. Nevertheless, the points of confluence we have presented in this chapter have, we hope, gone some way to show how Religious Studies can complement and enrich other approaches to conspiracism. But approaching from a Religious Studies perspective also reveals some issues with how we deal with the people who subscribe to such ideas—which is, after all, the subject of this volume. From our brief survey—and indeed, many other chapters in this volume—we see that there is a great deal of similarity between conspiracist and religious belief in terms of narrative structure, cognitive and psychological mechanisms, group dynamics, and even social demographics. Yet how the topics are treated in the media, by governments, and by academia, is very different in the two cases. We see few papers critiquing the cognitive errors that give rise to belief in Jesus' divinity, and fewer white papers written on how to stop Christianity spreading. On the other hand, we rarely see scholars of conspiracy theories openly advocating for the importance of such narratives in the public sphere. Conspiracy theories are treated along the lines of "cults" and "extremism"—that is, as social problems.

They may be so, although mostly in conjunction with other issues and rarely on their own. Seeing them in conjunction with "religion" may help. The comparison with religion makes it clear that conspiracy theories—like religion—may be irrational; but we should consider irrationality as more or less, not always dangerous, and not as a feature of conspiracy theorists nor religious people but of human beings. Academic work that is analytic and even-handed is possible and contributes to a social policy that is ultimately safer for all concerned.

Notes

1. Popper, Karl. 1966. *The Open Society and Its Enemies, Vol 2*. London: Routledge and Keagan Paul, 94.
2. For instance, Oliver, J. Eric, and Thomas J. Wood. 2014. "Paranoid Style(s) of Mass Opinion." *American Journal of Political Science* 58(4): 952–966.
3. Barrett, Justin, and Jonathan Lanman. 2008. "The Science of Religious Beliefs." *Religion* 38(2): 110.
4. Springer, Martin. 2008. *Contemporary Western Ethnography and the Definition of Religion*. London: Bloomsbury.
5. See for instance Cusack, Carole. 2012. *Invented Religions*. Farnham, UK: Ashgate.

6. Barron, David, Kevin Morgan, Tony Towell, Boris Altemeyer, and Viren Swami. 2014. "Associations between Schizotypy and Conspiratorial Ideation." *Personality and Individual Differences* 70: 158.

7. Campbell, Colin. 1972. "The Cult, the Cultic Milieu and Secularisation." In *A Sociological Yearbook of Religion in Britain*, ed. Michael Hill. London: SCM Press, 119–136.

8. Sutcliffe, Stephen. 2003. *Children of the New Age: A History of Spiritual Practices.* London: Routledge.

9. For a telling example, see Introvigne, Massimo. 2016. *Satanism: A Social History.* Leiden, Netherlands: Brill.

10. See Asprem, Egil, and Asbjørn Dyrendal. 2015. "Conspirituality Reconsidered: How New and How Surprising is the Confluence of Spirituality and Conspiracy Theory?" *Journal of Contemporary Religion* 30(3): 367–382.

11. See Asprem, Egil, and Dyrendal, Asbjørn. 2018. "Close Companions? Esotericism and Conspiracy Theories." In *Brill Handbook of Conspiracy Theory and Contemporary Religion*, eds. Asbjørn Dyrendal, David G. Robertson, and Egil Asprem. Leiden, Netherlands: Brill. Forthcoming.

12. See for instance Farias, Miguel, Gordon Claridge, and Mansur Lalljee. 2005. "Personality and Cognitive Predictors of New Age Practices and Beliefs." *Personality and Individual Differences* 39(5): 979–989.

13. Aird, Rosemary L., James G. Scott, John McGrath, Jake M. Najman, and Abdullah Al Mamun. 2010. "Is the New Age Phenomenon Connected to Delusion-like Experiences? Analysis of Survey Data from Australia." *Mental Health, Religion & Culture* 13(1): 37–53

14. Mason, Fran. 2002. "A Poor Person's Cognitive Mapping." In *Conspiracy Nation*, ed. Peter Knight. New York: New York University Press, 49–50.

15. Barkun, Michael. 2013. "Messages from Beyond: Prophecy in the Contemporary World." In *Prophecy in the New Millennium: When Prophecies Persist*, eds. Sarah Harvey and Suzanne Newcombe. Farnham, UK: Ashgate, 17.

16. Robertson, David G. 2016. *Conspiracy Theories, UFOs and the New Age: Millennial Conspiracism.* London: Bloomsbury, 145.

17. Robertson, David G. 2013. "(Always) Living in the End Times: The 'Rolling Prophecy' of the Conspiracy Milieu." In *Prophecy in the New Millennium: When Prophecies Persist*, eds. Sarah Harvey and Suzanne Newcombe. Farnham, UK: Ashgate, 207–219.

18. Thompson, Damien. 2005. *Waiting for the Antichrist: Charisma and Apocalypse in a Pentecostal Church.* London: Oxford University Press, 26–31

19. Festinger, Leon, Henry W. Riecken, and Stanley Schachter. 1956. *When Prophecy Fails: A Social and Psychological Study of a Modern Group That Predicted the Destruction of the Modern World.* Minneapolis: <<<REFO:BK>>>University of Minnesota Press.

20. Jenkins, Timothy. 2016. *Of Flying Saucers and Social Scientists: A Re-Reading of When Prophecy Fails and of Cognitive Dissonance.* New York: Palgrave Pivot.

21. Zeller, Benjamin. 2014. *Heaven's Gate: America's UFO Religion.* New York: New York University Press, 205–208.

22. Repp, Martin. 2005. "Aum Shinrikyo and the Aum Incident." In *Controversial New Religions*, eds. James R. Lewis and Jesper Aagaard Petersen. Oxford: Oxford University Press, 153–194; Robertson, David G. 2017. "Hermeneutics of Suspicion: Scientology and Conspiracism." In *Handbook of Scientology*, eds. James R. Lewis and Kjersti Hellesøy. Leiden, Netherlands: Brill, 300–318; Robertson, *Conspiracy Theories, UFOs and the New Age.*

23. Popper, *The Open Society.*

24. Jameson, Frederik. 1990. "Cognitive Mapping." In *Marxism and the Interpretation of Culture*, eds. Cary Nelson and Lawrence Grossberg. Champaign, IL: University of Illinois Press, 356.

25. Bromley, David G. 1997. "Constructing Apocalypticism." In *Millenniums, Messiahs, and Mayhem: Contemporary Apocalyptic Movements*, eds. Thomas Robbins and Susan J. Palmer. New York: Routledge, 31–46.

26. Uscinski, Joseph E., and Joseph M. Parent. 2014. *American Conspiracy Theories*. Oxford: Oxford University Press, 130–153.

27. Robertson, David G. 2014. "Transformation: Whitley Strieber's Paranormal Gnosis." *Nova Religio* 18(1): 58–78.

28. See for instance Butter, Michael. 2014. *Plots, Designs, and Schemes: American Conspiracy Theories from the Puritans to the Present*. Berlin: De Gruyter, 113–166.

29

The Credulity of Conspiracy Theorists

Conspiratorial, Scientific, and Religious Explanation Compared

BRIAN L. KEELEY

I offer that there are two mutually contradictory views concerning conspiracy thinking in our current culture, often reflecting the overall view one has of these theories and theorists. On the positive side, conspiracy theories are seen to reflect a healthy and natural skepticism, particularly directed toward the common wisdom or toward the narrative promulgated by the "movers and shakers" or the "powers that be" in a given society. In this view, conspiracy theorists play a crucial tonic role in society. They are the first to say that the emperor wears no clothes. They are the contrarians whose motto is "that many people can't be right"—who sometimes, at least, turn out to be right. At the very least, by refusing to accept what they're told hook, line, and sinker, they apply an important epistemic pressure without which we would slip first into complacency and then into error.

On the negative side, conspiracy theorists are seen to be the opposite of skeptical and steadfast. As the old saw goes, it's a virtue to be open-minded, but not so open-minded that your brains fall out. This negative view sees the conspiracy theorist as an ideologue or zealot, bordering on the paranoid, never trusting anything they hear. Or, rather, only trusting those claims that fit their preexisting, cynical world-view in which dark and mysterious forces have it in for the "little guy."

The more positive stance toward conspiracy theorists sees them as having many of the virtues of scientists, of taking an objective and unconventional approach to understanding the world. In this view, conspiracy theorists should be seen as proposing (often counterintuitive) hypotheses to explain the events of the social world and following the evidence where it leads, regardless of the outcome.

The more negative stance accuses conspiracy theorists of being insufficiently scientific in their method. Instead of lacking an agenda—as an unbiased and objective scientist would—conspiracy theorists come to their explanation with a conclusion already in mind.

I want to explore here the relationship between what I will call "conspiratorial explanation" and what philosophers of science traditionally study under the rubric of scientific explanation. By considering the kinds of explanations conspiracy theorists offer and comparing them to the kinds of explanations offered in the name of science, I hope to explore the strengths and weaknesses of both. One theme I hope to develop is that much of what attracts people to conspiracy theories is that they— at least superficially—sport many of the virtues of good scientific explanation. However, they often undermine these virtues in interesting ways. By exploring this class of social explanations, we can learn about what are the limits and hazards of scientific explanations.

In exploring the relationship between scientific and conspiratorial explanation, I will often find it useful to invoke a *third* class of explanation: supernatural or religious explanation. There are those in our Western world, but also elsewhere and in Western history, who seek to explain events in the world not by exclusive reference to natural phenomena, nor by the activity of secular conspiratorial forces, but by the activity of supernatural agency. So, consider the outbreak of a deadly disease in some population of people. Scientists might explain it by positing a role for poor hygiene of the water supply combined with a chance introduction of a pathogen. The conspiracy theorists might point to the introduction of the pathogen by a powerful, clandestine organization after undermining the water infrastructure (and stockpiling a supply of clean water). The religious explanation might seek to explain the outbreak as God's punishment on what they propose was a transgressive population of the insufficiently devout. All three of these explanations would need to be fleshed out to be more than just caricature, but right now I just want to begin by giving the flavor of each.[1]

Some Initial Stage Setting

Before continuing, it will help to clarify a few points and terminology. First, what is a conspiracy theory? In what follows, I take a conspiracy theory to be a proposed explanation of some historical event (or events) in terms of the significant causal agency of a relatively small group of persons—the conspirators—acting in secret. I take it for granted that conspiracy theories deserve the appellation "theory," because they proffer explanations of the events in question. A given conspiracy theory proposes *reasons* why the event occurred. Further, a conspiracy theory need not propose that the conspirators are all-powerful, only that they have played some pivotal role in bringing about the event.[2] The conspirators can be seen as merely setting events in motion. Indeed, it is often because the conspirators are not omnipotent that they must act in secret, for if they acted in public, others would move to obstruct them. Third, the group of conspirators must be small, although the upper bounds are necessarily vague. Technically speaking, a conspiracy of one is no conspiracy at all, but rather the actions of a lone agent.

Next, there is a useful bit of terminology discussed by philosopher Matthew Dentith,[3] which he credits to historian Daniel Pipes.[4] Pipes observes that "Conspiracy theories have a way of growing on a person, to the point that they become a way of seeing life itself. This is *conspiracism*, the *paranoid style*, or the *hidden-hand mentality.*"[5] From this, Dentith takes the terms *conspiracism* and *conspiracist*, which is meant to capture the contemporary pejorative sense of conspiracy theory, as when one derides a proffered explanation by responding, "Oh, that's just a conspiracy theory!" As Dentith puts it, "A conspiracist is someone who believes in the existence of conspiracies without good reason. The terms 'conspiracism' and 'conspiracist', then, are pejorative labels which reflect a pathological belief in conspiracies *sans* evidence."[6] When trying to diagnose what might be going wrong in some cases of conspiracy theorizing, it is important not to conflate conspiracy theory *simpliciter*, on one hand, with "wacky" or "unwarranted" or "wrong-headed" (or whatever pejorative appeals to you) conspiracy theories, because to do so risks begging the question at hand. Concluding that conspiracy theories are unwarranted is rendered tautological if "conspiracy theory" is glossed as those conspiracy theories that are clearly wrong.

Next, when evaluating the warrant of conspiracy theories, there are two different ways in which a given conspiratorial explanation can be found epistemically wanting, as represented by the terms *generalism* and *particularism*.[7] According to the *generalist*, the credibility of any given conspiracy theory can be assessed without considering particular conspiracy theories; instead, conspiracy theories should be judged as a class.[8] In this view, conspiratorial thinking qua conspiracy thinking is itself irrational. The *particularist*, however, denies that the rationality of conspiracy theories can be assessed without first considering particular conspiracy theories. That is to say, the particularist claims that no matter our views about conspiracy theories generally, we cannot dismiss particular conspiracy theories; rather, we must evaluate them on their individual merits.[9] In general, I will take a particularist approach to conspiracy theories. As with scientific theories, they vary in their plausibility.

Further, the charge of conspiracism is a knock against a person, a charge that a given individual suffers the opposite of epistemic virtue—that they are guilty of a kind of *epistemic viciousness*.[10] While this may well be an interesting line of argument to pursue, I choose to focus instead on the merit of the *theories* proposed rather than on judging the rationality of those who propose the theories. I do this for a number of reasons, but primarily for two. First, it is not clear to me that the rubric "conspiracy theorist" defines a coherent class of persons (whether epistemically virtuous or vicious). If the particularist approach to conspiracy theories is correct, then we are warranted in believing in *some* conspiracy theories (Watergate, Iran–Contra, the plot to assassinate Caesar), even while lacking warrant in others. Indeed, as Charles Pigden likes to stress, given that it is generally agreed that the history books are full of conspiracies that all rational and historically informed individuals ought to believe, we are all "conspiracy theorists," at least with respect to some theories.[11]

Another reason for paying more attention to the theories rather than the theorists is the general principle that the evaluation of the two are largely independent. As Henry Kissinger is purported to have said, "Even paranoids have real enemies." I am more interested in figuring out *what* to believe than *who* to believe.

Anomalies as a Starting Point

With the stage set, I now turn to some points of comparison between different forms of explanation. The first point of comparison between the three kinds of explanation is one that they share, and that is where the various kinds of explanation often start: anomalies. An anomaly is something that deviates from what is standard, normal, or expected. "Standard, normal, or expected" *by what*? In general, by some currently accepted explanation. The previous explanation explains what has happened and why; any events that do not fit that explanation will thus stand out as anomalous. This in turn might be taken to be the irritating grain of sand over which a new, beautiful pearl (a new explanation) may be created. As I have discussed elsewhere,[12] a common starting point for conspiracy theories is two different kinds of errant data left unexplained by the "official story" of what was supposed to have happened in an event. The first is *contradictory data*: Data that is seen to be contradicted by the official story, for example, 9/11 conspiracy theories that begin by observing that the melting point of structural steel is significantly higher than the burning temperature of aviation turbine fuel (and, hence, that the planes alone could not have been responsible for the collapse of the World Trade Center towers). The second is *unaccounted-for* data: data that is just left unexplained by the official story. For example, after the 1995 Oklahoma City bombing of the Murrah Federal Building, images of two suspects were created and distributed by law enforcement agencies. The drawing of John Doe #1 turned out to be a rather good likeness of Timothy McVeigh, a man eventually found guilty and executed for his role in the bombing. The person depicted in John Doe #2 was never officially identified or explained by the prosecutors. Mismatches such as these between the official account of an event and other data surrounding the event are often the starting point of conspiracy theories challenging the official account.

However, this is far from a feature that distinguishes conspiracy explanations from scientific and religious ones. The history of science is rife with examples of new explanations starting from a robust observation that fails to fit the predictions of preceding, accepted explanations, be it the anomalous orbital dynamics of the planet Mercury (relative to Newtonian mechanics), the anomalous weight gain of heated metals (relative to phlogistonic chemistry) or Dr. Semmelweis's observation of differential mortality rates due to childbed fever in different maternity wards (relative to pre–germ theory explanations of disease).[13] Similarly, the entry point to supernatural explanation is often an anomalous observation or fact that points to the existence and intervention of supernatural agency. Reports of miracles (as discussed by David Hume, see footnote #8) or the accurate pronouncements of prophets are presented as unexpected (by non-supernatural explanations) events in need of a more transcendent explanation. Another example will be discussed below while discussing the motivation for Intelligent Design explanations of biological diversity. These accounts begin with the proposal that observed organisms demonstrate a greater degree of functional organization than evolution by natural selection would lead us to believe. In all of these famous cases and many others, the spur to scientific revolution or supernatural explanation is something anomalous relative to our previous best understanding. Therefore, on this point, conspiracy theory is on par with other forms of explanation.

Naturalism and Supernaturalism

One feature of scientific explanations is that they are naturalistic. Naturalism with respect to a given domain, in general, is the belief that the tools and concepts of natural science are necessary to come to an understanding of the phenomena within that domain. Naturalism concerning the explanation of events, then, is the belief that these events are amenable to natural scientific explanation, whereas an anti-naturalist concerning such events believes that there is good reason to doubt that natural science is going to help us to come to an understanding of at least some crucially important aspects of such events.[14] For example, a naturalist explanation would be one amenable to experimentation or observation, at least in principle. Further, the forces proposed in a naturalist explanation must fall within the set of forces recognized by natural science—no magic allowed.

In his 1993 book *Philosophical Naturalism*, David Papineau puts the issue this way:

> Philosophical problems are characterized by a special kind of difficulty, a difficulty which means that they cannot be solved, as scientific problems normally are, simply by the uncovering of further empirical evidence. Rather they require some conceptual unraveling, a careful unpicking of implicit ideas, often culminating in the rejection of assumptions we didn't realize we had. But still, despite these differences, there is clearly a sense in which philosophical thinking of this kind is part and parcel of the construction of scientific theories. Even if there is no direct involvement with empirical evidence, the task of the philosopher is to bring coherence and order to the total set of assumptions we use to explain the empirical world.

The question at issue is whether *all* philosophical theorizing is of this kind. Naturalists will say that it is. Those with a more traditional attitude to philosophy will disagree.[15]

What Papineau observes for philosophy as a whole also applies to explanations more generally. When trying to explain the events of the world, one can be a naturalist and take the position that those events ought to be explained using the tools and concepts of science. One can also reject naturalism in this context and take the position that science and its concepts will not be sufficient to explain the events of the world.

On the issue of naturalism, scientific and religious explanations are most pointedly at odds. For those religious views that propose the active engagement of God (or other supernatural forces) in the world, naturalism is a nonstarter.[16] For example, when explaining the origin of biological diversity, we find a conflict between naturalist explanations (invoking evolution by natural selection) and non-naturalist ones positing the intervention of a supernatural, intelligent designer.[17]

The issue of naturalism presents the conspiracy theorist with a choice concerning whether the conspiratorial explanations will be naturalist. A conspiracy theory positing humans doing human things (albeit in secret and with a high degree of coordination) cleaves to a naturalist approach. However, naturalism places a constraint on conspiratorial explanation: the proposed conspirators cannot grow unnaturally powerful. They cannot have what are effectively supernatural abilities to operate undetected or to otherwise carry out their conspiracy. Conspiratorial explanations that propose that government conspirators have access to technologies well beyond what current science seems to be capable of—I'm thinking of hologram projectors capable of making hundreds of people think they saw something happen, or long-distance mind-control devices capable of achieving similar ends—run the risk of veering away from naturalism in their explanations.

Along similar lines, a conspiracy theory that involves extraterrestrials with powers far beyond the comprehension of contemporary science starts to run into problems on this count. Naturalism, as it is normally understood, is relativized to current natural science. If one posits scientifically and technologically advanced extraterrestrials, then verifying naturalism becomes difficult, to say the least. For example, science fiction legend Arthur C. Clarke proposes that, "Any sufficiently advanced technology is indistinguishable from magic."[18] If Clarke is right, then for all intents and purposes, positing advanced extraterrestrials is not epistemically distinguishable from positing supernatural agents (and, hence, violates naturalism).

But this discussion reveals an ambiguity in the idea of naturalism that is often obscured in debates between theists and natural scientists concerning naturalism. Let's return to debates over the origin of biological diversity of life on earth. The naturalists propose that such diversity can be fully explained by reference to the natural forces of selection, mutation, and so on, all processes well within the grasp of current science. Against this view, proponents of Intelligent Design (ID) propose that such naturalistic explanation is insufficient; the observed facts of biological life on earth require invoking an extremely powerful (and intelligent) designer. Is this designer necessarily supernatural? Generally, ID theorists say no, as when philosopher William Dembski (an ID proponent) argues that the search for signs of design are central to SETI (Search for Extraterrestrial Intelligence).[19] (SETI is thoroughly naturalistic, even if some worry that it is a fool's errand; SETI is looking for other natural agents in the universe. . . it's not looking for God.) But of course, if they want ID taught in U.S. public schools, given recent court rulings, Intelligent Design proponents would need to say this sort of thing, even if they don't believe that in their heart of hearts.

However, if Clarke is right, then it becomes difficult to reject the hypothesis that life on earth was influenced by an advanced alien race (far more advanced scientifically and technologically than we currently are) on the grounds that such a posit is non-naturalist. After all, is the natural science invoked by naturalism *current* natural science or natural science in principle, including future natural science that may propose all sorts of forces and concepts that might be anathema now?

Finally, returning to the distinction between particularism and generalism, one can use the above discussion of conspiracy theory and its relationship to naturalism to carve out a subset of conspiracy theories about which one might draw a conclusion both generalist and negative. If one is motivated by a desire that good explanation be naturalist, then one can remain a particularist about naturalist conspiracy theories while rejecting as unwarranted those conspiracy theories that invoke agents with supernatural powers of control or remaining secret. That is, one might draw a *general* conclusion about supernatural conspiracy theories by arguing that they should all be treated the same as supernatural religious explanation.

Falsification

Another feature of scientific explanation that can be applied to conspiratorial explanation is one most famously associated with philosopher of science, Karl Popper.[20] According to Popper, one hallmark of genuine science that sets it apart from other human endeavors is that scientific forms of explanation make risky predictions. Further, if those predictions turn out to be false, then this would falsify the theory that generated it and indicate that it needs to be reworked or changed in some way. So, to the extent that psychiatric analysis (Freudian, Jungian, Adlerian, etc.) does not make concrete predictions that would lead to its rejection, it is not science. Einstein's theory of general relativity predicts that the relative positions of the so-called "fixed stars" would change under the conditions of an eclipse, a risky prediction famously confirmed in 1922.

Conspiracy theories potentially run afoul of the condition that legitimate scientific theorizing be falsifiable. If, for a given conspiracy theory, all potentially falsifying evidence can be construed as supporting, or at worst as neutral evidence, then that conspiracy theory is by hypothesis unfalsifiable. In favor of conspiracy theorists, it should be noted that this unfalsifiability requirement is not as ad hoc as it might initially seem, due to the active nature of the investigated. It is not ad hoc to suppose that false and misleading data will be thrown your way when one supposes that there is somebody out there actively throwing that data at you. As evidenced by any number of twentieth-century U.S. government-sponsored activities (take your pick), we have reason to believe that there exist forces with both motive and capacity to carry out effective disinformation campaigns.

My claim here is that unfalsifiability is only a reasonable criterion in cases where we do not have reason to believe that there are powerful agents seeking to steer our investigation away from the truth of the matter. Falsifiability is a perfectly fine criterion in the case of natural science when the target of investigation is neutral with respect to our queries, but it seems much less appropriate in the case of the phenomena covered by conspiracy theories. President Richard Nixon and Colonel Oliver North both actively sought to divert investigations into their respective activities, and both could call upon significant resources to maintain their conspiracies. They saw to it that investigators were thwarted in many of their early attempts to uncover what they accurately suspected was occurring. Strictly hewing to the dogma of falsifiability in these cases would have led to a rejection of conspiracy theories at too early a point in the investigations, and may have left the conspiracies undiscovered.

All of this underlines the point that, by their nature, conspiratorial explanations generally engage *social* behavior of purposive agents, whereas the natural sciences typically restricts its studies to non-agents (or at least agents lacking an agenda to interfere with their investigations). The fact of the matter is that the scientific study of human agents by humans is fraught and methodologically contested, whether it be social psychology, economic behavior, or sexuality. When your research subjects can read your results and explanations of their behavior—and then respond with changed behavior—science gets a lot more difficult, and the easy proclamations of natural science (including falsification) go by the wayside. So, on this point, conspiratorial explanation is in good company.

While falsification shouldn't be used uncritically as a critique of conspiratorial explanation, it takes things too far to propose that the presence of countervailing evidence is itself evidence in favor of the conspiracy. To the extent that conspiracy theories are the only theories for which evidence *against* them is taken to be evidence *for* them (because that just goes to show how much "they" want us to reject the conspiracy theory), this is not a good epistemic stand to take.

Conclusion

So where does the above discussion of the comparison of conspiracy theorizing with other forms of explanation leave us? Unfortunately, there isn't space here to *fully* analyze the credibility of conspiratorial explanatory strategies. However, I believe I have shown that there is not an easy path to either of the caricatures of conspiracy theorists broached in the opening of this chapter. Conspiracy theory explanations share features with both scientific and religious forms of explanation. By the same token, there are points of difference between these kinds of explanation as well. Further, these similarities and differences can be viewed as positive or negative for one's evaluation of conspiracy theories, depending on what one thinks of scientific or religious explanation. And a general critical examination of the virtues and vices of scientific and religious explanatory strategies is another thing that would require far more than a short book chapter to examine. Instead, what I have endeavored to do here is explore some of the points of contact between these various kinds of explanation. Further, I believe I have shown that conspiracy theories are not entirely dissimilar to these other modes of explanation, about which philosophy of science, religious studies, and allied academic disciplines have spilled much ink on understanding, both with a mind to defend them and to disparage them, depending on the view of the scholar in question.

Notes

1. For more on the relationship between conspiracy theories and religious explanation, see Keeley, Brian L. N.d. "Is a Belief in Providence the Same as a Belief in Conspiracy?" In *Brill Handbook of Conspiracy Theory and Contemporary Religion*, eds. Egil Asprem, Asbjørn Dyrendal, and David G. Robertson. Leiden, Netherlands: Brill. Forthcoming; Keeley, Brian L. 2007. "God as the Ultimate Conspiracy Theory." *Episteme: A Journal of Social Epistemology* 4(2): 135–149.
2. Although, as I'll discuss below, sometimes given conspiracy theorists might overplay the power of their proposed conspirators and this may lead them into epistemic difficulties.
3. Dentith, Matthew R. X. 2014. *The Philosophy of Conspiracy Theories*. London: Palgrave Macmillan.
4. Pipes, Daniel. 1997. *Conspiracy: How the Paranoid Style Flourishes and Where It Comes From*. New York: Free Press.
5. Ibid., 22. As Dentith (2014) discusses, the term "paranoid style" comes from Richard Hofstadter (1964. "The Paranoid Style in American Politics." *Harper's Magazine*, 77–86), but its current formulation in the social science literature on conspiracy theories owes more to Pipes' reformulation of the concept than it does to Hofstadter's initial discussion.
6. Dentith, *The Philosophy of Conspiracy Theories*, 33. Emphasis in the original text.
7. The credit for posing this useful distinction goes to Buenting, Joel and Jason Taylor. 2010. "Conspiracy Theories and Fortuitous Data." *Philosophy of the Social Sciences* 40(4): 567–578.
8. In this way, generalism about conspiracy theories mimics David Hume's analysis of the credibility of miracles in Book X of *An enquiry concerning human understanding*, according to which the very features that makes some event a miracle also renders it literally incredible (Hume,

David. [1748] 2011. *An Enquiry Concerning Human Understanding*. Hollywood, FL: Simon and Brown.) See also Keeley, Brian L. 1999. "Of Conspiracy Theories." *Journal of Philosophy* 96(3): 109–126.

9. For more on this distinction see Dentith, Matthew R. X., and Brian L. Keeley. N.d. "The Applied Epistemology of Conspiracy Theories: An Overview." In *Routledge Handbook on Applied Epistemology*, eds. David Coady and James Chase. London: Routledge. Forthcoming.

10. Cassam, Quassim. 2016. "Vice Epistemology." *The Monist* 99(2): 159–80; Pigden, Charles R. 2016. "Are Conspiracy Theorists Epistemically Vicious?" In *Blackwell Companion to Applied Philosophy*, eds. Kasper Lipert-Rasmussen, Kimberley Brownlee, and David Coady. Chichester, U.K.: Wiley Blackwell, 120–132.

11. Charles Pigden explores the notion that all historically-literate people ought to be conspiracy theorists (2016. "Complots of Mischief." In *Conspiracy Theories: The Philosophical Debate*, ed. David Coady. Burlington, VT: Ashgate Publishing Company, 139–66). Coady develops the idea in useful ways as well (Coady, David. 2007. "Are Conspiracy Theorists Irrational?" *Episteme* 4(2): 193–204).

12. Keeley, "Of Conspiracy Theories."

13. Although this last story might be more mythic than is appreciated. See Tulodziecki, Dana. 2013. "Shattering the Myth of Semmelweis." *Philosophy of Science* 80(5): 1065–1075.

14. As noted, naturalism is a position that can be taken with respect to many domains. For example, one might advocate naturalism (or non-naturalism) concerning ethics depending on whether you think science (and science alone) ought to be our guide to right and wrong. Or one might be a naturalist (or non-naturalist) concerning the nature of the mind. One's stands on these views need not be connected; one might be a naturalist about ethics, but a non-naturalist about the mind.

15. Papineau, David. 1993. *Philosophical Naturalism*. Oxford: Blackwell Publishers: 3. Emphasis in the original.

16. For religious views that do not propose an ongoing active role for supernatural agency— Deism comes to mind—the situation will be different, of course.

17. Cf. Johnson, Phillip. 2001. "Evolution as Dogma: The Establishment of Naturalism." In *Intelligent Design and its Critics: Philosophical, Theological and Scientific Perspectives*, ed. Robert T. Pennock. Cambridge: The MIT Press, 59–76; Pennock, Robert T. 2001. Naturalism, Evidence, and Creationism: The Case of Phillip Johnson." In *Intelligent Design and its Critics: Philosophical, Theological and Scientific Perspectives*, ed. Robert T. Pennock. Cambridge: The MIT Press, 77–98.

18. This is known as "Clarke's Third Law." See. Clarke, Arthur C. 1973. *Profiles of the Future*. New York: Harper and Row.

19. For example, see Dembski, William A. 2004. "The Logical Underpinnings of Intelligent Design." In *Debating Design: From Darwin to DNA*, ed. William A. Dembski and Michael Ruse. Cambridge: Cambridge University Press, 311–330.

20. Popper, Karl R. 1959. *The Logic of Scientific Discovery*. New York: Harper & Row.

30

Empowerment as a Tool to Reduce Belief in Conspiracy Theories

JAN-WILLEM VAN PROOIJEN

Are conspiracy theories harmless entertainment? Research suggests that quite often they are not. What people believe drives their behavior; and if people believe conspiracy theories for which there is little evidence, the behavior that follows may be irrational and harmful. For instance, people who believe in conspiracy theories about the pharmaceutical industry are less likely to have children vaccinated.[1] People who believe that climate change is a hoax are less willing to reduce their carbon footprints.[2] Conspiracy theories directly accuse other groups in society of unethical and often criminal behavior, and may therefore be a breeding ground for aggression and conflict between groups.[3] Finally, conspiracy theories drive political choices in favor of populist political candidates who portray mainstream politicians as part of the "corrupt elites."[4]

It therefore makes sense for policymakers to try and reduce the appeal of conspiracy theories among the public. But in practice, this might be easier said than done. Not only do large numbers of regular citizens believe conspiracy theories, but also it is relatively difficult to falsify conspiracy theories. Through motivated reasoning, believers selectively embrace evidence or expert testimonies that support their theory (e.g., engineers and architects stating that, on 9/11 the impact of the airplanes could not cause the Twin Towers to collapse in this manner). In doing so they ignore, trivialize, or consider part of the conspiracy, evidence or expert testimonies to the contrary (e.g., all the engineers and architects who disagree with the "9/11 for truth" movement and see no evidence for controlled demolition). Indeed, reducing the appeal of conspiracy theories among deeply convicted believers, who are active on conspiracy theorist websites, may be a difficult if not impossible task.

This does not mean that providing rational arguments is useless. Besides such deeply convicted believers, a large group of citizens is more moderate and hence susceptible to both conspiratorial and nonconspiratorial explanations of societal events. Interventions to promote nonconspiratorial reasoning might well be effective, at least to some extent, among this large group of citizens. For instance, research suggests that providing rational arguments can decrease conspiracy theories.[5] Moreover, stimulating analytic thinking makes people less conspiratorial in their beliefs.[6] One may wonder, however, whether such a reflective, analytic approach is the most effective method to combat conspiracy theories. Providing rational arguments does not address the root cause of conspiracy theories: the negative emotions that people experience when they feel powerless and out of control.

The idea that feelings of powerlessness are at the basis of conspiracy theories has been first raised in the famous essay on "The Paranoid Style in American Politics" by Richard Hofstadter, who proposed that citizens who feel powerless or voiceless are particularly susceptible to conspiracy theories.[7] According to Hofstadter, such conspiracy theories facilitate comprehension of complex but distressing events by simplifying them into explanations that place blame on the evil schemes of powerful conspiracies. Subsequent research indeed found that when people feel powerless, or experience a lack of control over their environment, they are more likely to believe conspiracy theories.[8] Such powerless feelings may be either structural or incidental. For instance, citizens may feel that they have structurally little control over political decision making, as often seen in allegations that authorities do not listen to their concerns. Also more incidentally, distressing events decrease people's feeling that they can control their own fate. It is therefore not surprising that distressing events—incidents such as a terrorist strike or a natural disaster, but also ongoing events such as an economic crisis or climate change—prompt citizens to look for conspiratorial explanations.

Feelings of powerlessness are associated with a set of negative emotions that predict conspiracy theories, including anxiety and uncertainty.[9] These negative emotions increase a desire among people to make sense of their social environment, and make them vigilant toward possible threats. When distrusted and powerful groups are salient—such as governmental institutions—this vigilance may manifest itself in conspiracy theories. Put differently, the negative emotions that are associated with feelings of powerlessness put people in a suspicious, information-seeking state of mind that facilitates conspiratorial explanations for distressing events. Research indeed suggests that feelings of uncertainty increase belief in conspiracy theories, but only if the conspiracy involves groups that perceivers consider immoral.[10] Likewise, these sense-making desires have been found to predict conspiracy theories mainly when conspiratorial explanations for distressing events are salient.[11]

If feelings of powerlessness increase belief in conspiracy theories, might the reverse also be true—that is, do feelings of empowerment *decrease* belief in conspiracy theories? Empowerment refers to the feeling that one is in control over one's own life and can influence relevant decisions that shape one's future. Just like feelings of powerlessness are related with negative emotions, including fear, anxiety, and uncertainty, feelings of empowerment are likely to decrease such negative emotions and instead foster hope, optimism, and confidence in the future. Such positive emotions may stimulate citizens to perceive their social environment in a less suspicious state of mind. In the following, I first present evidence that empowerment indeed reduces conspiracy theories. Then, I will introduce procedural justice as a practical tool for decision makers to empower citizens and therefore reduce conspiracy theories.

Empowerment and Conspiracy Theories

Various studies investigated the influence of being out of control on conspiracy theories using experimental methods. In these studies, research participants were randomly assigned to one of two conditions: Participants were asked to perform a writing exercise, and for half of the participants this exercise entailed describing an incident from their own life in which they felt completely in control. For the other half, the exercise entailed describing an incident from their own life in which they felt not at all in control. Through this procedure, participants briefly relive an experience in which they felt either in, or out of, control. After the writing exercise, participants responded to questions in which they indicate their belief in conspiracy theories. These studies found that people believe conspiracy theories more strongly after writing about an incident in which they felt out of control than after writing about an incident in which they felt in control.[12] These findings often are interpreted as evidence that feeling out of control—a core element of powerlessness—increases belief in conspiracy theories. But how solid is the proof for this assertion based on these experiments? After all, an alternative interpretation could be that reliving an experience where one had full control *reduces* conspiracy theories. The only way to find out who is changing their beliefs—the participants who relive a high versus a low control experience—is to include a third condition that is more neutral about feelings of control.

One study, conducted in Amsterdam, included such a neutral baseline condition.[13] Besides writing about an incident in which participants experienced high or low control, a third group of participants wrote about what they had for dinner the night before—a topic that does not explicitly focus on feelings of control. After that, participants were reminded of controversial policy that was reported widely in the Dutch news at the time the study was conducted. The policy pertained to the construction of a new underground metro line directly through the Amsterdam historical center. Although citizens had voted against this project in a referendum, authorities moved forward with it anyway. Moreover, the project was over budget and behind schedule. At the time the study was conducted, public hostility against this project had reached its peak as the underground constructions caused unforeseen damage to house foundations. Some of the old houses had to be evacuated as they literally were sinking into the ground. How did the control manipulation influence belief in conspiracy theories about this project—such as theories that Amsterdam city council members were bribed by the construction companies—among Amsterdam residents?

In keeping with previous research, participants who relived a high control experience believed such conspiracy theories less strongly than participants who relived a low control experience. Of interest, however, was how the participants in the neutral baseline condition responded to the questionnaire. These participants did not differ in their conspiracy beliefs from participants in the low control condition, and expressed stronger conspiracy beliefs than participants in the high control condition. These findings suggest that, apparently, reliving a high control experience may *reduce* people's belief in conspiracy theories. This is not to say that experiencing a low sense of control is unrelated to conspiracy theories. In all likelihood, the low control and neutral conditions did not differ, given that base-rate control levels were already quite low in this experiment. All participants were reminded of unpopular and controversial policy that had harmful consequences within their city. More importantly, the conclusion that follows from this experiment is that empowering people—by reliving an experience in which participants had full control—reduces belief in conspiracy theories.

In addition, findings on the relationship between education and conspiracy theories support a role for empowerment in reducing conspiracy theories. Specifically, one common finding is that citizens are more likely to believe conspiracy theories if they are low as opposed to high educated.[14] Why does high education reduce the likelihood that people believe conspiracy theories? Education is a long-term transformative experience for any individual, and hence one cannot explain the effects of education with a single variable. One frequently noted effect of education is increased cognitive complexity. Through education, people become better equipped to detect nuances across judgment domains; moreover, people learn not to simplify the complex problems that they encounter but instead reflect analytically on them. Besides cognitive complexity, high education also increases one's self-esteem. Furthermore, people with high education tend to get better jobs and higher incomes (i.e., high social class), implying a less marginalized position in society. Of particular importance for the present discussion, an additional effect of high education is that it is empowering. Through education, people learn how to independently solve problems, and they learn how to effectively influence their social environment. As such, highly educated people experience more control in their everyday lives.

One study examined why high education predicts decreased belief in conspiracy theories, and specifically investigated four possible mediators: cognitive complexity, self-esteem, social class, and feelings of powerlessness.[15] The relationships between these variables were investigated in two surveys within the Netherlands, one with a high sample size (over 4,000 participants) and the other being a representative sample of the Dutch population. The results revealed no evidence for a role of self-esteem. Furthermore, the role of social class was small and inconsistent between both surveys. The other two variables, however, accounted for the relationship between education and conspiracy beliefs very well. As compared with people with low education levels, people with high education levels have higher cognitive complexity—as reflected in better analytic thinking skills and a reduced tendency to see societal problems as simple—reducing the likelihood that they believe conspiracy theories. Furthermore—and of particular importance for the present purposes—people with high education levels also felt more in control of their own lives, reducing their belief in conspiracy theories. Put differently, education empowers people, and therefore education buffers against the temptation to embrace simplistic conspiracy theories when making sense of complex societal events.

While these empowering effects of education are promising and in line with the main argument presented here, they offer little practical added value for policymakers who wish to implement interventions to reduce conspiracy theories among the public. Education is a rather long-term strategy, and both the public and policymakers already widely recognize the value of providing good education to children. If anything, these insights add an additional reason why supporting good education is important. How can policymakers empower the public more imminently, thereby decreasing the appeal of conspiracy theories?

Procedural Justice

The field of procedural justice asserts that people evaluate authorities based on the quality of their decision-making procedures. More specifically, procedural justice refers to the extent to which people believe that authorities use fair or unfair decision-making procedures. Empirical research suggests that perceived procedural justice has impactful consequences for how citizens respond to the outcomes of decision-making processes. For instance, if people believe that procedures were fair, they subsequently are more likely to accept unfavorable decisions, experience more positive and less negative emotions, and trust decision makers more, as compared to when people believe that procedures were unfair.[16] In the following I propose that procedural justice is empowering and that authorities can reduce the appeal of conspiracy theories by implementing procedural justice principles in decision making.

In a classic paper, Leventhal noted that people evaluate six criteria to determine whether not they evaluate decision-making procedures as fair.[17] These criteria are as follows:

(1) *Consistency*—people consider procedures as fair if they are applied consistently across persons and over time.

(2) *Bias suppression*—decision-making authorities should be independent and have no personal self-interest at stake in the decision at hand

(3) *Accuracy*—authorities should collect as much information as possible before making a decision, and base themselves on a full assessment of the available information. Moreover, authorities should retain transparent records of the information considered, so that they can be monitored and held accountable.

(4) *Correctability*—there should be proper appeal procedures in place to correct for possible mistakes or oversights in the decision-making process.

(5) *Representativeness*—the decision-making process must take the concerns, values, and opinions into account of the parties that are affected by the outcome of the decision-making process; and

(6) *Ethicality*—decision-making procedures should be compatible with fundamental moral and ethical values (for instance, they should not contain deception or invasion of privacy).

These six criteria inspired various interventions to increase perceived procedural justice among the public. One of the most well known and frequently replicated effects in procedural justice research is "voice." People evaluate procedures that allow them an opportunity to voice their opinion as fairer than procedures that deny them such an opportunity.[18] Voice procedures most directly address the representativeness criterion, but may also help satisfy other criteria such as accuracy and ethicality. After being allowed voice, people evaluate the outcome of the decision-making process as fairer, feel more satisfied, experience their relationship with the decision maker more positively, and perform better at tasks.[19] Other procedural justice interventions that have comparable effects are to consistently use the same procedures, to take all the available information into account, and to provide proper justifications for decisions.[20]

One explanation of these effects is that people feel empowered when authorities make an effort to be a procedurally fair decision maker. An important distinction here is between decision versus process control.[21] Decision control refers to the extent to which people can directly influence the outcome of a decision-making process. Process control refers to the extent to which people feel actively involved, and taken seriously, in the decision-making procedures that lead to these outcomes. In practice, providing all citizens with decision control is not always feasible. For instance, different recipients of a decision-making process often have conflicting interests, and it is impossible for decision makers to satisfy the wishes of all parties involved. But still, authorities can increase process control by ensuring that Leventhal's six procedural justice criteria are met, for instance by actively displaying an interest in the opinions of all the involved parties, by being transparent, and by being consistent between persons.

These empowering effects are resonated in relational models of procedural justice.[22] The relational models assert that while people to some extent value procedural justice for instrumental reasons (e.g., being able to voice an opinion increases the chance for a desired outcome), they particularly value procedural justice for symbolic reasons. People typically see group authorities as representative of a larger community, and hence the way authorities treat people is diagnostic for their standing within this community. If authorities use fair procedures, people feel respected and empowered as full-fledged members of their community; but if authorities use unfair procedures, people feel disrespected and disempowered within their community. As such, procedural justice has important symbolic value to people by informing them of the extent to which they are worthy members of a valuable community.

One implication of these symbolic concerns is that people appreciate procedural justice even when faced with unfavorable decisions. In fact, a large body of research reveals that procedural justice shapes perceptions of outcome fairness particularly when outcomes are unfavorable. When outcomes are favorable, people consider the outcome fair regardless of the procedure; but people only find an unfavorable outcome fair when they believe the preceding procedure was fair.[23] Furthermore, people consider procedural justice more important than receiving favorable outcomes.[24] Finally, being allowed voice positively shapes perceptions of justice, even when it is clear that one's opinion did not influence the final decision.[25] People can hence experience decision-making procedures as empowering even when they receive an unfavorable decision, and this strongly influences people's appraisals of the decision-making process.

Given the link between empowerment and conspiracy theories, it is likely that when citizens believe that powerful authorities acted in a procedurally fair manner, they are less likely to believe conspiracy theories that implicate these authorities as part of a corrupt network. Indeed, the effects of procedural justice are closely associated with the psychological basis of conspiracy theories. For instance, feeling powerless suppresses any positive effects of voice procedures.[26] Moreover, procedural justice regulates negative emotions, particularly feelings of subjective uncertainty.[27] This insight has direct implications for conspiracy theories: The extent to which authorities act fairly or unfairly has been shown to influence conspiracy beliefs particularly when people feel uncertain.[28] Finally, conspiracy theories are strongly related with distrust, and it is well-known that perceived procedural justice is closely associated with how much people trust decision makers.[29]

One study directly tested the relationship between procedural justice and belief in conspiracy theories.[30] The study took place in an organizational setting, and hence investigated organizational conspiracy theories (i.e., employees' beliefs that managers conspire to reach malevolent goals). With a questionnaire, employees rated their supervisors on four different leadership styles. The first was *despotic* leadership: the extent to which a leader is punitive and unwilling to tolerate criticism. The second leadership style was laissez-faire leadership, which is characterized by a lack of leadership—laissez-faire leaders do not intervene unless absolutely necessary. The third leadership style was *charismatic* leadership: Charismatic leaders inspire employees to internalize the organization's goals as their own. The fourth and final leadership style was *participative* leadership. This latter style is relevant for the present purposes, as participative leaders try to actively involve employees in important decision-making processes by asking for their inputs and opinions. Put differently, participative leaders try to implement procedural justice principles as central part of their leadership strategy.

The results revealed that both despotic and laissez-faire leadership predicted increased belief in organizational conspiracy theories among employees. These leadership styles are both destructive—either actively (despotic) or passively (laissez-faire)—and are disempowering by causing feelings of job insecurity. These destructive styles are hence counterproductive if one's goal is to reduce conspiracy theories. Charismatic leadership, in turn, was unrelated to organizational conspiracy beliefs. While charismatic leadership exerts positive effects on a range of other variables—such as intrinsic motivation—people are equally likely to perceive charismatic versus uncharismatic leaders as part of a conspiracy. Participative leadership, however, was associated with decreased belief in organizational conspiracy theories. This is evidence indicating that leaders who make procedural justice a signature of their leadership style successfully manage to decrease conspiracy theories among followers.

While the study on participative leadership is the first to suggest that implementing procedural justice principles may be an effective strategy to reduce conspiracy beliefs, also other evidence points to a relationship between procedural justice and belief in conspiracy theories. For instance, it has been noted that conspiracy theorists often call for greater transparency.[31] Apparently, conspiracy theorists evaluate the transparency of decision-making processes to be unacceptably low, which suggests a link between belief in conspiracy theories and perceived procedural injustice. Relatedly, belief in conspiracy theories is positively related with support for democratic principles.[32] Conspiracy theorists hence express an increased need to voice their opinion in political decision making, suggesting a belief that politicians do not listen enough to them. This assumption is in line with Hofstadter's notion that conspiracy theorists often feel voiceless.[33] Taken together, this suggests that conspiracy theorists often perceive procedural injustice in public governance.

Overcoming Irrationality

Conspiracy theories are prevalent and impactful in our society. Most of the effects of conspiracy theories are harmful. Belief in such theories may lead to negative emotions, irrational health behaviors, decreased civic virtue, hostility, aggression, and radicalization. There is good reason for policymakers to develop interventions that reduce conspiracy theories among the public. In the present contribution, my aim was to highlight empowerment as tool to reduce conspiracy theories. This tool might be more effective than trying to rationally refute conspiracy theories. Many conspiracy theories are not rational to begin with, and moreover, rational reasoning is often not the root cause of conspiracy theories. Instead, negative emotions cause conspiracy theories, and empowering citizens may transform these negative emotions into a more constructive mindset that includes hope and optimism. In order to empower citizens, authorities may effectively implement procedural justice principles in their decision-making processes. Ensuring that all procedural justice criteria are met hence may contribute to a less paranoid society.

Notes

1. Jolley, Daniel, and Karen M. Douglas. 2014. "The Effects of Anti-Vaccine Conspiracy Theories on Vaccination Intentions." *PLoS ONE* 9(2). DOI: 10.1371/journal.pone.0089177.
2. Jolley, Daniel, and Karen M. Douglas. 2014. "The Social Consequences of Conspiracism: Exposure to Conspiracy Theories Decreases Intentions to Engage in Politics and to Reduce One's Carbon Footprint." *British Journal of Psychology* 105(1): 35–56; van der Linden, Sander. 2015. "The Conspiracy-Effect: Exposure to Conspiracy Theories (About Global Warming) Decreases Pro-Social Behavior and Science Acceptance." *Personality and Individual Differences* 87: 171–173.
3. Abalakina-Paap, Marina, Walter G. Stephan, Traci Craig, and W. Larry Gregory. 1999. "Beliefs in Conspiracies." *Political Psychology* 20(2): 637–647; Swami, Viren, Rebecca Coles, Stefan Stieger, Jakob Pietschnig, Adrian Furnham, Sherry Rehim, and Martin Voracek. 2011. "Conspiracist Ideation in Britain and Austria: Evidence of a Monological Belief System and Associations between Individual Psychological Differences and Real-World and Fictitious Conspiracy Theories." *British Journal of Psychology* 102(2): 443–463.
4. van Prooijen, Jan-Willem, André P.M. Krouwel, and Thomas V. Pollet. 2015. "Political Extremism Predicts Belief in Conspiracy Theories." *Social Psychological and Personality Science* 6(5): 570–578.
5. Orosz, Gábor, Péter Krekó, Benedek Paskuj, István Tóth-Király, Beáta Böthe, and Christine Roland-Lévy. 2016. "Changing Conspiracy Beliefs through Rationality and Ridiculing." *Frontiers in Psychology* 7:1525.
6. Ståhl, Tomas, and Jan-Willem van Prooijen. 2018. "Epistemic Rationality: Skepticism Toward Unfounded Beliefs Requires Sufficient Cognitive Ability and Motivation to be Rational." *Personality and Individual Differences* 122: 155–163; Swami, Viren, Martin Voracek, Stefan Stieger, Ulrich S. Tran, and Adrian Furnham, A. 2014. "Analytic Thinking Reduces Belief in Conspiracy Theories." *Cognition* 133(3): 572–585.
7. Hofstadter, Richard. 1964. "The Paranoid Style in American Politics." In *The Paranoid Style in American Politics and Other Essays*, ed. Richard Hofstadter. New York: Knopf, 3–40.
8. Whitson, Jennifer A., and Adam D. Galinsky. 2008. "Lacking Control Increases Illusory Pattern Perception." *Science* 322(5898): 115–117; Abalakina-Paap, Stephan, Craig, and Gregory, "Beliefs in Conspiracies."
9. Douglas, Karen M., Robbie M. Sutton, and Aleksandra Cichocka. 2017. "The Psychology of Conspiracy Theories." *Current Directions in Psychological Science* 26(2): 538–542; van Prooijen, Jan-Willem. 2016. "Sometimes Inclusion Breeds Suspicion: Self-Uncertainty and Belongingness Predict Belief in Conspiracy Theories." *European Journal of Social Psychology* 46(3): 267–279.

10. van Prooijen, Jan-Willem, and Nils B. Jostmann. 2013. "Belief in Conspiracy Theories: The Influence of Uncertainty and Perceived Morality." *European Journal of Social Psychology* 43(1): 109–115.

11. Marchlewska, Marta, Aleksandra Cichocka, A., and Malgorzata Kossowska, 2017. "Addicted to Answers: Need for Cognitive Closure and the Endorsement of Conspiracy Theories." *European Journal of Social Psychology.* DOI: 10.1002/ejsp.2308.

12. Whitson and Galinsky, "Lacking Control Increases Illusory Pattern Perception"; Sullivan, Daniel, Mark J. Landau, and Zachary K. Rothschild. 2010. "An Existential Function of Enemyship: Evidence that People Attribute Influence to Personal and Political Enemies to Compensate for Threats to Control." *Journal of Personality and Social Psychology* 98(3): 434–449.

13. van Prooijen, Jan-Willem, and Michele Acker. 2015. "The Influence of Control on Belief in Conspiracy Theories: Conceptual and Applied Extensions. *Applied Cognitive Psychology* 29(5): 753–761.

14. van Prooijen and Acker, "The Influence of Control on Belief in Conspiracy Theories"; Douglas, Karem M., Robbie M. Sutton, Mitchell J. Callan, Rael J. Dawtry, and Annelie J. Harvey. 2016. "Someone Is Pulling the Strings: Hypersensitive Agency Detection and Belief in Conspiracy Theories." *Thinking and Reasoning* 22(1): 57–77; van Prooijen, Krouwel, and Pollet, "Political Extremism Predicts Belief in Conspiracy Theories."

15. van Prooijen, Jan-Willem. 2017. "Why Education Predicts Decreased Belief in Conspiracy Theories." *Applied Cognitive Psychology* 31(1): 50–58.

16. Brockner, Joel, and Batia M. Wiesenfeld. 1996. "An Integrative Framework for Explaining Reactions to Decisions: Interactive Effects of Outcomes and Procedures." *Psychological Bulletin* 120(2): 189–208; Tyler, Tom R., and E. Allan Lind. 1992. "A Relational Model of Authority in Groups." In *Advances in Experimental Social Psychology vol. 25*, ed. Mark P. Zanna. San Diego: Academic Press, 115–292; van den Bos, Kees, and E. Allen Lind. 2002. "Uncertainty Management by Means of Fairness Judgments." In *Advances in Experimental Social Psychology vol. 34*, ed. Mark P. Zanna. San Diego, CA: Academic Press, 1–60; van Prooijen, Jan-Willem, Kees van den Bos, and Henk A.M. Wilke. 2004. "The Role of Standing in the Psychology of Procedural Justice: Towards Theoretical Integration." *European Review of Social Psychology* 15(1): 33–58.

17. Leventhal, G. S. 1980. "What Should Be Done with Equity Theory? New Approaches to the Study of Fairness in Social Relationships. In *Social Exchange: Advances on Theory and Research*, eds. Kenneth J. Gergen, Martin S. Greenberg, and Richard H. Willis. New York: Plenum, 27–54.

18. Folger, Robert. 1977. "Distributive and Procedural Justice: Combined Impact of 'Voice' and Improvement on Experienced Inequity." *Journal of Personality and Social Psychology* 35(2): 108–119.

19. Brockner and Batia, "An Integrative Framework for Explaining Reactions to Decisions"; Tyler and Lind, "A Relational Model of Authority in Groups"; van den Bos and Lind, "Uncertainty Management by Means of Fairness Judgments"; van Prooijen, van den Bos, and Wilke, "The Role of Standing in the Psychology of Procedural Justice."

20. van Prooijen, Jan-Willem, Tomas Ståhl, Daniel Eek, and Paul A. M. Van Lange. 2012. "Injustice for All or Just for Me? Social Value Orientation Predicts Responses to Own Versus Other's Procedures." *Personality and Social Psychology Bulletin* 38(10): 1247–1258; Van Prooijen, Jan-Willem, Kees van den Bos, E. Allan Lind, and Henk A. M. Wilke. 2006. "How do People React to Negative Procedures? On the Moderating Role of Authority's Biased Attitudes." *Journal of Experimental Social Psychology* 42(5): 632–645; van den Bos and Lind, "Uncertainty Management by Means of Fairness Judgments"; Folger, Roger, and Chris Martin. 1986. "Relative Deprivation and Referent Cognitions: Distributive and Procedural Justice Effects." *Journal of Experimental Social Psychology* 22(6): 531–546.

21. Houlden, Pauline, Stephen LaTour, Laurens Walker, and John Thibaut. 1978. "Preference for Modes of Dispute Resolution as a Function of Process and Decision Control." *Journal of Experimental Social Psychology* 14(1): 13–30.

22. Tyler and Lind, "A Relational Model of Authority in Groups."

23. Brockner and Wiesenfeld, "An Integrative Framework."

24. Tyler, Tom R. 1987. "Conditions Leading to Value Expressive Effects in Judgments of Procedural Justice: A Test of Four Models." *Journal of Personality and Social Psychology* 52(2): 333–344.

25. Lind, E. Allan, Ruth Kanfer, and P. Christopher Earley. 1990. "Voice, Control, and Procedural Justice: Instrumental and Noninstrumental Concerns in Fairness Judgments." *Journal of Personality and Social Psychology* 59(5): 952–959.

26. van Prooijen, Jan-Willem, Kees Van den Bos, and Henk A.M. Wilke. 2007. "Procedural Justice in Authority Relations: The Strength of Outcome Dependence Influences People's Reactions to Voice." *European Journal of Social Psychology* 37(6): 1286–1297.

27. van den Bos and Lind, "Uncertainty Management by Means of Fairness Judgments."

28. van Prooijen and Jostmann, "Belief in Conspiracy Theories."

29. van den Bos, Kees, Henk A. M. Wilke, and E. Allan Lind. 1998. "When Do We Need Procedural Fairness? The Role of Trust in Authority." *Journal of Personality and Social Psychology* 75(6): 1449–1458.

30. van Prooijen, Jan-Willem, and Reinout E. de Vries. 2016. "Organizational Conspiracy Beliefs: Implications for Leadership Styles and Employee Outcomes." *Journal of Business and Psychology* 31(4): 479–491.

31. Clarke, Steve. 2002. "Conspiracy Theories and Conspiracy Theorizing." *Philosophy of the Social Sciences* 32(2): 131–150.

32. Swami, Coles, Stieger, Pietschnig, Furnham, Rehim, and Voracek. "Conspiracist Ideation in Britain and Austria."

33. Hofstadter, "The Paranoid Style in American Politics."

31

Conspiracy Theories for Journalists

Covering Dubious Ideas in Real Time

JOSEPH E. USCINSKI

When it comes to conspiracy theories, there are many things that scholars purport to know that are not so. For example, scholars continually make claims about the amount of conspiracy theorizing relative to other time periods, but most such claims are nothing more than speculation. Journalists are no different on this score, except that their ideas reach far more people. That so many dubious claims about conspiracy theories are reported is particularly troubling given that much of the fixation on conspiracy theories stems from concerns about people believing dubious things. In trying to thwart conspiracy theories, journalists make a lot of dubious assumptions without evidence. There are many fallacies, unsupported claims, and blind assertions reported about conspiracy theories in mainstream news outlets.

An overarching goal of this volume is to help journalists understand what researchers do and do not know, so that their reporting on the topic can be improved. Here I provide basic guidelines for journalists writing about conspiracy theories. In doing so, I highlight several of the volume's main themes.

Avoid Tarring Parties or Ideologies with the Conspiracy Theory Brush

It is comforting for one to believe that their political competitors are particularly prone to conspiracy theorizing. It may be true in some instances, but the accusations tend to get far ahead of the evidence.[1]

In the United States, it has been a longstanding assumption that conservatives and Republicans are more taken to conspiracy theories than liberals and Democrats. Surveying the mass public doesn't find much evidence for this. There are studies showing that conservatives are more likely to believe conspiracy theories than liberals, but the differences are not very large and certainly not large enough to justify the rhetoric.[2] And, such studies are becoming outnumbered by studies showing that conspiracy theorizing is equal between the left and right.[3] Whatever the latest poll or study shows, it is unlikely to show major differences between conservatives and liberals, meaning that conspiracy theorizing is less about political affiliation or ideology and more about something else. When differences between the left and right arise, it may be because of situational rather than dispositional factors; for example, parties that lose tend to believe and share more conspiracy theories because of their precarious situation.[4]

People in minor or extremist parties are more likely to believe in conspiracy theories.[5] But, it may be that such people recognize that their political views are unpopular, and this leads them to concoct conspiracy theories to explain why their ideas fail to blossom. Their conspiracy beliefs may not be so much about their extreme political views but rather the fact that their ranks are outnumbered.

Avoid One-Sided Coverage of Conspiracy Theories

If scientists assume that conspiracy theories are a priori bad, then they will design studies that link them to negative outcomes, meanwhile ignoring whatever benefits they might offer. The literature review by Michael Wood and Karen Douglas in Chapter 16 shows that much of the scholarly work on conspiracy theories takes as an underlying assumption that conspiracy theories should be subdued if not eliminated. If journalists assume the same, then the information environment will be the result of cherry-picking. The valence associated with conspiracy theories was first addressed by Peter Knight and Michael Butter in Chapter 2: They show how the literature has struggled to overcome some of the negative assumptions about conspiracy theorists made by early researchers. This theme is addressed again by Martin Orr and Ginna Husting in Chapter 5, by Matthew Dentith in Chapter 6, and by Juha Räikkä and Lee Basham in Chapter 7, who show how the term can be weaponized and used to demean or exclude. Chapter 12 by Steven Smallpage suggests that we as a society still need to better understand how conspiracy theories differ from other parts of our politics, particularly because American society tends to find conspiracy theorists to be odious.

Both scholars and journalists should consider the positive aspects of conspiracy theories and consider that removing them from society (if such a thing could be done) may present unintended consequences. Also, journalists should tread gently on conspiracy theories and theorists. There is a common trope in recent news reporting: "look at the latest stupid conspiracy theory and the idiots who believe it." Such stories have become a mainstay in recent journalism, but they may do more harm than good by bringing to the fore ideas that have few followers and needlessly castigating people who are already on the fringe of society.

Have a Clear Definition

Journalists should have a clear definition in mind when writing about conspiracy theories and be upfront with it. Why does a particular idea count or not count as a conspiracy theory? Definitions should be applied evenly.

As Jesse Walker discussed in Chapter 2, if we dilute *conspiracy theory* to mean any idea we don't like, then the term will always have a negative connotation. If partisans define conspiracy theory as false ideas promulgated by opposing partisans, then they are likely to accept the conspiracy theories promulgated by their co-partisans but castigate opposing partisans for doing the same. How news sources and scholars define conspiracy theory becomes particularly important given how the term is valenced.

Separate Beliefs and Uses

Most of the studies performed by psychologists examine the correlates of conspiracy belief. Very few scholars examine the uses of conspiracy theories, especially by those who stand to profit financially or politically from them. It is easy to hoist the attributes found to drive conspiracy theorizing in laboratory studies onto professional conspiracy theorists such as Alex Jones, or politicians who use conspiracy theories, but much of this research may not apply.

The use of conspiracy theories, as opposed to belief in them, is touched upon by Alfred Moore in Chapter 7, Matthew Atkinson and Darin DeWitt in Chapter 8, and by Ted Goertzel in Chapter 15. Goertzel, for example, examines celebrities who seem to both believe conspiracy theories and use them to promote pet causes. This volume's section on conspiracy theories across the world focuses almost exclusively on the uses of conspiracy theories by high-ranking politicians: Scott Radnitz looks at conspiracy theories in weak states (Chapter 23), Ilya Yablokov in Russia (Chapter 24), Turkay Nefes in Turkey (Chapter 26), and Tanya Filer in Argentina (Chapter 27). Alfred Moore and Darin DeWitt and Matthew Atkinson, consider how the forces that drive individual belief interact with the incentives for elites to use conspiracy theories (Chapters 7, 8, and 21), but more work, particularly in the area of theory building, needs to be done. In short, journalists should be careful not to misapply what we know about mass beliefs to individuals, especially elite actors.

Avoid Claims of Mental Illness

Mainstream news often refers to conspiracy theorists with language implying mental illness.[6] It is obvious that some people who believe in conspiracy theories are ill. However, the overwhelming majority of people who believe conspiracy theories are not ill in any way. Even though studies link anomie, anxiety, schizotypy, and delusional ideation to conspiracy theorizing, these studies are addressing tendencies rather than clinical illnesses. Journalists should be careful not to imply illness where none exists; it contributes to unnecessary stigmatization.

Don't Blame the Internet

Journalists (and scholars for that matter) often assume that the Internet drives conspiracy theorizing. The evidence, however, is not so clear. Conspiracy theories existed and prospered long before the Internet (and long before other communication technologies, for that matter). For example, belief in Kennedy assassination conspiracy theories has declined in the United States since the rollout of the Internet.[7]

Social media is often credited as an incubator for conspiracy theories, but social media may not be as kind as is often assumed. On any given day there are numerous new conspiracy theories concocted and shared on social media. However, the vast majority of these attract few followers and die on the vine. If the Internet were as conducive to the transmission of conspiracy theories as is often claimed, and if people were as affected by social media in the ways often discussed in journalistic accounts, then nearly everybody would believe indiscriminately in millions of conspiracy theories. But this' thankfully, is not the case. People are fickle with their conspiracy beliefs; just because they are exposed to a conspiracy theory does not mean they will believe it.[8]

Chapter 21 by Darin Dewitt, Matthew Atkinson, and Drew Wegner addresses the prevailing frameworks for understanding the transmission of conspiracy theories. Journalists tend to assume that conspiracy theories travel akin to herd behavior—people just indiscriminately adopt conspiracy beliefs as they see other people adopt those beliefs—but there is little evidence that conspiracy theories travel this way. It is therefore important that journalists (and scholars, too) not make assumptions about how conspiracy theories traverse from person to person, or about how the Internet affects conspiracy theorizing, until scientists fully study and understand these processes.

Don't Hit the Panic Button

Journalists always think that the high point of conspiracy theorizing is now. If this were true, then conspiracy theories would perpetually be on the rise, and we would have by now gone off the conspiracy theory cliff. Conspiracy theories certainly seem more prominent, relevant, and impactful in 2017 than in some previous years. But there is no evidence yet that people are more prone to believing conspiracy theories than they were in previous periods.

Salon.com claimed that conspiracy theories made their "big comeback" in 2017, despite having published dozens of articles about prominent conspiracy theories in 2016.[9] *The Atlantic* claimed that 2015 was the "age of conspiracy."[10] In 2013, *New York Times* editor Andrew Rosenthal saw a poll on U.S. conspiratorial beliefs and summed it up in five words: "No Comment Necessary: Conspiracy Nation."[11] Two years prior, the *New York Daily News* claimed "America is becoming a conspiratocracy. The tendency for a small slice of the population to believe in devious plots has always been with us. But conspiracies have never spread this swiftly across the country. They have never lodged this deeply in the American psyche. And they have never found as receptive an audience."[12] In 2010, *The Times* columnist David Aaronovitch was confident the West was "currently going through a period of fashionable conspiracism."[13] The *Boston Globe* argued that the "golden age of conspiracy theory" was in 2004.[14] In 1994, the *Washington Post* claimed that Bill Clinton's first term "marked the dawn of a new age of conspiracy theory" when only two years earlier it had posited that we then lived "in an age of conspiracy theories."[15] In 1977, the *Los Angeles Times* concluded the United States had set a world record: "we have become as conspiracy prone in our judgments as the Pan-Slav nationalists in the 1880s Balkans."[16] The *New York Times* believed 1964 was the age of conspiracy theories because they had "grown weedlike in this country and abroad."[17]

The problem here is that journalists are sometimes prone to making claims that seem true, but are merely assertions based on subjective personal experiences. It is hypocritical for journalists to attack other's ideas as unfounded, and then assert unfounded ideas of their own.

Improving the Information Environment

Donald Trump has incessantly attacked the news media, even Fox News at times, for what he has perceived as unfair coverage. Trump has a point. There are many documented instances of the media getting stories wrong, and outside of conservative outlets, the visible errors seem to go in the same direction.[18] Trust in news media has been waning for some time now; this is not new to the Trump era. Much of this has to do with structural forces: the introduction of cable television, cable news channels, the Internet, and online news sources. Technology has allowed more choice, and people have responded by choosing the news their ideologies prefer (if they prefer to consume news at all). But, some of this has to do with the behavior of the traditional news media itself. Much how Jan-Willem van Prooijen argued in Chapter 30, that conspiracy theories should be fought with better government, I argue here that conspiracy theories should be fought with better journalism overall.

Newsrooms need to have ideological diversity. This is vitally important with left/right ideology, but applies to other ideologies as well. Better work comes from environments where the people don't all think alike. But also, it is difficult for a person to trust a news source where the journalists all share an opposing ideology, all donate to the opposing party, and all vote the opposite way.

News outlets, particularly cable news and soft news programming, need to limit the commentary and conjecture. Too many talking heads spout party-line talking points and show little grasp of any given issue. This leads to arguments about party, ideology, and political strategy, rather than toward problem solving and the unbiased weighing of alternatives. Why are "political strategists" discussing tax rates, foreign policy, or terrorism, rather than people who study these issues? There are thousands of available authoritative experts who can share meaningful facts and expertise; I suggest that news outlets begin utilizing them more.

Just the same, our traditional news outlets, newspapers, need to feature less opinion and commentary. Too much opinion masquerades as news reporting simply because it has a news outlet's name attached to it. Also, news outlets should not endorse candidates. If objectivity is a norm, then political endorsements clearly violate it.

Mistakes happen. The problem is that the mistakes in news reporting can be very visible, but the corrections, if they ever come, are often buried and arrive too late. News outlets need to be upfront and honest with their corrections, perhaps by placing them on a dedicated section of their front page, or a dedicated webpage, or in a regular on-air segment. And, not only should mistakes be corrected and made public, but misleading or out-of-context stories should be corrected as well. Trust should not come without accountability.

Fact checking has become an important part of journalism in recent years, and fact-checking outlets such as Politifact have become ubiquitous. Yet, as it is currently practiced by news outlets worldwide, fact checking is little more than ideological political commentary.[19] Without a set methodology or an ideologically diverse set of fact checkers, fact checking outlets have devolved into opinion news; they are not about simply *checking facts*. This is unfortunate, because fact checking would provide a value if it were done transparently and with a standardized methodology.

Conspiracy theories are often wrong and present many problems for society. What can or should be done about them? Cass Sunstein addressed this question directly by suggesting that conspiracy theories could be eliminated by government through taxation or by an outright ban.[20] He also suggested sending government agents into conspiracy chat rooms to disrupt conspiracy theorists' conversations. None of these seem like viable policy options. Social scientists have attempted to prevent or correct conspiracy beliefs in a variety of ways, with varied results.[21] However, researchers have not been very clear about who should try to dissuade people from their conspiracy theories, and for what reasons. There seems to be an assumption underlying much of this work that a world without conspiracy theories would be a better place, but there needs to be consideration of what could happen if the powerful had the power to rid citizens of their conspiracy beliefs. Such a solution would have Orwellian consequences.

A more inclusive and transparent government, for example, would lessen the need for conspiracy theories. Achieving this is a difficult proposition, but one that could solve the problem: if the powerful were less able to conspire because of greater transparency and citizen involvement, then conspiracy theories would have less value.

Conspiracy theories tell us about our darkest fears. They also tell us about what we value most. It is easy to shut the door on people who disagree with us, especially when those disagreements devolve into accusations of conspiracy. A little bit of understanding, and some empathy, will go a long way toward lessening both the need for and the dangers of conspiracy theories.

Notes

1. Heer, Jeet. 2017. "No, Liberals Are Not Falling for Conspiracy Theories Just Like Conservatives Do." *New Republic.* https://newrepublic.com/article/142828/no-liberals-not-falling-conspiracy-theories-just-like-conservatives (Accessed December 28, 2017); Gerson, Michael. 2017. "The Conservative Mind Has Become Diseased." *The Washington Post.* https://www.washingtonpost.com/opinions/the-conservative-mind-has-become-diseased/2017/05/25/523f0964-4159-11e7-9869-bac8b446820a_story.html?utm_term=.1c5d05d73238 (Accessed December 28, 2017); Roberts, David. 2016. "Why Conspiracy Theories Flourish on the Right." Vox.com. https://www.vox.com/2015/12/10/9886222/conspiracy-theories-right-wing (Accessed December 28, 2017); Rosenberg, Paul. 2016. "Conspiracy Theories are for Losers: Science Explains Why Conservatives See Sneaky Cabals in Every Defeat." *Salon.* https://www.salon.com/2016/03/19/conspiracy_theories_are_for_losers_science_explains_why_conservatives_see_sneaky_cabals_in_every_defeat/ (Accessed December 28, 2017).
2. Miller, Joanne M., Kyle L. Saunders, and Christina E. Farhart. 2016. "Conspiracy Endorsement as Motivated Reasoning: The Moderating Roles of Political Knowledge and Trust." *American Journal of Political Science* 60(4): 824–844.
3. Oliver, Eric, and Thomas Wood. 2014. "Conspiracy Theories and the Paranoid Style (S) of Mass Opinion." *American Journal of Political Science* 58(4): 952–966; Uscinski, Joseph E., Casey Klofstad, and Matthew Atkinson. 2016. "What Drives Conspiratorial Beliefs? The Role of Informational Cues and Predispositions." *Political Research Quarterly* 69(1): 57–71; Uscinski, Joseph E., and Joseph M. Parent. 2014. *American Conspiracy Theories.* Oxford: Oxford University Press.
4. Ibid.
5. Ibid.; van Prooijen, Jan-Willem, André P. M. Krouwel, and Thomas V. Pollet. 2015. "Political Extremism Predicts Belief in Conspiracy Theories." *Social Psychological and Personality Science* 6(5): 570–578. DOI: 10.1177/1948550614567356.
6. Krugman, Paul. 2008. "Crazy Conspiracy Theorists." [Blog] *The Conscience of a Liberal.* Available at https://krugman.blogs.nytimes.com/2008/12/22/crazy-conspiracy-theorists-2/ (Accessed December 28, 2017).
7. CBSNews.com Staff. 1998. "CBS Poll: JFK Conspiracy Lives." *CBSNews.com.* https://www.cbsnews.com/news/cbs-poll-jfk-conspiracy-lives/ (Accessed December 28, 2017); Swift,

Art. 2013. "Majority in U.S. Still Believe JFK Killed in a Conspiracy." *Gallup.com*. http://news. gallup.com/poll/165893/majority-believe-jfk-killed-conspiracy.aspx (Accessed December 28, 2017).

8. Uscinski, Joseph E., Darin DeWitt, and Matthew Atkinson. 2018. "Conspiracy Theories and the Internet." In *The Brill Handbook of Conspiracy Theory and Contemporary Religion*, eds. Egil Asprem, Asbjorn Dyrendal, and David Robertson. Leiden, Netherlands: Brill; Uscinski, Klofstad, and Atkinson, "What Drives Conspiratorial Beliefs?"

9. Rosenberg, Paul. 2017. "Conspiracy Theory's Big Comeback: Deep Paranoia Runs Free in the Age of Donald Trump." *Salon*. https://www.salon.com/2017/01/01/conspiracy-theorys-big-comeback-deep-paranoia-runs-free-in-the-age-of-donald-trump/ (Accessed December 28, 2017).

10. LaFrance, Adrienne. 2015. "Going Online in the Age of Conspiracy Theories." *The Atlantic*. https://www.theatlantic.com/technology/archive/2015/10/going-online-in-the-age-of-conspiracy-theories/411544/ (Accessed December 27, 2017).

11. Rosenthal, Andrew. 2013. "No Comment Necessary: Conspiracy Nation." [Blog] *Taking Note*. Available at https://takingnote.blogs.nytimes.com/2013/01/17/no-comment-necessary-conspiracy-nation/ (Accessed December 28, 2017).

12. Jacobsen, Annie. 2011. "The United States of Conspiracy: Why, More and More, Americans Cling to Crazy Theories." *New York Daily News*. http://www.nydailynews.com/opinion/united-states-conspiracy-americans-cling-crazy-theories-article-1.949689 (Accessed December 28, 2017).

13. Aaronovitch, David. 2010. *Voodoo Histories: The Role of Conspiracy Theory in Shaping Modern History*. New York: Riverhead Books.

14. McMahon, Darrin M. 2004. "Conspiracies So Vast: Conspiracy Theory Was Born in the Age of Enlightenment and Has Metastasized in the Age of the Internet. Why Won't It Go Away?" *The Boston Globe*. http://archive.boston.com/news/globe/ideas/articles/2004/02/01/conspiracies_so_vast/ (Accessed December 28, 2017).

15. Cannon, Lou. 1991. "Gary Sick's Lingering Charges." *The Washington Post*. https://www.washingtonpost.com/archive/opinions/1991/05/13/gary-sicks-lingering-charges/b8bc811c-7046-4eb8-87e7-1645667d0e6b/?utm_term=.d27322727d89 (Accessed December 28, 2017); Krauthammer, Charles. 1991. "A Rash of Conspiracy Theories." *Washington Post*. https://www.washingtonpost.com/archive/opinions/1991/07/05/a-rash-of-conspiracy-theories/62f0ada3-a717-4653-a1ba-672d3931f75d/?utm_term=.cd83213f725f (Accessed December 28, 2017); Thomas, Kenn. 1994. "Clinton Era Conspiracies! Was Gennifer Flowers on the Grassy Knoll? Probably Not, but Here Are Some Other Bizarre Theories for a New Political Age." *The Washington Post*. https://www.washingtonpost.com/archive/opinions/1994/01/16/clinton-era-conspiracies-was-gennifer-flowers-on-the-grassy-knoll-probably-not-but-here-are-some-other-bizarre-theories-for-a-new-political-age/52f44fe4-ba8e-4f9a-a119-c1d526fad4b4/?utm_term=.bd0fc0eaa81f (Accessed December 28, 2017).

16. Geyer, Georgie Anne. 1977. "The Rewriting of History to Fit Our Age of Conspiracy." *The Los Angeles Times*.

17. The New York Times. 1964. "The Warren Commission Report." *The New York Times*. http://www.nytimes.com/1964/09/28/the-warren-commission-report.html (Accessed December 28, 2017).

18. Concha, Joe. 2017. "Media Shows Why It's So Mistrusted after Falsified Trump Fish-Feeding 'Story.'" *The Hill*. http://thehill.com/opinion/white-house/358983-media-shows-why-its-so-mistrusted-after-falsified-trump-fish-feeding (Accessed December 28, 2017).

19. Uscinski, Joseph E. 2015. "The Epistemology of Fact Checking (Is Still Naïve): Rejoinder to Amazeen." *Critical Review* 7(2): 243–252. DOI: 10.1080/08913811.2015.1055892; Uscinski, Joseph E., and Ryden W. Butler. 2013. "The Epistemology of Fact-Checking." *Critical Review* 25(2): 162–180. DOI: 10.1080/08913811.2013.843872.

20. Sunstein, Cass R. 2014. *Conspiracy Theories and Other Dangerous Ideas.* New York: Simon and Schuster; Sunstein, Cass R., and Adrian Vermeule. 2009. "Conspiracy Theories: Causes and Cures." *Journal of Political Philosophy* 17(2): 202–227.

21. Douglas, Karen M., and Daniel Jolley. 2017. "Prevention Is Better Than Cure: Addressing Anti-Vaccine Conspiracy Theories." *Journal of Applied Social Psychology* 47(8): 459–469; Nyhan, Brendan, Jason Reifler, and Peter A. Ubel. 2013. "The Hazards of Correcting Myths About Health Care Reform." *Medical Care* 51(2): 127–132.

REFERENCES

Aaronovitch, David. 2010. *Voodoo Histories: The Role of Conspiracy Theory in Shaping Modern History*. New York: Riverhead Books.

Abad-Santos, Alexander. 2012. "Yes, Half of Republicans Think ACORN, Which Doesn't Exist, Stole the Election." *The Atlantic*. https://www.theatlantic.com/politics/archive/2012/12/yes-half-republicans-think-acorn-which-doesnt-exist-stole-election/320846/ (Accessed December 27, 2017).

Abalakina-Paap, Marina, Walter G. Stephan, Traci Craig, and W. Larry Gregory. 1999. "Beliefs in conspiracies." *Political Psychology* 20(2): 637–647.

Abramowitz, Alan. 2013. *The Polarized Public: Why American Government Is So Dysfunctional*. Boston: Pearson.

Adamic, Lada, and Natalie Glance. 2005. *The Political Blogosphere and the 2004 US Election: Divided They Blog*. In *Proceedings of the 3rd International Workshop on Link Discovery*. New York: ACM. DOI: 10.1145/1134271.1134277.

Adler, Jonathan. 2017. "Nancy MacLean Responds to Her Critics." *Washington Post*. https://www.washingtonpost.com/news/volokh-conspiracy/wp/2017/07/20/nancy-maclean-responds-to-her-critics/?utm_term=.aef727858117 (Accessed December 7, 2017).

Adorno, Theodor W., Else Frenkel-Brunswik, Daniel J. Levinson, and R. Nevitt Sanford. 1950. *The Authoritarian Personality: Part Two*. New York: Wiley.

Adrianova, Anna. 2016. "Putin's Maverick Adviser Defies Nabiullina With $64 Billion Plan." *Bloomberg*. https://www.bloomberg.com/news/articles/2016-10-30/putin-s-maverick-adviser-defies-nabiullina-with-64-billion-plan (Accessed November 26, 2017).

Agustín, Laura. 2007. *Sex at the Margins: Migration, Labour Markets and the Rescue Industry*. New York: Zed Books.

Agustín, Laura. 2008. "The Shadowy World of Sex Across Borders." *The Guardian*, November 19, 2008.

Ahmed, A. 2013. "The Haqqanis, Revered for Soviet Fight, Losing Favor among Countrymen." *International New York Times*, November 7, 2013.

Aird, Rosemary L., James G. Scott, John McGrath, Jake M. Najman, and Abdullah Al Mamun. 2010. "Is the New Age Phenomenon Connected to Delusion-like Experiences? Analysis of Survey Data from Australia." *Mental Health, Religion & Culture* 13(1): 37–53

Aldrich, John H. 1995. *Why Parties?: The Origin and Transformation of Political Parties in America*. Chicago: University of Chicago Press.

Alexander, David. 1990. "Giving the Devil More Than His Due." *The Humanist*, March/April, 5–15.

Allport, Gordon W. and Leo Joseph Postman. 1947. *The Psychology of Rumor*. New York: H. Holt and Company.

Amano, Yukiua. 2015. *The Fukushima Daiichi Accident: Report by the Director General.* Vienna: International Atomic Energy Agency.

American Association for the Advancement of Science. 2012. "Statement by the AAAS board of directors on labeling of genetically modified foods." http://www.aaas.org/sites/default/files/AAAS GM statement.pdf (Accessed December 9, 2015).

American Psychiatric Association. 2013. *Diagnostic and Statistical Manual of Mental Disorders: DSM-5.* 5th ed. Arlington: American Psychiatric Association.

American Psychological Association. 2013. "Understanding Sexual Orientation and Gender Identity." http://www.apa.org/helpcenter/sexual-orientation.aspx. Accessed May, 19, 2018.

Anderson, Monica. 2015. "Amid Debate over Labeling GM Foods, Most Americans Believe They're Unsafe." *Pew Research Center.* http://www.pewresearch.org/fact-tank/2015/08/11/amid-debate-over-labeling-gm-foods-most-americans-believe-theyre-unsafe/ (Accessed December 28, 2017).

Anonymous. 2013. "Turkish Politics: Justice or Revenge?" *The Economist.* https://www.economist.com/news/europe/21583312-harsh-verdicts-are-handed-down-ergenekon-trial-justice-or-revenge (Accessed December 21, 2017).

Applegate, Debby. 2006. *The Most Famous Man in America. The Biography of Henry Ward Beecher.* New York: Doubleday.

Appleton, Sheldon. 2000. "Trends: Assassinations." *Public Opinion Quarterly* 64(4): 495–522.

Aras, Bulent. 2009. "Turkey's Rise in the Greater Middle East: Peace-building in the Periphery." *Journal of Balkan and Near Eastern Studies* 11(1): 29–41.

Archibold, Randal C. 2008. "In Smaller Numbers, Marchers Seek Immigrants' Rights." *New York Times*, May 2, 2008.

Arnold, Gordon B. 2008. *Conspiracy Theory in Film, Television and Politics.* Westport, CT: Praegar.

Arnsdorf, Issac. 2016. "Kelly Corners Brazile on Leaked Town Hall Question." *Politico Magazine.* https://www.politico.com/story/2016/10/megyn-kelly-donna-brazile-wikileaks-230064 (Accessed December 27, 2017).

Arpi, Ivar. 2016. "It's Not Only Germany that Covers Up Mass Sex Attacks by Migrant Men. . . Sweden's Record is Shameful." [Blog] *Coffee House.* Available at https://blogs.spectator.co.uk/2016/12/not-germany-covers-mass-sex-attacks-migrant-men-swedens-record-shameful/ (Accessed December 27, 2017).

Arrow, Kenneth Joseph. 1963. *Social Choice and Individual Values.* New Haven: Yale University Press.

Asprem, Egil, and Asbjørn Dyrendal. 2015. "Conspirituality Reconsidered: How New and How Surprising Is the Confluence of Spirituality and Conspiracy Theory?" *Journal of Contemporary Religion* 30(3): 367–382.

Asprem, Egil, and Asbjørn Dyrendal. 2018. "Close Companions? Esotericism and Conspiracy Theories." In *Brill Handbook of Conspiracy Theory and Contemporary Religion*, eds. Egil Asprem, Asbjørn Dyrendal, and David G. Robertson. Leiden, Netherlands: Brill. Forthcoming.

Associated Press. 2013. "Argentinian Looting Spreads amid Police Strikes." *The Guardian.* https://www.theguardian.com/world/2013/dec/10/argentinian-looting-spreads-police-strikes (Accessed April 8, 2017).

Atkinson, Matthew D., Darin DeWitt, and Joseph E. Uscinski. 2017. "How Conspiracy Theories Helped Power Trump's Disruptive Politics." *Vox.com.* https://www.vox.com/mischiefs-of-faction/2017/5/2/15517266/conspiracy-theories-trump-populism (Accessed December 27, 2017).

Atkinson, Matthew, Darin DeWitt, and Joseph E. Uscinski. 2017. "Conspiracy Theories in the 2016 Election." In *Conventional Wisdom, Parties, and Broken Barriers in the 2016 Election*, eds. Jennifer C. Lucas, Christopher J. Galdieri, and Tauna S. Sisco. Lanham, MD: Lexington Books, 163–180.

Ayto, John. 1999. *Twentieth Century Words. The Story of the New Words in the English Language over the Last Hundred Years.* Oxford: Oxford University Press.

Azari, Julia R., and Jennifer K. Smith. 2012. "Unwritten Rules: Informal Institutions in Established Democracies." *Perspectives on Politics* 10(1): 37–55.

Bacon Jr., Perry. 2007. "Foes Use Obama's Muslim Ties to Fuel Rumors About Him." *Washington Post*, November 29, 2007.

Baer, Marc David. 2013. "An Enemy Old and New: The Dönme, Anti-Semitism, and Conspiracy Theories in the Ottoman Empire and Turkish Republic." *Jewish Quarterly Review* 103(4): 523–555.

Bailyn, Bernarnd. 1967. "Foreword." In *The Ideological Origins of the American Revolution*. Cambridge: Belknap.

Baker, Jeffrey. 2008. "Mercury, Vaccines, and Autism: One Controversy, Three Histories." *American Journal of Public Health* 98(2): 144–153.

Bale, Jeffrey M. 2007. "Political Paranoia v. Political Realism: On Distinguishing between Bogus Conspiracy Theories and Genuine Conspiratorial Politics." *Patterns of Prejudice* 41(1): 45–60.

Balmforth, Tom. 2014. "From the Fringes toward Mainstream: Russian Nationalist Broadsheet Basks in Ukraine Conflict." *Radio Free Europe/Radio Liberty.* https://www.rferl.org/a/26534846.html (Accessed November 26, 2017).

Baltimore Police Department. 2015. "Credible Threat to Law Enforcement." https://scribd.com/doc/263262264/Credible-Threat (Accessed December 17, 2017).

Banerjee, Abhijit V. 1992. "A Simple Model of Herd Behavior." *The Quarterly Journal of Economics* 107(3): 797–817.

Bar-Tal, Daniel, and Dikla Antebi. 1992. "Siege Mentality in Israel." *International Journal of Intercultural Relations* 16(3): 251–275.

Barkan, Ross. 2015. "'Their Greed Has No End': Bernie Sanders Makes a Surprise Appearance in Manhattan." *The Observer.* http://observer.com/2015/10/their-greed-has-no-end-bernie-sanders-makes-a-surprise-appearance-in-manhattan/ (Accessed December 27, 2017).

Barker, David C. 2002. *Rushed to Judgment: Talk Radio, Persuasion, and American Political Behavior.* New York: Columbia University Press.

Barker, David C., and Christopher Carman. 2012. *Representing Red and Blue: How the Culture Wars Change the Way Citizens Speak and Politicians Listen.* New York: Oxford University Press.

Barkun, Michael A. 2003. *Culture of Conspiracy: Apocalyptical Visions in Contemporary America.* Berkeley: University of California Press.

Barkun, Michael. 2013. "Messages from Beyond: Prophecy in the Contemporary World." In *Prophecy in the New Millennium: When Prophecies Persist*, eds. Sarah Harvey and Suzanne Newcombe. Farnham, UK: Ashgate, 17–26.

Barkun, Michael. 2016. "Conspiracy Theories as Stigmatized Knowledge." *Diogenes* October. DOI: 10.1177/0392116669288.

Baron, David, Kevin Morgan, Tony Towell, Boris Altemeyer, and Viren Swami. 2014. "Associations between Schizotypy and Belief in Conspiracist Ideation." *Personality and Individual Differences* 70(November): 156–159.

Barrett, Justin, and Jonathan Lanman. 2008. "The Science of Religious Beliefs." *Religion* 38(2): 110.

Bartels, Larry M. 2002. "Beyond the Running Tally: Partisan Bias in Political Perceptions." *Political Behavior* 24(2): 117–150.

Bartlett, Jamie, and Carl Miller. 2010. *The Power of Unreason: Conspiracy Theories, Extremism and Counter-terrorism.* New York: Demos.

Basham, Lee. 2003. "Malevolent Global Conspiracy." *Journal of Social Philosophy* 34(1): 91–103.

Basham, Lee. 2011. "Conspiracy Theory and Rationality." In *Beyond Rationality: Contemporary Issues*, eds. Carl Jensen and Rom Harré. Newcastle on Tyne, UK: Cambridge Scholars Publishing, 49–88.

Basham, Lee. 2016. "The Need for Accountable Witnesses: A Reply to Dentith." *Social Epistemology Review and Reply Collective* 5(7): 6–13.

Basham, Lee. 2017. "Pathologizing Open Societies: A Reply to the *Le Monde* Social Scientists." *Social Epistemology Review and Reply Collective* 6(2): 59–68.

Bates, Daniel. 2017. "EXCLUSIVE: Hillary Supporter Harvey Weinstein Thinks a 'Right Wing Conspiracy Out to Get Me' Is Reason He has been revealed as Serial Sexual Harasser." *The Daily Mail*. http://www.dailymail.co.uk/news/article-4953450/Harvey-Weinstein-right-wing-conspiracy-sex-shame.html (Accessed December 28, 2017).

Batey, Mark, and Adrian Furnham. 2008. "The Relationship between Measures of Creativity and Schizotypy." *Personality and Individual Differences* 45(8): 816–821.

Bauer, Raymond A., and David B. Gleicher. 1953. "Word-of-Mouth Communication in the Soviet Union." *Public Opinion Quarterly* 17(3): 297–310.

BBC Russian. 2007. "*Putin sravnil opponentov s shakalami.*" *BBC Russian.* http://news.bbc.co.uk/hi/russian/russia/newsid_7105000/7105258.stm (Accessed December 21, 2017).

Beauchamp, Zack. 2017. "Democrats are Falling for Fake News About Russia: Why Liberal Conspiracy Theories are Flourishing in the Age of Trump." *Vox.com*. https://www.vox.com/world/2017/5/19/15561842/trump-russia-louise-mensch (Accessed December 27, 2017).

Becker, Jo. 2009. "The Road to Championing Same-Sex Marriage." *New York Times*, August 19, 2009.

Behrens, Erik, Franziska U. Schwarzkopf, Joke F. Lübbecke, and Claus W. Böning. 2012. "Model Simulations on the Long-term Dispersal of 137 Cs Released into the Pacific Ocean off Fukushima." *Environmental Research Letters* 7(3): 034004.

Beissinger, Mark R. 2013. "The Semblance of Democratic Revolution: Coalitions in Ukraine's Orange Revolution." *American Political Science Review* 107(3): 574–592.

Bellafante, Ginia. 2011. "Murder and Melodrama: An Obsessive Killer is Revealed in a Stylish Whodunit." *New York Times*, 20 June 2011.

Beltrame, J. 1996. "Did CIA Touch Off Epidemic of Crack?: Tie with Contras Claimed." *The Gazette* (Montreal, Quebec), September 21, 1996.

Belzer, Richard, and David Wayne. 2017. *Corporate Conspiracies: How Wall Street Took Over Washington*. New York: Skyhorse.

Benjamin, Walter. 2003. "The Paris of the Second Empire in Baudelaire." In *Walter Benjamin: Selected Writings. Volume 4: 1938–1949*, eds. Howard Eiland and Michael W. Jennings. Cambridge: Cambridge University Press.

Bennett, David H. 1995: *The Party of Fear: From Nativist Movements to the New Right in American History*. New York: Vintage Books.

Bennett, W. Lance, and Shanto Iyengar. 2008. "A New Era of Minimal Effects? The Changing Foundations of Political Communication." *Journal of Communication* 58(4): 707–731.

Berinsky, Adam J. 2015. "Rumors and Health Care Reform: Experiments in Political Misinformation." *British Journal of Political Science* 47(2):241–262. DOI: 10.1017/S0007123415000186.

Berinsky, Adam J. 2017. "Telling the Truth About Believing the Lies? Evidence for the Limited Prevalence of Expressive Survey Responding." *The Journal of Politics* 80(1). DOI: 10.1086/694258.

Berinsky, Adam. 2009. *In Time of War: Understanding American Public Opinion from World War II to Iraq*. Chicago: University of Chicago Press.

Berinsky, Adam. 2012. "The Birthers Are (Still) Back." *YouGov: What the World Thinks*. https://today.yougov.com/news/2012/07/11/birthers-are-still-back/ (Accessed December 28, 2017).

Berinsky, Adam. 2012. "Rumors, truths, and reality: A study of political misinformation." Massachusetts Institute of Technology. Manuscript.

Berman, Ari. 2016. "The Democratic Primary Wasn't Rigged." *The Nation*. https://www.thenation.com/article/the-democratic-primary-wasnt-rigged/ (Accessed December 27, 2017).

Bernardi, Daniel Leonard, and Pauline Hope Cheong. 2012. *Narrative Landmines: Rumors, Islamist Extremism, and the Struggle for Strategic Influence*. Piscataway, NJ: Rutgers University Press.

Bessi, Alessandro, Mauro Coletto, Goerge Alxeandru Davidescu, Antonio Scala, Guido Caldarelli, and Walter Quatrociocchi. 2015. "Science vs Conspiracy: Collective Narratives in the Age of Misinformation." *PloS ONE* 10(2). DOI: 10.1371/journal.pone.0118093.

Best, Joel. 1999. *Random Violence: How We Talk about New Crimes and New Victims*. London: University of California Press.

Bharath, Deepa. 2016. "'Gandhi of Grain' Visits Soka University for Talk on Genetically Modified Crops, Globalization." http://www.ocregister.com/2016/04/28/gandhi-of-grain-visits-soka-university-for-talk-on-genetically-modified-crops-globalization/ (Accessed November 30, 2017).

BIA News Center. 2005. "Doğrudur, Derin Devlet Vardır." http://bianet.org/bianet/siyaset/58067-dogrudur-derin-devlet-vardir (Accessed December 22, 2017).

Bilewicz, Michał, and Anna Stefaniak. 2013. "Can a Victim be Responsible? Antisemitic Consequences of Victimhood-Based Identity and Competitive Victimhood in Poland." In *Responsibility: An Interdisciplinary Perspective*, ed. Barbara Bokus. Lexem.

Bilewicz, Michał, and Grzegorz Sędek. 2015. "Conspiracy Stereotypes. Their Sociopsychological Antecedents and Consequences." In *The Psychology of Conspiracy*, eds. Michał Bilewicz, Aleksandra Cichocka, and Wiktor Soral. London and New York: Routledge, 3–22.

Bilewicz, Michał, and Ireneusz Krzemiński. 2010. "Anti-Semitism in Poland and Ukraine: The Belief in Jewish Control as a Mechanism of Scapegoating." *International Journal of Conflict and Violence* 4(2): 234–243.

Bilewicz, Michał, et al. n.d. "Conspiracy Divide. How Endorsement of Conspiracy Theories Affect Social Distance to Conspiracy Believers and Non-Believers After Societal Trauma." Forthcoming.

Bilewicz, Michał, Mikolaj Winiewski, Miroslaw Kofta, and Adrian Wojcik. 2013. "Harmful Ideas: The Structure and Consequences of Anti-Semitic Beliefs in Poland." *Political Psychology* 34(6): 821–839.

Birchall, Clare. 2006. *Knowledge Goes Pop: From Conspiracy Theory to Gossip.* Oxford: Berg.

Bischoping, Katherine, and Howard Schuman. 1992. "Pens and Polls in Nicaragua: An Analysis of the 1990 Preelection Surveys." *American Journal of Political Science* 36(2): 331–350.

Bishop, Bill. 2008. *The Big Sort.* New York: Houghton Mifflin.

Bjerg, Ole, and Thomas Presskorn-Thygesen. 2016. "Conspiracy Theory: Truth Claim or Language Game?" *Theory, Culture & Society* 34(1): 137–159.

Blake, Andrew. 2017. "Alex Jones Says He's Working with Secret Service to Protect Donald Trump from Assassination Plots." *The Washington Times.* https://www.washingtontimes.com/news/2017/dec/7/alex-jones-says-hes-working-secret-service-protect/ (Accessed December 28, 2017).

Blanusa, Nebojsa. 2011. *Teorije zavjera I hrvatska politicka zbilja 1980–2007.* Zagreb: Plejada.

Blitz, Matt. 2017. "The Real Story Behind the Myth of Area 51." http://www.popularmechanics.com/military/research/a24152/area-51-history/ (Accessed December 27, 2017).

Bloom, Paul. 2010. *How Pleasure Works: The New Science of Why We Like What We Like.* New York: Random House.

Bloss, Cinnamon S., Justin Stoler, Kimberly C. Brouwer, and Cynthia Cheung. 2017. "Public Response to a Proposed Field Trial of Genetically Engineered Mosquitoes in the United States." *JAMA* 318(7): 662–664.

Blumgart, Jake. 2013. "What's the Matter with Portland?" [Blog] *Medical Examiner.* Available at http://www.slate.com/articles/health_and_science/medical_examiner/2013/05/portland_fluoride_vote_will_medical_science_trump_fear_and_doubt.html (Accessed December 28, 2017).

Bock, Alan W. 1993. "Ambush at Ruby Ridge." http://reason.com/archives/1993/10/01/ambush-at-ruby-ridge (Accessed December 28, 2017).

Bode, Leticia, and Emily K. Vraga. 2015. "In Related News, That Was Wrong: The Correction of Misinformation through Related Stories Functionality in Social Media." *Journal of Communication* 65(4): 619–638. DOI: 10.1111/jcom.12166.

Bogart, Laura M., and Sheryl Thorburn. 2005. "Are HIV/AIDS Conspiracy Beliefs a Barrier to HIV Prevention among African Americans?" *JAIDS Journal of Acquired Immune Deficiency Syndromes* 38(2): 213–218.

Boltanski, Luc. 2014. *Mysteries and Conspiracies: Detective Stories, Spy Novels and the Making of Modern Societies.* Trans. C. Potter. Cambridge: Polity Press.

Bonilla-Silva, Eduardo 2014. *Racism Without Racists: Color-Blind Racism and the Persistence of Racial Inequality in America* (4th ed.). Lanham, MD: Rowman and Littlefield.

Bonner, Michelle D. 2014. "'Never Again': Transitional Justice and Persistent Police Violence in Argentina." *International Journal of Transitional Justice* 8(2): 235–255.

Borchers, Callum. 2016. "How on Earth Is the Media Supposed to Cover Trump's Wacky JFK-Cruz Conspiracy Theory?" *The Washington Post*. https://www.washingtonpost.com/news/the-fix/wp/2016/05/03/how-on-earth-is-the-media-supposed-to-cover-trumps-wacky-jfk-cruz-conspiracy-theory/?utm_term=.59bc512984ce (Accessed December 27, 2017).

Bordia, Prashant, and Nicholas DiFonzo. 2002. "When Social Psychology Became Less Social: Prasad and the History of Rumor Research." *Asian Journal of Social Psychology* 5(1): 49–61.

Bordia, Prashant, and Nicholas DiFonzo. 2005. "Psychological Motivations in Rumor Spread." In *Rumor Mills: The Social Impact of Rumor and Legend*, eds. Gary Alan Fine, Véronique Campion-Vincent, and Chip Heath. New York: Transaction Publishers, 87–101.

Bordia, Prashant, Kohyar Kiazad, Simon Lloyd D. Restubog, Nicholas DiFonzio, Nicholas Stenson, and Robert L. Tang. 2014. "Rumor as Revenge in the Workplace." *Group & Organization Management* 39(4): 363–388.

Bortin, Meg. 2006. "Muslims 'Still in Denial' About 9/11, Pew Survey Finds." *International Herald Tribune*. http://www.nytimes.com/2006/06/22/world/europe/22cnd-pew.html (Accessed December 21, 2017).

Bosley, Sarah. "Mbeki Aids Policy 'Led to 330,000 Deaths'." *The Guardian*. https://www.theguardian.com/world/2008/nov/27/south-africa-aids-mbeki (Accessed December 1, 2017).

Bost, Preston R. 2015. "Crazy Beliefs, Sane Believers: Toward a Cognitive Psychology of Conspiracy Ideation." *Skeptical Inquirer* 39(1): 44–49.

Bost, Preston R., and Stephen G. Prunier. 2013. "Rationality in Conspiracy Beliefs: The Role of Perceived Motive." *Psychological Reports: Sociocultural Issues in Psychology*. 113 (1): 118–128.

Bost, Preston R., Stephen G. Prunier, and Allen J. Piper. 2010. "Relations of Familiarity with Reasoning Strategies in Conspiracy Beliefs." *Psychological Reports* 107(2): 593–602.

Boudry, Maarten, and Johan Braeckman. 2011. "Immunizing Strategies and Epistemic Mechanisms." *Philosophia* 39(1): 145–161.

Bourne, Tom, Laure Wynants, Mike Peters, Chantal Van Audenhove, Dirk Timmerman, Ben Van Calster, and Maria Jalmbrant. 2015. "The Impact of Complaints Procedures on the Welfare, Health and Clinical Practise of 7926 Doctors in the UK: A Cross-Sectional Survey." *BMJ Open* 5(1): 1–13.

Bowley, Graham. 2010. "At Brown, Spotlight on the President's Role at a Bank." *New York Times*, March 2, 2010.

Boyer, Paul, and Stephen Nissenbaum. 1974. *Salem Possessed: The Social Origins of Witchcraft*. Cambridge: Harvard University Press.

Boykoff, Maxwell T., and Jules M. Boykoff. 2007. "Climate Change and Journalistic Norms: A Case-study of US Mass-media Coverage." *Geoforum* 38(6): 1190–1204. DOI: 10.1016/j.geoforum.2007.01.008.

Bratich, Jack Zeljko. 2004. "Trust No One (on the Internet): The Cia-Crack-Contra Conspiracy Theory and Professional Journalism." *Television & New Media* 5(2): 109–139.

Bratich, Jack Zeljiko. 2008. *Conspiracy Panics: Political Rationality and Popular Culture*. New York: State University of New York Press.

Brenner, David J., Richard Doll, Dudley T. Goodhead, Eric J. Hall, Charles E. Land, John B. Little, Jay H. Lunbin, Dale L. Preston, R. Julian Preston, Jerome S. Puskin, Elain Ron, Rainer K. Sachs, Jonathan M. Samet, Richard B. Setlow, and Marco Zaider. 2003. "Cancer Risks Attributable to Low Doses of Ionizing Radiation: Assessing What we Really Know." *Proceedings of the National Academy of Sciences* 100(24): 13761–13766. DOI: 10.1073/pnas.2235592100.

Brewer, Mark, and Jeffrey Stonecash. 2007. *Split: Class and Cultural Conflict in American Politics*, Washington, D.C.: CQ Press.

Briones, Rowena, Xiaoli Nan, Kelly Madden, and Leah Waks. 2011. "When Vaccines Go Viral: An Analysis of HPV Vaccine Coverage on YouTube." *Health Communication* 27(5): 478–485. DOI:10.1080/10410236.2011.610258.

Britt, Donna. 1996. "Finding the Truest Truth." *Washington Post*, 16 November 1996.

Brockner, Joel, and Batia M. Wiesenfeld. 1996. "An Integrative Framework for Explaining Reactions to Decisions: Interactive Effects of Outcomes and Procedures." *Psychological Bulletin* 120(2): 189–208.

Bromley, David G. 1997. "Constructing Apocalypticism." In *Millenniums, Messiahs, and Mayhem: Contemporary Apocalyptic Movements*, eds. Thomas Robbins and Susan J. Palmer. New York: Routledge, 31–46.

Bromwich, Jonah Engel. 2017. "How the Murder of a D.N.C. Staff Member Fueled Conspiracy Theories." *New York Times*. https://www.nytimes.com/2017/05/17/us/seth-rich-dnc-wikileaks.html

Broniatowski, David A., Karen M. Hilyard, and Mark Dredze. 2016. "Effective Vaccine Communication During the Disneyland Measles Outbreak." *Vaccine* 34(28): 3225–3228. DOI: 10.1016/j.vaccine.2016.04.044.

Brotherton, Robert, Christopher C. French, and Alan D. Pickering. 2013. "Measuring Belief in Conspiracy Theories: The Generic Conspiracist Beliefs Scale." *Frontiers in Psychology* 4(May). DOI: 10.3389/fpsyg.2013.00279 (Accessed December 18, 2017).

Brotherton, Robert, and Christopher C. French. 2014. "Belief in Conspiracy Theories and Susceptibility to the Conjunction Fallacy." *Applied Cognitive Psychology* 28(2): 238–248.

Brotherton, Robert, and Silan Eser. 2015. "Bored to Fears: Boredom Proneness, Paranoia, and Conspiracy Theories." *Personality and Individual Differences* 80(July): 1–5. DOI: 10.1016/j.paid.2015.02.011.

Brotherton, Robert, and Christopher C. French. 2015. "Intention Seekers: Conspiracist Ideation and Biased Attributions of Intentionality." *PLoS ONE* 10(5). DOI: 10.1371/journal.pone.0124125.

Brotherton, Robert. 2015. *Suspicious Minds: Why We Believe Conspiracy Theories*. New York: Bloomsbury.

Brown, Elizabeth Nolan. 2015. "The War on Sex Trafficking Is the New War on Drugs." https://reason.com/archives/2015/09/30/the-war-on-sex-trafficking-is (Accessed December 17, 2015).

Brown, Kim. 2004. "ExxonMobil Sued Over 55-Acre Oil Spill in Newtown Creek." *Queens Chronicle*, July 8, 2004.

Brown, Roger H. 1971. *The Republic in Peril: 1812*. New York: W.W. Norton.

Brückweh, Kerstin, Dirk Schumann, Richard F. Wetzell, and Benjamin Ziemann, eds. 2012. *Engineering Society. The Role of the Human and Social Sciences in Modern Societies, 1880–1980*. Basingstoke, UK: Palgrave Macmillan.

Bruder, Martin, Peter Haffke, Nina Nouripanah, and Roland Imhoff. 2013. "Measuring Individual Differences in Generic Beliefs in Conspiracy Theories across Cultures: The Conspiracy Mentality Questionnaire." *Frontiers in Psychology* 4(April). DOI: 10.3389/fpsyg.2013.00225.

Brulle, Robert J. 2014. "Institutionalizing Delay: Foundation Funding and the Creation of U.S. Climate Change Counter-Movement Organizations." *Climatic Change* 122(4): 681–694. DOI: 10.1007/s10584-013-1018-7.

Bruno, Jonathan. 2017. "Vigilance and Confidence: Jeremy Bentham, Publicity, and the Dialectic of Trust and Distrust." *American Political Science Review* 111(2): 295–307.

Bryan, Bob. 2016. "Krugman: It's Looking More and More Like the Election was Swung by the FBI in Virtual 'Alliance with Putin.'" *Business Insider*. http://www.businessinsider.com/paul-krugman-fbi-putin-comey-2016-11 (Accessed December 27, 2017).

Bryan, Bob. 2017. "Krugman: 'We Arguably Do Not Have a Legitimate President or Administration.'" *Business Insider*. http://www.businessinsider.com/paul-krugman-tweets-james-comey-trump-russia-investigation-2017-5 (Accessed December 27, 2017).

Bryant, Kenzie. "The Celebrity Conspiracy Theories That Just Won't Quit." *Vanity Fair*. https://www.vanityfair.com/style/2017/02/best-celebrity-conspiracy-theories-2017 (Accessed December 28, 2017).

Bryant, Kenzie. 2016. "Taylor Swift, Tom Hiddleston, and the Arrival of the Celebrity Conspiracy Economy." https://www.vanityfair.com/style/2016/09/taylor-swift-tom-hiddleston-celebrity-conspiracy-theories (Accessed December 27, 2017).

Brysse, Keynyn, Naomi Oreskes, Jessica O'Reilly, and Michael Oppenheimer. 2013. "Climate Change Prediction: Erring on the Side of Least Drama?" *Global Environmental Change* 23(1): 327–337. DOI: 10.1016/j.gloenvcha.2012.10.008.

Buenting, Joel, and Jason Taylor. 2010. "Conspiracy Theories and Fortuitous Data." *Philosophy of the Social Sciences* 40(4): 567–578.

Bullock, John G., Alan S. Gerber, Seth J. Hill, and Gregory A. Huber. 2015. "Partisan Bias in Factual Beliefs about Politics." *Quarterly Journal of Political Science* 10(4): 519–578.

Bunzel, John H. 1967. *Anti-Politics in America: Reflections on the Anti-Political Temper and Its Distortions of the Democratic Process*. New York: Knopf.

Burns, Dan. 2014. "Straddling the Vaccine Lines." http://www.ageofautism.com/2014/08/book-debut-thimerosal-let-the-science-speak-by-robert-f-kennedy-jr.html (Accessed on November 29, 2017).

Burns, John F. 2011. "London Protesters Identify with New York Counterparts and Worry of Similar Fate." *New York Times*, November 16, 2011.

Butler, Lisa D., Cheryl Koopman, and Philip G. Zimbardo. 1995. "The Psychological Impact of Viewing the Film 'JFK': Emotions, Beliefs, and Political Behavioral Intentions." *Political Psychology* 16(2): 237–257.

Butter, Michael, and Maurus Reinkowski, eds. 2014. *Conspiracy Theories in the United States and the Middle East: A Comparative Approach*. Berlin/Boston: de Gruyter.

Butter, Michael, and Peter Knight. 2016. "Bridging the Great Divide: Conspiracy Theory Research for the 21st Century." *Diogenes* (October). DOI: 10.1177/0392116669289.

Butter, Michael. 2014. *Plots, Designs, and Schemes: American Conspiracy Theories from the Puritans to the Present*. Berlin/Boston: Walter de Gruyter.

Byford, Jovan. 2001. *Conspiracy Theories: A Critical Introduction* [Proquest ebook]. New York, Basingstoke, Hampshire [England]: Palgrave Macmillan.

Byford, Jovan. 2014. "Beyond Belief: The Social Psychology of Conspiracy Theories and the Study of Ideology." In *Rhetoric, Ideology and Social Psychology: Essays in Honour of Michael Billig*, eds. Charles Antaki and Susan Condor. New York: Routledge/Taylor & Francis Group, 83–93.

Campbell, Angus, Philip E. Converse, Warren E. Miller, and Donald E. Stokes. 1960. *The American Voter*. New York: Wiley.

Campbell, Colin. 1972. "The Cult, the Cultic Milieu and Secularisation," In *A Sociological Yearbook of Religion in Britain*, ed. Michael Hill. London: SCM Press, 119–136.

Campbell, James. 2016. *Polarized: Making Sense of a Divided America*. Princeton: Princeton University Press.

Campoy, Ana. 2016. "A Conspiracy Theory about Sex and Gender is Being Peddled Around the World by the Far Right." *Quartz*. https://qz.com/807743/conservatives-have-created-a-fake-ideology-to-combat-the-global-movement-for-lgbti-rights/ (Accessed June 15, 2017).

Canadian Radiation Protection Bureau. 2015. *Special Environmental Radiation in Canada Report on Fukushima Accident Contaminants: Surveillance of Fukushima Emissions in Canada March 2011 to June 201*. http://www.hc-sc.gc.ca/ewh-semt/contaminants/radiation/impact/fukushima-eng.php (Accessed December 29, 2017).

Cannon, Lou. 1991. "Gary Sick's Lingering Charges." *The Washington Post*. https://www.washingtonpost.com/archive/opinions/1991/05/13/gary-sicks-lingering-charges/b8bc811c-7046-4eb8-87e7-1645667d0e6b/?utm_term=.d27322727d89 (Accessed December 28, 2017).

Caplan, Bryan. 2011. *The Myth of the Rational Voter: Why Democracies Choose Bad Policies*. Princeton: Princeton University Press.

Caplan, David. 2017. "Donna Brazile: Passing Potential Town Hall Topics to Clinton Camp 'A Mistake I Will Forever Regret.'" http://abcnews.go.com/Politics/donna-brazile-passing-debate-questions-clinton-camp-mistake/story?id=46218677 (Accessed December 27, 2017).

Caprettini, Gian Paolo. 1983. "Peirce, Holmes, Popper." In *Sign of Three. Dupin, Holmes, Peirce*, ed. Umberto Eco and Thomas A. Sebeok. Bloomington: Indiana University Press, 135–153.

Carey, Benedict. 2001. "Red Flags at a College, but Tied Hands." *New York Times*, January 11, 2001.

Carmines, Edward G., and James A. Stimson. 1989. *Issue Evolution: Race and the Transformation of American Politics*. Princeton: Princeton University Press.

Carpenter, Ted Galen, and Barbara Conry, eds. 1998. *NATO Enlargement: Illusions and Reality*. Washington, D.C.: Cato Institute.

Cassam, Quassim. 2015. *Bad Thinkers*. Ed. Brigid Hains. Available at: http://aeon.co/magazine/philosophy/intellectual-character-of-conspiracy-theorists/.

Cassam, Quassim. 2016. "Vice Epistemology." *The Monist* 99(2): 159–180. DOI: 10.1093/monist/onv034.

Cassidy, David. 2013. "The Reinhart and Rogoff Controversy: A Summing Up." *The New Yorker*, 26 April 2013.

Cave, Damien. 2011. "Mexico Crash Kills a Leader in Drug Fight." *New York Times*, November 12, 2011.

CBOS. 2015. *Zainteresowanie polityką i poglądy polityczne w latach 1989–2015. Deklaracje ludzi młodych na tle ogółu badanych*. http://www.cbos.pl/SPISKOM.POL/2015/K_135_15.PDF (Accessed December 22, 2017).

CBSNews.com Staff. 1998. "CBS Poll: JFK Conspiracy Lives." *CBSNews.com*. https://www.cbsnews.com/news/cbs-poll-jfk-conspiracy-lives/ (Accessed December 28, 2017).

Chait, Jonathan. 2008. "Dead Left." http://www.newrepublic.com/article/books/dead-left (Accessed December 20, 2017).

Chait, Jonathan. 2017. "Donald Trump Has Finally Erased the Line Between Conservatism and Conspiracy Theories." *New York Magazine*. http://nymag.com/daily/intelligencer/2017/08/trump-erases-the-line-between-conservatism-and-conspiracy.html (Accessed December 18, 2017).

Chan, Man-pui Sally, Christopher R. Jones, Kathleen Hall Jamieson, and Dolores Albarracín. 2017. "Debunking: A Meta-Analysis of the Psychological Efficacy of Messages Countering Misinformation." *Psychological Science* 28(11): 1531–1546.

Chen, Jing, Michael W. Cooke, Jean-Francois Mercier, Brian Ahier, Marc Trudel, Greg Workman, Malcolm Wyeth, and Robin Brown. 2015. "A Report on Radioactivity Measurements of Fish Samples from the West Coast of Canada." *Radiation Protection Dosimetry* 163(2): 261–266. DOI: 10.1093/rpd/ncu150.

Chen, Jing. 2013. "Evaluation of Radioactivity Concentrations From the Fukushima Nuclear Accident in Fish Products and Associated Risk to Fish Consumers." *Radiation Protection Dosimetry* 157(1):1–5. DOI: 10.1093/rpd/nct239.

Chen, Jing. 2015. "Issues and Challenges of Radiation Risk Communication to the Public." *Radiation Emergency Medicine* 4(1): 11–15.

Chester, A., K. Starosta, C. Andreoiu, R. Ashley, A. Barton, J.-C. Brodovitch, M. Brown, T. Domingo, C. Janusson, H. Kucera, K. Myrtle, D. Ridell, K. Scheel, A. Slomon, and P. Voss. 2013. "Monitoring Rainwater and Seaweed Reveals the Presence of 131I in Southwest and Central British Columbia, Canada Following the Fukushima Nuclear Accident in Japan." *Journal of Environmental Radioactivity* 124(October): 205–213. DOI: 10.1016/j.jenvrad.2013.05.013.

Chigwedere, Pride, George R. Seage III, Sofia Gruskin, Tun-Hou Lee, and M. Essex. 2008. "Estimating the Lost Benefits of Antiretroviral Drug Use in South Africa." *JAIDS Journal of Acquired Immune Deficiency Syndromes* 49(4): 410–415. DOI: 10.1097/QAI.0b013e31818a6cd5.

Chomsky, Noam. 1995. *Necessary Illusions: Thought Control in Democratic Societies*. Toronto: House of Anasi Press.

Chomsky's Philosophies. 2016. "Noam Chomsky—Conspiracy Theories." YouTube Video, 9:27. Posted May 8, 2016. https://www.youtube.com/watch?v=JirrKIQfOmk&t=314s (Accessed December 31, 2017).

Christie, Chris. n.d. http://www.rescuepost.com/Files/Christie.pdf (December 17, 2017).

Chwe, Michael Suk-Young. 2013. *Rational Ritual: Culture, Coordination, and Common Knowledge.* Princeton: Princeton University Press.

Cichobłazińska, Anna. 2013. "Gender Ideology Destroys a Cradle of Humankind—A Family. Interview with Dariusz Oko." *Sunday Catholic Weekly.* http://sunday.niedziela.pl/artykul.php ?lg=gb&nr=&dz=spoleczenstwo&id_art=00672 (Accessed June 15, 2017).

Cichocka, Aleksandra, Marta Marchlewska, Agnieszka Golec de Zavala, and Mateusz Olechowski. 2016 "'They Will Not Control Us': In-Group Positivity and Belief in Intergroup Conspiracies." *British Journal of Psychology* 107(3): 556–576.

Cichocka, Aleksandra, Marta Marchlewska, and Agnieszka Golec de Zavala. 2016. "Does Self-love or Self-hate Predict Conspiracy Beliefs? Narcissism, Self-esteem and the Endorsement of Conspiracy Theories." *Social Psychological and Personality Science* 7(2): 157–166.

Cichocka, Aleksandra. 2016. "Understanding Defensive and Secure In-Group Positivity: The Role of Collective Narcissism." *European Review of Social Psychology* 27(1): 283–317.

Cillizza, Chris. 2017. "Donald Trump was a Conspiracy-theory Candidate. Now He's on the Edge of Being a Conspiracy-theory President." *The Washington Post.* https://www.washingtonpost. com/news/the-fix/wp/2017/03/04/donald-trump-was-a-conspiracy-theory-candidate-now-hes-on-the-verge-of-being-a-conspiracy-theory-president/?utm_term=.bb2c4993027e (Accessed December 18, 2017).

Clark, William Roberts, Matt Golder, and Sona Nadenichek Golder. 2017. *Principles of Comparative Politics.* Washington, D.C.: CQ Press.

Clarke, Arthur C. 1973. *Profiles of the Future.* New York: Harper and Row.

Clarke, James W. 2012. *Defining Danger: American Assassins and the New Domestic Terrorists.* New Brunswick: Transaction Publishers.

Clarke, Steve. 2002. "Conspiracy Theories and Conspiracy Theorizing." *Philosophy of the Social Sciences* 32(3): 131–50.

Clover, Charles. 2016. *Black Wind, White Snow. The Rise of Russia's New Nationalism.* New Haven: Yale University Press.

CNN Wire Staff. 2010. "Mullen: Debt is Top National Security Threat." http://www.cnn.com/ 2010/US/08/27/debt.security.mullen/index.html (Accessed December 30, 2017).

CNN. 2011. "Medical Journal: Study Linking Autism, Vaccines is 'Elaborate Fraud'." http://edition.cnn. com/2011/HEALTH/01/06/autism.vaccines/?hpt=T1 (Accessed on November 18, 2017).

Coady, David. 2003. "Conspiracy Theories and Official Stories." *International Journal of Applied Philosophy* 17(2): 197–209.

Coady, David. 2006. "Rumour Has It." *International Journal of Applied Philosophy* 20(1): 41–53.

Coady, David. 2006. *Conspiracy Theories and Official Stories.* Ed. David Coady. Hampshire, UK: Ashgate.

Coady, David. 2007. "Are Conspiracy Theorists Irrational?" *Episteme* 4(2): 193–204.

Coady, David. 2012. *What to Believe Now: Applying Epistemology to Contemporary Issues.* Chichester, UK: Wiley-Blackwell.

Coady David. 2016. "Complots of Mischief." In *Conspiracy Theories: The Philosophical Debate,* ed. David Coady. Burlington, VT: Ashgate Publishing Company, 139–66.

Coady, David. 2017. "Cass Sunstein and Adrian Vermeule on Conspiracy Theories." *Argumenta.* DOI: 10.23811/56.arg2017.coa.

Cochin, Augustin. 1909. *La Crise de l'Histoire Révolutionnaire: Taine et M. Aulard.* Paris: Honoré Champion.

Cohen, Michael D., James G. March, and Johan P. Olsen. 1972. "A Garbage Can Model of Organizational Choice." *Administrative Science Quarterly* 17(1): 1–25.

Cohen, Stephen F. 2001. *Failed Crusade: America and the Tragedy of Post-communist Russia.* London: W.W. Norton.

Colby, William, and Peter Forbath. 1978. *Honorable Men: My Life in the CIA* New York: Simon & Schuster.

Collier, Peter, and David Horowitz, eds. 2004. *The Anti-Chomsky Reader.* New York: Encounter Books.

Concha, Joe. 2017. "Media Shows Why It's So Mistrusted After Falsified Trump Fish-feeding 'Story.'" *The Hill.* http://thehill.com/opinion/white-house/358983-media-shows-why-its-so-mistrusted-after-falsified-trump-fish-feeding (Accessed December 28, 2017).

Conroy, Bill. 2012. "Drug-related Homicides in the US Average at Least 1,100 a Year." https://narcosphere.narconews.com/notebook/bill-conroy/2012/03/drug-war-related-homicides-us-average-least-1100-year (Accessed December 28, 2017).

Converse, Philip E. 2006. "The Nature of Belief Systems in Mass Publics (1964)." *Critical Review* 18(1–3): 1–74.

Cook, John, Dana Nuccitelli, Sarah A. Green, Mark Richardson, Bärbel Winkler, Rob Painting, Robert Way, Peter Jacobs, and Andrew Skuce. 2013. "Quantifying the Consensus on Anthropogenic Global Warming in the Scientific Literature." *Environmental Research Letters* 8(2): 024024. DOI: 10.1088/1748-9326/8/2/024024.

Cook, John, Naomi Oreskes, Peter T. Dolan, William R.L. Anderegg, Bart Verheggen, Ed W. Maibach, J. Stuart Carlton, Stephan Lewandowsky, Andrew G. Skuce, and Sarah A. Green. 2016. "Consensus on Consensus: A Synthesis of Consensus Estimates on Human-Caused Global Warming." *Environmental Research Letters* 11(4): 1–8.

Cook, Steven A. 2007. *Ruling but Not Governing: The Military and Political Development in Egypt, Algeria, and Turkey.* Baltimore: Johns Hopkins University Press.

Cooper, John R., Keith Randle, and Ranjeet S. Sokhi. 2003. *Radioactive Releases in the Environment: Impact and Assessment.* West Sussex, UK: John Wiley & Sons.

Cooper, Milton William. 1991. *Behold a Pale Horse.* Flagstaff, AZ: Light Technology Publications.

Cooperman, Alan, Gregory Smith, Jessica Hamar Martinez, and Katherine Ritchey. 2015. *Catholics Divided Over Global Warming.* Washington, D.C.: Pew Research Center.

Coppins, Mckay. 2017. "How the Left Lost its Mind." *The Atlantic.* https://www.theatlantic.com/politics/archive/2017/07/liberal-fever-swamps/530736/ (Accessed December 27, 2017).

Corbin, Clara. 2015. "No Issue More Important than This." https://www.amazon.com/Thimerosal-Evidence-Supporting-Immediate-Neurotoxin-ebook/product-reviews/B0140EFEWK/ref=cm_cr_arp_d_viewopt_kywd?ie=UTF8&reviewerType=all_reviews&pageNumber=1&filterByKeyword=conspiracy (Accessed November 29, 2017).

Cordero, Carrie. 2017. "How to Understand Kushner's 'Back-Channel.'" Politico Magazine. https://www.politico.com/magazine/story/2017/06/06/how-to-understand-kushners-back-channel-215232 (Accessed December 27, 2017).

Cowell, Alan, and Burns, John F. 2012. "Cameron Dismisses Accusations of Deal with Murdoch Family." *New York Times,* June 15, 2012.

Cox, Gary W., and Mathew D. McCubbins. 2005. *Setting the Agenda: Responsible Party Government in the U.S. House of Representatives.* Cambridge: Cambridge University Press.

Craciun, Catrinel, and Adriana Baban. 2012. "'Who Will Take the Blame?': Understanding the Reasons Why Romanian Mothers Decline HPV Vaccination for Their Daughters." *Vaccine* 30(48): 6789–6793. DOI: 10.1016/j.vaccine.2012.09.016.

Cribb, Esme. 2017. "Dept. Of Energy Boosts Perry: 'Winning' Fight against Climate Scientists." http://talkingpointsmemo.com/livewire/perry-energy-department-boost-climate-skeptic-column (Accessed December 24, 2017).

Cristina Fernández de Kirchner. 2015. "Cristina Kirchner Anunció La Creación de La Agencia Federal de Inteligencia (Ex Side)." YouTube video, 1:00. Posted January 26, 2015. https://www.youtube.com/watch?v=OBYn8W8uupA (Accessed December 22, 2017).

Crocker, Jennifer, Riia Luhtanen, Stephanie Broadnax, and Bruce Evan Blaine. 1999. "Belief in U.S. Government Conspiracies against Blacks among Black and White College Students: Powerlessness or System Blame?" *Personality and Social Psychology Bulletin* 25(8): 941–953.

Cubitt, Geoffrey. 1989. "Conspiracy Myths and Conspiracy Theories." *Journal of the Anthropological Society of Oxford* 20(1): 18.

Cubitt, Geoffrey. 1993. *The Jesuit Myth: Conspiracy Theory and Politics in Nineteenth Century France.* Oxford: Clarendon Press.

Cull, Nicholas J., Vasily Gatov, Peter Pomerantsev, Anne Applebaum, Alistair Showcross. 2017. "Soviet Subversion, Disinformation and Propaganda: How the West Fought Against It." London: LSE Consulting.

Cullen, Jay T., and Ken Buesseler. 2014. *Today on Your Call.* By Rose Aguilar. 91.7 WKLAW FM, January 16, 2014.

Cullen, Jay T. 2017. [Blog] *Marine Chemist.* Available at http://www.dailykos.com/user/ MarineChemist/history (Accessed December 29, 2017).

Culp-Ressler, Tara. 2015. "How Chris Christie Became a Hero of the Anti-Vax Movement." https://thinkprogress.org/how-chris-christie-became-a-hero-of-the-anti-vax-movement-43c61a9563ae/ (Accessed December 17, 2017).

Cusack, Carole. 2012. *Invented Religions.* Farnham, UK: Ashgate.

Dachel, Anne. 2014. "Thimerosal: Let The Science Speak by Robert F. Kennedy, Jr. & Drs. Martha Herbert and Mark Hyman Debuts August 4." http://www.ageofautism.com/2014/07/ thimerosal-let-the-science-speak-by-robert-f-kennedy-jr-debuts-august-4.html (Accessed November 29, 2017).

Dagnall, Neil, Kenneth Drinkwater, Andrew Parker, Andrew Donovan, and Megan Parton. 2015. "Conspiracy Theory and Cognitive Style: A Worldview." *Frontiers in Psychology* 6(February): 206.

Dahl, Robert Alan. 1961. *Who Governs?: Democracy and Power in an American City.* New Haven: Yale University Press.

Daniel Pipes. 1997. *Conspiracy: How the Paranoid Style Flourishes and Where It Comes From.* New York: Free Press.

Darwin, Hannah, Nick Neave, and Joni Holmes. 2011. "Belief in Conspiracy Theories. The Role of Paranormal Belief, Paranoid Ideation and Schizotypy." *Personality and Individual Differences* 50(8): 1289–1293.

Daston, Lorraine, and Peter Galison. 2010. *Objectivity.* 2nd ed. New York: Zone Books.

Davies, Norman. 2005. *God's Playground. A History of Poland: Volume II: 1795 to the Present.* Oxford: Oxford University Press.

Davis, David Brion. 1970. *The Slave Power Conspiracy and the Paranoid Style.* Baton Rouge: Louisiana State University Press.

Davis, David Brion, ed. 1971. *The Fear of Conspiracy: Images of Un-American Subversion from the Revolution to the Present.* Ithaca: Cornell University Press.

Dawisha, Karen. 2015. *Putin's Kleptocracy: Who Owns Russia?* New York: Simon and Schuster.

Daybreak North, CBC News. 2015. "Fukushima Nuclear Pollution Hasn't Hit B.C. Shore, Says Researcher Jay Cullen." http://www.cbc.ca/news/canada/british-columbia/fukushima-nuclear-pollution-hasn-t-hit-b-c-shore-says-researcher-jay-cullen-1.2990947 (Accessed December 29, 2017).

Dean, Cornelia. 2008. "No Admission for Evolutionary Biologist at Creationist Film." *The New York Times.* http://www.nytimes.com/2008/03/21/science/21expelledw.html?mtrref=www.google.com&gw h=C729F9A07E34EEBE2DC2567F684FC52B&gwt=pay (Accessed December 28, 2017).

Dean, Jodi. 1998. *Aliens in America: Conspiracy Cultures from Outerspace to Cyberspace.* Ithaca: Cornell University Press.

Debenedetti, Gabriel. 2017. "Democrats Shaken and Angered by Brazile Book." *Politico Magazine.* https://www.politico.com/story/2017/11/05/brazile-democrats-clinton-sanders-dnc-244574 (Accessed December 27, 2017).

deHaven-Smith, Lance, and Matthew T. Witt. 2013. "Conspiracy Theory Reconsidered Responding to Mass Suspicions of Political Criminality in High Office." *Administration & Society* 45(13): 267–295.

deHaven-Smith, Lance. 2006. "When Political Crimes Are Inside Jobs: Detecting State Crimes against Democracy." *Administrative Theory & Praxis* 28(3): 330–355.

deHaven-Smith, Lance. 2010. "Beyond Conspiracy Theory: Patterns of High Crime in American Government." *American Behavioral Scientist* 53(6): 795–825.

deHaven-Smith, Lance. 2013. *Conspiracy Theory in America*. Austin: University of Texas Press.

Delasara, Jan. 2000. *PopLit, Popcult and 'The X-Files': A Critical Exploration*. Jefferson, NC: McFarland, 2000.

Delingpole, James. 2009. "Climategate: The Final Nail in the Coffin of 'Anthropogenic Global Warming?'" [Blog] *GlobalClimateScam.com*. Available at http://www.globalclimatescam.com/causeeffect/climategate-the-final-nail-in-the-coffin-of-anthropogenic-global-warming/ (Accessed December 30, 2017).

DelReal, Jose A. 2016. "Here Are 10 More Conspiracy Theories Embraced by Donald Trump." *The Washington Post*. https://www.washingtonpost.com/news/post-politics/wp/2016/09/16/here-are-10-more-conspiracy-theories-embraced-by-donald-trump/?utm_term=.217633487e52 (Accessed December 27, 2017).

Dembski, William A. 2004. "The Logical Underpinnings of Intelligent Design." In *Debating Design: From Darwin to DNA*, ed. William A. Dembski and Michael Ruse. Cambridge: Cambridge University Press, 311–330.

Dentith, M. R. X. 2017. "Conspiracy Theories on the Basis of the Evidence." *Synthese* (August): 1–19.

Dentith, Matthew R. X. 2014. *The Philosophy of Conspiracy Theories*. London: Palgrave Macmillan.

Dentith, Matthew R. X. 2016. "When Inferring to a Conspiracy Might Be the Best Explanation" *Social Epistemology*. 30(5–6): 572–591.

Dentith, Matthew R. X. 2017. "The Problem of Conspiracism." *Argumenta*. DOI: 10.23811/58.arg2017.den.

Dentith, Matthew R. X., and Martin Orr. 2017. "Secrecy and Conspiracy." *Episteme*: 1–18. DOI: 10.1017/epi.2017.9.

Dentith, Matthew R. X., and Brian L. Keeley. n.d. "The Applied Epistemology of Conspiracy Theories: An Overview." *Routledge Handbook on Applied Epistemology*, eds. David Coady and James Chase. London: Routledge. Forthcoming.

Dickey, Bronwen. 2017. "Climb Aboard, Ye Who Seek Truth!" http://www.popularmechanics.com/culture/a21919/conspiracy-theory-cruise/ (Accessed December 12, 2017).

Diethelm, Pascal, and Martin McKee. 2009. "Denialism: What Is It and How Should Scientists Respond?" *The European Journal of Public Health* 19(1): 2–4. DOI: 10.1093/eurpub/ckn139.

DiFonzo, Nicholas. 2008. *The Watercooler Effect: A Psychologist Explores the Extraordinary Power of Rumors*. New York: Avery.

DiFonzo, Nicholas. 2010. "Ferreting Facts or Fashioning Fallacies? Factors in Rumor Accuracy." *Social and Personality Psychology Compass* 4(11): 1124–1137.

DiFonzo, Nicholas, and Prashant Bordia. 1998. "A Tale of Two Corporations: Managing Uncertainty During Organizational Change." *Human Resource Management (1986–1998)* 37(3–4): 295.

DiFonzo, Nicholas, and Prashant Bordia. 2000. "How Top PR Professionals Handle Hearsay: Corporate Rumors, Their Effects, and Strategies to Manage Them." *Public Relations Review* 26(2): 173–90.

DiFonzo, Nicholas, and Prashant Bordia. 2007. "Rumor, Gossip and Urban Legends." *Diogenes* 54(1): 19–35.

DiFonzo, Nicholas, and Prashant Bordia. 2007. "Rumors Influence: Toward a Dynamic Social Impact Theory of Rumor." In *The Science of Social Influence: Advances and Future Progress*, ed. Anthony R. Pratkanis. Philadelphia: Psychology Press, 271–296.

DiFonzo, Nicholas, and Prashant Bordia. 2007. *Rumor Psychology: Social and Organizational Approaches*. Washington, D.C.: American Psychological Association.

DiFonzo, Nicholas, Jerry Suls, Jason W. Beckstead, Martin J. Bourgeois, Christopher M. Homan, Samuel Brougher, Andrew J. Younge, and Nicolas Terpstra-Schwab. 2014. "Network Structure Moderates Intergroup Differentiation of Stereotyped Rumors." *Social Cognition* 32(5): 409.

DiGrazia, Joseph. 2017. "The Social Determinants of Conspiratorial Ideation." *Socius* 3 (February): 1–9.

Dixit, Avinash K., and Barry J. Nalebuff. 1993. *Thinking Strategically: The Competitive Edge in Business, Politics, and Everyday Life*. New York: W.W, Norton.

Dixon, Ruth M., and Jonathan A. Jones. 2015. "Conspiracist Ideation as a Predictor of Climate-Science Rejection: An Alternative Analysis." *Psychological Science* 26(5): 664–666. DOI: 10.1177/0956797614566469.

Dobbs, Michael. 2008. "Dr. Obama and Dr. McCain." *Washington Post*, April 22, 2008.

Domingo, José, and Jordi Giné Bordonaba. 2011. "A Literature Review on the Safety Assessment of Genetically Modified Plants." *Environment International* 37(4): 734–742.

Dominus, Susan. 2001. "The Crash and Burn of an Autism Guru." http://www.nytimes.com/2011/04/24/magazine/mag-24Autism-t.html?_r=1 (Accessed December 20, 2017).

Donadio, Rachel. 2013. "Vatican Bank Looks to Shed its Image as an Offshore Haven." *New York Times*, May 31, 2013.

Donald, David Herbert. 1996. *Lincoln*. New York: Simon and Schuster.

Donovan, Robert J. 1996. *Conflict and Crisis: The Presidency of Harry S. Truman, 1945–1948*. Columbia, MO: University of Missouri Press.

Douglas, Karen, and Robbie Sutton. 2011. "Does It Take One to Know One? Endorsement of Conspiracy Theories Is Influenced by Personal Willingness to Conspire." *British Journal of Social Psychology* 50(3): 544–552. DOI: 10.1111/j.2044-8309.2010.02018.x.

Douglas, Karen M., and Daniel Jolley. 2014. "The Effects of Anti-Vaccine Conspiracy Theories on Vaccination Intentions." *PLoS ONE* 9(2): e89177.

Douglas, Karen, and Robbie Sutton. 2015. "Climate Change: Why the Conspiracy Theories Are Dangerous." *Bulletin of the Atomic Scientists* 71(2): 98–106.

Douglas, Karen M., and Ana C. Leite. 2017. "Suspicion in the Workplace: Organizational Conspiracy Theories and Work-Related Outcomes." *British Journal of Psychology* 108(3): 486–506.

Douglas, Karen M., and Daniel Jolley. 2017. "Prevention Is Better Than Cure: Addressing Anti-Vaccine Conspiracy Theories" *Journal of Applied Social Psychology* 47(8): 459–469. DOI: 10.1111/jasp.12453.

Douglas, Karen M., Robbie M. Sutton, and Aleksandra Cichocka. 2017. "The Psychology of Conspiracy Theories." *Current Directions in Psychological Science* 26(6): 538–542. DOI: 10.1177/0963721417718261.

Douglas, Karen M., Robbie M. Sutton, Mitchell J. Callan, Rael J. Dawtry, and Annelie J. Harvey. 2016. "Someone is Pulling the Strings: Hypersensitive Agency Detection and Belief in Conspiracy Theories." *Thinking and Reasoning* 22(1): 57–77.

Draper, Theodore. 1991. *A Very Thin Line: The Iran-Contra Affairs*. New York: Hill and Wang.

Dredze, Mark, David A. Broniatowski, and Karen M. Hilyard. 2016. "Zika Vaccine Misconceptions: A Social Media Analysis." *Vaccine* 34(30): 3441–3442. DOI: 10.1016/j.vaccine.2016.05.008.

Drobnic Holan, Angie, and Louis Jacobson. 2011. "Michele Bachmann Says HPV Vaccine Can Cause Mental Retardation." http://www.politifact.com/truth-o-meter/statements/2011/sep/16/michele-bachmann/bachmann-hpv-vaccine-cause-mental-retardation/ (Accessed December 28, 2017).

Drucker, David M. 2017. "Romney was Right about Russia." http://www.cnn.com/2017/07/31/opinions/obama-romney-russia-opinion-drucker/index.html (Accessed December 27, 2017).

Duckitt, John, and Chris G. Sibley. "Personality, Ideology, Prejudice, and Politics: A Dual-Process Motivational Model." *Journal of Personality* 78(6): 1861–1894.

Dugin, A. 2000. *Osnovy geopolitiki*. Moscow: Arktogeia-tsentr.

Dulles, Allen. "Plan Dallesa po unichtozheniiu SSSR (Rossii)." http://www.russkoedelo.org/mysl/miscellaneous/dulles_plan.php (Accessed November 26, 2017).

Dunlap, Riley E., and Aaron M. McCright. 2008. "A Widening Gap: Republican and Democratic Views on Climate Change." *Environment: Science and Policy for Sustainable Development* 50(5): 26–35. DOI: 10.3200/ENVT.50.5.26–35.

Dunn, John. 1988. "Trust and Political Agency." In *Trust: Making and Breaking Cooperative Relations*, ed. Diego Gambetta. Oxford: Basil Blackwell, 73–93.

Durkheim, Emile. [1897] 1951. *Suicide: A Study in Sociology.* Trans. John A. Spaulding and George Simpson. Glencoe, IL: Free Press.

Durnford, Dana R. 2010. "NEPTUNE Canada Was My Business Model Stolen by University of Victoria B.C." YouTube, 6:53, BeautifulGirlByDana. Available at: https://www.youtube.com/ watch?v=iKCGsphnmhc (Accessed December 29, 2017).

Durnford, Dana R. 2011. "Giving a Kid Toothpaste is Child Abuse." YouTube, 12:31, BeautifulGirlByDana. Available at: https://www.youtube.com/watch?v=XhVp4i36yaA (Accessed December 29, 2017).

Durnford, Dana R. 2013. "Proof Directed Energy Weapons Took Down the Twin Towers." YouTube, 24:11. BeautifulGirlByDana. Available at: https://www.youtube.com/watch?v=0TtNJdXWkpo (Accessed December 29, 2017).

Dwyer, Paula. 2016. "Everything Is 'Rigged." *Chicago Tribune.* http://www.chicagotribune.com/ news/opinion/commentary/ct-elizabeth-warren-bernie-sanders-system-rigged-20160204- story.html (Accessed December 27, 2017).

Dyrendal, Asbjorn. 2015. "Confluence of Spirituality and Conspiracy Theory?" *Journal of Contemporary Religion* 30(3): 367–82.

Earnest, Josh. 2015. "Press Briefing by Press Secretary Josh Earnest." *The White House,* February 3, 2015. https://obamawhitehouse.archives.gov/the-press-office/2015/02/03/press-briefing- press-secretary-josh-earnest-232015 (Accessed December 17, 2017).

Edelson, Jack, Alexander Alducin, Christopher Krewson, James A. Sieja, and Joseph E. Uscinski. 2017. "The Effect of Conspiratorial Thinking and Motivated Reasoning on Belief in Election Fraud." *Political Research Quarterly* 70(4). DOI: 10.1177/1065912917721061.

Editorial Board. 2015. "Argentina's President Resorts to Anti-Semitic Conspiracy Theories." *Washignton Post.* https://www.washingtonpost.com/opinions/conspiracy-theory/2015/ 04/23/0d2d07ca-e90b-11e4-aae1-d642717d8afa_story.html?utm_term=.5d938bcb85f7 (Accessed December 27, 2017).

Ehrenfreund, Max. 2016. "What Is Hillary Clinton Trying to Say with This Ad About Donald Trump and Putin?" *Washington Post.* https://www.washingtonpost.com/news/wonk/wp/ 2016/08/07/what-is-hillary-clinton-trying-to-say-with-this-ad-about-donald-trump-and- putin/?utm_term=.593955d33239 (Accessed December 27, 2017).

Eichenwald, Kurt. 2014. "The Plots to Destroy America." *Newsweek.* http://www.newsweek.com/ 2014/05/23/plots-destroy-america-251123.html (Accessed December 21, 2017).

Einstein, Katherine Levine, and David M. Glick. 2015. "Do I Think BLS Data are BS? The Consequences of Conspiracy Theories." *Political Behavior* 37(3): 679–701.

Ellick, Adam B., and Huma Imtiaz. 2010. "Pakistani's Death in London sets off Unrest in Karachi." *New York Times,* September 18, 2010.

Enders, Adam M., and Steven M. Smallpage. 2016. "Obama was Right: Conspiracy Theorists are More Likely to Oppose Gun Control." [Blog] Monkey Cage. Available at https://www. washingtonpost.com/news/monkey-cage/wp/2016/01/19/obama-was-right-conspiracy- theorists-are-more-likely-to-oppose-gun-control/?utm_term=.ea822330d0aa (Accessed December 29, 2017).

Enders, Adam M., Steven M. Smallpage, and Robert N. Lupton. 2017. "Are All `Birthers' Conspiracy Theorists? On the Relationship Between Conspiratorial Thinking and Political Orientations." *British Journal of Political Science* 5(4): 952–966.

Energy News. 2014. "Newspaper: Strontium-90 From Fukushima Found Along West Coast of N. America—"Plutonium. . . Might be in the Plume"—Scientist: There Needs to be More Monitoring. . . No Sign radioactive Releases From Plant are Going to Stop." http://enenews. com/newspaper-strontium-90-from-fukushima-detected-along-west-coast-of-n-america- months-ago-plutonium-might-be-in-the-plume-scientist-no-sign-releases-from-plant-are- going-to-stop-there/ (Accessed December 29, 2017).

Energy News. 2015. "Man Arrested Over Fukushima-related YouTube Videos—Charged with Criminal Harassment of University Scientists—Professor: I Certainly Don't Want to

Jeopardize the Prosecution (VIDEO)." http://enenews.com/man-arrested-fukushima-related-youtube-videos-charged-criminal-harassment-university-scientists-professor-dont-jeopardize-prosecution-video (Accessed December 29, 2017).

Ennis, Stephen. 2014. "Russian TV Sees US Plot behind Ukraine and IS Militants." *BBC News.* http://www.bbc.com/news/world-europe-29368707 (Accessed December 21, 2017).

Enten, Harry. 2017. "Most People Believe in JFK Conspiracy Theories." https://fivethirtyeight.com/features/the-one-thing-in-politics-most-americans-believe-in-jfk-conspiracies/ (Accessed December 27, 2017).

Etkind, Alexander, and Ilya Yablokov. 2017. "Global Crises as Western Conspiracies: Russian Theories of Oil Prices and the Ruble Exchange Rate." *Journal of Soviet and Post-Soviet Politics and Society* 3(2).

Farias, Miguel, Gordon Claridge, and Mansur Lalljee. 2005. "Personality and Cognitive Predictors of New Age Practices and Beliefs." *Personality and Individual Differences* 39(5): 979–989.

Farrell, Henry, and Steven Teles. 2017. "Even the Intellectual Left is Drawn to Conspiracy Theories About the Right. Resist Them." [Blog] *Vox.* October 9, 2017. Available at https://www.vox.com/the-big-idea/2017/7/14/15967788/democracy-shackles-james-buchanan-intellectual-history-maclean (Accessed December 7, 2017).

Farrell, Stephen. 2007. "From Iraq's Rumor Mill, a Conspiracy of Badgers." *New York Times,* July 31, 2007.

Fein, Steven. 1996. "Effects of Suspicion on Attributional Thinking and the Correspondence Bias." *Journal of Personality and Social Psychology* 70(6): 1164–1184.

Feldman, Susan. 2011. "Counterfact Conspiracy Theories." *International Journal of Applied Philosophy* 25(1): 15–24.

Fenster, Mark. 1999. *Conspiracy Theories: Secrecy and Power in American Culture.* Minneapolis: University of Minnesota Press.

Fenster, Mark. 2008. *Conspiracy Theories: Secrecy and Power in American Culture.* Rev. ed. Minneapolis: University of Minnesota Press.

Fenster, Mark. 2009. "On His Book *Conspiracy Theories: Secrecy and Power in American Culture (Revised and Updated Edition)."* http://rorotoko.com/interview/20090120_fenster_mark_on_conspiracy_theories_secrecy_power_american_culture/ (Accessed December 22, 2017).

Fernández de Kirchner, Cristina. 2013. "Todo lo que falta lograr, sólo se puede hacer en democracia." https://www.casarosada.gob.ar/informacion/archivo/26950-todo-lo-que-falta-lograr-solo-se-puede-hacer-en-democracia-afirmo-la-presidenta (Accessed April 8, 2017).

Fernández de Kirchner, Cristina. 2015. "18F The Baptism of Fire of the Judicial Party." http://www.cfkargentina.com/18f-the-baptism-of-fire-of-the-judicial-party/2/ (Accessed July 4, 2016).

Fernández de Kirchner, Cristina. 2015. "AMIA y la denuncia del fiscal Nisman." http://www.cfkargentina.com/amia-y-la-denuncia-del-fiscal-nisman/ (Accessed May 15, 2015).

Festinger, Leon, Henry W. Riecken, and Stanley Schachter. 1956. *When Prophecy Fails: A Social and Psychological Study of a Modern Group That Predicted the Destruction of the Modern World.* Minneapolis: University of Minnesota Press.

Festinger, Leon. 1957. *A Theory of Cognitive Dissonance.* Stanford: Stanford University Press.

Fetzer, Jim, and Mike Palecek. 2015. *Nobody Died at Sandy Hook.* Moon Rock Books.

Filer, Tanya, and Fredheim, Rolf. 2016. "Sparking Debate? Political Deaths and Twitter Discourses in Argentina and Russia." *Information, Communication & Society* 19(11): 1539–1555.

Filer, Tanya. 2015. "The Conspiratorial Queue? Perceptions of 'anti-Government' Aesthetics." *Conspiracy and Democracy.* http://www.conspiracyanddemocracy.org/blog/the-conspiratorial-queue-perceptions-of-anti-government-aesthetics/ (Accessed May 20, 2015).

Filkins, Dexter. 2006. "Votes Counted. Deals Made. Chaos Wins." *New York Times,* April 30, 2006.

Finchelstein, Federico. 2014. "Returning Populism to History." *Constellations* 21(4): 467–482.

Fine, Gary Alan, and Nicholas DiFonzo. 2011. "Uncertain Knowledge." *Contexts* 10(3): 16–21.

Fine, Gary Alan, and Patricia A. Turner. 2001. *Whispers on the Color Line: Rumor and Race in America*. Berkeley and Los Angeles: University of California Press.

Fiorina, Morris P., and Kenneth A. Shepsle. 1989. "Formal Theories of Leadership: Agents, Agenda Setters, and Entrepreneurs." In *Leadership and Politics: New Perspectives in Political Science*, ed. B. D. Jones. Kansas: University of Kansas Press, 17–40.

Fisher, Nicholas S., Karine Beaugelin-Seiller, Thomas G. Hinton, Zofia Baumann, Daniel J. Madigan, and Jacqueline Garnier-Laplace. 2013. "Evaluation of Radiation Doses and Associated Risk From the Fukushima Nuclear Acccident to Marine Biota and Human Consumers of Seafood." *Proceedings of the National Academy of Sciences* 110(26): 10670–10675. DOI: 10.1073/pnas.1221834110.

Fisher, Nicholas S., Scott W. Fowler, and Daniel J. Madigan. 2015. "Perspectives and Reflections on the Public Reaction to Recent Fukushima related Radionuclide Studies and a Call for Enhanced Training in Environmental Radioactivity." *Environmental Toxicology and Chemistry* 34(4): 707–709. DOI: 10.1002/etc.2860.

Fisman, Ray, and Tim Sullivan. 2016. *The Inner Lives of Markets: How People Shape Them—And They Shape Us*. New York: PublicAffairs, 67.

Flynn, D. J., Brendan Nyhan, and Jason Reifler. 2017. "The Nature and Origins of Misperceptions: Understanding False and Unsupported Beliefs About Politics." *Political Psychology* 38(S1): 127–150.

Folger, Robert. 1977. "Distributive and Procedural Justice: Combined Impact of "Voice" and Improvement on Experienced Inequity." *Journal of Personality and Social Psychology* 35(2): 108–119.

Folger, Roger, and Chris Martin. 1986. "Relative Deprivation and Referent Cognitions: Distributive and Procedural Justice Effects." *Journal of Experimental Social Psychology* 22(6): 531–546.

Foner, Eric. 1995. *Free Soil, Free Labor, Free Men: The Ideology of the Republican Party Before the Civil War*. New York: Oxford University Press.

Fontanella-Khan, Amana. 2016. "Fethullah Gülen: Turkey Coup May Have Been 'Staged' by Erdoğan Regime." *The Guardian*. https://www.theguardian.com/world/2016/jul/16/fethullah-gulen-turkey-coup-erdogan (Accessed December 21, 2017).

Fores, Betsi. 2012. "Jack Welch: 'Chicago Guys Will Do Anything,' Including Cook Unemployment Rate." *The Daily Caller*. http://dailycaller.com/2012/10/05/jack-welch-chicago-guys-will-do-anything-including-cook-unemployment-rate/ (Accessed December 29, 2017).

Fox News. "ACORN Fires More Officials for Helping 'Pimp,' and 'Prostitute' in Washington Office." http://www.foxnews.com/story/2009/09/11/acorn-fires-more-officials-for-helping-pimp-prostitute-in-washington-office.html (Accessed December 27, 2017).

Fox, Richard Wightman. 1999. *Trials of Intimacy. Love and Loss in the Beecher-Tilton Scandal*. Chicago: University of Chicago Press.

Francis. 2015. *Laudato Si' [Encyclical Letter]*. http://w2.vatican.va/content/francesco/en/encyclicals/documents/papa-francesco_20150524_enciclica-laudato-si.html (Accessed December 19, 2017).

Frank, Lawrence. 2003. *Victorian Detective Fiction and the Nature of Evidence: The Scientific Investigations of Poe, Dickens and Doyle*. Basingstoke, UK: Palgrave Macmillan.

Frankovic, Kathy. 2016. "Belief in Conspiracies Largely Depends on Political Identity." https://today.yougov.com/news/2016/12/27/belief-conspiracies-largely-depends-political-iden/ (Accessed December 27, 2017).

Franks, Bradley, Adrian Bangerter, and Martin W. Bauer. 2013. "Conspiracy Theories as Quasi-Religious Mentality: An Integrated Account from Cognitive Science, Social Representations Theory, and Frame Theory." *Frontiers in Psychology* 4(July). DOI: 10.3389/fpsyg.2013.00424.

Fredericks, Bob. 2017. "Roy Moore Accuser Admits Altering Yearbook Entry." *The New York Post*. https://nypost.com/2017/12/08/roy-moore-accuser-admits-altering-yearbook-entry/ (Accessed December 28, 2017).

Freedman, Alix M. 1991. "Rumor Turns Fantasy into Bad Dream." *The Wall Street Journal*, May 10, 1991.

Freely, Maureen. 2007. "Why They Killed Hrant Dink." *Index on Censorship* 36(2): 15–29.

Freeman, Daniel, and Jason Freeman. 2017. "Are We Entering a Golden Age of the Conspiracy Theory?" *The Guardian*. https://www.theguardian.com/science/blog/2017/mar/28/are-we-entering-a-golden-age-of-the-conspiracy-theory (Accessed December 18, 2017).

Freeman, Daniel and Richard P. Bentall. 2017. "The Concomitants of Conspiracy Concerns." *Social Psychiatry and Psychiatric Epidemiology* 52(5): 595–604. DOI: 10.1007/s00127-017-1354-4.

French, David. 2017. "The Seth Rich Conspiracy Theory Is Shameful Nonsense." *National Review*. http://www.nationalreview.com/article/447903/sean-hannity-seth-rich-conspiracy-theory-disgrace (Accessed December 21, 2017).

Freudenburg, William R., and Violetta Muselli. 2010. "Global Warming Estimates, Media Expectations, and the Asymmetry of Scientific Challenge." *Global Environmental Change* 20(3): 483–491. DOI: 10.1016/j.gloenvcha.2010.04.003.

Friedman, Thomas L. 2013. "From Beirut to Washington." *New York Times*, October 20, 2013.

Fukuyama, Francis. 1995. *Trust: The Social Virtues and the Creation of Prosperity*. New York: Free Press.

Funk, Cary, and Brian Kennedy. 2016. "The New Food Fights: U.S. Public Divides Over Food Science." http://www.pewinternet.org/2016/12/01/the-new-food-fights (Accessed December 21, 2017).

Furnham, Adrian. 2013. "Commercial Conspiracy Theories: A Pilot Study." *Frontiers in Psychology* 4(June). DOI: 10.3389/fpsyg.2013.00379.

Gaines, Brian, James Kuklinski, Paul Quirk, Buddy Peyton, and Jay Verkuilen. 2007. "Same Facts, Different Interpretations: Partisan Motivation and Opinion on Iraq." *Journal of Politics* 69(4):957–974.

Galer, Sophia S. 2017. "The Accidental Invention of the Illuminati Conspiracy." http://www.bbc.com/future/story/20170809-the-accidental-invention-of-the-illuminati-conspiracy (Accessed December 27, 2017).

Galison, Peter. 2015. "The Journalist, the Scientist, and Objectivity." In *Objectivity in Science. New Perspectives from Science and Technology Studies*, ed. Flavia Padovani, Alan Richardson, and Jonathan Y. Tsou. Cham: Springer, 57–75.

Gambetta, Diego. 2009. *Codes of the Underworld: How Criminals Communicate*. Princeton: Princeton University Press.

Gangarosa, E. J., A. M. Galazka, C. R. Wolfe, L. M. Phillips, E. Miller, R. T. Chen, and R. E. Gangarosa. 1998. "Impact of Anti-Vaccine Movements on Pertussis Control: The Untold Story." *The Lancet* 351(9099): 356–361. DOI: 10.1016/S0140-6736(97)04334-1.

Gee, Oliver. 2016. "Schools: France Vows to Fight Terror Conspiracy Theories." https://www.thelocal.fr/20160209/france-takes-up-fight-against-conspiracy-theories-in-schools (Accessed December 27, 2017).

Gentry, Curt. 1992. *J. Edgar Hoover: The Man and the Secrets*. New York: Plume.

Georgakopoulos, Thordoris. 2017. "What Greeks Believe in 2017." https://www.dianeosis.org/en/2017/04/greeks-believe-in-2017/ (Accessed January 9, 2017).

Gerber, Alan, and Gregory Huber. 2010. "Partisanship, Political Control, and Economic Assessments." *American Journal of Political Science* 54(1):153–173.

Gerson, Michael. 2017. "The Conservative Mind Has Become Diseased." *The Washington Post*. https://www.washingtonpost.com/opinions/the-conservative-mind-has-become-diseased/2017/05/25/523f0964-4159-11e7-9869-bac8b446820a_story.html?utm_term=.1c5d05d73238 (Accessed December 28, 2017).

Geyer, Georgie Anne. 1977. "The Rewriting of History to Fit Our Age of Conspiracy." *The Los Angeles Times*.

Gibson, James L. 2011. "Political Intolerance in the Context of Democratic Theory." In *Oxford Handbook of Political Science*, ed. Robert E. Goodin. Oxford: Oxford University Press, 323–341.

Gillis, Justin. 2013. "Unlocking the Conspiracy Mindset." *The New York Times*, February 21, 2013.

Gillon, Steven. 2017. "Why the Public Stopped Believing the Government about JFK's Murder." www.history.com/news/why-the-public-stopped-believing-the-government-about-jfks-murder (Accessed December 21, 2017).

Ginzburg, Carlo. 1990. *Clues, Myths, and the Historical Record*. Trans. John Tedeschi and Anne C. Tedeschi. Baltimore: John Hopkins Press.

Girodano, Dom. 2015, "Rick Santorum on Pope Francis' Letter on Climate Change: 'Leave The Science To The Scientist.'" http://philadelphia.cbslocal.com/2015/06/01/rick-santorum-on-pope-francis-letter-on-climate-change-leave-the-science-to-the-scientist/ (Accessed December 19, 2017).

Gneezy, Uri, and Aldo Rustichini. 2000. "A Fine is a Price." *The Journal of Legal Studies* 29(1):1–17.

Göçek, Fatma Muge. 2011. *The Transformation of Turkey: Redefining State and Society from the Ottoman Empire to the Modern Era*. New York: IB Tauris.

Goertzel, Ted. 1994. "Belief in Conspiracy Theories." *Political Psychology* 15(4): 731–742.

Goertzel, Ted. 2010. "Conspiracy Theories in Science." *EMBO Reports* 11(7): 493–499.

Goertzel, Ted. 2011. "The Conspiracy Meme." *The Skeptical Inquirer* 35(1). https://www.csicop.org/SI/show/the_conspiracy_meme (December 30, 2017).

Goertzel, Ted, and Ben Goertzel. 1995. *Linus Pauling: A Life in Science and Politics*. New York: Basic Books.

Goldberg, Robert Alan. 2001. *Enemies Within: The Culture of Conspiracy in Modern America*. New Haven: Yale University Press.

Golden, Tim. 1996. "Though Evidence is Thin, Tale of CIA and Drugs Has a Life of Its Own." *The New York Times*, October 21, 1996.

Goldenberg, Suzanne. 2014 "Jeb Bush May be 'The Smart Brother'—But He's as Much of a Climate Denier as any Conservative." *The Guardian*, December 16, 2014.

Goldenberg, Suzanne. 2015. "Republicans' Leading Climate Denier Tells the Pope to Butt out of Climate Debate." *The Guardian*, June 11, 2015.

Golec de Zavala, Agnieszka, Aleksandra Cichocka, and Irena Iskra-Golec. 2013. "Collective Narcissism Moderates the Effect of In-group Image Threat on Intergroup Hostility." *Journal of Personality and Social Psychology* 104(6): 1019–1039.

Golec de Zavala, Agnieszka, Aleksandra Cichocka, Roy Eidelson, and Nuwan Jayawickreme. 2009. "Collective Narcissism and its Social Consequences." *Journal of Personality and Social Psychology* 97(6): 1074–1096.

Golec de Zavala, Agnieszka, and Aleksandra Cichocka. 2012. "Collective Narcissism and Anti-Semitism in Poland." *Group Processes and Intergroup Relations* 15(2): 213–229.

Goñi, Uki, and Jonathan Watts. 2015. "Argentina President: US 'Vulture Funds' Backed Nisman before His Death." *The Guardian*. https://www.theguardian.com/world/2015/apr/21/argentina-president-fernandez-alberto-nisman (April 19, 2017).

Goodlee, Fiona, Jane Smith, and Harvey Macrovitch. 2011. "Wakefield's Article Linking MMR Vaccine and Autism was Fraudulent." Editorial, *British Medical Journal* 342: c7452.

Goodman, J. David, and Vivian Yee. 2013. "'I was just sure they just wanted to kill this group of Persians.'" *New York Times*, November 15, 2013.

Goodson, Larry P. 2001. *Afghanistan's Endless War: State Failure, Regional Politics, and the Rise of the Taliban*. Seattle: University of Washington Press.

Gorbachev, Mikhail. 2010. "Tsel'iu moeï zhizni bylo unichtozhenie kommunizma." *Newsland*. https://newsland.com/user/4297656659/content/gorbachiov-tseliu-moei-zhizni-bylo-unichtozhenie-kommunizma/4074611 (Accessed November 26, 2017).

Gorvett, Jon. 2006. "Talking Turkey: Turkey's 'Deep State' Surfaces in Former President's Words, Deeds in Kurdish Town." *Washington Report on Middle East Affairs* 25(1): 37–41.

Graham, David A. 2016. "Deliberate Disenfranchisement of Black Voters." *The Atlantic*. https://www.theatlantic.com/politics/archive/2016/07/north-carolina-voting-rights-law/493649/ (Accessed December 27, 2017).

Gray, Matt C. 2010. *Conspiracy Theories in the Arab World: Sources and Politics*. London: Routledge.

Green, Donald P., Bradley Palmquist, and Eric Schickler. 2004. *Partisan Hearts and Minds: Political Parties and the Social Identities of Voters*. New Haven: Yale University Press.

Greenfield, Leah. 1992. *Nationalism: Five Roads to Modernity*. Cambridge: Harvard University Press.

Gregory, T. Ryan. 2008. "Evolution as Fact, Theory, and Path." *Evolution: Education and Outreach* 1(1): 46–52. DOI: 10.1007/s12052-007-0001-z.

Gribbin, William. 1974. "Antimasonry, Religious Radicalism, and the Paraniod Style of the 1820s." *History Teacher* 7(2): 239–254.

Grice, H. Paul. 1975. "Logic and Conversation. The William James Lectures." In *Syntax and Semantics* Vol.3, eds. P. Cole and J. L. Morgan. New York: Academic Press, 41–58.

Grimes, David Robert. 2016. "On the Viability of Conspiratorial Beliefs." *PLoS ONE* 11(1). DOI: 10.1371/journal.pone.0147905.

Grzesiak-Feldman, Monika, and Agnieszka Haska. 2012. "Conspiracy Theories Surrounding the Polish Presidential Plane Crash Near Smolensk, Russia." http://deconspirator. com/2012/ 11/22/conspiracy-theories-surrounding-the-polish-presidentialplane-crash-near-smolensk-russia (Accessed December 22, 2017).

Grzesiak-Feldman, Monika and Anna Ejsmont. 2008. "Paranoia and Conspiracy Thinking of Jews, Arabs, Germans, and Russians in a Polish sample." *Psychological Reports* 102(3): 884–886.

Grzesiak-Feldman, Monika, and Hubert Suszek. 2008. "Conspiracy Stereotyping and Perceptions of Group Entitativity of Jews, Germans, Arabs, and Homosexuals by Polish Students." *Psychological Reports* 102(3): 755–758.

Grzesiak-Feldman, Monika, and Monika Irzycka. 2009. "Right-Wing Authoritarianism and Conspiracy Thinking in a Polish Sample." *Psychological Reports* 105(2):389–393.

Grzesiak-Feldman, Monika. 2013. "The Effect of High-Anxiety Situations on Conspiracy Thinking." *Current Psychology: A Journal for Diverse Perspectives on Diverse Psychological Issues* 32(1): 100–118.

Grzesiak-Feldman, Monika. 2015. "Are the High Authoritarians More Prone to Adopt Conspiracy Theories? The Role of Right-Wing Authoritarianism in Conspiratorial Thinking." In *The Psychology of Conspiracy*, eds. Michał Bilewicz, Aleksandra Cichocka, and Wiktor Soral. London and New York: Routledge: 99–121.

Guida, Michalengelo. 2008. "The Sèvres Syndrome and 'Komplo' Theories in the Islamist and Secular Press." *Turkish Studies* 9(1): 37–52.

Haberman, Maggie, and Jonathan Martin. 2017. "Trump Once Said the 'Access Hollywood' Tape Was Real. Now He's Not Sure." *New York Times*. https://www.nytimes.com/2017/11/28/us/ politics/trump-access-hollywood-tape.html (Accessed December 1, 2017).

Hagen, Kurtis. 2011. "Conspiracy Theories and Stylized Facts." *The Journal for Peace and Justice Studies* 21(2): 3–22.

Hagen, Kurtis. 2018. "Conspiracy Theorists and Monological Belief Systems." *Argumenta*. https:// www.argumenta.org/issues/ DOI: 10.23811/57.arg2017.hag

Haider-Markel, Donald, and Mark Joslyn. 2008. "Beliefs About the Origins of Homosexuality and Support for Gay Rights: An Empirical Test of Attribution Theory." *Public Opinion Quarterly* 72(2): 291–310.

Hale, Mike. 2009. "The Week Ahead: March 8–March 14: Film." *New York Times*, March 8, 2009.

Halpern, Michael. "A Conspiracy Theory Researcher Falls Victim to Conspiracy Theories: Intimidated Journal to Retract Lewandowsky Paper." [Blog] *Union of Concerned Scientists: Science for a Healthy Planet and Safer World*. Available at https://blog.ucsusa.org/michael-halpern/ a-conspiracy-theory-researcher-falls-victim-to-conspiracy-theories-intimidated-journal-to-retract-lewandowsky-paper-457 (Accessed December 24, 2017).

Hamada, Nobuyuki, and Haruyuki Ogino. 2012. "Food Safety Regulations: What we Learned From the Fukushima Nuclear Accident." *Journal of Environmental Radioactivity* 111(September): 83–99. DOI: 10.1016/j.jenvrad.2011.08.008.

Hamsher, J. Herbert, Jesse D. Geller, and Julian B. Rotter. 1968. "Interpersonal Trust, Internal-External Control, and the Warren Commission Report." *Journal of Personality and Social Psychology* 9(3): 210–215.

Hannam, Peter. 2014. "'Conspiracist' Climate Change Study Withdrawn Amid Legal Threats." *The Sydney Morning Herald*. http://www.smh.com.au/environment/climate-change/

conspiracist-climate-change-study-withdrawn-amid-legal-threats-20140401-35xao.html (Accessed December 24, 2017).

Hanyok, Robert. 2001. "Skunks, Bogies, Silent Hounds, and the Flying Fish: The Gulf of Tonkin Mystery, 2–4 August 1964" *Cryptologic Quarterly* 19(1).

Harambam, Jaron, and Stef Aupers. 2014. "Contesting Epistemic Authority: Conspiracy Theories on the Boundaries of Science." *Public Understanding of Science* 24(4): 466–480.

Hardin, Russell. 1993. "The Street-level Epistemology of Trust." *Politics & Society* 21(4): 505–529.

Harmon, Amy. 2014. "A Lonely Quest for Facts on Genetically Modified Crops." *New York Times.* https://www.nytimes.com/2014/01/05/us/on-hawaii-a-lonely-quest-for-facts-about-gmos. html?_r=0 (Accessed December 28, 2017).

Headquarters, Emergency Disaster Countermeasures; National Police Agency, Japan. 2015. "Damage Situation and Police Countermeasures Associated with 2011 Tohoku District—Off the Pacific Ocean Earthquake." http://www.npa.go.jp/news/other/earthquake2011/pdf/ higaijokyo_e.pdf (Accessed December 29, 2017).

Healy, Jack. 2012. "Iraq Turns Justice into a Show, and Terror Confessions a Script." *New York Times,* January 8, 2012.

Heath, Yuko, and Robert Gifford. 2006. "Free-Market Ideology and Environmental Degradation:The Case of Belief in Global Climate Change." *Environment and Behavior* 38(1): 48–71. DOI: 10.1177/0013916505277998.

Hedlund, Stefan. 2005. *Russian Path Dependence: A People with a Troubled History.* London and New York: Routledge.

Heer, Jeet. 2017. "No, Liberals Are Not Falling for Conspiracy Theories Just Like Conservatives Do." *New Republic.* https://newrepublic.com/article/142828/no-liberals-not-falling-conspiracy-theories-just-like-conservatives (Accessed December 28, 2017).

Heins, Volker. 2007. "Critical Theory and the Traps of Conspiracy Thinking." *Philosophy Social Criticism* 33(7): 787–801.

Henig, Jess. 2008. "Acorn Accusations: McCain Makes Exaggerated Claims of 'Voter Fraud.' Obama Soft-pedals His Connections." http://www.factcheck.org/2008/10/acorn-accusations/ (Accessed December 27, 2017).

Herman, Ed. 1966. "The Propaganda Model Revisited." http://musictravel.free.fr/political/political7.htm (Accessed June 5, 2016).

Herman, Edward, and Noam Chomsky. 2011. *Manufacturing Consent.* New York: Pantheon.

Herman, Edward S., and Noam Chomsky. 1988. *Manufacturing Consent: The Political Economy of the Mass Media.* New York: Pantheon.

Herndon, Thomas, Michael Ash, and Robert Pollin. 2013. "Does high public debt consistently stifle economic growth? A critique of Reinhart and Rogoff. *Cambridge Journal of Economics* 38(2): 257–279.

Hetherington, Marc J., and Thomas J. Rudolph. 2015. *Why Washington Won't Work: Polarization, Political Trust, and the Governing Crisis.* Chicago: University of Chicago Press.

Higgins, Andrew. 2013. "Change Comes Slowly for Bulgaria, Even with EU Membership." *New York Times,* December 25, 2013.

Hill, Kyle. 2013. "Why Portland is Wrong About Water Fluoridation." [Blog] *But Not Simpler.* Available at https://blogs.scientificamerican.com/but-not-simpler/why-portland-is-wrong-about-water-fluoridation/ (Accessed December 28, 2017).

Hirschhorn, Norbert, and Stella Aguinaga Bialous. 2001. "Second Hand Smoke and Risk Assessment: What Was In It for the Tobacco Industry?" *Tobacco Control* 10(4): 375–382. http://tobaccocontrol.bmj.com/content/10/4/375.full (Accessed December 30, 2017).

Hirschman, Albert. 1982. *Shifting Involvements: Private Interest and Public Action.* Princeton: Princeton University Press.

Hjekmgaard, Kim. 2017. "How Fake News Could Put German Election at Serious Risk." *USA Today.* https://www.usatoday.com/story/news/world/2017/02/01/german-election-fake-news/ 97076608/ (Accessed December 27, 2017).

Hochschild, Jennifer, and Katherine Einstein. 2015. *Do Facts Matter? Information and Misinformation in American Politics*. Norman: University of Oklahoma Press.

Hofstadter, Richard. 1964. "The Paranoid Style in American Politics and Other Essays." *Harper's Magazine*. https://harpers.org/archive/1964/11/the-paranoid-style-in-american-politics/ (Accessed December 29, 2017).

Hofstadter, Richard. 1964. *The Paranoid Style in American Politics, and Other Essays*. Cambridge: Harvard University Press.

Hogg, Michael, and Dominic Abrams. 1990. *Social Identifications: A Social Psychology of Intergroup Relations and Group Processes*. Florence, KY: Routledge.

Hogue, William M. 1976. "The Religious Conspiracy Theory of the American Revolution: Anglican Motive." *Church History* 4(3): 277–292.

Hollingworth, Robert M., Leonard F. Bjeldanes, Michael Bolger, Ian Kimber, Barbara Jean Meade, Steve L. Taylor, and Kendall B. Wallace. 2003. "The Safety of Genetically Modified Foods Produced through Biotechnology." *Toxicological Sciences* 71(1): 2–8. DOI: 10.1093/toxsci/71.1.2.

Horton, Richard. 2004. "The Lessons of MMR." *Lancet* 363(9411): 747–749.

Horvath, Robert. 2013. *Putin's Preventive Counter-Revolution: Post-Soviet Authoritarianism and the Spectre of Velvet Revolution*. London and New York: Routledge.

Horwitz, Steven. 2017. "Confirmation Bias Unchained." *Social Science Research Network*: 5. https://papers.ssrn.com/sol3/papers.cfm?abstract_id=3007751 (Accessed December 7, 2017).

Houlden, Pauline, Stephen LaTour, Laurens Walker, and John Thibaut. 1978. "Preference for Modes of Dispute Resolution as a Function of Process and Decision Control." *Journal of Experimental Social Psychology* 14(1): 13–30.

Howlett, Caitlin. 2015. "For the Love of Grain." [Blog] *Green Lifestyle*. Available at http://www.greenlifestylemag.com.au/node/20438 (Accessed November 30, 2017).

Hubbell, Webb. 1997. *Friends in High Places: Our Journey from Little Rock to Washington, D.C.* New York: William Morrow.

Huff, Ethan A. 2016. "How Monsanto Invaded, Occupied and Now CONTROLS Government Regulators." https://www.naturalnews.com/054636_Monsanto_federal_regulators_corporate_collusion.html (Accessed December 28, 2017).

Hughes, Ken. n.d. "A Rough Guide to Richard Nixon's Conspiracy Theories." https://millercenter.org/the-presidency/educational-resources/a-rough-guide-to-richard-nixon-s-conspiracy-theories (Accessed December 28, 2017).

Hulme, Mike. 2009. *Why We Disagree About Climate Change: Understanding Controversy, Inaction and Opportunity*. Cambridge: Cambridge University Press.

Hume, David. 1739. *A Treatise of Human Nature*.

Hume, David. [1748] 2011. *An Enquiry Concerning Human Understanding*. Hollywood, FL: Simon and Brown.

Hume, Mark. 2015. "Canadian Researcher Targeted by Hate Campaign Over Fukushima Findings." *The Globe and Mail*. http://www.theglobeandmail.com/news/british-columbia/canadian-researcher-targeted-by-hate-campaign-over-fukushima-findings/article27060613/ (Accessed December 29, 2017).

Hume, Mark. 2015. "Charges Laid Against B.C. Man Who Called for Death of Fukushima Researcher." *The Globe and Mail*. http://www.theglobeandmail.com/news/british-columbia/charges-laid-against-bc-man-who-called-for-death-of-fukushima-researcher/article27136264/ (Accessed December 29, 2017).

Hunt, George P. 1966. "A Matter of Reasonable Doubt." *Life Magazine*, November, 48.

Hunter, James Davison. 1991. *Culture Wars: The Struggle to Define America*. New York: Basic Books.

Hunter. 2015. "In 2009, Chris Christie sent letter endorsing anti-vaxxer conspiracy theory." https://dailykos.com/story/2015/02/02/1361766/-In-2009-Chris-Christie-sent-letter-endorsinganti-vaxxer-conspiracy-theory (Accessed February 2, 2015).X

Huntington, Samuel P. 1983. *American Politics: The Promise of Disharmony*. Cambridge: Harvard University Press.

Hurley, Patrick T., and Peter A. Walker. 2004. "Whose Vision? Conspiracy Theory and Land-Use Planning in Nevada County, California." *Environment and Planning* 36(9):1529–1547.

Hurriyet. 2005. "Ecevit: Turkiye'de Bir Derin Devlet Olayi Var." http://www.hurriyet.com.tr/ecevit-turkiyede-bir-derin-devlet-olayi-var-3544213 (Accessed December 22, 2017).

Hurriyet. 2013. "Turkish Prime Minister Vows to Increase Police Force." *Hurriyet*. http://www.hurriyetdailynews.com/turkish-prime-minister-vows-to-increase-police-force.aspx?pageID=238&nID=49006&NewsCatID=338 (Accessed December 21, 2017).

Hurst, Sarah, Oren Dorell, and George Petras. 2017. "Suspicious Russian Deaths: Sacrificial Pawns or Coincidence?" *USA Today*. https://www.usatoday.com/pages/interactives/suspicious-russian-deaths-sacrificial-pawns-or-coincidence/ (Accessed December 27, 2017).

Husting, Ginna, and Martin Orr. 2007. "Dangerous Machinery: 'Conspiracy Theorist' as a Transpersonal Strategy of Exclusion." *Symbolic Interaction* 30(2): 127–150.

Hylid, Anders, Michael Stellfeld, and Jan Wohlfahrt. 2003. "Association between Thimerosal-Containing Vaccine and Autism." *Journal of the American Medical Association* 290(13): 1763–1766.

Icke, David. 2010. *Human Race Get Off Your Knees: The Lion Sleeps No More*. Isle of Wight, UK: David Icke Books Ltd.

Igor', Panarin. 2010. *Pervaia Informatsionnaia Voĭna: Razval SSSR*. St. Petersburg, Russia: Piter.

Iliukhin, Viktor. 2017. "Obviniaetsia El'tsin." http://www.viktor-iluhin.ru/node/328 (Accessed November 26, 2017).

IMDb. "Manufacturing Consent: Noam Chomsky and the Media." At http://www.imdb.com/title/tt0104810/quotes (Accessed December 1, 2017).

Imhoff, Roland, and Martin Bruder. 2013. "Speaking (Un-)Truth to Power: Conspiracy Mentality as a Generalised Political Attitude." *European Journal of Personality* 28(1): 25–43. DOI: 10.1002/per.1930.

Inhofe, James M. 2003. "Sen. Inhofe Delivers Major Speech on the Science of Climate Change." https://www.inhofe.senate.gov/epw-archive/press/bsen-inhofe-delivers-major-speech-on-the-science-of-climate-change/b-icatastrophic-global-warming-alarmism-not-based-on-objective-sciencei-ipart-2/i (Accessed December 20, 2017).

Inhofe, James M. 2012. *Greatest Hoax: How the Global Warming Conspiracy Threatens Your Future* [Kindle Edition]. Washington D.C.: WND Books.

Inhofe, James M. 2012. *The Greatest Hoax: How the Global Warming Conspiracy Threatens Your Future*. Washington, D.C.: WND Books.

Inouye, Daniel K., and Lee H. Hamilton. 1988. *Report of the Congressional Committees Investigating the Iran-Contra Affair* [Abridged ed.]. New York: Times Books.

Inskeep, Steve. 2013. "Hamid Karzai Lives in a 'World of Paranoia and Conspiracy.'" *NPR.org*. http://www.npr.org/2013/11/21/246492072/hamid-karzai-lives-in-a-world-of-paranoia-and-conspiracy (Accessed December 21, 2017).

Intergovernmental Panel on Climate Change (IPCC). 2014. *Climate Change 2014: Synthesis Report*, Fifth Assessment Report of the Intergovernmental Panel on Climate Change, Geneva.

Introvigne, Massimo. 2016. *Satanism: A Social History*. Leiden, Netherlands: Brill.

Investor's Business Daily. 2017. "Deep State Run Amok? Deomcrats and Hillary Clinton Paid for FBI's Dossier on Trump." https://www.investors.com/politics/editorials/deep-state-run-amok-democrats-and-hillary-paid-for-fbis-dossier-on-trump/ (Accessed December 27, 2017).

Jacobsen, Annie. 2011. "The United States of Conspiracy: Why, More and More, Americans Cling to Crazy Theories." *New York Daily News*. http://www.nydailynews.com/opinion/united-states-conspiracy-americans-cling-crazy-theories-article-1.949689 (Accessed December 28, 2017).

Jacobson, Mark. 2007. "American Jeremiad: A harrowing ride up the proverbial creek and into the beating, bleeding heart of RFK Jr." http://nymag.com/news/politics/27340/ (Accessed December 20, 2017).

Jaffe, Alexandra. 2015. "Paul: Vaccines can cause 'profound mental disorders.'" http://www.cnn.com/2015/02/02/politics/rand-paul-vaccine-effects/index.html (Accessed December 17, 2017).

Jameson, Frederik. 1990. "Cognitive Mapping." In *Marxism and the Interpretation of Culture*, eds. Cary Nelson and Lawrence Grossberg. Champaign, IL: University of Illinois Press.

Jarrett, Gregg. 2017. "Did the FBI and the Justice Department Plot to Clear Hillary Clinton, Bring Down Trump?" http://www.foxnews.com/opinion/2017/12/15/gregg-jarrett-did-fbi-and-justice-department-plot-to-clear-hillary-clinton-bring-down-trump.html (Accessed December 27, 2017).

Jenkins, Timothy. 2016. *Of Flying Saucers and Social Scientists: A Re-Reading of When Prophecy Fails and of Cognitive Dissonance*. New York: Palgrave Pivot.

Jenkins, William. 1995. "Review of Behind the Mask of Chivalry: The Making of the Second Ku Klux Klan." *Journal of Social History* 29(1): 218–220.

Jensen, Tom. 2013. "Democrats and Republicans Differ on Conspiracy Theory Beliefs." https://www.publicpolicypolling.com/polls/democrats-and-republicans-differ-on-conspiracy-theory-beliefs/ (Accessed December 27, 2017).

Jerit, Jennifer, and Jason Barabas. 2012. "Partisan Perceptual Bias and the Information Environment." *Journal of Politics* 74(3): 672–684.

Johansen, Mathew P., Elizabeth Ruedig, Keiko Tagami, Shigeo Uchida, Kathryn Higley, and Nicholas A. Beresford. 2015. "Radiological Dose Rates to Marine Fish From the Fukushima Daiichi Accident: The First Three Years Across the North Pacific." *Environmental Science & Technology* 49(3): 1277–1285. DOI: 10.1021/es505064d.

Johnson, Loch K. *A Season of Inquiry: Congress and Intelligence*. Chicago: Dorsey Press.

Johnson, Phillip. 2001. "Evolution as Dogma: The Establishment of Naturalism." In *Intelligent Design and its Critics: Philosophical, Theological and Scientific Perspectives*, ed. Robert T. Penncock. Cambridge: The MIT Press, 59–76.

Jolley, Daniel, and Karen M. Douglas. 2014. "The Effects of Anti-Vaccine Conspiracy Theories on Vaccination Intentions." *PLoS ONE* 9(2). DOI: 10.1371/journal.pone.0089177.

Jolley, Daniel, and Karen M. Douglas. 2014. "The Social Consequences of Conspiracism: Exposure to Conspiracy Theories Decreases Intentions to Engage in Politics and to Reduce One's Carbon Footprint." *British Journal of Psychology* 105(1): 35–56.

Jolley, Daniel, Karen M. Douglas, and Robbie M. Sutton. 2017. "Blaming a Few Bad Apples to Save a Threatened Barrel: The System-Justifying Function of Conspiracy Theories." *Political Psychology* (February). DOI: 10.1111/pops.12404.

Jolley, Daniel. 2013. "Are Conspiracy Theories just Harmless Fun?" *The Psychologist* 26(1): 60–62.

Jones, Roger. 2014 "Froniers Retraction Controversy." [Blog] *Understanding Climate Risk*. Available at https://2risk.wordpress.com/2014/04/17/frontiers-retraction-controversy/ (Accessed December 24, 2017).

Joslyn, Mark, and Donald Haider-Markel. 2014. "Who Knows Best? Education, Partisanship, and Contested Facts." *Politics & Policy* 42(6):919–947.

Jost, John T., and Orsolya Hunyady. 2003. "The Psychology of System Justification and the Palliative Function of Ideology." *European Review of Social Psychology* 13(1): 111–153.

Kaftan, Liudmila. 2004. "'Zamestitel' glavy administratsii Prezidenta RF Vladislav Surkov: Putin ukrepliaet gosudarstvo, a ne sebia." *Komsomol'skaia Pravda*, http://www.kp.ru/daily/23370/32473/ (Accessed November 26, 2017).

Kahan, Dan, and Donald Braman. 2006. "Cultural Cognition and Public Policy." *Yale Law & Policy Review* 24(1): 147–170.

Kahan, Dan M. 2013. "Ideology, Motivated Reasoning, and Cognitive Reflection." *Judgment & Decision-Making* 8(4): 407–424.

Kahan, Dan M. 2015. "Climate-Science Communication and the Measurement Problem." *Advances in Political Psychology* 36(S1): 1–43. DOI: 10.1111/pops.12244.

Kahan, Dan, Ellen Peters, Maggie Wittlin, Paul Slovic, Lisa Larrimore Ouellette, Donald Braman, and Gregory Mandel. 2012. "The Polarizing Impact of Science Literacy and Numeracy on Perceived Climate Change Risks." *Nature Climate Change* 2(10): 732–735.

Kaiser, eds. 2007. *Conspiracy in the French Revolution*. Manchester: Manchester University Press.

Kalichman, Seth. 2009. *Denying Aids: Conspiracy Theories, Pseudoscience, and Human Tragedy.* New York: Springer Science & Business Media.

Kaplan, Sarah. 2017. "The Truth About Vaccines, Autism, and Robert F. Kennedy Jr's Conspiracy Theory." *The Washington Post.* https://www.washingtonpost.com/news/speaking-of-science/wp/2017/01/10/the-facts-about-vaccines-autism-and-robert-f-kennedy-jr-s-conspiracy-theory/?utm_term=.d877704de0d1 (Accessed December 27, 2017).

Kasinof, Laura. 2011. "As Yemen Teeters from Political Unrest, a Humanitarian Crisis May Not Be Far Off." *New York Times,* June 28, 2011.

Kata, Anna. 2010. "A Postmodern Pandora's Box: Anti-Vaccination Misinformation on the Internet." *Vaccine* 28(7): 1709–1716.

Kaufman, Scott. 2014. "Noam Chomsky: Reagan was an 'extreme racist' who re-enslaved African Americans." [Blog] *Rawstory.* Available at https://www.rawstory.com/2014/12/noam-chomsky-reagan-was-an-extreme-racist-who-re-enslaved-african-americans/ (Accessed December 12, 2017).

Kavakci, Merve. 2009. "Turkey's Test with Its Deep State." *Mediterranean Quarterly* 20(4): 83–97.

Kawilarang, Harry. 2006. *Quotations on Terrorism.* Victoria, Canada: Trafford Publishing.

Kay, Aaron C., Jennifer A. Whitson, Danielle Gaucher, and Adam D. Galinsky. 2009. "Compensatory Control: Achieving Order through the Mind, Our Institutions, and the Heavens." *Current Directions in Psychological Science* 18(5): 264–268.

Kay, Jonathan. 2011. *Among the Truthers: A Journey Through America's Growing Conspiracist Underground.* New York: HarperCollins.

Keeley, Brian L. 1999. "Of Conspiracy Theories." *The Journal of Philosophy* 96(3): 109–126.

Keeley, Brian L. 2007. "God as the Ultimate Conspiracy Theory." *Episteme: A Journal of Social Epistemology* 4(2): 135–149.

Keeley, Brian L. n.d.. "Is a Belief in Providence the Same as a Belief in Conspiracy?" In *Brill Handbook of Conspiracy Theory and Contemporary Religion,* eds. Egil Asprem, Asbjørn Dyrendal, and David G. Robertson. Leiden, Netherlands: Brill. Forthcoming.

Keller, Bill. 2013. "The Revolt of the Rising Class." *New York Times,* July 1, 2013.

Kelly, C. 2013. "Thinking Beyond the Creationists and the Darwinists." *Texas Monthly,* February, 25B.

Kelly, Michael. 1995. "The Road to Paranoia." *New Yorker,* June, 60–75.

Kelman, David. 2015. *Counterfeit Politics: Secret Plots and Conspiracy Narratives in the Americas.* Lewisburg, PA: Bucknell University Press.

Kennedy, Jr., Robert F. 2005. "Deadly Immunity: Government Cover-up of a Mercury/Autism Scandal." http://robertfkennedyjr.com/articles/deadly_immunity.2005.html (Accessed December 20, 2017).

Kennedy, Jr., Robert F. 2014. *Thimerosal: Let the Science Speak,* New York: Skyhorse.

Kennedy, Jr., Robert F. 2015. Foreword to *Vaccine Whistleblower: Exposing Autism Research Fraud at the CDC.* Kevin Barry. New York: Skyhorse.

Kennedy, Jr., Robert F. 2015. "Letter to the Editor." *New York Times,* July 10, 2015.

Kennedy, Jr., Robert F. 2017. "Praise for *Corporate Conspiracies*." https://www.amazon.com/Corporate-Conspiracies-Wall-Street-Washington-ebook/dp/B01HLN69K8/ref=sr_1_1?ie=UTF8&qid=1511971225&sr=8-1&keywords=Belzer+corporate+conspiracies (Accessed November 29, 2017).

Kinder, Donald R., and Cindy D. Kam. 2010. *Us Against Them: Ethnocentric Foundations of American Opinion.* Chicago: University of Chicago Press.

Kinder, Donald R., and Nathan P. Kalmoe. 2017. *Neither Liberal nor Conservative: Ideological Innocence in the American Public.* Chicago: University of Chicago Press.

Kingdon, John W. 1984. *Agendas, Alternatives, and Public Policies.* Boston: Little, Brown.

Kingsley, Patrick. 2017. "Erdogan Claims Vast Powers in Turkey After Narrow Victory in Referendum." *New York Times,* April 16. https://www.nytimes.com/2017/04/16/world/europe/turkey-referendum-polls-erdogan.html (Accessed December 21, 2017).

Kingsley, Patrick, and Sam Jones. 2011. "Osama Bin Laden Death: The Conspiracy Theories." https://www.theguardian.com/world/2011/may/05/osama-bin-laden-conspiracy-theories (Accessed December 27, 2017).

Kirkland, Anna. 2016. *Vaccine Court: The Law and Politics of Injury*. New York: NYU Press.

Kirkpatrick, David D. 2013. "Secret Recordings Reveal Mubarak's Frank Views on a Range of Subjects." *New York Times*, September 23, 2013.

Kirkpatrick, David D. and Mayy el Sheikh. 2012. "Egypt's New President is Being Undercut by State-run Media." *New York Times*, July 14, 2012.

Klaehn, Jeffrey. 2002. "A Critical Review and Assessment of Herman and Chomsky's 'Propaganda Model'." *European Journal of Communication* 17(2): 147–182.

Klar, Samara, and Yanna Krupnikov. 2016. *Independent Politics*. Cambridge: Cambridge University Press.

Klausnitzer, Ralf. 2007. *Poesie und Konspiration: Beziehungssinn und Zeichenökonomie von Verschwörungsszenarien in Publizistik, Literatur und Wissenschaft 1750–1850*. Berlin: de Gruyter.

Klein, Naomi. 2007. *The Shock Doctrine: The Rise of Disaster Capitalism*. New York: Metropolitan Books.

Kliegman, Julie. 2014. "Jerry Brown Says "virtually no Republican" in Washington accepts climate change science." *Tampa Bay Times PolitiFact*, May 18, 2014.

Kloor, Keith. 2014. "Robert Kennedy Jr.'s Belief in Autism-Vaccine Connection, and its Political Peril." *The Washington Post*, July 18, 2014.

Kluger, Jeffrey. 2017. "Why So Many People Believe Conspiracy Theories." *Time*. http://time.com/4965093/conspiracy-theories-beliefs/ (Accessed December 28, 2017).

Knight, P.G. 1997. "Naming the Problem: Feminism and the Figuration of Conspiracy." *Cultural Studies* 11(1): 40–63. DOI: 10.1080/09502389700490031.

Knight, Peter. 1999. "Everything Is Connected: Underworld's Secret History of Paranoia." *MFS Modern Fiction Studies* 45(3): 811–836.

Knight, Peter. 2000. *Conspiracy Culture: From Kennedy to the X-Files*. London: Routledge.

Knight, Peter, ed. 2003. *Making Sense of Conspiracy Theories*. Santa Barbara, CA: ABC-CLIO.

Knopf, Terry Ann. 1975. *Rumors, Race, and Riots*. New York: Transaction Publishers.

Kofta, Mirosław, and Grzegorz Sędek. 2005. "Conspiracy Stereotypes of Jews during Systemic Transformation in Poland." *International Journal of Sociology* 35(1): 40–64.

Kofta, Mirosław, et al. n.d. "What Breeds Conspiracy Beliefs? The Role of Political Powerlessness and Meaninglessness in the Belief in Jewish Conspiracy." Forthcoming.

Kossowska, Małgorzata, and Marcin Bukowski. 2015. "Motivated Roots of Conspiracies: The Role of Certainty and Control Motivation in Conspiracy Thinking." In *The Psychology of Conspiracy*, eds. Michał Bilewicz, Aleksandra Cichocka, and Wiktor Soral. London and New York: Routledge, 145–161.

Koziński, Agaton. 2014. "Wybuch w salonce, sztuczna mgła, bomba termobaryczna. . . Smoleńskie teorie spiskowe [Explosion, artificial mist, fuel-air bomb. . . Smolensk conspiracy theories]." *Polska The Times*. http://www.polskatimes.pl/artykul/3399133,wybuch-w-salonce-sztuczna-mgla-bomba-termobaryczna-smolenskie-teorie-spiskowe-galeria,id,t.html (Accessed 15 June 2017).

Kramer, Roderick M. 1998. "Paranoid Cognition in Social Systems: Thinking and Acting in the Shadow of Doubt." *Personality and Social Psychology Review* 2(4): 251–275.

Kramer, Roderick M., and Dana Gavrieli. 2005. "The Perception of Conspiracy: Leader Paranoia as Adaptive Cognition." In *The Psychology of Leadership: New Perspectives and Research*, eds. David M. Messick and Roderick M. Kramer. Mahwah, NJ and London: Taylor & Francis, 241–274.

Kramer, Roderick M., and Jennifer Schaffer. 2014. "Misconnecting the Dots: Origins and Dynamics of Outgroup Paranoia." In *Power, Politics, and Paranoia. Why People are Suspicious of Their Leaders*, eds. Jan-Willem van Prooijen and Paul A. M. van Lange. Cambridge: Cambridge University Press, 199–217.

Krauthammer, Charles. 1991. "A Rash of Conspiracy Theories." *Washington Post*. https://www.washingtonpost.com/archive/opinions/1991/07/05/a-rash-of-conspiracy-theories/62f0ada3-a717-4653-a1ba-672d3931f75d/?utm_term=.cd83213f725f (Accessed December 28, 2017).

Krekó, Péter. 2015. "Conspiracy Theory as Collective Motivated Cognition." In *The Psychology of Conspiracy*, eds. Michał Bilewicz, Aleksandra Cichocka, and Wiktor Soral. London and New York: Routledge, 62–75.

Kruglanski, Arie W., and Donna M. Webster. 1996. "Motivated Closing of the Mind: 'Seizing' and 'Freezing.'" *Psychological Review* 103(2): 263–283.

Krugman, Paul. 2008. "Crazy Conspiracy Theorists." [Blog] *The Conscience of a Liberal*. Available at https://krugman.blogs.nytimes.com/2008/12/22/crazy-conspiracy-theorists-2/ (Accessed December 28, 2017).

Krugman, Paul. 2012. "Nobody Understands Debt." *New York Times*, January 1, 2012.

Krugman, Paul. 2015. "Debt is Good." *New York Times*, August 21, 2015.

Kryshtanovskaya, Olga, and Stephen White. 2005. "The Rise of the Russian Business Elite." *Communist and Post-Communist Studies* 38(3): 293–307.

Kuklinski, James, Paul Quirk, Jennifer Jerit, David Schweider, and Robert Rich. 2000. "Misinformation and the Currency of Democratic Citizenship." *Journal of Politics* 62(3):790–815.

Kunda, Ziva. 1990. "The Case for Motivated Reasoning." *Psychological Bulletin* 108(3): 480–498.

Kuran, Timur. 1991. "Now Out of Never: The Element of Surprise in the East European Revolution of 1989." *World Politics* 44(1): 33.

Kuran, Timur. 1997. *Private Truths, Public Lies: The Social Consequences of Preference Falsification*. Cambridge: Harvard University Press.

Kutler, Stanley. 1999. *Abuse of Power: The New Nixon Tapes*. New York: Free Press.

Kuvakin, Ilya. 2015. "Dvorkovich dopustil zagovor protiv Rossii kak prichinu padeniia tsen na neft'. *RBC*. http://www.rbc.ru/economics/17/02/2015/54e2760b9a7947ea2a641f0a (Accessed November 26, 2017).

L.A. Times staff and Associated Press. 2017. "Fox News Retracts Story Alleging DNC Staffer Seth Rich Leaked Information to WikiLeaks Before Death." *Los Angeles Times*. http://www.latimes.com/politics/washington/la-na-essential-washington-updates-fox-news-retracts-story-alleging-dnc-1495565128-htmlstory.html (Accessed December 21, 2017).

Ladd, Jonathan M. 2011. *Why Americans Hate the Media and How It Matters*. Princeton: Princeton University Press.

LaFrance, Adrienne. 2015. "Going Online in the Age of Conspiracy Theories." *The Atlantic*. https://www.theatlantic.com/technology/archive/2015/10/going-online-in-the-age-of-conspiracy-theories/411544/ (Accessed December 27, 2017).

LaFrance, Adrienne. 2017. The Normalization of Conspiracy Theories: People Who Share Dangerous Ideas Don't Necessarily Believe Them." *The Atlantic*. https://www.theatlantic.com/technology/archive/2017/06/the-normalization-of-conspiracy-culture/530688/ (Accessed December 27, 2017).

Lahsen, Myanna. 1999. "The Detection and Attribution of Conspiracies: The Controversy Over Chapter 8." In *Paranoia within Reason: A Casebook on Conspiracy as Explanation*, ed. George Marcus. Chicago: University of Chicago Press.

Landman, Anne and Stanton A. Glantz. 2009. "Tobacco Industry Efforts to Undermine Policy-Relevant Research." *American Journal of Public Health* 99(1): 45–58. DOI: 10.2105/ajph.2007.130740.

Landrum, Ashley R., Robert B. Lull, Heather Akin, and Kathleen Hall Jamieson. 2016. "Making It About Morals: Pope Francis Shifts the Climate Change Debate." https://ssrn.com/abstract=2997490.

Lanning, Kenneth V. 1989. "Satanic, Occult, Ritualistic Crime: A Law Enforcement Perspective." *The Police Chief*, October, 62–84.

LaRouchePac. 2012. "Britain's Thermonuclear War and Russia's Warning." [Blog] *LaRouchePac*. Available at http://archive.larouchepac.com/node/22617 (Accessed December 28, 2017).

LaRouchePac. 2016. "It Was Your Bloody Hand that Unleashed 9/11, Queen Elizabeth!" [Blog] *LaRouchePac*. Available at https://larouchepac.com/20160421/it-was-your-bloody-hand-unleashed-911-queen-elizabeth (Accessed December 28, 2017).

Laruelle, Marlene. 2016. "The Izborsky Club, or the New Conservative Avant-Garde in Russia." *Russian Review* 75(4): 626–644.

Laruelle, Marlene. 2016. "The Three Colours of Novorossiya, or the Russian Nationalist Mythmaking of the Ukrainian Crisis." *Post-Soviet Affairs* 32(1): 55–74.

Lasswell, Harold D. 1986. *Psychopathology and Politics*. Chicago: University of Chicago Press.

Lauerman. 2017. "Correcting Our Record." https://www.salon.com/2011/01/16/dangerous_immunity/ (Accessed November 30, 2017).

Lausen, Lukas, and Nicolas Stuehlinger. 2017. "The Populists Can Be Beaten. Here's How." *The New Statesman*. https://www.newstatesman.com/2017/03/populists-can-be-beaten-heres-how (April 11, 2017).

Layman, Geoffrey. 2001. *The Great Divide: Religious and Cultural Conflict in American Party Politics*. New York: Columbia University Press.

Lee, Trymaine. 2007. "Sorrow and Reflection in Killer's Housing Project." *New York Times*, January 25, 2007.

Legacy World Travel. n.d. "Conspira-Sea Cruise." Legendary World Travel http://www.divinetravels.com/ConspiraSeaCruise.html (Accessed December 12, 2017).

Leman, Patrick J., and Marco Cinnirella. 2013. "Beliefs in Conspiracy Theories and the Need for Cognitive Closure." *Frontiers in Psychology* 4(June). https://doi.org/10.3389/fpsyg.2013.00378 (Accessed December 18, 2017).

Lemon, Don. 2014. "The Mystery of Flight 370: The Theory of Black Holes." YouTube, 1:02. Talking Points Memo TV. Available at: https://www.youtube.com/watch?v=ZpVd7k1Uw6A (Accessed December 17, 2017).

Lenard, Patti Tamara. 2008. "Trust Your Compatriots, but Count Your Change: The Roles of Trust, Mistrust, and Distrust in Democracy." *Political Studies*, 56(2) 2008: 312–332.

Lenard, Patti Tamara. 2012. *Trust, Democracy, and Multicultural Challenges*. University Park: Pennsylvania State University Press.

Lenz, Gabriel S. 2013. *Follow the Leader?: How Voters Respond to Politicians' Policies and Performance*. Chicago: University of Chicago Press.

Leopold, Jason. 2015. "Fearing a 'Catastrophic Incident,' 400 Federal Officers Descended on the Baltimore Protests." https://news.vice.com/article/fearing-a-catastrophic-incident-400-federal-officers-descended-on-the-baltimore-protests (Accessed December 17, 2017).

Lepore, Jill. *New York Burning: Liberty, Slavery, and Conspiracy in Eighteenth-century* Manhattan. New York: Vintage.

Lester, Grant, Beth Wilson, Lynn Griffin, and Paul E. Mullen. 2004. "Unusually Persistent Complainants." *The British Journal of Psychiatry* 184(4): 352–356. DOI: 10.1192/bjp.184.4.352.

Levada-Center. 2017. "Druz'ia' i 'vragi' Rossii." *Levada-tsentr*. https://www.levada.ru/2017/06/05/druzya-i-vragi-rossii-2/ (Accessed November 26, 2017).

Leventhal, G. S. 1980. "What Should Be Done with Equity Theory? New Approaches to the Study of Fairness in Social Relationships." In *Social Exchange: Advances on Theory and Research,* eds. Kenneth J. Gergen, Martin S. Greenberg, and Richard H. Willis. New York: Plenum, 27–54.

Levy, Clifford J. 2007. "Party's Triumph Raises Question of Putin's Plans." *New York Times*, January 15, 2007.

Levy, Neil. 2007. "Radically Socialized Knowledge and Conspiracy Theories." *Episteme* 4(2): 181–192. DOI: 10.3366/epi.2007.4.2.181.

Lewandowsky, NotStephan. "Lewandowsky's Downfall." Video, 3:49. April 25, 2014. https://www.youtube.com/watch?v=bL_QWRgj_-k (Accessed November 9, 2017).

Lewandowsky, Stephan. 2010. "Climate Debate: Opinion Vs. Evidence." http://www.abc.net.au/news/2010-03-11/33178 (Accessed December 24, 2017).

Lewandowsky, Stephan. 2010. "No Climate Change Alternatives." http://www.abc.net.au/news/2010-08-12/35848 (Accessed December 24, 2017).

Lewandowsky, Stephan. 2011. "Bitten by a Sock Puppet, but the Climate Is Still Changing." *ABC News*. http://www.abc.net.au/news/2011-03-28/lewandowsky/45638 (Accessed December 24, 2017).

Lewandowsky, Stephan. 2014. "Recursive Fury Goes Recurrent." [Blog] *Shaping Tomorrow's World*. Available at http://www.shapingtomorrowsworld.org/rf1.html (Accessed December 24, 2017).

Lewandowsky, Stephan. 2014. "The Analysis of Speech." [Blog] *Shaping Tomorrow's World*. Available at http://www.shapingtomorrowsworld.org/rfspeech.html (Accessed December 24, 2017).

Lewandowsky, Stephan. 2014. "The Frontiers Expert Panel." [Blog] *Shaping Tomorrow's World*. Available at http://www.shapingtomorrowsworld.org/xp.html (Accessed December 24, 2017).

Lewandowsky, Stephan. "Revisiting a Retraction." [Blog] *Shaping Tomorrow's World*. Available at http://www.shapingtomorrowsworld.org/rf3.html (Accessed December 24, 2017).

Lewandowsky, Stephan, and Dorothy Bishop. 2016. "Don't Let Transparency Damage Science." *Nature* 529(7587) 459.

Lewandowsky, Stephan, Elisabeth A. Lloyd, and Scott Brophy. 2017. "When Thuncing Trumps Thinking: What Distant Alternative Worlds Can Tell Us About the Real World." *Argumenta*. DOI: 10.23811/52.arg2017.lew.llo.bro.

Lewandowsky, Stephan, Gilles E. Gignac, and Klaus Oberauer. 2013. "The Role of Conspiracist Ideation and Worldviews in Predicting Rejection of Science." *PLoS ONE* 8(10). DOI: 10.1371/journal.pone.0075637.

Lewandowsky, Stephan, Gilles E. Gignac, and Klaus Oberauer. 2015. "The Robust Relationship between Conspiracism and Denial of (Climate) Science." *Psychological Science* 26(5): 667–670.

Lewandowsky, Stephan, Gilles E. Gignac, and Klaus Oberauer. 2015. "Correction: The Role of Conspiracist Ideation and Worldviews in Predicting Rejection of Science." *PLoS ONE* 10(8). DOI: 10.1371/journal.pone.0134773.

Lewandowsky, Stephan, James S. Risbey, and Naomi Oreskes. 2015. "On the Definition and Identifiability of the Alleged "Hiatus" in Global Warming." *Scientific Reports* 5(November): 16784. DOI: 10.1038/srep16784.

Lewandowsky, Stephan, Jasmes S. Risbey, and Naomi Oreskes 2016. "The "Pause" in Global Warming: Turning a Routine Fluctuation into a Problem for Science." *Bulletin of the American Meteorological Society* 97(5): 723–733. DOI: 10.1175/bams-d-14-00106.1.

Lewandowsky, Stephan, James S. Risbey, Michael Smithson, Ben R. Newell, and John Hunter. 2014. "Scientific Uncertainty and Climate Change: Part I. Uncertainty and Unabated Emissions." *Climatic Change* 124(1–2): 21–37. DOI: 10.1007/s10584-014-1082-7.

Lewandowsky, Stephan, James S. Risbey, Michael Smithson, Ben R. Newell, and John Hunter. 2014. "Scientific Uncertainty and Climate Change: Part II. Uncertainty and Mitigation." *Climatic Change* 124(1–2): 39–52. DOI: 10.1007/s10584-014-1083-6.

Lewandowsky, Stephan, John Cook, and Elisabeth Lloyd. 2016. "The 'Alice in Wonderland' Mechanics of the Rejection of (Climate) Science: Simulating Coherence by Conspiracism." *Synthese* 195(1): 1–22. DOI: 10.1007/s11229-016-1198-6.

Lewandowsky, Stephan, John Cook, Klaus Oberauer, and Michael Marriott. 2013. "Recursive Fury: Conspiracist Ideation in the Blogosphere in Response to Research on Conspiracist Ideation." *Frontiers in Psychology* 4(73). DOI: 10.3389/fpsyg.2013.00073.

Lewandowsky, Stephan, John Cook, Klaus Oberauer, Scott Brophy, Elisabeth Lloyd, and Michael Marriott. 2015. "Recurrent Fury: Conspiratorial Discourse in the Blogosphere Triggered by Research on the Role of Conspiracist Ideation in Climate Denial." *Journal of Social and Political Psychology* 3(1): 142–178. DOI: 10.5964/jspp.v3i1.443.

Lewandowsky, Stephan, Klaus Oberauer, and Gilles E. Gignac. 2013. "NASA Faked the Moon Landing—Therefore, (Climate) Science Is a Hoax: An Anatomy of the Motivated Rejection of Science." *Psychological Science* 24(5): 622–633. DOI: 10.1177/0956797612457686.

Lewandowsky, Stephan, Mark C. Freeman, and Michael E. Mann. 2017. "Harnessing the Uncertainty Monster: Putting Quantitative Constraints on the Intergenerational Social Discount Rate." *Global and Planetary Change* 156(C): 155–166. DOI: 10.1016/j.gloplacha.2017.03.007.

Lewandowsky, Stephan, Michael E. Mann, Linda Bauld, Gerard Hastings, and Elizabeth F. Loftus. 2013. "The Subterranean War on Science." *APS Observer* 26(9).

Lewandowsky, Stephan, Naomi Oreskes, James S. Risbey, Ben R. Newell, and Michael Smithson. 2015. "Seepage: Climate Change Denial and Its Effect on the Scientific Community." *Global Environmental Change* 33(July): 1–13. DOI: 10.1016/j.gloenvcha.2015.02.013.

Lewandowsky, Stephan, Timothy Ballard, Klaus Oberauer, and Rasmus Benestad. 2016. "A Blind Expert Test of Contrarian Claims About Climate Data." *Global Environmental Change* 39(C): 91–97. DOI: 10.1016/j.gloenvcha.2016.04.013.

Lewandowsky, Stephan, Ulrich K. H. Ecker, Collen M. Seifert, Norbert Schwarz, and John Cook. 2012. "Misinformation and Its Correction: Continued Influence and Successful Debiasing." *Psychological Science in the Public Interest* 13(3): 106–131. DOI: 10.1177/1529100612451018.

Lewandowsky, Stephan, Ulrich K. H. Ecker, and John Cook. 2017. "Beyond Misinformation: Understanding and Coping with the 'Post-Truth' Era." *Journal of Applied Research in Memory and Cognition* 6(4): 353–369. DOI: 10.1016/j.jarmac.2017.07.008.

Lewandowsky, Stephan, Werner G. K. Stritzke, Klaus Oberauer, and Michael Morales. 2009. "Misinformation and the 'War on Terror': When Memory Turns Fiction into Fact." In *Terrorism and Torture: An Interdisciplinary Perspective,* eds. Werner G. K. Stritzke, Stephan Lewandowsky, David Denemark, and Joseph Clare. Cambridge: Cambridge University Press, 179–203.

Lewandowsky, Stephan, Werner G. K. Stritzke, Klaus Oberauer, and Michael Morales. 2005. "Memory for Fact, Fiction, and Misinformation: The Iraq War 2003." *Psychological Science* 16(3): 190–195. DOI:10.1111/j.0956-7976.2005.00802.x.

Lewicki, R. J., McAllister, D. J., and Bies, R. J., 1998. "Trust and Distrust: New Relationships and Realities." *The Academy of Management Review* 23(3): 438–458.

Li, Nan, Joseph Hilgard, Dietram A. Scheufele, Kenneth M. Winneg, and Kathleen Hall Jamieson. 2016. "Cross-Pressuring Conservative Catholics? Effects of Pope Francis' Encyclical on the U.S. Public Opinion on Climate Change." *Climatic Change* 139(3–4): 367–380. DOI: 10.1007/s10584-016-1821-z.

Lind, Dara. "Waco and Ruby Ridge: The 1990s Standoffs Haunting the Oregon Takeover, Explained." *Vox.com.* https://www.vox.com/2016/1/5/10714746/waco-ruby-ridge-oregon (Accessed December 28, 2017).

Lind, E. Allan, Ruth Kanfer, and P. Christopher Earley. 1990. "Voice, Control, and Procedural Justice: Instrumental and Noninstrumental Concerns in Fairness Judgments." *Journal of Personality and Social Psychology* 59(5): 952–959.

Lindsey, Ursula. 2013. "Tall Tales in Egypt." *New York Times,* September 1, 2013.

Linkins, Jason. 2009. "Ben Stein Dropped as University of Vermont Commencement Speaker." *Huffington Post.* https://www.huffingtonpost.com/2009/02/03/ben-stein-dropped-as-univ_n_163586.html (Accessed December 28, 2017).

Linnekin, Baylen, and Juie Kelly. 2016. "Unless a Federal Court Acts Fast, Vermont's GMO Labeling Law Will Wreak Havoc on the Nation's Food Supply Next Week." http://reason.com/archives/2016/06/25/court-must-put-a-halt-now-to-vermonts-gm (Accessed December 27, 2017).

Lippmann, Walter. 1922. *Public Opinion.* New York: Free Press.

Lippmann, Walter. 1927. *The Phantom Public.* New York: Macmillan.

Lipset, Seymour Martin, and Earl Raab. 1970. *The Politics of Unreason: Right-Wing Extremism in America, 1790–1970.* New York: Harper.

Lipset, Seymour Martin. 1955. "The Sources of the Radical Right." In *The New American Right,* ed. Daniel Bell. New York: Criterion Books.

Lipton, Peter. 2004. *Inference to the Best Explanation.* 2nd ed. London: Routledge.

Litvinenko, Alexander, and Yuri Felshtinsky. 2007. *Blowing Up Russia: The Return of the KGB.* London: Gibson Square Books.

Lobato, Emilio, Jorge Mendoza, Valerie Sims, and Matthew Chin. 2014. "Examining the Relationship between Conspiracy Theories, Paranormal Beliefs, and Pseudoscience Acceptance among a University Population." *Applied Cognitive Psychology* 28(5): 617–625. DOI: 10.1002/acp.3042.

LoBianco, Tom. 2016. "Report: Aide Says Nixon's War on Drugs Targeted Blacks, Hippies." http://www.cnn.com/2016/03/23/politics/john-ehrlichman-richard-nixon-drug-war-blacks-hippie/index.html (Accessed December 28, 2017).

Loewenthal, Leo, and Norbert Gutermann. 1949. *Prophets of Deceit: A Study of the Techniques of the American Agitator.* New York: Harper.

Luhmann, Niklas. 1979. *Trust and Power.* Toronto: John Wiley and Sons.

Lukas, J. Anthony. 1988. *Nightmare: The Underside of the Nixon Years.* New York: Penguin.

Lupia, Arthur. 1994. "Shortcuts Versus Encyclopedias: Information and Voting Behavior in California Insurance Reform Elections." *American Political Science Review* 88(1): 63–76.

Luxmoore, J. 2014. "Polish Church Declares War on Gender Ideology. A Pastoral Letter by Polish Bishops Has Caused Backlash from Some Who See Attack as a 'Witch Hunt'." https://www.osv.com/ (Accesssed Decmber 22, 2017).

MacAskill, Ewan. 2014. "Putin Calls Internet a 'CIA Project' Renewing Fears of Web Breakup." *Guardian.* https://www.theguardian.com/world/2014/apr/24/vladimir-putin-web-breakup-internet-cia (Accessed November 26, 2017).

MacGregor, Karen. 2000. "Conspiracy Theories Fuel Row over AIDS Crisis in South Africa." http://www.independent.co.uk/news/world/africa/conspiracy-theories-fuel-row-over-aids-crisis-in-south-africa-699302.html (Accessed December 27, 2017).

MacLean, Nancy. 2017. *Democracy in Chains: The Deep History of the Radical Right's Stealth Plan for America.* New York: Viking.

Madan, Monique O. 2017. "Professor Who Said Sandy Hook Massacre Was a Hoax Loses Suit to Get His Job Back." *Miami Herald.* http://www.miamiherald.com/news/local/education/article189261704.html (Accessed December 28, 2017).

Maddaus, Gene. 2017. "Harvey Weinstein Hired Investigators to Spy on Accusers, New Yorker Reports." *Variety.* http://variety.com/2017/film/news/harvey-weinstein-spies-accusers-1202608495/ (Accessed December 28, 2017).

Madden, Kelly, Xiaoli Nan, Rowena Briones, and Leah Waks. 2012. "Sorting through Search Results: A Content Analysis of HPV Vaccine Information Online." *Vaccine* 30(25): 3741–3746. DOI: 10.1016/j.vaccine.2011.10.025.

Maddow, Rachel. 2016. "Trump Can't Resist a Conspiracy Theory: Todd." Video, 3:44, 2016. http://www.watchable.com/shows/12164-rachel-maddow/videos/85601-trump-can-t-resist-a-conspiracy-theory-todd (Accessed December 27, 2017).

Malka, Ariel, Jon A. Krosnick, and Gary Langer. 2009. "The Association of Knowledge with Concern about Global Warming: Trusted Information Sources Shape Public Thinking." *Risk Analysis* 29(5): 633–647. DOI: 10.1111/j.1539-6924.2009.01220.x.

Manchester, Julia. 2017. "Trump Promotes Hannity's 'Deep State' Monologue." *The Hill.* http://thehill.com/media/338241-trump-shares-hannity-tweet-on-monologue-calling-for-leakers-to-be-jailed (Accessed December 21, 2017).

Mandik, Pete. 2007. "Shit Happens." *Episteme* 4(2): 205–218. DOI: 10.3366/epi.2007.4.2.205.

Mann, Thomas E., and Norman J. Ornstein. 2016. *It's Even Worse Than It Looks: How the American Constitutional System Collided with the New Politics of Extremism.* New York: Basic Books.

Mansbridge, Jane. 2009. "A 'Selection Model' of Political Representation." *The Journal of Political Philosophy* 17(4): 369–398.

March, Luke. 2002. *The Communist Party in Post-Soviet Russia.* Manchester, UK: Manchester University Press.

Marchlewska, Marta, Aleksandra Cichocka, A., and Malgorzata Kossowska, 2017. "Addicted to Answers: Need for Cognitive Closure and the Endorsement of Conspiracy Theories." *European Journal of Social Psychology.* DOI: 10.1002/ejsp.2308.

Marchlewska, Marta, et al. n.d. "In Search of an Imaginary Enemy: Catholic Collective Narcissism and the Endorsement of Gender Conspiracy Beliefs." Forthcoming.

Marcotte, Amanda. 2015. "4 Reasons Right-wingers are Embracing Vaccine Trutherism." https://www.salon.com/2015/02/07/4_reasons_right_wingers_are_embracing_vaccine_trutherism_partner/ (Accessed December 17, 2017).

Marcus, George, ed. 1999. *Paranoia within Reason.* Chicago: University of Chicago Press.

Marietta, Morgan, David Barker, and Todd Bowser. 2015. "Fact-Checking Polarized Politics: Does the Fact-Check Industry Provide Consistent Guidance on Disputed Realities?" *The Forum: A Journal of Applied Research in Contemporary Politics* 13(4): 577–596.

Markram, Henry. "Rights of Human Subjects in Scientific Papers." [Blog] *Frontiers Blog.* Available at https://www.frontiersin.org/blog/Rights_of_Human_Subjects_in_Scientific_Papers/830 (Accessed December 24, 2017).

Marks, John. 1979. *The Search for the 'Manchurian Candidate': The CIA and Mind Control.* New York: Times Books.

Marrs, Jim. 2015. *Population Control: How Corporate Owners Are Killing Us.* New York: William Morrow.

Marshall, Colin. 2013. "Noam Chomsky Schools 9/11 Truther; Explains the Science of Making Credible Claims." [Blog] *Open Culture.* Available at http://www.openculture.com/2013/10/noam-chomsky-derides-911-truthers.html (Accessed December 1, 2017).

Mashuri, Ali, and Esti Zaduqisti. 2015. "The Effect of Intergroup Threat and Social Identity Salience on the Belief in Conspiracy Theories over Terrorism in Indonesia: Collective Angst as a Mediator." *International Journal of Psychological Research* 8(1): 24–35.

Mason, Fran. 2002. "A Poor Person's Cognitive Mapping." In *Conspiracy Nation,* ed. Peter Knight. New York: New York University Press.

Masood, Salman. 2012. "After Cabinet Officials, Next on the Docket for Pakistan's Chief Justice is His Son." *New York Times,* June 7, 2012.

Mathis-Lilley, Ben. 2016. "Watch Hillary Shred Trump on Releasing His Taxes." [Blog] *The Slatest.* Available at http://www.slate.com/blogs/the_slatest/2016/09/26/hillary_clinton_s_effective_shot_at_trump_over_tax_releases.html (Accessed December 27, 2017).

McAdams, David. 2014. *Game-Changer: Game Theory and the Art of Transforming Strategic Situations.* New York. W.W. Norton.

McCarthy, Charles. 1903. "The Antimasonic Party, A Study of Political Antimasonry in the United States, 1827–1840." In *Annual Report . . . for the Year 1902, 1.* Washington, D.C.: American Historical Association.

McCarthy, Justin. 2014. "Trust in Mass Media Returns to All-Time Low." http://news.gallup.com/poll/176042/trust-mass-media-returns-time-low.aspx (Accessed December 20, 2017).

McCarty, Nolan, Keith T. Poole, and Howard Rosenthal. 2006. *Polarized America: The Dance of Ideology and Unequal Riches.* Cambridge: MIT Press.

McConnachie, James, and Robin Tudge. 2005. *A Rough Guide to Conspiracy Theories.* New York: Rough Guides.

McCright, Aaron M., and Riley E. Dunlap. 2010. "Anti-reflexivity: The American Conservative Movement's Success in Undermining Climate Science and Policy." *Theory, Culture & Society* 27(2–3): 100–133. DOI: 10.1177/0263276409356001.

McGirk, James. 2012. "Jesse Ventura Suspects a Conspiracy About His Show About Conspiracies." *The Atlantic.* https://www.theatlantic.com/entertainment/archive/2012/12/jesse-ventura-suspects-a-conspiracy-about-his-show-about-conspiracies/266361/ (Accessed December 28, 2017).

McHoskey, John W. 1995. "Case Closed? On the John F. Kennedy Assassination: Biased Assimilation of Evidence and Attitude Polarization." *Basic and Applied Social Psychology* 17(3): 395–409.

McKee, Martin, and Pascal Diethelm. 2010. "How the Growth of Denialism Undermines Public Health." *BMJ: British Medical Journal* 341(1): 1309–1311.

McKenzie-McHarg, Andrew, and Rolf Fredheim. 2017. "Cock-ups and Slap-downs: A Quantitative Analysis of Conspiracy Rhetoric in the British Parliament 1916–2015." *Historical Methods: A Journal of Quantitative and Interdisciplinary History* 50(3): 156–169.

McKenzie-McHarg, Andrew. 2018. *The Hidden History of Conspiracy Theory.* Princeton: Princeton University Press.

McKeown, Elaine. 2014. "Climate Deniers Intimidate Journal into Retracting Paper that Finds They Believe Conspiracy Theories." *Scientific American.* https://www.scientificamerican.com/article/climate-deniers-intimidate-journal-into-retracting-paper-that-finds-they-believe-conspiracy-theories/ (Accessed December 24, 2017).

McKeown, Elaine. 2014. "Editors Resign as Retraction Scandal Deepens at Science Journal that Caved In to Intimidation from Climate Deniers." [Blog] *Huffington Post Blog.* Available at https://www.huffingtonpost.com/elaine-mckewon/why-this-is-a-dark-time-for-the-field-of-climate-science_b_5174083.html (Accessed December 24, 2017).

McLaren, Lindsay, Steven Patterson, Salima Thawer, Peter Faris, Deborah McNeil, Melissa Potestio, and Luke Shwart. 2016. "Measuring the Short-Term Impact of Fluoridation Cessation on Dental Caries in Grade 2 Children Using Tooth Surface Indices." *Community Dentistry and Oral Epidemiology* 44(3): 274–282. DOI: 10.1111/cdoe.12215.

McLean, Iain. 2001. *Rational Choice and British Politics: An Analysis of Rhetoric and Manipulation from Peel to Blair.* Oxford: Oxford University Press.

McMahon, Darrin M. 2004. "Conspiracies So Vast: Conspiracy Theory Was Born in the Age of Enlightenment and Has Matastasized in the Age of the Internet. Why Won't It Go Away?" *The Boston Globe.* http://archive.boston.com/news/globe/ideas/articles/2004/02/01/conspiracies_so_vast/ (Accessed December 28, 2017).

McMahon, Paula. 2017. "Jury rules against fired FAU prof James Tracy in free speech case." *SunSentinel,* Dec. 11. http://www.sun-sentinel.com/local/palm-beach/fl-reg-james-tracy-fau-closings-20171208-story.html.

Meacher, Michael. 2003. "This War on Terrorism Is Bogus." *The Guardian.* https://www.theguardian.com/politics/2003/sep/06/september11.iraq (Accessed December 20, 2017).

Media Matters Staff. 2016. "Trump Advisor Roger Stone Claims Clinton Was Placed on 'Oxygen Tank' Immediately After Presidential Debate." [Blog] *Media Matters for America.* Available at https://www.mediamatters.org/video/2016/09/27/trump-adviser-roger-stone-claims-clinton-was-placed-oxygen-tank-immediately-after-presidential/213346 (Accessed December 27, 2017).

Media Matters Staff. 2016. "Trump Ally Roger Stone on Hillary Clinton: 'Bitch Can Hardly Stand UP.'" [Blog] *Media Matters for America.* Available at https://www.mediamatters.org/blog/2016/10/25/trump-ally-roger-stone-hillary-clinton-bitch-can-hardly-stand/214090 (Accessed December 27, 2017).

Meek, James Gordon. 2008. "FBI Was Told to Blame Anthrax Scare on Al Qaeda by White House Officials." *New York Daily News,* 2 August 2008.

Mele, Alfred. 2001. *Self-Deception Unmasked.* Princeton: Princeton University Press.

Mele, Christopher. 2017. "Minnesota See Largest Outbreak of Measles in Almost 30 Years." *New York Times,* May 5, 2017.

Melley, Timothy. 2000. *Empire of Conspiracy: The Culture of Paranoia in Postwar America.* Ithaca: Cornell University Press.

Merlan, Ann. 2016. "Sail (Far) Away: At Sea with America's Largest Floating Gathering of Conspiracy Theorists." https://jezebel.com/sail-far-away-at-sea-with-americas-largest-floating-1760900554 (Accessed December 12, 2017).

Merton, Robert. 1968. "The Self-Fulfilling Prophecy." *Social Theory and Social Structure. 1968 Enlarged Edition.* New York: Free Press.

Michael, Meron Tesfa. 2002. "Africa Bites the Bullet on Genetically Modified Food Aid." http://www.worldpress.org/Africa/737.cfm (Accessed December 27, 2017).

Mickey, Robert, Steven Levitsky, and Ahmad Way. 2017. "Is America Still Safe for Democracy: Why the United States Is in Danger of Backsliding." *Foreign Affairs* 96: 20–29.

Mikkelson, Barbara. 2014. "Flashing Headlights Gang Initiation." https://snopes.com/crime/gangs/lightsout.asp (Accessed December 17, 2017).

Mikkelson, David. 2015. "Sandy Hook Exposed." https://www.snopes.com/politics/guns/newtown.asp (Accessed December 20, 2017).

Miller, D. A. 1989. *The Novel and the Police*. Berkley: University of California Press.

Miller, Joanne M., Kyle L. Saunders, and Christina E. Farhart. 2016. "Conspiracy Endorsement as Motivated Reasoning: The Moderating Roles of Political Knowledge and Trust." *American Journal of Political Science* 60(4): 824–844.

Miller, Jon D. 1998. "The Measurement of Civic Scientific Literacy." *Public Understanding of Science* 7(3): 203–223. DOI: 10.1088/0963-6625/7/3/001.

Miller, Jon D. 2004. "Public Understanding of, and Attitudes toward, Scientific Research: What We Know and What We Need to Know." *Public Understanding of Science* 13(3): 273–294. DOI: 10.1177/0963662504044908.

Miller, Manjari Chatterjee. 2013. *Wronged by Empire: Post-Imperial Ideology and Foreign Policy in India and China*. Palo Alto: Stanford University Press.

Miller, Nick. 2015. "Crash Conspiracy Theories Alive and Well Organised: Mh17: One Year On." *The Age* 2015: 12. Web.

Miller, Stuart. 2012. "Brooklyn Pipeline Project Raises a Host of Worries." *New York Times*, August 30, 2012.

Mills, C. Wright. 1940. "Situated Actions and Vocabularies of Motive." *American Sociological Review* 5(6): 904–913.

Mindich, David T. Z. 1998. *Just the Facts: How "Objectivity" Came to Define American Journalism*. New York: New York University Press

Mirowsky, J., and C.E. Ross. 1983. "Paranoia and the Structure of Powerlessness." *American Sociological Review* 48(2): 228–239.

Mishler, William, and Richard Rose. 2005. "What are the Political Consequences of Trust? A Test of Cultural and Institutional Theories in Russia." *Comparative Political Studies* 38(9): 1050–1078.

MIT Technology Review. 2014. "Data Mining Reveals How Conspiracy Theories Emerge on Facebook." *Technology Review.* [Blog] *arXiv.* Available at https://www.technologyreview.com/s/525616/data-mining-reveals-how-conspiracy-theories-emerge-on-facebook/ (Accessed December 17, 2017).

Mocanu, Delia, Luca Rossi, Qian Zhang, Marton Karsai, and Walter Quattrociocchi. 2015. "Collective Attention in the Age of (Mis)information." *Computers in Human Behavior* 51: 1198–1204.

Morey, Richard D., Christopher D. Chambers, Peter J. Etchels, Christine R. Harris, Rink Hoekstra, Daniël Lakens, Stephan Lewandowsky, Candice Coker Morey, Daniel P. Newman, Felix D Schönbrodt, Wolf Vanpaemel, Eric-Jan Wagenmakers, and Rolf A. Zwann. 2016. "The Peer Reviewers' Openness Initiative: Incentivizing Open Research Practices through Peer Review." *Royal Society Open Science* 3(1). DOI: 10.1098/rsos.150547.

Moscovici, Serge. 1987. "The Conspiracy Mentality." In *Changing Conceptions of Conspiracy*, ed. Carl F. Graumann, and Serge Moscovici. New York: Springer-Verlag, 151–169.

Moynihan, Colin. 2011. "Fight on Islamic Center Flares Anew as Ex-firefighter Takes Case to Court." *New York Times*, March 16, 2011.

Muirhead, Russell, and Nancy L. Rosenblum. 2016. "Speaking Truth to Conspiracy: Partisanship and Trust." *Critical Review* 28(1): 63–88.

Mullen, Paul E., and Grant Lester. 2006. "Vexatious Litigants and Unusually Persistent Complainants and Petitioners: From Querulous Paranoia to Querulous Behaviour." *Behavioral Sciences & the Law* 24(3): 333–349. DOI: 10.1002/bsl.671.

Munro, Geoffrey D., Carrie Weih, and Jeffrey Tsai. 2010. "Motivated Suspicion: Asymmetrical Attributions of the Behavior of Political Ingroup and Outgroup Members." *Basic and Applied Social Psychology* 32(2): 173–184.

Musgrave, Paul. 2017. "Donald Trump is Normalizing Paranoia and Conspiracy Thinking in U.S. Politics." *Washington Post*. https://www.washingtonpost.com/posteverything/wp/2017/01/12/donald-trump-has-brought-us-the-american-style-in-paranoid-politics/?utm_term=.1f1f6c9963e5 (Accessed December 21, 2017).

Mutz, Diana, and Byron Reeves. 2005. "The New Videomalaise: The Effects of Televised Incivility on Political Trust." *American Political Science Review* 99(1) 2005: 1–15.

Nacol, Emily C. "The Risks of Political Authority: Trust, Knowledge and Political Agency in Locke's *Second Treatise*." *Political Studies* 59(3): 580–595.

Narochnitskaia, Nataliia. 2007. *"Nataliia Narochnitskaia: 'My dolzhny stat' natsiei."* http://www.narochnitskaia.ru/in-archive/nataliya-narochnitskaya-quot-myi-dolzhnyi-stat-natsiey-quot.html?view=full (Accessed November 26, 2017).

National Academies of Science. 2010. *Advancing the Science of Climate Change.* Washington, D.C.: The National Academies Press.

National Science Board. 2014. Science and Engineering Indicators 2014 (No. NSB 14-01) *National Science Foundation*. Arlington, VA: National Science Foundation.

Nattrass, Nicoli. 2012. "How Bad Ideas Gain Social Traction." *The Lancet* 380(9839): 332–333. DOI: 10.1016/S1040-6736(12)61238-0.

Nattrass, Nicoli. 2013. "Understanding the Origins and Prevalence of AIDS Conspiracy Beliefs in the United States and South Africa." *Sociology of Health & Illness* 35(1):113–129. DOI: 10.1111/j.1467-9566.2012.01480.x.

Nazaryan, Alexander. 2017. "Russian Plot to Elect Trump Included Jill Stein, According to Latest Gleeful Twitter Theory." *Newsweek*. http://www.newsweek.com/donald-trump-jr-jill-stein-putin-russia-senate-639422 (Accessed December 27, 2017).

Nefes, Turkay Salim. 2012. "The History of the Social Constructions of Dönmes (Converts)." *Journal of Historical Sociology* 25(3): 413–439.

Nefes, Turkay Salim. 2013. "Political Parties' Perceptions and Uses of Anti-Semitic Conspiracy Theories in Turkey." *The Sociological Review* 61(2): 247–264.

Nefes, Turkay Salim. 2013. "Ziya Gökalp's Adaptation of Emile Durkheim's Sociology in his Formulation of the Modern Turkish Nation." *International Sociology* 28(3): 335–350.

Nefes, Turkay Salim. 2014. "Rationale of Conspiracy Theorizing: Who Shot the President Chen Shui-bian?" *Rationality and Society* 26(3): 373–394.

Nefes, Turkay Salim. 2015. "Scrutinizing Impacts of Conspiracy Theories on Readers' Political Views: A Rational Choice Perspective on Anti-Semitic Rhetoric in Turkey." *The British Journal of Sociology* 66(3): 557–575.

Nefes, Turkay Salim. 2017. "The Impacts of the Turkish Government's Conspiratorial Framing about the Gezi Park Protests." *Social Movement Studies* 16(5): 610–622. DOI: 10.1080/14742837.2017.1319269.

Neville, Delvan R., A. Jason Phillips, Richard D. Brodeur, and Kathryn Higley. 2014. "Trace Levels of Fukushima Disaster Radionuclides in East Pacific Albacore." *Environmental Science & Technology* 48(9): 4739–4743. DOI: 10.1021/es500129b.

Newheiser, Anna Kaisa, Miguel Farias, and Nicole Tausch. 2011. "The Functional Nature of Conspiracy Beliefs: Examining the Underpinnings of Belief in the Da Vinci Code Conspiracy." *Personality and Individual Differences* 51(8): 1007–1011. DOI: 10.1016/j.paid.2011.08.011.

Nicholls, Robert J., et al. 2011. "Sea-Level Rise and Its Possible Impacts Given a 'Beyond 4 C World' in the Twenty-First Century." *Philosophical Transactions of the Royal Society of London A: Mathematical, Physical and Engineering Sciences* 369(1934): 161–181.

Nicolia, Alessandro, Albert Manzo, Fabio Veronesi, and Daniele Rosellini. 2013. "An Overview of the Last 10 Years of Genetically Engineered Crop Safety Research." *Critical Reviews in Biotechnology* 34(1): 77–88. http://www.agrobio.org/bfiles/fckimg/Nicolia%202013.pdf (Accessed December 1, 2017).

Nordland, Rod. 2009. "Sunnis and Shiites See an Omen for Reconciliation in Iraq." *New York Times*, August 23, 2009.

Norman, Eric B., Christopher T. Angell, and Perry A. Chodash. 2011. "Observations of Fallout From the Fukushima Reactor Accident in San Francisco Bay Area Rainwater." *Plos ONE* 6(9). DOI: 10.1371/journal.pone.0024330.

North, Douglass C. 1990. *Institutions, Institutional Change, and Economic Performance.* Cambridge: Cambridge University Press.

Norton, Michael, and Samuel Sommers. 2011. "Whites See Racism as a Zero-Sum Game That They Are Now Losing." *Perspectives on Psychological Science* 6(3): 215–218.

Nye, Russel B. 1972. "The Slave Power Conspiracy: 1830–1860." In *Conspiracy: The Fear of Subversion in American History*, eds. Richard O. Curry and Thomas M. Brown. New York: Holt, Rinehart, and Winston.

Nyhan, Brendan. 2009. "9/11 and Birther Misperceptions Compared." [Blog] *The Blog.* Available at https://www.huffingtonpost.com/brendan-nyhan/911_and_birther_misperceptions_b_726561.html (Accessed December 20, 2017).

Nyhan, Brendan. 2012. "Enabling the Jobs Report Conspiracy Theory." *Columbia Journalism Review,* October 16, 2012. http://www.cjr.org/united_states_project/enabling_the_jobs_report_conspiracy_theory.php?page=all#sthash.OLFq8PWf.dpuf (Accessed October 30, 2014).

Nyhan, Brendan. 2017. "Why More Democrats Are Now Embracing Conspiracy Theories." *New York Times.* https://www.nytimes.com/2017/02/15/upshot/why-more-democrats-are-now-embracing-conspiracy-theories.html (Accessed December 29, 2017).

Nyhan, Brendan, and Jason Reifler. 2010. "When Corrections Fail: The Persistence of Political Misperceptions." *Political Behavior* 32(2): 303–330.

Nyhan, Brendan, and Jason Reifler. 2015. "Does Correcting Myths about the Flu Vaccine Work? An Experimental Evaluation of the Effects of Corrective Information." *Vaccine* 33(3): 459–464.

Nyhan, Brendan, Eric McGhee, John Sides, Seth Masket, and Steven Greene. 2012. "One Vote out of Step? The Effects of Salient Roll Call Votes in the 2010 Election." *American Politics Research* 40(5): 844–879.

Nyhan, Brendan, Jason Reifler, and Peter A. Ubel. 2013. "The Hazards of Correcting Myths About Health Care Reform." *Medical Care* 51(2): 127–132.

Nyhan, Brendan, Jason Reifler, Sean Richey, and Gary L. Freed. 2014. "Effective Messages in Vaccine Promotion: A Randomized Trial." *Pediatrics* 133(4): e835–e842. DOI: 10.1542/peds.2013-2365.

O'Grady, Siobhán. 2016. "Conspiracy Theorists Think Hillary Clinton Has a Body Double. She's Not Alone." *Foreign Policy.* http://foreignpolicy.com/2016/09/12/conspiracy-theorists-think-hillary-clinton-has-a-body-double-shes-not-alone/ (Accessed December 27, 2017).

O'Loughlin, John, Gerard Toal, and Vladimir Kolosov. 2017. "The Rise and Fall of 'Novorossiya': Examining Support for a Separatist Geopolitical Imaginary in Southeast Ukraine." *Post-Soviet Affairs* 33(2) 2017: 124–144.

O'Neill, Onora. 2002. *A Question of Trust: The BBC Reith Lectures.* Cambridge: Cambridge University Press.

Oliver, Eric J., and Thomas Wood. 2014. "Conspiracy Theories and the Paranoid Style(s) of Mass Opinion." *American Journal of Political Science* 58(4): 952–966.

Oliver, Eric, and Thomas Wood. 2014. "Medical Conspiracy Theories and Health Behaviors in the United States." *JAMA Internal Medicine* 174(5): 817–818. DOI: 10.1001/jamainternmed.2014.190.

Olmsted, Kathryn S. 1996. *Challenging the Secret Government: The Post-Watergate Investigations of the CIA and FBI.* Chapel Hill: University of North Carolina Press.

Olmsted, Kathryn S. 2009. *Real Enemies: Conspiracy Theories and American Democracy, World War I to 9/11.* Oxford: Oxford University Press.

Onlooker1001. 2009. "*Podlye plany Khodorkovskogo i YuKOSa v otnoshenii Rossii.*" YouTube video, 10:05. Posted December 12, 2009. https://www.youtube.com/watch?v=jIv-aaiOaHw (Accessed November 26, 2017).

Oppenheimer, Jerry. 2015. *RFK Jr.: Robert F. Kennedy, Jr. and the Dark Side of the Dream.* New York: St. Martin's Press.

Oreskes, Naomi. 2004. "The Scientific Consensus on Climate Change." *Science* 306(5702):1686. DOI: 10.1126/science.1103618.

Oreskes, Naomi, and Erik Conway. 2010. *Merchants of Doubt: How a Handful of Scientists Obscured the Truth on Issues from Tobacco Smoke to Global Warming.* London: Bloomsbury Press.

Orosz, Gábor, Péter Krekó, Benedek Paskuj, István Tóth-Király, Beáta Böthe, and Christine Roland-Lévy. 2016. "Changing Conspiracy Beliefs Through Rationality and Ridiculing." *Frontiers in Psychology* 7: 1525.

Orr, Martin, and Ginna Husting. 2007. "Dangerous Machinery: 'Conspiracy Theorist' as a Transpersonal Strategy of Exclusion." *Symbolic Interaction* 30(2): 127–50.

Osher, Christopher N. 2010. "Bike Agenda Spins Cities toward U.N. Control, Maes Warns." *Denver Post.* https://www.denverpost.com/2010/08/03/bike-agenda-spins-cities-toward-u-n-control-maes-warns/ (Accessed December 28, 2017).

Osmundson, Joseph. 2011. "'I Was Born This Way': Is Sexuality Innate and Should it Matter?" *LGBTQ Policy Journal at the Harvard Kennedy School* 1: 15–27.

Ostrom, Elinor. 1990. *Governing the Commons: The Evolution of Institutions for Collective Action.* Cambridge: Cambridge University Press.

Ostrom, Elinor. 2010. "Beyond Markets and States: Polycentric Governance of Complex Economic Systems." *American Economic Review* 100(3): 641–72.

Ott, Brian L. 2017. "The Age of Twitter: Donald J. Trump and the Politics of Debasement." *Critical Studies in Media Communication* 34(1): 59–68. DOI: 10.1080/15295036.2016.1266686.

Oushakine, Seguei. 2009. *The Patriotism of Despair: Nation, War and Loss in Russia.* Ithaca: Cornell University Press.

Oxford English Dictionaries. 2016. "Word of the Year: 2016." https://en.oxforddictionaries.com/word-of-the-year/word-of-the-year-2016 (Accessed December 30, 2017).

Pagán, Victoria E. 2012. *Conspiracy Theory in Latin Literature.* Austin: University of Texas Press.

Papineau, David. 1993. *Philosophical Naturalism.* Oxford: Blackwell Publishers.

Parent, Joseph, and Joseph Uscinski. 2016. "People Who Believe in Conspiracy Theories are More Likely to Endorse Violence." [Blog] Monkey Cage. Available at https://www.washingtonpost.com/news/monkey-cage/wp/2016/02/05/are-conspiracy-theorists-plotting-to-blow-up-the-u-s/?utm_term=.395c94e7c119 (Accessed December 28, 2017).

Park, Bill. 2008. "Turkey's Deep State: Ergenekon and the Threat to Democratisation in the Republic." *The RUSI Journal* 153(5): 54–59.

Parry, Geraint. 1976. "Trust, distrust and consensus." *British Journal of Political Science* 6(2): 129–142.

Parry, Richard Lloyd. 2001. "Al-Qa'ida Almost 'immune to attack' Inside its Hi-tech Underground Lair." *The Independent,* November 27, 2001.

Pasek, Josh, Gaurav Sood, and Jon A. Krosnick. 2015. "Misinformed About the Affordable Care Act? Leveraging Certainty to Assess the Prevalence of Misperceptions." *Journal of Communication* 65(4): 660–673. DOI: 10.1111/jcom.12165.

Pasek, Josh. 2017. "It's Not My Consensus: Motivated Reasoning and the Sources of Scientific Illiteracy." *Public Understanding of Science.* DOI: 10.1177/0963662517733681.

Patel, David. 2013. "Preference Falsification, Revolutionary Coordination, and the Tahrir Square Model." *Annual Proceedings of the Wealth and Well-Being of Nations* 4: 61–71.

Paterson, Tony. 2014. "Ukraine Crisis: Angry Angela Merkel Questions Whether Putin is in Touch with Reality." *Telegraph.* http://www.telegraph.co.uk/news/worldnews/europe/ukraine/10673235/Ukraine-crisis-Angry-Angela-Merkel-questions-whether-Putin-is-in-touch-with-reality.html (Accessed 26 November 2017).

Patricknelson750. 2015. "Neoliberalism Is a Conspiracy of the Rich." [Blog] *patricknelson750.* Available at https://patricknelson750.wordpress.com/2015/01/06/neoliberalism-is-a-conspiracy-of-the-rich/ (Accessed May 26, 2017).

Pearlstein, Rick Facebook page. Accessed December 7, 2017. https://www.facebook.com/photo.php?fbid=10105442217265045&set=a.10101400332564385.1073741830.27435697&type=3&theater.

Peffley, Mark, and Jon Hurwitz. 2010. *Justice In America: The Separate Realities of Blacks and Whites.* Cambridge: Cambridge University Press.

Pelkmans, Mathijs, and Rhys Machold. 2011. "Conspiracy Theories and Their Truth Trajectories." *Focaal—Journal of Global and Historical Anthropology* 59(March): 66–80.

Pennock, Robert. 2001. Naturalism, Evidence, and Creationism: The Case of Phillip Johnson." In *Intelligent Design and its Critics: Philosophical, Theological and Scientific Perspectives,* ed. Robert T. Penncock. Cambridge: The MIT Press, 77–98.

Pérez-Peña, Richard. 2012. "Sandusky's Adopted Son, Claiming Abuse, Offered to Testify at Trial." *New York Times,* June 22, 2012.

Pérez-Peña, Richard. 2012. "Ousted Head of University is Reinstated in Virginia." *New York Times,* June 27, 2012.

Perlmutter, David D., and Nicole Smith Dahmen. 2008. "(In)Visible Evidence: Pictorially Enhanced Disbelief in the Apollo Moon Landings." *Visual Communication* 7(2): 229–251.

Peskin, Allan. 1999. *Garfield.* Kent, OH: Kent State University Press.

Pesta, Abigail. 2016. "What Drives Someone to Confront Grieving Families?" http://www.cosmopolitan.com/politics/a58661/young-women-killed-gun-truthers/ (Accessed December 28, 2017).

Petrocik, John R. 1996. "Issue Ownership in Presidential Elections, with a 1980 Case Study." *American Journal of Political Science* 40(3): 825–850.

Pettit, Philip. 2012. *On the People's Terms: A Republic Theory and Model of Democracy.* Cambridge: Cambridge University Press.

Pew Research Center. 2017. "Public Trust in Government, 1958–2017." http://www.people-press.org/2017/05/03/public-trust-in-government-1958-2017/ (Accessed December 20, 2017).

Pfau, Michael. 2005. *The Political Style of Conspiracy: Chase, Sumner, and Lincoln.* East Lansing: Michigan State University Press.

Pigden, Charles. 1995. "Popper Revisited, or What is Wrong with Conspiracy Theories?" *Philosophy of the Social Sciences* 25(1): 3–34.

Pigden, Charles. 2007. "Conspiracy Theories and Conventional Wisdom." *Episteme* 4(2): 219–232.

Pigden, Charles R. 2016. "Are Conspiracy Theorists Epistemically Vicious?" In *Blackwell Companion to Applied Philosophy,* eds. Kasper Lipert-Rasmussen, Kimberley Brownlee, and David Coady. Chichester, UK: Wiley Blackwell, 120–132.

Pioneer Press. 2013. "Retired UMD Professor Theorizes that Government Behind Newtown Massacre." *Twin Cities Pioneer Press,* January 4. https://www.twincities.com/2013/01/04/retired-umd-professor-theorizes-that-government-behind-newtown-massacre/.

Pipes, Daniel. 1996. *The Hidden Hand: Middle East Fears of Conspiracy.* Basingstoke: Macmillan.

Pipes, Daniel. 1997. *Conspiracy: How the Paranoid Style Flourishes and Where It Comes From.* New York: Free Press.

Plait, Phil. 2013. "Antivaccine Megachurch Linked to Texas Measles Outbreak." [Blog] *Bad Astronomy.* Avaiable at http://www.slate.com/blogs/bad_astronomy/2013/08/26/antivax_communities_get_measles_outbreaks_linked_to_denial_of_vaccines.html (Accessed December 27, 2017).

Plotkin, Mariano Ben. 2002. *Mañana es San Perón: A Cultural History of Perón's Argentina.* Wilmington, DE: Scholarly Resources.

Popper, Karl R. 1959. *The Logic of Scientific Discovery.* New York: Harper & Row.

Popper, Karl R. 1966. *The Open Society and Its Enemies, Vol. 2: The High Tide of Profecy: Hegel, Marx, and the Aftermath.* 5th edition. London and New York: Routledge & Kegan Paul.

Popper, Karl R. [1963] 2002. *Conjectures and Refutations.* London: Routledge.

Povinec, Pavel P., Katsumi Hirose, and Michio Aoyama. 2013. *Fukushima Accident: Radioactivity Impact on the Environment.* Amsterdam: Elsevier.

Powell, Michael. 2013. "The Quashing of a Case against a Christie Ally." *New York Times*, October 11, 2013.

Pozner, Lenny, and Veronique Pozner. 2015. "Sandy Hook Massacre 3rd Anniversary: Two parents target FAU conspiracy theorist." *SunSentinel*, December 10. http://www.sun-sentinel.com/opinion/commentary/sfl-on-sandy-hook-anniversary-two-parents-target-fau-professor-who-taunts-family-victims-20151210-story.html.

Prasad, Jamuna. 1935. "The Psychology of Rumour: A Study Relating to the Great Indian Earthquake of 1934." *British Journal of Psychology* 26(1): 1–15.

Proctor, Robert. 2011. *Golden Holocaust: Origins of the Cigarette Catastrophe and the Case for Abolition*. Berkeley and Los Angeles: University of California Press.

Public Health Service, U.S. Dept. of Health and Human Services. 1999. "Thimerosal in Vaccines: A Joint Statement of the American Academy of Pediatrics and the Public Health Service," *Morbidity and Mortality Weekly Report* 48(26): 563–565.

Puiggrós, Rodolfo. 1974. "El nuevo peronismo en la universidad. Declaraciones a *Confirmado*, 12 de Junio 1973." *La Universidad Del Pueblo*. Buenos Aires: Crisis.

Putin, Vladimir. 2005. "Annual Address to the Federal Assembly of the Russian Federation." http://archive.kremlin.ru/eng/speeches/2005/04/25/2031_type70029type82912_87086.shtml (Accessed November 26, 2017).

Putin, Vladimir. 2014. "Address by President of the Russian Federation, Official Internet Resources of the President of Russia, March 18, 2004." http://en.kremlin.ru/events/president/news/20603 (Accessed December 30, 2017).

Putin, Valdimir. 2015. "Federal Security Service Board Meeting." http://en.kremlin.ru/events/president/news/49006 (Accessed December 21, 2017).

Putnam, Hillary. 2002. *The Collapse of the Fact/Value Dichotomy and Other Essays*. Cambridge: Harvard University Press.

Putnam, Robert D., Robert Leonardi, and Raffaella Y. Nanetti. 1994. *Making Democracy Work: Civic Traditions in Modern Italy*. Princeton: Princeton University Press.

Raab, Marius Hans, Nikolas Auer, Stefan A. Ortlieb, and Claus-Christian Carbon. 2013. "The Sarrazin Effect: The Presence of Absurd Statements in Conspiracy Theories Makes Canonical Information Less Plausible." *Frontiers in Psychology* 4(July): 453. DOI: 10.3389/fpsyg.2013.00453.

Radnitz, Scott. 2016. "Paranoia with a Purpose: Conspiracy Theory and Political Coalitions in Kyrgyzstan." *Post-Soviet Affairs* 32(5): 474–489.

Räikkä, Juha. 2009. "On Political Conspiracy Theories." *Journal of Political Philosophy* 17(2): 185–201.

Räikkä, Juha. 2014. *Social Justice in Practice: Questions in Ethics and Political Philosophy*. New York: Springer.

Räikkä, Juha. 2018. "Conspiracies and Conspiracy Theories: An Introduction." *Argumenta* 5. DOI: 10.23811/51.arg2017.rai.

Rainsford, Sarah. 2008. "'Deep State Plot' Grips Turkey." *BBC*. http://news.bbc.co.uk/1/hi/world/europe/7225889.stm (Accessed December 22, 2017).

Raphael, Lutz. 1996. "Die Verwissenschaftlichung des Sozialen als methodische und konzeptionelle Herausforderung für eine Sozialgeschichte des 20. Jahrhunderts." *Geschichte und Gesellschaft* 22(2): 165–193.

Readfearn, Graham. 2014. "Science Journal Set to Retract Paper Linking Climate Change Scepticism to Conspiracy Theorists after Sceptics Shout Libel." [Blog] *Desmogblog: Clearing the PR Pollution that Clouds Climate Science*. Available at https://www.desmogblog.com/2014/03/20/science-journal-retracts-paper-showing-how-climate-change-sceptics-were-conspiracy-theorists-after-sceptics-shout (Accessed December 24, 2017).

Reedy, Justin, Chris Wells, and John Gastil. 2014. "How Voters Become Misinformed: An Investigation of the Emergence and Consequences of False Factual Beliefs." *Social Science Quarterly* 95(5):1399–1418.

Regina, V. 2016. "Dana Ryan Durnford: Reasons for Judgement of The Honourable Judge R. Sutton." *The Japan Times*. https://www.japantimes.co.jp/news/2016/09/23/national/crime-legal/canada-activist-found-guilty-harassing-scientists-fukushima-fallout/ (Accessed December 29, 2017).

Reinhart, Carmen, and Kenneth Rogoff. 2010. "Growth in a Time of Debt." *American Economic Review* 100(2): 573–578.

Reinhart, Carmen, Vincent Reinhart, and Kenneth Rogoff. 2012. "Public Debt Overhangs: Advanced Economy Episodes Since 1800." *Journal of Economic Perspectives* 26(3):69–86.

Remizov, Mikhail. 2014. "Zhertva krymskoï kampanii." *Izvestiia*. http://iz.ru/news/567486 (Accessed November 26, 2017).

Repp, Martin. 2005. "Aum Shinrikyo and the Aum Incident." In *Controversial New Religions*, eds. James R. Lewis. and Jesper Aagaard Petersen. Oxford: Oxford University Press, 153–194.

Representative Maxine Waters to Attorney General Janet Reno, personal correspondence. August 30, 1996. https://www.narconews.com/darkalliance/drugs/library/32.htm (Accessed December 30, 2017).

Reuters Staff. "Turks Believe Cleric Gulen was Behind Coup Attempt: Survey." *Reuters.com*. http://www.reuters.com/article/us-turkey-security-survey-idUSKCN1060P1 (Accessed December 21, 2017).

Revkin, Andrew. 2003. "Politics Reasserts Itself in the Debate Over Climate Change and Its Hazards." *New York Times*, August 5, 2003.

Riker, William H. 1982. *Liberalism Against Populism: A Confrontation Between the Theory of Democracy and the Theory of Social Choice*. Long Grove, IL: Waveland Press.

Riker, William H. 1986. *The Art of Political Manipulation*. New Haven: Yale University Press.

Risbey, James S., and Stephan Lewandowsky. 2017. "Climate Science: The 'Pause' Unpacked." *Nature* 545(7652): 37–39. DOI: 10.1038/545037a.

Risbey, James S., Stephan Lewandowsky, Clothilde Langlais, Didier P. Monselesan, Terence J. O'Kane, and Naomi Oreskes. 2014. "Well-Estimated Global Surface Warming in Climate Projections Selected for Enso Phase." *Nature Climate Change* 4(9): 835–840. DOI:10.1038/nclimate2310.

Risbey, James S., Stephan Lewandowsky, John R. Hunter, and Didier P. Monselesan. 2015. "Betting Strategies on Fluctuations in the Transient Response of Greenhouse Warming." *Philosophical Transactions of the Royal Society A: Mathematical, Physical and Engineering Sciences* 373(2055). DOI:10.1098/rsta.2014.0463.

Roberts, David. 2016. "Why Conspiracy Theories Flourish on the Right." Vox.com. https://www.vox.com/2015/12/10/9886222/conspiracy-theories-right-wing (Accessed December 28, 2017).

Robertson, David G. 2013. "(Always) Living in the End Times: The 'Rolling Prophecy' of the Conspiracy Milieu." In *Prophecy in the New Millennium: When Prophecies Persist*, eds. Sarah Harvey and Suzanne Newcombe. Farnham, UK: Ashgate, 207–219.

Robertson, David G. 2014. "Transformation: Whitley Strieber's Paranormal Gnosis." *Nova Religio* 18(1): 58–78.

Robertson, David G. 2016. *Conspiracy Theories, UFOs and the New Age: Millennial Conspiracism*. London: Bloomsbury.

Robertson, David G. 2017. "Hermeneutics of Suspicion: Scientology and Conspiracism." In *Handbook of Scientology*, eds. James R. Lewis and Kjersti Hellesøy. Leiden, Netherlands: Brill, 300–318.

Robertson, David G. 2017. "The Hidden Hand: Why Religious Studies Need to Take Conspiracy Theories Seriously." *Religion Compass* 11(3–4): e12233.

Robison, Will. 2016. "Hillary Clinton: Jimmy Kimmel Discusses Pickle Jar Conspiracy." http://ew.com/article/2016/08/26/hillary-clinton-jimmy-kimmel-pickle-jar-conspiracy/ (Accessed December 27, 2017).

Rock, David. 1992. *Authoritarian Argentina: The Nationalist Movement, Its History and Its Impact*. Berkeley: University of California Press.

Rohan, Tim. 2013. "Groups Want Bad Image of Penn State to Go Away." *New York Times,* September 17, 2013.

Roisman, Joseph. 2006. *The Rhetoric of Conspiracy in Ancient Athens.* Berkeley: University of California Press.

Romer, Thomas, and Howard Rosenthal. 1978. "Political Resource Allocation, Controlled Agendas, and the Status Quo." *Public Choice* 33(4): 27–43.

Roos, J. Micah. 2014. "Measuring science or religion? A measurement analysis of the National Science Foundation sponsored science literacy scale 2006–2010." *Public Understanding of Science* 23(7): 797–813. DOI: 10.1177/0963662512464318.

Root, Wayne Allyn. 2010. "Obama's Agenda: Overwhelm the System." *Las Vegas Review Journal.* http://www.reviewjournal.com/opinion/obamas-agenda-overwhelm-the-system/ (Accessed December 20, 2017).

Rosbalt.RU. 2014. "Strelkov: Surkov vedet Rossiiu k pozornoi kapituliatsii v Novorossii i Krymu." *Rosbalt.* http://www.rosbalt.ru/ukraina/2014/12/23/1351475.html (Accessed November 26, 2017).

Rosenberg, Paul. 2016. "Conspiracy Theories Are for Losers: Science Explains Why Conservatives See Sneaky Cabals in Every Defeat." *Salon.* https://www.salon.com/2016/03/19/conspiracy_theories_are_for_losers_science_explains_why_conservatives_see_sneaky_cabals_in_every_defeat/ (Accessed December 28, 2017).

Rosenberg, Paul. 2017. "Conspiracy Theory's Big Comeback: Deep Paranoia Runs Free in the Age of Donald Trump." *Salon.* https://www.salon.com/2017/01/01/conspiracy-theorys-big-comeback-deep-paranoia-runs-free-in-the-age-of-donald-trump/ (Accessed December 28, 2017).

Rosenblum, Nancy. 2008. *On the Side of the Angels. An Appreciation of Parties and Partisanship.* Princeton: Princeton University Press.

Rosenthal, Andrew. 2013. "No Comment Necessary: Conspiracy Nation." [Blog] *Taking Note.* Available at https://takingnote.blogs.nytimes.com/2013/01/17/no-comment-necessary-conspiracy-nation/ (Accessed December 28, 2017).

Rosnow, Ralph L. 1991. "Inside Rumor: A Personal Journey." *American Psychologist* 46(5): 484.

Ross, Lee. 1977. "The Intuitive Psychologist and His Shortcomings: Distortions in the Attribution Process." *Advances in Experimental Social Psychology* 10(C): 173–220.

Rossi, Vincent, Erik Van Sebille, Alexander Sen Gupta, Véronique Garçon, and Matthew H. England. 2013. "Multi-decadal Projections of Surface and Interior Pathways of the Fukushima Cesium-137 Radioactive Plume." *Deep Sea Research Part I: Oceanographic Research Papers* 80(October): 37–46. DOI: 10.1016/j.dsr.2013.05.015.

Rostovskii, Mikhail. 2016. "Nikolai Patrushev: 'Mirovoe soobshchestvo dolzhno skazat' nam spasibo za Krym'." *Moskovskii Komsomolets.* http://www.mk.ru/politics/2016/01/26/nikolay-patrushev-mirovoe-soobshhestvo-dolzhno-skazat-nam-spasibo-za-krym.html (Accessed November 26, 2017).

Rothschild, Zachary K., Mark J. Landau, Daniel Sullivan, and Lucas A. Keefer. 2012. "A Dual-Motive Model of Scapegoating: Displacing Blame to Reduce Guilt or Increase Control." *Journal of Personality and Social Psychology* 102(6): 1148–1163.

Rovere, Richard H. 1959. *Senator Joe McCarthy.* New York: Harper Colophon.

Rowley, Hazel. 2001. *Richard Wright: The Life and Times.* New York: Henry Holt.

Rubin, Alissa J. 2009. "Prospect of More U.S. Troops Worries a Wary Afghan Public." *New York Times,* November 7, 2009.

Rubin, Elizabeth. 2009. "Karzai in his Labyrinth." *New York Times Magazine.* http://www.nytimes.com/2009/08/09/magazine/09Karzai-t.html?pagewanted=all (Accessed December 21, 2017).

Rumsfeld, Donald. 2001. *Meet the Press.* By Tim Russert. NBC, December 2, 2001.

Ryon, Holly S., and Marci E. J. Gleason. 2014. "The Role of Locus of Control in Daily Life." *Personality and Social Psychology Bulletin* 40(1): 121–131.

Saad, Lydia. 2015. "U.S. Views on Climate Change Stable after Extreme Winter." *Gallup* News. http://news.gallup.com/poll/182150/views-climate-change-stable-extreme-winter.aspx (Accessed December 28, 2017).

Sacks, Brianna. 2017. "Roy Moore Just Blamed His Sexual Misconduct Allegations on Lesbians, Gays, and Socialists." https://www.buzzfeed.com/briannasacks/roy-moore-just-blamed-the-lgbt-community-for-the-sexual?utm_term=.uxQxLLdJN9#.arrAwwL5Gm (Accessed December 28, 2017).

Sakwa, Richard, ed. 2005. *Chechnya: From Past to Future*. London: Anthem Press.

Sakwa, Richard. 2014. *Putin and the Oligarch: The Khodorkovsky-Yukos Affair*. New York: I.B. Tauris.

Salisbury, S. 1998. "Still on Trail of CIA Links to Drug-runners." *The Philadelphia Inquirer*, July 7, 1998.

Sanders, Bernie. n.d. "Issues: Reforming Wall Street." https://berniesanders.com/issues/reforming-wall-street/ (Accessed December 12, 2017).

Sanger, David E. 2017. "Putin Ordered 'Influence Campaign' Aimed at U.S. Election, Report Says." *New York Times*. https://www.nytimes.com/2017/01/06/us/politics/russia-hack-report.html (Accessed December 21, 2017).

Santora, Marc. 2009. "7 Blasts around Baghdad kill at least 24." *New York Times*, June 23, 2009.

Sapountzis, Antonis, and Susan Condor. 2013. "Conspiracy Accounts as Intergroup Theories: Challenging Dominant Understandings of Social Power and Political Legitimacy." *Political Psychology* 34(5): 731–752.

Sarlo, Beatriz. 2012. "La 'filosofía del lenguaje' K." *La Nación*. http://www.lanacion.com.ar/1456937-la-filosofia-del-lenguaje-k (Accessed December 22, 2017).

Savage, Charlie. 2012. "Report by House Democrats Absolves Administration in Gun Trafficking Case." *New York Times*, January 31, 2012.

scarc. 2009. "Linus Pauling and the Search for UFOs." [Blog] *The Pauling Blog*. Available at: https://paulingblog.wordpress.com/tag/conspiracy-theory/ (Accessed December 1, 2017).

Schattschneider, E. E. 1960. *The Semi-Sovereign People: A Realist's View of Democracy*. New York: Holt, Rinehart and Winston.

Schell, Jonathan. 1976. *The Time of Illusion: An Historical and Reflective Account of the Nixon Era*. New York: Vintage.

Schier, Steven. 2016. *Polarized: The Rise of Ideology in American Politics*. Lanham, MD: Rowman & Littlefield.

Schiller, Daniel. 1981. *Objectivity and the News. The Public and the Rise of Commercial Journalism*. Philadelphia: University of Pennsylvania Press.

Schmidt, Michael S. 2011. "Heat Wave and Fasting Add to Woes of Iraqis." *New York Times*, August 3, 2011.

Schofield, Norman. 2006. *Architects of Political Change*. Cambridge: Cambridge University Press.

Schorn, Daniel. 2006. "The Priory of Sion: Is the 'Secret Organization' Fact or Fiction?." https://www.cbsnews.com/news/the-priory-of-sion/ (Accessed December 27, 2017).

Schudson, Michael. 1978. *Discovering the News. A Social History of American Newspapers*. New York: Basic Books.

Schudson, Michael. 1998. *The Good Citizen: A History of Civic Life*. New York: Free Press.

Schudson, Michael. 2001. "The Objectivity Norm in American Journalism." *Journalism* 2(2): 149–170.

Schultheis, Emily. 2012. "Santorum: I never believed global warming 'hoax'." https://www.politico.com/blogs/burns-haberman/2012/02/santorum-i-never-believed-global-warming-hoax-113739 (Accessed December 19, 2017).

Schulteis, Emily. 2016. "Jill Stein Announces Plans for Leftover Recount Money." https://www.cbsnews.com/news/jill-stein-announces-plans-for-leftover-recount-money/ (Accessed December 27, 2017).

Schwartz, Barry. 1987. *George Washington: The Making of an American Symbol*. New York: Free Press.

Seitz, Frederick. 1994. *Global Warming and Ozone Hole Controversies: A Challenge to Scientific Judgment.* Washington, D.C.: George C. Marshall Institute.

Seitz, Frederick. 1994. *On the Frontier: My Life in Science.* College Park, MD: American Institute of Physics.

Sengupta, Somini. 2009. "Bangladeshi Premier Faces a Grim Crucible with Notes of Defiance." *New York Times,* March 14, 2009.

Shaheen, Kareem. 2017. "Turkey's Opposition Begins 250-mile Protest March over MP's Imprisonment." *The Guardian.* https://www.theguardian.com/world/2017/jun/15/turkeys-opposition-begins-protest-march-over-mps-imprisonment-enis-berberoglu   (Accessed December 22, 2017).

Shane, Scott, and Michael D. Shear. 2013. "Visions of Drones Swarming the Skies Touch Bipartisan Nerve." *New York Times,* March 9, 2013.

Shane, Scott. 2009. "C.I.A. is Cagey about '63 Files Tied to Oswald." *New York Times,* October 17, 2009.

Shapiro, Dina. 2011. "The Risk of Disease Stigma: Threat and Support for Coercive Public Heath Policy." Presented at APSA Pre-Conference on Political Communication of Risk.

Shapiro, Ian. 2017. "Collusion in Restraint of Democracy: Against Political Deliberation." *Daedalus* 146(3): 77–84.

Shapiro, Robert, and Yaeli Bloch-Elchon. 2008. "Do the Facts Speak for Themselves? Partisan Disagreement as a Challenge to Democratic Competence." *Critical Review* 20(1): 115–139.

Sharma, Megha, et al. 2017. "Zika Virus Pandemic: Analysis of Facebook as a Social Media Health Information Platform." *American Journal of Infection Control* 45(3): 301–302. DOI:10.1016/j.ajic.2016.08.022.

Sharma, Megha, Kapil Yadav, Nitika Yadav, and Keith C. Ferdinand. 2017. "Zika Virus Pandemic: Analysis of Facebook as a Social Media Health Information Platform." *American Journal of Infection Control* 45(3): 301–302. DOI: 10.1016/j.ajic.2016.08.022.

Shear, Michael D. 2013. "A Sleeper Scandal Awakens, Post-election." *New York Times,* May 22, 2013.

Shelbourne, Mallory. 2016. "Trump Claims Voter Fraud without Evidence, Says 'I Won the Popular Vote.'" *The Hill.* http://thehill.com/homenews/campaign/307622-trump-i-would-have-won-popular-vote-if-people-had-not-voted-illegally (Accessed December 27, 2017).

Shepsle, Kenneth A. 1979. "Institutional Arrangements and Equilibrium in Multidimensional Voting Models." *American Journal of Political Science* 23(1): 27–59.

Shepsle, Kenneth A. 2003. "Losers in Politics (and How They Sometimes Become Winners): William Riker's Heresthetic." *Perspectives on Politics* 1(2): 307–315.

Shepsle, Kenneth A. 2017. *Rule Breaking and Political Imagination.* Chicago: University of Chicago Press.

Shermer, Michael. 2004. "Then a Miracle Occurs." https://michaelshermer.com/2004/05/then-a-miracle-occurs/ (Accessed December 28, 2017).

Shermer, Michael. 2011. *The Believing Brain.* New York: Times Books.

Shibutani, Tamotsu. 1966. *Improvised News: A Sociological Study of Rumor.* Indianapolis: Bobbs-Merrill.

Shils, Edward. 1956. *The Torment of Secrecy: The Background and Consequences of American Security Politics.* New York: Free Press.

Shironin, Valeriĭ. 2010. *Agenty perestroĭki.* Moscow: Ėksmo.

Shiva, Vandana. 1988. "Reductionist Science as Epistemological Violence." In *Science, Hegemony and Violence: A Requiem for Modernity,* ed. Ashis Nandy. Oxford: Oxford University Press.

Shiva, Vandana. 2017. "Peddling Poisons and Selling Seeds of Suicide." http://vandanashiva.com/?p=554 (Accessed November 30, 2017).

Shklar, Judith. 1989. "Liberalism of Fear." In *Liberalism and the Moral Life,* by Nancy L. Rosenblum, 21–38. Cambridge, Massachusetts: Harvard University Press.

Shlapentokh, Vladimir. 1991. "A Glut of Conspiracy Theories." *Los Angeles Times.* http://articles.latimes.com/1991-04-16/local/me-17_1_conspiracy-theorie   (Accessed   December 21, 2017).

Shwed, Uri, and Peter S. Bearman. 2010. "The Temporal Structure of Scientific Consensus Formation." *American Sociological Review* 75(6): 817–840. DOI: 10.1177/0003122410388488.

Siever, Larry, J. 2002. "Schizotypy: Implications for Illness and Health." *American Journal of Psychiatry* 159(4): 683–684.

Simmons, William Paul, and Sharon Parsons. 2005. "Beliefs in Conspiracy Theories among African Americans: A Comparison of Elites and Masses." *Social Science Quarterly* 86(3): 582–598.

Simon, Arthur M., and Joseph E. Uscinski. 2012. "Prior Experience Predicts Presidential Performance." *Presidential Studies Quarterly* 42(3): 514–548. DOI: 10.1111/j.1741-5705.2012.03991.x.

Simons, Herbert W. 1994. "'Going Meta': Definition and Political Applications." *Quarterly Journal of Speech* 80(4): 468–81.

Sinaceur, Marwan. 2010. "Suspending Judgment to Create Value: Suspicion and Trust in Negotiation." *Journal of Experimental Social Psychology* 46(3): 543–550.

Sirajuddin, S. 2010. "Quotation of the Day." *New York Times,* May 26, 2010.

Sleek, Scott. "Inconvenient Truth Tellers: What Happens When Research Yields Unpopular Findings." *APS Observer* 26(9).

Smallpage, Steven M., Adam M. Enders, and Joseph E. Uscinski. 2017. "The Partisan Contours of Conspiracy Theory Beliefs." *Research and Politics* 4(4): 1–7. DOI: 10.1177/2053168017746554.

Smith, A. R, K. J. Thomas, E. B. Norman, D. L. Hurley, B. T. Lo, Y. D. Chan, P. V. Guillaumon, and B. G. Harvey. 2014. "Measurements of Fission Products From the Fukushima Daiichi Incident in San Francisco Bay Area Air Filters, Automobile Filters, Rainwater, and Food." *Journal of Environmental Protection* 5(3): 207–221. DOI: 10.4236/jep.2014.53025.

Smith, Ben. 2008. "E-Mails, Conspiracy Rumors Plague Palin." https://www.politico.com/story/2008/09/e-mails-conspiracy-rumors-plague-palin-013307 (Accessed October 14, 2009).

Smith, John N., Robin M. Brown, William J. Williams, Marie Robert, Richard Nelson, and S. Bradley Moran. 2015. "Arrival of the Fukushima Radioactivity Plume in North American Continental Waters." *Proceedings of the National Academy of Sciences* 112(5): 1310–1315. DOI: 10.1073/pnas.1412814112.

Smith, John N., Vincent Rossi, Ken O. Buesseler, Jay T. Cullen, Jack Cornett, Richard Nelson, Alison M. Macdonald, Marie Robert, and Jonathan Kellogg. 2017. "Recent Transport History of Fukushima Radioactivity in the Northeast Pacific Ocean." *Environmental Science & Technology* 51(18): 10494–10502. DOI: 10.1021/acs.est.7b02712.

Smith, Marc A., Lee Rainie, Ben Shneiderman, and Itai Himelboim. 2014. *Mapping Twitter Topic Networks: From Polarized Crowds to Community Clusters.* Pew Center Research 20. http://www.pewinternet.org/2014/02/20/part-2-conversational-archetypes-six-conversation-and-group-network-structures-in-twitter/ (Accessed December 20, 2017).

Smith, Nicholas, and Anthony Leiserowitz. 2012. "The Rise of Global Warming Skepticism: Exploring Affective Image Associations in the United States over Time." *Risk Analysis* 32(6): 1021–1032.

Sniderman, Paul M. 2000. "Taking Sides: A Fixed Choice Theory of Political Reasoning." In *Elements of Reason: Cognition, Choice, and the Bounds of Rationality,* eds. Samuel L. Popkin, Arthur Lupia, and Matthew D. McCubbins. Cambridge: Cambridge University Press, 67–84.

Snyder, Michael. 2013. "28 Signs That The West Coast Is Being Absolutely Fried With Nuclear Radiation From Fukushima." [Blog] *Activist Post.* Available at http://www.activistpost.com/2013/10/28-signs-that-west-coast-is-being.html (Accessed December 29, 2017).

Soral, Wiktor, and Mirosław Kofta. n.d. "In-Group as a Shield: Existential Threat to the In-Group Increases Accessibility of Group Agency-Related Traits." Forthcoming.

Soral, Wiktor, and Monika Grzesiak-Feldman. 2015. "Socjo-psychologiczne wyznaczniki wiary w spisek smoleński [Socio-psychological antecedents of belief in Smolensk conspiracy]." In *Uprzedzenia w Polsce [Prejudice in Poland],* eds. Anna Stefaniak, Michal Bilewicz, and Mikolaj Winiewski. Warsaw: Liberi Libri: 285–304.

Specter, Michael. 2014. "Seeds of Doubt: An Activist's Controversial Crusade Against Genetically Modified Crops." *The New Yorker,* August 25.

Spence, Andrew Michael. 1974. *Market Signaling: Informational Transfer in Hiring and Related Screening Processes*. Cambridge: Harvard University Press.

Springer, Martin. 2008. *Contemporary Western Ethnography and the Definition of Religion*. London: Bloomsbury.

Ståhl, Tomas, and Jan-Willem van Prooijen,. 2018. "Epistemic Rationality: Skepticism Toward Unfounded Beliefs Requires Sufficient Cognitive Ability and Motivation to be Rational." *Personality and Individual Differences* 122: 155–163.

Stanovich, K. E., and R. F. West. 2000. "Individual Differences in Reasoning: Implications for the Rationality Debate?" *Behavioral and Brain Sciences* 23(5): 645–665.

Starbird, Kate. 2017. "Examining the Alternative Media Ecosystem Through the Production of Alternative Narratives of Mass Shooting Events on Twitter." In *ICWSM*: 230–239.

Starikov, Nikolaĭ. 2009. *Zapad protiv Rossii: Za chto nas nenavidiat?* Muscow. Ėksmo.

Stauffer, Vernon. 1918. *New England and the Bavarian Illuminati*. Diss. New York: Columbia University Press.

Steig, Eric. "O'Donnellgate." [Blog] *O'Donnellgate*. Available at: http://www.realclimate.org/index.php/archives/2011/02/odonnellgate/ (Accessed December 24, 2017).

Stein, Jeff. 2017. "Donna Brazile's Bombshell About the DNC and Hillary Clinton Explained." *Vox.com*. https://www.vox.com/policy-and-politics/2017/11/2/16599036/donna-brazile-hillary-clinton-sanders (Accessed December 27, 2017).

Steinhauser, George, Alexander Brandl, and Thomas E. Johnson. 2014. "Comparison of the Chernobyl and Fukushima Nuclear Accidents: A Review of the Environmental Impacts." *Science of the Total Environment* 470(February): 800–817. DOI: 10.1016/j.scitotenv.2013.10.029.

Stewart III, Charles. 2016. "Donald Trump's 'Rigged Election' Talk Is Changing Minds. Democrats' Minds, That Is." [Blog] *The Monkey Cage*. Available at https://www.washingtonpost.com/news/monkey-cage/wp/2016/10/19/donald-trumps-rigged-election-talk-is-changing-minds-democrats-minds-that-is/?utm_term=.5e072a8490ee (Accessed December 27, 2017).

Stieger, Stefan, Nora Gumhalter, Ulrich S. Tran, Martin Voracek, and Viren Swami. 2013. "Girl in the Cellar: A Repeated Cross-Sectional Investigation of Belief in Conspiracy Theories about the Kidnapping of Natascha Kampusch." *Frontiers in Psychology* 4(May): 297.

Stiglitz, Joseph. "Bleakonomics." *New York Times*. http://www.nytimes.com/2007/09/30/books/review/Stiglitz-t.html?_r=1&oref=slogin (Accessed December 20, 2017).

Stollberg, Janine, Immo Fritsche, and Anna Bäcker. 2015. "Striving for Group Agency: Threat to Personal Control Increases the Attractiveness of Agentic Groups." *Frontiers in Psychology* 6(649): 1–13.

Streckfuss, Richard. 1990. "Objectivity in Journalism: A Search and a Reassessment." *Journalism & Mass Communication Quarterly* 67(4): 973–983.

Sturgis, Patrick, and Nick Allum. 2004. "Science in Society: Re-Evaluating the Deficit Model of Public Attitudes." *Public Understanding of Science* 13(1): 55–74. DOI: 10.1177/0963662504042690.

Sullivan, Daniel, Mark J. Landau, and Zachary K. Rothschild. 2010. "An Existential Function of Enemyship: Evidence that People Attribute Influence to Personal and Political Enemies to Compensate for Threats to Control." *Journal of Personality and Social Psychology*, 98(3): 434–449.

Sun, Lena H. 2017. "Anti-vaccine Activists Spark a State's Worst Measles Outbreak in Decades." *The Washington Post*, 5 May 2017.

Sunstein, Cass R. 2014. *Conspiracy Theories and Other Dangerous Ideas*. New York: Simon and Schuster.

Sunstein, Cass R. 2014. *On Rumors: How Falsehoods Spread, Why We Believe Them, and What Can Be Done*. Princeton: Princeton University Press.

Sunstein, Cass, and Adrian Vermeule. 2008. "Conspiracy Theories." John Olin Program in Law and Economics, Working Paper No. 387. Available at https://chicagounbound.uchicago.edu/law_and_economics/119/ (Accessed January 9, 2017).

Sunstein, Cass R., and Adrian Vermeule. 2009. "Conspiracy Theories: Causes and Cures." *Journal of Political Philosophy* 17(2): 202–227.

Sutcliffe, Stephen. 2003. *Children of the New Age: A History of Spiritual Practices.* London: Routledge.

Sutton, Robbie M., and Karen M. Douglas. 2014. "Examining the Monological Nature of Conspiracy Theories." In *Power, Politics, and Paranoia: Why People Are Suspicious of Their Leaders,* eds. Jan-Willem van Prooijen and Paul A. M. van Lange. Cambridge: Cambridge University Press, 254–272.

Swami, Viren. 2012. "Social Psychological Origins of Conspiracy Theories: The Case of the Jewish Conspiracy Theory in Malaysia." *Frontiers in Psychology* 3:1–9. DOI: 10.3389/fpsyg.2012.00280.

Swami, Viren, and Rebecca Coles. 2010. "The Truth is Out there: Belief in Conspiracy Theories." *The Psychologist* 23(7): 560–563.

Swami, Viren, Jakob Pietschnig, Ulrich S. Tran, Ingo W. Nader, Stefan Stieger, and Martin Voracek. 2013. "Lunar Lies: The Impact of Informational Framing and Individual Differences in Shaping Conspiracist Beliefs About the Moon Landings." *Applied Cognitive Psychology* 27(1): 71–80.

Swami, Viren, and Adrian Furnham. 2014. "Political Paranoia and Conspiracy Theories." In *Power, Politics, & Paranoia: Why People Are Suspicious of Their Leaders,* eds. Jan-Willem van Prooijen and Paul A. M. Lange. Cambridge: Cambridge University Press, 218–236.

Swami, Viren, Tomas Chamorro-Premuzic, and Adrian Furnham. 2010. "Unanswered Questions: A Preliminary Investigation of Personality and Individual Difference Predictors of 9/11 Conspiracist Beliefs." *Applied Cognitive Psychology* 24(6): 749–761.

Swami, Viren, Rebecca Coles, Stefan Stieger, Jakob Pietschnig, Adrian Furnham, Sherry Rehim, and Martin Voracek. 2011. "Conspiracist Ideation in Britain and Austria: Evidence of a Monological Belief System and Associations between Individual Psychological Differences and Real-World and Fictitious Conspiracy Theories." *British Journal of Psychology* 102(3): 443–463.

Swami, Viren, Martin Voracek, Stefan Stieger, Ulrich S. Tran, and Adrian Furnham. 2014 "Analytical Thinking Reduces Belief in Conspiracy Theories." *Cognition* 133(3): 572–585.

Swami, Viren, Adrian Furnham, Nina Smyth, Laura Weis, Alixe Lay, Angela Clow. 2016. "Putting the Stress on Conspiracy Theories: Examining Associations between Psychological Stress, Anxiety, and Belief in Conspiracy Theories." *Personality and Individual Differences* 99(September): 72–76.

Swami, Viren, Laura Weis, Alixe Lay, David Barron, and Adrian Furnham. 2016. "Associations Between Belief in Conspiracy Theories and the Maladaptive Personality Traits of the Personality Inventory for DSM-5." *Psychiatry Research* 236(28): 86–90.

Swift, Art. 2013. "Majority in U.S. Still Believe JFK Killed in a Conspiracy." *Gallup.com.* http://news.gallup.com/poll/165893/majority-believe-jfk-killed-conspiracy.aspx (Accessed December 28, 2017).

Taber, Charles S., and Milton Lodge. 2006. "Motivated Skepticism in the Evaluation of Political Beliefs." *American Journal of Political Science* 50(3): 755–769.

Taguieff, Pierre-André. 2005. *La Foire aux illumines. Ésotérisme, théorie du complot, extrémisme.* Paris: Mille et une nuits.

Tani, Maxwell. 2016. "The Conspiracy Candidate? 13 Outlandish Theories Donald Trump Has Floated on the Campaign Trail." *Busness Insider.* http://www.businessinsider.com/donald-trump-birther-conspiracy-theories-2016-9 (Accessed December 27, 2017).

Tashman, Brian. 2012. "James Inhofe Says the Bible Refutes Climate Change." http://www.rightwingwatch.org/post/james-inhofe-says-the-bible-refutes-climate-change/ (Accessed December 20, 2017).

Tavernise, Sabrina. 2009. "Pakistanis View Market Blast with Disbelief, and Seek Places to put Blame." *New York Times,* November 4, 2009.

Tavernise, Sabrina. 2010. "U.S. Heads a Cast of Villains in Pakistan's Conspiracy Talk." *New York Times,* May 6, 2010.

Tavernise, Sabrina, and Abdul Waheed Wafa. 2009. "UN Official Acknowledges 'Widespread Fraud' in Afghan Election." *New York Times.* http://www.nytimes.com/2009/10/12/world/asia/12afghan.html (Accessed December 21, 2017).

Taylor, Jon. 2017. "Kyrie Irving is Back on His Flat-Earth Theory Nonsense." *Sports* https://www.si.com/nba/2017/11/01/kyrie-irving-celtics-flat-earth-theory (Accessed December 27, 2017).

Thalmann, Katharina. 2014. "'John Birch Blues': The Problematization of Conspiracy Theory in the Early Cold-War Era." *COPAS* 15(1). https://copas.uni-regensburg.de/article/view/182 (Accessed December 18, 2017).

The Council of the Federation. 2014. "Stenogramma trista sorok sed'mogo (vneocherednogo) zasedaniia Soveta Federatsii, Moscow." *The Council of the Federation.* http://council.gov.ru/media/files/41d4c8b9772e9df14056.pdf (Accessed November 26, 2017).

The Daily Beast. 2014. "MH370's Kookiest Conspiracies." https://www.thedailybeast.com/mh370s-kookiest-conspiracies (December 17, 2017).

The New York Times. 1964. "The Warren Commission Report." *The New York Times.* http://www.nytimes.com/1964/09/28/the-warren-commission-report.html (Accessed December 28, 2017).

Theriault, Sean M. 2008. *Party Polarization in Congress.* New York: Cambridge University Press.

Theriault, Sean M. 2013. *The Gingrich Senators: The Roots of Partisan Warfare in Congress.* Oxford: Oxford University Press.

Thomas, Kenn. 1994. "Clinton Era Conspiracies! Was Gennifer Flowers on the Grassy Knoll? Probably Not, But Here Are Some Other Bizarre Theories for a New Political Age." *The Washington Post.* https://www.washingtonpost.com/archive/opinions/1994/01/16/clinton-era-conspiracies-was-gennifer-flowers-on-the-grassy-knoll-probably-not-but-here-are-some-other-bizarre-theories-for-a-new-political-age/52f44fe4-ba8e-4f9a-a119-c1d526fad4b4/?utm_term=.bd0fc0eaa81f (Accessed December 28, 2017).

Thomas, Ronald R. 1999. *Detective Fiction and the Rise of Forensic Science.* Cambridge: Cambridge University Press.

Thomas, Stephen B., and Sandra C. Quinn. 1991. "The Tuskegee Syphilis Study, 1932 to 1972: Implications for HIV Education and AIDS Risk Education Programs in the Black Community." *American Journal of Public Health* 81(11): 1498–1505.

Thompson, Damien. 2005. *Waiting for the Antichrist: Charisma and Apocalypse in a Pentecostal Church.* London: Oxford University Press.

Thomson, Robert, Naoyo Ito, Hinako Suda, Fangyu Lin, Yafei Liu, Ryo Hayasaka, Ryuzo Isochi, and Zian Wang. 2012. "Trusting Tweets: The Fukushima Disaster and Information Source Credibility on Twitter." *Proceedings of the 9th International Conference on Information Systems for Crisis Response and Management.*

Time Magazine. n.d. "Conspiracy Theories." http://content.time.com/time/specials/packages/completelist/0,29569,1860871,00.html (Accessed December 28, 2017).

Tolz, Vera. 2001. *Russia.* London: Arnold.

Topaz, Jonathan. 2015. "Christie Causes Stir with Vaccination Comments." https://www.politico.com/story/2015/02/chris-christie-vaccinations-114825 (Accessed December 17, 2015).

Topping, Alexandra. 2014. "Jane Austen Twitter Row: Two Plead Guilty to Abusive Tweets." *The Guardian.* https://www.theguardian.com/society/2014/jan/07/jane-austen-banknote-abusive-tweets-criado-perez (Accessed December 24, 2017).

Tracy, James. 2015. "Medical Examiner: More Questions than Answers." In *Nobody Died at Sandy Hook: It Was A FEMA Drill to Promote Gun Control,* eds. Jim Fetzer and Mike Palecek. Moon Rocks Books, 19–28

Tracy, James. 2015. "FAU Professor Questions whether Sandy Hook Massacre Was Staged." *SunSentinel,* December 14. http://www.sun-sentinel.com/opinion/commentary/sfl-former-fau-professor-questions-whether-sandy-hook-massacre-was-staged-20151214-story.html.

Trofimov, Dmitri. "2014. Pakistan Leader's Predicament Shows Power of 'Deep State.'" *Wall Street Journal*. https://www.wsj.com/articles/pakistan-leaders-predicament-shows-power-of-deep-state-1410282028 (Accessed December 21, 2017).

Trope, Yaacov, Benjamin Gervey, and Nira Liberman. 1997. "Wishful Thinking from a Pragmatic Hypothesis-Testing Perspective." In *The Mythomanias: The Nature of Deception and Self-Deception*, ed. M. Myslobodsky. Mahwah, NJ: Lawrence Erlbaum, 105–131.

Trump, Donald. 2012. Twitter Post. November 6, 2012. 11:15am, https://twitter.com/realdonaldtrump/status/265895292191248385?lang=en.

Truth-or-Fiction.com. 2017. "Alex Jones Appointed White House Press Secretary—Fiction!" https://www.truthorfiction.com/alex-jones-white-house-press-secretary/ (Accessed December 20, 2017).

Tsygankov, Andrei P. "Finding a Civilisational Idea: 'West,' 'Eurasia,' and 'Euro-East' in Russia's Foreign Policy." *Geopolitics* 12(3): 375–399.

Tulodziecki, Dana. 2013. "Shattering the Myth of Semmelweis." *Philosophy of Science* 80(5): 1065–1075.

Tupy, Marian. 2017. "Europe's Anti-GMO Stance Is Killing Africans." http://reason.com/archives/2017/09/05/europes-anti-gmo-stance-is-killing-afric (Accessed December 27, 2017).

Turner, Patricia A. 1993. *I Heard It Through the Grapevine: Rumor in African American Culture*. Berkeley and Los Angeles: University of California Press.

Tyler, Tom R. 1987. "Conditions Leading to Value Expressive Effects in Judgments of Procedural Justice: A Test of Four Models." *Journal of Personality and Social Psychology* 52(2): 333–344.

Tyler, Tom R., and E. Allan Lind. 1992. "A Relational Model of Authority in Groups." In *Advances in Experimental Social Psychology vol. 25*, ed. Mark P. Zanna. San Diego: Academic Press, 115–292.

U.S. Congress. Senate Select Committee to Study Governmental Operations with Respect to Intelligence Activities. 1976. 94th Cong., 2nd sess., *Final Report*, Part II. Washington, D.C.: Government Printing Office.

U.S. Congress. Senate Select Committee to Study Governmental Operations with Respect to Intelligence Activities. 1976. 94th Cong., 2nd sess., *Final Report*, Part III. Washington, D.C.: Government Printing Office.

U.S. Congress. Senate, Select Committee on Intelligence and the Subcommittee on Health and Scientific Research of the Committee on Human Resources. 1977. *Joint Hearings on Project MKULTRA, the CIA's Program of Research in Behavioral Modification*, 95th Cong., 1st sess. Washington, D.C.: Government Printing Office.

U.S. Congress. Senate. Senate Select Committee to Study Governmental Operations with Respect to Intelligence Activities. 1974. 94th Cong., 2nd sess., *Interim Report: Alleged Assassination Plots Involving Foreign Leaders*. New York: W.W. Norton.

U.S. Federal Bureau of Investigations. 2011. *National Gang Threat Assessment: Emerging Trends*, National Gang Intelligence Center, Washington, D.C.

U.S. Office of the Inspector General, Central Intelligence Agency.1998. *Allegations of Connections between CIA and the Contras in Cocaine Trafficking to the United States, Volume II: "The Contra Story."* https://www.cia.gov/library/reports/general-reports-1/cocaine/contra-story/contents.html (Accessed 5 February 2015).

Ullmann-Margalit, Edna. 2004. "Trust, Distrust, and In Between." In *Distrust*, ed. Russell Hardin, New York: Russell Sage Foundation, 60–82.

United Nations Scientific Committee on the Effects of Atomic Radiation. 2013. *Levels and Effects of Radiation Exposure Due to the Nuclear Accident After the 2011 Great East Japan Earthquake and Tsunami*. https://reliefweb.int/sites/reliefweb.int/files/resources/13-85418_Report_2013_Annex_A.pdf (Accessed December 29, 2017).

United Press International. 2000. "Mbeki Says CIA had Role in HIV/AIDS Conspiracy." Reproduced at *Padraig O'Malley Blog*. Available at: https://www.nelsonmandela.org/omalley/index.php/site/q/03lv03445/04lv04206/05lv04302/06lv04303/07lv04308.htm (Accessed December 1, 2017).

Unknown. 1865. "Conspiracy." *The Vermont Journal*, April 22, 1865.

Unknown. 1881. "Guiteau. a Sensational Report Exploded-Complete Failure of the Conspiracy Theory." *Boston Journal*, July 6, 1881.

Unknown. 1881. "Likely to Live." *St. Louis Globe-Democrat* (St. Louis, Missouri), July 7, 1881.

Unknown. 1881. "The Assassin." *Boston Journal*, July 5, 1881.

Unknown. 2001. "Bin Laden's Mountain Fortress." *Times of London*, November 29, 2001.

Unknown. n.d. *"Rech' prezidenta SShA B. Klintona."* http://militera.lib.ru/science/kapitanetz/08.html (Accessed November 26, 2017).

Uscinski, Joseph E. 2013. "Placing Conspiratorial Motives in Context: The Role of Predispositions and Threat, a Comment on Bost and Prunier (2013)." *Psychological Reports* 115(2):612–617.

Uscinski, Joseph E. 2014. *The People's News: Media, Politics, and the Demands of Capitalism.* New York: New York University Press.

Uscinski, Joseph E. 2015. "The Epistemology of Fact Checking (Is Still Naïve): Rejoinder to Amazeen." *Critical Review* 7(2): 243–252. DOI: 10.1080/08913811.2015.1055892.

Uscinski, Joseph E. 2016. "If Trump's Rhetoric around Conspiracy Theories Follows Him to the White House, It Could Lead to the Violation of Rights on a Massive Scale." [Blog] *Impact of American Politics & Policy Blog*. Available at: http://blogs.lse.ac.uk/usappblog/2016/03/30/if-trumps-rhetoric-around-conspiracy-theories-follows-him-to-the-white-house-it-could-lead-to-the-violation-of-rights-on-a-massive-scale/ (Accessed December 27, 2017).

Uscinski, Joseph E. 2016. "Lots of Americans Agree with Donald Trump About 'Rigged Elections.'" *The Washington Post*. https://www.washingtonpost.com/news/monkey-cage/wp/2016/08/08/lots-of-americans-agree-with-donald-trump-about-rigged-elections/?utm_term=.ed91fd2bdcd9 (Accessed December 27, 2017).

Uscinski, Joseph E. 2016. "Will Trump Become Conspiracy Theorist in Chief?" *Newsweek*. http://www.newsweek.com/trump-become-conspiracy-theorist-chief-442847 (Accessed December 18, 2017).

Uscinski, Joseph, and Ryden Butler. 2013. "The Epistemology of Fact Checking." *Critical Review* 25(2): 162–180.

Uscinski, Joseph E., and Joseph M. Parent. 2014. *American Conspiracy Theories*. Oxford: Oxford University Press.

Uscinski, Joseph E., and Santiago Olivella. 2017. "The Conditional Effect of Conspiracy Thinking on Attitudes toward Climate Change." *Research & Politics* 4(4). DOI: 10.1177/2053168017743105.

Uscinski, Joseph E., Casey Klofstad, and Matthew Atkinson. 2016. "What Drives Conspiratorial Beliefs? The Role of Informational Cues and Predispositions." *Political Research Quarterly* 69(1): 57–71.

Uscinski, Joseph E., Darin DeWitt, and Matthew Atkinson. 2018. "Conspiracy Theories and the Internet." In *The Brill Handbook of Conspiracy Theory and Contemporary Religion*, eds. Egil Asprem, Asbjorn Dyrendal, and David Robertson. Leiden, Netherlands: Brill.

Uscinski, Joseph E., Karen Douglas, and Stephan Lewandowsky. 2017. "Climate Change Conspiracy Theories." *Oxford Research Encyclopedia of Climate Science*: 1–43. DOI: 10.1093/acrefore/9780190228620.013.328.

Uslaner, Eric. 1999. "Democracy and Social Capital." *Democracy and Trust*, ed. Mark E. Warren, Cambridge: Cambridge University Press.

van Deth, Jan W. 2007. "Norms of Citizenship." In *Oxford Handbook of Political Behavior*, by Russell J. Dalton and Hans-Dieter Klingerman, 402–417. Oxford: Oxford University Press.

Van De Walle, Steven, and Frédérique Six. 2014. "Trust and Distrust as Distinct Concepts: Why Studying Distrust in Institutions is Important." *Journal of Comparative Policy Analysis: Research and Practice* 16(2): 158–174.

van den Bos, Kees, and E. Allen Lind. 2002. "Uncertainty Management by Means of Fairness Judgments." In *Advances in Experimental Social Psychology vol. 34*, ed. Mark P. Zanna. San Diego, CA: Academic Press, 1–60.

van den Bos, Kees, Henk A. M. Wilke, and E. Allan Lind. 1998. "When Do We Need Procedural Fairness? The Role of Trust in Authority." *Journal of Personality and Social Psychology* 75(6): 1449–1458.

van der Linden, Sander. 2015. "The Conspiracy-effect: Exposure to Conspiracy Theories (About Global Warming) Decreases Pro-social Behavior and Science Acceptance." *Personality and Individual Differences* 87(December): 171–173.

van der Tempel, Jan, and James E. Alcock. 2015. "Relationships between Conspiracy Mentality, Hyperactive Agency Detection, and Schizotypy: Supernatural Forces at Work?" *Personality and Individual Differences* 82(August): 136–141.

van Prooijen, Jan-Willem. 2012. "Suspicions of Injustice: The Sense-Making Function of Belief in Conspiracy Theories." In *Justice and Conflicts*, eds. Elisabeth Kals and Jürgen Maes. Berlin, Heidelberg: Springer-Verlag Berlin Heidelberg, 121–32.

van Prooijen, Jan-Willem. 2016. "Sometimes Inclusion Breeds Suspicion: Self-Uncertainty and Belongingness Predict Belief in Conspiracy Theories." *European Journal of Social Psychology* 46(3): 267–279.

van Prooijen, Jan-Willem. 2017. "Why Education Predicts Decreased Belief in Conspiracy Theories." *Applied Cognitive Psychology* 31(1): 50–58.

van Prooijen, Jan-Willem, and Nils B. Jostmann. 2013. "Belief in Conspiracy Theories: The Influence of Uncertainty and Perceived Morality." *European Journal of Social Psychology* 43(1): 109–115.

van Prooijen, Jan-Willem, and Eric van Dijk. 2014. "When Consequence Size Predicts Belief in Conspiracy Theories: The Moderating Role of Perspective Taking." *Journal of Experimental Social Psychology* 55(November): 63–73.

van Prooijen, Jan-Willem, and Paul A. M. van Lange. 2014. "The Social Dimensions of Belief in Conspiracy Theories." In *Power, Politics, and Paranoia: Why People Are Suspicious of Their Leaders*, eds. Jan-Willem van Prooijen and Paul A M van Lange. Cambridge: Cambridge University Press, 237–253.

van Prooijen, Jan-Willem, and Michele Acker. 2015. "The Influence of Control on Belief in Conspiracy Theories: Conceptual and Applied Extensions. *Applied Cognitive Psychology* 29(5): 753–761.

van Prooijen, Jan-Willem, and Andre P. M. Krouwel. 2015. "Mutual Suspicion at the Political Extremes: How Ideology Predicts Belief in Conspiracy Theories." In *The Psychology of Conspiracy*, eds. Michał Bilewicz, Aleksandra Cichocka, and Wiktor Soral. London and New York: Routledge, 79–98.

van Prooijen, Jan-Willem, and Reinout E. de Vries. 2016. "Organizational Conspiracy Beliefs: Implications for Leadership Styles and Employee Outcomes." *Journal of Business and Psychology* 31(4): 479–491.

van Prooijen, Jan-Willem, Kees van den Bos, and Henk A. M. Wilke. 2004. "The Role of Standing in the Psychology of Procedural Justice: Towards Theoretical Integration." *European Review of Social Psychology* 15(1): 33–58.

van Prooijen, Jan-Willem, Kees Van den Bos, and Henk A. M. Wilke. 2007. "Procedural Justice in Authority Relations: The Strength of Outcome Dependence Influences People's Reactions to Voice." *European Journal of Social Psychology* 37(6): 1286–1297.

van Prooijen, Jan-Willem, Karen M. Douglas, and Clara De Inocencio. 2017. "Connecting the Dots: Illusory Pattern Perception Predicts Belief in Conspiracies and the Supernatural." *European Journal of Social Psychology*. DOI: 10.1002/ejsp.2331.

van Prooijen, Jan-Willem, Kees van den Bos, E. Allan Lind, and Henk A. M. Wilke. 2006. "How do People React to Negative Procedures? On the Moderating Role of Authority's Biased Attitudes." *Journal of Experimental Social Psychology* 42(5): 632–645.

van Prooijen, Jan-Willem, Tomas Ståhl, Daniel Eek, and Paul A. M. Van Lange. 2012. "Injustice for All or Just for Me? Social Value Orientation Predicts Responses to Own Versus Other's Procedures." *Personality and Social Psychology Bulletin* 38(10): 1247–1258.

van Prooijen, Jan-Willem., André P. M. Krouwel, and Thomas V. Pollet. 2015. "Political Extremism Predicts Belief in Conspiracy Theories." *Social Psychological and Personality Science* 6(5): 570–578.

Volkov, Vadim. 2016. *Violent Entrepreneurs: The Use of Force in the Making of Russian Capitalism.* Ithaca: Cornell University Press.

Wagner, Richard E. 1996. "Pressure Groups and Political Entrepreneurs: A Review Article." *Public Choice* 1(1): 161–170.

Wakefield, Andrew ed. 2010. *Callous Disregard: Autism and Vaccines: The Truth Behind a Tragedy.* New York: Skyhorse Publishing.

Wakefield, Andrew, S. H. Murch, A. Anthony, J. Linnell, D. M. Casson, M. Malik, M. Berelowitz, A. P. Dhillon, M. Thomson, P. Harvey, A. Valentine, S. E. Davies, and J. A. Walker-Smith. 1998. "RETRACTED: Ileal Lymphoid Nodular Hyperplasia, Non-specific Colitis, and Pervasive Developmental Disorder in Children." *Lancet* 351(9):637–641.

Wald, Matthew L. 2008. "Controversy Dogs Inquiry on Bridge Collapse." *New York Times,* January 30, 2008.

Walker, Jesse. 2013. *The United States of Paranoia: A Conspiracy Theory.* New York: Harper Collins.

Walker, Jesse. 2015. "What I Saw at the Conspiracy Theory Conference." [Blog] *Hit and Run.* Available at http://reason.com/blog/2015/03/18/what-i-saw-at-the-conspiracy-theory-conf (Accessed December 28, 2017).

Walker, Jesse. 2016. "Donald Trump Loves Conspiracy Theories. So Do His Foes." *Chicago Tribune* http://www.chicagotribune.com/news/opinion/commentary/ct-donald-trump-russia-conspiracy-theories-20160815-story.html (Accessed December 27, 2017).

Walsh, Declan. 2012. "A Personal Quest to Clarify bin Laden's Last Days Yields Vexing Accounts." *New York Times,* March 8, 2012.

Walsh, Declan. 2012. "Fallout of bin Laden Raid: Aid Groups in Pakistan are Suspect." *New York Times,* May 3, 2012.

Walsh, Declan. 2013. "A Fiery Preacher's Arrival Shakes Pakistani Politics." *New York Times,* January 13, 2013.

Walsh, Nick Paton. 2005. "Russia Says Spies Work in Foreign NGOs." *The Guardian,* May 13, 2005.

Walch, Tad. 2006. "BYU Action on Jones Lamented." *Deseret News,* September 14. https://www.deseretnews.com/article/645200780/BYU-action-on-Jones-lamented.html.

Walch, Tad. 2006. "BYU Professor in Dispute over 9/11 Will Retire." *Deseret News,* Oct. 22. https://www.deseretnews.com/article/650200587/BYU-professor-in-dispute-over-911-will-retire.html.

Wanklyn, Alastair. 2015. "Anti-nuclear Firebrand's Case Heads to Canadian Court Over Death Threats Against Fukushima Environmental Scientists." *The Japan Times.* November 17, 2015.

Wanklyn, Alastair. 2016. "Canada Activist Found Guilty of Harassing Scientists Over Fukushima Fallout." *The Japan Times.* https://www.japantimes.co.jp/news/2016/09/23/national/crime-legal/canada-activist-found-guilty-harassing-scientists-fukushima-fallout/ (Accessed December 29, 2017).

Warner, Benjamin R., and Ryan Neville-Shepard. 2014. "Echoes of a Conspiracy: Birthers, Truthers, and the Cultivation of Extremism." *Communication Quarterly* 62(1): 7.

Warren, James. 2010. "Blagojevich Trial Shines a Light on Real Politics." *New York Times,* July 2, 2010.

Warren, Mark E. 1999. "Democratic Theory and Trust." *Democracy and Trust,* ed. Mark E. Warren. Cambridge: Cambridge University Press, 310–345.

Watson, Traci. 2001. "Conspiracy Theories Find Menace in Contrails." *USA Today.* https://usatoday30.usatoday.com/weather/science/2001-03-07-contrails.htm (Accessed December 20, 2017).

Watts, Duncan J. 2017. "Should Social Science be More Solution-oriented?" *Nature Human Behaviour* 1: 0015.

Webb, Edward. 2011. "Resisting Anamnesis: A Nietzschean Analysis of Turkey's National History Education." *Journal of Contemporary European Studies* 19(4): 489–500.

Webb, Gary. 1998. *Dark Alliance: The CIA, the Contras, and the Crack Cocaine Explosion.* New York: Seven Stories Press.

Weber, Elke U., and Paul C. Stern. 2011. "Public Understanding of Climate Change in the United States." *American Psychologist* 66(4): 315–328. DOI: 10.1037/a0023253.

Weber, Max. 1946. "Science as a Vocation." In *Max Weber: Essays in Sociology*, eds. H. H. Gerth and C. Wright Mills. New York: Oxford University Press.

Weingast, Barry R. 1979. "A Rational Choice Perspective on Congressional Norms." *American Journal of Political Science* 23(2): 245–262.

Wesseler, Justus, et al. 2017. "Foregone Benefits of Important Food Crop Improvements in Sub-Saharan Africa." *PLoS ONE* 12(7). DOI: 10.1371/journal.pone.0181353.

West, Harry G., and Todd Sanders, eds. 2003. *Transparency and Conspiracy: Ethnographies of Suspicion in the New World Order.* Durham: Duke University Press.

West, Lindy. 2016. "Donald and Billy on the Bus." *The New York Times*, October 8, 2016.

White, John Kenneth. 2002. *The Values Divide: American Politics and Culture in Transition.* Washington, D.C.: CQ Press.

White, Jonathan, and Lea Ypi. 2011. "On Partisan Political Justification." *American Political Science Review* 105(2): 381–396.

Whitson, Jennifer A., and Adam D. Galinsky. 2008. "Lacking Control Increases Illusory Pattern Perception." *Science* 322(3): 115–117.

Whitson, Jennifer A., Adam D. Galinsky, and A. Kay. 2015. "The Emotional Roots of Conspiratorial Perceptions, System Justification, and the Belief in the Paranormal." *Journal of Experimental Social Psychology* 56(January): 89–95.

Wicker, Tom. 1971. "The Tradition of Objectivity in the American Press: What's Wrong with It." *Proceedings of the Massachusetts Historical Society, Third Series* 84, 87.

Wikipedia. "Nancy MacLean." https://en.wikipedia.org/wiki/Nancy_MacLean (Accessed December 7, 2017).

Wikipedia. "Not Evil, Just Wrong." https://en.wikipedia.org/wiki/Not_Evil_Just_Wrong (Accessed May 25, 2017).

Wilkinson, Will. "Bernie Sanders Is Right the Economy Is Rigged. He's Dead Wrong About Why." *Vox.com.* https://www.vox.com/policy-and-politics/2016/7/15/12200990/bernie-sanders-economy-rigged (Accessed December 12, 2017).

Williams, Carol J. 2014. "Turkish Government Sacks 350 Police Carrying Out Corruption Probe." *Los Angeles Times.* http://articles.latimes.com/2014/jan/07/world/la-fg-wn-turkey-corruption-police-sacked-20140107 (Accessed December 21, 2017).

Wilson, Andrew. 2005. *Virtual Politics: Faking Democracy in the Post-Soviet World.* New Haven: Yale University Press.

Wilson, Kuman, Ed Mills, and Dory Ross. 2003. "Association of Autistic Spectrum Disorder and the Measles, Mumps, and Rubella Vaccine: A Systematic Review of Current Epidemiological Evidence." *Archives and Adolescent and Pediatric Medicine* 157(7):628–634.

Wilson, Rick K. 2011. "The Contribution of Behavioral Economics to Political Science." *Annual Review of Political Science* 14(June): 201–223.

Wilstein, Matt. 2017. "Bill O'Reilly Lashes Out at Critics in Conspiracy-Laden Glenn Beck Interview." *The Daily Beast.* https://www.thedailybeast.com/bill-oreilly-lashes-out-at-critics-in-conspiracy-laden-glenn-beck-interview (Accessed December 28, 2017).

Winer, Stuart. 2013. "Turkish Deputy PM Blames Jews for Gezi Protests." *Times of Israel.* http://www.timesofisrael.com/turkish-deputy-pm-blames-jews-for-gezi-protests/ (Accessed December 21, 2017).

Winiewski, Mikołaj, and Michał Bilewicz. 2015. "Antysemityzm: Dynamika i psychologiczne uwarunkowania [Anti-semitism: Dynamics and psychological antecedents]." In *Uprzedzenia w Polsce [Prejudice in Poland]*, eds. Anna Stefaniak, Michal Bilewicz, and Mikolaj Winiewski. Warsaw: Liberi Libri: 15–40.

Winiewski, Mikołaj, et al. n.d. *Prejudice in Poland in 2017.* Forthcoming.

Witkowska, Marta, et al. n.d. "Historia est Magistra Vitae? The Impact of Historical Victimhood on Current Conspiracy Beliefs." Forthcoming.

Wolf, Bryon Z. 2017. "Trump Embraces Deep State Conspiracy Theory." http://www.cnn.com/2017/11/29/politics/donald-trump-deep-state/index.html (Accessed December 27, 2017).

Wolfgang, Ben. 2015. "Jeb Bush, Rick Santorum Say Pope Should Stay out of Climate Change Debate." *Washington Times*, June 17, 2015.

Wood, Gordon S. 1982. "Conspiracy and the Paranoid Style: Causality and Deceit in the Eighteenth Century" *The William and Mary Quarterly* 39(3): 401–441.

Wood, Michael, et al. 2012. "Dead and Alive. Beliefs in Contradictory Conspiracy Theories." *Social Psychological and Personality Science* 3(6): 767–773. DOI: 10.1177/1948550611434786.

Wood, Michael J. 2016. "Conspiracy Suspicions as a Proxy for Beliefs in Conspiracy Theories: Implications for Theory and Measurement." *British Journal of Psychology* 108(3): 507–527.

Wood, Michael J. 2016. "Some Dare Call It Conspiracy: Labeling Something a Conspiracy Theory Does Not Reduce Belief in It." *Political Psychology* 37(5): 695–705.

Wood, Michael J., and Karen M. Douglas. 2015. "Online Communication as a Window to Conspiracist Worldviews." *Frontiers in Psychology* 6(June): 836.

Wood, Michael J., and Karen M. Douglas. 2013. "'What About Building 7?' a Social Psychological Study of Online Discussion of 9/11 Conspiracy Theories." *Frontiers in Psychology* 4(July). DOI: 10.3389/fpysg.2013.00409.

Wood, Michael J., Karen M. Douglas, and Robbie M. Sutton. 2012. "Dead and Alive: Beliefs in Contradictory Conspiracy Theories." *Social Psychological and Personality Science* 3(6): 767–773. DOI: 10.1177/1948550611434786.

Wootton, David. 2016. *The Invention of Science. A New History of the Scientific Revolution.* London: Penguin, 2016.

Wright, Thomas L., and Jack Arbuthnot. 1974. "Interpersonal Trust, Political Preference, and Perceptions of the Watergate Affair." *Personality and Social Psychology Bulletin* 1(1): 168–170.

Yablokov, Ilya. 2014. "Pussy Riot as Agent Provocateur: Conspiracy Theories and the Media Construction of Nation in Putin's Russia." *Nationalities Papers: The Journal of Nationalism and Ethnicity* 42(4): 622–636.

Yablokov, Ilya. 2015. "Conspiracy Theories as Russia's Public Diplomacy Tool: The Case of 'Russia Today' (RT)." *Politics* 35(3–4): 301–315.

Yardley, Jim. 2013. "Grim Task Overwhelms Bangladeshi DNA Lab." *New York Times*, May 31, 2013.

Yelland, Linda M., and William F. Stone. 1996. "Belief in the Holocaust: Effects of Personality and Propaganda." *Source: Political Psychology Political Psychology* 17(3): 551–562.

Yılmaz, Hakan. 2011. "Euroscepticism in Turkey: Parties, Elites, and Public Opinion." *South European Society and Politics* 16(01): 185–208.

Yoder, E. 1996. "The CIA-Crack Scandal Myth." *Denver Post*, October 6, 1996.

YouGov, and Leverhulme Trust Conspiracy and Democracy Project. *Conspiracy (Argentina).* YouGov, 2016.

Zaller, John. 1992. *The Nature and Origins of Mass Opinion.* Cambridge: Cambridge University Press.

Zap, Claudine. 2013. "Professor Won't Back Down from Newtown Massacre Conspiracy Theory." Yahoo News, January 9, 2013, http://news.yahoo.com/blogs/lookout/professor-won-t-back-down-newtown-massacre-conspiracy-183530799.html.

Zaza, Peter. 2017. "Naomi Klein—Female Chomsky and 9–11 Apologist." [Blog] *Rense.com.* Available at: http://www.rense.com/general78/naom.htm (Accessed December 1, 2017).

Zeller, Benjamin. 2014. *Heaven's Gate: America's UFO Religion.* New York: New York University Press.

Zimmerman, Malia. 2017. "Slain DNC Staffer's Father Doubts WikiLeaks Link as Cops Seek Answers." *Fox News*. http://www.foxnews.com/politics/2017/01/10/slain-dnc-staffers-father-doubts-wikileaks-link-as-cops-seek-answers.html (Accessed December 21, 2017).

Zonis, Marvin, and Craig M. Joseph. 1994. "Conspiracy Thinking in the Middle East" Political *Psychology*. 15(3): 443–459.

Zucca, Constanza, and Fred Frenter. 2014. "Retraction of Recursive Fury: A Statement." [Blog] *Frontiers Blog*. Available at https://www.frontiersin.org/blog/Retraction_of_Recursive_Fury_A_Statement/812/all_blogs (Accessed December 24, 2017).

Zwierlein, Cornel, and Beatrice de Graaf. 2013. "Security and Conspiracy in Modern History." *Historical Social Research/Historische Sozialforschung* 38(1): 7–45.

Zygar, Mikhail. 2016. *All the Kremlin's Men*. New York: PublicAffairs.

INDEX

Lightning Source UK Ltd.
Milton Keynes UK
UKHW041602240121
377501UK00015B/621